Public Administration

An Action Orientation

Seventh Edition

ROBERT B. DENHARDT
University of Southern California

JANET V. DENHARDT
University of Southern California

TARA A. BLANC
Arizona State University

WADSWORTH
CENGAGE Learning

Australia • Brazil • Mexico • Singapore • Spain • United Kingdom • United States

Public Administration: An Action Orientation, Seventh Edition
Robert B. Denhardt, Janet V. Denhardt, and Tara A. Blanc

Publisher: Suzanne Jeans

Executive Editor: Carolyn Merrill

Acquiring Sponsoring Editor: Anita Devine

Development Editor: Michael B. Kopf, S4Carlisle Publishing Services

Assistant Editor: Patrick Roach

Media Editor: Laura Hildebrand

Brand Manager: Lydia LeStar

Marketing Development Manager: Kyle Zimmerman

Rights Acquisitions Specialist: Jennifer Meyer Dare

Art and Design Direction, Production Management, and Composition: Cenveo Publisher Services

Manufacturing Planner: Fola Orekoya

Cover Image: Rachelle Antoinette

For product information and technology assistance, contact us at
Cengage Learning Customer & Sales Support, 1-800-354-9706

For permission to use material from this text or product, submit all requests online at **www.cengage.com/permissions**. Further permissions questions can be emailed to **permissionrequest@cengage.com**.

Library of Congress Control Number: 2012943892

ISBN-13: 978-1-133-93921-4

ISBN-10: 1-133-93921-X

Wadsworth
20 Channel Center Street
Boston, MA 02210
USA

Cengage Learning is a leading provider of customized learning solutions with office locations around the globe, including Singapore, the United Kingdom, Australia, Mexico, Brazil and Japan. Locate your local office at **international.cengage.com/region**.

Cengage Learning products are represented in Canada by Nelson Education, Ltd.

For your course and learning solutions, visit **www.cengage.com**.

Purchase any of our products at your local college store or at our preferred online store **www.cengagebrain.com**.

Instructors: Please visit **login.cengage.com** and log in to access instructor-specific resources.

Printed in the United States of America
1 2 3 4 5 6 7 16 15 14 13 12

For all our children

CONTENTS

PREFACE

The seventh edition of *Public Administration: An Action Orientation* updates the text by taking it through President Obama's first term and into his second term, following a very close election. It discusses the implications of the recent economic crisis, explores the resulting budget deficits at all levels of government as well as the increase in the national debt, considers the possible ramifications of the Obama health care reform effort, and covers recent political moves to limit collective bargaining for public employees.

Most notably, the book has been revised to more completely examine performance in government, on the one hand, and efforts to engage citizens in the work of public and nonprofit organizations, on the other hand. Placed in the context of the history of reform in the field, we now have extended our discussion of management reforms such as the New Public Management, updated material on advances in information and communication technology, and given more emphasis to performance management systems. In addition, we have included important new material dealing with leadership, organizational theory, and bureaucracy; expanded the discussion of special purpose governments, including school districts; and given a closer look at the increasingly important connection between public administration and civic action or citizenship. We particularly emphasize new efforts to promote transparency, collaboration, and participation in public and nonprofit organizations, with much of this discussion centering on the New Public Service. We have once again reordered the chapters to create a more logical progression of material given the large number of revisions since the organization of the previous edition. Additionally, new vignettes asking "What Would You Do?" give students the opportunity to think about and discuss their responses to specific and realistic challenges in public service. Finally, we have inserted in each chapter a reference to CourseReader.

CourseReader for *Public Administration: An Action Orientation*

ISBN-13: 9781133939214 (Public Administration: An Action Orientation with Printed Access Card for CourseReader)

CourseReader 0-30 PAC ISBN-13: 9781133350385 (Printed Access Card)

CourseReader 0-30 IAC ISBN-13: 9781133350378 (Instant Access Code)

In addition to reviewing important public administration issues, we have selected certain readings that highlight the focus of each chapter. Assigning readings can often be a difficult process. Within each chapter, you will come across reading assignments that are easily accessible within the Cengage Learning CourseReader. We have designed the CourseReader selections to tie in seamlessly with the section material. Keeping in mind that we must make the most of the time today's busy students can allocate to extra reading, we've handpicked one selection per chapter that will add the most to their study, reinforce the concepts from the text, and help them apply what they've learned to events around them. You may assign the questions that accompany the readings as graded or completion-based homework or use them to spark in-class discussion.

CourseReader is an easy-to-use and affordable option to create an online collection of readings for your course, and this is the first and only introductory book to political science offering a customizable e-reader. You may assign the readings we've recommended for each chapter without any additional setup, or you can choose to create and customize a reader specifically for your class from the thousands of text documents and media clips within CourseReader. You can also

- add your own notes and highlight sections within a reading.
- edit the introductions to the readings.
- assign due dates using the pop-up calendar.
- easily organize your selections using the drag-and-drop feature.

You can view a demo of CourseReader at www.cengage.com/coursereader.

Companion Website for *Public Administration: An Action Orientation*
ISBN 13: 9781133938712

Students will find open access to tutorial quizzes for every chapter, while instructors have access to the Instructor's Manual for *Public Administration: An Action Orientation.*

Instructor's Manual for *Public Administration: An Action Orientation* online
ISBN 13: 9781133949145

The Instructor's Manual includes an introduction on teaching public administration, ideas on preparing and designing a syllabus, a section on using supplementary textbooks, an overview and test bank including multiple-choice, true/false, and essay questions for each chapter, and a section on ideas for class activities.

Like previous editions, the seventh edition contains subtle but telling differences from other books in the field. We assume that students in an introductory course in public administration don't want to learn about the profession only in the abstract, but are interested in influencing the operations of public agencies, as managers from the inside or as citizens from the outside. They want to acquire the skills necessary for changing things for the better.

For this reason, it is important that the text not only introduce students to the scholarly literature of public administration, but also that it helps them develop the insights and abilities that will make them more effective and responsible actors. This book contains a good deal of material that is basic to working in or with public organizations. At the same time, the discussion attends to the complex and often confounding values that distinguish work in the public sector. Most significant, however, is the focus on personal values and interpersonal skills that are crucial to effecting change in public organizations.

Another feature of the book is its balanced attention to the work of managers at all levels of government and in nonprofit organizations. Although the federal government is a powerful model for the study of public administration, managers of state and local agencies are important actors in the governmental process, and their work is acknowledged and examined as well. Similarly, we show how managers of associations, nonprofit and "third-sector" organizations, and even traditionally private organizations are now confronting the same issues faced by administrators in the public sector. In fact, we frequently use the term *public organizations* to describe all such groups involved in the management of public programs.

This edition also gives proper attention to the global dimensions of public administration today. No longer is administrators' work confined to their own organizations or even to their own jurisdictions. The complexity of modern life means, among other things, that administrators must be attentive to developments around the world as well as to those at home. Decisions made in a foreign capital may affect the work of a public administrator even more significantly than those made only miles away. Today, knowledge of international affairs and comparative issues is important not only to those who work in other countries but also to all who work in public administration.

Public Administration: An Action Orientation remains distinctive in its treatment of the ethics of public service. The topic of ethics is thoroughly covered in a separate chapter, and references to ethical concerns appear throughout the text. Ethical issues cannot be separated from action. Indeed, every act of every public servant, at whatever level of government or in any related organization, has an important ethical dimension. For this reason, we have made a strong effort to discuss the ethical considerations that are a part of all administrative activities.

Finally, *Public Administration: An Action Orientation* was the first text on this subject to be fully integrated with the Internet resources that are available to assist public administrators and those studying public administration. In each chapter, we highlight "networking" resources available to students, including websites that contain material that supplements the text, provides examples and case studies, and links the student to other materials available online.

In this text we talk about action, but we also invite students to act. At the end of each chapter are self-diagnostic materials and exercises (cases, simulations, discussion points, and so on) designed to supplement students' cognitive learning with behavioral practice. These activities impart a sense of not only what public administration looks like to the impartial observer, but also what it feels like to the manager or private individual engaged in public action. Students have opportunities to test, practice, and improve their skills. We have included a list of key terms and definitions in the glossary and have recommended additional readings in each chapter. There are very exciting possibilities in public administration today. Working to solve important public problems, sensing the human drama involved in such work, and gaining the satisfaction of doing something really worthwhile make being involved in public organizations quite fascinating. The perspective adopted here—focusing on the experiences of people acting in the real world of public organizations and on the skills needed for managerial success—permits a lively and interesting presentation of the field. We particularly hope to convey, in a personal and direct manner, the challenges and rewards of public service.

ACKNOWLEDGMENTS

Many people contributed to this book. From our work with members of the American Society for Public Administration, the National Academy of Public Administration, the International City Management Association, and the Alliance for Innovation, we have gained special appreciation of the complexity of public management and of the dedication and hard work required for public service. We hope we have conveyed the commitment and concern that guide the work of the best public managers; they deserve great credit and respect.

In the first edition of the text, Bob's colleagues in the Department of Public Administration at the University of Missouri-Columbia were a great source of help and support. In subsequent editions, good colleagues and friends at the University of Colorado, the University of Delaware, Arizona State University, and the University of Southern California have made important contributions.

We wish to thank the reviewers who provided invaluable feedback on the sixth edition for our use in creating this new edition. They are Marcus Castro, University of La Verne; William Riggs, Texas A&M International University; Cryshanna Jackson, Youngstown State University; Willie Britt, Golden Gate University; and Bradley Best, Buena Vista University.

Finally, this book is dedicated to all of our children, who have been a constant source of joy, wonderment, and pride. Thanks to all.

Robert B. Denhardt, Janet V. Denhardt, and Tara A. Blanc

ABOUT THE AUTHORS

Robert B. Denhardt is Senior Fellow in the Sol Price School of Public Policy at the University of Southern California, Regents Professor Emeritus at Arizona State University, and Distinguished Visiting Scholar at the University of Delaware. Dr. Denhardt is a past president of the American Society for Public Administration and a member of the National Academy of Public Administration. He has published twenty-two books, including *The Dance of Leadership, The New Public Service, Managing Human Behavior in Public and Nonprofit Organizations, Theories of Public Organization, Public Administration: An Action Orientation, In the Shadow of Organization,* and *The Pursuit of Significance*.

Janet V. Denhardt is the Chester A. Newland Professor of Public Administration in the Sol Price School of Public Policy at the University of Southern California. Her teaching and research interests focus on organization theory, organizational behavior, and leadership. Her most recent book, *The Dance of Leadership,* was preceded by *The New Public Service, Managing Human Behavior in Public and Nonprofit Organizations,* and *Street-Level Leadership: Discretion and Legitimacy in Front-Line Public Service*. Prior to joining the faculty at the University of Southern California, Dr. Denhardt taught at Arizona State University and Eastern Washington University and served in a variety of administrative and consulting positions.

Tara A. Blanc is a lecturer in the School of Public Affairs at Arizona State University. Her teaching and research interests are primarily in the areas of public service, civic and political engagement, leadership, and public service ethics. Formerly the associate director of the Cronkite/Eight Poll at Arizona State University, she codirects a public opinion poll for ASU's Morrison Institute for Public Policy and provides consulting services on projects involving public opinion research, planning, and communication.

CHAPTER 1

PERSONAL ACTION IN PUBLIC ORGANIZATIONS

Public administration is concerned with the management of public programs. Public administrators work at all levels of government, both at home and abroad, and they manage nonprofit organizations, associations, and interest groups of all kinds. The substantive fields within which public managers work range across the varied interests of government and public affairs, from defense and national security to social welfare and environmental quality, from the design and construction of roads and bridges to the exploration of space, and from taxation and financial administration to human resources management. Though public administration varies tremendously in its scope and substance, those who work in public organizations share certain commitments. Among these, none is more important than a commitment to public service.

In this book, we examine the work of public administrators in many different kinds of organizations and define the political and historical context within which public and nonprofit organizations operate. We examine the commitments that underlie the notion of public service and the opportunities and constraints they place on public action. We examine the many technical fields, such as planning, budgeting, personnel, and evaluation, with which public administrators must be familiar and consider the personal and interpersonal talents needed by successful public managers. Most importantly, we emphasize the knowledge, skills, and values that *you* will need to be both effective and responsible as you act in the public interest.

Although we introduce many different areas of public administration, we do so from a particular point of view that provides a unifying theme in our examination of administrative work in public and nonprofit organizations. This point of view holds that there is something very special about public administration: your work in public service is distinguished by its pursuit of democratic values, and this concern affects nearly everything you do as a public manager. As a public administrator, you are obligated not only to achieve efficiency and effectiveness, but also to be responsive to the many bodies that help define the public interest: elected officials, members of the legislature, client or constituent groups, and citizens generally. This special obligation requires that you be ever mindful of managerial concerns, political concerns, and ethical concerns and that you develop structures and processes that take into account all three. The result is a particularly complicated approach to getting things done, but one that has special rewards. From service to the public, you may gain a very special sense of accomplishment and personal satisfaction, one that comes from helping others and from pursuing the public interest.

What Is Public Administration?

We have already described public administration as the management of public programs. But to elaborate on this definition, it helps to know a little history. Happily, there is only a little history to learn because public administration, at least in this country, is a relatively young field of study. Of course, people have been engaged in the management of public programs for thousands of years. (For example, imagine the administrative headaches involved in building the Egyptian pyramids!) However, the self-conscious study of public administration is a fairly recent development, often dated to the work of French and German scholars in the late nineteenth century. Public administration as we know it today in the United States began as the study of government administration, and that study began as part of late-nineteenth-century efforts to reform governmental operations. Most scholars and practitioners date the beginnings of the deliberate study of public administration in this country to an 1887 essay written by Woodrow Wilson (then scholar, later president). Although some have recently questioned the influence Wilson had on the field, there is no question that his essay marks the symbolic beginning of American public administration.

Wilson's essay was basically reformist in nature, and highly practical. It was designed to address the inefficiency and open corruption that had become a part of government during the late 1880s and to suggest certain remedies within the administration of government. Wilson argued that although scholars and practitioners had focused on political institutions (such as Congress or the presidency), too little attention had been paid to administrative questions—the questions of how the government actually operates. The result, according to Wilson, was that it was becoming "harder to run a constitution than to frame one" (Wilson, 1887, p. 200). Wilson first wanted the work of government agencies to be accomplished more effectively. He felt that such organizations would operate best if they pursued the private sector's commitment to efficient or "businesslike" operations. Wilson, of course, wrote in a period during which business, industry, and technology were developing in rapid and surprising new ways. Like others, he admired the managerial philosophies that business seemed to be developing. Among these notions, Wilson particularly favored the idea of concentrating power in a single authority atop a highly integrated and centralized administrative structure. His recommendation of a strong chief executive has been echoed by writers (and chief executives!) even to the present.

The men and women who followed Wilson in discussions of what came to be called public administration were very practical people, concerned with reforming governmental structures and making them more efficient. But they were also quite careful to place these concerns within the context of democratic government. How might the principles of democracy, including such lofty ideals as liberty and justice, be extended throughout government and throughout society? Indeed, Leonard D. White, one of the most thoughtful of the early writers, commented that "the study of public administration…needs to be related to the broad generalizations of political theory concerned with such matters as justice, liberty, obedience, and the role of the state in human affairs" (White, 1948, p. 10). As we will see, a continued concern for operating efficiently while at the same time operating in a way consistent with democratic values marks the field of public administration even today.

Values of Democracy

Because their commitment to democratic values so clearly affects the work of those in public and nonprofit organizations in this country, it may be helpful to briefly review some of the key commitments we associate with democratic governance. The term *democracy* well reflects its roots: the Greek words *demos,* meaning "people," and *kratis,* meaning "authority." Generally speaking, democracy refers to a political system in which the interests of the people at large prevail. However, it is clear that within these broad parameters there are many different conceptions of democracy. For example, at the end of World War II, representatives of the United States, Great Britain, France, and Russia met to consider the "democratization" of Germany. Yet, it soon became apparent that the Russian idea of democracy was quite different from the Western view. While Westerners associated democracy with such ideas as free elections, freedom of the press, freedom of movement, and the freedom to criticize the government, the Russians had quite a different conception. For them, democracy did not necessarily mean government by or of the people, but rather whether government policy is carried out *in the interest* of the people.

Even today, the term *democratic* is used in many different ways by many different people. For example, North Korea, a highly authoritarian state, claims aspects of democracy such as a multiparty system. In the American experience, however, there is general agreement that democracy refers to a political system—a way of ordering power and authority in which decision-making power is widely shared among members of the society. Or to put it in terms of control, democracy is a system in which many ordinary citizens exercise a high degree of control over their leaders. (In either case, the opposite would be an *oligarchy,* government by the few, or an *autocracy,* government by one.)

But democracy is defined not only in terms of processes or procedures (for example, rule by many), but also by several important cultural values that are typically pursued in a democratic society. Among these, three—individualism, equality, and liberty—have been of special importance to those who have helped shape the American idea of democracy. The first is *individualism,* the idea that the dignity and integrity of the individual is of supreme importance. Individualism suggests that achieving the fullest potential of each individual is the best measure of the success of our political system. It is the idea of individualism that is reflected in the familiar phrasing of the Declaration of Independence—that all persons are endowed by their Creator with certain inalienable rights and that it is the purpose of government to secure those rights.

Second is the idea of *equality,* which does not mean that all persons are equal in their talents or possessions, but that each individual has an equal claim to life, liberty, and the pursuit of happiness. In this view, each person should be seen as an end, not as a means; no one should be a mere tool of another. Moreover, equality in the field of government would suggest that differences in wealth or position are not sufficient reasons for giving one group preference over another. In a democracy, each one has an equal claim to the attention of the system and should be able to expect just outcomes.

A third central value of a democratic society is *liberty,* or freedom. This idea suggests that the individual citizen of a democracy should have a high degree of self-determination. You should have the maximum opportunity to select your own purposes in life and to choose the means to accomplish them. Liberty is more than just the absence of constraints; it suggests the freedom to act positively in pursuit of one's own ends. Only by allowing individuals the freedom to choose, it is argued, will social progress occur.

The influence of these themes on the development of public administration is undeniable, although, as we will see, people differ over the degree to which they influence the day-to-day operations of public agencies. Similarly, the way in which democracy has been operationalized in the American political tradition has had important influences on the operation of public organizations. For example, take the traditional separation of legislative, executive, and judicial functions. The primary task of the legislative branch is to make policy through the enactment of legislation, the primary task of the executive branch is the faithful execution or implementation of policy, and the primary task of the judicial branch is the interpretation of the law, especially as it relates to constitutional guarantees.

David Rosenbloom of American University has argued that these three functions of government are related to three views of the role of public administrators in American society (Rosenbloom, 1993, p. 15):

1. The *managerial approach* to public administration, which Rosenbloom connects to the executive function, emphasizes the management and organization of public organizations. As with Wilson, this view sometimes suggests that management in the public sector is very much like that in the private sector; that is, it is primarily concerned with efficiency.

2. The *political approach* to public administration, related to the legislative function in government, is more concerned about ensuring constitutional safeguards, such as those already mentioned. Efficiency becomes less a concern than effectiveness or responsiveness.

3. Finally, the *legal approach* to public administration, related to the judicial function, emphasizes the administrator's role in applying and enforcing the law in specific situations. It is also concerned with the adjudicatory role of public organizations.

Although we will examine these various approaches in more detail as we move through the book, it is important to understand at the outset that all actions of public administrators take place within an important political context: a commitment to democratic ideals and practices. Yet, today, that ideal is somewhat tarnished. Americans' trust in government has been steadily declining over the last several decades. Questions are being raised not only about the quality and productivity of government, but also about the responsiveness of government to the people (see the box "Public Administration in History: The Democratic Dream"). This tension will be a persistent theme as we examine contemporary approaches to the study and practice of public administration. Borrowing a phrase from earlier times, the task of public administrators today is still to "make democracy suitable for modern conditions." Doing so in a time of confusion and mistrust will be a special challenge to those in public administration as we move through the twenty-first century. Restoring trust in government and public service is not merely a responsibility of elected officials; it is a responsibility of appointed administrators as well. Keep this in mind as we examine the various approaches and techniques that are appropriate to public administration today.

Public Administration in History

THE DEMOCRATIC DREAM

The predominant American political belief—attained, pretended, or otherwise—from before the establishment of the republic and throughout the nation's history has been the democratic dream, nominally based on some version of popular representation and governance. Virtually every political structure and reform has been predicated on some mode of the democratic, egalitarian ethos, even as they oscillated back and forth between its Jeffersonian and Hamiltonian poles. Indeed, to imagine a widespread domestic political movement (and probably foreign policy initiative) that does not in some very visible manner drape itself in the sacred vestment of democracy is inconceivable.

It is in this ambience that American political philosophies, politics themselves, and even certain professions (e.g., public administration) were created and nurtured. Not surprisingly, public service and public administration in the United States have shared a similar democratic coloration. From the early days of the professional public administrator—when Woodrow Wilson temporarily partitioned "politics" and "administration" into separate entities—we find a solid stream of democratic theory underpinning and underlining contemporary public administration.

But the Constitution cannot serve as a singular political poultice for whatever ails the body politic. Within the country at large, there is a tangible sense that as often as appeals are made to the nation's democratic benchmarks, these are more calls to a fading faith than references to reality. Americans are apparently disenchanted with their politics, both in terms of substance and process. Our public life is rife with discontent. Americans do not believe they have much to say about how they are governed and do not trust government to do the right thing.

SOURCE: Reprinted by permission from *Democracy and the Policy Sciences* by Peter deLeon, State University of New York Press, © 1997, State University of New York. All rights reserved.

Contrasting Business and Public Administration

One issue, however, deserves further comment up front. Even though work in public and nonprofit organizations is guided by commitments to democratic ideals, it is also involved with management, and, for that reason, public administration is often confused with business management. Indeed, such confusion has occasionally been prominent in the field of public administration. (As we have already seen, early writers in the field often suggested that government should become more like business, a sentiment heard even today.) Certainly, there are some similarities between business and public administration. Managers across all sectors—public, private, and nonprofit—are involved in questions of organizational design, the allocation of scarce resources, and the management of people. But most observers would agree that the primary distinction between business and public service is that business is primarily concerned with making a profit, while public service is concerned with delivering services or regulating individual or group behavior in the public interest. All would agree that the context of public and nonprofit management significantly alters the work itself. Nonprofit management is characterized by ambiguity, pluralistic decision making, and visibility (see the box "Exploring Concepts: Public Administration Is Different from Business").

Exploring Concepts

PUBLIC ADMINISTRATION IS DIFFERENT FROM BUSINESS

- The objectives are much more ambiguous.
- There are multiple decision centers.
- Public administrators operate with much greater visibility.

Ambiguity One difference between public administration and business management lies in the purposes to be served. In most businesses, even those with service objectives, the bottom-line profit is the basic measure of evaluating how good a job the organization is doing. In turn, the performance of individual managers can, in many cases, be directly measured in terms of their unit's contribution to the overall profit of the company. This is not true of public or nonprofit agencies, where the objectives of the organization may be more ambiguous and where making or losing money is not the main criterion for success or failure.

Often the objectives of public and nonprofit organizations are stated in terms of service; for example, an agency's mission may be to protect the quality of the environment or to provide an adequate level of rehabilitative services to the disabled. Yet, such service objectives are much harder to specify and to measure. What does "quality" mean with respect to the environment? What level of service to the disabled is "adequate"? The difficulty of specifying objectives such as these makes it harder to assess the performance of government agencies and, in turn, their managers. Moreover, most businesses wouldn't tolerate a money-losing operation in a depressed area, but a public or nonprofit organization, though equally attentive to the money being spent, might well consider meeting human needs more important than the financial "bottom line."

Pluralistic Decision Making A second difference between work in public service and in business is that public service, at least in a democratic society, requires that many groups and individuals have access to the decision process. As a result, decisions that might be made rapidly by one individual or a small group in a business might, in a public or nonprofit organization, require input from many diverse groups and organizations. Consequently, it is difficult to speak of specific decision centers in government. W. Michael Blumenthal, a business executive who became secretary of the treasury, described the situation this way:

> If the President said to me, you develop [an economic policy toward Japan], Mike, the moment that becomes known there are innumerable interest groups that begin to play a role. The House Ways and Means Committee, the Senate Finance Committee, and every

member on them and every staff member has an opinion and seeks to exert influence. Also, the Foreign Relations Committee, the oversight committees, and then the interest groups, business, the unions, the State Department, the Commerce Department, OMB, Council of Economic Advisers, and not only the top people, but all their staff people, not to speak of the President's staff and the entire press. (Blumenthal, 1983, p. 30)

The pluralistic nature of public decision making has led many business executives who have worked in the public or nonprofit sectors to comment that this feature makes public and nonprofit management much more difficult than management in the private sector. But, as Blumenthal points out, "the diversity of interests seeking to affect policy is the nature and essence of democratic government" (Blumenthal, 1983, pp. 30–31). Many have also found that this aspect of public service is particularly challenging and rewarding.

Visibility Finally, managers in public and nonprofit organizations seem to operate with much greater visibility than their counterparts in industry. Public service in a democratic society is subject to constant scrutiny by both the press and the public. The media seem to cover everything you do, and this may be a mixed blessing. On the one hand, media coverage enables the leaders of the organization to communicate rapidly to external and internal audiences. On the other hand, the media's constant scrutiny of policy positions and their labeling of inconsistencies and policy differences as weaknesses can be limiting to free discussion of issues in their formulation stage. And, of course, the occasional intrusions of the press into even the most mundane personal matters can be excessive; one local newspaper even reported a problem a new city manager was having with his refrigerator! Yet, executives in government realize that it is essential to a democratic society that their work be visible to the public and subject to the interest and control of the citizenry. Indeed, one of the current concerns of public executives is how to increase the "transparency" of their work, something we will explore in more detail later.

What Would You Do?

You have just been appointed city manager of a city of 30,000 in the upper Midwest. While the economy of the area is generally stable, there is talk of one of the area's major industrial firms moving out, taking much-needed jobs from the community. On the other hand, that firm has been a persistent contributor to pollution in the area. The city council seems evenly divided on whether to make an effort to keep the firm and its jobs or simply let it go. In your first six months on the job, what would you do?

Thinking about Public Administration Today

With this background, we can now think more carefully about how the field of public administration has traditionally been described and how we might develop an action orientation toward the study of public administration suitable to a contemporary world. In terms of definition, many early writers spoke of administration as a function of government, something that occurred in many shapes and forms throughout government. There were obviously administrative activities performed in the executive branch, but there were also administrative functions performed in the legislative and judicial branches. Some even noted that from time to time any single official might engage in both legislative and administrative functions.

Somewhat later, public administration was viewed as merely concerned with the activities of the executive agencies of government. In the words of an early text, public administration is concerned with the "operations of the administrative branch only" (Willoughby, 1927, p. 1). By the 1950s, such a perspective was so firmly entrenched that the leading text of that period stated, "By public administration is meant, in common usage, the activities of the executive branches of national, state, and local governments; independent boards and commissions set up by Congress and state legislatures; government corporations; and certain other agencies of a specialized character" (Simon et al., 1950, p. 7). Modern definitions of public administration have returned to the traditional view, giving attention to administrative officials in all branches of government and even focusing on those in nonprofit organizations.

For our purposes, a formal definition of the field may be less important than trying to discover how public administration is experienced by those in the "real world." Our commitment to an action orientation suggests that we try to determine the kinds of activities engaged in by public administrators and the environmental factors that help to shape their work. We have already seen how the ambiguity of service objectives, the pluralistic nature of governmental decision making, and the visibility of management in the public and nonprofit sectors create a context in which managerial work is significantly different from that in other settings. From the standpoint of the real-world administrator, the things that really make the difference in the way you operate are not whether you are employed by a government agency, but whether you work under circumstances that feature an ambiguity of objectives, a multiplicity of decision centers, and high public visibility.

Networking

The leading national organization for those in the field of public administration is the American Society for Public Administration. See www.aspanet.org. Other related organizations with helpful websites include the National Academy of Public Administration at www.napawash.org; the Association for Public Policy Analysis and Management at www.appam.org; the International City Management Association at www.icma.org; the American Political Science Association at www.apsanet.org; the Alliance for Nonprofit Management at www.allianceonline.org; the Independent Sector at www.independentsector.org; and the Academy of Management, Public and Nonprofit Division at http://division.aomonline.org/pnp/.

Publicness These features in turn all derive from the simple fact that the public or nonprofit manager is pursuing public purposes. In terms of the actions and experiences of the public administrator, therefore, we may say that it is the "publicness" of the work of the public or nonprofit manager that distinguishes public administration from other similar activities. This view of the administrator's role suggests that, as a public or non-profit manager, you must operate with one eye toward managerial effectiveness and the other toward the desires and demands of the public. It recognizes that you are likely to experience an inevitable tension between efficiency and responsiveness as you work in governmental or nongovernmental organizations, a tension that will be absolutely central to your work.

Let us highlight some of the implications of this orientation. Many commentators point out that the distinction between public and private management is no longer simply a distinction between business and government or between profit and service. In fact, more and more frequently, we encounter situations in which traditionally public organizations are pursuing enhanced revenues (profits?), and traditionally private organizations are concerned with the provision of services. What is important is not merely what is being sought, but rather whose interest is being served. On this basis, a private enterprise is one in which private interests privately arrived at are paramount. A public organization, on the other hand, is one in which public interests publicly arrived at are paramount.

There is a trend in our society for greater openness and responsiveness on the part of many organizations. Most associations and nonprofit organizations would fit this mold, and managers in those organizations must certainly be attentive to both efficiency and responsiveness. But many corporations as well are finding it important to open their decision-making processes to public scrutiny and involvement. The range of organizations engaged in public service (and the applicability of public and nonprofit management) seems ever-increasing.

Certainly this trend has become even more important over the last couple of decades as more and more public problems require building collaborations or networks involving public, private, and nonprofit organizations (O'Leary & Bingham, 2009). In part this result has come about as government staffing has been decreased and more and more services are contracted out to private and nonprofit organizations. In part it has come about because the complexities of the problems we face require the involvement of many groups. Building networks of organizations to address public problems obviously makes solutions more difficult. "As more public programs are delivered by private and nonprofit actors, and as many more public programs rely on intricate public-private-nonprofit partnerships, it is ever harder to make sure the right dots are connected well" (Kettl, 2009, p. 26). Similarly, these arrangements make issues of responsibility and accountability more difficult as well, but they do represent the changing face of public administration that you will encounter.

The Global Context   We need to also recognize that changing economic conditions have combined with technological developments to mean that public administration is no longer bound by national borders, as the traditional definitions of the field implied. Today the international dimensions of public administration are more important than ever. Understanding the activities of political and administrative officials in other countries is important not only for those who will spend part of their careers outside the United States, but also for those who will work at home. Increasingly, city managers, even in small communities, find that to be effective in local economic development activities, they must be experts in international business. But global interdependencies will affect us in other ways as well; for example, the deforestation in Brazil, Africa, and the Philippines will directly affect the quality of our own environment. And, of course, we cannot overlook our obligation to help reduce poverty and hunger throughout the world.

Several diverse—indeed, competing—views have emerged relating to this globalization trend. They range from a critical perspective, in which the trend is seen as an attempt by developed nations to introduce Western values into other regions, to what supporters believe to be a chance to extend employment opportunities and wealth creation into impoverished nations. This latter view suggests that, over time, all of us in the global village will benefit from the forces of globalization and the internationalization of economic markets.

The impact of globalization on public administration should not be underestimated. However, relating to the internationalization process is a pattern that carries perhaps even greater implications: decentralization. Central governments increasingly are handing over new powers and responsibilities to local and regional authorities. And in many cases, these jurisdictions lack the capacity and resources to deal effectively with their newfound authority.

To better understand these trends, and what they mean for public administration, the development of more globalized, comparative forms of analysis and practice will be critical. We will require both an understanding of international issues and a way of more effectively managing with global issues in our own communities. So as we continue to live in our "global village," we will be challenged to deal with opportunities and threats that defy national boundaries. Our systems of governance, consequently, will need to reflect our concern for the public interest—both at home and abroad.

We now have a notion of the complexity of work in the public and nonprofit sectors—the complexity inherent in the technical work of governmental and nongovernmental agencies, but, even more important, the complexity of the political and ethical context in which managers operate. Indeed, as noted before, this complexity will provide a theme that ties together many aspects of your work as an administrator. The way you set objectives, the way you develop budgets and hire personnel, the way you interact with other organizations and with your own clientele, the way you evaluate the success or failure of your programs—all of these aspects of your work as an administrator, and many more, are directly affected by the fact that you will be managing in the public interest.

What Do Public Administrators Do?

An action orientation to public administration requires that we focus on what public and nonprofit managers actually do—how they act in real-world situations. How do they spend their time? What skills do they require to do their work well? What are the rewards and frustrations of public service? From the perspective of the administrator, we can ask, what characterizes the most effective and responsible public or nonprofit management? What are the demands on administrators? What are the satisfactions that public managers draw from their work?

We will approach these issues by concentrating on the skills managers need to accomplish their work. In a classic article in the *Harvard Business Review*, Robert Katz provided the first major descriptions of the general skills all managers need: conceptual, technical, and human (Katz, 1974):

1. Conceptual skills include the ability to think abstractly, especially in regard to the manager's concept of the organization. This category also involves the ability to see the organization as a whole, how all the parts or functions work and fit together, and how making a change in one part will affect other parts. Conceptual skills also include the ability to see how the organization, or parts of it, relate to the organization's environment.

2. Technical skills refer to an understanding of, and proficiency in, the methods, processes, and techniques for accomplishing tasks. These are, for example, the skills of an accountant who can conduct an audit or develop an income statement or the skills of a mechanic who can repair an engine.

3. Human skills involve the capacity to work effectively as a member of a group or the ability to get others to work together effectively. ("Others" may include subordinates, superiors, managers at the same level, or virtually anyone with whom one might work on a given project or assignment.)

All these skills are important to managers, but they are not equally important to all managers. Katz makes a strong argument that technical skills are most important to managers at the supervisory level who manage day-to-day operations but become less and less important as the level of management increases. On the other hand, conceptual skills are most important to top-level managers who must deal with the organization as a whole rather than with just one or a few parts of it. Conceptual skills are less important at the middle-management level and least important at the supervisory level.

Human skills, however, maintain a constant, high level of importance; they are critical regardless of one's level. How managers' human skills are employed may vary from level to level (for example, top managers lead more meetings than supervisory managers), but as a category, human skills remain the one constant for managerial success. In this book, we will consider the knowledge and values associated with public management (conceptual skills), the techniques public managers require in such areas as budgeting and personnel (technical skills), and the personal and interpersonal qualities that help managers work effectively with others (human skills).

An Inventory of Public Management Skills

One way to elaborate on an action approach is to create an inventory of the skills and competencies required for successful public and nonprofit management. There are many ways such an inventory can be constructed. One of the best ways is to talk with public and nonprofit managers about their work, as we suggest in exercise 1 at the end of the chapter. Several research studies have sought to answer this question by identifying the skills that are critical to managerial success. Of these studies, an early study by the federal government's Office of Personnel Management (OPM) is particularly helpful (Flanders & Utterback, 1985). The OPM study was based on information gathered from a large number

Networking

Websites dealing with management issues at the federal level include the Office of Personnel Management at www.opm.gov and those services listed at www.usa.gov. You might also be interested in the websites of the following: *Governing* magazine at www.governing.com; the *Chronicle of Philanthropy* at www.philanthropy.com; *Government Executive* magazine at www.govexec.com; and *The Public Manager* at www.thepublicmanager.org.

of highly effective federal managers and produced a description of the broad elements of managerial performance at the supervisory, managerial, and executive levels.

According to the OPM study, the competencies of managers include being sensitive to agency policies and national concerns; representing the organization and acting as a liaison to those outside the organization; establishing organizational goals and the processes to carry them out; obtaining and allocating necessary resources to achieve the agency's purposes; effectively utilizing human resources; and monitoring, evaluating, and redirecting the work of the organization. But the OPM researchers recognized that managerial excellence requires not only doing the job, but doing it well. For this reason, they developed a set of skills, attitudes, and perspectives that seemed to distinguish the work of highly successful managers.

Different skills are required at different levels. As managers move up the organizational ladder, they must accumulate increasingly broader sets of skills. The researchers suggest, for example, that first-line supervisors must apply communication skills, interpersonal sensitivity, and technical competence to ensure effective performance on their own part and within the work unit. In addition, their actions must begin to reflect those characteristics in the next ring: leadership, flexibility, an action orientation, and a focus on results.

Middle managers, on the other hand, must demonstrate all these characteristics of effectiveness and begin to acquire the skills listed in the outer ring: a broad perspective, a strategic view, and environmental sensitivity. Executives at the highest levels of public service who are responsible for the accomplishment of broad agency objectives must demonstrate the full complement of effectiveness characteristics to be most successful. Clearly, a wide diversity of skills, regardless of how the job is constructed or of the style in which it is executed, will be essential to your success as a manager.

A more recent study by the OPM elaborated the core qualifications expected of the highest-level government executives, in this case focusing on those characterizing the Senior Executive Service. This study first presented five executive core qualifications: leading change, leading people, results driven, business acumen, and building coalitions. These qualifications were complemented by six "competencies": interpersonal skills, oral communication skills, integrity or honesty, written communication skills, continual learning, and public service motivation (http://www.opm.gov/ses/recruitment/qualify.asp).

Voices of Public Administrators

Studies such as that of the OPM are helpful in understanding what you need to know and what you must be able to do to be successful in public administration. But how does it actually "feel" to work in a public or nonprofit organization? The best way to answer this question is to let some public servants speak for themselves. Not long ago, we spoke to two outstanding professionals in the field of public administration about their views of the field and their feelings about their work. The following accounts are based on those interviews. Jan C. Perkins served for many years as city manager of Fremont, California. When asked about her motivations for entering the field of public administration, this was her reply:

> I was interested in improving the quality of life for all people and increasing the access of women and minorities. I believed that I could have the most impact by being involved in local government at a management level.
>
> The most rewarding aspects of my work have been being able to articulate the mission of the city and focus my resources and efforts in effectively meeting that mission, solving the problems of residents, and seeing employees grow and develop.
>
> Those considering public service careers should understand that managing in the public arena is different from that in a private corporation. It requires a commitment to values such as providing quality services for all and dealing with all people on an equal level. It is very important that people who enter the public service do so with a high standard of ethical behavior and an ability to deal honestly and directly with all people.

Michael Stahl works for the federal government in the Environmental Protection Agency. He reflected on his motivations for public service:

> I entered public service because I viewed (and still do) government as an instrument to solve social problems. Democratic government can be a tremendous positive force in society, and in spite of recent political rhetoric and prevailing political ideology, I am convinced that the institutions and programs of government are of vital importance to the nation and that public service is a noble calling.
>
> If you are considering a career in the public service, take the time to reflect on your motivation for entering the public service, because there are right reasons and wrong reasons. You are entering for the right reasons if you want to make a contribution to the solution of social problems, promote democratic values and ethical standards in using the powers of government, and if the concept of serving the public good is a passion. You are entering for the wrong reasons if you are looking for public adulation and recognition for your accomplishments, seeking material or financial rewards as compensation for your hard work, or expecting to acquire levels of power and change the world according to your own plan. Those entering for the wrong reasons will be bitterly disappointed. Yet, for those whose passion is to contribute to the public good, government service can represent the single most satisfying way of translating your passion into ideas and events for improving the quality of life for scores of people.

CourseReader Assignment

Log in to **www.cengage.com** and open CourseReader to access the reading:

Read "Confessions of a Public Service Junkie" and "The Value of Public Service."

What does this article say about the passions and commitments that motivate public servants? How important is it to you to "make a difference"?

Obviously, these professionals take very seriously their commitment to serving others. In making such a commitment, they participate in a long and proud tradition. Indeed, public service has historically been considered one of the highest callings in our society and has been even more highly regarded in other countries, such as France and Japan.

Without question, the idea of serving others has enormous appeal, in part because of the great joy and satisfaction it brings. Those working in public organizations experience almost daily the rewards of public service.

Why Study Public Administration?

Students come to introductory courses in public administration for many different reasons. Many students recognize the vast array of positions in government (and elsewhere) that require training in public administration and hope that the course will provide basic information and skills that will move them toward careers as public or nonprofit managers. These students seek to understand the field of public administration, but also to sharpen their own skills as potential administrators. (See the box "Exploring Concepts: Why Study Public Administration?")

Exploring Concepts

WHY STUDY PUBLIC ADMINISTRATION?

- To prepare for administrative positions
- To combine technical and managerial training
- To help business and government interact
- To influence public organizations as a citizen

Other students, whose interests lie in technical fields as wide-ranging as engineering, teaching, natural resources, social work, and the fine arts, recognize that at some point in their careers their jobs may involve management in the public sector. The engineer may become director of a public works department; the teacher may become school principal; the natural resources expert may be asked to run an environmental quality program; the social worker may administer a welfare program; or the fine arts major may direct a publicly supported gallery or museum. In these cases, and others like them, the individual's technical expertise may need to be complemented by managerial training.

Networking

The National Association of Schools of Public Affairs and Administration is the accrediting body for programs in public administration and pursues other educational matters. See its home page at www.naspaa.org and see a list of NASPAA-accredited Master of Public Administration programs at http://www.naspaa.org/accreditation/NS/roster.asp.

Other students may have no expectations whatsoever of working in a public agency, but they recognize that as corporate executives, as businesspeople, or merely as citizens, they are likely to be called upon to interact with those in public organizations. Someone who owns a small business might wish to sell products or services to a city, a county, or some other governmental body; partners in an accounting firm might seek auditing contracts with a local or state government; or a construction firm might bid on the design and construction of a new public building. In each case, knowledge of the operations of public agencies would be not only helpful but essential.

A final group of students, a group overlapping any of the previous three, might simply recognize the importance of public agencies in the governmental process and the impact of public organizations on their daily lives. They might wish to acquire the knowledge and skills that would enable them to more effectively analyze and influence public policy. Some will find the world of public administration a fascinating field of study in its own right and pursue academic careers in public affairs. Because understanding the motives for studying public administration will also give us a more complete view of the variety and importance of managerial work in the public sector, we will examine each in greater detail.

CourseReader Assignment

Log in to www.cengage.com and open CourseReader to access the reading:

Read "The Public Sector as a Career Choice: Antecedents of an Expressed Interest in Working for the Federal Government," by Dennis Doverspike et al. There are many reasons that people choose to work in public administration, and many of these have to do with their commitment to public service and their wanting to make a difference in their communities. Others have to do with their personal experiences growing up.

Consider your own motivations and those of your friends. What has stimulated your interest in public administration? Might you consider a career in federal, state, or local government or in a nonprofit organization? What might affect your choice? How important is it to you to make a difference in your community?

Preparing for Administrative Positions

You may be among those who wish to use the introductory public administration course as a stepping-stone to a career in public service. If so, you will find that these careers take many forms. We sometimes make distinctions among program managers, staff managers, and policy analysts. *Program managers* range from the executive level to the supervisory level and are in charge of particular governmental or nongovernmental programs, such as those in environmental quality or transportation safety. Their job is to allocate and monitor human, material, and financial resources to meet the service objectives of their agency. *Staff managers,* on the other hand, support the work of program managers through budgeting and financial management, personnel and labor relations, and purchasing and procurement. Meanwhile, *policy analysts* provide important information about existing programs through their research into the operations and impacts of the programs; moreover, analysts help bring together information about new programs, assess the possible effects of different courses of action, and suggest new directions for public policy. Managers and analysts may work with the chief executive, with the legislature, with officials at other levels of government, and with the public in framing and reframing public programs.

As we will see, the work of public and nonprofit organizations also encompasses a wide variety of substantive areas. Think for a moment of the range of activities the federal government engages in. The federal government touches upon nearly every aspect of American life, from aeronautics, air transportation, and atmospheric sciences; to helping the homeless, juvenile delinquents, and migrant workers; to working with waste management, wage standards, and water quality. In each area, skilled managers are called upon to develop, implement, and evaluate government programs. But the work of managers at the federal level represents only a part of the work of those trained in public administration.

At the state and local levels of government, and in the nonprofit sector, even more opportunities exist. As we will see in Chapter 2, although there is only one federal government in this country, there are almost 89,000 state and local governments (these include cities, counties, and special districts) and more than 1.5 million nonprofit organizations. State and local government employment in this country amounts to almost 15 million persons (compared to under 3 million civilians employed at the federal level), and nearly 15 million people work for nonprofit organizations.

Obviously, the work of government at the state and local levels is different from that at the federal level. State and local governments, for example, do not directly provide for the national defense; however, most have police forces, which the federal government does not have. There are also other positions at the state and local levels that do not have exact counterparts at the federal level. For example, the president or chancellor of your state university is a public administrator with significant and unusual responsibilities; the city manager in a local community is a professional administrator appointed by a city council to manage the various functions of local government.

And public service is not limited to work in government. Beyond employment in federal, state, or local government, those trained in public administration will find many other opportunities. Directors of nonprofit organizations at the state and local levels, as well as those in similar associations at the national level, often find that the skills required for their jobs—skills that combine managerial training with an understanding of the political system—are the skills developed in public administration courses. Again, to demonstrate the breadth of these activities, we might note that there are large numbers of nonprofit associations at the national level alone, ranging from well-known groups such as the American Medical Association or the American Bar Association, to trade groups such as the American Frozen Food Institute and the National Association of Bedding Manufacturers, to professional associations such as the American Society for Public Administration and those representing a particular field of interest, such as the Metropolitan Opera Guild. There is even an association of association executives: the American Society of Association Executives. Beyond these groups at the national level, there are numerous nonprofit groups operating at state and local levels—for example, local United Way organizations, local food banks, art leagues, or historic preservation groups.

Finally, those with training in public administration may work in a private corporation's public affairs division. Because of the increasing interaction across private, public, and nongovernmental sectors, corporations and nonprofit organizations often need special assistance in tracking legislation, developing and monitoring government contracts, and influencing the legislative or regulatory process. Thus, the combination of managerial and political skills possessed by someone with training in public administration can be highly valuable. The career possibilities in the field of public administration are seemingly endless.

Combining Technical and Managerial Training

Many students seek positions in public service as a primary career objective, whereas many others see the possibility of work in public administration as secondary, but nonetheless important, to their main field of interest. As noted, the work of government spans many areas; consequently, the people who work for government (one out of every six people in this country) come from a wide variety of professional backgrounds. There are engineers who work in the Defense Department and for NASA at the federal level, in state highway departments, and in local public works departments. People interested in natural resources may work for the U.S. Forest Service and the Environmental Protection Agency, in state conservation departments, and in local parks departments. Medical personnel may work for the Veterans Administration or the National Institute for Mental Health, for state health departments, and for local hospitals and health offices.

Governments at all levels hire social workers, planners, personnel specialists, accountants, lawyers, biologists, law enforcement officers, educators, researchers, recreation specialists, and agricultural specialists, just to mention a few. To illustrate the magnitude of federal government employment, over 725,000 work in national defense and foreign affairs, over 700,000 people work in the postal service, 340,000 are employed in health care, and 124,000 financial administrators work for the federal government (http://www2 .census.gov/govs/apes/09fedfun.pdf).

As mentioned earlier, people who have worked for some time within a technical field in a public organization are often promoted to managerial positions. A surgeon may become chief of surgery, a water pollution specialist may be asked to direct a pollution control project, or a teacher may become a school principal. Despite having started out in a technical field, these individuals find themselves in a managerial position; they are public administrators. Some people may desire promotion to a managerial position; others may not. (There are some jurisdictions in which continued advancement practically requires moving into an administrative position.) But whatever one's motivation, the new administrator soon discovers a completely new world of work. Now the most pressing questions are not the technical ones, but rather those having to do with management, with program planning and design, with supervision and motivation, and with balancing scarce resources. Often the situation is quite bewildering; it's almost as if one has been asked to change professions in midcareer from technical expert to public manager.

So many people from technical fields find themselves in managerial positions in the public sector that many of them seek training in public administration. For this reason, it is no longer unusual for students majoring in technical fields to take courses in public administration or for students to combine undergraduate training in a technical field with graduate training in public administration (even at midcareer). This, then, is a second reason for studying public administration: to prepare for the eventuality that work in a technical field of interest might lead you to a managerial position in the public sector.

Interaction of Business and Government

Even for students who never work for a public agency of any type, understanding the processes of policy formulation and implementation can be enormously helpful. One of the most important trends in American society is the increasing interaction of business and government. Clearly, the decisions of government affect the environment in which business operates, but government also specifically regulates many businesses and, of course, serves as the biggest single customer of business.

Those in business recognize that governmental decisions affect the economic climate. Most obvious are the effects of governmental decisions at the federal level. Consider, for example, the impact of government economic pronouncements on the stock market. State and local governments, however, also affect the business climate. The governors of many states have begun major campaigns to attract industry to their states, providing not only information and advice but also specific incentives for plants and industries that might relocate. Similar activities are being undertaken in more and more local communities, as cities recognize that they are in competition for economic development. At a minimum, business recognizes that the political climate of any locality directly affects the area's economic climate.

But the influence of government on business is more specific. At the federal level, major regulatory agencies, such as the Federal Communications Commission and the Federal Trade Commission, provide specific guidelines in which certain businesses must operate. Moreover, requirements of agencies such as the Environmental Protection Agency and the Occupational Safety and Health Administration restrict the operations of business so as to ensure the quality of air and water and the safety of working conditions. Similarly, at the state level, some agencies directly regulate specific businesses, while others act more generally to prevent unfair or unsafe practices. Even at the local level, through licensing and zoning practices, public organizations directly regulate business practice.

Government is also important as a consumer of business products and services. At the federal level, over $550 billion is spent each year on goods and services; in the Department of Defense alone, the figure is over $354 billion per year (http://www.census.gov/prod/2010pubs/cffr-09.pdf). Business is attentive to its customers, so it is not surprising that business is attentive to government!

For all these reasons, people in business are becoming increasingly aware of the need to understand in detail the work of government—how policies are made, how they are implemented, and how they may be influenced. Not only are more and more businesses developing public affairs offices to specialize in governmental operations, track policy developments, and attempt to influence policy, but they are also placing a greater premium on having executives at all levels who understand how government agencies operate. Even if you plan a career in business, understanding the work of public organizations is an essential part of your training.

Influencing Public Organizations

Any of the motives for studying public administration we have discussed so far may bring you to an introductory course. There is, however, another more general reason you may wish to study public administration: to understand one important aspect of the governmental process so you can deal effectively with public issues that directly affect your life. We are all affected by the work of governmental and nongovernmental organizations, so it is helpful, and sometimes even essential, to understand the operations of these organizations.

We have become so accustomed to the pervasiveness of public service and the range of its influence that we sometimes forget just how often our lives are touched by public and nonprofit organizations. Imagine a typical day: We wake up in the morning to the sounds of a commercially regulated radio station or National Public Radio coming over a patented and Federal Communications Commission–registered clock radio operating on power supplied by either a government-regulated power company or a public utility. We brush our teeth with toothpaste produced under a government patent and trust that it has been judged safe (if not effective) by a federal agency. We use municipally operated water and sewer systems without thinking of the complexity of their operation. We dress in clothes produced under governmental restrictions and eat food prepared in accordance with government regulations and inspected by the government. We drive on a public highway, following government-enforced traffic laws, to a university substantially funded by federal, state, and sometimes local dollars to study from books copyrighted and catalogued by the Library of Congress. Though the day has hardly begun, our lives already have been touched by public organizations in a multitude of ways.

The importance of public administration in daily life is tremendous; consequently, the decisions made by governmental and nongovernmental officials (and not just elected officials) can affect us directly. Imagine, for example, that one day you discover that the loan program that is helping to finance your college education is being reviewed and will likely be revised in such a way that you will no longer be eligible for funding. In this case, you might well want to take some action to maintain your eligibility. Obviously, knowing something about the operations of government agencies, especially some of the ways administrative decisions can be influenced, would be of great help.

As citizens affected by the public service, understanding the operations of public and nonprofit organizations is helpful; it is even more important if one becomes personally involved in some aspect of the governmental process. For those reading this book, such involvement is actually rather likely. Indeed, if you are a college graduate, regardless of your major or field of interest, chances are quite good that at some point in your life you will engage in some kind of formal governmental activity. You may be elected to local, state, or national office; you may be asked to serve on a board or commission; or your advice concerning government operations in your area may be sought in other ways. You may also become involved in the work of nonprofit organizations or charities in your local community. In any of these cases, a thorough knowledge of the structure and processes of public organizations, both government and nonprofit organizations, will be of great importance.

Finally, those who are interested in understanding the work of public or nonprofit organizations may indeed find the field of public administration interesting from a more academic standpoint: studying and commenting on the operations of government and nonprofit organizations contribute to our understanding of the process of policy development and support the work of those in public organizations. The opportunities for academic careers in public administration, positions involving teaching and research, are many, and you may find yourself drawn to those opportunities. Even here, however, one begins with a concern for action.

What Would You Do?

You are the executive director of the Parents Anonymous organization in your area. Your organization is devoted to preventing child abuse and strengthening families. Recently one of your traditional sources of funding was terminated. You are faced with the prospect of reducing staff (and services) or coming up with new revenues. What would you do?

Making Things Happen

Of the many reasons to learn about public and nonprofit organizations, one theme seems to tie together the various interests: an interest in making things happen. Whether you are preparing for a career in the public sector with the possibility that you might someday manage a public agency, or simply preparing to influence the course of public policy and its implementation as it directly affects you or your business, your interest is in taking action and influencing what goes on in public and nonprofit organizations. It's one thing to gain knowledge of the field in the abstract, but most students want to learn those things that will make them more effective *actors* in the governmental process. Some of the more prominent actors are discussed in the box "Public Administration in History: Public Service: A Distinguished Profession."

Public Administration in History

PUBLIC SERVICE: A DISTINGUISHED PROFESSION

For my part, when I think of government service, in uniform and out, I think of individual men and women of genuine distinction who have served this country over the years and also of the amazing diversity of a service that can range from defending our borders to delivering our mail, curing disease to exploring outer space. I was looking at a civil service publication the other day containing an alphabetical list of well-known employees through the years "and found it began with a career civil servant named Neil Armstrong who went on TDY (temporary duty) to the moon" and concluded several pages later with Walt Whitman, the poet, who worked in the Department of the Interior and the U.S. Attorney [General's office]. How's that for diversity? Incidentally, the group also included four Nobel Prize winners and several important inventors, including Alexander Graham Bell, who among his other associations worked for the Census Bureau. There also were some other familiar names of people who shared your proud profession: Clara Barton, Washington Irving, Abraham Lincoln, Charles Lindbergh, Knute Rockne, Harry Truman, and James Whistler, to name but a few.

In my own experience, as one who served the federal government for some years, I look back on those periods as among the most exciting, challenging, and thoroughly demanding in life. I have often said, and still say, that I never worked harder than I did in my years as a public servant. I worked alongside some of the finest, most competent, thoroughly committed people I have ever known. I realize this does not comport with everything that you read in the papers or see on television, but I never miss a chance to point it out. My own experience in government left me with an abiding respect for the men and women who serve this nation as public employees.

SOURCE: Norman R. Augustine, Chairman and Chief Executive Officer of Martin Marietta Corporation, Address to the Federal Executive Board, Denver, Colorado, April 26, 1989. Text provided by the Council for Excellence in Government, Washington, D.C.

This book is geared toward action, toward how to make things happen in public service. Our perspective will be that of the actor, not the scholar, although an understanding of the world of administrative action is the basis for good scholarship as well. Action first requires a base of knowledge; there are certain things that you simply need to know about government and the administrative process to be effective. There are also value questions that must be settled in the course of making and carrying out public decisions. And, finally, there are both technical and interpersonal skills you must acquire to be effective in working with others in your chosen field. Selecting an action orientation, therefore, commits you to emphasizing all three areas: the knowledge, values, and skills that will help you to become more effective and responsible in your work with "real-life" public organizations.

Issues in Public Administration Theory and Practice

Throughout the chapters to come, our primary emphasis will be on action—those things that real-world actors do to be successful in public and nonprofit organizations. But action never stands alone. Without some degree of reflection, action is sterile and unguided. For this reason, we will outline two themes that have traditionally characterized work in public organizations and that continue to be of great importance today. As such, these themes—of politics and administration and of bureaucracy and democracy—provide a part of the intellectual and practical context of public administration. Although our purpose is to simply introduce these two themes, we suggest that they are most often manifest in contemporary public administration as a tension between efficiency and responsiveness. This tension is absolutely central to the work of public administrators today, and we will return to it frequently in our discussions of administrative action.

Politics and Administration

Even though the supposed dichotomy between politics and administration is one of the oldest issues in public administration, it continues to hold great relevance for administrators today. You will recall that an early essay by Woodrow Wilson framed the initial study of public administration in this country. In addition to emphasizing businesslike practices, Wilson was concerned with isolating the processes of administration from the potentially corrupting influences of politics. He wrote, "Administration lies outside the proper sphere of politics. Administrative questions are not political questions. Although politics sets the tasks for administration, it should not be suffered to manipulate its offices" (Wilson, 1887, p. 210). In other words, although policies were to be debated and decided by politicians, they were to be carried out by a politically neutral, professional bureaucracy. In this way, the everyday conduct of government would be isolated from the potentially corrupting influence of politics.

Other early writers joined Wilson in talking, at least analytically, about the distinction between politics (or policy) and administration. More practical reformers went further, creating governmental forms, such as the council-manager plan for local government, that were based on a separation of policy and administration. As we will see later, in this form of government, the council presumably makes the policy and the city manager carries it out. The council is engaged in politics (or policy) and the manager in administration.

Over the first few decades of this century, however, the distinction between policy and administration was increasingly broken down, even in council-manager governments. Managers found that they had expertise that was needed by policy makers and began to be drawn into the policy process. By about the middle of the century, Paul Appleby of Syracuse University would write simply, "Public administration is policy-making" (Appleby, 1949, p. 170).

The increasing involvement of administrators in the policy process was in part attributable to the fact that the operations of government—and in contemporary society, of nonprofit organizations—were becoming more complex, and the technical and professional skills needed to operate public agencies were dramatically increasing. As people with such skills and expertise became a part of public organizations, they were inevitably called upon to present their views. At the same time, the legislative branches of government (at all levels) found it difficult to be knowledgeable about every detail of government and, consequently, were forced to rely more and more on the expertise of those in public agencies. Additionally, the complexity of government meant that legislative bodies often found it necessary to state laws in general terms, leaving those within government agencies with considerable discretion to interpret those laws as they saw fit and, therefore, make policy daily.

Ensuring Accountability   The acknowledgment of the interaction of politics and administration does not make the question of their relationship any easier. If public administrators make policy, how can we be sure that the policies they make are responsible to the people (as we would expect in a democratic society)? Presumably, legislators must be at least somewhat responsive, or, come the next election, they will no longer be legislators. But what of administrators?

What Would You Do?

You have served three years as head of your state's human services agency. In general, your relationship with the governor has been quite good, and your relationship with the legislature (which is dominated by the governor's party) has been congenial as well. Recently, however, there has been a move in the legislature to reduce funding for a child-care program you think is essential to finding and maintaining employment for women on welfare. What would you do?

Traditionally, the answer was that the administrators were accountable to the legislators, who, in turn, were accountable to the people. But even that argument is somewhat tricky today. Those in public and nonprofit agencies do indeed both work with and report to legislatures (or boards), but they also shape public opinion through the information they provide. They mobilize for support inside and outside government and bargain with a variety of public and private groups. To a certain extent, they act as independent agents.

For this reason, more contemporary discussions of accountability (which we will elaborate on in Chapter 4) place an emphasis on measures that would supplement accountability to the legislature by either seeking a strong subjective sense of responsibility on the part of administrators or by providing structural controls to ensure responsibility. As we will see, some people have tried to assert professional standards in public and nonprofit organizations, while others have developed codes of ethics and standards of professional practice. Others have sought greater legislative involvement in the administrative process or more substantial legislative review. Still others have described mechanisms such as public participation in the administrative process or surveys of public opinion that would bring the administrator in closer alignment with the sentiments of the citizenry (something we will discuss further in Chapter 11).

The relationship between politics (or policy) and administration will be a theme that recurs throughout the remainder of this book. Although the classic dichotomy between politics and administration has become less distinct as the role of public administrators in the policy process has become more apparent, the question of the relationship between politics and administration remains central, simply because it goes to the heart of what public administration is all about. If public organizations differ from other organizations in our society, that difference must surely rest in the way public organizations participate in and respond to the public interest. But that issue merely leads us to another: the relationship between bureaucracy and democracy.

Bureaucracy and Democracy

A second theme that grew from early discussions of public administration had to do with the potential for conflict between democracy and bureaucracy. Let's start once again with democracy. One writer has defined the moral commitments of a democracy in terms of three standards. First, democratic principles assume that the individual is the primary measure of human value and that the development of the individual is the primary goal of a democratic political system. Second, democratic morality suggests that all persons are created equal—that differences in wealth, status, or position should not give one person or group an advantage over another. Third, democratic morality emphasizes widespread participation among the citizens in the making of major decisions (Redford, 1969, p. 8).

Set against these tenets of democracy are the ideals of bureaucratic management. The early scholars and practitioners in public administration were, of course, writing at a time when businesses were growing rapidly and beginning to use more complicated technologies and new ways of organizing appropriate to those technologies. To some extent the public sector looked to the field of business for models of organization. It found that the growth of large-scale business had led to the development of large and complex bureaucratic organizations, organizations that were built around values quite different from those of democracy. (Although the term *bureaucracy* is often used in a pejorative sense, as in "bureaucratic red tape," we will use it here in its more neutral and scientific sense: as a way of organizing work.) Consequently, the bureaucratic model of organizing was brought into the public sector.

The values of bureaucracy included first the need to bring together the work of many individuals in order to achieve purposes far beyond the capabilities of any single individual. Second, bureaucratic systems were to be structured hierarchically, with those at the top having far greater power and discretion than those at the bottom. Third, bureaucratic organization generally assumes that power and authority flow from the top of the organization to the bottom rather than the other way around. (We will examine the concept of bureaucracy in greater detail in Chapter 5.)

In contrast to the democratic value of individuality, there stood the bureaucratic value of the group or organization; in contrast to the democratic values of equality, there stood the bureaucratic hierarchy; and in contrast to the democratic values of participation and involvement, there stood the bureaucratic value of top-down decision making and authority.

How these values were to be reconciled became a difficult issue for early scholars and practitioners in the field of public administration, as it continues to be today. A variety of questions are raised. For example, is it proper for a democratic government to carry out its work through basically authoritarian organizations? The key issue turns out to be an emphasis on efficiency as the sole measure of agency success.

Efficiency versus Responsiveness

Those in public administration have long wrestled with the issues of politics and administration and of democracy and bureaucracy. Public and increasingly nonprofit managers have begun to experience these tensions more frequently in the day-to-day problems they face in terms of efficiency versus responsiveness. Indeed, in a sense, the two earlier issues seem to have dissolved into the single issue of efficiency versus responsiveness. On the one hand, there is the hope that public and nonprofit organizations will operate in the most efficient way possible, getting things done quickly and at the least cost to taxpayers and donors. On the other hand, public managers must be constantly attentive to the demands of the citizenry, whether those demands are expressed through the chief executive, through the legislature, or directly.

A practical and contemporary expression of this difficulty is presented in case study number 5 at the end of the chapter. (You might want to read it now.) The case relates a dispute that arose in the course of developing a new housing loan program. Although the case presents several different issues, most students reviewing the case focus their attention on the different interpretations that John and Carol have of their work. At first glance, John appears to be solely interested in doing things efficiently, while Carol appears to be much more concerned with responding to the needs of the client group. The case appears to be a classic illustration of the tension between efficiency and responsiveness, and indeed it is. But at a deeper level, the case also illustrates how complex the issues really are. You might say, for example, that John was trying to be efficient in response to the demands of those clients who had been waiting for their loans to be processed. You might also say that Carol, through her educational efforts, was helping to ensure a more efficient, long-term operation.

The main point, of course, is that in public organizations, you may frequently encounter difficulties in reconciling efficiency and responsiveness. A key to resolving the ethical questions raised in situations such as that faced by John and Carol is (1) understanding the various moral values represented on each side of the equation and then (2) engaging in ethical deliberation (and perhaps dialogue) to arrive at a proper approach to the problem. Interestingly enough, in this particular case, the real-life characters represented by John and Carol got together and talked through the differences in their respective approaches. The result was a course of action they both agreed on, one they felt met their obligations to be both efficient and responsive. In the real world, dialogue sometimes works!

To summarize this point, the themes of politics and administration and of bureaucracy and democracy have marked much of the history of the field of public administration. Today these themes seem often to manifest in the tension between efficiency and responsiveness. Are public agencies to concentrate only on creating the desired outcomes in the most efficient manner possible? Or should such agencies be responsive to the public interest and the public will, even though the public interest and the public will may not have been explicitly articulated by elected officials, especially those in the legislature? Time after time, you'll find evidence of this tension in discussions on public policy, human resources management, budgeting and financial management, and so on. The tension between efficiency and responsiveness remains an "unsolved mystery" of public administration. But perhaps for that reason, it is a tension that helps make public administration such a fascinating and dynamic field.

Summary and Action Implications

As noted, our focus in this book is on the individual administrator or the individual citizen seeking to influence public policy through the agencies of government or through other public and nongovernmental organizations. We consider in some detail the institutions, processes, and techniques required for work in the public and nonprofit sectors. But, most importantly, we examine the "real world" of public administration, the world as experienced by the administrator.

That world, as we have seen, is one for which you will need to develop certain capabilities to operate effectively and responsibly. Among these we include an understanding of the institutions and processes of government; an appreciation of the values underlying public service; technical skills in such areas as program design, budgeting, and personnel; interpersonal skills in communications, leadership, and decision making; and a capacity to "put it all together" to integrate knowledge, skills, and values appropriately.

Ideally, in studying the issues discussed in this book, you will develop a good sense of the political context of public administration; a sound understanding of your role in both policy development and policy implementation; a sensitivity to the moral and ethical questions inherent in the notion of public service; technical competence in areas such as planning and program development, budgeting, personnel, and performance management; facility with interpersonal relationships (including leadership, decision making, and communications); and the self-confidence and self-awareness to act effectively and responsibly in real-life situations. Though public administration in the abstract sometimes appears lifeless and remote, the real world of the practicing public administrator is a quite lively and interesting place, filled with challenging problems and unique opportunities.

STUDY QUESTIONS

1. Discuss some of the career opportunities available to those trained in public administration.

2. "One of the most important trends in American society is the increasing interaction of business and government." This quotation signals the need for better recognition and understanding of the interactions between business and government. Discuss the importance of this interaction and why a clear understanding of the relationship between the public and private sector is necessary.

3. The differences between public administration and business management are profound. Explain how the two fields are alike and how they differ. Why are the two terms not interchangeable?

4. How did early scholars, such as Woodrow Wilson, view the role of public administration in a democracy?

5. The term *democracy* can be interpreted in a variety of ways. What significant concepts helped form the democratic society within which American government operates?

6. What is the role of "publicness" in defining the work of public and nonprofit managers?

CASES AND EXERCISES

1. Interview a public administrator. Locate one or more people who work as managers or analysts in a public or nonprofit organization and interview them. The interviewees might work for a public university, local government, state or federal agency, or nonprofit organization. They might be a university administrator, a city manager or department director (public works or parks and recreation), a county official (such as a county clerk), a manager in state government (perhaps someone in a welfare office or a highway department), a federal government manager (in a local office of a department such as Social Security, Agriculture, or the Federal Aviation Administration), or someone who works in a local, state, or national nonprofit association. They might be a program manager, a staff manager, or a policy analyst.

   Ask the people you interview to describe their jobs, including the range of responsibilities they have and the knowledge, values, and skills that are important to them in their work. The following are some examples of questions you might want to ask:
   - Describe the work you do and how you came to this position. What is your educational and work background?
   - What impact does the work you do have on the community/state/nation/ and so on?
   - What do you find different or unusual about working in a public organization? How do you think your job compares to other jobs at a comparable level in business or industry?
   - What knowledge, values, and skills are important to your work? For instance, if you were hiring someone to take your place, what would you look for?

2. Consider the following case. As an administrative assistant in the Department of Finance of a midsize suburban community, you are asked by the director to contract with an accounting firm to audit the books of the ten major city departments. You develop a request for bids, advertise in the local newspaper, and send written notices to all the local accounting firms. In response, you receive five proposals, four from local firms and one from a Big Eight accounting firm based in a nearby city. The proposals are essentially the same with respect to cost and expected quality of work.

However, one firm, Jones and Denham, appears to have considerably more experience, having done similar audits locally in the past. Having gathered all the information you feel you need to make a decision, you make an appointment to report to the director early Tuesday morning. At lunch on Monday, however, a friend who knows you are working on the auditing contract casually mentions that a certain Mr. Howard of the Firm T. P. Howard and Co. is the brother-in-law of the mayor. T. P. Howard and Co. is one of the five firms that have submitted bids for the auditing contract. Later that afternoon, you receive a call from the mayor, asking for a report on the auditing contract. What do you say to the mayor? What do you recommend be done about the contract? What does this case say about the relationship between business and government?

3. Consider the following case. There wasn't much that David Wood couldn't do. He was an excellent teacher, a dedicated scholar, and a good department chair. He had been called to the chancellor's office to comment on a new curriculum proposal, one his faculty and he had discussed, and one they firmly opposed. The chancellor began the meeting by commenting on the excellent administrative work that David had been doing and on the possibility that he might be considered for a deanship that was opening up soon. David had always wanted to be a dean. He voiced very mild objection to the curriculum proposal and then promised to try to convince his faculty to support it.

   Moving from an academic position into an administrative position or from any technical position into an administrative position puts you in a different world, one with greater complexity and different pressures. What are some of the factors that affect those holding managerial jobs as opposed to technical jobs?

4. Consider the following case. Recently fraternities and sororities at a major mid-western university were informed that the property tax classification for their houses was being changed from "residential" to "commercial," a change that would increase the assessed values of the properties from 19 percent to 32 percent and would cost the Greek houses thousands of dollars in new taxes. The Greeks felt the change was inappropriate because, as one member stated, "There's not a fraternity or sorority on campus that makes a profit." On the other hand, a county official pointed out that the houses contain more than "four dwelling units," as the law describes it. Moreover, fraternities and sororities are probably not residential enterprises and are definitely not agricultural ones (as specified in the law), so they are relegated to the third "catch-all" category, "commercial and all others."

   If you were advising the Greek organizations as to how they might seek relief, what would you recommend? What kind of action should they take? Where should an appeal originate? How might it proceed?

5. As you consider the following case, remember the discussion under "Efficiency versus Responsiveness" earlier in this chapter. John Taylor and Carol Langley worked for a local, nonprofit community development agency. Following a rather massive reorganization of the agency in which a number of new programs were taken on, John was asked to supervise a new housing loan program and Carol was asked to assist

him. The program was designed to provide low-interest loans to people in rehabilitating housing in certain parts of the city. Although John and Carol had experience in related areas, neither was familiar with this particular program. To make matters worse, seminars to provide help in establishing such programs had been held some months earlier. John and Carol were simply given a manual and told to begin.

The program involved a number of new activities and took considerable time to set up. For example, it was necessary to train new housing inspectors to coordinate their inspection activities with those provided by the city government, and relationships had to be established with the other public and nonprofit agencies that would provide information about the applicants being processed.

John soon began receiving considerable pressure to complete the processing of the first group of applications within a brief period of time. For one thing, the first group of applicants consisted of some forty people who had originally applied for other programs but had been turned down. Because their applications had been on file in the agency for as long as one year, they were quite anxious to have their applications processed quickly. Initial visits and phone calls from several of the applicants made John quite aware of their feelings. In addition, however, John knew that this particular loan program would have a significant impact on the community and that, consequently, his doing an efficient job under these difficult circumstances would be important both to the agency and to his own future in public service.

Carol recognized the necessity to do the work as quickly as possible, but she also felt a special obligation to the applicants themselves. She took seriously the agency director's comment that the agency could use this opportunity to help "educate" the applicants about the procedures involved in such projects. She felt it was very important to check periodically on the inspections, cost estimates, loan amounts, financial information, and terms and conditions of the loans. Unlike John, who spent most of his time in the office, she talked frequently with the applicants, many of whom she knew personally from her previous position in the agency.

For each applicant, John and Carol were to accumulate a complete file of information about the financial status and rehabilitation project the applicant had in mind. This file was to be received and signed by the applicant, then forwarded to the federal regional office of HUD for further action.

John felt the process could be completed more quickly if Carol would simply get the applicants to sign a blank set of forms that could be kept at the office. When information was received regarding a loan, the appropriate items could be entered on the signed forms, bypassing the time involved reviewing each form with the applicant. Also, this procedure would eliminate the often lengthy process of coordinating several office visits to discuss the material.

When John asked Carol to obtain the signed forms, she refused. Not only was she concerned that the applicants see and understand the materials before signing, but she was also afraid that getting people to sign blank forms might be illegal. When she talked with John's supervisor about the request, she was told that the procedure was not illegal and had been used before by people in the regional office. Do you agree with John or Carol? Why? What should happen next?

FOR ADDITIONAL READING

Balutis, Alan P., Terry F. Buss, and Dwight Ink. *Transforming American Governance: Rebooting the Public Square*. Armonk, NY: M.E. Sharpe, 2011.

Ban, Carolyn. *How Do Public Managers Manage?* San Francisco: Jossey-Bass, 1995.

Bevir, Mark. *Democratic Governance*. Princeton, NJ: Princeton University Press, 2010.

Bevir, Mark. *The Sage Handbook of Governance*. Thousand Oaks, CA: Sage Publications, 2011.

Bowman, James S., Jonathan P. West, and Marcia A. Beck. *Achieving Competencies in Public Service: The Professional Edge*. 2nd ed. Armonk, NY: M.E. Sharpe, 2009.

Cayer, Joseph N., and Louis F. Weschler. *Public Administration: Social Change and Adaptive Management*. 2nd ed. San Diego, CA: Birkdale Publishers, 2003.

Frederickson, H. George. *The Spirit of Public Administration*. San Francisco: Jossey-Bass, 1997.

Hal, Rainey G. *Understanding and Managing Public Organizations*. 3rd ed. San Francisco: Jossey-Bass, 2003.

Kettl, Donald F. *The Next Government of the United States: Why Our Institutions Fail Us and How to Fix Them*. New York: W. W. Norton, 2009.

King, Cheryl Simrell. *Government Is Us 2.0*. Armonk, NY: M.E. Sharpe, 2011.

King, Cheryl Simrell, and Lisa A. Zanetti. *Transformational Public Service: Portraits of Theory in Practice*. Armonk, NY: M.E. Sharpe, 2005.

Koppell, Jonathan G. S. *World Rule: Accountability, Legitimacy, and the Design of Global Governance*. Chicago; London: University of Chicago Press, 2010.

McNabb, David E. *The New Face of Government: How Public Managers Are Forging a New Approach to Governance*. Boca Raton, FL: CRC Press, 2009.

Meier, Kenneth J., and Laurence J. O'Toole, Jr. *Bureaucracy in a Democratic State: A Governance Perspective*. Baltimore, MD: Johns Hopkins University Press, 2006.

Menzel, Donald C., and Harvey L. White. *The State of Public Administration: Issues, Challenges, and Opportunities*. Armonk, NY: M.E. Sharpe, 2011.

O'Leary, Rosemary, and Lisa B. Bingham. *The Collaborative Public Manager: New Ideas for the Twenty-First Century*. Washington, DC: Georgetown University Press, 2009.

O'Leary, Rosemary, David Van Slyke, and Soonhee Kim. *The Future of Public Administration around the World: The Minnowbrook Perspective*. Washington, DC: Georgetown University Press, 2010.

Peters, Guy B., and Jon Pierre, eds. *Handbook of Public Administration*. Thousand Oaks, CA: Sage Publications, 2003.

Pollitt, Christopher. *The Essential Public Manager*. Maidenhead, England: Open University Press, 2003.

Rabin, Jack, W. Bartley Hildreth, and Gerald Miller. *Handbook of Public Administration*. 3rd ed. Boca Raton, FL: CRC/Taylor & Francis, 2007.

Rainey, Hal G. *Understanding and Managing Public Organizations*. 4th ed. San Francisco: Jossey-Bass, 2009.

Rosenbloom, David H., and Howard E. McCurdy, eds. *Revisiting Waldo's Administrative State: Constancy and Change in Public Administration*. Washington, DC: Georgetown University Press, 2006.

Rutgers, Mark R., ed. *Retracing Public Administration*. Amsterdam: Elsevier, 2003.

Stivers, Camilla. *Democracy, Bureaucracy and the Study of Public Administration*. Boulder, CO: Westview Press, 2000.

APPENDIX

Office of Personnel Management List of Core Executive Qualifications

Leading Change

Competency	Description
Vision	Takes a long-term view and acts as a catalyst for organizational change; builds a shared vision with others. Influences others to translate vision into action.
External Awareness	Identifies and keeps up to date on key international policies and economic, political, and social trends that affect the organization. Understands near-term and long-range plans and determines how to best be positioned to achieve a competitive business advantage in a global economy.
Creativity and Innovation	Develops new insights into situations and applies innovative solutions to make organizational improvements; creates a work environment that encourages creative thinking and innovation; designs and implements new or cutting-edge programs/processes.
Strategic Thinking	Formulates effective strategies consistent with the business and competitive strategy of the organization in a global economy. Examines policy issues and strategic planning with a long-term perspective. Determines objectives and sets priorities; anticipates potential threats or opportunities.
Continual Learning	Grasps the essence of new information; masters new technical and business knowledge; recognizes own strengths and weaknesses; pursues self-development; seeks feedback from others and opportunities to master new knowledge.
Resilience	Deals effectively with pressure; maintains focus and intensity and remains optimistic and persistent, even under adversity. Recovers quickly from setbacks. Effectively balances personal life and work.
Flexibility	Is open to change and new information; adapts behavior and work methods in response to new information, changing conditions, or unexpected obstacles. Adjusts rapidly to new situations warranting attention and resolution.
Service Motivation	Creates and sustains an organizational culture which permits others to provide the quality of service essential to high performance. Enables others to acquire the tools and support

they need to perform well. Shows a commitment to public service. Influences others toward a spirit of service and meaningful contributions.

Leading People

Competency	Description
Conflict Management	Identifies and takes steps to prevent potential situations that could result in unpleasant confrontations. Manages and resolves conflicts and disagreements in a positive and constructive manner to minimize negative impact.
Leveraging Diversity	Recruits, develops, and retains a diverse high-quality work-force in an equitable manner. Leads and manages an inclusive workplace that maximizes the talents of each person to achieve sound business results. Respects, understands, values, and seeks out individual differences to achieve the vision and mission of the organization. Develops and uses measures and rewards to hold self and others accountable for achieving results that embody the principles of diversity.
Team Building	Inspires, motivates, and guides others toward goal accomplishments. Consistently develops and sustains cooperative working relationships. Encourages and facilitates cooperation within the organization and with customer groups; fosters commitment, team spirit, pride, trust. Develops leadership in others through coaching, mentoring, rewarding, and guiding employees.
Integrity/Honesty	Instills mutual trust and confidence; creates a culture that fosters high standards of ethics; behaves in a fair and ethical manner toward others, and demonstrates a sense of corporate responsibility and commitment to public service.

Building Coalitions/Communication

Competency	Description
Oral Communication	Makes clear and convincing oral presentations to individuals or groups; listens effectively and clarifies information as needed; facilitates an open exchange of ideas and fosters atmosphere of open communication.
Written Communication	Expresses facts and ideas in writing in a clear, convincing, and organized manner.

Influencing/Negotiating	Persuades others; builds consensus through give and take; gains cooperation from others to obtain information and accomplish goals; facilitates "win-win" situations.
Partnering	Develops networks and builds alliances, engages in cross-functional activities; collaborates across boundaries, and finds common ground with a widening range of stakeholders. Utilizes contacts to build and strengthen internal support bases.
Political Savvy	Identifies the internal and external politics that impact the work of the organization. Approaches each problem situation with a clear perception of organizational and political reality, recognizes the impact of alternative courses of action.
Interpersonal Skills	Considers and responds appropriately to the needs, feelings, and capabilities of different people in different situations; is tactful, compassionate, and sensitive, and treats others with respect.

Results Driven

Competency	Description
Accountability	Assures that effective controls are developed and maintained to ensure the integrity of the organization. Holds self and others accountable for rules and responsibilities. Can be relied upon to ensure that projects within areas of specific responsibility are completed in a timely manner and within budget. Monitors and evaluates plans, focuses on results and measuring attainment of outcomes.
Problem Solving	Identifies and analyzes problems; distinguishes between relevant and irrelevant information to make logical decisions; provides solutions to individual and organizational problems.
Decisiveness	Exercises good judgment by making sound and well-informed decisions; perceives the impact and implications of decisions; makes effective and timely decisions, even when data are limited or solutions produce unpleasant consequences; is proactive and achievement oriented.
Customer Service	Balances interests of a variety of clients; readily readjusts priorities to respond to pressing and changing client demands. Anticipates and meets the need of clients; achieves quality end-products; is committed to continuous improvement of services.
Entrepreneurship	Identifies opportunities to develop and market new products and services within or outside of the organization. Is willing to take risks; initiates actions that involve a deliberate risk to achieve a recognized benefit or advantage.

Technical Credibility	Understands and appropriately applies procedures, requirements, regulations, and policies related to specialized expertise. Is able to make sound hiring and capital resource decisions and to address training and development needs. Understands linkages between administrative competencies and mission needs.

Business Acumen

Competency	Description
Financial Management	Demonstrates broad understanding of principles of financial management and marketing expertise necessary to ensure appropriate funding levels. Prepares, justifies, and/or administers the budget for the program area; uses cost-benefit thinking to set priorities; monitors expenditures in support of programs and policies. Identifies cost-effective approaches. Manages procurement and contracting.
Human Resources Management	Assesses current and future staffing needs based on organizational goals and budget realities. Using merit principles, ensures staff is appropriately selected, developed, utilized, appraised, and rewarded; takes corrective action.
Technology Management	Uses efficient and cost-effective approaches to integrate technology into the workplace and improve program effectiveness. Develops strategies using new technology to enhance decision making. Understands the impact of technological change on the organization.

SOURCE: https://www.opm.gov/deu/Handbook_2003/DEOH-MOSAIC-5.asp

CHAPTER 2

THE POLITICAL CONTEXT OF PUBLIC ADMINISTRATION

Your involvement in public organizations, whether in your career or as a private citizen, will inevitably center on the development, implementation, and evaluation of public policies. You may work for an agency charged with devising new approaches to familiar problems, you may want to see that a particular policy or proposal is framed in a way that is consistent with your beliefs, or you may simply want to better understand the implications of a particular direction in national, state, or local public policy. In any case, it will be helpful for you to know how public policies are designed and put into practice.

Talk of public policy is, of course, quite familiar. From one day to another, we hear criticisms of the U.S. policy in the Middle East, proposals for new initiatives in health care, calls for a more effective drug enforcement policy, challenges to a school district's approach to violence in the schools, ideas for changing a city's policy toward the homeless, or proposals for altering an organization's hiring practices. Uses of the term *policy* are varied, and the process by which policies are developed is even more complex.

We may think of a policy as a statement of goals and intentions with respect to a particular problem or set of problems, a statement often accompanied by a more detailed set of plans, programs, or instructions for pursuing those goals. Public policies are authoritative statements made by legitimate governmental actors (the chief executive, the legislature, public agencies) or nongovernmental actors (nonprofit organizations, foundations, quasi-governmental organizations, private corporations) about important, and sometimes not so important, public problems. We expect decision makers at all levels to spend considerable time and energy dealing with such topics as foreign affairs, health, education, employment, the economy, civil rights, the environment, energy, transportation, housing, agriculture, law enforcement, and myriad other issues. But in each of these areas, *public policy* is simply what an agency or an entire network of public, private, and nonprofit organizations decides to do or not do.

Organizations in all sectors are deeply involved in carrying out public policy—executing or "implementing." But these organizations are also involved in developing policy. Governmental and nongovernmental organizations play an important role in shaping public policy. Proposals are written and submitted by agency personnel; testimony and other expert advice are presented; and representatives of various agencies, especially political appointees who head agencies, often seek to build public support for particular ideas. Those in government agencies, and increasingly in nonprofit organizations, are often asked to elaborate on or clarify legislative intentions, and, in doing so, they continue the process of policy development.

Moreover, public, private, and nonprofit organizations not only develop policies that guide their own activities, but they also seek to influence the course of public policy on behalf of their members or other constituencies. Many such groups limit their activities to providing public information and seeking to indirectly affect the formation of policies in their area of interest. But others are far more direct, employing lobbyists and others whose specific job is to influence the policy process.

To understand the conduct of specific public and nonprofit organizations in the policy process, you must have some understanding of the context in which these organizations operate. That context is not merely physical; it includes the beliefs and values that shape our expectations of the organizations as well as the structures we have developed to try to maintain those values. In large part, the complexity of the policy process in this country is the result of the Founding Fathers' fear of concentrated power, a fear they sought to allay by organizing the federal government into three branches—executive, legislative, and judicial—so that no one branch could exert itself above the others. In this formulation, the primary task of the legislative branch is to make the laws, the primary task of the executive branch is to carry out the laws, and the primary task of the judicial branch is to interpret the laws. As we will see, our political system has evolved in such a way that the relations between and among the various branches, and between governmental and nongovernmental institutions, remain a central issue in conducting public programs. This chapter focuses on the relations between public administrators and the executive, the legislature, and the judiciary as they work together to seek important policy goals.

Administrative Organizations and Executive Leadership

As we saw in Chapter 1, public administrators work in federal, state, and local governments and in nonprofit organizations and associations. But, understandably, the federal government, simply by virtue of its size and the range of its activities, has become the model against which others are often judged. For that reason, we begin our discussion of the political context of American public administration by examining the development of the national administrative system and the role of the chief executive in that system.

Again it is helpful to begin with a brief historical review, primarily because some of the arguments that characterized discussions of administration in the early days of our nation are quite similar to those that continue to confront us. Take, for example, the difference between the Federalist view, expressed most forcefully by Alexander Hamilton, and that of the Jeffersonians, led by (you guessed it!) Thomas Jefferson. Hamilton and his Federalist colleagues argued for a strong centralized government, staffed and managed by men of wealth, class, and education. "The Federalist preference for the executive branch was a faithful reflection of their distrust of the people. An intelligent perception of sound public policy, in their view, could come only from well-educated men of affairs, men with trained minds and broad experience—in short from the upper classes" (White, 1948, p. 410).

The Jeffersonians, on the other hand, saw the administration of government as intimately connected to the problem of extending democracy throughout the nation. They thus preferred a more decentralized approach to the executive function and sought formal legal controls on the executive so that executive power would not be abused (Caldwell, 1964). These democratic views reached their pinnacle in the administration of

Andrew Jackson, known for its openness to the "common man." But the Jacksonian era was also notable for extension and formalization of the administrative apparatus of government; the administration of government began to form "a link between the nation's political authorities and its citizens" (Crenson, 1975, p. 10; see also Nelson, 1982).

Despite these developments, the president's role as chief executive officer, the head of the federal bureaucracy, was not clearly established until well into the twentieth century, when Franklin Roosevelt was able to assert his administrative management of the executive branch and to set a model for all the presidents who have followed him. Some changes were inevitable: the growing size and scope of governmental activity simply required greater attention to management and organization. Other changes reflected a greater understanding of the administrative process and how the work of government might be accomplished more effectively.

In 1936, President Roosevelt appointed a committee on administrative management, chaired by Louis Brownlow, that included a number of respected scholars and practitioners in the emerging field of public administration. The Brownlow committee concluded that "the president needs help" and recommended a series of possible steps to improve the president's management of the executive branch (Karl, 1963). Though initially sidetracked in the wake of the president's attempt to "pack" the Supreme Court, the major recommendations of the Brownlow committee were finally approved in the Reorganization Act of 1939. This act authorized the president to take the initiative in reshaping and reorganizing the executive branch, subject only to congressional veto. The Reorganization Act also allowed President Roosevelt to create the Executive Office of the President, composed of six assistants, to give the president the help he needed. (The Executive Office of the President continues today, but now it employs about 2,000 people.)

All presidents since Roosevelt have continued to assert their executive power in various ways. President Nixon sought to further centralize managerial power in the White House; President Carter sought greater managerial responsiveness through the Civil Service Reform Act. President Reagan and the first President Bush pursued the same ends by extending political control further into the bureaucracy while also developing programs to reduce costs and increase productivity.

President Clinton acted on his promises to streamline government and improve quality and productivity through implementation of the National Performance Review (NPR), an initiative aimed at increasing trust in government through a broad range of improvements in government quality and productivity as well as through reductions in the size of government. First presented in 1993 and implemented over several years, the NPR made hundreds of recommendations aimed at cutting red tape and regulations, empowering federal employees to make decisions while holding them accountable for results, and emphasizing service to "customers." Although the NPR ended in January 2001, the larger "Reinventing Government" movement of which it was a part has become a central theme in discussions of public and nonprofit reform, which will be discussed in more detail in later chapters.

President George W. Bush introduced substantial changes in management practices through the President's Management Agenda (PMA), an initiative aimed at improving management and performance through strategic management of human capital, budget and performance integration, improved financial performance, expanded e-government, and competitive sourcing. However, his reforms did not stop with management practices. Bush's decisions on national intelligence, including the establishment of the new Department of Homeland Security and his initiatives in international affairs (primarily the Iraq and Afghanistan interventions), constituted "the most far-reaching reorganization of the executive branch since the National Security Act of 1947" (Pfiffner, 2007, pp. 14–15) and gave him a great deal of success in extending presidential powers.

Whereas his predecessors came into office with high-profile plans for reforming government, President Obama's approach has been much more subdued. The global economic problems and contentious political environment that marked the beginning of the Obama administration may have led the new president toward a more pragmatic approach to management changes (Vlk, 2011). Early efforts focused on reforms in government contracting and outsourcing, the creation of a performance management initiative, the increased use of technology to connect with citizens, and a drive toward increasing transparency by making huge amounts of government data available online. One strategy that President Obama has employed is that of "setting broad principles on big issues—the stimulus, climate change, health care reform—and then tossing the debate back to Congress to resolve" (Kettl, 2010, p. 287). And while this strategy has drawn a great deal of criticism, it resulted in a stimulus package, the adoption of health-care reform, and "some movement on climate change" (Kettl, 2010, p. 287).

Neither President Obama nor Mitt Romney said very much during their 2012 presidential campaigns about management reform in the federal government, but both face the difficult problem of reducing the deficit and curbing spending. Obama is seeking a balanced tax plan that involves spending cuts and making sure the wealthiest Americans pay their fair share of taxes.

One important tool that presidents have employed is the *executive order*, a presidential mandate directed to and governing, with the effect of law, the actions of government officials and government agencies. Over time, the executive order has become a chief instrument of presidential power. President Obama, for example, used one of his early executive orders (no. 13507, April 8, 2009) to create the White House Office of Health Reform to coordinate his administration's efforts to reform the nation's health-care system. In this case and many others like it, the president essentially makes law by decree, occasionally in direct opposition to the wishes of Congress and constituent groups.

Another way in which presidents increasingly have sought to expand their authority is through the use of high-level appointees, termed "czars," who are assigned responsibility for specific policy issues. These appointees "have the president's trust as well as his ear, and thus the ability to effect significant change on the important policy task to which they have been assigned" (Villalobos & Vaughn, 2010, p. 5). However, because they are not subject to Senate approval and report only to the president, critics charge that these czars hold too much power (Buss, Balutis, & Ink, 2011). President Obama in particular came under fire from Congress and the media for the number of czars he appointed, although some observers argue that Obama's use of czars did not differ dramatically from that of his immediate predecessor.

In fact, czars have been used by nearly every president since Franklin Roosevelt, when the creation of the Executive Office of the President in 1939 opened the door for such appointments, although the use of czars in the ensuing decades was limited until the Clinton administration. The number of czars grew exponentially under George W. Bush, a practice that has been continued in the Obama administration. Villalobos and Vaughn (2010) note that, together, Bush and Obama represent a significant shift in the use of these appointees, and they argue that this "rise of presidential policy czars has not occurred in isolation, but rather is part of a comprehensive pattern that includes centralization/politicization, signing statements, executive orders, secrecy, etc., that reflects the increasing untenability of the role and responsibility of the American presidency" (p. 31).

The president, as chief executive officer of the federal government, exercises power over an enormous and wide-ranging set of public organizations. In 2010, there were some 2.8 million civilians employed by the federal government and another 1.6 million uniformed military personnel (http://www.opm.gov/feddata/HistoricalTables/TotalGovernmentSince1962.asp). In addition, the federal government supports and pays for a wide variety of activities in which the actual work is performed by someone other than a federal civil servant. The Department of Defense, for example, supervises almost 2 million persons in private industry who are involved, directly or indirectly, in defense-related work.

Administrative Organizations

You are probably already familiar with many of the agencies of government at the federal level; however, several types are particularly important: (1) the Executive Office of the President; (2) the cabinet-level executive departments; (3) a variety of independent agencies, regulatory commissions, and public corporations; and (4) administrative agencies that support the work of the legislature and the judiciary.

The Executive Office of the President   The various administrative bodies located in the Executive Office of the President both advise the president and assist in formulating and implementing national policy. Several offices have come to play especially important policy roles. The Office of Management and Budget (OMB), for example, assists the president in preparing the budget, submitting it to Congress, and administering it. OMB is also involved in reviewing the management of various agencies, suggesting changes in structures and procedures, and searching out capable executives for service in government. The National Security Council is charged with integrating domestic, military, and foreign policy; it is made up of the president, vice president, and secretaries of state and defense and is directed by the national security adviser. Finally, the Council of Economic Advisers consists of three economists who develop proposals to "maintain employment, production, and purchasing power." The council also develops a variety of economic reports.

Obviously, all of these groups, and others in the Executive Office of the President, are used in different ways by different presidents according to the personality of the president and the particular issues that are most pressing at that time. Some presidents, such as Reagan and Bush, have relied very heavily on their staffs, whereas others, such as Carter, have been much more personally involved in management and policy development.

Networking

To locate information about the executive branch of the federal government, check out the following websites: www.whitehouse.gov and http://www.usa.gov/Agencies/Federal/ Executive.shtml. For access to executive orders, go to http://www.whitehouse.gov/ briefing-room/presidential-actions/executive-orders.

Cabinet-Level Executive Departments   These agencies are among the most visible, if not always the largest, of the federal executive agencies. There are currently fifteen cabinet-level departments. They are the Departments of Defense, Health and Human Services, Treasury, Agriculture, Interior, Transportation, Justice, Commerce, State, Labor, Energy, Housing and Urban Development, Education, Veterans Affairs, and—the newest— Homeland Security, established by the Homeland Security Act of 2002. Several departments, such as Treasury and State, date back to the nation's founding; others were created by Congress as needed.

Each cabinet-level department is headed by a secretary, who, along with a group of top-level staff people, is appointed by the president with the approval of the Senate. Each cabinet-level department is organized into smaller units, such as offices, services, administrations, branches, and sections. The Department of Health and Human Services, for example, includes the Public Health Service, which in turn includes the Food and Drug Administration, the National Institutes of Health, and the Centers for Disease Control and Prevention. In early 2012, President Obama elevated the head of the Small Business Administration to cabinet-level status. Obama also announced plans to merge the Department of Commerce, the Small Business Administration, the Office of the United States Trade Representative, the Export-Import Bank, the Overseas Private Investment Corporation, and the United States Trade and Development Agency (Harrison & Khazan, 2012). President Obama can be expected to continue this plan into his second term, although there are likely to be few other reorganizations. In any case, we should note that though each department is headquartered in Washington, D.C., their offices are, of course, spread across the country. Indeed, just over 10 percent of the federal workforce lives in or around the District of Columbia.

The cabinet-level secretaries, along with a few others, such as the director of the Office of Management and Budget and the ambassador to the United Nations, constitute the president's cabinet, a group that some presidents have used sparingly and primarily for formal matters and others have employed extensively for help and advice. Inevitably, a president will come to rely informally on certain advisers, cabinet members, or others outside the formal inner circle for advice and consultation. Historically, for example, President Kennedy relied heavily on the advice of his brother, Robert, during the Cuban Missile Crisis, even though as attorney general his brother held no formal position that would involve him in foreign affairs.

Independent Agencies, Regulatory Commissions, and Public Corporations   A variety of *independent agencies* have been created intentionally outside the normal cabinet

What Would You Do?

You are in charge of the federal government's effort to assess the scientific, technical, and socioeconomic impact of greenhouse gas emissions and to understand the potential for climate change caused by these emissions. Your agency has recently been accused of "sugarcoating" the data to protect the administration from potential political damage. What would you do?

organization. Some are engaged in staff functions in support of other agencies. The Office of Personnel Management, for example, oversees the federal personnel function, and the General Services Administration oversees the government's property. Other agencies have simply not been viewed as appropriate to include in cabinet-level departments; among these are the Environmental Protection Agency and the Small Business Administration. With rare exceptions, these independent agencies are directed by persons appointed by the president with the confirmation of the Senate.

Regulatory commissions, examples of which would be the Federal Communications Commission and the Consumer Product Safety Commission, are formed to regulate a particular area of the economy and are structured quite differently. But typically, they are headed by a group of individuals (variously called directors, commissioners, or governors) appointed by the president and confirmed by the Senate. These persons are protected in various ways from removal by the president; in some cases, their terms of appointment overlap presidential terms. Presumably, the regulatory commissions are to perform their tasks independently and objectively, free from undue influence either by the political incumbent or by the affected clientele. As we will see later, however, the nature of regulatory work makes this task exceedingly difficult. (Note that not all regulatory bodies are located outside the cabinet departments; for instance, the Food and Drug Administration is part of the Department of Health and Human Services.)

Public corporations are employed where the objective of the agency is essentially commercial, where the work of the agency requires greater latitude than would be typical, and where the agency will acquire at least a portion of its funding in the marketplace (Moe, 2001; Walsh, 1978). The Tennessee Valley Authority, which has provided power in the Tennessee Valley for well over fifty years, is a classic example of a public corporation. Somewhat more recent additions to the growing list of government corporations include the U.S. Postal Service and the National Railroad Passenger Corporation (AMTRAK), both established in 1970.

Agencies Supporting the Legislature and the Judiciary   Both the legislative and judicial branches require considerable direct administrative support for their members (legislative staff, committee staff, and court administrators). There are also several specific agencies attached to the legislative branch that are of special significance. You are probably already familiar with the Government Printing Office and the Library of Congress. But, although less is known about the Government Accountability Office (GAO), its duties have become increasingly important. Established in 1921 and headed by the comptroller general, the GAO is responsible for auditing funds to see that they are properly spent. In recent years, however, the agency's mission has broadened to include formal program evaluations within various agencies. The GAO studies the way federal money is spent and advises Congress and executive agencies on ways to improve the efficiency and responsiveness of government. Finally, Congress is supported by the Congressional Budget Office, an agency that supports the budget process and whose operations we will examine more carefully in Chapter 7.

The State Level

The organization of state governments varies considerably, according to each state's policy interests and political development; however, there is little question that state government in this country is "big business." In fact, if you compare the revenues of state governments with those of the largest private companies in America, the results are striking. California would rank thirteenth just above Bank of America, and New York would be fortieth just behind Boeing. Even Hawaii, a small state, would still rank in the top 500 (http://money.cnn .com/magazines/fortune/fortune500/2012/full_list/; http://www2.census.gov/govs/statetax/ 11staxrank.pdf).

Recent efforts to decrease federal involvement in domestic policy have combined with a general growth in the range of activities undertaken at the state level to support a vast increase in state activity. Between 1980 and 2008, state government employment rose from 3.7 million to 5.2 million, with an even more dramatic rise in state expenditures, from $4.3 billion in 2008 to $18.7 billion in 2008 (http://www.census.gov/compendia/ statab/cats/state_local_govt_finances_employment.html). From time to time, states in fact play an important role in the redistribution of governmental power. For example, in the mid-1990s, states were central to the federal government's move to reform the nation's welfare system, a reform agenda that led to the devolution of many public assistance programs and a further expansion in the role of state government. Similarly, the states have been important actors in the most recent debates concerning health care, especially concerning the role of states in funding and executing various proposals.

The organization and structure of state governments in many ways mirror the organization and structure of the national government, but there are some distinctive features. You should note, for example, the large number of elected administrative officials in most state governments. In most states, the people elect not only the governor and lieutenant governor, but also the attorney general, the secretary of state, and the state treasurer. Many states still elect the head of the Department of Agriculture by popular vote, and it is not uncommon to have members of various boards and commissions (for instance, the Public Service Commission) elected by the public. Obviously, the corresponding offices at the federal level are filled by presidential appointment. (The large number of elected officials at the state and local level is a carryover from a period in which democratic tendencies in this country were especially strong and it was felt that nearly all major officials of government should be elected directly by the people.)

In addition, many state departments do not report directly to the governor, but rather to boards or commissions isolated from executive control in the same way as regulatory commissions at the federal level. For example, a Department of Conservation may report to a commission appointed by the governor for periods exceeding those of the governor and, indeed, may have dedicated sources of revenue essentially outside the governor's budgetary control. Obviously, under such circumstances, the governor's power as chief executive is severely limited.

Networking

For information about state governments, start with http://www.usa.gov/Agencies.shtml. Also see the Council of State Governments at www.csg.org.

Despite structural limitations on gubernatorial powers, contemporary governors exercise a broad range of political and executive influence that enable them to play a major, even central role in the operations of state government. In recent years, these powers have even had an impact on national policy making, particularly in the welfare and health-care reform agendas mentioned previously. For example, the Massachusetts health-care system enacted when Mitt Romney was governor of that state became a model for similar federal legislation, even though Romney later became an opponent of the Obama health-care plan. Most important, governors play a key symbolic role, helping to set the political agenda and to focus the attention of other political and administrative actors on a limited number of special topics. Many governors have accumulated special powers with respect to the budget process through which they are able to dramatically affect the allocation of state resources and to mediate policy disputes among executive agencies (Bowman & Kearney, 1986, p. 54).

Beyond these somewhat informal powers, the strength of the governor's formal executive powers is often gauged by three measures: the presence or absence of the item veto, the ability of the governor to reorganize state agencies, and the number of other elected officials. All state governors have the power to veto legislation. Most states also give the governor the power of an item veto (also called "line-item veto"), the capacity to veto specific items within an appropriations bill (as opposed to accepting all or nothing), which is a helpful tool in shaping legislation according to the governor's preferences. (During his final term, President Clinton, himself a former governor, supported passage of the line-item veto at the federal level. The federal provision, however, was ultimately invalidated by the Supreme Court in *Clinton v. City of New York* [1998].) The gubernatorial power to reorganize is more limited. Roughly half the states require either statutory or even constitutional action to reorganize. Finally, as we have seen, nearly all states have a variety of statewide elected officials in addition to the governor and lieutenant governor. Indeed, most states have between four and eight agencies that are controlled by individuals elected statewide rather than appointed.

The growing importance of state government suggests that governors will likely continue to assert their executive leadership role and will seek greater control by reorganizing the executive branch. So far, however, relatively few structural moves have been made. However, some procedural changes have occurred; for example, many states have moved in the direction of more clearly establishing the governor's leading role in the budgetary process and establishing centralized management improvement programs.

Although the organization of government varies considerably from state to state, most states have a variety of substantive agencies concerned with state and local needs (Natural

Resources, Highways and Transportation, and so on), as well as several agencies, such as the Department of Social Services, that largely administer programs funded by the federal government. These agencies are likely to be assisted by a central management support unit, called an Office of Administration or a similar title, that provides budget, personnel, and other general services. As mentioned, if there is one trend in the reorganization of state agencies, that trend would seem to be the creation of a greater number of state departments devoted to economic development. In some cases, these departments seek to coordinate many economic development activities; in others, there is a more specific focus on small business or on providing incentives for industrial location or relocation.

The Local Level

According to the most recent data available, there are over 89,000 local governments (see Table 2.1). Many of these are municipalities, cities, and towns of varying sizes offering a full range of services; others are counties, typically more limited in their role but still embracing a variety of governmental functions. But most are *special districts*, created to serve one particular function, such as education, fire protection, or parks and recreation. (Only special districts have substantially increased in numbers over the past several years.)

Cities   American cities are organized in three ways. The *mayor-council* form is used by about 47 percent of all municipalities, about 57 percent of those with a population over 250,000, and two-thirds of those with a population over 1 million (ICMA, 2010). In all cases, both the council and mayor are elected, the latter either by direct

TABLE 2.1

Number of Governmental Units, by Type of Government, 2007

Federal	1
State	50
Local	89,476
County	3,033
Municipal	19,492
Township and town	16,519
School district	13,051
Special district	37,381
Total	89,527

SOURCE: U.S. Bureau of the Census, *Statistical Abstract of the United States, 2011* (http://www.census.gov/compendia/statab/cats/state_local_govt_finances_employment.html).

popular vote or a council election. One variation of the mayor-council form features a strong mayor with almost total administrative authority, including for preparation and administration of the budget. Policy making in this form is a joint endeavor of the mayor and council. The weak mayor type places primary administrative control, including for most appointments and development of the budget, in the hands of the council.

The power of the mayor as chief executive is obviously greater in the strong mayor system, and, consequently, that system is used in most large, industrial cities. At least in a formal sense, however, several large cities, including Chicago, still maintain a weak mayor system, although even under such circumstances, a particular mayor may assert considerable strength. The legendary Mayor Richard Daley of Chicago, for example, was able to utilize a well-oiled political machine to assert substantial administrative power. Though he operated in a weak mayor system, Daley was unquestionably a strong mayor.

A recent variation on the mayor-council form is the use of a professionally trained chief administrative officer (sometimes called a "deputy mayor") to oversee the administrative operations of city government (as in Los Angeles, New Orleans, Washington, D.C.). We find this administrative arrangement in many big cities, where mayors are often more interested in campaigning and in working with external constituencies and like to have someone else oversee the internal management of the city. But city administrators are also being hired in an increasing number of smaller mayor-council communities as well, mostly in an effort to bring professional expertise to local government.

The *council-manager* form of local government is of special interest. It represents a structural effort to solve the classic question of the relationship between politics (or policy) and administration. In this form, the city council, usually five to seven people, has responsibility for making policy, including passing appropriations and supervising in a general way the administration of city government. The primary executive responsibility, however, lies with a full-time professionally trained city manager; the mayor has no involvement in the administration of the city and performs primarily ceremonial duties and legislation. In its classic formulation, therefore, the council-manager form is designed so that the council makes policy and the city manager carries it out.

The council-manager plan was first tried in Staunton, Virginia, in 1908, and a few years later it was adopted in Dayton, Ohio, with great success. Several reform organizations, such as the National Municipal League, felt the council-manager plan would be a good way to insulate the management of city government from the vagaries of local politics and consequently added their endorsement.

Networking

For information about local and tribal governments, see http://www.usa.gov/Agencies.shtml. See also the National League of Cities at www.nlc.org; the National Civic League at www.ncl.org; the U.S. Conference of Mayors at www.usmayors.org; and the International City Management Association at http://icma.org.

The number of council-manager governments has grown steadily throughout this century and continues to increase. Today, some 52 percent of American communities employ the plan. Whereas the mayor-council system is associated with larger, industrialized, and heterogeneous cities, the council-manager plan is most frequently found in medium-sized cities. Over 60 percent of American cities with populations between 25,000 and 250,000 operate with the plan, and 32 percent of the cities with a population below 5,000 have adopted it. Although a number of large cities, such as Phoenix, San Antonio, and Kansas City, use the plan, it is more rare among cities over 1 million in population. The council-manager form continues to grow, however, with the number of council-manager adoptions outrunning those of the mayor-council form by three to one over the past twenty years. Those favoring the council-manager plan usually argue that it emphasizes professional expertise and administrative accountability; those favoring the mayor-council plan emphasize its adaptability and its responsiveness to community needs. As a result, more than 89 million Americans now live in communities with council-manager governments (Council-Manager System, 2006).

A small number of American cities use the *commission* form of government. Under this form, the people elect a set of commissioners. Each acts as a council member but also as director of a particular city department; for example, one commissioner might head the Parks Department and another the Public Works Department. The commission form is fading; we find it today primarily in smaller rural communities, although it is still found in places such as Portland, Oregon, the last remaining large city using the form.

Counties   Counties (or variations, such as parishes in Louisiana) are found in nearly every state and range in population from very small to huge. Once considered an unexplored area of local government, counties are emerging as important actors in the modern governmental system. Counties have traditionally provided a range of services in behalf of state government, a role that has expanded considerably in the last decades. In addition, counties have recently assumed a wide range of new services (such as mass transit, mental health, waste disposal, and police services) that, for one reason or another, cannot be offered by individual municipalities.

The traditional form of county government has been a combination of a county commission and a series of elected administrative officials, such as sheriff, auditor, treasurer, and so on. An emerging trend in county government, however, is the use of appointed county administrators, similar in many ways to the city manager at the municipal level. Still another type of county government, also increasing in use, involves the combination of a city council and an elected executive. In this system, a chief executive is elected by the people and holds powers similar to that of a governor in a state system. For example, the elected executive often has veto power over council actions. Trends toward a greater range of activities, especially in the social services, combined with the increasing professionalism of county government make this often overlooked area one of the most interesting arenas for public service today.

Native American Tribes   Native American tribes have a special relationship with the U.S. government. This relationship was first articulated by Supreme Court Justice Marshall in three decisions between 1827 and 1832 known as the Marshall Trilogy. In these decisions, Marshall acknowledged that American Indians had inherent rights to possess and use their land and that they had sovereignty to run their own affairs. But even though they were seen as nations, the tribes were not foreign nations. They could not sell their land without the consent of the federal government. And the federal government had responsibilities to protect Indian land from incursions from the states and others. Marshall described this relationship as similar to guardianship.

This relationship has evolved over the last 150 years. Influenced greatly by European settlers' desire to move westward, Congress made treaties, fought wars, and otherwise moved Indians out of the way of western expansion. Despite efforts to assimilate Indians into the dominant culture, many Indians have clung to their heritage and maintained their tribal governance systems. Today, the Department of the Interior recognizes more than 500 tribes who have sovereignty over their internal affairs, and tribal management is emerging as a growing and significant field in public administration. Not only do those engaged in tribal administration need to understand the special circumstances surrounding tribal governance, but also public administrators who work near or with tribes need to be aware of the legal history that has led to Native American rights that are unique in America.

Special Purpose Governments   Finally, we should note again the large number of special districts, or special purpose governments, that operate in the United States. Some exist at the local level: limited-purpose districts, which may operate in the areas of natural resources, fire protection, libraries, schools, housing and community development, and so forth, are typically governed by an appointed part-time governing board and a full-time general manager or executive director who plays the most significant role in the operation of the district. Critics claim that the proliferation of special districts causes fragmentation and lack of coordination, but others argue that such districts remain important because they are "close to the people."

The largest group of special districts are school districts. There are roughly 14,000 local school districts in the United States, serving over 79 million students—62 million kindergarten, elementary, and secondary students and 17 million postsecondary students (http://nces .ed.gov/programs/digest/d10/tables/dt10_001.asp?referrer=report). School districts employ over 8 million teachers, administrators, and other staff to provide elementary and secondary education to the nation's school children, making educators the largest single category of public employees in the nation.

School districts vary in their size, organizational structure, governance, and mix of federal, state, and local funding sources. One significant trend, however, is the takeover of local school systems by local governments. About a dozen of the largest school districts in the country are now under the control of local governments. Boston's mayor was given control of the schools in 1992, Chicago's in 1995, and New York's in 2002. Washington, D.C.'s mayor has been successful in taking over the school system, and mayors in other major cities are now considering such a move. The Los Angeles mayor, however, suffered a setback in his efforts to control the schools when a California court declared unconstitutional a law giving the mayor substantial control over schools. The mayor has nonetheless been active in the school quality issue.

Other major types of special purpose governments include public nonprofit corporations such as economic development corporations and housing finance corporations at the local and state levels. For example, the City of Baltimore Development Corporation is a nonprofit corporation chartered by the city to promote economic development by attracting new business and assisting new and growing companies. Similarly, the City of Houston recently handed management of its convention and arts venues to a government corporation. Housing finance corporations may, for example, issue housing bonds, offer tax-exempt financing, or extend other assistance to facilitate the development of low-income housing and address other housing needs.

Nonprofit Organizations and Associations   Increasing numbers of institutions in the American system of public policy fall between what we think of as the "public sector" and the "private sector." These institutions may be described as belonging to an independent or third sector of our economy. For the most part, independent-sector organizations do not have the distribution of profits to shareholders as one of their major objectives. They exist instead to meet the needs of the public at large, a particular portion of the public, or the needs and interests of their own members (Boris, 1999; Salamon, 1999). Technically, *nonprofit organizations* are defined as those prohibited by law from distributing surplus revenues (profits) to individuals (typically, members). Such organizations may in fact make a profit; however, the profit must be used for the purposes of the organization.

Nonprofit organizations may include churches, educational institutions, civic organizations, schools and colleges, charitable organizations, social and recreational groups, health and human service organizations, membership organizations (including labor unions and fraternal organizations), conservation and environmental groups, mutual organizations (including farmers' cooperatives), trade associations, community chests, youth activities (such as Boy Scouts), community betterment organizations, advocacy groups of all kinds, and many others. In 2009, the total number of tax-exempt nonprofit organizations, including public charities, private foundations, and other nonprofits such as fraternal organizations and civic leagues, exceeded 1.5 million.

While private nonprofit organizations account for about 9 percent of employment in the United States (depending again on how you count), the voluntary effort that is expended in support of these groups makes their impact far greater. Nearly 27 percent of American adults devote volunteer time to such organizations, an investment of time that has been estimated as the equivalent of over $200 billion a year (http://nccs.urban.org/statistics/quickfacts.cfm). Over the last twenty-five years, the third sector has been the fastest-growing segment of our economy.

During the past decade, nonprofit organizations have taken a leading role in the delivery of public services. As mentioned previously, change in the federal welfare system has led to the devolution of services to the state and local levels (a trend we will explore later), where networks of agencies, many of which are nonprofits, manage the implementation of public programs (Light, 2000). The current system has been characterized as "an extended chain of implementation," in which recipients of public support in some cases will "not even encounter a government employee—federal, state, or local" (Kettl, 2000, pp. 492–493). Moreover, nonprofits have become active in other areas of service delivery, including hospitals, museums, colleges and universities, the performing arts, religion, advocacy, and research (Boris, 1999).

Nonprofit organizations can be categorized in many ways, but perhaps most easily according to their purposes and sources of financial support. Some nonprofits are *charitable* or *public benefit organizations*, which provide services to the public at large or to some segment of the public. These organizations, such as social service organizations or art museums, may receive some funding from government and some from private contributions; they are generally tax-exempt under federal statutes. Other nonprofits are *advocacy organizations*, groups that espouse a particular cause and seek to lobby for that cause, or *mutual benefit organizations*, which produce benefits primarily for their members. The former would include groups like Common Cause and the Sierra Club; the latter would include trade associations, professional organizations, labor unions, and others that directly promote the interests of their own members. Obviously, however, from these examples, the line between the two is not completely clear. Finally, *churches* are obviously charitable organizations, but are they are difficult to classify in the categories mentioned.

Networking

For information on nonprofit organizations, see the Alliance for Nonprofit Management at www.allianceonline.org and CompassPoint Nonprofit Services at http://www.compasspoint .org/. See also the following sites for information on foundations: www.cof.org and www .foundations.org.

Indeed, the entire "independent sector" is sometimes difficult to categorize. For one thing, the distinctions among the three sectors are not clear, even to the point that a particular individual might find the same service provided by one or more sectors. For example, you can play golf at a municipal course (public sector), a private driving range (private sector), or a country club (independent sector). Furthermore, the sources of funding are often intermixed. For example, both governments (public sector) and private corporations (private sector) often contribute financial support to local chambers of commerce.

The fact that nonprofit organizations are required to pursue a public interest is reflected in their legal structure (and tax-exempt status). Typically, so that government can feel that a public purpose is being carried out, the organization must be governed by a board of trustees (or directors or commissioners), whose purpose, at least in legal terms, is to promote and protect the public interest (Boris, 1999; Salamon, 1999). Such persons will also likely establish the mission and operating policies, hire an executive director, and generally oversee fiscal and programmatic operations. The executive director is responsible for day-to-day operations and often becomes the organization's chief spokesperson. Most nonprofit associations are highly dependent on their executive director's leadership. More and more, such persons (and other major staff persons in nonprofit organizations) are coming from a background in public administration.

Relationships with the Legislative Body

In examining the political context of public organizations, we have thus far emphasized the importance of executive leadership. For example, we noted the emergence of the president as the chief executive officer of our national government and the pivotal role of the chief executive in state and local governments and in nonprofit organizations and associations. But although we tend to associate public agencies with the executive branch of government, there are numerous administrative bodies associated with the legislative and judicial branches. More importantly, wherever agencies are located, their role in the policy process will be especially clear in their relationship with the legislature. In discussing the relationship between public agencies and legislative bodies, we will focus much more directly on the policy process.

The Policy Process

Before we examine the role of public and nonprofit organizations in developing public policy, we should review the process by which public policies are developed. We may think of the policy process as involving five stages: agenda setting, policy formulation, policy legitimation, policy implementation, and policy evaluation and change. (See the box "Exploring Concepts: Stages in the Policy Process.") Whereas public and nonprofit organizations are the primary actors in implementing public policy (indeed, most of this book focuses on ways to effectively carry out public policy), they are also significant players in the first two phases.

Exploring Concepts

STAGES IN THE POLICY PROCESS

1. Agenda setting
2. Policy formulation
3. Policy legitimation
4. Policy implementation
5. Policy evaluation and change

SOURCE: Michael E. Kraft and Scott R. Furlong, *Public Policy: Politics, Analysis, and Alternatives*, 2nd ed. (Washington, DC: CQ Press, 2007), pp. 80–85.

Agenda Setting   Obviously, before policies are acted upon, they must get the attention of major decision makers. From among all the many and competing claims on their time and interests, decision makers must select issues that will be given priority and those that will be filtered out. Through the *agenda-setting* phase, certain problems come to be viewed as needing action, whereas others are postponed. Naturally, there is a great deal of ebb and flow in what is considered most important. In the 1970s and 1980s, U.S. foreign policy was dominated by concerns for Soviet movement into such areas as the Middle East; in the 1990s attention shifted to a variety of "flash points" such as Somalia and Bosnia. More recently, foreign policy has focused on Afghanistan and Iraq, Iran and North Korea. Similarly, any particular issue area can gain or decline in prominence over time, as has the attention to energy policy over the last twenty years.

Many people contribute to setting the public policy agenda. The president, for example, has a special claim on the attention of the American people and their elected representatives; a presidential speech or press conference can significantly affect what decision makers see as important. But there are many others whose actions can give certain topics greater or lesser visibility. Members of Congress, executive branch officials, political parties, interest groups, the media, and the general public can all significantly shape the question of what will be considered important. Think, for example, how concern for teen pregnancy has been recently brought to public awareness. Who have been the leaders in shaping public opinion on this issue?

The agenda-setting process may be viewed as the confluence of three streams of events: policy recognition, policy generation, and political action (Kingdon, 1995). The first, *policy recognition*, has to do with the way certain topics emerge as significant issues that demand action. As you can well imagine, decision makers are subject to many influences in choosing what items are significant. They may respond to particular indicators that come to public view, such as an increase in air traffic problems or a rise in unemployment. Or they may get feedback on current programs that indicates some need to reassess the status of a particular issue. Finally, some items are brought to the policy agenda by events that simply demand attention, such as AIDS in Africa or the damage brought about by hurricanes, tsunamis, or other natural disasters.

Networking

See the home pages of various "think tanks" such as the Brookings Institution at www .brookings.edu and the American Enterprise Institute at www.aei.org. Especially interesting is the site for the Urban Institute at www.urban.org.

There are many ways people try to affect the degree of attention given to particular items. Sometimes called *policy entrepreneurs*, those who are willing to invest personal time, energy, and often money in pursuit of particular policy changes can use a variety of personal tactics, such as publicity campaigns, direct contacts with decision makers (letters, phone calls), petition drives, and many others. Or they can involve themselves in major institutions, such as the media, political parties, or interest groups, that provide access to decision makers. Election campaigns, for example, often help clarify or focus the policy agenda.

A second phase of the agenda-setting process may occur almost simultaneously. At the same time that attention is focusing on a particular issue, it is likely that many will be involved in trying to *generate solutions* to the problem. Ideas may come from decision makers themselves, members of their staffs, experts in the bureaucracy, members of the scientific community, policy think tanks (such as the Brookings Institution or the American Enterprise Institute), or from the public generally. Typically, proposed solutions swirl around through speeches and articles, papers, and conversations until a few ideas begin to gain special currency. Most often these will be the ideas that not only seem to correctly address the problem, but also seem to be politically acceptable.

A third stream of events affecting the policy agenda is concerned with *political action*. For a proposal to reach the top of the policy agenda, it must be consistent with emerging political realities. Items that are consistent with the prevailing political climate, those that are favored by the incumbent administration and legislative majority, and those that have interest group support (or at least lack organized opposition) are more likely to reach the top of the agenda. These political realities, the proposed ideas or solutions, and the recognition of particular topics represent streams that must come together at just the right moment for action to occur. The windows of opportunity for policy action are narrow, and it takes great skill in managing the various streams so that one's interests are best served.

Policy Formulation   Formulation of public policy involves the development of formal policy statements (legislation, executive orders, administrative rules, and so on) that are viewed as legitimate. Again, we will focus here on policy making by the legislature and on the role of public administrators in the legislative process. The basics of how a bill becomes law are well known. At the federal level and in most state governments, a bill is introduced and referred to a committee (and perhaps a subcommittee), hearings are held, the committee reports to the larger body, a vote is taken in both houses, a conference committee works out any differences in the two versions, and the bill is sent to the chief executive for signature. In most other jurisdictions, a similar, though often simplified, approach is used. In any case, the complexity of the legislative process, and the fact that many different decision points must be passed before anything is final, mean there are many occasions when those seeking to shape legislative outcomes can seek to exert their influence.

The president, of course, has both formal and informal means of influencing legislation, most notably through program initiatives and budget proposals. Others in the government, including many agency personnel, interact with Congress on a regular basis and may also affect policy outcomes. At the same time, those outside the government—from individual citizens to well-organized interest groups—also seek access and influence. Agency personnel become involved in the legislative process in several ways. In many cases, agencies actually send program proposals to the legislature for its consideration. Such proposals are usually submitted to the legislative leadership and then passed on to the appropriate committee chairs. Though a member of Congress will actually be the one to introduce the proposed legislation, that person may depend on those in the agency for background information and other support. Whether or not legislation has been submitted by an agency, agency personnel will often be called upon to provide testimony regarding particular proposals. As you might imagine, those who staff major public agencies constitute an important source of expertise concerning public issues. For example, it's hard to imagine a group of people better able to understand the tax laws of a particular state than those who work in the state revenue department.

Over time, the relationship between agency personnel and representatives of Congress (either members or staff) can become quite strong. After all, the two groups share common interests and concerns, along with representatives of certain interest groups. A subcommittee on aging, a senior citizen's lobbying organization, and the Social Security Administration, for example, are likely to agree on the need to protect Social Security benefits.

When the interactions among such interest groups, agency personnel, and members of Congress become especially frequent and intense, the resulting alliances are sometimes called *iron triangles*. These coalitions can often exert great, possibly even unwarranted, influence.

You should be aware of some of the special considerations facing public administrators at the local level and in nonprofit organizations as they are called upon for advice and help during the process of policy development. As noted, the council-manager form of government was actually founded on a separation of policy and administration—the council made policy and the city manager carried it out. Over time, however, many city managers have become valued by their councils for their expertise in local government and frequently find themselves commenting on or even proposing particular policies. While this situation is quite at odds with the theory underlying council-manager government, it is the reality in most council-manager cities. The same is true of executives in nonprofit organizations and associations. Such situations are not without risk, however, for a delicate balance must be maintained between the executive and legislative functions. Council or board members who feel that their policy-making territory has been intruded upon may exercise another of their council prerogatives: firing the manager or executive!

Policy Legitimation   Kraft and Furlong (2007) define policy legitimation as "giving legal force to decisions or justifying policy action" (p. 86). Legitimation, as the authors point out, may be seen as both simple and complex. When a policy is approved by a recognized authority (such as when a bill is passed), then we may talk about a simple process of legitimation. But the authors suggest that legitimation is more about acceptance of a new policy by the broader public. The process of policy acceptance should, therefore, be considered from the legal aspect, political culture and values, and the level of popular support. Many times, the authors suggest, politicians bring in actors or other celebrities to testify in front of congressional committees. Frequent public meetings and public hearings as well as participation of citizen advisory bodies are other ways to legitimize policies.

The authors give the Nuclear Waste Policy Act of 1992 as an example of adopting a law that was not embraced by the public or interest groups. Since lawmakers were "rushing" to adopt the new law, they underestimated public unwillingness to accept the new piece of legislation. The act was revised when "Congress voted to study only one possible site in the nation, at Yucca Mountain in Nevada" (p. 87). But this revision again was not embraced by the public or interest groups, and it was especially opposed by prominent politicians from Nevada. As a result, almost twenty years later, President Obama stopped funding for Yucca Mountain and initiated an alternative process for identifying repositories for nuclear waste.

The whole process of legitimation, according to Kraft and Furlong (2007, pp. 87–88), is mostly political. They suggest that lawmakers ask questions before they decide to adopt a policy. Referring to public opinion poll data, considering the views of interest groups, initiating a broad political debate, and developing an ethical analysis of the issue are only some of the many ways to achieve policy legitimation.

Policy Implementation   Members of public and nonprofit organizations play important roles in building the policy agenda and shaping legislative policy, but they are also involved in policy making as part of the implementation process. By its very nature, legislation is general and lacking in detail. Legislators cannot foresee all the individual questions that might come up in implementing a program. Moreover, legislators don't want to tie the hands of program managers by being too restrictive. Consequently, legislation typically leaves a great deal of discretion to public managers in working out the details of a particular program. The Federal Trade Commission, for example, is instructed to prevent deceptive advertising, but it has to decide what is deceptive; the Occupational Safety and Health Administration is asked to define and set safety standards for the workplace, but it must define more clearly what that means (Meier, 1987, p. 52). In these and many other cases, managers develop administrative rules or policies to give detail to the legislation or to fill in the gaps, and, in effect, they make policy.

Policy implementation is the "set of activities directed toward putting a program into effect" (Jones, cited in Kraft & Furlong, 2007, pp. 82–83). According to Kraft and Furlong, policy implementation includes organization, interpretation, and application. Organization refers to the use of resources and methods to administer a particular program. Interpretation involves translating the language of regulation (or law) into language understandable to the affected parties. Application is the "routine provision of services, payments, or other agreed upon program objectives or instruments" (pp. 82–83). Policy implementation is the stage of policy process in which the public sees concrete governmental actions or interventions. Implementation involves following the rules imposed in the law (or the regulation), developing program details, and then putting them into effect.

A classic case involving the Environmental Protection Agency (EPA) illustrates the latitude administrators are often given by Congress (and other legislative bodies) and the difficulties it can cause (Reich, 1985). The EPA was required by law to develop national standards limiting the emission of hazardous air pollutants so as to provide an "ample margin of safety" to protect the public health. But there was no definition in the legislation of "ample." The EPA was left with the task of identifying standards. This question was especially problematic in the case of a copper smelter in Tacoma, Washington. The EPA determined that, in the absence of any controls on emissions of arsenic from the plant, four new cases of cancer each year could be expected. Even with the very best control equipment, there would still be one new case each year. On the other hand, requiring actions to eliminate the threat would cost the company so much money that it could not afford to continue operations and its annual $23 million payroll would be lost to the Tacoma community. Obviously, then EPA administrator William Ruckelshaus faced a difficult exercise of discretion. (We'll see in Chapter 7 what he did.)

There have been several recent debates concerning the amount of discretion given to administrative agencies. Some analysts argue that broad grants of discretion amount to an abdication of legislative power; others point to the advantages of depending on the expertise and flexibility residing in the agencies or with the executive. Currently, the trend appears to be in the direction of greater detail in federal legislation, though occasionally less so at other levels. In any case, there inevitably remain many opportunities for the exercise of administrative discretion.

Policy Evaluation and Change   Policy evaluation "is an assessment of whether policies are working well" (Kraft & Furlong, 2007, p. 84). Policy evaluation asks whether the policy that is implemented has met the goals and the objectives of the legislation. Cost-benefit analysis is one of the most frequently used methods for evaluating policies, but there are many others. Evaluation may involve more than technical considerations; many times, it may involve "political judgments about a program's worth, decisions that are likely to be of great interest to all policy actors involved. In this sense, programs are continually, if often informally, evaluated by members of Congress, interest groups, think tanks, and others" (p. 85).

The purpose of policy evaluation is to determine whether a certain program is effective, that is, whether it produces the intended results. After the evaluation stage, changes in the policy may be introduced that can expand, reduce, or eliminate the program. But most programs undergo continuous incremental changes in an effort to make the policy more effective and more responsive. In this sense, the policy process actually never ends.

Types of Policy

The government develops and carries out several different types of policies, and the involvement of public and nonprofit organizations in the policy process varies somewhat according to type. We will examine four types: regulatory, distributive, redistributive, and constituent policy (Meier, 1987). (See the box "Exploring Concepts: Types of Public Policy.") These classifications are not precise, however, and indeed, many agencies work in several different areas at the same time.

Exploring Concepts

TYPES OF PUBLIC POLICY

1. Regulatory
2. Distributive
3. Redistributive
4. Constituent

Regulatory Policy *Regulatory policy* is designed to limit the actions of persons or groups so as to protect the general public or a substantial portion of the public. For example, people are prohibited from selling certain drugs, polluting the air and water, and engaging in monopolistic business practices. One form of regulation simply focuses on illegal criminal activity; it is a crime to do certain things. State and local governments have special responsibilities in this area, and certain federal agencies, such as the Drug Enforcement

Administration, are active here as well. Another form of regulation focuses on American business and seeks to ensure fair and competitive practices. Indeed, the first major regulatory effort in this country came in 1887, when the federal government created the Interstate Commerce Commission to regulate the railroads. Similar regulatory agencies today monitor securities (Securities and Exchange Commission), commodity exchanges (Commodity Futures Trading Commission), and labor relations (National Labor Relations Board), among others.

A modern regulatory area is concerned with access to certain goods available to the public generally, such as the airwaves (regulated by the Federal Communications Commission) or clean air and water (regulated by the Environmental Protection Agency). Other regulatory bodies focus on protecting health and safety in such areas as consumer protection (Consumer Product Safety Commission), air travel (Federal Aviation Administration), food (Food and Drug Administration), and workplace safety (the Occupational Safety and Health Administration).

Although federal regulation of economic activities has seen several waves of growth through the past century (Ripley & Franklin, 1987), the last two decades have seen somewhat of a movement in the opposite direction. Late in the Carter administration and extending through the Reagan administration, there were several efforts to deregulate certain industries. The Civil Aviation Board was disbanded in 1984, and over the following decade significant areas of transportation, telecommunications, and banking were deregulated. Moreover, regulations were eliminated or enforcement slowed down in areas such as workplace, auto, and consumer products safety.

During the 1990s, however, as many federal agencies relaxed their regulatory grip, a few attempted to expand their authority. The Environmental Protection Agency sought to set standards for pesticide and cancer risk, while the Occupational Safety and Health Administration created guidelines for reducing violent crime in retail locations open at night (Niskanen, 2001). The Food and Drug Administration attempted to expand its jurisdiction to the tobacco industry by establishing nicotine as a drug, which would have given federal regulators the power to control tobacco products. This move, however, was challenged by the tobacco companies, and in 2000 the Supreme Court ruled against the federal government, calling the FDA's attempt to assert jurisdiction in this area "impermissible" (Kessler, 2001, p. 384). These actions took place during the Clinton administration, which focused its efforts on regulatory changes in several areas, including the environment, corporate tax shelters, civil rights, trade, transportation, the securities market, banking, food, drugs, and health-care insurance. The administration used its National Performance Review to eliminate or rework a number of federal regulations.

Many of the regulatory activities undertaken by the George W. Bush administration were in response to crises, resulting in rules related to financial institutions, homeland security procedures, corporate governance, and energy. Two other Bush initiatives—No Child Left Behind and the addition of a drug benefit to Medicare—also involved new regulatory programs (DeMuth, 2011). The Bush administration also established two sets of guidelines: one for scientific peer review and the other related to conducting regulatory analysis, which imposed additional obligations for regulatory agencies but at the same time "reinvigorated the regulatory review process, exhibiting a willingness to return regulations that do not meet analytical requirements" (Dudley, 2004–2005, p. 9).

The Obama administration approved slightly fewer rules than did the Bush administration in its first years, although the number of "significant" rules—those costing $100 million or more—increased. The Obama White House has focused on regulations related to health-care and financial reforms, deep-water oil drilling, the environment, and food recalls. It also has stepped up enforcement of existing rules (Drajem & Dodge, 2011; *The Economist*, 2011). As the administration proceeded, however, there were signs that it was working toward balancing its regulatory activities with concerns for potential impacts on a weakened economy (Meckler & Lee, 2011).

Distributive Policy   *Distributive policy*, perhaps the most common form of government policy, uses general tax revenues to provide benefits to individuals or groups, often by means of grants or subsidies. If the country faces a large agricultural surplus, for example, the federal government may provide incentive payments to farmers to not produce crops that would add to the surplus. Similarly, the federal government provides direct grants to state and local governments for a variety of purposes. Finally, governments often create "public goods" that all citizens can enjoy. In some cases, such as national defense, the good is provided for all; in others, such as city, state, or national parks, it is anticipated that some citizens will use the benefit and others will not. (In Chapter 3, we will examine the growing trend toward employing user fees for certain of these traditionally public goods.) Unlike regulatory agencies, which are often at odds with the clientele group they are seeking to regulate, agencies that carry out distributive policies often develop close relationships with their constituencies and, in turn, with interested members of Congress. The growth of veterans' benefits over the past several decades is an almost classic example of the operation of such a subgovernment. The Department of Veterans Affairs is now one of the largest federal agencies and provides a broad range of health benefits, educational assistance, pensions, and insurance for veterans. Such a development would not have been possible without its close relationship with veterans' groups (such as the American Legion and the Veterans of Foreign Wars) and with the veterans' committees in Congress.

Redistributive Policy   *Redistributive policies* take taxes from certain groups and give them to another group. On rare occasions, redistribution is from the less-well-off to the better-off; many charge that capital gains proposals are of this type. Redistribution is, however, generally thought of as benefiting less advantaged groups at the perceived expense of the advantaged. Among major redistributive policies are those that deal with (1) income stabilization, helping to support those who are unemployed or retired; (2) social welfare, providing either direct payments to individuals or supporting state and local efforts for the indigent; and (3) health-care programs, such as Medicaid and Medicare. Most federal agencies active in the redistributive area are located in the Department of Health and Human Services, which claims its mission to be "the United States government's principal agency for protecting the health of all Americans and providing essential human services, especially for those who are least able to help themselves" (http://www.hhs.gov/about/).

Since redistributive policies are often (though sometimes incorrectly) viewed in win-lose terms—that is, if one group benefits, another will surely lose—they generate perhaps more intense discussion than any other area of public policy. Despite this controversy, every American president since Roosevelt and prior to Reagan has supported some major redistributive effort. Presidents Reagan and George H. W. Bush, however, took the opposite position, seeking to limit and even reduce redistributive programs. The reform agenda also influenced President Clinton, whose pledge to "end welfare as we know it" resulted in legislation placing a five-year cap on public assistance and tying welfare benefits to a work requirement. President George W. Bush continued this trend by advancing a $1.3 trillion tax cut and encouraging Congress to trim federal spending. In addition, President Bush implemented a faith-based initiative designed to employ private and nonprofit organizations in the delivery of social services, under which federal, state, and local governments sought to recruit, train, and assist religious groups to provide a broad array of social services. The Obama administration did an about-face, taking on the issue of economic inequality through its efforts to pass the health-care bill—the first major social legislation in decades—and a push for increased taxes on the wealthiest Americans. These moves signaled the Obama administration's commitment to moving the country away from the "hands-off" legacy of the Reagan years (Leonhardt, 2010). Clearly President Obama's tax plan for rolling back the Bush tax cuts for the wealthiest Americans will continue this trend.

Constituent Policy   *Constituent policies* (Lowi, 1972, p. 300) are intended to benefit the public generally or to serve the government. Foreign and defense policies are good examples of the first set of constituent policies, as well as good examples of the operations of a significant subgovernment. The Air Force had lobbied since the 1960s to build the B-1 bomber as a mainstay of our air defense. In 1978, President Carter was able to "kill" the B-1; however, only three years later, a combination of Department of Defense officials, representatives from the defense industry (especially contractors), and congressional supporters of increased military capabilities helped President Reagan resurrect the B-1. Incidentally, although more than a hundred B-1 bombers were built and were in service at one time, even today the B-1 remains controversial, with some proposals to retire the final sixty-six bombers facing opposition from military analysts and politicians, especially those with bombers based in their home states (http://www.time.com/time/nation/article/0,8599,2000020,00.html).

The other set of constituent policies are those directed toward the agencies of government itself. Legislation affecting the structure and function of government agencies, as well as policies governing their operations, falls in this area. President Carter was especially interested in policies impacting government agencies and was instrumental in such changes as a reorganization of the federal personnel system and a reemphasis on affirmative action in hiring practices. Presidents Reagan and George H. W. Bush were more interested in matters of technical efficiency and problems of waste in government. President Clinton, early in his term, expressed an interest in managerial issues, pledging to implement some version of Total Quality Management in the federal government, as he had done in Arkansas, and later developed the National Performance Review to make government work better and cost less (a topic we will examine in detail later). More recently, President George W. Bush placed an emphasis on developing more efficient, businesslike practices of government through a top-down performance system tied to the budget. President Obama has engaged in what has been called a "stealth revolution" in the way government works, quietly emphasizing new technology, the use of White House czars for different policy areas, and new levels of openness and transparency (Kettl, 2011).

Sources of Bureaucratic Power

There are several reasons governmental agencies have become so influential in the policy process. First, those who staff the agencies constitute an enormous source of expertise with respect to their areas of interest. No president, governor, mayor, or legislator could ever be expected to gain comparable expertise in all areas. Consequently, to make informed decisions, elected officials must often rely on those in the various agencies. It is often said that information is power; the information that is stored in government agencies is a distinct source of power.

What Would You Do?

You are testifying before a congressional committee in support of an increase in your agency's budget so that you can better investigate intellectual property claims involving software development. It is clear that one member of the committee, who is very supportive of the increase, really doesn't understand what's going on, and if he did, he might not support the budget increase. What would you do?

Second, as noted earlier, legislation is often both inevitably and intentionally vague, leaving considerable discretion to the administrator. In some cases, legislators simply wish to defer to the expertise of those in the agencies to provide detailed rules and interpretations. In others, they are recognizing the necessity of some flexibility in administering public programs. In still others, they are responding to the pressures of the legislative process itself, where specificity leads to disputes and vagueness can often promote agreement. Administrative discretion is also necessary because changing conditions necessitate changing policies, and it is not always possible to wait for new laws to be passed.

Third, flexibility is also needed as new information is discovered. For example, a few years ago, the surgeon general sent a brochure to all households in the country outlining the latest information about AIDS, an action not mandated by Congress but, in the judgment of the surgeon general, required by emerging events.

Through their expertise and discretionary power, those in public agencies help shape public policy. But there are more active and more political ways in which certain agencies become involved in the policy process. Whereas all agencies participate in making policy at some level, some agencies clearly are more politically adept than others. The Department of Defense and the Department of Veterans Affairs, for example, both wield considerable power, whereas the Government Printing Office has little.

The power, influence, and, in turn, the resources an agency is able to generate depend on several factors, some external to the agency, some internal. Obviously, shifts in public opinion concerning the agency's tasks are likely to affect the support the agency receives. The National Aeronautics and Space Administration has experienced wide variations in public support over the years, riding a crest of popularity with the first lunar landing but later coming under special scrutiny in the wake of the *Challenger* disaster. More recently, the agency has been fighting for a new identity following the end of the shuttle program. Not surprisingly, there seems to be a close correlation between favorable public opinion concerning an agency's area of interest and the support it receives from Congress.

More specific support comes from clientele groups, members of the legislature, and others in the executive branch. We have already noted the support certain agencies receive from clientele groups who benefit from the agencies' actions. Obviously, the larger and more powerful the supporters of the agency are, the more powerful the agency is likely to be. But agencies also develop opposition, which can be damaging to their programs. The Environmental Protection Agency (EPA), for example, interacts with many different groups, including businesses, state environmental agencies, members of the scientific community, and groups like the Sierra Club or the National Wildlife Federation; the EPA is likely to receive support from some groups and opposition from others.

Special support can also come from individual members of the legislature who decide, for whatever reason, to champion an agency's cause. But, as we have seen, the combination of congressional and clientele support can lead to the development of "subgovernments" within particular policy areas. These subgovernments come about, in part, because each group has something to give and something to gain from the relationship. The agency can provide quick and favorable responses to congressional requests for help as well as rulings favorable to clientele groups. In return, the agency might receive support for expansion of its budget and programs.

Support may also come from other members of the executive branch. Presidential support is obviously important, whether it is diffuse support of an agency's general work or more specific, such as in a president's support for stem cell research, increased drug enforcement, or a particular new weapons system. But agencies are also attentive to their relationships with other agencies. The development of a new state park may raise environmental issues, economic development issues, and health issues. The parks department will clearly fare better if all the relevant groups and agencies are "on board."

For nonprofit organizations, the capacity to influence public policy tends to be limited as much by informal as formal mandates. Although federal law does set guidelines for the use of public and charitable resources for lobbying purposes, some nonprofit leaders assume that these limitations prevent them from representing their constituents' interests in policy decision making. Or they refrain from taking a stand on issues so as not to isolate themselves from opposing parties. Philanthropy groups, such as the Independent Sector with its Charity Lobbying in the Public Interest initiative, have launched campaigns to encourage nonprofit leaders to be more proactive in their lobbying and to expand the advocacy role of nonprofits in the public policy process. The Internal Revenue Service has assisted in this effort by making available a simplified set of guidelines from the federal tax code that nonprofits can use to map their lobbying strategies.

In addition to the external sources of bureaucratic power, there are several internal sources of power. We have already noted the importance of the *information and expertise* of agency personnel. Especially in highly technical areas, such as medicine or agricultural economics, agency personnel are likely to be far more knowledgeable than many others involved in setting policies and priorities. If they can employ their expertise credibly, demonstrating effective performance over time, the agency will surely benefit.

Networking

For information on the advocacy role of nonprofit organizations, see Center for Lobbying in the Public Interest at www.clpi.org. A copy of the *Nonprofit Lobbying Guide* can be downloaded at http://www.independentsector.org/lobby_guide.

Agencies are also likely to benefit by their *cohesion*—the degree to which members are uniformly committed to the organization and its goals. An agency that is seen as divided over major issues will suffer a loss of credibility. Conversely, a sense of unity within an agency is likely to make the agency more effective, both internally and externally.

Finally, agencies benefit from strong and effective *leadership*. For example, as secretary of state in the Obama administration, Hillary Clinton played a strong leadership role in U.S. policy in the Middle East and elsewhere, while using her political experience and skills in dealing effectively with Congress. Similarly, Secretary of Defense Bob Gates enjoyed widespread respect from members of both political parties.

The power of particular agencies, therefore, is the result of interaction between the agency and its environment, a process to which the agency brings certain strengths, but it must also exercise considerable skill to reach its goals. The external support an agency can generate and the internal combination of its knowledge, cohesion, and leadership affect the amount of power and influence it can command.

Legislative Supervision: Structural Controls

Whatever an agency's degree of power and influence, however, that power and influence must be exercised judiciously. The agency is a creation of the legislature, and its programs are always subject to the legislature's review, alteration, and even termination. Obviously, most governmental programs (and the agencies that administer them) first take shape in the legislative process. In response to public demands, and perhaps also executive leadership, Congress or a state legislature or a city council or a board of directors passes legislation or policies to correct a particular problem. The problems vary widely, from federal environmental policy to state education requirements to local trash collection practices to the establishment of local health centers, but in most cases legislation authorizes the program. Typically, especially in larger jurisdictions, money to operate the program is authorized separately through an appropriations process. With a program authorized and money appropriated, the building (or expansion) of a public organization can commence.

Networking

For information on Congress, see www.loc.gov/index.html for the Library of Congress; www.house.gov for the House; and www.senate.gov for the Senate.

Legislation is, however, somewhat limited as a device for controlling the day-to-day activities of public organizations, especially at the federal and state levels. Remember that legislation is usually intentionally vague at some points, but legislation can be used as a control device. After a program is under way, legislation may be passed to prevent members of the executive branch from taking certain actions (Meier, 1987, pp. 140–141). For example, the Boland Amendment sought to prevent covert action in support of the Contras in Nicaragua in the mid-1980s. Whereas legislation authorizing programs must inevitably be somewhat general, legislative prohibitions on administrative actions can be quite specific. In 2007, the Congress sought legislative means to stop the Bush "surge" of troops being sent to Iran. However, as both these cases demonstrated, members of an administration may go to great lengths to reinterpret legislation to avoid even fairly specific prohibitions.

Legislative Veto   One specific device legislatures employ to control public agencies is the *legislative veto*, a statutory provision that essentially says that any action proposed by the executive (or administrative agency) under provisions of a particular piece of legislation is subject to the approval or disapproval of Congress (or some portion of Congress), usually within thirty to ninety days. For example, legislation might authorize a new highway program but require legislative consent to undertake specific projects. The legislative veto was first used in the 1930s to permit the president to reorganize, subject to review by Congress. In the 1970s and early 1980s, however, the legislative veto began to be used in many other areas.

In one case, Congress gave the Immigration and Naturalization Service the power to regulate immigration but retained the power to reverse its decisions. In this case that found its way to the Supreme Court as *Immigration and Naturalization Services v. Chadha* (1983), the Court ruled the legislative veto unconstitutional. The Court argued that the constitutional process for passing legislation requires the involvement of the president and that actions under a legislative veto provision violate the separation of powers by failing to involve the executive.

Despite the unconstitutionality of the legislative veto, the interest of Congress in controlling the work of administrative agencies has not diminished. Indeed, Congress has found a variety of ways to get around the *Chadha* ruling, either informally, by adding detailed rules to legislative authorizations, or by simply continuing to include veto provisions in legislation despite the Court's ruling. In the 1996 Congressional Review Act, Congress approved a legislative review process that, although providing a veto alternative, would not be open to the types of legal challenges that limited previous procedures (Cooper, 2000, p. 172).

It should be noted that the question of legislative control over administrative agencies is not limited to the federal government. At the state level, the use of the legislative veto has been growing rapidly, and many states have adopted the veto either in the form of legislation or as part of state administrative procedures. Moreover, while state courts have reinforced the principles of *Chadha* (the *Chadha* ruling in a federal case does not itself limit the use of the legislative veto at the state level), state lawmakers continue to employ vetolike actions in their processes of legislative review (Cooper, 2000, p. 172).

Sunset Laws   Another control device that legislatures employ to assess the performance of agencies and to eliminate those that are not successful is the *sunset law.* Sunset laws are based on the assumption that certain governmental programs should periodically terminate, to continue only after an evaluation of the program's effectiveness and a specific vote by the legislature. A classic case on the problem of program continuation is the military commissary system, which was created to provide foodstuffs to the cavalry on the Western Plains in the 1800s. The program continues today, although nearly all military commissaries are within ten miles of two or more supermarkets!

Sunset laws became popular in the late 1970s and early 1980s, after the state of Colorado, at the urging of Common Cause, passed a set of laws requiring that certain regulatory agencies be terminated at a given point unless given new life by the legislature. Soon dozens of other states and many municipalities passed general sunset laws, applying termination dates to a set of programs, or included sunset provisions in legislation creating new programs. Proposals containing sunset provisions were also presented at the federal level.

The purpose of specifying a particular life span for a program is to force careful evaluation of the program at some future point. Critics of automatic terminations point out several problems, not the least of which is the cost of evaluations and the burden to the legislature and legislative staff if all programs were periodically evaluated in great detail. Questions also arise about whether sunset legislation actually changes our assumptions about continuing most programs; for example, no one would seriously anticipate that a police or fire department would be eliminated. Finally, critics point out that most programs are reviewed periodically anyway and that highly ineffective programs are often eliminated even without "sunset" provisions.

A recent example of a sunset provision occurred when a sunset deadline for the Bush tax cuts was reached. In 2001, Congress acted to phase in key elements of the Bush administration's $1.3 trillion tax cut over a ten-year period, but it established a sunset deadline for the end of the tenth year. When that deadline arrived in 2011, Congress, as part of the debt ceiling debate, had to act positively to maintain the cuts, though they still remained a significant political issue.

Sunshine Laws   These examples of constraints on the operation of government agencies are closely related to *sunshine laws,* which require various agencies, especially regulatory agencies, to conduct business in public view (except under specific conditions). For example, Florida's Government-in-the-Sunshine Law provides the public the right of access to governmental proceedings at the state, county, and municipal levels, as well as in other political subdivisions, such as authorities and special districts. This law requires that any gathering of two or more members of any board or commission be subject to the requirements of the Sunshine Law if they discuss any matter that will, in the foreseeable future, come before that board for action. The three basic requirements of the law are that (1) meetings must be open to the public, (2) reasonable notice of such meetings must be given, and (3) minutes of the meetings must be taken. In effect, the law prohibits members of any board or commission from having informal or casual discussions of board business outside an open public meeting for which reasonable notice was given.

All fifty states now have "sunshine" provisions for their own legislative bodies, administrative agencies, and local governments. In all these cases, the legislative body, in expressing its concern for the public's right to be informed about the public's business, has exercised control over a broad range of administrative agencies.

Agency Conduct   A final mechanism through which legislative bodies formally exert control over administrative agencies is passage of broad legislation to govern agency conduct. Such legislation, applicable to all agencies, might affect administrative procedures, contracting or purchasing arrangements, human resources management, or other areas. A good example is the continuing congressional interest in access to governmental information. Following World War II, governmental agencies, probably in keeping with the military mentality of the war years, could legally classify as "confidential" all records for which there was "good cause" to hold them secret. As you can imagine, it was not difficult to come up with all kinds of "good causes" or reasons to withhold records. The practice of keeping secrets became so widespread that one congressional investigating group found that the Pentagon had classified as secret the construction of the bow and arrow and the fact that water runs downhill! Similarly, the General Services Administration had decided that photographs could not be taken in federal buildings without permission of the janitor (Archibald, 1979, p. 314).

What Would You Do?

You are the superintendent of schools in an urban school district. The mayor has approached you about using two of your high school gyms to house a nighttime recreational basketball league for inner-city youth. You are concerned that there could be serious damage to the gyms themselves and that the school buildings nearby would become a target for graffiti. What would you do?

As a result of findings such as these, and in the belief that the public has the right to information gathered by the government, Congress passed the Freedom of Information Act (FOIA) in 1966. The law was based on the assumption that the public has the right to know, except in clearly defined and exceptional cases; in other words, it tried to prevent those in the executive branch from classifying documents for ill-defined purposes. Implementation of the new law was hindered by confusion about certain parts and by some agency officials who still tried to maintain as much secrecy as possible. These problems were addressed in a series of amendments in 1974, 1986, and 1996. The amendments required agencies to respond to inquiries quickly and even sought to penalize government officials who hid government records from the public.

Although problems with the act have persisted, nearly all federal agencies have now implemented the FOIA provisions. In fact, processing and responding to FOIA requests have become a substantial activity in federal agencies. The importance of doing so has been reinforced by the Obama administration in a memo to federal agencies stating: "The Freedom of Information Act should be administered with a clear presumption: In the face of doubt, openness prevails. The Government should not keep information confidential merely because public officials might be embarrassed by disclosure, because errors and failures might be revealed, or because of speculative or abstract fears" (http://www .whitehouse.gov/the_press_office/FreedomofInformationAct/).

Legislative Supervision: Oversight

In addition to the "structural" mechanisms for legislative control, the legislature also exercises continuing supervision of administrative agencies through what is called the oversight function. Each house of Congress has a government operations committee charged with overseeing the activities of all government agencies, including their relationships with other levels of government. In addition, each of the other congressional committees exercises oversight responsibility with respect to its particular area of interest and expertise (such as defense, welfare, the post office). Oversight is especially connected to the legislative and appropriations processes, but it may occur at any time. For this reason, it is not unusual to see a cabinet secretary, complete with charts and documents, testifying before a congressional committee that is interested in his or her programs.

Holding hearings is probably the most visible oversight activity of Congress, at times assuming a circuslike atmosphere. The Iran-Contra hearings, for example, were essentially an investigation of the activities of the National Security Council, an executive agency, but they became the arena for considerable political infighting concerning the Reagan administration's conduct of foreign policy. The exposure that hearings provide members of Congress is obvious. Politicians from Harry Truman to Fred Thompson have built national reputations through their involvement in congressional hearings. But hearings can also provide excellent opportunities for administrative officials at the federal, state, and local levels, and in nonprofit organizations, to tell their side of the story, to help educate members of the legislature and the public generally, and to build support for their programs. Consequently, most agencies devote considerable time and attention to legislative relations, often—at the federal level—working through a legislative liaison office or—at the state and local levels—on a more individual basis.

Perhaps the most extraordinary example of legislative oversight of the executive occurred in 1998–1999, when Congress impeached, and then acquitted, President Clinton on charges stemming from an adulterous affair with a White House intern. The House of Representatives approved two articles of impeachment against the president, claiming that he perjured himself in his testimony before a federal grand jury and that he obstructed justice by interfering with the investigation of the independent council, Ken Starr. However, the Senate voted to acquit the president on both articles of impeachment, a decision that in many ways brought to a close eight years of allegations and investigations.

Nationally, Congress can also exercise oversight through its staff agencies, most of which were significantly enhanced by legislation in the early 1970s that created the Congressional Budget Office (CBO). The CBO was charged with furnishing certain program information to Congress. At about the same time, Congress shifted the focus of the GAO from its traditional financial auditing to program evaluations. Now, in addition to holding hearings, Congress can exercise oversight responsibility through staff evaluations of agency operations by requesting information from the Congressional Budget Office or by initiating audits or program evaluations by the GAO. Although legislative staff capabilities at the state and local levels are considerably less and often focused more on policy development than oversight, all levels of government have witnessed a general increase in legislative staff over the last twenty years.

Finally, there are myriad informal relationships between legislators and those in executive agencies. In fact, such nonstatutory controls may be the most common form of congressional oversight.

Despite the array of oversight activities available to members of Congress and despite the increased staff resources committed to oversight, questions remain concerning the effectiveness of legislative oversight of executive branch operations. Part of the problem is simply that many legislators have relatively little interest in oversight activities. Instead, they tend to focus on policy issues, recognizing that they are much more likely to build their reputations in the policy arena than in oversight. Moreover, interest in oversight activities is likely to vary from time to time, increasing in times of crisis or public outcry, when new and different program requests are forthcoming from an agency or when a member feels a particular agency has not been responsive to constituent groups. Generally, when a member has high confidence in a set of leaders and tends to agree with policies, the motivation for oversight decreases; conversely, when trust is low or when the member's favored programs are being ignored, the incentive for oversight is greater.

Legislative Supervision: Casework

Legislators also interact with those in public agencies on an individual basis, usually on behalf of their constituents. Obviously, legislators who wish to be reelected must be attentive to requests for information or influence from those in their districts. On the other side of the coin, individual citizens have come to expect that they can and should receive help from their senator or representative in dealings with government. Thus, members of the legislature receive a multitude of requests for assistance, from someone who needs help to collect Social Security benefits to someone who hopes to influence the award of a particular governmental contract. Intervention on behalf of individuals or groups that need assistance with or access to government agencies is called *legislative casework*.

At the federal level, providing services for constituents has become one of the most time-consuming and important activities for Congress members. Requests for assistance are typically handled by congressional staff members who specialize in casework. If the request requires an inquiry into an agency activity, the staffer will likely approach the agency's congressional liaison office or perhaps go directly to the agency head or a regional office. In most instances, inquiries are responded to promptly, and information about the case and any necessary explanations of the agency's action are returned quickly to the member of Congress.

Federal officials, in both the legislature and the agencies, feel the process is useful not only in providing a mechanism for review, but also in clarifying agency policies and procedures and assessing agency performance. Occasionally, however, there is pressure to "bend the rules" or to use political favoritism. Several years ago, for example, Congressman Daniel Flood of Pennsylvania was charged with conspiracy, bribery, and perjury in connection with his efforts to obtain certain federal grants and loans for a hospital in his district.

Casework activities seem less routine and institutionalized at the state and local levels. Here there appear to be both benefits and costs. On the one hand, casework activities serve to "humanize" the bureaucracy; on the other, there are disadvantages in the disruption of administrative processes and in the possibility of political influence. Certainly in the more highly professionalized governmental agencies, agency heads view legislators' involvement positively.

In many European countries and in some American states and localities, the legislature's casework function has been paralleled or even turned over to the office of the *ombudsman*, a permanent office that receives complaints and acts on behalf of citizens in securing information, requesting services, or pursuing grievances. Many other jurisdictions have created similar, though less formal, structures, such as public advocates, citizens' assistance offices, and so on.

Relationships with the Judiciary

The doctrine of separation of powers underlies the relationship between administrative agencies and the judiciary, a relationship that derives from the legal foundations of administrative actions. Agencies are created through legislative acts that define an agency's structure and scope of authority. Although the authority invested in agencies is primarily administrative, or executive, in nature, legislative bodies also delegate quasi-legislative and quasi-judicial responsibilities to agencies, giving them the unique ability to perform functions of all three branches of government. As we saw in previous sections, the executive and legislative branches employ various devices to serve as a check on agency conduct. The judiciary also plays an important role in this process by interpreting legislative mandates and delegation to agencies and reviewing the appropriateness of agency actions (Hall, 2006).

Actions that are quasi-legislative elaborate the details of legislation (rule making) while those that are quasi-judicial involve proceedings that produce some type of order (adjudication). Another area in which the courts may become involved concerns *agency discretion*. Because informal actions constitute the vast majority of what agencies do, they often require a substantial amount of discretion. Judicial review may be used to ensure that this discretion is used appropriately, although such review is limited.

Quasi-Legislative Action

As we have noted, most legislation is necessarily and intentionally general, leaving considerable room for interpretation or discretion on the part of the administrator. For example, an agency might be required by law to set safety standards for nuclear-powered electric utilities but receive little guidance about which specific standards should be employed. The agency would seek to determine appropriate standards and then develop rules to govern implementation of the legislation. *Rule making* is concerned with establishing general guidelines that would apply to a class of people or a class of actions in the future.

At the federal level, rule making by administrative agencies, as well as many other aspects of administrative law, is governed by the Administrative Procedure Act (APA). (Similar statutes exist in each state to provide the legal framework for administrative actions.) Adopted in 1946, the act seeks to ensure that agencies keep the public informed about their organization, procedures, and rules; that there is public participation in rule making; that there are uniform standards for formal rule making and adjudication; and that the extent of judicial review is defined (Funk, Lubbers, & Pou, 2008, p. 2).

Challenges to the APA have centered on issues of regulatory reform, including efforts by Congress to curb the powers of administrative agencies. The courts, however, remain favorable to the APA and in recent years have sustained the act's administrative framework. So while the legislative debate goes on, the APA continues to be the primary guide for the practice of administration.

In most cases, rule making is fairly straightforward, involving notice, comment, and steps to ensure an adequate record; in others, legislation requires greater detail and great formality in the rule-making process. Food and Drug Administration regulations and others that involve high risks require a formal rule-making process. Formal rule-making procedures require that the agency issue its rule only after trial-type hearing procedures are completed.

Networking

For the Supreme Court, go to www.supremecourt.gov/. For legal research on issues of administrative law, go to http://public.findlaw.com/library/pa-administrative-law.html.

Several important provisions have been added to the APA, including measures that reduced regulatory demands in some circumstances involving smaller for-profit, non-profit, and public-sector organizations. The first of these changes appeared in the APA as part of the Regulatory Flexibility Act (RFA) in 1980. Under the RFA, administrative agencies not only must take into account the impact of new regulations on smaller agencies but also must ensure a requisite level of flexibility in the rules to accommodate agency compliance and reporting without adding to administrative costs. In 1996, Congress expanded the RFA by adding three statutes and approving a legislative review process for proposed regulations. With the review process, lawmakers would now have a window of opportunity to adopt a "resolution of disapproval" prior to final decision making (Cooper, 2000, p. 139).

The Negotiated Rulemaking Act of 1990 created mechanisms for resolving disputes that would not require formal legal processes. Essentially, negotiated rule making brings together various parties involved in a particular issue to discuss potential rules and to try to arrive at a consensus in advance of the structure and content of those rules. Like other forms of dispute resolution, such as mediation or arbitration, no agency is forced to use these techniques; however, many public agencies find it helpful to do so (Funk, Lubbers, & Pou, 2008).

Quasi-Judicial Action

In addition to rule making, agencies can make policy through the use of *adjudication*, or proceedings that produce orders relating to individual cases. For example, following the issuance of safety standards for nuclear power plants, an administrator might have to decide if a particular plant has met those standards. Similarly, an administrator might have to decide if a specific individual is eligible for workers' compensation. In such cases, the administrator is making decisions that determine one's status under the law. The substantive decisions are obviously important, but so are the procedures under which they are resolved. For example, a woman denied welfare support might request a hearing to argue her case before a final decision is made. The administrator's decision to grant or refuse the hearing represents a type of adjudication.

In quasi-judicial administrative actions, there is a desire that citizens be treated fairly and not subjected to arbitrary decisions. This issue involves questions about who has the right to a hearing, at what stage in the process is a hearing appropriate, and what procedural rules should apply (Barry & Whitcomb, 2005, p. 8). Consequently, where standards of due process are applied, notice of the proposed action must be given, there must be a chance for the affected party to respond, and there must be an independent decision maker and an opportunity for appeal.

CourseReader Assignment

Log in to **www.cengage.com** and open CourseReader to access the reading:

Read "Judicial Review of Administrative Action," by Logan E. Sawyer III. We have examined the relationship between administrative agencies and the judiciary, a relationship that is quite complex but very important. One aspect of that relationship is judicial review of administrative actions.

How do you understand the role of discretion and regulation on behalf of administrative agencies? What is the role of the courts in reviewing discretion and regulation? What position with respect to the courts' review of administrative action would you take if you were a member of the Supreme Court? What position would you take if you were head of an administrative agency?

Agency Discretion

Most observers agree that in order to do their jobs effectively, public administrators need a certain amount of discretion, or "the authority to choose between two or more alternatives" (Hall, 2006, p. 34). However, excessive discretion can lead to arbitrariness and the violation of individual rights, while too little discretion can result in inflexibility. Informal agency action carries few procedural restrictions in terms of protecting individuals, which, in turn, places little restraint on discretion, and in certain areas discretion is accorded to administrators by law. Consequently, administrators often have considerable latitude in making judgments.

Judicial Review

The courts may review administrative actions (in rule making, adjudication, or other areas) through *judicial review*. Such review typically occurs when a party "suffering legal wrong because of agency action, or adversely affected or aggrieved by agency action" seeks judicial remedy (5 U.S.C., Section 702). The court reviews the case in light of constitutional, statutory, and executive provisions and determines the appropriateness of the administrative action. Courts may find unlawful and set aside agency actions that are unconstitutional, that extend beyond the limits of statutory authority, that are "arbitrary, capricious, or an abuse of discretion," or that are procedurally unfair or without substantive justification (5 U.S.C., Section 706).

The authority of the court to review administrative action is derived from both statute and common law. The APA stipulates that judicial review can be denied when statutory provisions prohibit review and when "agency action is committed to agency discretion by law" (5 U.S.C., Section 701), although the latter has been interpreted narrowly by the courts (Hall, 2006). One of the key aspects of the relationship between the courts and agencies is the amount of deference the courts should give agencies in their interpretation of statutes. This question applies to an agency's interpretation of both the "scope of its jurisdiction" and the "substantive provisions" under its originating statute (Heinzerling & Tushnet, 2006, p. 378). This is a particularly thorny issue when Congress is unclear in its intent with regard to an agency's jurisdiction. However, following the Supreme Court's finding in *Chevron v. National Resources Defense Council* (1984), if a statute is silent or ambiguous with respect to the issue at hand, the agency's interpretation of the statute must be upheld if its interpretation is a reasonable one.

The deference to administrators underlying *Chevron* stems from the Court's belief that an administrative agency responsible for implementing a piece of legislation has the most knowledge of the policy and of existing legislation concerning the issue. The courts may ultimately disagree with the agency interpretation, but they start with a heavy presumption that the agency was correct. Although *Chevron* has been called into question, subsequent Supreme Court decisions have reinforced the doctrine of judicial deference to administrative agencies. On the other hand, the courts have established parameters for *Chevron*, limiting the standard to regulatory measures and to circumstances in which the administering agency clearly acts within the confines of the statute. The courts have maintained that petitions regarding administrative issues, but whose primary concerns relate to legal matters such as contracts, should be viewed as "a question of law clearly within the competence of the courts" (Cooper, 2000 p. 254). Despite these limitations, the courts have been consistent in reinforcing the *Chevron* doctrine.

That is not to say that courts always rule in favor of the administrative agency. Of particular interest are those cases in which the court determines that the agency has misinterpreted (or gone beyond) the intent of the legislation. For example, the statute creating the Occupational Safety and Health Administration (OSHA) charged the agency with developing a standard for toxic substances in the workplace "which assures, to the extent feasible, that no employee will suffer material impairment even if such employee has regular exposure to the hazard for the period of his working life" (Cooper, 1983, p. 192). After extensive studies, OSHA determined that exposure to the toxic substance benzene created a risk of cancer and other health hazards and set a standard accordingly.

In response, the American Petroleum Institute sought judicial review that led the courts to a discussion of two issues. A lower court focused on legislative intent, finding that the phrase "to the extent feasible" in the legislation meant that a standard had to be both technologically and economically feasible. For this reason, the court set aside the OSHA standard. The Supreme Court concentrated on the health aspects of the case, with the majority concluding that existing standards were not dangerous and the new standard was not necessary. The justices who dissented argued that the Court should not substitute its own judgment on the technical merits of the case for that of experts within the agency. The case illustrates several of the most important difficulties that face the courts in reviewing administrative actions (Cooper, 2000).

The courts have acted not only to review agency actions but also to compel agency action "unlawfully withheld or unreasonably delayed" (5 U.S.C., Section 706). In one example, the Food and Drug Administration received a petition from a group of death row inmates to determine whether the materials used for lethal injections were safe and painless or whether they might leave the prisoner conscious but paralyzed, a witness to his or her own slow death. The FDA argued that it did not have jurisdiction to review the practices of state corrections systems in cases such as this; however, on review, the circuit court in 1983 concluded that the FDA did indeed have jurisdiction. The court wrote, "In this case FDA is clearly refusing to exercise enforcement discretion because it does not wish to become embroiled in an issue so morally and emotionally troubling as the death penalty. As a result of the FDA's inaction, appellants face the risk of cruel execution" (Cooper, 1985, p. 649). However, in a 2004 case involving an attempt to force the Bureau of Land Management to take action to protect wilderness lands in Utah from damage by off-road vehicles, the Supreme Court ruled that such attempts are limited to cases in which an agency fails to take a discrete action that is required by law.

Closely related to the FDA's failure to undertake an investigation are cases in which the agency refuses to make rules or delays the issuance of rules required by statute. But there also have been several cases in which agencies have been found to have exceeded their authority in rescinding previously established rules.

Concerns for Due Process

At the heart of our system of jurisprudence is the assurance that people will be treated fairly, that they have a right to present arguments and evidence in their own behalf, and that those who make the decisions will be unbiased and impartial. With regard to issues of due process in administrative adjudication—whether a hearing is required, at what point, and the format of the hearing—some patterns have emerged in the Supreme Court's evaluation of administrative matters. During the 1950s, 1960s, and early 1970s, the Court sought to protect the rights of citizens from arbitrary action on the part of administrative agencies by requiring that a person be allowed an opportunity to challenge a proposed action before being made to suffer serious harm. The Court would not allow cost or inconvenience to the agency as an excuse for causing harm to an individual.

Through the 1970s and 1980s, however, the Supreme Court, under the leadership of Chief Justice Warren Burger, began to alter its approach to administrative due process, treating administrative hearings not as a means of protection, but as devices for fact-finding. Most frequently, the Court has employed a "balancing test," weighing the interests of the individual (rather narrowly defined), the value of additional safeguards, and the government's interest (including the fiscal and administrative burdens that additional procedural safeguards might impose). (See the box "Public Administration in History: The Spotted Owl and Agency Interpretation of the Law.") As a result, it has become much more difficult for someone who feels that adequate protections have not been provided to prevail in the courts (Cooper, 2000).

The flexibility in administrative law for due process has contributed to a variety of alternative dispute resolution (ADR) strategies, namely, mediation and arbitration. The adoption of the Alternative Dispute Resolution Act of 1990 helped remove many of the barriers administrators face to such alternative approaches. For the most part, ADR strategies are easier to employ in less complex cases. Yet ADR should not be used to obtain settlements that fail to protect the public interest. The spirit and letter of the agreement must be clear or else face considerable challenge, and potential failure, during the implementation stage.

The Courts and Agency Administration

Over the last twenty years, one of the most dramatic developments in the relationship between administrative agencies and the judiciary is the direct involvement of federal district courts (and some state courts) in agency administration, including decisions on spending, personnel, organization, and management. This involvement has come about through court rulings in *administrative equity* cases, wherein individual rights, such as the prohibition against cruel and unusual punishment, have been violated by state and local administrative organizations.

Two landmark cases in the early 1970s set precedents for such rulings. In the first, prisoners in the Arkansas penitentiary system alleged a large number of abuses, including dangerous and unhealthy conditions in the prisons. The court ruled that confinement in the Arkansas system amounted to cruel and unusual punishment and ordered corrections officials to devise a plan to remedy the problems. Similarly, in Alabama a federal district court judge found "intolerable and deplorable" conditions in that state's largest mental health facility and ordered corrective actions. The court also established a constitutional right to treatment, detailing actions required to meet that constitutional standard (Gilmour, 1982, pp. 26–29).

Public Administration in History

THE SPOTTED OWL AND AGENCY INTERPRETATION OF THE LAW

When a court reviews an agency's construction of the statute it administers, it is confronted with two questions.

First, always, is the question of whether Congress has directly spoken to the precise question at issue. If the intent of Congress is clear, that is the end of the matter; for the court, as well as the agency, must give effect to the unambiguously expressed intent of Congress.

If, however, the court determines Congress has not directly addressed the precise question at issue, the court does not simply impose its own construction of the statute, as would be necessary in the absence of an administrative interpretation. Rather, if the statute is silent or ambiguous with respect to the specific issue, the question for the court is whether the agency's answer is based on a permissible construction of the statute.

Given the ubiquity of ambiguity in regulatory statutes, *Chevron* looked like a recipe for judicial acquiescence to agency interpretations. It hasn't worked out that way.

Sometimes, to be sure, the Court gives full scope to the doctrine announced in *Chevron*. Other times, however, the Court virtually ignores the *Chevron* test. Most importantly, only three years after *Chevron*, the Court opened up further opportunities for exceptions to the doctrine of deference to agency interpretation.

Babbitt v. Sweet Home Chapter of Communities for a Great Oregon—the celebrated Spotted Owl case—illustrates the indeterminacy of the *Chevron* doctrine. At issue was the meaning of the term *harm* in the Endangered Species Act. The act prohibits the "taking" of endangered animals and defines "take" to mean "to harass, harm, pursue, hunt, shoot, wound, kill, trap, capture, or collect." According to Secretary of the Interior Bruce Babbitt, "harm" includes destruction of habitat that has the effect—although not the purpose—of harming endangered wildlife. Oregon business interests challenged this interpretation as contrary to the statute.

The fundamental problem in administrative law is that a congressional majority typically favors some federal response to a problem, but no congressional majority favors any particular response. Rather than do nothing, Congress adopts general language and leaves it to the agencies—and the courts—to make the controversial choices. The Endangered Species Act is a good illustration of this. Congress knew quite well that habitat destruction poses the biggest threat to endangered species. Congress also knew, however, that regulating habitat destruction would conflict with economic development. So Congress waffled.

The only clear intention Congress had regarding habitat destruction is a clear intention to have no clear intention. The problem calls less for lawyerly interpretations of authoritative language than for a policy decision made by an institution that is familiar with the problem and is held politically accountable. The agency has the advantage (over) the courts on both counts.

SOURCE: Donald A. Dripps, *Trial* 32, no. 2 (February 1996): 70–71. Reprinted with permission of the author.

The involvement of courts in the management of public agencies is especially well illustrated in a federal judge's order demanding reform of the New Orleans Parish Prison. In addition to ordering adequate medical services, improved security, and development of recreational facilities, the judge directed that "the management and operation of the prison be improved immediately," that a professional penologist be hired to manage the prison, and that personnel practices (filling vacancies, raising wages, etc.) be improved in specific ways. Although court actions such as this have obviously corrected constitutional inequities, there are questions as to whether the courts are well suited for involvement in the details of administration. Moreover, many states and localities argue that court-ordered expenditures of funds on projects such as desegregation or prison reform take money away from other needed services, such as education, social welfare, or mental health. For these reasons, the Supreme Court has taken steps to limit the involvement of courts in the work of administrative agencies, requiring carefully tailored plans of limited duration based on specific constitutional violations.

Summary and Action Implications

This chapter has explored the political context of public administration, including things you will simply need to know to operate effectively in or with public or nonprofit organizations. The material in this chapter (and in Chapters 3 and 4) constitutes a knowledge base on which to build your action skills. Understanding the political context of work in the public sector will enhance the effectiveness of your actions.

Public managers, and their counterparts in nonprofit organizations, work in many different institutional settings, but those institutions all reflect important political values that lie at the heart of a democratic system. Whether at the federal, state, or local level, in the governmental or nongovernmental sector, a democracy's values, especially a concern for operating in the public interest, affect the structure of public and nonprofit organizations. For example, the division of powers at the federal level expresses a fear of concentrated power; similarly, the council-manager plan expresses one way to view the relationship between politics and administration. Finally, the structure of nonprofit organizations reflects their operation in the public interest. Knowing something about how democratic values are reflected in the structure of the various organizations and knowing something about the role of executive leadership in administrative organizations will enable you to act with greater confidence and authority.

As a manager or analyst, you may have important interactions with a legislative body, either the national Congress, a state legislature, a local city council, or a nonprofit organization's board of directors. Those serving in the public interest participate in one way or another in nearly all policy areas—a situation that our political system encourages. The distinction Woodrow Wilson suggested between politics (or policy) and administration no longer accurately describes the relationship between the legislative and the executive branches. Today, the legislature and the various agencies of government share in the policy process, either working together in developing policy or making separate decisions in different realms.

As a manager or analyst, you will also deal with the legislature in many other ways. Most importantly, the legislature will establish the tasks your agency or association will undertake and provide human and financial resources to carry them out. Moreover, the legislative body will exercise continuing, although sometimes intermittent, supervision over your work. Thus, you may spend a great deal of time developing effective working relationships with those in the legislature.

The involvement of the courts in the work of administration is both intense and inevitable. For this reason, your understanding of the legal system and your ability to interact with legal and judicial officials will improve your effectiveness as a public manager. Whether you are dealing with the legislative body or the courts, your relationship with either need not be adversarial. Indeed, in many cases, the legislature and the courts can help to substantially improve administrative practices.

By now you should be coming to realize that your behavior as a public or nonprofit manager is bounded by a vast and complicated network of relationships in which you are but one of many players. Within this network, you must be attentive to questions of executive leadership, legislative intent and oversight, and judicial interpretation. The world of the public administrator is indeed complex!

STUDY QUESTIONS

1. What do we mean by the term *public policies?*

2. Describe how the president's role in the administration of government has changed since the framing of the Constitution.

3. Describe the administrative system at the federal level.

4. State and local governments have been designed to operate similarly to the national level; however, both have distinct structures for administering government initiatives. Explain each level's structure and the different approaches to operating the government bureaucracy.

5. Describe the policy process and the actors who play significant roles in shaping administrative issues.

6. What are the four types of policy? Define and give examples.

7. How do agencies maintain a power base within the government?

8. Describe some of the structural controls on bureaucratic power and how government, as a whole, benefits from these controls.

9. Discuss several ways the legislative and judicial branches interact with the bureaucracy. Explain why these interventions are necessary and useful.

CASES AND EXERCISES

1. We have discussed the various powers, both formal and informal, that affect the governor's ability to exercise executive power in the administration of state government. Among the informal powers that governors exercise are political powers (including agenda setting), budgetary powers, and executive leadership.

Among the formal powers are the presence or absence of an item veto and the ability of the governor to reorganize state agencies. Another indicator of gubernatorial power is the number of other elected statewide officials. Analyze the power of the governor in your state, giving special attention to the governor's power to exercise executive leadership over the agencies of state government. How do your governor's executive powers compare to those of the president of the United States? How do they compare to those of your local mayor?

2. Attend a meeting of a congressional or state legislative committee, your local city council, or the board of directors of a local nonprofit organization. Watch the pattern of interaction between elected members of the legislative body and full-time administrators. (The latter may be agency staff called to testify, legislative support staff, a city manager or executive director, or many others.) What strengths does each side bring to the exchange? What is the level of cooperation or competition? If possible, try to follow up with the administrator to see how he or she felt about the interchange. To what extent did the legislative body set a clear direction for the administrator's ensuing actions? What discretion did the administrator have (or claim to have) following the meeting?

3. Consider the following case: Billie Jackson was the leader of a nonprofit, economic development corporation in a small community in Colorado. For six years, Billie had been trying to interest members of the city council in purchasing an abandoned downtown hotel for conversion to a city-owned long-term care facility. Billie felt strongly that the community needed such a facility and that the city had a golden opportunity to meet that need through purchase of the hotel. The problem was that several extremely conservative members of the council felt differently. In their view, the city shouldn't get into providing social services, especially where the need might be met by a private firm at some point in the future. Moreover, they felt the cost of the purchase and renovations would be more than the community could bear.

The hotel issue was once again on the council agenda, and Billie was determined to make the strongest appeal possible. With the help of a nearby university, she had prepared a lengthy report documenting the need for the facility and the desirability of purchasing the hotel. Just as she was beginning her presentation, one of the conservative council members said, "Mrs. Jackson, we have heard more on this topic than we care to. I just don't want to go through all this again. I move to table the issue indefinitely." The motion to table carried by a quick and somewhat confused voice vote.

Assume the role of Billie Jackson. What is your immediate response? What would you do in the days and weeks that followed? Would you continue to pursue the issue? Why or why not?

FOR ADDITIONAL READING

Anderson, James E. *Public Policymaking: An Introduction*. 6th ed. Boston: Houghton Mifflin, 2006.

Balutis, Alan P., Terry F. Buss, and Dwight Ink. *Transforming American Governance: Rebooting the Public Square*. Armonk, NY: M.E. Sharpe, 2011.

Barry, Donald D., and Howard R. Whitcomb. *The Legal Foundations of Public Administration*. Lanham, MD: Rowman & Littlefield Publishers, 2005.

Beckett, Julia, and Heidi O. Koenig, eds. *Public Administration and Law*. Armonk, NY: M.E. Sharpe, 2005.

Boris, Elizabeth T., and C. Eugene Steuerle, eds. *Nonprofits and Government: Collaboration and Conflict*. Washington, DC: Urban Institute, 1999.

Cooper, Phillip J. *By Order of the President: The Use and Abuse of Executive Direct Action* (Studies in Government and Public Policy). Lawrence: University Press of Kansas, 2002.

Cooper, Phillip J. *Cases on Public Law and Public Administration*. Belmont, CA: Thomson/Wadsworth, 2005.

Cooper, Phillip J. *Public Law and Public Administration*. 4th ed. Belmont, CA: Thomson/Wadsworth, 2007.

Cooper, Phillip J. *The War against Regulation* (Studies in Government and Public Policy). Lawrence: University Press of Kansas, 2009.

deLeon, Peter. *Democracy and the Policy Sciences*. Albany: State University of New York Press, 1997.

Frederickson, H. George, John Nalbandian, and International City/County Management Association. *The Future of Local Government Administration: The Hansell Symposium*. Washington, DC: International City/County Management Association, 2002.

Funk, William F., Jeffrey S. Lubbers, and Charles Pou, Jr., eds. *Federal Administrative Procedure Sourcebook*. 4th ed. Chicago: ABA Publishing, 2008.

Hall, Daniel E. *Administrative Law: Bureaucracy in a Democracy*. 3rd ed. Upper Saddle River, NJ: Pearson Prentice Hall, 2006.

Heinzerling, Lisa, and Mark V. Tushnet. *The Regulatory and Administrative State: Materials, Cases, Comments*. New York: Oxford University Press, 2006.

Kettl, Donald F. *The Global Public Management Revolution*. 2nd ed. Washington, DC: Brookings Institution Press, 2005.

Kettl, Donald F., Steven Kelman, and IBM Center for the Business of Government. *Reflections on 21st Century Government Management. 2008 Presidential Transition Series*. Washington, DC: IBM Center for the Business of Government, 2007.

Kraft, Michael E., and Scott R. Furlong. *Public Policy: Politics, Analysis, and Alternatives*. 2nd ed. Washington, DC: CQ Press, 2007.

Light, Paul C. *Making Nonprofits Work: A Report on the Tides of Nonprofit Management Reform*. Washington, DC: Brookings Institution Press, 2000.

Meier, Kenneth J. *Politics and the Bureaucracy*. 2nd ed. Pacific Grove, CA: Brooks/Cole, 1987.

Menzel, Donald C., and Harvey L. White. *The State of Public Administration: Issues, Challenges, and Opportunities*. Armonk, NY: M.E. Sharpe, 2011.

Nalbandian, John. *Professionalism in Local Government: Transformation in Roles, Responsibilities and Values of City Managers*. San Francisco: Jossey-Bass, 1991.

Peters, B. Guy. *American Public Policy: Promise and Performance*. 7th ed. Washington, DC: CQ Press, 2007.

Piotrowski, Suzanne J., and David Rosenbloom. "Nonmission-Based Values in Results-Oriented Public Management: The Case of Freedom of Information." *Public Administration Review* 62, no. 6 (2002): 643–657.

Reich, Robert. *Locked in the Cabinet*. New York: Alfred A. Knopf, 1997.

Renz, David O., and Robert D. Herman. *The Jossey-Bass Handbook of Nonprofit Leadership and Management*. 3rd ed. San Francisco: Jossey-Bass, 2010.

Ripley, Randall B., and Grace A. Franklin. *Congress, the Bureaucracy, and Public Policy*. 4th ed. Pacific Grove, CA: Brooks/Cole, 1987.

Roberts, Nancy C., and Paula J. King. *Transforming Public Policy*. San Francisco: Jossey-Bass, 1996.

Rosenbloom, David H. *Administrative Law for Public Managers*. Boulder, CO: Westview Press, 2003.

Salamon, Lester M. *America's Nonprofit Sector: A Primer*. 2nd ed. New York: Foundation Center, 1999.

Salamon, Lester M. *The State of Nonprofit America*. Washington, DC: Brookings Institution Press, 2002.

Svara, James H. *Official Leadership in the City: Patterns of Conflict and Cooperation*. New York: Oxford University Press, 1990.

Svara, James H. *The Facilitative Leader in City Hall: Reexamining the Scope and Contributions*. Boca Raton, FL: CRC Press, 2009.

CHAPTER 3

THE INTERORGANIZATIONAL CONTEXT
OF PUBLIC ADMINISTRATION

As a manager, you will interact not only with many others at your level of government or the independent sector, but also with those throughout our system of governance at the federal, state, and local levels. More and more, public administrators recognize that managing an agency requires paying attention to what happens in other organizations and that relations with those outside the agency are just as important as relations with those inside. This chapter examines the interorganizational context in which public administrators operate.

The traditional focus in public administration has been the agency, and that is the focus we have largely taken so far. However, given the "transformation of governance" that has occurred during the past couple of decades, it may be more helpful to focus not on the individual agency, but on the *relationships* among many different groups: public, private, and nonprofit (Kettl, 2009). Indeed, today more than ever, the effectiveness of public programs depends on the ability of various agencies to cooperate in processes of service delivery. This development is explored further in the box "Exploring Concepts: Transformation of Governance" later in this chapter.

Government resources, from federal grants for public assistance to local funding for health and human services, go to a variety of actors, and although the funding usually contains guidelines and performance objectives, the implementing agencies often have a certain amount of leeway for running the program or for forging relationships with other groups to deliver the services.

For example, Temporary Assistance for Needy Families (TANF), the federal welfare program that replaced Aid to Families with Dependent Children (AFDC) under the Personal Responsibility and Work Opportunity Reconciliation Act of 1996, provides funding to the states for public assistance and welfare-to-work initiatives (Plotnick et al., 2011). The states in turn rely on a variety of local government, for-profit, and nonprofit organizations for service delivery. These organizations may provide the services themselves, or they may contract with other organizations (again, public, private, or nonprofit) for carrying out the programs. In many cases, an individual or family may receive an array of public assistance without ever coming into contact with a government employee (Kettl, 2000, 2009).

Another example of intergovernmental and interorganizational cooperation is in the area of emergency management and disaster relief. Hurricane Katrina was the single most destructive and costly natural catastrophe in U.S. history. In August 2005, the hurricane struck the Gulf Coast, affecting four states: Alabama, Florida, Mississippi, and Louisiana. Immediately after the disaster, forty-two states and the District of Columbia received presidential emergency declarations to shelter the evacuees. The Federal Emergency Management

Agency (FEMA, which became part of the Department of Homeland Security in March 2003), in coordination with the American Red Cross, state and local governments, nongovernmental organizations, local communities, and businesses, worked (and still works) on relief and recovery of the regions hit by the hurricane. FEMA provided $6 billion to the direct victims for housing and other assistance. An additional $4.8 billion in federal funds was reimbursed to the states for "mission assignments." According to FEMA, "The U.S. Small Business Administration has approved more than $10.4 billion in disaster loans to homeowners, renters and businesses as a result of damages caused by the hurricane. More than $15.3 billion has been paid out to National Flood Insurance Program policyholders" (Pittman, 2009, p. 149). What was most striking, however, was the failure of various public and private agencies to effectively coordinate services to the victims of the hurricane. Katrina made policy makers reevaluate the emergency management programs on national and state levels, but it also provides a significant example of the importance of interorganizational cooperation and coordination (Liu et al., 2011).

These examples illustrate the complexity of the interactions triggered by federal policies and natural disasters. But equally complex relationships can develop as a result of a local initiative. A local community that wants to attract new industry might develop a coalition of government, business, labor, and education groups to promote the city's image and to work with groups at other levels of government. These groups might include a state department of economic development to help contact prospective employers wishing to relocate. Or the city might request that the state or federal government designate a particular area in the city as an *enterprise zone*, thus permitting special tax incentives and other benefits for businesses willing to locate there. Again, a variety of government and nongovernment entities are involved in the task of economic development.

One can easily understand why the effectiveness of many public programs depends on the quality of the relationships among various organizations (Bevir, 2011; Goldsmith & Eggers, 2004). Some analysts for this reason emphasize the importance of the *interorganizational networks* that develop in various policy areas. Obviously, the various groups and organizations involved in any policy arena do not report to a

CourseReader Assignment

Log in to **www.cengage.com** and open CourseReader to access the reading:

Read "Public Management in Intergovernmental Networks: Matching Structural Networks and Managerial Networking," by Kenneth J. Meier and Lawrence J. O'Toole, Jr. As we have seen, public administrators interact with a wide variety of other groups and organizations both inside and outside government. We have pointed out that networks of organizations—public, private, and nonprofit—are increasingly involved in the development and implementation of public policy. This trend amounts to a change from intergovernmental relations to interorganizational relations.

What are some of the factors that contribute to an increase in network governance? What are some of the advantages to working through networks? What are some of the disadvantages? Can you think of examples of public policies in your own area that are being carried out by such networks?

single director, nor are they structured in a typically hierarchical fashion. Rather, they are ==loosely joined systems that often have overlapping areas of interest, duplication of effort, and lack of coordination== (see the box "Exploring Concepts: Networks and Network Management"). Hult and Walcott (1990) wrote, "Governance networks link structures both within and across organizational boundaries. Like governance structures, networks may be permanent or temporary, formal or informal. They may be consciously designed, emerge unplanned from the decisions of several actors, or simply evolve. A given governance structure may be part of one or several networks" (p. 97).

Whether the growing dependence on such systems is a helpful development is a matter of some debate. Many experts have suggested that the use of intermediaries in the delivery of services is a major reason for the difficulties many programs encounter. On the other hand, many such networks have proven enormously stable over time, and others have capitalized on the inherent flexibility and adaptability of such systems. In any case, because interorganizational networks are such an important part of the management of public programs, they deserve our attention.

Exploring Concepts

NETWORKS AND NETWORK MANAGEMENT

The first type is a *service implementation network* that governments fund to deliver services to clients. Collaboration is critical because these networks are based on joint production of services, often for vulnerable citizens like the elderly, families on welfare, or the mentally ill. Integration of services is critical so clients will not fall through the cracks. The second type of network is an *information diffusion network*, whose central purpose is to share information across governmental boundaries to anticipate and prepare for problems that involve a great deal of uncertainty, such as earthquakes, wildfires, and hurricanes.

The third type of network (which often grows out of an information diffusion network) is a *problem solving network*. The purpose of this network is to solve a proximate problem like the response to the attack on the World Trade Center and the Pentagon on 9/11. The problem that the managers confront demands immediate attention and shapes the nature of the response and the set of interorganizational relations that emerge. Past cooperative relationships prove useful in managing a problem solving network.

The fourth type of network is a *community capacity building network*, whose purpose is to build social capital in a community so that it is better able to deal with a variety of ongoing and future problems, such as substance abuse among youth. An effective community capacity building network allows a town or city to be more resilient and responsive when new problems emerge, as when methamphetamine emerged from drug labs to ravage certain communities.

Managing networks that do not have a hierarchical chain of command but which rely on trust and reciprocity as the levers of collaboration makes the tasks of managers much different

(Continued)

(Continued)

from those in organizations. These tasks must be performed by network managers, like Coast Guard Vice Admiral Thad Allen, who led the recovery of New Orleans and the Gulf Coast in the wake of the devastation of Hurricane Katrina. But the tasks must also be performed by the managers of organizations who are part of a network, for example, the local police chief with a DARE (Drug Abuse Resistance Education) program in district schools that is part of a substance abuse prevention network but also manages a police department.

…The first task [that leads to effective network management] is the *management of accountability*. With no chain of command, this is a critical issue that both network managers and managers of organizations in a network must successfully negotiate. Key issues are determining who is responsible for what and how to respond to free riders who don't contribute their fair share but continually demand more resources.

The second task is the *management of legitimacy*, which is more critical for networks than for organizations. A public organization is created by law to serve a particular purpose. A network is usually a cooperative venture that must continually negotiate its legitimacy, particularly if, as is often the case, its boundaries cross the public, private, and nonprofit sectors. Managers of organizations in networks must continually work to convince their stakeholders that their work with other organizations in the larger network continues to be valuable and worthwhile.

Management of conflict is the third task of network managers. Conflict can develop from differing goals among the organizations in the network, and the result cannot be resolved by commands issued from on high. It is important that network managers listen to the voices of their members and provide mechanisms for conflict resolution. These devices help to create dispute resolution mechanisms for conflicts that arise between managers of network organizations and network managers.

SOURCE: H. Brinton Milward and Keith G. Provan, "A Manager's Guide to Choosing and Using Collaborative Networks," Washington, DC: IBM Endowment for the Business of Government, 2006 (www.businessofgovernment.org/pdfs/ProvanReport.pdf).

The Development of Intergovernmental Relations

To operate public programs effectively and responsibly, you must understand the relationships among levels of government. There are various ways to define the relationship between a larger comprehensive unit of government and its constituent parts. A *confederation,* for example, is a system in which the constituent units grant powers to the central government but do not allow it to act independently. A unitary system is one in which all powers reside with the central government and various units derive their powers from that unit. France and Sweden, for instance, are characterized by unitary systems, as is the relationship between states and localities in the United States; localities hold only those powers specified or permitted by the state.

The relationship between our national government and the states, however, is *federal*. It involves a division of powers between the two levels of government, federal and state.

unitary
govt

(Local governments exist under the legal framework of the states.) As you know, some powers are granted specifically to the central government (to conduct foreign relations, to regulate interstate commerce, and so on); some are reserved by the states (to conduct elections, to establish local governments, and so on); and some are held by both levels (to tax, to borrow money, to make laws, and so on). (This system of governance is also referred to as federalism.) A federal structure has many advantages. It allows for diversity and experimentation, but it can also lead to the development of a highly complex intergovernmental system, a fact of life with important implications for the management of public programs.

The term *intergovernmental relations* is often used to encompass all the complex and interdependent relationships among those at various levels of government as they seek to develop and implement public programs. The importance of intergovernmental relations has been recognized in several structural developments. At the federal level, a permanent Advisory Commission on Intergovernmental Relations was established in 1959 and continued to operate until the mid-1990s. All states and nearly all major cities have a coordinator for intergovernmental relations (though the specific titles vary). Finally, many scholars and practitioners have begun to emphasize the managerial processes involved in intergovernmental relations by employing the term *intergovernmental management.*

A key to understanding intergovernmental relations in this country involves understanding the changing patterns used to fund public programs. Although intergovernmental relations consist of much more than money, financial questions are inevitably at the core of the process. Thus, definitions of various types of *grants*, or transfers of money (and property) from one government to another, are a helpful starting place.

Some grants give more discretion to the recipient than do others. *Categorical grants* or *project grants* are spent for only a limited purpose, such as building a new sewage treatment plant. Categorical grants have historically been the predominant form of grants in this country; however, in recent years, many categorical grants have been consolidated into *block grants,* which are used for nearly any purpose within a specific functional field, such as housing, community development, education, or law enforcement. For example, the recipient government might spend a law enforcement grant on police training, new equipment, or crime prevention programs. Finally, *revenue sharing* makes funds available for use by the recipient government in any way its leaders choose (within the law).

Grants may also be classified in terms of how they are made available. A *formula grant* employs a specific decision rule indicating how much money any given jurisdiction will receive. Typically, the decision rule is related to the purpose of the grant (for example, money for housing might be distributed to qualified governments based on the age and density of residential housing). A project grant, on the other hand, makes funds available on a competitive basis. Those seeking aid must submit an application for assistance for review and approval by the granting agency.

Grants may also be categorized as to the purposes they serve. *Entitlement grants* provide assistance to persons meeting certain criteria, such as age or income—for example, TANF or Medicaid. *Operating grants* are used in the development and operation of specific programs, such as those in education or employment and job training. *Capital grants* are used in construction or renovation, as in the development of the interstate highway system.

Networking

Some basic information on federal-state-local interactions can be found at www.usa.gov or www.whitehouse.gov. For coverage of the changing roles of state and local government, go to *Governing* magazine at www.governing.com.

Finally, grants may vary according to whether they require matching funds from the recipient agency. Some federal grants require the state or locality to put up a certain percentage of the money for the project; in the case of the interstate highway system, states contribute one dollar for every nine dollars of federal money. Other grants require different matching amounts, and some require no matching at all. Different types may be combined in different ways to create quite a variety of grant possibilities. A specific grant might be made available on a competitive basis strictly for use in programs for job training and may require local matching funds.

What Would You Do?

You are a member of a task force that has been asked to consider ways your local parks and recreation service could be delivered at less cost to the city. You have been considering alternatives such as special charges, citizen involvement in service delivery, and limitations on services. But you strongly feel that parks and recreation are essential functions of local government and should be protected from cuts. What would you do?

Dual Federalism

Historically, the various grant types have been employed in different ways and in different times. The earliest period in our country's intergovernmental history, a period that lasted well into the twentieth century, was characterized by what has been called *dual federalism*. Both federal and state governments sought to carve out their own spheres of power and influence, and there was relatively little intergovernmental cooperation—indeed, there was substantial conflict.

However, some programs cut across the strict divisions of federal, state, and local responsibility associated with dual federalism. A notable example is the Morrill Act of 1862, which granted land to universities to establish agricultural programs and was the basis for the eventual development of "land-grant" colleges. It was important in the development of higher education, but it also set a precedent in the structure of its grants (Nathan et al., 1987). No longer were grants made in a fairly open-ended fashion; specific instructions were attached, requiring that they be used for "agriculture and the mechanical arts." In addition, new reporting and accounting requirements were added as a condition of receiving the grants.

FIGURE 3.1

Images of American Federalism

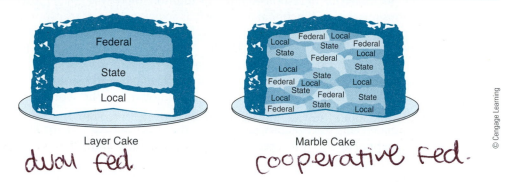

Layer Cake

dual fed.

Marble Cake

cooperative fed.

The adoption of grant programs such as the Morrill Act was accompanied by considerable anguish, because some saw such programs as a drastic departure from the dual federalism they preferred. The Morrill Act itself, signed by President Lincoln, had previously been vetoed by President Buchanan, who commented: "Should the time arrive when the State governments shall look to the Federal Treasury for the means of supporting themselves and maintaining their systems of education and internal policy, the character of both Governments will be greatly deteriorated" (Nathan et al., 1987, p. 25).

In any case, the period of dual federalism was marked by considerable conflict among the various levels of government. The federal government sought to deal effectively with the increasingly broad issues being raised in a more complex, urbanized society by developing new grant programs in such areas as highway construction and vocational education. The states, though they appreciated federal money, were cautious of federal interference in their spheres of responsibility. The localities, though creatures of the state and dependent on state grants of authority or money, sought to build their own political base. The resulting pattern of federalism resembled a layer cake, with three levels of government working parallel to one another but rarely together (see Figure 3.1).

Cooperative Federalism

If the layer cake was the prevailing image associated with dual federalism, the marble cake was the image for the period that followed, notable for its increasing complexity and interdependence. As opposed to the conflict and division of the earlier period, the emerging era of *cooperative federalism* was characterized by greater sharing of responsibilities. The marble cake image implied a system in which roles and responsibilities were intermixed in a variety of patterns—vertical, horizontal, and even diagonal (see Figure 3.1).

The great impetus for the development of cooperative federalism was the Roosevelt program for economic recovery following the Great Depression. Although the majority of President Roosevelt's programs were national in scope and could have been national in execution, a political choice was made to operate many of the programs through the states and their localities. The pattern of intergovernmental relations that emerged revealed a dramatically increased federal role, accompanied almost paradoxically by greater federal, state, and local sharing of responsibilities. In addition, there was greater attention to vertical relationships within functional areas such as social welfare or transportation.

The pattern of federal, state, and local relations that emerged from the New Deal is illustrated by several key programs. The first was the Federal Emergency Relief Administration, which provided grants to states for both direct and work relief. It also revitalized many weak state relief agencies. A variety of public works and employment security programs also supplemented relief efforts. The best known was the Works Progress Administration (WPA), a program that used federal money to hire state-certified workers for locally initiated construction projects. Finally, the Social Security Act of 1935 brought the federal government into direct relief for the poor, disabled, and unemployed, an area that had previously been reserved for states and cities.

Through the middle part of the twentieth century, the structure of the various grant programs initiated at the federal level featured the following:

1. A federal definition of the problem
2. A transfer of funds, primarily to the states (rather than localities)
3. A requirement that plans for use of funds be submitted to the federal government
4. A requirement for state matching funds
5. A requirement for federal review and audit of the programs (Nathan et al., 1987)

For the most part, these grant programs were categorical—that is, directed to a particular category of activity, such as public works. Indeed, the use of categorical grants as the primary mechanisms for federal-to-state transfers continued until the 1970s. Throughout this period, various groups appointed to review the state of intergovernmental relations returned the same verdict: the federal government and the states should begin "cooperating with or complementing each other in meeting the growing demands on both" (cited in Nathan et al., 1987, p. 33). Today, the principle of cooperative federalism is well established.

Picket-Fence Federalism

Through the 1960s, 1970s, and 1980s, there were dramatic shifts in the pattern of intergovernmental relations. Nowhere were these shifts more striking than in the contrast between the activism of the Kennedy and Johnson years and the cutbacks of the Reagan and Bush years. President Johnson used the phrase "creative federalism" to describe his approach to intergovernmental relations, which included a huge increase in the number and amount of federal grants available to states, localities, and other groups. The new federal programs focused mainly on urban problems and problems of the disadvantaged. Medicaid, for example, the largest of the new grant programs, provided funds to states to assist in medical care for low-income people. (Medicaid is largely administered by the states [eligibility requirements vary from state to state], but it also requires state matching funds, which became a fiscal problem for many states.) But there were also new programs in education aimed directly at school districts, new programs in employment and training run by cities and other independent providers, and new programs in housing and urban development in major metropolitan areas.

Probably the most publicized domestic program of the Johnson years was the "War on Poverty," launched with the passage of the Economic Opportunity Act of 1964. The War on Poverty and other Johnson programs were significant for both their size and shape. Substantially more aid was aimed directly at local governments, school districts, and various nonprofit groups, as opposed to the previous pattern of aid primarily to states. In addition, there were requirements for detailed planning and for streamlined budgeting systems, as well as demands for public participation in management of the programs. Finally, and most importantly, the majority of new programs involved project grants, requiring grant applications for specific purposes. States and localities began to spend enormous amounts of time playing the federal grant game trying to obtain grants, searching for matching funds, and trying to meet planning and reporting requirements. As a result, intergovernmental relations took on an increasingly competitive tone (Wright, 1988, pp. 81–90).

Throughout this period, the intergovernmental system was becoming increasingly dominated by the relationships among professionals within various substantive areas at various levels of government. For example, the relationship among mayor, governor, and president might be less important than that involving a local health department official, someone from a state department of health, and the manager of a federal program in health care. A new image emerged, replacing the "cakes" of earlier periods—that of *picket-fence federalism*. The horizontal bars of the fence represented the levels of government, and the vertical slats represented various substantive fields, such as health, welfare, education, employment, and training (see Figure 3.2).

President Nixon's administration brought about a reaction against many of the developments we have just described. Claiming that programs of the Great Society were too detailed to administer effectively at the local level and that subgovernments were coming to dominate the intergovernmental system, Nixon proposed what he termed a "New Federalism" that would reestablish greater local autonomy in the use of federal funds. Although a part of his program involved administrative changes, lessening certain requirements, the most notable changes President Nixon proposed involved changes in the structure of grant programs.

One way to return power to state and local leaders—especially elected leaders as opposed to program professionals—was through general revenue sharing. The Nixon plan for general revenue sharing involved transfers of money from the federal government to states and localities to use for any purpose they wished. The funds were distributed based on a complex formula, but once in the hands of the state or local political leadership, they could be used for tax reduction, transportation, community development, law enforcement, or any other area. First passed in 1972, the Nixon revenue-sharing program provided approximately $6 billion a year for five years and was continued through the Nixon, Ford, Carter, and early Reagan years before being eliminated in 1986.

The Nixon administration also sought to consolidate large numbers of categorical grants into block grants, two of which were passed. The Comprehensive Employment and Training Act (CETA) provided funds to local "prime sponsors," usually a local government or group of governments, for manpower training. Which specific programs would be developed was up to the prime sponsor at the local level. Similarly, two weeks after President Nixon resigned, President Ford signed the Community Development Block

FIGURE 3.2
Picket-Fence Federalism

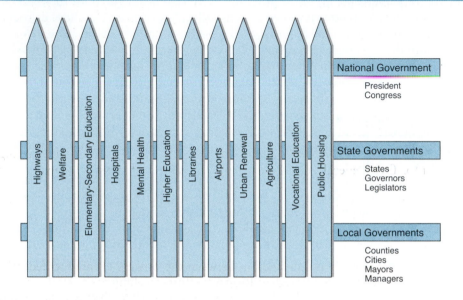

The Big Seven Public Interest Groups

1. Council of State Governments
2. National Governors Association
3. National Conference of State Legislatures
4. National Association of Counties

5. National League of Cities
6. U.S. Conference of Mayors
7. International City Management Association

SOURCE: From *Understanding Intergovernmental Relations*, 4th edition, by D. Wright © 2003. Reprinted with permission of the author.

Grant program (CDBG) consolidating several categorical grant programs, including urban renewal and the model cities program. Despite these successes in altering the pattern of federal grants, the Nixon and Ford years actually increased the total amount of aid available to states and localities.

The dependency of state and especially local governments on federal aid became more apparent during the administration of President Carter. The Carter years saw few dramatic departures in intergovernmental relations, continuing the general revenue sharing and block grants of the Nixon administration, though there was a greater tendency to target funds through categorical grants. Among the more important initiatives were expansion of public service employment under CETA, so that local government jobs would be filled by the unemployed, and passage of the Urban Development Action Grant program to stimulate economic development in distressed cities.

As a former governor, President Carter was attentive to the needs of state and local governments to more effectively operate intergovernmental programs, so he proposed a series of administrative steps for improving intergovernmental management. In this effort,

Grants- decrease beaucracy at federal level, equalize states, he worked closely with a group of seven major public interest groups, known as the PIGs, that were active in the intergovernmental system. These included such groups as the Council of State Governments, the National League of Cities, the National Governors Association, and others. Later in the Carter years, however, a new mood of fiscal restraint, combined with Carter's own fiscal conservatism, was something states and localities found difficult to handle. From the standpoint of state and local governments, the reductions of the late Carter years were just the beginning.

The Reagan and First Bush Years

The Reagan and the first Bush administrations brought major structural changes in the pattern of fiscal federalism, including the elimination of general revenue sharing and a reworking of the block grant system. However, these years were more significant primarily because of both administrations' efforts to reduce the size of the federal government through a variety of tax and spending cuts and to return responsibility for major areas, especially social welfare, to the states.

An ideological commitment to decrease the size and influence of the federal government and to recognize the distinction between the powers granted to federal and state governments undergirded President Reagan's efforts to eliminate federal funding and federal regulation of state and local activity wherever possible. One way he proposed to do this was by turning back responsibility for a variety of federal programs, and the resources to pay for them, to the states. President Bush employed the same ideology, using the term *turnovers* rather than *turnbacks*. These kinds of proposals became intertwined with President Reagan's 1981 efforts to reduce taxes through *supply-side economics*, an approach based on the idea that decreased taxes and spending will stimulate capital investment and, in turn, economic growth (Stone & Sawhill, 1984). Because the Reagan administration protected the defense budget, it sought the majority of the cuts in federal grant programs and general government operations.

State and local officials decried the depth of the Reagan administration's cuts and its failure to make available any revenue sources to pick up the slack, especially since the tax cuts failed to produce the expected economic growth. Concerns were increasingly voiced that efforts to balance the budget were especially damaging to the poor—for example, by reducing eligibility for Aid to Families with Dependent Children (AFDC) (Nathan et al., 1987, pp. 52–57). Although the public was concerned about excessive spending, it became clear that neither Congress nor the public considered spending for social welfare, environmental protection, and infrastructure maintenance excessive. Consequently, by the middle of the second Reagan term, eligibility requirements for AFDC were restored; Congress funded the environmental Superfund to clean up toxic wastes and repair leaking underground tanks at a significantly higher level than the president requested; and the Highway Trust Fund for highway improvement was passed despite Reagan's veto. On the other hand, reductions continued in specific areas, particularly in general revenue sharing. Revenue sharing for the states had been eliminated early in the Reagan administration; in 1986 revenue sharing for local governments was ended as well.

President Bush continued the Reagan approach to federalism, including the strategy of turning various programs over to the states. Bush made important but largely symbolic gestures to the states and localities, partly because he could do little else. The budget deficit continued unabated, which led to the Budget Enforcement Act (BEA) of 1990. Under the BEA, any legislation that exceeds the budget ceiling in its category will trigger an across-the-board cut in that category. When this legislation was combined with the savings and loan bailout, there was little enthusiasm left for expanding domestic spending, including state and local aid.

The Clinton Presidency

During the Clinton administration, the philosophical foundation of New Federalism remained in place, with a focus on regulatory reform and shifting decision-making authority to state and local governments. However, the character and scope of this devolution of power were interpreted in vastly different ways by the president, the Republican House, and the more moderate leadership in the Senate. In the latter years of the Clinton administration, state and local governments offered their own ideas on federalism and intergovernmental relations. Such diverse viewpoints generated a number of questions concerning not only the state of federalism but also the implications for government practice.

Early on, President Clinton left little doubt as to his administration's position on intergovernmental relations, a position characterized by sensitivity to state and local governments. Within months of taking office, the administration identified the removal of burdensome federal regulations as a primary objective. President Clinton issued executive orders that prevented federal agencies from imposing mandates without financial support. Although administrative agencies gained regulatory powers, central review was continued to ensure that new regulations were in line with the president's priorities. The president reinforced his stance with another order that established a system of state and local review of intergovernmental regulations.

The Clinton administration's New Federalist philosophy also was evident in programmatic areas, such as its drive to "end welfare as we know it." The administration transformed the nation's system of public assistance by turning to mainly market forces for public well-being and placing service delivery into the hands of nongovernmental actors. Key provisions included putting time limits on benefits, tying welfare to work requirements, giving authority for welfare programs to state governments, and limiting or eliminating access to public assistance for legal immigrants and the disabled. This philosophy also was apparent in the Empowerment Zone/Enterprise Community Program, the Clinton administration's main community and economic development initiative, and the Goals 2000: Educate America Act, its key education initiative. Both involved efforts to expand state and/or local discretion (Walker, 1996), reinforcing the belief that reducing federal regulations and handing decision-making power to state and local governments would place those closest to a given issue in a better position to effect innovation and change.

Vice President Al Gore's National Performance Review (NPR) and related efforts further advanced the Clinton administration's position on intergovernmental relations by focusing on a variety of alternative strategies for managing public programs. These strategies, which echoed Osborne and Gaebler's (1992) *Reinventing Government*, injected a spirit of entrepreneurship into the federal government. Gore's NPR called for "a new customer service contract with the American people, a new guarantee of effective, efficient, and responsive government," along with several practical measures that affected intergovernmental relations, such as collapsing categorical grants into more flexible funding streams and removing unfunded federal mandates.

Regulatory reform and removing unfunded mandates also became key issues for the 104th Congress. As heralded in the Republican Contract with America, conservatives argued that federal agencies placed too great a burden on state and local administrations by imposing regulations without adequate financial resources for their implementation. With assistance from the Clinton administration, Republican lawmakers revised two measures from the preceding Congress into the Unfunded Mandates Reform Act of 1995, under which the cost of any future mandate would need to be spelled out by the Congressional Budget Office. The act also raised the president's executive orders mentioned above to a statutory level, binding agencies by law to find less expensive, more flexible ways of instituting regulations.

During President Clinton's second term, however, ties with the Republican Congress degenerated into political gridlock. Though the two camps did come together on measures to eliminate the federal deficit and reform the nation's welfare system, the prevailing environment was one of partisan extremism. Moreover, even the hallmarks of the period failed to gain support among many state and local governments that, while recognizing the need for fiscal constraint and welfare reform, remained concerned that the cost of the measures would fall primarily on the subnational levels of administration.

The impact of NPR and "reinventing government" also remains in question. While a variety of federal agencies implemented reform during both Clinton terms, many were fraught with political and administrative challenges. Reinvention, compared to many political reform movements, has had a fairly long life span. Examples can be found at all levels of government, and in the nonprofit sector, as reformers strive to create a more responsive, entrepreneurial, and results-based system of governance. On the other hand, a growing number of scholars and practitioners have taken issue with the assumptions underlying the reform agenda. Although few would dispute the value of making federal agencies more responsive or of ensuring effectiveness in delivering public services, many have come to recognize that productivity and performance should not be the only measures of success.

The Bush Administration

The political conditions associated with the election of George W. Bush in 2000—his agenda to streamline the government, increase the role of nongovernmental organizations in the policy process, and shift to more market-based models of service delivery, coupled with the passage of the 1995 Unfunded Mandates Reform Act—hinted at the possibility of a move away from federal policy centralization. Unlike many of his recent predecessors, President Bush did not offer specific proposals signaling his philosophy on federalism. In practice, however, the administration appeared to have been less concerned with federalism and more focused on efforts to extend the role of the federal government (Nathan, 2006).

While some Bush administration initiatives were devolutionary in nature, such as a state-driven change in Medicaid policy and grant consolidations of community development, the Bush era was characterized primarily by its expansion of centralizing actions, in some instances overturning "cooperative federalism frameworks that had evolved over many years" in favor of "a more insistent, demanding federal role" to accomplish policy and political goals (Posner, 2007, p. 408). This emphasis on less cooperative and more coercive kinds of policy tools—what we might call *coercive federalism*—was not new, as the use of mandates and preemptions of state and local authority had been increasing since the 1970s (Kincaid, 1990). The continuation of this trend was evident in many of the Bush administration's actions, including its approach to homeland security, education, Medicare, and the administration of elections.

The attacks of September 11, 2001, and the effects of Hurricane Katrina in 2005 resulted in several proposals and directives by the Bush administration aimed at centralizing emergency preparedness and response. For example, the Department of Homeland Security, created under President Bush in response to 9/11, developed federal standards for thirty-six areas of emergency planning and response that cover fifteen types of emergencies. Another measure, the Real ID Act of 2005, established federal standards for driver's licenses, requiring proof of identity and lawful status, security features to be incorporated into each card, and security standards for offices that issue licenses. Residents in states that do not comply by January 2013 will lose acceptance of their driver's licenses by federal entities, including security personnel in airports. In response to problems in mobilizing National Guard troops in the aftermath of Hurricane Katrina, a rider to the 2007 Defense Authorization Act gave presidents the authority to federalize the National Guard without the permission of a governor in times of natural disasters.

Despite a Republican history of supporting local control of schools, the Bush administration in 2001 proposed the No Child Left Behind Act (NCLB), which created federal requirements for testing and accountability and, thus, a stronger federal role in education policy. Under the act, while standards are set by the individual states, schools receiving federal funds must administer a statewide standardized test each year to all students, students must make "adequate yearly progress" in test scores, and schools must provide highly qualified teachers for all students. NCLB marked "an expansion of federal authority over programmatic aspects of education and raises the expectations of federal policy by emphasizing equal educational outcomes" (Sunderman, 2009, p. 11).

President Bush also supported the Medicare Prescription Drug, Improvement, and Modernization Act of 2003 (MMA), "the largest expansion of the federal role in health care since 1965" (Conlan & Dinan, 2007, p. 282). The act expanded Medicare to include prescription drug coverage that would be administered by private health plans. It also included a major restructuring of the program, relying heavily on private insurance for benefit delivery and increasing beneficiary cost-sharing responsibilities. The new drug benefit provision, known as Medicare Part D, shifted drug coverage for low-income beneficiaries from Medicaid to Medicare, thus relieving states of some prescription drug coverage costs for these "dual eligibles." This shift, however, was offset by added administrative costs as states became responsible, along with the Social Security Administration, for determining who qualifies for assistance, increasing administrative costs. States also were required to pay back the Medicaid savings on these dual eligibles, which, in essence, levied a federal tax on state Medicaid spending (Matthews, 2004).

The controversy over the 2000 presidential election led to the passage of the Help America Vote Act (HAVA), which President Bush signed into law in October 2002. The act created new federal standards and provided federal funding aimed at regulating significant aspects of the administration of state and local elections. Requirements covered voting systems, provisional ballots, and access to polling places for the disabled. The act also required centralization of statewide voter databases and uniform processes for vote definitions. Although the act is centralized in nature, much of the implementation was framed in a devolutionary way, as key decisions on defining several of the requirements were left to the states (Posner, 2007). An interesting commentary on the broader trends in governance can be found in the "Exploring Concepts" box "Transformation of Governance: Globalization, Devolution, and the Role of Government."

Exploring Concepts

TRANSFORMATION OF GOVERNANCE: GLOBALIZATION, DEVOLUTION, AND THE ROLE OF GOVERNMENT

Over the last generation, American government has undergone a steady, but often unnoticed, transformation. Its traditional practices and institutions have become more marginal to the fundamental debates. Meanwhile, new processes and institutions—often nongovernmental ones—have become more central to public policy. In doing the people's work to a large and growing degree, American governments share responsibility with other levels of government, with private companies, and with nonprofit organizations.

This transformation has two effects. First, it has strained the traditional roles of all the players. For decades, we have debated privatizing and shrinking government. While the debate raged, however, we incrementally made important policy decisions. Those decisions have rendered much of the debate moot. Government has come to rely heavily on for-profit and nonprofit organizations for delivering goods and services ranging from antimissile systems to welfare reform. It is not that these changes have obliterated the roles of Congress, the president, and the courts. State and local governments have become even livelier. Rather, these changes have layered new challenges on top of the traditional institutions and their processes.

Second, the new challenges have strained the capacity of governments—and their nongovernmental partners—to deliver high-quality public services. The basic structure of American government comes from the New Deal days. It is a government driven by functional specialization and process control. However, new place-based problems have emerged: How can government's functions be coordinated in a single place? Can environmental regulations flowing down separate channels (air, water, and soil) merge to form a coherent environmental

(Continued)

(Continued)

policy? New process-based problems have emerged as well: How can hierarchical bureau-cracies, created with the presumption that they directly deliver services, cope with services increasingly delivered through multiple (often nongovernmental) partners? Budgetary control processes that work well for traditional bureaucracies often prove less effective in gathering information from nongovernmental partners or in shaping their incentives. Personnel systems designed to insulate government from political interference have proven less adaptive to these new challenges, especially in creating a cohort of executives skilled in managing indirect government.

Consequently, government at all levels has found itself with new responsibilities but without the capacity to manage them effectively. The same is true of its nongovernmental partners. Moreover, despite these transformations, the *expectations* on government—by citizens and often by government officials—remain rooted in a past that no longer exists. Citizens expect their problems will be solved and tend not to care who solves them. Elected officials take a similar view: They create programs and appropriate money. They expect government agencies to deliver the goods and services. When problems emerge, their first instinct is to reorganize agencies or impose new procedures—when the problem often has to do with organizational structures and processes that no longer fit reality. The performance of American government—its effectiveness, efficiency, responsiveness, and accountability— depends on cracking these problems.

SOURCE: Donald F. Kettl, "Transformation of Governance: Globalization, Devolution and the Role of Government." *Public Administration Review* 60, no. 6 (November/December 2000): 488–497. Reprinted by permission.

Obama and Federalism

The economic crisis in 2008 and a commitment to enacting health-care reform legisla-tion prompted a great deal of activity by the Obama administration, resulting in several national initiatives and inciting widespread concerns about policy centralization and the expansion of the federal government's role. While some initiatives involved coercive feder-alism strategies, the administration also turned to a variety of cooperative tools, following a path "that was far more nuanced and cooperative than that suggested by early expec-tations" (Conlan & Dinan, 2011, p. 421) in its attempts to promote economic recovery, regulate the financial industry, and reform health care.

President Obama gave an early indication regarding his approach to federalism in a memorandum early in 2009 directing agencies to preempt state law only in cases with a sufficient legal basis for doing so. The memorandum also included restrictions on includ-ing statements of preemption in regulations and directed agencies to conduct a review of regulations enacted over the previous ten years that included preemptive statements to determine if preemption was justified. Another memo in 2011 directed agencies to work with state, local, and tribal governments to create greater administrative flexibility and reduce burdens created by federal regulations (Metzger, 2011).

The American Recovery and Reinvestment Act (ARRA), also known as the Recovery Act, enacted shortly after President Obama took office, looked to the intergovernmental system to play a key role in recovery. The ARRA provided critical relief for state and local budgets hit hard by the recession of 2008, including funding for existing federal aid programs in education, community development, and social services. The use of established programs was aimed at enabling faster state and local spending, although it did little to promote innovation and reform (Conlan & Dinan, 2011). The ARRA also included flexible funding related to Medicaid and education, aimed at reducing the impact of the rapid decline in state and local revenues and minimizing layoffs of government employees. These funds, however, were restricted by maintenance-of-effort requirements, under which states could not reduce services covered under Medicaid or reduce education funding to below FY 2006 levels. The ARRA also imposed requirements on states to use the funds immediately or lose them, and it included extensive requirements regarding transparency and accountability.

Although historically the states played a major role in the oversight of financial products, the 2008 economic crisis prompted calls for major reforms in the regulation of financial institutions. In 2010 President Obama signed into law the Dodd-Frank Wall Street Reform and Consumer Protection Act, which overturned a Bush administration policy of preempting state authority over federally chartered national banks to protect consumers and maintain competition. The act essentially safeguarded existing state laws and reaffirmed state authority to enforce federal consumer protection laws even as it created a more powerful regulatory effort at the federal level. Although initial versions of the bill included an expansion of federal preemption, the Obama administration intervened to help protect state authority (Conlan & Dinan, 2011).

The Obama administration's health-care reform initiative, which resulted in the Patient Protection and Affordable Care Act of 2010 (ACA), took aim at overhauling the nation's health insurance system. ACA imposed sweeping new federal requirements and expanded coverage to 32 million of the nation's 55 million uninsured. Although the provision requiring individuals to have a minimum level of coverage generated the most controversy, the greatest impact on the states came from a significant expansion of Medicaid and the establishment of health exchanges. Although the federal government would cover most of these costs, the states would assume a portion of these along with increased administrative costs. States also are required to maintain existing eligibility and benefit levels for Medicaid and the Children's Health Insurance Program (Metzger, 2011). In short, while the states will have some flexibility and maintain some major responsibilities, the ACA represents a sweeping centralization effort at the federal level.

While the initiatives advanced by the Obama administration clearly involve the expansion of federal authority, they also are notable for the extent to which "states are offered central roles to play in the new federal regimes, with broad grants of authority and federal funds to entice their participation" (Metzger, 2011, p. 599). This "hybrid" model of intergovernmental relations "mixes money, mandates, and flexibility in new and distinctive ways" (Conlan & Dinan, 2011, p. 443). However, in the face of mounting federal deficits and rising ideological and political polarization, it remains to be seen whether such an approach is sustainable. Certainly a key issue for President Obama will be whether he can achieve deficit reduction while also getting Congress to pass programs for innovation, infrastructure, and education.

Judicial Influence

One final point relates to the role of the judiciary in shaping intergovernmental relations. Through the 1990s, students of federalism became increasingly aware of the role of the judiciary, especially the Supreme Court, in defining the relationship between the federal government and the states. Although the recent judicial activism has produced varied results, with the scope of federal authority limited in some cases and reaffirmed in others, an important outcome has emerged. The Court has once again established itself as "a conscious arbiter of the respective powers of the national government and the states" (Wise, 2001, p. 343).

At issue has been Congress's constitutional authority to regulate activities at the state level. For much of the twentieth century, the Commerce Clause, which gives Congress the power to regulate trade between the states, has been the center point of federal legislation. However, regulations also have been imposed under the Fourteenth Amendment, which grants Congress the power to enforce by appropriate legislation the rights provided in the amendment. Regardless of its legal basis, federal regulatory authority has been allowed to expand virtually unchecked by the Court since the 1940s. In fact, some scholars of federalism began to wonder whether any boundaries would be established to limit the scope of the federal government relative to the states (see Wise, 1998, 2001). The tides began to change, however, during the 1990s.

Among the first key decisions setting parameters on Congress's regulatory power was *Gregory v. Ashcroft* (1991). In this case, the Court ruled that the Missouri constitution's rule that state judges must retire at age seventy does not violate the federal Age Discrimination Act, as the Equal Employment Opportunity Commission had ruled. "The significance of this [the *Gregory* ruling] is that it bars individuals and groups who wish to use federal statutes of general applicability adopted under the Commerce Clause to attack state regulation in federal court from doing so, unless Congress makes it clear that the statute applies to the states" (Wise, 2001, p. 344). Justice O'Connor, in her opinion, emphasized the constitutional principle of dual sovereignty and the importance of maintaining a certain degree of state authority.

Congress's regulatory power under Commerce came into question again in *United States v. Lopez* (1995) and *United States v. Morrison* (2000). In *Lopez,* the Court considered a challenge to federal restrictions placed on handgun possession in a school zone. The *Morrison* case focused on provisions in the Violence Against Women Act, which allow victims of violent crimes motivated by gender to seek federal civil action. The Supreme Court ruled in both cases that Congress had overstepped its regulatory jurisdiction because the statutes were not consistent with the authority afforded under the Commerce Clause. At the heart of the Court's decisions was the premise that clear lines must be established between national and state powers and that, under Commerce, these lines must be limited to matters of interstate trade.

Of course, the *Lopez* and *Morrison* decisions focused primarily on restoring a balance of regulatory power between the national government and state governments. The recent judicial activism, however, also can be seen on issues of administration, such as in *New York v. United States* (1992) and *Printz v. United States* (1997), where the Court placed restrictions on Congress's ability to compel state and local actors to implement federal statutes.

The *New York* case involved a challenge from local governments against the Low-Level Radioactive Waste Policy Act, which required state and regional authorities in certain circumstances to assume ownership of radioactive waste and commanded them to implement provisions of the federal legislation. The Court ruled unconstitutional both alternatives, stating that Congress must not view state and local governments as "mere political subdivisions...[or] regional offices" (Wise, 1998, p. 95) of the national government and must afford the level of state sovereignty guaranteed under the Tenth Amendment.

In *Printz,* the Court reviewed a challenge to provisions of the Brady Handgun Violence Prevention Act, which mandated background checks on prospective buyers and required local law enforcement officers to serve as entities of the national government in executing the regulation. The federal government, in an interesting twist, argued that unlike in *New York,* the Brady Act did not place responsibility on the states for policy making and that, given the rewards, the cost to the states would be minimal. The Court disagreed. In its rejection of the federal claim, the Court stated that *New York* established, in very clear terms, that Congress cannot command state officials to execute or administer federal regulations, nor can the national government bypass the *New York* limitations by directly enlisting state actors.

However, the decisions cited here should not be taken as a complete shift toward state sovereignty. Several recent rulings, including *Davis v. Monroe County Board of Education* (1999), *Saenz v. Roe* (1999), and *Sabri v. United States* (2004), have reinforced the national government's capacity to monitor state activities.

In *Davis,* for example, the Court reaffirmed Congress's authority to establish state liability for certain actions as part of the states' agreement to receive federal funding. The majority of the justices ruled that, under the Spending Clause, Congress could use its control over appropriations to enforce constitutional rights—in this case, the guarantee against third-party discrimination in public schools—as long as the language in the funding program remained clear enough so that states would have adequate notice of the federal requirements.

The main issue in *Saenz* was the state of California's revision to its welfare laws to set a twelve-month residency requirement for certain levels of public assistance. Although the Court had previously invalidated residency requirements for eligibility (in *Shapiro v. Thompson* [1969]), Secretary Saenz, of California's Department of Social Services, claimed that the new welfare reform provisions did not exclude new arrivals from welfare benefits but simply maintained their assistance levels to those of the states where they resided previously. The Court disagreed, ruling that the Fourteenth Amendment does not assign levels of citizenship according to length of residence but instead links citizenship with residence generally. Although the Court appreciated California's desire to reduce the cost of welfare benefits, a majority determined that fiscal efficiency could not be allowed to outweigh citizen guarantees against discrimination.

In the *Sabri* case, Sabri was accused of offering bribes to a Minneapolis councilman to facilitate city construction projects. The constitutional question before the Court was whether Congress could criminalize such bribes under its spending power. Even though it was not possible to establish a direct link between the bribes and a particular federal project, the Court held that the federal government could act to safeguard the integrity of local government administration involved in federally funded projects.

When taken as a whole, the decisions cited here present a mixed image of federalism. On one hand, the Court clearly has reconsidered its deference to Congress on issues of intergovernmental relations, a practice it had followed throughout the twentieth century, setting restraints on the scope of federal power. On the other hand, federal regulatory authority in other areas has been reaffirmed, particularly under the Spending Clause and the Fourteenth Amendment. Despite the significance of these decisions in themselves, the implications go even further. Indeed, the most significant outcome is that the Court appears to have reassumed its responsibility for judicial review on questions of federal-state authority, which it had all but abandoned in *Garcia v. San Antonio Metropolitan Transit Authority* (1985). (The *Garcia* case will be discussed in more detail in the next section.) Given not only the nature of the decisions but the mere fact that the judiciary has been willing to intervene, we can be assured that the Supreme Court once again has become the "arbiter-in-chief" in our federal system (Wise, 1998, p. 98).

The State and Local Perspective

We have described the system of intergovernmental relations primarily from the federal perspective, but states and localities are also major actors in the intergovernmental system, both as they participate in federal programs and as they interact state to state, state to locality, and locality to locality. Here, also, intergovernmental relations have seen great changes. Although budgetary shifts have created serious problems for state and local governments, the governments have proven remarkably well equipped to deal with these dilemmas, both financially and administratively.

Funding Patterns

As we noted earlier, federal aid to state and local governments began as early as the Civil War with the passage of the Morrill Act, establishing land-grant colleges. Soon after, federal aid was extended to agriculture, highways, and public health, among other areas. During the Great Depression, federal aid also went to income security and social welfare. But the most significant increases in federal grants occurred after World War II. There has been a dramatic increase in federal funding of state and local activities over the last fifty years. In 1960, transportation received the largest amount of federal funding, but by 1970 there had been significant increases in funding for education, training, employment, and social services. Since 1980, changes in the relative amounts among functions reflect large increases in grants for health (primarily Medicaid) and for income security. Funding for health care alone increased dramatically over the last two decades, from $43.9 billion in 1990 to $290.2 billion in 2010.

Over the last twenty years, federal dollars have amounted to approximately 20 percent of the amount spent by state governments. But that share increased to 25 percent in 2010, as the federal government sought to assist states and local governments in getting through

Block + categorical Grants?

the recession. Specifically, as noted above, the federal government provided additional support through the American Recovery and Reinvestment Act (Recovery Act), enacted in February 2009. Federal grants to state and local governments increased from $538.0 billion in 2009 to $608.4 billion in 2010 and were estimated to be $625.2 billion in 2011. These amounts were used by state and local governments to maintain earlier service levels in the education, health-care, energy, water, and other programs, and to avoid greater cuts to state services and increases in taxes. Since state and local governments usually recover at a slower rate than other sectors, they will continue to face fiscal difficulties for the foreseeable future. However, the 2012 budget proposed a decrease in the overall amounts of federal grant funding because most of the funds provided under the Recovery Act will have been spent (Office of Management and Budget, 2012).

Without question, the last several decades have presented a variety of fiscal challenges to state and local governments. One surprising development, however, is that the states have proven capable of managing their new responsibilities far better than many predicted. Indeed, although the federal government has a huge deficit, most states have continued to operate with balanced budgets over the last decade typically relying much more on spending cuts then raising new revenues.

Once considered a weak link in the federal system, over the last thirty years, states have dramatically increased their capacities. Although there are still considerable variations in states' powers, most states have undertaken important institutional reforms (such as developing legislative audits), expanded the scope and professionalism of their operations (to include new services in areas such as energy planning and conservation or new programs in areas such as performance management), and demonstrated remarkable fiscal restraint.

The states also are moving into areas of responsibility once thought to rest at the federal level. International trade is one area where shifting roles already seem to be taking place. Whereas the federal government has traditionally played the leading (if not the exclusive) role in foreign affairs, economic forces are precipitating much greater state and local activity in the international arena. For example, all states have offices of economic development involved in some way with international economic development. Through such units, the states provide local businesses with seminars and conferences on how to market themselves overseas. Over forty states also maintain permanent offices overseas, with some of the larger states having offices in several countries.

Preemptions and Mandates

Preemptions   As discussed previously, although our federal system of government establishes certain federal powers, reserves certain powers to the states, and permits certain actions at both levels, there has long been controversy about the exact definitions of these categories. Intense controversy surrounds the issue of the right of the federal government to preempt the traditional powers of states and localities or to coerce states and localities into doing (or not doing) certain things.

As a case in point, the Fair Labor Standards Act (FLSA) of 1938 set the minimum wage and the maximum hours that could be worked before overtime pay was required.

The act originally applied only to the private sector, but 1974 amendments applied it to all state and local governments. Many state and local officials argued against the amendments, citing the difficulties in applying the standards to government—for example, how do you measure the hours a firefighter works in off-and-on shifts of several days' duration? Soon the amendments were challenged in court, and, in the case of *National League of Cities v. Usery* (1976), the Supreme Court decided that the functions of "general government" were part of the powers "reserved" to the states by the Tenth Amendment and therefore could not be regulated by the federal government. Consequently, the FLSA did not apply.

Networking

For data relating to federal funding to state and local governments, go to the 2012 *Statistical Abstract of the United States* at http://www.census.gov/compendia/statab/ or to the 2013 budget at the Office of Management and Budget at http://www.whitehouse.gov/omb/budget/Overview/.

The Court's ruling in many ways raised as many questions as it answered, especially around the issue of what could be included under the notion of "general government." The confusion persisted until, nearly ten years later, the Court reviewed a case that sought to determine whether the San Antonio transit authority was performing "general government" functions and was therefore exempt from the Fair Labor Standards Act.

In *Garcia v. San Antonio Metropolitan Transit Authority* (1985), however, the Court went beyond the narrow question of whether transit is a general government function and decided that, under its responsibilities to regulate commerce, Congress did in fact have the power to intervene in the affairs of state and local governments.

The effect of *Garcia*, a direct reversal of the Court's earlier position in the *Usery* case, was to remove questions about the scope of the federal government's powers from the realm of judicial inquiry. The Court essentially held that states have sufficient input into the national legislative process, through the election of members of Congress and the influence of their governors and mayors, to protect themselves politically from burdensome legislation. That being the case, the question of whether the federal government could act in areas previously believed reserved to the states should be decided through legislation rather than judicial action. The rights of the states were, therefore, viewed as raising political rather than judicial questions.

A similar argument was developed by the Court in *South Carolina v. Baker* (1988), a case viewed by many at the time as putting a nail in the coffin of the Tenth Amendment rights of the states. *South Carolina* asked whether the federal government had the right to dictate the form of bonds issued by the states. The Court not only answered "yes," but it also indicated that the federal government had the right to tax income earned on tax-exempt bonds. Obviously, if the federal government had this right, then the states would have to compete directly with private firms issuing bonds. Although political leaders tried to assure the bond market that the federal government would not try to balance its budget by intruding on the states' abilities to issue tax-exempt bonds, several such proposals were introduced in Congress. As you can imagine, states and localities were incensed at this intrusion into a critical area of state financing, but, again, the states were precluded from a judicial remedy and asked to rely on their political power to see that Congress did not act to tax state and local bonds.

The *Garcia* and *South Carolina* cases open the door for the federal government to move into areas once thought to be the purview of state and local governments. Certainly, state and local officials, who have seen the federal government act in areas from rat control to minimum drinking ages, have been skeptical of the self-restraint of Congress. At a minimum, *Garcia* and *South Carolina* set a precedent for expanded federal action directed at state and local governments.

We should not, however, rush to judgment, because many of the Supreme Court rulings handed down in the past decade have been decided by 5–4 votes, and in several key cases, the majority has clearly reaffirmed the sovereignty of state governments (for example, *New York v. United States* [1992], *Seminole Tribe of Florida v. Florida* [1996], *Printz v. United States* [1997], and *Alden v. Maine* [1999]). In fact, a recent commentary on emerging judicial federalism noted that majority opinion maintained the theme "that state sovereignty may not be invaded, not only because it is rooted in the nation's constitutional structure, but also because such invasion undermines the very operation of American democracy" (Wise, 2001, p. 354).

These cases deal with the powers of the federal government over states and localities, but somewhat less complex issues have been raised with respect to the powers of the states over local governments. As noted, our intergovernmental system does not allocate separate spheres of power to state and local governments, but rather treats local governments merely as "creatures of the state," having only those powers granted by the state. In what has come to be known as *Dillon's Rule*, Judge John Dillon declared in 1868 that municipalities had only those powers granted in their charters, those fairly implied by the expressed powers, and those essential to the purposes of their being granted a charter. In other words, Dillon's Rule allowed for state control over all but a narrow range of local activities. Dillon's Rule has been somewhat relaxed, especially in states that permit cities greater autonomy through *home-rule* provisions, but the powers of local government continue to derive directly from the actions of the state.

There are various mechanisms involved in the relationship between the federal government and the states and between the states and localities. *Preemptions* involve the federal government preempting state action traditionally associated with the lower level of government. For example, the federal Nutrition Labeling and Education Act of 1990 preempted many state and local laws regarding food labeling. Such assumptions of power have been particularly significant in the last few years. For example, federal preemptions of state and local authority more than doubled after 1970. More than 50 percent of the preemption statutes enacted in the entire history of our country were enacted in the last twenty years. Not even Ronald Reagan, despite his rhetoric promising a return of more power to the states, was exempt from this trend, endorsing federal limits on the regulation of business, as well as restraints in health and the environment (Kincaid, 1990, p. 149).

As we have seen, President Obama, recognizing the limitations that preemptions place on the states, issued a memorandum on May 20, 2009, requiring executive offices to limit preemptions of state power. In part the memorandum read:

> The purpose of this memorandum is to state the general policy of my Administration that preemption of State law by executive departments and agencies should be undertaken only with full consideration of the legitimate prerogatives of the States and with a sufficient legal basis for preemption. Executive departments and agencies should be mindful that in our Federal system, the citizens of the several States have distinctive circumstances and values, and that in many instances it is appropriate for them to apply to themselves rules and principles that reflect these circumstances and values. (Presidential Memorandum, May 20, 2009)

Mandates The *New York* and *Printz* cases deal with what are called *direct orders*, requirements or restrictions enforced by one government upon another (the federal government on states and localities, the states on the cities). Direct orders might include a federal requirement that cities meet certain clean water standards or a state requirement that a city pay part of the costs of certain welfare programs. Another way control can be exercised over another government is through conditions tied to grants-in-aid. These conditions are typically of the type parents use with children: "You can go outside to play after you have cleaned your room." Conditions of aid might require land-use planning or an assurance of making facilities accessible to the handicapped prior to a capital construction project.

Because cities derive their powers from the states, most state requirements are direct orders. But most federal requirements are conditions-of-aid tied to a particular grant program. "Conditions-of-aid" are of two varieties. *Cross-cutting requirements* are rules that apply to most, if not all, grant programs. For instance, the federal government requires environmental impact statements before undertaking capital projects, certain personnel provisions in agencies receiving grant funds, and compliance with civil rights legislation. Other conditions-of-aid are program-specific, applicable only to the particular program. They may include rules about program planning, implementation, and evaluation. For example, a particular program might prescribe certain maximum salaries for individuals employed under the grant or some form of citizen participation in program design (most federal programs have this latter requirement).

What Would You Do?

> You are in charge of a coalition combating domestic violence. The various nonprofit organizations that are the primary service delivery groups in this area have complained to you that a new state initiative to stop human trafficking will have the effect of reducing their capacity to help current victims of domestic violence and abuse. What would you do?

Congress imposes such conditions-of-aid requirements under the Spending Clause of the Constitution. For the terms to be valid, though, federal lawmakers must clearly state the conditions in the legislation, making certain that state and local governments are aware of the requirements. The legality of Congress using funding conditions as a way of advancing regulatory and administrative objectives has been reaffirmed in several Supreme Court decisions, notably *Cedar Rapids Community School District v. Garret* (1999) and *Davis v. Monroe County Board of Education* (1999).

The term *mandate* has been used to embrace both conditions-of-aid and direct orders, in either case an order requiring a government to do something it might not otherwise do. And mandates often require states or localities to spend money they would not otherwise spend. Today it is estimated that federal mandates cost state and local governments an estimated $100 billion a year. State spending mandated by the recent immigration bills alone is estimated to be over $1 billion. Moreover, states and cities claim that mandates unduly impinge upon the autonomy of their level of government. Consequently, mandates have become a source of considerable frustration for those on the receiving end. The argument continues today by mayors and governors across the country—the mayors concerned with both federal and state mandates, and the governors concerned primarily with federal mandates.

For nonprofits, mandates tend to be a part of daily life. The key difference is that where a local government may have mandates from a relatively narrow number of sources, such as the federal and state levels, a nonprofit agency often will face direct orders or conditions-of-aid requirements from each of its funding sources, and the larger the funder (and funding amount), the greater the burden. Those in the nonprofit sector sometimes speak of mandates as the "golden handcuffs"—the funding is great, but grant-maker demands usually place an excessive administrative strain on the organization. As Paul Light concluded, the situation has been exacerbated in recent years by trends in nonprofit management reform: "Unfortunately, the nonprofit sector is caught in the middle of an unrelenting contest between competing philosophies and advocates of reform, all of which produce significant motion back and forth across different reform ideologies" (Light, 2000, p. 45). The varying philosophical positions can become manifested in an array of reporting standards and administrative procedures imposed by grant makers.

The United Way of America, for example, plays a leading role in establishing guidelines for performance (or "outcome") management by nonprofit organizations, and an increasing number of local United Ways have set reporting standards for agencies receiving grants. Similarly, many foundations (large and small) have made interagency partnerships an eligibility requirement for grant programs. If a nonprofit service provider wants to apply for a grant, the leadership must show how the agency will "collaborate" with other nonprofits, government, and even for-profit firms.

At the federal level, every president since Nixon has pledged to reduce the burden of mandates on states and local governments. In his 1992 State of the Union address, President Bush said, "We must put an end to unfinanced Federal Government mandates…If Congress passes a mandate, it should be forced to pay for it and to balance the cost with savings elsewhere. After all, a mandate just increases someone else's burden, and that means higher taxes at the state and local level" (Bowman & Pagano, 1992, p. 4). However, shortly after the president made his remarks, he signed a budget agreement that contained twenty new mandates expected to cost state and local governments about $17 billion over the next five years.

An important step forward was taken in March 1995, when President Clinton signed the Unfunded Mandates Reform Act (UMRA) of 1995, presumably an effort to limit the effects of federally imposed mandates. Although this legislation does not provide federal funding for all mandated activities, it does require that Congress recognize the implications of mandates for state and local activities and, in some cases, authorize funding for such mandates. According to Gullo (2004), UMRA increased the amount of information that federal agencies are required to provide Congress when proposing a bill that will impose costs for state, local, and tribal governments. UMRA also gives Congress the authority to defeat or alter a bill that would impose costs for state, local, and tribal governments above the 2011 threshold of $71 million for intergovernmental mandates.

However, there seem to be a variety of "loopholes" through which Congress might avoid funding. Although most state and local government associations (such as the Big Seven Public Interest Groups) actively supported the act, most also realize that it provides limited relief from federally imposed mandates. Also, the act does nothing about mandates imposed on local governments by state governments.

And, according to many, unfunded mandates continue. For example, the Bush administration received criticism from educational groups as well as state and local officials for the presumably unfunded mandates required by the No Child Left Behind Act. Similarly, the Obama administration was criticized for including unfunded mandates in the Patient Protection and Affordable Care Act, the president's health-care reform act and a signature piece of his legislative agenda. In both cases, lawsuits were filed by a number of states seeking remedy from these supposedly unfunded mandates.

Subnational Relationships

Even focusing on state and local activities, we find the federal government involved in some way—at a minimum, in providing funds for states and localities. But important intergovernmental activity also occurs at the subnational level: state to state, state to local, and local to local.

State to State   Relationships between and among states are mentioned several times in the U.S. Constitution, most notably in the requirement that states recognize the rights and privileges of citizens of other states and give "full faith and credit" to the public acts and legal proceedings of other states. Some of the most important intergovernmental relationships involving various state governments are not based in constitutional doctrine, however, but are rather the result of political practices over the years.

Relationships among states are not without conflict. States may differ over census counts (important in determining the number of representatives in Congress), shifting state boundaries (as when a river changes course), and a variety of substantive policy issues (such as the rights to underground water or the degree to which dumping pollutants into a river affects water quality in states downstream). In addition, states must increasingly compete with one another for economic development; for example, California recently established the Governor's Office of Business and Economic Development, which is designed to serve as California's single point of contact for economic development and job creation efforts. "GO-Biz offers a range of services to business owners including: attraction, retention and expansion services, site selection, permit streamlining, clearing of regulatory hurdles, small business assistance, international trade development, assistance with state government, and much more" (http://business.ca.gov/AboutUs.aspx).

States also cooperate. There are many opportunities for officials in one state to seek the advice of those in other states with respect to policy alternatives or new administrative arrangements. Many organizations, including the Council of State Governments, the National Governors Association, the National Council of State Legislators, and groups that bring together state officials in personnel, budgeting, purchasing, social welfare, health, and so forth, have been created to help officials share information and expertise. These groups, along with the Washington offices of various states, constitute an important lobbying group in Washington.

One way the states come together to resolve potential disputes or work together on common problems is through *interstate compacts*. These agreements have historically been bilateral, involving only two states; however, increasingly, they involve a number of states within a region or even all fifty states. Originally used to resolve boundary disputes, interstate compacts today cover a wide variety of topics, most arising from the fact that today's policy problems do not confine themselves neatly to the borders of one state. Imagine, for example, the common interests of people in several states sharing the same underground water supply. Think also of the problems that are of interest to all who live in metropolitan areas, such as Cincinnati or Kansas City, that cross the boundaries of two or even more states. It is not uncommon in such areas to find interstate compacts covering air and water pollution, transportation, law enforcement, and so on.

States may also use interstate compacts to symbolize their agreement to cooperate in especially important policy areas. For example, Arizona, California, Nevada, and other southwestern states have a definite interest in ensuring access to water from the Colorado River. The states' governments follow compacts dating back to 1922, which lay out strict guidelines on access rights and water usage. In cases such as this, an interstate compact provides a way for states to formalize resolution of a dispute or to work together without involving the federal government.

State to Local   We have seen that the relationship between states and localities is unitary—that is, local governments have only those powers granted by the state. However, the nature of the powers may vary considerably. Most cities operate under some form of *charter,* the local government equivalent of a constitution. But a state may grant charters in several ways. Some states develop *special charters* for each individual local government; others take exactly the opposite approach and grant a *general charter* for local government. The *classified charter* approach seeks to avoid the restrictive nature of the special charter and the rigidity of the general charter by granting charters to various classes of cities. For example, all cities over 1 million in population might be designated Class A and have one set of charter provisions, whereas cities from 250,000 to 1 million might be Class B and have a different set of provisions. A final means of chartering cities, called home rule, permits cities to write their own charters, within very broad state guidelines and generally subject to voter approval.

Home rule obviously provides the greatest flexibility for local governments in terms of basic structure; however, even under home rule, there is substantial state involvement in local government affairs. For one thing, the states are an important source of funding for local activities. Indeed, at a time when federal aid has leveled somewhat, state aid to local governments has increased dramatically. Between 1980 and 2004, for example, state aid to local governments increased from about $83 billion to over $379 billion, with most of that targeted for education and lesser amounts for welfare, highways, and other purposes (U.S. Census, www.census.gov/govs/www/estimate.html). But more severe economic times have led to a change in direction, as many states have sought to balance their own budgets by decreasing aid to local governments. For example, in 2011, Governor John Kasich (R) of Ohio proposed cutting aid to local governments by up to 50 percent and limiting state colleges and universities to 3.5 percent tuition increases. The cuts would cost counties, municipalities, and townships $167 million in the first year, an amount local officials described as "devastating."

What Would You Do?

You are city manager for a medium-sized community in the Northwest. The state legislature is considering a bill intended to prevent underage drinking. It would require local police departments in the state to perform additional spot inspections of bars and restaurants serving alcohol after midnight. Although you think the cause is an important one, you simply don't have the resources in your police department to do this. The state is not willing to provide more money. What would you do?

But states do not only provide money; they also regulate local government activities. State governments tell local governments what taxes they can levy, what services they can provide, and what types of management systems they must employ. In doing so, states provide needed uniformity, as in the case of highway signs, and ensure minimum standards of performance, as in education or welfare programs. Because states have virtually unlimited power over local governments, there is an obvious temptation to compel local governments to assume new responsibilities. In most states, there are twenty to thirty statutes that impose substantial financial burdens on local governments. The total number of mandates or regulations may number in the thousands (Berman, 1992, p. 53).

Just as states complain about federal mandates, many local officials view state mandates as unnecessary intrusions on local prerogatives. The mandates may require local expenditures that might not otherwise be made. Recently, localities have complained especially about *sneaky mandates*, actions that are required of local governments by the inaction of state governments. For example, Georgia failed to pick up prisoners housed "temporarily" in county jails, resulting in overcrowding in jails, to say nothing of the additional financial burden on the counties. There is, however, new sympathy for localities in terms of mandates, and about one-third of the states now have requirements for at least partial reimbursements of expenses created by mandates.

Localities are not powerless in their relationship with the states, especially as they constitute an important base of political support for those in the legislatures. Local representatives and senators can and often do voice the local message loudly and clearly in the state legislature. Moreover, various patterns of state/local cooperation have emerged in the past several years. Many states, for example, have developed state-level commissions on intergovernmental relations. These state commissions bring together state and local officials to discuss problems in the intergovernmental system and devise ways to work together more effectively. Among the recommendations that have emerged are suggestions for greater local discretionary authority and for reductions in the number of state mandates.

Local to Local   In discussions of intergovernmental relations, there is an understandable tendency to focus on national patterns, but for those who work at the local level, relationships with other local governments are extremely important. One reason is that many citizens live in one jurisdiction, work in another, shop in another, and pay taxes to several. They naturally expect services, such as quality streets or law enforcement, to remain fairly constant as they move from one place to another.

From a political standpoint, the fragmentation of government, especially in urban areas, often means that problems are separated from the resources that might be employed to solve them. Wealthier cities have the money; poorer cities have the problems. But even where resources are evenly distributed, it is difficult to get several local governments together to resolve common problems. In such cases, citizens often turn to higher-level governments for help, thus taking the problem (and its solution) out of the hands of local authorities.

But many interlocal problems are resolved at the local level. Natural, though informal, patterns of cooperation develop, especially in the relationships among local professionals. The police chief in one community talks with other police chiefs, the health officer talks with other health officers, and so on. More formally, one government may actually purchase services from another, contracting for police or fire protection, wastewater treatment, or trash collection. Los Angeles County, for example, provides a variety of services to local governments through contract arrangements. Additionally, *councils of government* (COGs), oversight bodies representing various localities, may be created to help coordinate local affairs.

In recent years, partnerships between local governments have entered the information age as many cities and counties have started to share technological innovations across jurisdictions. In the city of Sunnyvale, California, for example, the local government worked with other municipalities and the Microsoft Corporation to develop online permitting software. The Silicon Valley Smart Permit initiative proved to be so successful that Sunnyvale has created a public-private partnership with a management firm and its e-government affiliate to market the application to other local authorities that are interested in enhancing their efficiency and responsiveness (Eggers, 2007; Mariani, 2001).

Finally, special districts may be created to solve problems that cross governmental boundaries. As mentioned in Chapter 2, special districts are local governments created for a specific purpose within a specific area (not necessarily coinciding with the boundaries of a city or county). Although special districts may promote coordination of health, education, or other services, they also add to the number of governments within a particular area. Thus, one city block may be governed by the city, a county, and several special districts. A resident may have difficulty figuring out which government can help with a particular problem. The difficulties in coordinating efforts are substantial, as are the problems of holding the various governments accountable.

Working with Nongovernmental Organizations

It is impossible to speak of intergovernmental relations without discussing the role of nongovernmental organizations (NGOs) in the policy process. Nonprofit, for-profit, and faith-based organizations have taken a leading role in the delivery of public services. NGOs can be found at all levels of governance and in a variety of policy areas. However, NGOs must be considered not only for their part in implementing public programs, but also for their growing influence in raising issues to the public agenda, lobbying for particular policy alternatives, and guiding political and administrative decision making. In many respects, even the term *intergovernmental relations* seems a bit outdated; perhaps we should opt for the more inclusive term *interorganizational relations*.

The use of NGOs in the delivery of public services has grown markedly in the last several years. Figure 3.3 compares, at the federal level, civilian employment and overall governmental expenditures. Between 1970 and 2004, government spending increased by over 400 percent, even holding inflation constant, but government employment grew only

FIGURE 3.3

Federal Spending and Payroll, 1970–2004 (in Billions of Dollars)

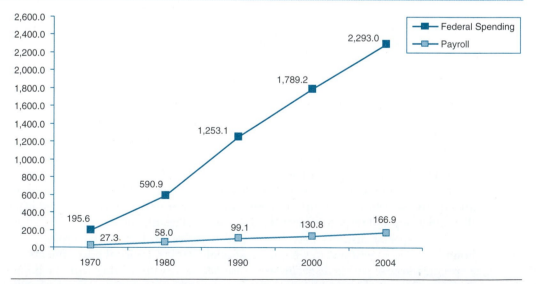

SOURCE (numbers): http://www.whitehouse.gov/omb/budget/fy2008/pdf/hist.pdf; and https://www.opm.gov/feddata/factbook/2005/factbook2005.pdf (p. 62).

about 25 percent, with practically no significant growth in the last twenty-five years. This substantial growth in federal programs, occurring without comparable growth in federal employment, is explained by the fact that parties other than the federal government are actually conducting the programs and delivering the services. Federal money, for example, goes to private firms, such as defense contractors or banks that administer school loan programs, and to nonprofit organizations, especially those that provide human services such as care for the homeless or disabled.

Much of the attention on NGOs tends to focus on the nonprofit sector, which we will discuss later in this chapter, but for-profits also deserve attention. Traditionally, business was seen as the antithesis to government, with clear boundaries between the public and private sectors. Today, we have experienced a significant blurring between sector lines, with only vague distinctions between for-profit firms and government agencies. Such involvement of private-sector firms in public programs, of course, isn't completely new. Defense and aerospace companies have contracted with government for decades, and for-profit prisons were actually the norm in the nineteenth century. In fact, many of our technological innovations stem from public-private partnerships. Increasingly, though, these partnerships can be found in areas once viewed as purely public in nature, including health and human services, trash collection, education, environmental protection, and parks and recreation (Rosenau, 2000; Sagawa & Segal, 2000).

Governments have entered into public-private partnerships to conserve revenues, to reduce crime in blighted areas, and to promote economic growth. We mentioned previously the partnership between Sunnyvale, California, and other municipalities with the Microsoft Corporation to create online permitting software. Other examples include an alliance between the city of Daytona Beach, Florida, and a private development firm to renovate a dilapidated boardwalk and build a beachfront hotel; a partnership between the state of Michigan and other states for correctional services; and relationships across the country between school districts and private computer firms to bring public school classrooms into the information age. In each case, the interorganizational relationships that arise are important to the success or failure of public programs.

Privatization and Contracting

The movement toward greater involvement of NGOs in the delivery of public services is partly ideological. Some people simply feel that services should be provided by those outside government wherever possible. But the movement has also been stimulated by recent restrictions on government spending and a resulting effort to find more efficient ways to conduct the public's business. Both motives have been discussed under the heading *privatization*—the use of NGOs to provide goods or services previously provided by government. It is important to be clear about its various meanings because the term is used several different ways.

In its broader sense, privatization refers to efforts to remove government from any involvement in either the design or conduct of a particular service. In Great Britain, for example, major industries such as steel or coal, once nationalized, are returning to private control, typically through direct sales to individuals, firms, or other groups. In the United

States, most such major industries, including most utilities, are already in private hands, so there are relatively few examples of such magnitude (the sale of Conrail and certain petroleum reserves are exceptions). There are many more limited examples of privatization, however; a city might, for example, sell a golf course to a country club development, thus ending the government's involvement in golf.

The rationale for removing government from a particular area varies. In some cases, people may feel that clients will receive more personal attention from a nongovernmental or private group, such as one that operates a drug abuse program or a day-care center. Others suggest that privatization enhances competition among service providers, thus ensuring that the new means of delivering services will provide higher quality at a lower cost to the client. Programs also can be turned over to the private sector because the programs seem inappropriate to government or because the private firm operates more efficiently.

Networking

To trace some innovative practices in government, check out the Alliance for Innovation at http://transformgov.org and the Ash Institute for Democratic Governance and Innovation at Harvard University's Kennedy School of Government program at www.ashinstitute.harvard .edu/Ash/index.htm. For innovations in nonprofit organizations, see the Leader to Leader material at http://www.hesselbeininstitute.org/.

Privatization is used in a more narrow sense (and more frequently) to refer to various devices through which a government retains a policy role regarding a particular service but engages someone else to actually deliver the service. For example, a federal agency might decide to contract with a private firm rather than handle computer programming itself; a state might contract with a nonprofit organization to deliver services to welfare recipients; or a local government might lease a public hospital to a private firm. In each case, the services would be spelled out in detail by the government and some, if not all, funding might be provided, but day-to-day operation of the program would be the responsibility of the for-profit or nonprofit agency.

During the past decade, government at all levels has explored a variety of mechanisms for privatizing public services, the most popular being the use of *contracting* (see the box "Take Action: Taking Contracting Seriously"). Supporters view fee-for-service and similar arrangements with NGOs as a more efficient method of service delivery, given the greater flexibility, different labor costs, and economies of scale offered by for-profit and nonprofit organizations. Some of the most publicized examples of contracting in recent years have been in human services, because the federal government shifted to state and local authorities (and in turn to NGOs) a larger role in the nation's welfare system.

For example, the state of Kansas used contracts to hand over most of its child welfare services to the private sector. Several years ago, government officials recognized that the state's foster care, adoption, and related programs simply had to change. "We had a failed child welfare system in this state," said State Representative Melvin Neufeld, who played

Take Action   TAKING CONTRACTING SERIOUSLY

A government that took contract management seriously would
- regard resources required to manage contracts as part of the cost of contracting, funded from the savings and performance improvements they are likely to produce.
- train contracting people, especially those developing contract requirements and doing contract management, in the selection and use of performance measures for contracts.
- take evaluation of contractor past performance seriously, as a method for incentivizing good performance, particularly for complex "relational" contracts where there is a danger the contractor will exploit the government after the award has been granted.
- look for ways to hire relatively young "doers" (such as software programmers, bench engineers) from industry to do stints as contract managers, to give government the technical expertise to manage technical contracts in situations where the government has few "doers" itself.
- reconceptualize—in terms of training and self-image—contract management as a high-level management job.

SOURCE: Donald F. Kettl and Steven Kelman, "Reflections on 21st Century Government Management," IBM *Center for The Business of Government* (2008 Presidential Transition Series); http://www.businessof government.org/report/reflections-21st-century-government-management (p. 45).

a key part in drafting the reform legislation. Excessive costs and declining effectiveness on the part of government agencies, coupled with newly elected conservative state leadership, prompted state officials to shift virtually the entire system of service delivery over to NGOs, mostly for-profit firms. Under the new system, state government contracts with lead agencies at a regional level, which in turn subcontract with NGOs to handle actual service delivery. State officials act mainly to administer the contracts and ensure standards for service quality (Gurwitt, 2000, p. 40).

But privatization of human services has its challenges. Even as supporters point to success stories, a closer look reveals major problems relating to sustainability. For example, next door to its thriving effort to supply welfare services in West Palm Beach, Lockheed Martin IMS struggled in Miami-Dade County. Although the company's costs exceeded $38 million in the same fiscal year, it failed to make a significant impact on caseloads. In fact, the county government has since handed the contract for welfare-to-work services over to a local community college (Walters, 2000).

In Kansas, the state's transformation of child and family services has come under attack not only from liberal critics, who argue that public welfare should not be left up to firms whose primary motive is profit, but also from the businesses themselves. *Governing* magazine reported that "Kansas's story isn't really about *privatization*: It's about a rushed, no-holds-barred effort to build a public-private social services system using managed-care principles, as well as its struggle to recover from the fallout" (Gurwitt, 2000, p. 40). What was the fallout? State officials have been forced to pick up the pieces from what can only be considered a managed-care revolution. Unlike other states, Kansas bypassed smaller-scale, experimental initiatives, choosing instead sweeping reforms. The change inside the state resulted in confusion, as state officials struggled to learn new roles as contract managers rather than caregivers. For private firms, the reforms opened a floodgate on newly created service networks and swamped many businesses that simply did not have the expertise or capacity to deal with the increased demands of public welfare programs (Cohen & Eimicke, 2008).

A more recent example of the difficulties of contracting for services concerns federal spending for grants and contracts in wartime. A bipartisan Commission on Wartime Contracting, which submitted its report in August 2011, found that at least one out of every six dollars of U.S. spending for grants and contracts in Iraq and Afghanistan has been wasted. "Tens of billions of taxpayer dollars have been wasted through poor planning, vague and shifting requirements, inadequate competition, substandard contract management oversight, lax accountability, weak interagency coordination, and subpar performance or outright misconduct by some contractors and federal employees" ("Reducing Waste and Wartime Contracts," 2011). The Department of Defense reported to the commission that the United States simply can't conduct prolonged military operations without contractor support, and indeed, the number of contractors in Iraq and Afghanistan has approximately equaled the number of U.S. military forces. But the commission concluded that poor planning, bad management, and weak accountability needed to be corrected in order to save money and produce more economical and effective outcomes.

States as well have continued to explore privatization through contracts and other devices. New Jersey governor Chris Christie created the state Privatization Task Force to explore opportunities for privatization but also to consider potential difficulties. The task force explored privatization efforts in other states, noting that Philadelphia mayor Ed Rendell saved $275 million by privatizing forty-nine city services. The task force identified similar savings as possible in New Jersey, but it also noted that care must be taken in the process of privatization. While the government has increasingly served as a broker of services, that new role bears special responsibilities. "The report took careful note of another key factor: the states most successful in privatization created a permanent, centralized entity to manage and oversee the operation, from project analysis and vendor selection to contracting and procurement. For governments that forgo due diligence, choose ill-equipped contractors and fail to monitor progress, however, outsourcing deals can turn into costly disasters" ("The Pros and Cons of Privatizing," 2010).

Contracts used to provide public services certainly have promise; however, alliances with NGOs may not always be effective. Nor should contracts be seen as the only mechanism. There are a variety of options for partnering with NGOs. A *franchise* can be awarded to a private firm to perform a certain service within a state or locality. The firm charges citizens directly for the services it provides. Typically, rates and performance standards are established by the government, and there is often some continuing regulation of the firm. Examples include electric power, taxi services, cable television, and emergency ambulance services. Similarly, governments may provide grants or subsidies to private or nonprofit organizations that are performing needed public services. The government provides full or partial support for activities that will benefit the community but that the local government, for financial or other reasons, does not wish to operate on its own. Examples include local government support for the arts, child care, or shelter for the homeless.

All levels of government have experimented with the use of *vouchers*, which are coupons citizens redeem for goods or services. The federal food stamp program, for example, provides recipients with vouchers to purchase food, but it permits the individual to choose both the supplier and the items to be purchased (within stated limits).

At the local level, many jurisdictions have explored the use of vouchers for education. But although proponents suggest it would lead to more effective, efficient options than the public schools, the issue has become one of the most controversial topics in current education policy.

Increased privatization means that public officials need to be attentive to the process of contracting for services. In the words of Ruben Berrios (2006), "The government purchases the expertise of private firms to provide services. The goal is to create a more effective and efficient delivery through a system that fosters and creates competition, provides better management, and helps reduce the size of the government" (p. 119). Although government contracts are not new, they create new relations between government organizations and private or nonprofit organizations. Cooper (2003) describes a shift from the traditional authority-based relations (vertical model) as in regulatory enforcement to negotiation relations (horizontal model) in today's public contract relationships:

> The vertical model is about authority relationships: the way that decisions get from the democratically appointed executives and down through agencies to the contracting officer who is ultimately authorized to negotiate for the needs of the community and then to commit its resources in a legally binding relationship.…The second model comes into play once the decision to contract for goods or services has been made and operates in tandem with the vertical model…contractual relationships are horizontal in character and operate from the base of mutual commitment in which, theoretically at least, the parties are equal. (Cooper, 2003, p. 48)

Recent trends with government contracting refer to so-called public-private partnerships, where the term "partnership" indicates more than cooperation. These partnerships may include long-term agreements for activities that are inherently considered governmental, such as commercial operation of prisons, or for including contractors in rule-making policy procedures (Cooper 2003, p. 57). Public-private partnerships and alliances operate between government agencies and for-profit companies and between government agencies and nonprofit organizations. Nonprofit organizations are a convenient choice for governments for at least two reasons: they are often fervently committed to providing assistance for people in need, and they have close relations with the communities. In addition, volunteers in these organizations often deliver public services for lower costs than if these services were provided by government agencies. However, government grants to nonprofit organizations impose additional administrative requirements for these organizations, frequently requiring more resources and paid personnel.

While public-private partnerships and alliances may provide better services for lower costs, they present a huge challenge for government officials. When entering a partnership with a for-profit company, public managers should be aware that these companies operate for making profit. "Whatever else is promised, the most common way in which for-profit firms seek to make money on government contracts for the same amount of money government is spending now to do the job itself, is to reduce personnel costs" (Cooper, 2003, p. 63). There are also moral issues related to government contracting. Berrios (2006) talks about some flaws that complement the contracting process: favoritism for companies that already have contracts with the government, preferences for large firms over small firms, and corrupt behavior of the government officials that in some instances grant contracts to private companies without following legal requirements. Finally, where government programs are run directly by government, responsibility for their success lies squarely with the government agency. But where such programs are actually delivered by those in the private or nonprofit sector, traditional mechanisms for control and accountability may not work. Maintaining a proper concern for democratic values such as equity and responsiveness may, in the long run, prove more difficult than the managerial challenges of creating appropriate interorganizational policy networks.

The Management of Nonprofit Organizations

As we have seen, nongovernmental organizations have become important players in public policy and administration. Unfortunately, many public administrators fail to appreciate the distinct challenges faced by these organizations, especially those in the nonprofit sector. In order to develop more effective interorganizational, cross-sector relations, it may be helpful to identify some of the key elements of organizational capacity within nonprofits.

Operational Leadership

Nonprofit management begins with effective leadership. By leadership, we mean an organization's internal systems for establishing a mission and vision to guide organizational action, for engaging in strategy making and planning as a way of setting goals and objectives, and for developing an operational structure to facilitate the translation of strategy into action.

Creating effective leadership systems in nonprofits starts with forging a sound mission and vision. The mission represents the purpose the organization will serve in its community. This vision is the guiding image of what members want the organization to become in the future (Bryson, 1995; Smith, Bucklin & Associates, 2000). Although these factors are critical in virtually all organizations, they are especially important in nonprofits. Independent-sector groups depend on a lot more than paid staff to carry out organizational objectives, including volunteers, donors, board members, and other resources. Without a strong sense of purpose or a clear vision for the future, nonprofit leaders will find it extremely difficult to build the "critical mass" necessary for success.

Of course, setting a mission and vision must be combined with sound planning—in particular, with the establishment of clear, measurable goals and objectives. A recent survey of nonprofits found that the "level of support and commitment to planning by the leadership of the organization is…a crucial element in an assessment of organizational capacity. If management neither plans nor possesses the support systems needed to enable planning (such as budgeting systems, planning models, information about past organizational experiences), then the issue of capacity is largely moot. Organizational survival generally requires planning and the development of a shared vision and goals" (Fredericksen & London, 2000, pp. 234–235).

Networking

To explore some of the aspects of nonprofit management, go to the Aspen Institute at www.aspeninstitute.org; and the Hauser Center for Nonprofit Organizations at Harvard University at www.ksghauser.harvard.edu. See Chapter 2 for a list of sites relating to the advocacy role of nonprofit organizations.

Leadership also involves building a solid organizational foundation that allows nonprofits to transform their strategy into action. For those working in the charitable sector, this often proves to be the most difficult task. Most nonprofits begin with an idea that translates very well into mission and vision. Things get much tougher, though, in trying to turn the idea into an organizational reality.

In fact, one of the biggest challenges confronting today's nonprofits involves creating effective, high-capacity systems of operation. Much of this challenge stems from an unwillingness on the part of government and foundation grant makers to provide funding for administrative costs. Nonprofit agencies could gain access to resources for programming and service delivery, but they struggled to find support for the basics of management: staff, equipment, technology, and related expenses. Fortunately, foundations have begun to realize that although restricting funding to program-related needs sounds good, it's impossible to deliver quality services without a well-developed administrative structure (Greene, 2001).

Resource Development

Speaking of financial support, resource development represents another key element of nonprofit management. Agencies in the independent sector receive their funding from a variety of sources, including fees and charges, government grants-in-aid, and private giving. According to the National Center for Charitable Statistics, of some 1.4 million nonprofit organizations registered with the IRS, nearly half have collected more than $25,000 in gross receipts. They reported more than $299 billion in revenues from charitable contributions during 2004, with 83 percent from individual contributions, 11 percent from private foundations, and 5 percent from corporations (*The Nonprofit Sector in Brief*, 2007).

These figures don't include funding from fees and government grants, which make up an additional $400 billion. With such a diverse revenue base, it might seem strange that a primary weakness of nonprofits (especially the smaller organizations) is to rely on a single source of support and not look beyond the next grant cycle for their funding. Successful nonprofits, on the other hand, diversify their revenue streams, balancing between grants, fees-for-service, and other sources.

Nonprofit organizations that are classified as either a public charity or private foundation under IRC 501(c)(3) benefit from their tax-exempt status, which allows taxpayers to deduct contributions as charitable donations. Some nonprofits also may receive discounts on postal rates, special provisions for financing, and various exemptions from state and local taxes.

To ensure sustainability, many nonprofits and their associations have developed innovative strategies for maintaining a sound financial base for the next generation. For example, the National Committee on Planned Giving has initiated the Leave a Legacy program, a nationwide effort to encourage people of all socioeconomic groups to include charitable contributions as part of their estates. The program in large part aims at attracting charitable contributions from the "baby boomer" generation, which over the next few decades will retire with unprecedented wealth. An important element of Leave a Legacy is its community-based focus; that is, a single organization cannot adopt the program, but instead the program brings together nonprofits from around a given community. Prospective donors are asked to work directly with the planned giving officers of the foundations or with estate planners to decide upon a charitable beneficiary.

As any nonprofit manager will tell you, resource development goes well beyond grants and other types of financial contributions. Although most people recognize the challenge nonprofits face in competing for donors, few appreciate the level of competition for other vital resources, such as in-kind support and volunteerism. Although charitable giving certainly remains central to a nonprofit organization's balance sheet, more and more nonprofits depend on in-kind contributions and the time, energy, and expertise of volunteers to meet their objectives. A study conducted by the Independent Sector found that while charitable giving by individuals has declined in recent years, more Americans are volunteering than ever before. In 2004, about 65 million volunteered in charitable organizations (http://www.urban.org/UploadedPDF/311373_nonprof t_sector.pdf).

Keys for successful resource development include being able to articulate a case for your organization, exploring a diverse array of support, identifying an appropriate development strategy and action plan, and ensuring effective implementation of the action plan. Most importantly, at the heart of the resource development strategy must be a commitment to building and maintaining relationships with funders, donors, and volunteers (Smith, Bucklin & Associates, 2000).

Financial Management

Running a nonprofit also depends on sound financial management. The benefits of being a charitable organization were discussed previously, but with these benefits come important requirements for accounting and public disclosure of financial transactions. For example, all IRC 501(c)(3) organizations must maintain open records and prepare financial reports for their stakeholders on a periodic basis. Many foundations and other grant makers ask grant recipients to undergo periodic audits, sometimes as an eligibility requirement. And charitable organizations with annual gross receipts of $25,000 or more must submit to the IRS each year a Form 990 (Return of Organizations Exempt from Income Tax), as well as disclosure statements to state and local tax authorities.

To satisfy these requirements, nonprofits must maintain detailed financial records. At the very least, this includes following basic accounting standards and procedures. But financial management includes much more than reporting. It should be at the heart of a nonprofit's strategic planning and management. Without the ability to generate clear, meaningful financial information and incorporate this information into organizational decision making, a nonprofit agency limits its overall capacity. Unfortunately, many nonprofits fail to follow established procedures, and some do not have in place even the simplest mechanisms for accounting. Small- to medium-sized nonprofits have the greatest need in this area.

The basics of financial management include monitoring the assets, liabilities, and net assets of the organization, as well as the revenues and expenses for established reporting periods. Moreover, nonprofit managers should make sure that the budget and financial management process is undertaken in coordination with the governing board. In many cases, such coordination is mandated in the articles of incorporation, but it also makes sense to have those responsible for setting the strategic direction informed on the organization's financial condition.

Board Governance

Most of the principles of nonprofit management discussed here have focused on the operational side of the organization. However, independent-sector agencies also must have an effective governance system. Nonprofit boards are, in some respects, even more vital to the organization than to the staff, because some smaller agencies rely on board members for performing day-to-day tasks. Regardless of an agency's size, its board represents the final decision-making body of the organization. By law, board members are bound (in the articles of incorporation) to ensure the fiscal and legal health of the agency.

The board is responsible for several important roles. These include setting the strategic direction for the organization, serving as champions in the external community, and overseeing organizational planning and implementation (Carver & Carver, 1996; Eadie, 2001). First, with regard to strategic direction, board members act as the primary source of vision, mission, and values for the agency. They ensure that these strategic factors become reflected in organizational action. An excellent example can be seen in Porter Hills Retirement Communities and Services, a nonprofit health-care provider in Grand Rapids, Michigan. The Executive Leadership Team at Porter Hills actually brings the outline of the Porter Hills mission, vision, and values into its strategy sessions and considers these principles prior to moving ahead on decisions. If a new venture, partnership, or internal change does not reflect the core principles of the organization, or doesn't coincide with where the board wants to be in the future, then the issue is either dropped or taken back to the board for direction.

Second, board members also must be the organization's champions in the community. They are the principal spokespeople, representing the organization on key issues, but also the role models for donations and volunteerism. In this capacity, the board should set the policies and procedures for the operational staff and leadership on strategies for external communication. Board members, consequently, must always be kept "in the loop" on factors affecting the organization.

A vital point here is that the board must speak with one voice, or it shouldn't speak at all. This means that board members should support decisions of the governance body once a consensus has been achieved. Too often, and particularly with smaller, community-based organizations, members of nonprofit boards go into the community and speak against other members or against the organization. This does nothing but send a signal to those listening that the disgruntled board member has failed to appreciate the core values of governance.

Third, the board must support the organization's leadership on issues of planning and implementation. The board should make sure that the organization has an effective and ongoing planning process and work with staff to establish priorities and goals. This doesn't mean that board members should try to manage day-to-day activities on the part of the staff. It does mean, though, that those on the operational side of the organization should coordinate and seek direction from the board on issues that are truly strategic in nature.

Nonprofit boards vary in size, with some organizations having fewer than ten members and others having more than fifty members (which is toward the extreme!). The composition of the board will reflect the history and mission of the organization, but most nonprofits strive to ensure that the governance system will reflect the diversity and values of the constituent community. Here are a few of the considerations relating to board size:

- What functions are required of the board?
- How many individuals, and in what roles, are needed to accomplish those functions?
- How many board committees are needed to accomplish the organization's goals?
- Are there sufficient individuals on the board to participate on board committees? (Smith, Bucklin & Associates, 2000, p. 29)

Boards are perhaps one of the most important components of effective nonprofit management. A high-impact board with an effective board chairperson can have an extraordinary influence on the organization's success. Unfortunately, the opposite is also true. Many a good nonprofit has been severely limited, and in some cases completely destroyed, because of an ineffective, divisive board.

Board-Staff Relations

Among the greatest challenges faced by nonprofits is the need to strike a balance in board-staff relations. As the previous discussion suggested, board members have a central role to play in the organization's strategy making and in representing the organization in the external community. However, once the parameters for action have been established, board members must step back and allow staff adequate room to achieve the goals and objectives. Frequently, boards (especially those consisting of inexperienced members) tend to micromanage the operational staff. This does little more than foster distrust and frustration, and, in many cases, it contributes to high staff turnover.

There are several keys to effective relationships. First, the board must set clear expectations for leadership and staff. At least once a year, board members should sit down with the executive director and lay out the goals and objectives for the coming term. Second, the expectations must be reinforced by lines of communication between board and staff. Communication channels should be maintained by the executive director, and in some rare events directly between the board and staff. Third, the board must reinforce success. As part of its oversight function, the governing board should be ready to celebrate the good work being done, not just sanction the shortcomings.

In many respects, the primary buffer between the board and staff is the executive director. Although some executive directors position themselves in ways that cut off the governance and operational sides of the agency, with very little direct involvement between board members and staff, this takes things a bit too far. The most effective relationships feature executive directors as the main conduits or brokers. Staff should be present, when appropriate, at board meetings, mainly to offer expertise and inform the board on key decisions; similarly, the board must provide oversight and guidance to the staff on key issues of agency strategy. How far to go on either side will depend on the organization, but it's up to the executive director and members of the leadership team to determine the appropriate balance.

Advocacy

The advocacy role of independent-sector organizations is perhaps the most overlooked and misunderstood aspect of nonprofit management. This stems from the fact that the federal tax code limits lobbying activities by charitable organizations, and, depending on the party affiliation or political position, some legislators and policy makers have frowned upon non-profit activism. But nonprofit organizations may, even under federal tax law, engage in advocacy as a way of amplifying the voice of their constituents in the policy process.

In 1976, Congress granted nonprofits the right to lobby in the public interest without having to worry about losing their status as tax-exempt organizations (Pub. L. 94–455, 1307 [1976], now codified under Section 501(c) of the federal tax code). While the IRS deliberated on the issue for more than a decade, in 1990 the federal tax code was revised to expand the advocacy rights of nonprofits. Under the 1976 tax law, nonprofits that choose to come under its jurisdiction must comply with the definition of lobbying as "the expenditure of money by the organization for the purpose of attempting to influence legislation. Where there is no expenditure by the organization for lobbying, there is no lobbying by the organization" (Smucker, 1999, p. 51).

The tax law establishes two types of lobbying: *direct* and *grassroots*. In direct lobbying, the organization communicates with legislators or other public officials on matters concerning legislation in which they have a role to play or with the nonprofit organization's own membership. In grassroots lobbying, the organization influences the legislative process by attempting to sway public opinion on policy issues. The tax law also establishes ceilings for expenditures that may be allocated to lobbying, based on the total level of tax-exempt expenditures for the organization.

As future nonprofit managers, you should explore the legal constraints before engaging in lobbying activities, but by no means should you shy away from attempting to influence policy decision making on behalf of your constituents. The law is on your side, and you certainly will have greater protection than you may have originally thought for lobbying without fear of threatening your organization's tax-exempt status.

Summary and Action Implications

Given the complexity of modern society, your work as a public administrator will likely involve a complex set of relationships with all kinds of external groups. Many of these groups will be agencies at other levels of government. Our federal system has evolved from a pattern in which the various levels of government were relatively distinct to a pattern in which funding and programmatic relationships are extremely intense.

The fact that public programs today operate through vast and complex webs of people and organizations—public, private, and nonprofit—means that new skills are required of the public manager. Any particular program may involve various levels of government, organizations from all sectors of society, and clients or citizens with many different interests and concerns. As a public manager, you must be able to identify the network that is or should be involved in a particular situation and assess the effectiveness of that network.

To make that judgment, you will need to consider several factors. The first is *communications*, the type of information that goes from one organization to another and how it is transmitted. Second, you might focus on *exchanges* of goods and services, money, and personnel among the organizations involved. Third, you might examine the *normative* aspect of the relationship—that is, what each organization expects of the other and what each is willing to contribute to the alliance. Examining these same categories may also suggest ways to improve the effectiveness of interorganizational relationships.

The interorganizational nature of modern public administration also has interesting implications for the interpersonal skills you must bring to the job. Increasingly, the government official responsible for a given program must be skilled in negotiating relationships with those outside the agency to ensure that the program proceeds effectively and responsibly. More and more, the public administrator works in a world in which older images of organizational hierarchy and control are quickly giving way to newer images of "managing in ambiguity" and "negotiating organizational boundaries." The interorganizational nature of public administration today has a direct effect on what skills managers need.

STUDY QUESTIONS

1. Although intergovernmental relations involve more than financial matters, funding programs have a significant role in the process. Define and give examples of the various kinds of grants and funding programs.

2. Compare and contrast dual federalism, cooperative federalism, and coercive federalism. Describe the approach to federalism used during the Clinton and Bush presidencies. How would you characterize the Obama approach?

3. In the last decade, states and localities have faced significant changes in funding from the federal government. Discuss the reasons for the changes and how they affect relations among the various levels.

4. How do governmental mandates and regulations affect operations at the state and local levels?

5. Government has been moving to "privatization" of some goods and services. How will this trend affect intergovernmental relations?

6. Explain the importance and use of contracting for services and goods.

CASES AND EXERCISES

1. Analyze the relationship between state and local governments in your state. What legal requirements govern state-local relationships? What, if any, bodies exist to help in intergovernmental cooperation? What kinds of mandates has the state imposed on local governments? What has been the reaction to these? How do you think state-local relations could be improved?

2. Divide the class into several groups of six to eight students each. Have one group assume the role of a granting agency charged, by legislation, with providing funds to local communities to help in projects that improve the economic potential of the community and assist low-income and disadvantaged groups in the community. Assume that the agency has $50 million to distribute, but that the legislation has given the granting agency the authority to determine all other details of the grant program.

   The agency group must first define as clearly as possible the intent of the legislation and then prepare guidelines outlining the types of projects that will be funded under the program. A written Request for Proposals (RFP) should then be prepared and distributed to a set of potential applicant communities, each represented by one of the other groups in the class. The RFP should contain, at a minimum, a description of the program, criteria by which proposals will be evaluated, examples of projects that might be funded, and instructions for submitting proposals for funding (including a deadline for applications).

   Each community group will then prepare a grant application to support a project or projects it wants for its community. Members of each community group may communicate with one representative of the agency designated as liaison to that community, but should not talk with other agency members. Community groups can communicate with one another if they wish. By the deadline contained in the RFP, all proposals should be submitted to the agency. The agency will then determine which, if any, projects will be funded and at what levels. The results should be communicated to all the communities.

   Following the exercise, the class as a whole should discuss the entire process. You might want to focus on issues such as these:

   - What is the role of the agency in defining the kinds of projects that will be funded?
   - What types of instructions are necessary to enable communities to compete fairly and effectively?
   - What was most attractive about the proposals that were funded?
   - For what reasons were other proposals not funded?
   - What effect on the final decisions did communications between the community and the liaison from the agency have?
   - Did "politics" play any role?

FOR ADDITIONAL READING

Bernstein, Susan R. *Managing Contracted Services in the Nonprofit Economy.* Philadelphia: Temple University Press, 1991.

Bevir, Mark. *The Sage Handbook of Governance.* Thousand Oaks, CA: Sage Publications, 2011.

Boris, Elizabeth T., and C. Eugene Steuerle. *Nonprofits and Government: Collaboration and Conflict.* Washington, DC: Urban Institute, 1999.

Cohen, Steven, and William B. Eimicke. *The Responsible Contract Manager: Protecting the Public Interest in an Outsourced World.* Washington, DC: Georgetown University Press, 2008.

Cook, Brian J. *Bureaucracy and Self-Government.* Baltimore: Johns Hopkins University Press, 1996.

Cooper, Phillip J. *Governing by Contract.* Washington, DC: CQ Press, 2003.

Cooper, Phillip J., and Chester A. Newland. *Handbook of Public Law and Administration.* San Francisco: Jossey-Bass, 1997.

Cooper, Phillip J., et al. *Public Administration for the Twenty-First Century.* Fort Worth, TX: Harcourt Brace College Publishers, 1997.

Eadie, D. C. *Extraordinary Board Leadership: The Seven Keys to High-Impact Governance:* Aspen Pub, 2001.

Gage, Robert W., and Myrna P. Mandell, eds. *Strategies for Managing Intergovernmental Policies and Networks.* Westport, CT: Greenwood Press, 1990.

Goldsmith, Stephen, and William D. Eggers. *Governing by Network: The New Shape of the Public Sector.* Washington, DC: Brookings Institution Press, 2004.

Katz, Michael B. *The Price of Citizenship: Redefining the American Welfare State.* New York: Metropolitan Books, 2001.

Kemp, Roger L., ed. *Privatization: The Provision of Public Services by the Private Sector.* Jefferson, NC: McFarland & Company, 1991.

Kettl, Donald F. *The Next Government of the United States: Why Our Institutions Fail Us and How to Fix Them.* New York: W. W. Norton, 2009.

Kettl, Donald F. *Sharing Power: Public Governance and Private Markets.* Washington, DC: Brookings Institution Press, 1993.

Levin, Martin, and Mary Sanger. *Making Government Work.* San Francisco: Jossey-Bass, 1994.

Light, Paul C. *Making Nonprofits Work: A Report on the Tides of Nonprofit Management Reform.* Washington, DC: Brookings Institution Press, 2000.

Light, Paul C. *Sustaining Innovation: Creating Nonprofit and Government Organizations That Innovate Naturally.* San Francisco: Jossey-Bass, 1998.

McLaughlin, Curtis. *The Management of Nonprofit Organizations.* New York: Wiley, 1986.

Peirce, Neal R., Curtis Johnson, and John Stuart Hall. *Citistates: How Urban America Can Prosper in a Competitive World.* Washington, DC: Seven Locks Press, 1993.

Peterson, Paul. *The Price of Federalism.* Washington, DC: Brookings Institution Press, 1995.

Plotnick, Robert, Marcia Meyers, Jennifer Romich, and Stephen Rathgab Smith, eds. *Old Assumptions, New Realities.* New York: Russell Sage, 2011.

Rusk, David. *Cities without Suburbs.* Baltimore: Johns Hopkins University Press, 1993.

Salamon, Lester M. *Partners in Public Service: Government-Nonprofit Relations in the Modern Welfare State.* Baltimore: Johns Hopkins University Press, 1995.

Vincent-Jones, Peter. *The New Public Contracting: Regulation, Responsiveness, Relationality.* New York: Oxford University Press, 2006.

PLANNING, IMPLEMENTATION, AND EVALUATION

Developing policies and programs, putting them into operation, and measuring their success or failure constitute an important and recurring cycle for public and nonprofit managers. For example, a new monitoring program is initiated in the Balkans. To support that policy, the U.S. Navy organizes a fleet of vessels to expand our presence in the Persian Gulf, while political and military leaders assess the operation and decide what to do next. Similarly, a new policy involves sending literature on AIDS to all households in the United States. A group in the surgeon general's office convenes to monitor the operation. Both the efficiency of the mailing and its effectiveness as an educational device are discussed. Meanwhile, a local parks and recreation department joins with nonprofit organizations to develop a program for handicapped athletes. After staff and money are acquired to support the program and it begins operations, the department director asks whether the program is worth the time and energy it seems to be taking from other tasks. Repeatedly, plans are made, policies and programs are implemented, and the work of the organization is evaluated (Birkland, 2011; Sabatier, 2007; Stone, 2011).

Recently these issues have taken on increased importance as managers in the public and nonprofit sectors have been asked to do with less, while at the same time providing more and better services. This situation has led many to call for "managing for results"—that is, clearly stating goals and objectives in terms of public outcomes, designing and implementing programs, and then measuring the performance of the government or other agency against established standards. The idea of "managing for results" or "performance management" suggests the importance of bringing together careful planning, implementation, and evaluation.

Although planning, implementation, and evaluation all require knowledge of the political and ethical context of public administration and certain personal and interpersonal skills, various technical aids have been developed during the past decade to assist the manager in these three areas. These technical aids include Web-based participative planning, strategic planning, and specific quantitative methods for measuring performance. Moreover, these techniques reflect a change in the way public and nonprofit organizations account for their actions. Citizens, lawmakers, and other advocacy groups increasingly hold agencies accountable not only for their efficiency in expending public and charitable resources, but also for their effectiveness in achieving public outcomes. Techniques such as *strategic planning* and *performance measurement* link the actions of public and nonprofit organizations with specific, measurable results. Through the use of such techniques, public administrators may account for both their own efforts and the impact those efforts have in each given policy area.

Networking

The Government Accountability Office website at www.gao.gov provides resources relating to managing for results. For additional resources on productivity and performance management, see the American Productivity and Quality Center at www.apqc.org.

Planning

On a daily basis, all managers engage in planning. But organizations, and indeed entire governments, engage in more formal planning processes, often involving a wide range of participants and the development of considerable data and other information. Planning typically leads to the development of alternative courses of action, and each must be examined to decide which way to go. Depending on the level of the problem, the process of examining and choosing among alternatives may involve the manager in either *policy analysis* or *program design* or both.

In a planning effort that captured the public's attention like few in recent memory, New York City was faced with the momentous task of deciding how to rebuild the devastated downtown area after the September 11, 2001, terrorist attacks. New York's Regional Planning Association convened the Civic Alliance to spearhead a participative planning process (see www.civic-alliance.org). The Civic Alliance is a coalition of approximately eighty-five different civic groups, businesses, universities, foundations, and community groups that joined together to solicit public comment and involvement and to provide recommendations to the Lower Manhattan Development Corporation, a joint city and state organization charged with the rebuilding and revitalization effort. Several different approaches were used to provide citizens with the opportunity to become involved and have their ideas heard in the process. For example, an event called "Listening to the City" employed both face-to-face dialogue and technology in one-day forums. More than 4,500 people participated in small roundtable discussions while a network of people with laptop computers recorded and immediately transmitted the ideas generated to a "theme team." The theme team identified key themes and concepts and reported them back to all of the participants. Participants also had electronic keypads to record their preferences and answers to specific questions. Subsequent to these forums, an additional 800 people exchanged approximately 10,000 messages in small virtual discussion groups and participated in numerous polls in online dialogue over a two-week period to express their views and preferences.

In the first phase of this project, 230 workshops and an interactive website were used to solicit answers to three primary questions: What have we lost? How have we changed? What should be done? In the subsequent phases, participants were asked to react to proposed designs for rebuilding on the site of the World Trade Center. Although the revitalization project is not completed, the process used in New York City illustrates the potential of using innovative strategies and approaches to garner public participation in large-scale planning projects.

Strategic Planning

Planning is not only used when responding to a crisis, but has been increasingly employed as an ongoing process in the public and nonprofit sectors. A number of writers have commented on the rapidity of the social and technological changes we are now experiencing and on the turbulence and complexity that such changes generate. In an effort to recognize and respond to such changes, many private corporations began programs in the 1960s and 1970s to systematically plan for future development. The success of these programs is now confirmed by the fact that more than half of publicly traded companies use strategic planning in some form. Strategic planning helps an organization match its objectives and capabilities to the anticipated demands of the environment to produce a plan of action that will ensure achievement of objectives (Andrews, 2012; Bryson, 2004; Greiner & Cummings, 2009).

We can differentiate strategic planning from more familiar long-range planning activities in several ways. Long-range planning primarily concerns establishing goals or performance objectives over a period of time; it is less concerned with specific steps that must be undertaken to achieve those goals. Strategic planning, on the other hand, implies that a series of action steps will be developed as part of the planning process and that these steps will guide the organization's activities in the immediate future. Strategic planning takes the future into account, but in such a way as to improve present decisions.

A second way that strategic planning differs from long-range planning is its special attention to environmental complexity. The organization is not assumed to exist in a vacuum; rather, both the organization's objectives and the steps to achieve them are seen in the context of the resources and constraints presented by the organization's environment.

A final distinction between the two types of planning is that strategic planning, especially in the public sector, is a process that must involve many individuals at many levels. As most managers know quite well, effective changes in organizational practices are most readily accomplished by involving all those who will be affected by the change. This general rule is especially applicable to changes generated through a process of strategic planning.

Public organizations undertake strategic planning efforts for many reasons: (1) to give clarity and direction to the organization, (2) to choose from among competing goals and activities, (3) to cope with expected shifts in the environment, and (4) to bring together the thoughts and ideas of all participants in the work of the organization. Most importantly, planning activities provide an opportunity for the widespread involvement of leaders and citizens in defining the direction of the community or the agency as it moves into the future, thus building trust and commitment.

Planning for Planning

As a manager, you may wonder whether such activities are appropriate for your jurisdiction or agency. Whatever your work—at any level of government or in a nonprofit organization—you will find precedents for planning. Many federal, state, and local agencies have begun strategic planning programs over the past several years, as have voluntary associations, human service organizations, and job training programs. The key seems to be that any organization is a candidate for strategic planning if, by allocation of resources, it can significantly influence either formulation or implementation of public policy.

You may, of course, question whether strategic planning is worth the costs in terms of consultant fees, research and data analysis, and time away from other duties. The best gauges for assessing costs are: (1) Is it likely that careful planning will lead to reduced operating costs or increased productivity over the long run? and (2) What might the organization lose in the absence of a more comprehensive and integrated approach to the future?

The latter question has become increasingly important to those in local governments, who now realize that they must compete with other communities in attracting industry, providing amenities, and maintaining the population base. The issue, however, must be treated differently when an administrative agency such as a state government department is considering planning. Although strategic planning might make the agency more competitive in attracting resources from the executive or legislature, this clearly should not be the purpose of planning. Rather, the agency should use strategic planning to involve key *stakeholders* in assessing the unit's work and the possibilities for improving its services. The process may indeed lead to requests for further funding, but it may also suggest ways to more effectively utilize existing resources or even ways to reduce the scope of activities.

What Would You Do?

You are a member of the management team of a medium-sized Florida oceanfront vacation and retirement community. You have been asked to make recommendations to the city council concerning elements that should be part of a new vision and an accompanying strategic plan for the city. What would you do?

Because of budgetary uncertainties, you may also question whether the time is right for planning activities. Some say that planning can't take place without solid information about funding levels. But the opposite argument is compelling—that planning is most essential in times of uncertainty, for these are exactly the times when you most need to be in control of your own destiny. Times of uncertainty do not mitigate the need for planning; they intensify it.

Managers in the public sector voice a related argument: that periodic changes in political leadership make planning more difficult than in private industry. Again, the opposite argument is compelling: in times of transition, planning can provide continuity. Even when new leadership wishes to change the directions specified in an earlier planning effort, changes can be made with greater clarity and aimed more readily toward critical concerns if a plan is in place.

Finally, you may wonder whether strategic planning efforts are consistent with your organization's commitment to democratic or participatory processes. Here lies the most significant difference between strategic planning in the public and private sectors. Whereas planning in the private sector may involve many people throughout an organization, it remains centered and directed at the top, because that is where the private interests of the firm are most clearly articulated. In the public sector, however, every effort must be made to significantly involve all those who play an important role in the jurisdiction or the agency. For example, a local government planning effort should involve not only elected leadership and city staff, but also many others with a stake in the outcome: unions, neighborhood associations, chambers of commerce, civic organizations, and so forth. Similarly, a state government agency's planning effort should involve people from all levels of the organization, members of constituent groups, elected officials, people from other agencies and other levels of government, and representatives of the general citizenry.

Strategic planning in the public sector must be a highly participatory process; consequently, this participation opens the possibility of building new understanding among various groups. Many communities that have engaged in strategic planning have found that the process brought together various groups in a way not previously possible. Strategic planning may therefore be undertaken to achieve both direction and commitment.

Organizing for Planning

The planning process can proceed in a number of different ways, but the most common approach is to form a central planning group to work closely with an outside consultant to obtain information and make commitments to various new directions. In a local community, the group might include the city's political leadership; representatives of the city administration (for example, the city manager); representatives of business, industry, and labor; members of neighborhood associations; and so on. For a federal or state agency, on the other hand, the major planning group might consist of the agency director, managers from the next organizational level below, and selected program directors. The planning group in a nonprofit organization might include the executive director, members of the board, staff members, and representatives of constituent groups.

Steps in Planning

Once it has been brought together, the planning group will want to give its attention to four primary concerns before developing action strategies (see the box "Exploring Concepts: Steps in Strategic Planning"). The group should consider (1) the organization's mission or objectives, (2) an assessment of the environment in terms of both opportunities and

Exploring Concepts

STEPS IN STRATEGIC PLANNING

1. Statement of mission or objectives
2. Environmental analysis
3. Assessment of strengths and weaknesses
4. Analysis of organizational leaders' values
5. Development of alternative strategies

constraints, (3) an examination of the organization's existing strengths and weaknesses, and (4) the values, interests, and aspirations of those important to the organization's future. Consideration of these issues will lead to several strategic alternatives—perhaps stated as "scenarios for the future"—and to the choice of a particular direction in which the organization should move. Finally, a set of action steps or implementation items will be developed to indicate what must be done immediately to put the organization in the proper position to face the future most effectively.

Statement of Mission or Objectives   Arriving at a concise, yet inclusive, mission statement of the organization is a difficult step in the planning process. Although most organizations have a general sense of their mission, questions often arise that cannot be readily answered in terms of stated objectives. Having a specific mission statement, however, provides an identity for the organization, as well as a guideline for future decisions and a standard against which to measure specific actions.

Because arriving at a mission statement may imply certain strategies, care should be taken to consider alternative approaches to the organization's goals. A mission statement might indicate, for instance, whether a city wishes to seek a broad industrial base or focus on particular types of businesses, such as tourism or high-tech industries. Similarly, a university mission statement might indicate whether the institution seeks a broad range of programs in all areas or a limited number of exceedingly high-quality programs. The mission statement of a state agency might comment on the desired range of clientele, responsiveness to changes in the environment, or quality of service. If there is doubt or debate about items, they should be carried forward as elements of strategy for later consideration.

Environmental Analysis   After developing a mission statement, the planning group should move to an analysis of the environment within which the organization operates. This assessment should include legal and political considerations, social and cultural trends, economic circumstances, technological developments, and, where appropriate, the organization's competitive or "market" position. Each area should be examined in terms of the present environment and how it is likely to change in the future. This assessment leads the group toward identifying possibilities for reducing constraints and extending opportunities.

Assessment of Strengths and Weaknesses   At this point, the planning group can turn its attention toward assessing the organization's existing capabilities—its strengths and weaknesses. The analysis should be as forthright and inclusive as possible, taking into account financial resources (including changing patterns of funding), human resources (including political and managerial strengths and weaknesses), the operation of both technical and organizational systems, and quality of work. This assessment of capabilities should relate as directly as possible to the stated mission of the organization. For example, an agency involved in facilities design and construction might want to consider the age and condition of facilities, the number and abilities of architects and engineers, the number and frequency of design projects, and the unit's standing among other similar organizations. Examining strengths and weaknesses should be accompanied by some attention to programs that might significantly improve capabilities in one or more areas.

Analysis of Organizational Leaders' Values A next step in preparing to develop strategic alternatives is to take into account the values, interests, and aspirations of those who will guide the organization into the future. People will respond to the same environmental and organizational analysis in different ways. In business, for example, some will be perfectly satisfied with the security of a stable market share, whereas others will be willing to take greater risks in the hope of greater payoffs. Leaders vary in terms of creativity, energy, and commitment. Yet, if a plan is to be effectively implemented, it must reflect the concerns and interests of those who will play major roles in shaping the future of the organization.

Development of Alternative Strategies At this point, the planning group can move to formulate alternative strategies. These strategies can take several forms; however, one useful way to proceed is to draw up alternative "scenarios of the future," indicating what the organization might look like five, ten, or twenty years into the future. The scenarios should indicate new directions the organization might take; pessimistic, realistic, and optimistic interpretations of its future; and factors likely to influence these future patterns. It is helpful to develop more than one scenario and then use them as competing viewpoints from which to debate the merits of various alternatives. From a thorough discussion of the scenarios, one or more strategies will emerge. The strategy should be chosen that most effectively moves the organization toward its mission, given environmental opportunities and constraints, organizational strengths and weaknesses, and the values, interests, and aspirations of the leadership. After developing the strategic orientation, the planning group should be pressed to identify specific action steps for implementing the strategy.

The Logic of Policy Analysis

One possible outcome of a formal planning process is that the need for new policies will be identified. (The need for new policies can be generated in other ways as well, many of which we discussed in Chapter 2.) A local group considering economic development issues might recognize the need for new tax incentives for industries interested in locating in the community. A state welfare department planning group might focus on the relationship between providing day care and job training. Or a nonprofit organization might decide there is a need for a new publications program. In each case, a problem is identified and the question arises as to whether a new approach to the problem—a new policy—might help.

Many issues may come up. Exactly what is the nature of the problem? What would we be trying to achieve with the new policy? What might be alternative approaches? What might we expect from each alternative? What criteria would we use to evaluate alternatives? Which alternative would best meet our criteria? Answering questions like these is the basis of analyzing public policies. We can therefore define *policy analysis* as the process of researching or analyzing public problems to give policy makers specific information about the range of available policy options and their advantages and disadvantages. There are several ways you might become involved in policy analysis. All managers engage almost daily in a sort of informal analysis of public policies; they encounter new problems and consider alternative policies. Often a more formal review of policy options is called for. Sometimes staff members perform the analysis; many public organizations employ policy analysts to work on just such problems. In other cases, another governmental agency may help; for example, the Office of Management and Budget, as well as its counterparts in many states, develops policy reports. Policy analysis might also be performed by legislative staff or legislative research groups. Finally, many analyses are performed by consultants, including university consultants, where the public manager acts as a client, issues the contract, monitors the work, and receives the final report. Even though, as a manager, you may not perform the analysis yourself, you must be able to distinguish between high-quality analysis and work of limited usefulness (Fischer, Miller, & Sidney, 2007; Iris, 2005; Kraft & Furlong, 2009; Sabatier, 2007; Stone, 2011).

Steps in Policy Analysis

Broadly speaking, most policy analyses attempt to follow a "rational" model of decision making, involving five major steps: (1) formulating the problem, (2) establishing criteria for evaluation, (3) developing policy alternatives, (4) considering the expected impact of the various alternatives, and (5) ranking the alternatives according to the established criteria. (See the box "Exploring Concepts: Steps in Policy Analysis.") As a simple illustration, think about how you might decide what would be the best route from home to work (Quade, 1989, pp. 33–34). If you assumed at the outset that the "best" route is the shortest, then you could simply lay out the alternative routes on a map and select the shortest. (Using a map would in effect create a "model" that would help in your analysis.) As in almost all policy analyses, however, there may be more than one criterion involved. For example, the shortest route might involve more traffic and take longer to drive. The shortest travel time might then constitute a second criterion, but it would require a more sophisticated model than a map, taking into account traffic congestion and perhaps other variables. Just thinking through the various complications that might arise in this "simple" example, you can get some sense of the difficulties you might encounter in moving through the five stages of a more comprehensive policy analysis.

Exploring Concepts

STEPS IN POLICY ANALYSIS

1. Defining the problem
2. Setting objectives and criteria
3. Developing alternatives
4. Analyzing various policies
5. Ranking and choosing

Defining the Problem   There are obviously many problems facing any public organization and, correspondingly, many opportunities to analyze policy alternatives. Someone, however, must decide about the problem and how the analysis will proceed. This someone—the *sponsor* of the analysis—may be a legislator, an elected chief executive, or an agency manager. But, in any case, the one who will perform the analysis—the *analyst*—should seek as clear a statement of the problem as possible and as much information about the nature of the problem and the range of solutions. Why has the problem surfaced? Who is affected? How does this problem relate to similar problems? What policy options have already been tried? What is the range of policies that would be feasible, both economically and politically? What resources are available to support the analysis?

Obviously, how the question is initially formulated will guide the analyst toward certain possibilities and away from others, so it is important at the outset to be as clear as possible without unnecessarily cutting off alternatives. The sponsor might ask, for example, "How can we provide adequate shelter for the homeless in our community this winter?" This statement permits exploring alternatives ranging from subsidizing existing shelters to building new shelters. If, however, certain options, such as building new shelters, are clearly out of the question due to time or money, then the analyst should be advised of these limitations.

Sometimes the problem is only vaguely understood at the outset, and part of the analyst's job is to develop a background statement or issue a paper that outlines the problem. In some cases, gathering information at the library will be helpful, especially in laying out the history of the problem, discovering approaches used in other jurisdictions, and becoming aware of technical developments in the field. The analyst may want to talk with other people, perhaps in other jurisdictions, to see what their experience has taught them. People in other governments, other levels of government, and other agencies at the same level can be helpful. The analyst can also gather information from those involved. In our example, the analyst would probably want to talk with those already involved in providing shelter. A statistical survey might even be possible. Finally, agency records and statistics might be helpful. Throughout these initial information-gathering efforts, the analyst wants to develop an idea of how different people and different groups perceive the problem and possible solutions.

Setting Objectives and Criteria   As we have seen, establishing objectives for a new policy or criteria for judging alternatives is often quite difficult. In some rare agencies, the existing values and preferences are clear enough to guide choices. The manager might be able to say, "It's worth much more to our agency to achieve Result A than Result B, C, or D. Therefore, whenever the choice presents itself, choose A." But in most policy areas, there are likely to be multiple and often conflicting objectives. To route a highway through an urban area, for example, one must consider factors such as the cost of the project, how many and who might use the highway, the number of houses and other properties that might be displaced, and the impact of noise and pollution on adjacent neighborhoods. How does one begin to rank all the factors?

There are other problems in selecting criteria. For example, criteria may differ among different levels of the organization. A constant problem for decision makers is to be sure that criteria used at one level are consistent with those at another level. A particular course of action might fit the criteria developed at one level, but so distort the use of resources at the next higher level as to make the choice inappropriate. Criteria must also be stated as completely as possible. An analyst might be told to seek a solution that maximizes output at minimum cost and then discover that no single alternative can meet both criteria. Which is more important?

Finally, choosing criteria depends on individual perspective. Most policy areas have many different stakeholders—people who are involved in and affected by the policy decision. These may include legislators, agency personnel, client groups, and other interest groups, and each group may feel quite differently about what is most important. In the design of a new highway, for example, a neighborhood association might place highest value on environmental concerns, while someone who lives in the suburbs might be most concerned with finding the shortest, quickest route to work. Different criteria compete for prominence in any policy analysis. And, often, which criteria receive greatest prominence is a political decision of legislators or high-ranking administrators.

Developing Alternatives Developing alternative policies is without question the most creative phase of policy analysis, for it is here that the analyst must move beyond easy solutions and develop innovative approaches to public problems. Different alternatives often derive from different assumptions about the problem. For example, should the welfare system be oriented toward providing support at home for impoverished mothers or should it enable mothers to work by providing day care? Should day care be addressed by building new centers or by providing tax credits or vouchers to subsidize attendance at existing centers? Obviously, answers to questions about alternative approaches to child support depend on interpretation of both the causes of poverty and the motivations of the mothers. To develop a complete range of alternatives, the analyst must assume the perspectives of many different stakeholders.

Another way to develop far-ranging alternatives is to consider the relationship between the particular problem and other similar issues. For example, adequate care for the homeless ties to issues of health care, financial support for housing, welfare policy, and perhaps such areas as mental health and Social Security. Again, alternatives that take the various interrelated concerns into account are likely to be generated if the analyst considers the views of many different stakeholders. Rather than saying, "How can my organization solve this problem?" the analyst should ask, "How can this problem be solved?"

Analyzing Various Policies Having generated a number of realistic policy alternatives, the analyst must now assess the likely impact of each alternative. How one analyzes the impact will vary according to the particular type of policy. In some policy areas, including some of major importance, limited information about possible impacts will be available. The analyst can only make intuitive judgments based on his or her experience and the experience of others. In other cases, however, one can gather specific data and analyze it by means of quantitative techniques. In the urban highway example, data could be gathered and analyzed to determine cost per mile, load-bearing capabilities, travel time for users, and a variety of other factors.

Occasionally, actual experiments with several policy options may be possible, sometimes with an experimental design similar to that used in the natural sciences. That is, the behavior of a particular target population may be compared to that of a control group when only one variable (the policy) is changed. Applied to large-scale social problems, such experiments may be quite costly, but they may also save considerable time and money in the long run. Sometimes it is appropriate to spend millions to save billions. (We should also note the ethical problems associated with providing a treatment expected to be beneficial to one group but intentionally denying it to another "control" group. Is it ethical to deny some people a treatment you think will be beneficial?) A less formal means of policy experimentation occurs when one state or locality tries a particular policy approach and makes the results available to other communities. Sometimes this form of experimentation is simply the result of different groups trying different programs, but sometimes it is conscious. When state and local groups pressured the Carter administration to move the management of the small cities' portion of the Community Development Block Grant program to the states, Wisconsin and Kentucky were asked to run the program on an experimental basis. Their success in tailoring programs to local needs led to legislation allowing all other states to assume administration of the program (Jennings et al., 1986; for more recent examples, see Beland & Waddan, 2012).

Ranking and Choosing The final step in the analytic process is to compare the impacts associated with various alternatives and the criteria for evaluation established earlier. Alternatives can then be ranked in terms of their respective impacts. When both the criteria and impact levels are fairly straightforward, a simple comparison of possible effects may readily show which choice should be made; other cases may be more complex. The highway construction example, for instance, might yield three or four alternative proposals and as many as twenty criteria by which to evaluate the alternatives. One way to treat such cases is to simply lay out the expected results of each alternative in terms of the various criteria, leaving the task of comparing the data and ranking the alternatives to the decision maker. Sometimes more sophisticated quantitative techniques are available to the analyst.

Costs and Benefits

One of the most straightforward quantitative techniques is the *cost-effectiveness* approach, which compares policies by quantifying their total costs and effects. Costs are usually measured in monetary terms, but effects may be measured in units of any type.

Typically, the cost-effectiveness approach takes one of two forms. First, the level of effectiveness can be fixed, and one can search for the alternative that achieves this level at the least cost. If, for example, we want to increase the number of houses in a community that get tested for radon by 25 percent, would it be cheaper to hire inspectors or to spend money on advertising so that homeowners would do the inspection themselves? A second approach fixes the budget amount and then asks which alternative will provide the highest level of effectiveness for that amount. If we want to spend no more than $50,000 a year on radon inspections, which two approaches will result in a higher number of inspections?

The cost-effectiveness model is widely used because it is quite flexible and does not demand the same degree of precision as other approaches. Cost-effectiveness is especially useful when the relative merits of competing proposals, such as different child-care delivery mechanisms, are being debated. It is not as useful in comparing questions of absolute merits, however, such as whether to allocate resources to early childhood programs or to radon testing. Moreover, the cost-effectiveness approach may be somewhat limited where criteria and impacts are more complex.

Closely related to cost-effectiveness is *cost-benefit* analysis. Essentially, the cost-benefit approach involves identifying and quantifying both the negative impacts (costs) and positive impacts (benefits) of a proposal, then subtracting one from the other to arrive at a measure of net benefit. In contrast to cost-effectiveness analysis, the cost-benefit approach seeks to establish both the total monetary costs and total monetary benefits of a proposal. The logic of cost-benefit analysis is obvious, but applying it to policy proposals that involve large expenditures and produce difficult-to-measure results can be quite complicated.

There are several advantages to cost-benefit analysis. If programs can be evaluated in terms of costs and benefits, the approach can result in rather precise recommendations. But even if it is difficult to calculate costs or benefits, focusing on the two areas may help clarify the manager's thinking about a proposal. Legislation often requires that cost-benefit analysis precede particular policy changes, especially in environmental or regulatory policy.

Several factors make it difficult to assess the costs and benefits of a particular program. First, the analyst will be asked to come up with measures of both costs and benefits and reduce them to a common unit of measure (usually money). But in analyzing a proposed new highway, can we accurately portray the fatality rate for similar highway segments as a measure of safety? And, if so, how can we translate the rate of fatalities into dollars? Second, we should always remember that the final calculated cost-benefit ratio is not the only basis for choosing one alternative over another. Despite the ratio of costs and benefits in our highway example, a particular level of fatalities may simply be considered too high, either politically or ethically.

Typically, costs are thought of as inputs and benefits as outputs. Costs might include one-time items such as research and development, buildings and facilities, land acquisition, equipment purchases, and so on. Costs might also include recurring budgetary items such as personnel, rent, maintenance, administrative overhead, insurance, and so forth. Because these expenditures take place over time, calculations usually take into account the time value of money—the fact that people generally are not as willing to pay for something in the future as in the present. Although the particular calculations are beyond the scope of this text, taking time into account enables us to answer questions such as whether Project A with low initial cost but high maintenance is better than Project B with high initial cost but low maintenance.

Benefits, based on outputs, include both positive and negative effects. (The negative effects of a program obviously might be calculated either as increases in cost or decreases in benefits. They are usually the latter.) Positive benefits might include reduction in disease or improved drinking water or increased highway safety. Negative benefits might include increased noise and pollution from constructing a new airport. Again, some effort to translate positive or negative benefits into monetary terms would have to be made.

Obviously, measuring outputs and translating them into dollars are exceedingly difficult tasks. For example, eliminating a disease might increase productivity, which could be measured, but also reduce pain and suffering, which would be more difficult to measure. Omitting these factors because they are hard to measure biases the analysis, but assigning a dollar value to them might do the same. Consequently, the quantitative presentation of costs and benefits is often accompanied by an explanation of additional qualitative considerations.

Other Quantitative Techniques

In addition to cost-effectiveness and cost-benefit approaches, there are many other techniques to aid policy analysis. It is not necessary to examine the mathematical formulas, but it is helpful to understand the logic they depend on. Let us examine the following payoff matrices with that goal in mind. Assume a simple example: hiring an office worker who will need proficiency in computer operation and budgeting. After interviewing two applicants, A and B, you feel that A is stronger (rated 1) than B in both areas. Your thoughts might be modeled as shown in Table 4.1.

TABLE 4.1		
Simple Payoff Matrix		
	Value Measures	
	Computers	Budgeting
Candidate A	1	1
Candidate B	2	2

© Cengage Learning

Your choice here is simple, because one candidate is clearly superior in both respects. But what if your decision appears to be structured as shown in Table 4.2?

TABLE 4.2		
Mixed Payoff Matrix		
	Value Measures	
	Computers	Budgeting
Candidate A	1	2
Candidate B	2	1

© Cengage Learning

Now there is no clear choice. Even if you thought computer skills were more important than budgeting skills, you couldn't choose, because Candidate A might be a little better with computers, but Candidate B may be much better in budgeting. To decide, you need either more sophisticated measures of ability or a way to weight the two factors, as we do in the example in Table 4.3.

TABLE 4.3			
Weighted Payoff Matrix			
	Value Measures		
	Computers	Budgeting	Combination
Candidate A	9	3	6.3 + 0.9 = 7.2
Candidate B	5	8	3.5 + 2.4 = 5.9
Weight	0.7	0.3	

© Cengage Learning

Here we measure the ability of each candidate in the two areas on a 10-point scale, with a higher score indicating higher proficiency. Because we have established that computer skills are more important than budgeting skills, we give those skills a higher weight (0.7 compared to 0.3). By multiplying the candidates' scores by the weights, we obtain a combined value measure for the two candidates, thus enabling us to choose the better candidate. (This classic example is adapted from Latane, 1963.)

We could extend the logic of the payoff matrix even further. One way is to combine scores under differing working conditions. Indeed, following the logic of the payoff matrix, we could accommodate large numbers of weighted variables, as might be involved in a large-scale policy analysis; the logic remains much the same. Remember that one can adopt different decision rules and that the choice of criteria is subjective.

Another tool of policy analysis is *decision analysis*, a technique for use where decisions are likely to be made sequentially and with some degree of uncertainty. Decision analysis is applicable to a variety of complex problems, such as choosing airport sites or developing plans for commercial breeder reactors, but the underlying logic is fairly straightforward and often quite helpful. Consider another classic illustration.

> The officer in charge of a U.S. embassy recreation program has decided to replenish the employees' club funds by arranging a fund-raising dinner. It rains nine days out of ten at the post, and he must decide whether to hold the dinner indoors or out. An enclosed pavilion is available but uncomfortable, and past experience has shown turnout to be low at indoor functions, resulting in a 60 percent chance of gaining $100 from a dinner held in the pavilion and a 40 percent chance of losing $20. On the other hand, an outdoor dinner could be expected to earn $500 unless it rains, in which case the dinner would lose about $10. (Stokey & Zechauser, 1978, p. 202)

Using decision analysis to structure the officer's dilemma involves first constructing a *decision tree* to show the various possible outcomes, given the risks associated with each (see Figure 4.1). Obviously, the decision tree lays out the options, probabilities of various occurrences, and anticipated outcomes in much the same way as a payoff matrix. It is easy to imagine how much more complicated the situation could become, however, with the addition of other variables or other decision options. Even in this simple case, matters might be complicated by other variables, such as whether the weather will be hot or cold, whether there are other ways to increase attendance (advertising and so on), and whether the commanding

FIGURE 4.1

Embassy Dinner Decision Tree

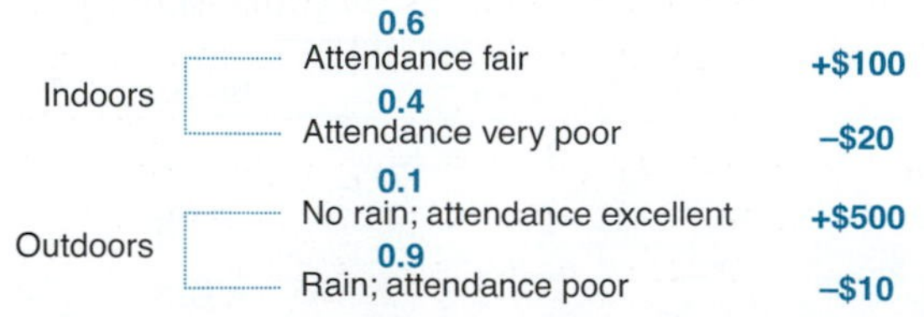

		0.6	
Indoors		Attendance fair	+$100
		0.4	
		Attendance very poor	−$20
		0.1	
Outdoors		No rain; attendance excellent	+$500
		0.9	
		Rain; attendance poor	−$10

© Cengage Learning

FIGURE 4.2
Chess Match Decision Tree

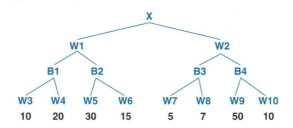

© Cengage Learning

officer prefers to be indoors or outdoors. You can imagine how much more serious are the sequences and variables involved in a decision concerning location of a nuclear facility.

And as if this weren't enough, consider what happens when you take into account competition from others. Let's imagine a chess match in which we have decided on some evaluation criterion, such as king safety or center control that we can measure. That is, we have identified a way to place a value on each outcome that might result from a given set of moves. Let's say that White is ready to move and has two options, W1 and W2, leading to the decision tree in Figure 4.2. (If we move W1, then Black can move either B1 or B2; if we move W2, then Black can move either B3 or B4; and so on. After evaluating all possible outcomes, we assigned the values shown across the bottom row.) We would obviously prefer to choose W2, and then have Black choose B4, so we could choose W9, the alternative with the highest value for us. But taking into account what Black is likely to do, we recognize that if we take W2, then Black will take B3, leading us to the two lowest payoffs. Recognizing this probability, we will instead take W1, expecting that Black will take B1, and we will have a satisfactory outcome.

Although our examples have been quite simple, their logic can support far more sophisticated applications of policy analysis. Moreover, the discipline these techniques impose makes them useful for even relatively simple applications. The models force us to examine our assumptions, structure the problem clearly and logically, and consider the full range of available options. The models also allow us to more effectively communicate our analysis to others.

That brings us to one final point. No matter how sophisticated the analysis and how rational its conclusions, a policy analysis must be effectively communicated to the actual decision makers. Communication is often quite difficult, because decision makers are extremely busy and have a variety of conflicting demands on their time and interests. Sometimes even those who are invited to do a policy analysis find themselves and their analysis swept aside by political or other considerations, and, indeed, that is the prerogative of major decision makers. A rational analysis is helpful in the decision process, but political considerations, in the positive sense, must also be taken into account before any actions are taken.

Bardach (2011) suggests that policy analysis is more art than science and emphasizes the importance of intuition as a complementary part of the methodology used for a policy analysis. He develops eight useful steps in the policy analysis process that can be used as a practical guide when constructing policy proposals.

1. Define the problem. A clear operational definition of the problem to be solved is a crucial step that gives "both a reason for doing all the work necessary to complete the project and a sense of direction for your evidence-gathering activity" (p. 1).
2. Assemble some evidence. Before gathering evidence, it is important for the analyst to think carefully about what is relevant to the problem. Pertinent literature review, applied best practices, and analogies are some of the sources for supporting the argument for the existing policy problem.
3. Construct the alternatives. When looking for alternatives, use a comprehensive and focused approach. The alternatives should address the problem and should be feasible.
4. Select the criteria. Commonly used evaluative criteria are efficiency, equality, equity, fairness, and justice. Commonly used practical criteria are legality, political acceptability, robustness, and improbability.
5. Project the outcomes. When analyzing the policy along with the policy proposal, think about results that will come in the future. For this step, it is most important to be realistic (not too optimistic, which is a common pitfall) in one's expectations for the future.
6. Confront the trade-offs. "As economics teaches us, trade-offs occur at the margin" (p. 48). In other words, it tells us how much extra money we should pay to receive an extra unit of some service.
7. Decide! With this step, the policy analyst makes a decision on which policy alternative to concentrate his or her attention.
8. Tell your story. This step implies that the intention of the analysis is to suggest a solution for a certain problem. The policy analyst should be aware that the clarity of the presentation of his or her analysis is very important.

Implementation

In the cycle of planning, implementation, and evaluation, implementation is the action phase. Once plans have been made and policies decided on, you must put them into operation. Financial and human resources must be allocated and mobilized, organizational structures and systems must be devised, and internal policies and procedures must be developed. During implementation, you may be involved in issuing and enforcing directives, disbursing funds, awarding grants and contracts, analyzing programmatic and operational problems, taking corrective action, and negotiating with citizens, business, and those in other public and nonprofit organizations.

Over the past 25 years, a body of literature dealing with the implementation process has emerged. Some of the literature merely uses new terms to talk about the general processes of administration in the public sector. Other parts of the literature focus on the relationship between policy development and program implementation. This literature specifically alerts us to the difficulty of effective program implementation and to how implementation may distort or even subvert the intent of policy makers. Most pointedly, one commentator has written, "It is hard enough to design public policies and programs that look good on paper. It is harder still to formulate them in words and slogans that resonate pleasingly in the ears of political leaders and the constituencies to which they are responsive. And it is excruciatingly hard to implement them in a way that pleases anyone at all, including the supposed beneficiaries or clients" (Bardach, 1977, p. 3).

A classic study of the relationship between policy and implementation was suggestively titled *Implementation: How Great Expectations in Washington Are Dashed in Oakland; or Why It's Amazing That Federal Programs Work at All* (Pressman & Wildavsky, 1973). *Implementation* described a particular economic development program in the Oakland, California, area that was less than successful. Pressman and Wildavsky concluded that "what seemed to be a simple program turned out to be a very complex one, involving many participants, a host of different perspectives, and a long and tortuous path of decision points that had to be cleared" (p. 94). Implementation was characterized by multiple and conflicting interests trying to influence the program's direction to suit their many and divergent needs. The major recommendation of the study seemed to be that people involved in designing public policies "pay as much attention to the creation of organizational machinery for executing a program as for launching one" (pp. 144–145).

This lesson has been clearly recognized in the literature of strategic planning. Plans remain sterile without implementation, so there has always been a close connection between planning and execution. As noted, planning is most beneficial where it can help make immediate decisions in light of future impact. Thus, a final step in any planning process is to arrive at a series of specific actions to take in the near future—the next six months, or the next year or two years—who does what, when, and to what effect. These steps, which may detail new policy positions or new organizational processes, will form a new action agenda for the community or the agency.

Organizational Design

Some of the classic approaches to implementation, formerly called "organization and management," focused on the structure and design of new organizations and their work processes or flows. The traditional organization chart expresses both the division of labor within an organization and the structure of command or control.

In the late 1930s, Luther Gulick advised managers developing new organizations that there were several ways they could divide work (Gulick, 1937, pp. 21–29). Among these were (1) purpose, (2) process, (3) people or things, or (4) place. Dividing work according to purpose might result in distinctions such as between providing education or controlling crime, while dividing work according to process might lead to a legal unit, a medical unit, or an engineering unit. One could also divide work according to the people served or the things being dealt with—for example, the Department of Veterans Affairs deals with all problems that veterans face, whether legal, medical, and so on. Finally, one may organize according to geographic area, as would a state welfare department that has regional or county offices.

Networking

Online resources and case studies relating to the planning and implementation of productivity initiatives can be found at the U.S. Conference of Mayors site at www.usmayors.org/uscm/best_practices. For information on scenario planning, go to the Global Business Network at www.gbn.com.

Gulick and his contemporaries also talked about the number of levels that would be appropriate to an organization. Obviously, many organizations are fairly "tall"—they have many levels; others are "flat"—they have relatively few levels. The number of levels is guided to a degree by the type of work and by the number of people who report to any one manager. The term *span of control* signifies the number of people that one individual supervises; although there are significant variations, depending on the type of work, it is generally considered difficult to supervise more than six to ten people.

In addition to developing organizational structures, early writers urged charting work processes as an aid to organizational design. *Process charting* or *flowcharting* can provide a graphic demonstration of the various steps in an operation, the people performing each step, and the relationships among these elements. Figure 4.3 shows a simple illustration of process charting, although charts can become far more sophisticated in actual applications. This process chart uses a variety of symbols to indicate different activities. The vertical lines set the basic framework of the chart. The columns show the flow of work from one person to another and vary depending on the complexity of the process and the degree of analysis desired. The column headings indicate the positions under study. In Figure 4.3, the ovals indicate a specific task (sorting, conferring, and so on); the circles indicate transportation of work from one person to another. The triangle indicates storage, a period during which operation is stationary. Finally, the rectangle indicates an inspection, usually to check for quality or quantity. As illustrated here, one can make notations on the chart to indicate the nature of particular steps in the process.

FIGURE 4.3
Process Charting

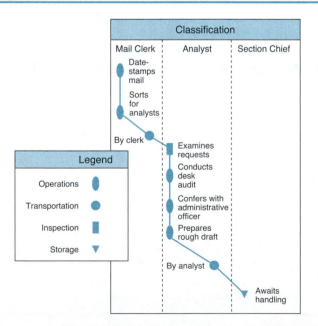

© Cengage Learning

Process charting is most useful where a considerable number of clerical or nonprofessional employees perform the same general classes of work and follow the same general sequence of operating steps. Although process charting is less useful in analyzing the work of professionals, there are possible applications here as well. For example, charting a professional operation may reveal bottlenecks, excessive periods of review, or excessive checkpoints that inhibit the flow of work. As with other techniques, process charting can become quite complex, but its logic is both simple and compelling. Process charting simplifies analysis because it sharply points out backtracking, excessive detail, unnecessary repetition, poor distribution of functions, and other administrative defects. For this reason, process charting has enjoyed a revival of interest by those implementing total quality management programs.

Systems Analysis

There are many other sophisticated devices that have been developed for analyzing the design and operations of both public and private organizations. Many of the approaches are based in *systems theory*, an effort to identify, in logical fashion, the interactions of various internal and external elements that impinge on an organization's operations. The systems approach has been used in a variety of fields, including physics, biology, economics, sociology, and information science, but the basic concepts are much the same regardless of discipline. Generally speaking, a *system* is a set of regularized interactions configured or bounded in a way that differentiates and separates them from other actions that constitute the systems environment. Thus, we can speak of a biological system, a physical system, an economic system, or a political system. Any such system receives *inputs* from its environment and then translates these through some sort of *conversion process* into *outputs* that are returned to the environment. These outputs in turn affect future inputs to the system through a *feedback loop*. Presumably, if the outputs of a system are valued by the environment, new inputs will be forthcoming and the organization will survive. A basic systems model is illustrated in Figure 4.4.

FIGURE 4.4
A Basic Systems Model

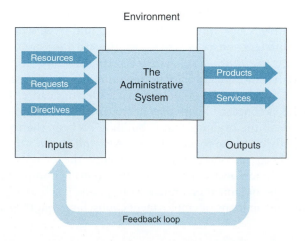

© Cengage Learning

Following this model, consider the operation of a thermostat. The thermostat takes in information about the heat in a room and then measures the heat against some standard. If the level of heat is below the standard, the thermostat causes more heat to be put out into the room. The additional heat becomes part of the environment and creates new information (feedback), which becomes part of the next input into the system.

The systems concept works similarly in human organizations. A business might receive input from its environment that customers are demanding more red shoes. A decision might be made to produce more red shoes, and those shoes would be part of the organization's output. The new red shoes become part of the environment and affect new inputs into the system, which might range from comments about the quality of the shoes to information that the demand has not yet been met. This new information guides the operation of the system in the future.

Like many of the other models we have discussed in this chapter, the systems approach has been used in highly sophisticated applications ranging from the analysis of organizational design and processes to the creation and modification of major weapons systems. Indeed, the first major applications of systems analysis occurred in the military during and soon after World War II. For some time thereafter, the Department of Defense was the major user of systems analysis, depending on a variety of contractors, most notably the RAND Corporation to help in applying systems analysis to a variety of problems. Yet, it is possible to apply systems logic to a variety of problems public organizations face, and, as with other techniques, the systematic discipline that the approach brings to problem solving is perhaps its greatest strength.

Systems analysis emphasizes the relationship between the organization and its environment, suggesting that public managers carefully consider factors in the environment that impinge on their operations. These factors include legal and political matters, support and opposition generated by interest groups and client organizations, human and financial resources, and applicable technology. Naturally, the environment also includes a large number of other organizations with which the agency interacts, such as the chief executive's office, the legislature, the budget office, related agencies at the same level of government, parallel agencies at other levels of government, and a variety of private and nonprofit groups and associations.

Many systems analysts tend to ignore what occurs within the system itself, preferring to think of it as a black box into which inputs go and from which outputs come. Others speak of several different subsystems that carry forward the organization's work. In a classic formulation, the *institutional subsystem* is responsible for adapting the organization to its environment and for anticipating and planning for the future. People involved in this activity generally constitute the organization's leadership cadre. The *technical subsystem*, on the other hand, is concerned with the effective performance of the organization's actual work. If the work of the organization is building rockets, the technical subsystem is the people who actually build the rockets. Finally, the *managerial subsystem* is concerned with providing the necessary resources for accomplishing the technical task, as well as mediating between the technical and institutional subsystems (Thompson, 1967, pp. 10–11).

Outputs of public organizations range from goods (such as highways or buildings) to services (such as student loans or employment counseling), but they also include regulations, adjudication, and support for other programs. To know the effect of their efforts, managers need some sort of feedback mechanism. Feedback often occurs naturally: clients write letters of appreciation; legislators inquire about program operations; a program may even become an issue during an election campaign. Sometimes, however, you will want to secure more systematic and accurate feedback, for which you can use devices such as questionnaire surveys, field testing, or spot checks of service provision. Recall that systems analysis helps focus on how an organization interacts with its environment; developing effective feedback mechanisms helps the manager in that process.

Reengineering

Over the past twenty years, many public administrators have adopted a more comprehensive, even radical technique for enhancing organizational performance, called *reengineering*. (Although the word *reengineering* has been used with decreasing frequency, the basic principles of reengineering are reflected in other approaches such as Six Sigma and have become a part of the core organizational processes in many agencies.) The central tenet of reengineering centers on redesigning work processes and organizational structures to be in line with agency outcomes. Through this technique, policy makers attempt to make public organizations more flexible and capable of responding to the dynamic conditions of contemporary society.

In some respects, reengineering builds upon systems theory and other analytic techniques in that it involves the recognition of core processes and the systemic context of staff behavior. However, the outcome of reengineering goes well beyond simply making alterations within the existing bureaucratic structure. Its goal is to overhaul rigid government agencies into what one author calls seamless organizations: "In contrast to the fragmented bureaucracies of the past, seamless organizations provide a smooth, transparent, almost effortless experience for their customers. Staff in seamless organizations perform the full job, in direct contact with their end users" (Linden, 1994, p. xii).

Implementation of a reengineering process begins with an identification of the organization's desired outcomes. These include the short- and long-term impacts the agency wants to achieve. Then the organization is redesigned around the core and support processes that will produce these outcomes. Given the hierarchical, inflexible nature of many public organizations, though, this is not as simple as it may seem.

Reengineering requires that public administrators change their current assumptions, those equating organization with traditional bureaucracy. Such a reorientation helps to transform work processes and agency structures to those driven by meaningful outcomes—a shift from segmentation to integration, from division of labor to seamless work (Linden, 1994).

Reengineering involves enhancing those activities that may be considered value-added—activities that give customers more of what they are willing to pay for and cutting functions that merely stand in the way. Of course, some functions remain crucial for the organization's success. Central administration activities such as budgeting, accounting, and quality inspections cannot simply be removed from the picture. On the other hand, these functions often hinder the completion of the more value-added activities. The key to successful reengineering is to separate the core processes from the other tasks, enabling the critical activities to be carried out more effectively (Hammer & Champy, 1993; Linden, 1994).

Evaluation

The sequence of planning, implementation, and evaluation is completed by asking whether the program goals and objectives have been achieved in a way that was both efficient and effective. Such evaluations may, however, operate at a variety of different levels. Some may respond to the legislature's interest in knowing whether the intended benefits of legislation were achieved; others may be designed to communicate to the public what is happening in areas of broad citizen interest; still others may be oriented toward improvements either in the design of the policy being implemented or in the way it was conducted. An understanding of contemporary approaches to evaluation requires attention to both the performance measurement movement mentioned earlier and more traditional program evaluation approaches. Whereas program evaluation offers insight into each policy or program's direction, effectiveness, and sustainability, performance measurement generates information concerning the organization or network as a whole. When combined within the framework of evaluation research, these strategies not only assist in the decision-making process but also improve the overall accountability of public organizations. In turn, evaluation research enhances legislative oversight and administrative control.

Several legislative groups conduct or sponsor evaluation research at the federal level. These include the Government Accountability Office (GAO), the Congressional Budget Office, and various legislative committees, primarily those concerned with the budget and oversight of specific programs. Executive agencies, such as the Office of Management and Budget and the Executive Office of the President, also conduct evaluation research. Much of this research, however, is sponsored by the agencies themselves, as managers seek to determine how they can better manage or generate greater productivity from their organizations.

There is also great interest in program evaluation at the state and local levels, although resources to support such activities have often been limited. State governments have developed analytic capabilities within the executive branch, often through the budget office. In recent years, many states have restructured their budgets to be in line with predetermined performance standards (see Chapter 10). This has enabled state governments to link fiscal resources to the desired results targeted by each agency. Evaluation research is then used to help a state government determine how successful it has been in achieving its performance goals. Consequently, state legislatures and citizens can now see what services and impacts were gained with public resources.

Again, at state and local levels and in most nongovernmental organizations, as at the federal level, a great deal of evaluation research is done as part of the agency's or program manager's ongoing responsibility. Public administrators increasingly must show not only the efficiency of their actions, but also the results of their actions within the broader stakeholder community. Examples of performance measurement and program evaluation range from complex, detailed, one-time studies to the ongoing, integrated monitoring of performance goals. Regardless of the level of sophistication, evaluation research offers important details to support the organization's overall strategic planning and to assist the organization in determining the direction of individual programs.

Program Evaluation

There are a variety of ways to classify the approaches to program evaluation, including outcome evaluations and process evaluations. *Outcome evaluations* are closely tied to the type of assessment in performance measurement; they focus on the results of program activity—that is, the extent to which a program meets its objectives in terms of impact on the environment (as described in the discussion of the United Way in Chapter 3). If the work of an organization is to improve adult literacy, then an evaluation might measure the number of individuals who learned to read. That information would likely then be related to program inputs to show, in a cost-benefit ratio (in this case, based on allocative efficiency), the number of individuals learning to read per thousand dollars spent. In general, an outcome evaluation seeks to determine whether X causes Y, where X is the activity of the program and Y is the desired outcome or goal. As you can imagine, outcome evaluations are particularly valuable to legislators, grant makers, and others concerned with the performance of various programs.

In contrast to outcome evaluations, *process evaluations* focus on ways that program implementation might be improved to better meet the program's objectives. The question here is what can be done to X, the program's management, to improve Y, the desired outcome. Whereas an evaluator interested in outcomes might spend a great deal of time developing systematic measures of program results, someone interested in process evaluation would analyze the organization and management of the agency's activities, including distribution of financial and human resources and design of service delivery mechanisms. Process evaluations also determine if legally prescribed processes are being followed and ensure that individual rights are not violated.

Relevant measures here would fall more on the input side and might include such items as workload measures or data on resource allocation. In such studies, it may be important to distinguish between *efficiency*

CourseReader Assignment

Log in to **www.cengage.com** and open CourseReader to access the reading:

Read "Children in Poverty: Can Public Policy Alleviate the Consequences?" by Aletha C. Huston, and "Prison Math: What Are the Costs and Benefits of Leading the World in Locking Up Human Beings?" by Veronique de Rugy. These two articles discuss the kinds of public policy issues that confront those in the public sector and in related organizations. The first article discusses policy options that might be available to help with the issue of children in poverty. The second article discusses the costs and benefits of a high prison population.

Discuss each case, emphasizing in the first the possible policy solutions that might be developed. What are the alternative policies, and what are the advantages and disadvantages of each? In the second case, consider the "mathematics" of the situation being evaluated here. What policy conclusions would your analysis of the situation suggest? How much are your recommendations guided by the data and how much by your personal values? How does one affect the other?

Quiz

Quiz

and *effectiveness*. Efficiency is concerned with the relationship between inputs and outputs, usually expressed in a ratio per unit of input. For example, a measure of streets paved per thousand dollars spent would be a measure of efficiency. Effectiveness, on the other hand, is concerned with the extent to which a program is achieving or failing to achieve its stated objectives. Effectiveness measures are outcome oriented; they focus on the real changes the program produces, such as a decrease in airline deaths.

Sometimes process evaluations occur after the fact—that is, upon completion of the program; but often they occur during program operation. Indeed, some process evaluations are almost continuous in their ongoing review of program operations. In either case, the information that emerges in the course of a process evaluation is likely to be of greatest interest to the program manager who hopes to improve his or her organization's performance.

Program evaluations may therefore be directed toward many different audiences and serve many different purposes. The specific kinds of information required vary from evaluation to evaluation. Eleanor Chelimsky, former head of the GAO's Program Evaluation and Methodology Division, lists the following types of information that may be developed retrospectively:

- Information on program implementation (such as the degree to which the program is operational, how similar it is across sites, whether it conforms to the policies and expectations formulated, how much it costs, how stakeholders feel about it, whether there are major problems of service delivery or of error, fraud, and abuse, and so on).
- Ongoing information on the current state of the problem or threat addressed by the program. (Is the problem growing? Is it diminishing? Is it diminishing enough so that the program is no longer needed? Is it changing in terms of its significant characteristics?)
- Information on program outcomes. (What happened as a result of program implementation?)
- Information on the degree to which the program made, or is making, a difference. (That is, what change in the problem or threat occurred that can be directly attributed to the program?)
- Information on the unexpected (as well as expected) effects of the programs. (For instance, was a program of drug education accompanied by an increase in the use of drugs?) (Chelimsky, 1985, pp. 8–9)

Evaluation Designs and Techniques

Approaches to the evaluation of public programs range from historical analysis to sophisticated experimental designs. Indeed, over the years, there has been a recurring debate over the proper approach to evaluation. Some argue that such research should be primarily qualitative, concerned with tracking program development and indicating forces that helped shape the program. Advocates of this approach tend to be most interested in process questions, such as reasons for success or failure and unanticipated consequences of the program; they ask, "What happened?" Others argue that program evaluations should, wherever possible, employ the most rigorous scientific methods appropriate to the subject matter, including the design and execution of formal experiments. These analysts tend to be more interested in program outcomes; they ask, "Does it work?" (Chelimsky, 1985, p. 14).

Whatever the approach, those involved in program evaluation must confront two challenges to the validity of their work. The first question, concerning *internal validity*, asks whether the approach measured what was intended. Was the design consistent with the goals of the program and the needs of the sponsor? Were the methods most appropriate for answering the questions that needed to be asked? Were the results as free from bias as possible? A second question, concerning *external validity*, asks to what extent the findings may be applicable to more general circumstances. What does the study say about similarly situated programs? Can the study be replicated and be expected to produce similar results? These and other questions can be directed toward the various techniques employed in evaluation research.

Qualitative Techniques   Many program evaluations depend on qualitative information derived from reading about the program, from interviewing important actors (including agency personnel, clients, and others), and sometimes from actually participating in the work of the program. The initial step in a qualitative evaluation project is usually to read everything available about the program, including background material on the subject of the program (flu vaccines, child nutrition, rapid transit systems, and so on), agency documents, operating procedures, internal memoranda, newspaper and magazine articles, articles on similar programs elsewhere, and reports issued by various concerned groups. The researcher would also likely make a few phone calls to identify the significant actors in the program and determine where the most important activities are taking place.

Following an initial reconnaissance, the analyst settles on a limited number of sites (schools, hospitals, highway systems, and so on) as the focus of the investigation. Most qualitative evaluations are largely exploratory, designed to explore a variety of hunches or intuitions about the program's operation. For these cases, the analyst will probably try to select sites that vary widely along several crucial dimensions. Some evaluations, however, are *hypothesis guided*, designed to demonstrate the plausibility of a particular hypothesis, so the analyst might choose a limited number of crucial sites that are especially illustrative of the issue under investigation.

What Would You Do?

You have been asked to assess the effectiveness of a new program aimed at reducing teen pregnancies by providing birth control information through the high schools. You have heard several suggestions about how to design the study—and some comments that it's simply impossible to measure something like this. What would you do?

Once the research sites have been chosen, the analyst may choose to gather most of his or her information through *intensive interviews*, detailed information-gathering sessions involving major actors both inside and outside the agency responsible for the program. Interviewing skills include establishing the interviewer's credentials, setting the proper climate, arranging questions effectively, asking reasonable but challenging questions, and keeping a good record of all that is said. Perhaps most important, the interviewer must keep the discussion on the subject, in a way that is neither obvious nor embarrassing to either party. Immediately following the interview, the interviewer should review and expand upon the notes taken during the interview session. These notes will form an important basis for drawing conclusions about the program.

An alternative means of gathering qualitative information is the use of a *participant-observer*, someone involved in either the target population or the agency itself who makes observations and draws conclusions based on firsthand data. For example, an evaluation of an antipoverty program in eastern Kentucky some years ago employed a participant-observer who lived in the community, talked daily with others in the community about the program, and reported back to the overall evaluation staff.

Either technique can be questioned with respect to both internal and external validity. Biased information and questions about internal validity can arise if the wrong people are chosen to interview or if those interviewed provide misleading information, intentionally or unintentionally. Participant-observers can affect the program's operation through their own presence, leading to outcomes far different from what would otherwise have happened. Questions concerning external validity (or generalizability) might be raised with either technique based on the choice of only a limited number of sites for investigation.

Quantitative Techniques   Policy evaluations often endeavor to approximate the scientific methods of the physical sciences, although such efforts are extremely difficult. In its classic formulation, an *experimental design* involves examination of two or more groups under carefully controlled conditions. One group, the *experimental group,* receives a treatment or intervention; in the case of program evaluation, members of the experimental group receive the benefits of the program being evaluated. Another group, the *control group,* consists of individuals who are as similar as possible to those in the experimental group and who act under the same general conditions, yet do not receive the intervention. Members of both groups are tested before and after the experimental intervention (pretest and posttest measures), and the results are compared. If the program has had either a positive or negative effect, the differences should show up in the data. We can illustrate the difficulties in designing a rigorous experimental design with respect to social programs by imagining that we are interested in analyzing the effectiveness of a new approach to mathematics education in the fourth grade. One classroom might be designated an experimental group and be taught using the new approach; another classroom might be designated the control group and be taught using traditional methods. The mathematical abilities of all students would be measured both before and after the period in which the new program was being taught. If the new technique is indeed more effective in educating children in mathematics, the posttest scores of the children in the experimental group should be higher than those of the children in the control group.

In a very general sense, this is an application of an experimental design to a social program, and you can easily imagine how similar designs might be used to measure other programs, ranging from immunizations to welfare incentives to highway designs. But we can observe difficulties in such designs, some of which relate to questions of internal validity. One might respond to the study by saying that students in the experimental group were smarter to begin with, or that the absence rate was higher among those in the control group. Or you might suggest that one teacher was better than the other, and that made the difference. Or even if the same teacher taught both groups, you might speculate that he or she taught the new material with more enthusiasm. Similar questions might be raised about external validity. For instance, if the results were obtained in a rural school, would they apply as well to an urban setting?

Some, if not all, of these questions could be anticipated by slightly altering the research design. For example, students could be randomly assigned to the two groups, thus eliminating any possibility of bias in the groups' composition. But questions such as these show the difficulty of achieving true experimental conditions in measuring social programs. For this reason, most evaluations of social programs are called quasi-experimental.

Quasi-experimental designs retain the requirement for systematic data gathering that should be part of any quantitative approach, but they free the researcher from some of the difficulties of developing experimental designs, such as the need for random assignment of subjects to various groups. Here again, different groups may be compared, but an essential task for the researcher is to separate the effects of a treatment from the effects of other factors. Only the effects caused by the treatment are of interest.

Quasi-experimental approaches not only are more adaptable to social situations, but they also better fit the situation in which program evaluators often find themselves—assigned to the evaluation long after the program has begun and having little influence on patterns of intervention. In such a case, a historical approach may be of special value. For example, one quasi-experimental design—*time series analysis*—involves making a number of observations about the target population both before and after the program intervention. (These observations may even be made retrospectively by gathering historical data.) In one case, basic information about neighborhood crime was evaluated for a period of years prior to the introduction of a new patrol pattern; then similar data evaluation followed after the new approach was introduced.

Summary and Action Implications

As a public manager, you will become quite familiar with the cycle of planning, implementation, and evaluation. In practice, the phases of the cycle will rarely appear as distinct as in our discussion, but you will still find that you must devote a portion of your time to each phase. In middle and upper management, the planning, implementation, and evaluation cycle will become especially complex because you will find yourself engaged in all three phases almost simultaneously. That is, you will be planning for one project at the same time that you are implementing a second and evaluating a third, and so on. Obviously, maintaining a good sense of the timing of the various projects and knowing when and how to shift from one to the next will be extremely important.

As we have seen, techniques have been developed to help you work through the typical problems you will encounter in each phase of the cycle. Although many of the techniques can be elaborated in highly complex ways, the logic on which they are based can be helpful in dealing even with fairly simple and immediate problems.

Throughout the planning, implementation, and evaluation cycle, you should remember that, whereas we have focused on technical aids to your administrative work, each of the three areas will be strongly affected by how you interact with the *people* in your organization (and elsewhere). Planning, implementation, and evaluation are human processes and are thus subject to people's shifting values, attitudes, and behaviors. In planning, implementation, and evaluation, as with budgeting, financial management, and personnel, techniques are successful only when you use them with full regard for democratic values, clear leadership, and humane management.

STUDY QUESTIONS

1. Planning is one aspect of the policy process. Discuss the various types of planning and their objectives.

2. In organizing a planning process, what are the primary concerns of the planning group?

3. Discuss the necessary steps for comprehensive policy analysis.

4. Identify some of the quantitative techniques used for policy analysis.

5. The second phase of the policy process is implementation of plans. Discuss some of the techniques available to help in the beginning stages of the implementation process.

6. Compare and contrast the several different subsystems that carry forward an organization's work.

7. What does the phrase "managing for results" mean? How might such a program be implemented?

8. What are the different types of evaluation approaches? Discuss the distinctions among them.

CASES AND EXERCISES

1. As a class or working in small groups, assume the role of a task force that the governor has asked to develop plans for a new university that the legislature has created in a rapidly expanding area in one corner of your state. Your plan should be based on whatever assumptions you wish to make by explicitly stating them in writing; however, all your assumptions should be consistent with the following guidelines:

a. Assume that you have full legal authority to develop the university, including the power to develop a full range of undergraduate programs and a limited number of graduate programs in areas of special interest to the state. Assume a high degree of political support within the corner of the state where the university will be built, and general support throughout the state, but assume major opposition from the state's leading public university.

b. Assume that the area where the new university is to be located already has a community college, which the university will take over, and a couple of small, private liberal arts colleges. Assume that the community college has 2,000 freshmen and sophomores and operates in two large buildings on a large tract of otherwise undeveloped land, which is sufficient to accommodate the new university.

c. Assume that the area in which the university will be built has traditionally had an agricultural and tourist-based economy but is experiencing rapid growth in high-tech industry, primarily because companies are attracted to the area's natural beauty and comfortable climate.

d. Assume that you can anticipate a budget starting at $112 million for the first year of operations (this is inclusive of the community college budget), but rising at a rate of $27 million a year for the next nine years. Assume also that there is adequate financing available for whatever new construction will be required during the first ten years of the university's existence.

e. Assume that you have full control over the curriculum of the university and authority to propose to the Coordinating Board on Higher Education any new program offerings. Assume, however, that the major university in the state will fight hard to protect its engineering and computer science programs from competition.

You should create a plan for development of the new university over the next ten years. You should take into account all aspects of development, including all academic programs, student services, administrative support (including the physical plant, personnel, and financial and accounting systems), capital construction, and intercollegiate athletics. You may wish to establish subcommittees or task forces to work on particular areas; however, all reports should be combined into a single planning document to be submitted to the governor's office.

2. Imagine that your city council is considering a proposed ordinance to require an 8 percent deposit on each beverage container sold in the city. Each beer can, soft drink bottle, or other container would carry a city sticker or imprint. Retailers would collect the deposit on each container sold and would be required to pay 8 cents for each empty container returned to the store. Proponents of the bill argue that it would help clean up the city and provide better recycling of containers. Opponents argue that the bill would be difficult for stores to adhere to and a nightmare for the city to enforce. Develop a research design—that is, a plan for conducting research—that would enable you to report to the city council on the potential costs and benefits of the proposed ordinance.

3. Complete the following exercise: You have been hired by Expert Analysis consulting firm to work on a project for New York City. The city has hired the firm to analyze the advisability of contracting out garbage collection, expanding city garbage collection capacity, or going to a twenty-four-hour collection system.

The city currently operates a sanitation department of 2,538 people using 781 garbage trucks of two different sizes. The large trucks carry 35 tons per trip and make two trips per day. The small trucks carry 15 tons and make three trips per day. There are 537 small trucks and 244 large trucks. The cost of one day for a large truck is $720 in wages for three people (eight-hour shift) and $200 for maintenance. The cost of one day for a small truck is $480 for wages for two people (eight-hour shift) and $150 for maintenance. The collective bargaining contract calls for a "shift differential" of 15 percent above the standard $30 per hour for the truck crews, if the crews work other than 6:00 a.m. to 3:00 p.m. The contract has three years to go before it expires. A recent study indicates that the amount of garbage to be collected in the city will increase 14 percent in the next year and 18 percent in the following year. The study also shows that many of the larger firms in the city are contemplating using a private garbage service, We-Haul, Inc., which has recently begun competing with the city. The study concludes that, although the amount of garbage to be collected will increase, the amount the city will be required to collect might decrease slightly or remain steady. A quick check of the maintenance records indicates that you can expect a 20 percent increase in maintenance costs for the large trucks and a 30 percent increase for the small trucks, if you operate twenty-four hours a day. You call the Tidy-Truck manufacturer and get a quote of $82,000 for a new large truck and $59,000 for a new small truck if you order this year. They expect a 6 percent price increase next year.

Just as you put down the phone, your liaison with the city calls to tell you that We-Haul, Inc. has offered to collect the additional garbage at a "special rate" for the city of $18 per ton for the first year and $20 per ton for the second year.

Making reasonable assumptions about information you may need, develop a recommendation as to whether the city should expand its service by buying more trucks and hiring more people, operate its service twenty-four hours a day, or contract with We-Haul, Inc. to pick up the increase.

SOURCE: This case was adapted from material provided by Barry Hammond of Slippery Rock University, Pennsylvania.

FOR ADDITIONAL READING

Abramson, Mark A., and Ann M. Kieffaber, eds. *New Ways of Doing Business*. Lanham, MD: Rowman & Littlefield, 2003.

Adler, Matthew D., and Eric A. Posner. *New Foundations of Cost-Benefit Analysis*. Cambridge, MA: Harvard University Press, 2006.

Andrews, Rhys. *Strategic Management and Public Service Performance*. New York: Palgrave Macmillan, 2012.

Bardach, Eugene. *A Practical Guide for Policy Analysis*. Washington, DC: CQ Press, 2011.

Beland, Daniel, and Alex Waddan. *The Politics of Policy Change*. Washington, DC: Georgetown University Press, 2012.

Bingham, Richard D., and Claire L. Felbinger. *Evaluation in Practice: A Methodological Approach*. 2nd ed. New York: Chatham House, 2001.

Birkland, Thomas A. *An Introduction to the Policy Process*. 3rd ed. Armonk, NY: M.E. Sharpe, 2011.

Boyne, George A., et al., eds. *Public Service Performance: Perspectives on Measurement and Management*. Cambridge, NY: Cambridge University Press, 2006.

Bryson, John M. *Strategic Planning for Public and Nonprofit Organizations: A Guide to Strengthening and Sustaining Organizational Achievement*. 3rd ed. San Francisco: Jossey-Bass, 2004.

Campbell, Heather E., and Elizabeth A. Corley. *Urban Environmental Policy Analysis*. Armonk, NY: M.E. Sharpe, 2012.

Chambers, Donald E. *Social Policy and Social Programs: A Method for Practical Public Policy Analysis*. Boston: Allyn & Bacon, 1999.

Fischer, Frank, Gerald Miller, and Mara S. Sidney. *Handbook of Public Policy Analysis: Theory, Politics, and Methods* (Public Administration and Public Policy). Boca Raton, FL: CRC/Taylor & Francis, 2007.

Forester, John. *Planning in the Face of Power*. Berkeley: University of California Press, 1989.

Geva-May, Iris. *Thinking like a Policy Analyst: Policy Analysis as a Clinical Profession*. New York: Palgrave Macmillan, 2005.

Goggin, Malcolm L., Ann O. Bowman, James P. Lester, and Laurence O'Toole, Jr. *Implementation Theory and Practice: Toward a Third Generation*. New York: HarperCollins, 1990.

Greiner, Larry E., and Thomas G. Cummings. *Dynamic Strategy-Making: A Real-Time Approach for the 21st Century Leader*. San Francisco: Jossey-Bass, 2009.

Hatry, Harry P., Therese van Houten, Margaret C. Plantz, and Martha Taylor Greenway. *Measuring Program Outcomes: A Practical Approach*. Alexandria, VA: United Way of America, 1996.

Julnes, Patria de Lancer. *Performance-Based Management Systems: Effective Implementation and Maintenance*. Boca Raton, FL: CRC Press, 2009.

Julnes, Patria de Lancer, and Marc Holzer. *Performance Measurement: Building Theory, Improving Practice* (Aspa Classics). Armonk, NY: M.E. Sharpe, 2008.

Kaufman, Roger. *Strategic Planning Plus: An Organizational Guide*. 2nd ed. Newbury Park, CA: Sage Publications, 1992.

Kearns, Kevin. *Managing for Accountability*. San Francisco: Jossey-Bass, 1996.

Keehley, Patricia, et al. *Benchmarking for Best Practices*. San Francisco: Jossey-Bass, 1996.

Koteen, Jack. *Strategic Management in Public and Nonprofit Organizations*. 2nd ed. Westport, CT: Praeger Publishers, 1997.

Kraft, Michael E., and Scott R. Furlong. *Public Policy: Politics, Analysis, and Alternatives*. Washington, DC: CQ Press, 2009.

Lejano, Raul P. *Frameworks for Policy Analysis: Merging Text and Context*. New York: Routledge, 2006.

Mintrom, Michael. *People Skills for Policy Analysts*. Washington, DC: Georgetown University Press, 2003.

Norris-Tirrell, Dorothy, and Joy A. Clay. *Strategic Collaboration in Public and Nonprofit Administration: A Practice-Based Approach to Solving Shared Problems*. Boca Raton, FL: CRC Press, 2010.

Peters, Guy B. *American Public Policy: Promise and Performance*. New York: Chatham House, 1999.

Poister, Theodore H. *Measuring Performance in Public and Nonprofit Organizations*. San Francisco: Jossey-Bass, 2003.

Rabin, Jack, W. Bartley Hidreth, and Gerald J. Miller, eds. *Handbook of Strategic Management*. New York: Marcel Dekker, 1989.

Sabatier, Paul A. *Theories of the Policy Process*. Boulder, CO: Westview Press, 2007.

Sylvia, Ronald, et al. *Program Planning and Evaluation for the Public Manager*. 2nd ed. Prospect Heights, IL: Waveland Press, 1997.

Vines, David. *Information Strategy and Public Policy*. Cambridge, MA: B. Blackwell, 1991.

Wholey, Joseph, Harry P. Hatry, and Kathryn Newcomer, eds. *Handbook of Practical Program Evaluation*. San Francisco: Jossey-Bass, 1994.

CHAPTER 5

BUDGETING AND FINANCIAL MANAGEMENT

Public budgeting and financial management are concerned with allocating limited resources to problems that governments and other public organizations face. Just as you establish a personal budget to track your income and expenses and, just as businesses create budgets to aid in decisions affecting profits and losses, so do public organizations employ budgets to help in planning and management. Public organizations must carefully and responsibly manage large amounts of money and other resources—taking in taxes and other revenues, purchasing goods and services, investing surplus funds, and managing debt wisely.

From the point of view of the manager or citizen trying to influence public policy, the budget is an extremely important tool for planning and control. To manage public programs effectively, you must be able to manage resources, both practically and politically. In this chapter we focus on the budget process from the standpoint of the individual public manager, examining how budget decisions are made and how you can influence budgetary outcomes. Although much of the budget process is highly charged politically, specific technical knowledge about budgeting systems will give you a distinct advantage.

The elaborate systems that public organizations have developed to manage their fiscal affairs are relatively recent. Prior to 1900, revenues were easily sufficient to cover the expenses of government, and financial management was merely record keeping. As the scope of government grew and new demands were placed on its resources, the need for more sophisticated systems of decision making became apparent. Moreover, repeated instances of corruption and waste made more effective control over the public's resources necessary.

In establishing its executive budget process through the Budgeting and Accounting Act of 1921, the federal government followed the lead of several local and state governments that had already taken similar actions. This municipal reform movement emphasized the budget process as a means of bringing order to public spending; consequently, by the 1920s, most big cities had established a formal budget process. Similar developments were also occurring at the state level. In 1910, Ohio became the first state to require an executive budget; within the next decade, similar actions took place in most other states. At the federal level, a special Commission on Economy and Efficiency, known as the Taft Commission, recommended establishing an executive budget in 1912; the recommendation was implemented nearly a decade later.

Since the 1920s, the federal budget has grown in both size and complexity, as have budgets at the state and local levels. This growth means that budgeting and financial management have come to involve far more than keeping a record of income and expenses. Today, how government spends its money affects many other areas of the economy; consequently, the budget is an instrument of fiscal policy. Moreover, the budget is a primary expression of government priorities; it constitutes a record of the decisions that are made concerning various public policies.

Networking

General information on budgeting and financial management can be found at www.gasb.org and at www.nasbo.org.

The Budget as an Instrument of Fiscal Policy

Budgets express the public policy choices of governments and others. Among these are choices with respect to the impact of the public sector on the economy. *Fiscal policy* is concerned with the impact of government taxation and spending on the economy generally. Before the Great Depression, little attention was paid to how the federal budget affected the economy, which was presumably regulated by the *business cycle*. Periods of economic growth featuring inflation and high employment were followed by periods of recession or depression featuring deflation and unemployment. Meanwhile, the federal government sought to balance its budget each year—that is, to make revenues and expenditures approximately equal.

Economists soon began to realize, however, that this pattern of government spending was influencing the economy in a negative way. In periods of economic growth, government revenues naturally increased. In an effort to balance the budget, taxes could be lowered to the level of expenditures; in periods of economic decline, the budget was balanced by lowering spending to meet the lower revenues. The unanticipated result was to increase citizens' income during good times and decrease their income in bad times—just the opposite of what would be desirable. Government taxation and spending had the effect of accentuating economic instability.

Economists such as the British scholar John Maynard Keynes argued, in contrast, that all else being equal, positive government action could lead to greater economic stability. A key to Keynes's analysis was the relationship between inflation and unemployment. Keynes noted that periods of rapid economic growth are typically accompanied by high inflation, which is harmful to individuals because it lowers their purchasing power, especially if they are on fixed incomes. On the other hand, periods of economic decline are typically accompanied by high unemployment, which not only hurts individuals but also lowers revenues for government. In either case, government action aimed at achieving greater stability might be both possible and desirable.

There are many ways the federal government can influence the economy, but one important way is simply by varying its own spending or, somewhat more indirectly, by raising or lowering taxes. The capacity of government spending patterns to influence the economy so dramatically is not hard to understand if you recognize the enormous role of government in the economy. The gross domestic product (GDP), the rate of inflation, and the rate of unemployment are the key indicators of economic health. *Gross domestic product*, a measure of total economic output, is measured by the market value of goods and services. Almost three-quarters of our current GDP is private in nature, but about one-quarter (about 24.7 percent in 2010) is based on government spending. Based on revenues, the U.S. federal government is the single largest organization in the world, almost 10 times the size of Walmart, Exxon, or Chevron (top three in the Fortune 500). Obviously, decisions at the federal level play an important role in the health and stability of the economy generally.

The key relationships are these: (1) If the economy is experiencing rapid growth—with high inflation and low unemployment—the government might seek to "cool off" the economy by taking money out of the economy through lowering spending, raising taxes, or both. This limits private demand and slows economic growth. On the other hand, (2) if the economy is experiencing recession or depression—with falling prices and high unemployment—the government might want to stimulate the economy by putting more money into circulation, through increasing spending, lowering taxes, or both. This stimulates private demand and increases economic growth. Creating a surplus, as might occur in the first case, would help restrain private spending during prosperity; creating a deficit, as might occur in the second case, might stimulate spending during a recession.

Cumulative state and local spending also affects the economy. State and local government expenditures constitute close to 12 percent of the GDP and must be taken into account in discussions of fiscal policy. If the federal government cuts taxes, but also cuts aid to states and localities, those governments may find it necessary to raise taxes themselves, thus offsetting any economic gains caused by lower federal taxes.

Patterns of spending in many states and in major cities do have some effect on the local economy, and consequently, state and local officials are becoming more cognizant of their role in fiscal policy and especially economic development. These governments, however, often don't have the tools or authority to make certain kinds of decisions. For example, all the states except Vermont have either constitutional or statutory provisions requiring a balanced budget. (Various political leaders, especially Republicans in Congress, have recently called for a balanced budget amendment at the federal level as a way to eliminate deficit spending; however, at this point, no legislation has passed.) Such a proposal, though attractive in a symbolic sense, would limit the flexibility of the federal government in seeking to influence the economy. In any case, it is clear that the budget process has important effects on the economy that must be anticipated when structuring overall patterns of public spending.

The Budget as an Instrument of Public Policy

Although the overall pattern of spending represented in a government budget has an important effect on the economy, individual entries in the budget represent important choices with respect to public policies of all types. The budget is, essentially, a measure of support (or lack of support) for specific programs. Those in favor are funded; those out of favor are not. For this reason, discussions of budgetary priorities are of special importance to political leaders, government officials at all levels, and representatives of various interests in society. As a manager, you will need to understand both where the money comes from and where the money goes.

Where the Money Comes From

Governments obtain funds either from their own sources or through transfers from other governments to operate programs deemed important. There are a variety of ways governments can raise their own revenues, including levying taxes and charging individuals or groups for specific services (see Figure 5.1). Because all public programs are affected by the way governments raise revenues, and because revenue administration is itself an important part of public administration, you will find it helpful to understand the way taxes are structured.

Developing tax policies requires attention not only to the level of taxes being taken from individuals or groups, but also to the fairness, efficiency, and simplicity of the tax system. Everyone agrees that the tax system should be fair and that everyone should pay

FIGURE 5.1

The Federal Government Receipts: Fiscal Year 2011

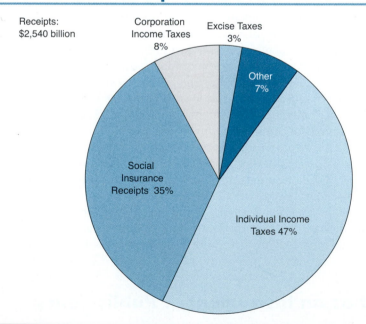

SOURCE: Analytical Perspectives, Budget of the US Government, FY 2013 (Table 15.1 Receipts by Source—Summary, p. 187), retrieved March 19, 2012, from www.whitehouse.gov/sites/default/files/omb/budget/fy2013/assets/receipts.pdf.

his or her "fair share." But what exactly does that mean? Some argue that people should pay according to the benefits they receive; others argue that those who have a greater ability to pay should in fact pay more.

One way to approach the issue is to think in terms of the relationship between one's tax rate and one's income (vertical-equity concept). A tax structure is *proportional* (or "flat") if it taxes everyone at the same effective tax rate. If an effective tax rate is applied to a $20,000 income (yielding $2,000) and the same rate is applied to a $200,000 income (yielding $20,000), even though the amounts differ, the tax is proportional to the amount of income. A tax is *progressive* if it taxes those with higher income at a higher effective tax rate. Income tax is often cited as progressive. For example, a person with a $20,000 income and tax rate of 10 percent will pay $2,000 in taxes; another individual with a $200,000 income might be taxed at 10 percent for the first $20,000 (yielding $2,000), 20 percent for the next $80,000 (yielding $16,000), and 50 percent for the remaining $100,000 of income (yielding $50,000). The total tax paid on $200,000 will be $68,000, or an effective rate of 34 percent. Finally, a tax is *regressive* (such as sales taxes) if it taxes those with lower incomes at a proportionally higher effective rate than those with higher incomes. For example, if an individual with a $20,000 income buys a car and pays $500 in taxes, then the effective tax rate for this individual relative to his income is 2.5 percent. If another individual with a $200,000 income buys the same car and pays $500 in taxes, then the effective tax rate for that individual relative to his income is 0.25 percent.

Individual Income Tax All methods of taxation involve application of a *tax rate* to a particular *tax base*; the product of these yields *tax revenue*. The individual income tax is the single most important tax in our country. It calls for individuals to add up all income from taxable sources, reduce that amount by certain deductions or exemptions, and then apply a tax rate to that base to arrive at the individual's income tax. The current federal income tax, for example, applies rates between 10 and 35 percent to six income brackets.

All advanced industrial nations use some form of income tax. In the United States, income tax is the primary source of revenue for the federal government and is used to a lesser extent in many states and some cities. In most cases, a higher rate is applied to higher incomes, making the income tax a progressive tax. For nearly thirty years after its passage in 1913, the federal income tax applied only to a fairly small number of high-income people. With the advent of World War II, deductions were reduced significantly and higher rates applied.

Managing the task of collecting income tax from everyone in the country is obviously difficult. Yet the Internal Revenue Service (IRS) has developed a relatively efficient mechanism for collection and does so at a cost of about one-half of 1 percent of the revenues produced. Key to the existing system is the requirement that each individual calculate his or her own tax liability. IRS auditors then select a few returns for closer inspection, concentrating on those with unusual features. The extent of compliance with tax regulations in this country, though far from complete, is considered comparatively high.

Corporation Income Tax The corporation income tax, also a progressive tax, actually predates the individual income tax by several years and, for most of the last century, was a key source of federal revenue. Its proponents justify it as a way of taxing capital accumulation that is not specifically distributed to individuals. Moreover, the corporation income tax is needed to support the individual income tax; without it, individuals could simply keep their income in corporations and avoid paying income taxes. Though most states have corporation income taxes, the tax is far more substantial at the federal level, currently at 35 percent, though there are many proposals to reduce the corporate tax in return for closing loopholes in the tax. Yet, even before these proposals, corporation income tax has been declining in contrast to other sources of revenue. Where it once yielded more revenue than the individual income tax, the corporation income tax has declined to only about one-tenth of federal revenues.

Payroll Taxes   Taxes on payrolls support a variety of Social Security and other social insurance programs, such as unemployment compensation and medical care for the aged. (Do not confuse these specific taxes with the general income taxes that may be deducted from a payroll check.) These programs are primarily financed by taxes paid either by the employer or by the employer and employee in equal amounts. Payroll taxes overall are regressive because there is a flat rate, with no deductions or exemptions, and maximum amounts above which taxes are not required. Payroll taxes at the federal level, which support social insurance, now constitute the second largest source of federal revenue.

Sales and Excise Taxes   Both sales and excise taxes are applied to goods and services. *Sales taxes* are applied to a broad range of goods and services at either retail or whole-sale levels and are a popular source of income at state and local levels. There are significant variations in sales tax rates and in items covered by sales taxes—for example, some jurisdictions exempt food, clothing, and medicine from sales tax. *Excise taxes* are applied to the sale of specific commodities such as gasoline, tobacco, or alcohol; they are the primary form of consumption tax at the federal level. Typically, excise taxes are applied at specific rates (such as two cents per gallon of gasoline), but they may be applied to the total sales price. Some excise taxes are, in effect, user charges that help support particular activities. Gasoline taxes, for instance, are typically used to support highway construction and maintenance. A major issue concerning sales and excise taxes is that of equity. Because the poor consume a greater portion of their income than the rich, the burden of consumption taxes tends to fall more heavily on the poor, so the taxes are regressive. These taxes also tend to penalize certain groups, such as those with large families or those just starting a household. On the other hand, these taxes tend to provide more stable revenues, something that is especially important at state and local levels.

Property Taxes   Taxes on personal property are widely used at the local level and provide about half of local government revenues. Administration of a property tax involves assessment of an individual's property, most often land and buildings, and then the application of a tax rate. About half the revenue generated by the property tax derives from residential property and half from businesses. Although the property tax is a proportional tax, it is progressive in its effect (those who spend more on housing pay more), administration is difficult and has often not been highly professional. Moreover, recent tax limitations have severely restricted the capacity of local governments to raise additional revenue through the property tax.

Other Revenue Sources   There are, of course, a variety of other sources of government revenues. Whereas public organizations have often charged fees for the use of specific government services, recent limitations on other tax revenues have made such charges increasingly attractive, especially at the local level. For example, fees for the use of parks and recreational facilities are becoming increasingly important. Another recent development in terms of revenues at the state level is the use of lotteries. Nearly half the states and several local governments now conduct lotteries, which provide a highly visible, but relatively small and unstable, source of funds. Lotteries are also highly regressive in their effect (because poorer citizens tend to play the lotteries more); indeed, they are more regressive than even the sales tax.

Nonprofit organizations, which lack the power to tax, derive revenues from quite different sources and, indeed, engage in a wide variety of efforts to support their programs. Obviously, membership organizations depend in large measure on member dues for revenue, but such organizations, along with many others, have recently sought to diversify revenues. Although grant funding remains an important source of revenue for many nonprofit organizations, recent reductions in federal social service programs have seriously limited grant opportunities for many nonprofits. Additional sources of funds include donations (from individuals, corporations, and foundations), sales of goods and services (from books to coffee cups), and joint enterprises involving commercial firms (such as insurance plans or "affinity" credit cards).

Networking

For the budget of the United States, and how to get to the budgets of other governments, see the Department of the Treasury at www.ustreas.gov. For details on the current fiscal year federal budget and access to historical budget data, go to www.gpoaccess.gov/usbudget/index.html.

Where the Money Goes

While government revenue figures are staggering, they hardly match up to the demands on governments at all levels. There simply isn't enough money to meet every need or cure every problem, even if money alone were the solution. Instead, difficult choices must be made each year about which programs will be funded and at what levels. The choices made through the public policy process are reflected in the government's budget. The budget, therefore, stands as a record of the government's priorities.

What Would You Do?

You are the director of motor vehicle registration for your state. Your agency, with offices scattered across the state, is responsible for registration and licensing of cars, trucks, and other motor vehicles. About six months into the fiscal year, the governor announces that all state agencies will have to finish the fiscal year with expenditures 5 percent less than originally budgeted. You have already spent half your yearly budget allocation, so the reduction means you actually have to cut spending by 10 percent over the next six months. What would you do?

But government priorities are always shifting. As new conditions arise, new programs are proposed and old programs are expanded or contracted. The emphasis the federal government gives to various areas sometimes has reflected the condition of the country and the world, as in the large percentage of national resources devoted to national defense during periods of international conflict.

We can also trace budgetary changes over shorter time spans to see the policy priorities of various presidents, governors, mayors, or other public officials. Restrictions, however, have been built into the federal budget over the years that somewhat limit the choices any president or Congress can make. For example, Congress has passed a variety of *entitlement programs* that provide specified benefits to those who meet certain eligibility requirements. For example, legislation might provide benefits to people above a certain age or below a certain income level. The implication, supported by several judicial rulings, is that individuals are entitled to or have a right to certain benefits (primarily social welfare benefits).

For these programs, Congress essentially agrees to provide whatever money is necessary from year to year to ensure a certain level of benefits to all eligible people. Legislation is typically written so that new action is not required each year to keep the program going. Only a projection of likely beneficiaries is needed to determine the level of expenditures for a given year. Unless Congress takes specific steps to limit benefits or eligibility—something that legislators are reluctant to do—funding of these programs is practically automatic.

These programs vary in size over time. In a recession, for example, unemployment would be high, and spending for unemployment compensation would rise. Similarly, the changing character of the population—for example, a larger number of older Americans—would also change the amount of money required to provide benefits to that group. Moreover, most entitlement programs have now been indexed to the cost of living (or related measures) so that benefit levels automatically rise with inflation. (Over the past decade, Congress has passed major expansions of indexing in Social Security and Medicare.) Expenditures for entitlement programs thus increase almost every year. The Congressional Budget Office (CBO) projects that under current law, federal spending on Medicare and Medicaid measured as a share of GDP will rise from 4 percent in 2007 to 12 percent in 2050 and 19 percent in 2082—which, as a share of the economy, is roughly equivalent to the total amount that the federal government spends today (CBO, 2007).

Such programs constituted just over 50 percent of the proposed fiscal year 2013 federal budget, with Social Security amounting to 20 percent of the entire budget. When they are combined with farm price supports (also indexed), interest on the national debt (which must be paid), and expenditures based on previous commitments, these so-called *uncontrollable expenditures* constitute almost two-thirds of the federal budget.

The remainder of the federal budget might be termed *discretionary spending*; meaning the president and Congress are open to make changes in this relatively small portion of the budget. This includes defense spending (about 18 percent) and domestic discretionary spending (only about 19 percent). These are the areas that generate the most difficult policy choices.

From Deficits to Surplus and Back

A great deal of political debate in the 1980s and early 1990s centered on strategies for controlling the federal deficit. However, by 2000, a booming economy and fiscal measures taken by Congress in the late 1990s changed the debate from how to control the deficit to ways to spend a growing budget surplus. To understand this change in fortune, it may be helpful to examine some of the deficit reduction methods employed by the federal government during the past decades.

Let's begin with the deficit. As noted, traditional economic theory does not necessarily disapprove of public borrowing; indeed, there may be benefits to deficit spending in particular years. But at some point, a growing deficit becomes unmanageable, especially as interest payments become a substantial part of government spending. Large deficits are generally thought to limit both short-term and long-term economic recovery, especially because they limit private investment. Moreover, large deficits contribute to an understandable lack of public confidence concerning their political leaders' ability to deal effectively with the budget.

The budget deficits of the Reagan years were substantial. The administration's accumulated debt exceeded that of all previous administrations combined. By 1984 it became clear that if no further actions were taken to reduce the deficit, by the end of the Reagan years, the accumulated deficit would total over $2.6 trillion. Interest payments alone would require one out of every six federal dollars. Facing this prospect, Congress passed the Gramm-Rudman-Hollings Act of 1985. Under this legislation, deficit targets were set for each of the next five budget years and aimed at reducing the deficit to zero in 1990 (though a later amendment pushed the target to 1992). Unfortunately, the president and Congress were overly optimistic in their economic projections and employed several questionable budget techniques to evade the restraints set by Gramm-Rudman-Hollings.

With the deficit still out of control in 1990, President Bush and Congress faced very difficult budget deliberations. For the 1990 budget, the Gramm-Rudman-Hollings law had targeted an annual deficit of no more than $110 billion. By October, when the fiscal year began, there was still no agreement on the budget. (As we will see, it is not unusual for a federal fiscal year to begin before the year's budget is approved.) Consequently, automatic, across-the-board spending cuts were applied to all federal agencies.

Finally, in late November, a deficit-reduction plan was approved that would bring the projected deficit below the Gramm-Rudman-Hollings target. The plan that was agreed to, however, contained a number of provisions that appeared to be budgetary "smoke and mirrors." The biggest reduction item was to simply maintain for another 130 days the across-the-board cuts that had been imposed in October. Many observers read this as a failure of the administration and Congress to come to grips with the hard choices that deficit reduction requires.

As part of the budget agreement, the Budget Enforcement Act (BEA) was passed to police the deficit even further. The BEA set annual ceilings on several categories of discretionary spending, with violation of the caps requiring across-the-board cuts. BEA also required that legislative actions affecting mandatory spending not increase the deficit in any year. (This is known as the "pay as you go" provision.) Though these provisions seem to have had the desired effect on the budget process, the deficit continued to grow, driven in part by incorrect economic assumptions and in part by increased spending for health-care programs and the savings and loan bailout.

Networking

Check out the National Debt Clock at www.brillig.com/debt_clock and the Department of the Treasury's FAQs about the budget at http://www.treasury.gov/Pages/default.aspx.

In 1997, the Clinton administration led a bipartisan effort in Congress to pass yet another landmark piece of legislation aimed at balancing the federal budget. The budget agreement was originally scheduled to eliminate the deficit by 2002, phasing in $121 billion in spending cuts over a five-year period. Much of the savings were planned to come from reductions in Medicare payments to health providers and hospitals. An additional $55 billion was to have been saved each year through mandates imposed on future spending bills. The budget agreement also featured $95 billion in tax cuts over the five years, including credits for higher education, relief for families with children, and reductions in capital gains.

When President Clinton signed the measure into law, few would have imagined that in less than three years the Congressional Budget Office would be projecting a budget surplus. But the federal government turned the tide, thanks to a variety of factors—including old-fashioned good luck. One of the most significant contributors to the government's change in fortune came in the "dot-com" craze of 1999–2000, as thousands of Internet companies went public on the stock market, leading to a dramatic increase in tax revenues and an overall expansion in the American economy. Reductions in military spending in the wake of the cold war also helped, as the government was able to invest its resources in more productive areas (Uchitelle, 2000, p. A1). The net outcome was a projected surplus of $81 billion, scheduled to materialize during the next decade. This is a far cry from the crisis years of the early 1980s.

The Bush Tax Plan   President George W. Bush seized upon the opportunity afforded by this emerging surplus to advance one of the key themes in his election platform: a reduction in federal taxes. Given the estimates early in the year from both the Congressional Budget Office and the president's Office of Management and Budget, few could stand in the way of the new administration's drive for sweeping tax reform.

The administration's original plan called for a $1.6 trillion cut in the federal income tax, but even the president's most ardent supporters on Capitol Hill cautioned that it would be extremely difficult to pass such an enormous reduction plan. Recognizing the importance of a victory on his administration's first key policy initiative, President Bush worked with lawmakers to pare down the original proposal and gain the necessary votes. The final measure, which was signed into law on June 7, 2001, featured a $1.3 trillion tax cut to be phased in over the next decade and a fundamental restructuring of federal income taxes.

Supporters of the plan said that reducing the tax burden on the American public, particularly with the projected federal surplus, was a way to return "an overcharge" to taxpayers and to curb federal spending. For example, House Majority Leader Dick Armey said, "The addicts are going to have to take the cure. We're no longer going to get stoned on the other people's money" (Stevenson, 2001, p. A1). Proponents also argued that the tax rebates, which the IRS began sending out in the summer of 2001, would help to stimulate an economy that had declined sharply in the preceding months.

Some of the central elements of the Bush plan included reducing personal income tax rates, phasing out the estate tax, increasing the child tax credit (and expanding the number of low-income families eligible for this credit), and increasing the contribution limits to 401(k) and individual retirement accounts. For nonprofits, the tax reduction plan that finally passed Congress lacked many of the provisions from the original Bush proposal that would have encouraged increases in charitable giving.

Critics of the Bush tax plan in the governmental sector predicted that it would prove to be too much, too soon. Senator Tom Daschle, who became majority leader when the Democrats took control of the Senate in June 2001, said, "We think this is good short-term politics. [But] it is disastrous long-term policy" (Stevenson, 2001, p. 26). Daschle and others suggested that the plan would not leave enough in reserve to cover the cost of upgrading the military, much less the substantial reforms to Social Security and Medicare that remained on the horizon. And even the president's own economic advisers moved away from their original optimism, saying that the more cautionary estimates of the federal surplus, which were released just weeks after the tax plan became law, would require Congress to revisit some of its main provisions.

Even so, President Bush succeeded in pushing through three more major tax cuts aimed at reducing revenue by $1.9 trillion over a ten-year period. Unfortunately, the surplus did not materialize, and spending far outstripped revenue to produce high levels of debt. During the Bush administration, economic recessions, terrorist attacks, and corporate scandals, coupled with the tax cuts and new spending for military action in Iraq and Afghanistan, put the federal government further and further into debt. Instead of the surplus forecasted at the beginning of the Bush administration, there were federal budget deficits each year beginning in 2002, and in January 2009, just before President Bush left office, the Congressional Budget Office projected a deficit of $1.2 trillion for FY 2009 based on a continuation of the Bush administration policies and the effects of the financial collapse of 2008 (Tritch, 2011). Overall, under the Bush administration the total federal debt increased from $5.7 trillion in January 2001 to $10.7 trillion in December 2008 (United States Department of the Treasury).

Obama and Economic Recovery   The deep recession spurred by the financial collapse in 2008 framed the context for the incoming Obama administration. One of President Obama's first acts was to sign into law the American Recovery and Reinvestment Act (ARRA) in February 2009, a $787 billion economic stimulus package that included spending on job preservation and creation, health care, education, and energy; investments in infrastructure; tax breaks; expanded unemployment benefits; and a host of other programs designed to halt further economic deterioration.

The new president, who began his term with a budget deficit that was larger than any since World War II, set out in his 2010 budget proposal to capitalize on what he called a "once in a generation" opportunity to reverse "an era of profound irresponsibility that engulfed both private and public institutions" (OMB 2009, p. 1). The budget proposal included measures intended to help jumpstart the economy and stabilize the country's financial system, including appropriations to buy toxic bank assets, expand a consumer loan program, and continue funding for the Troubled Asset Relief Program (TARP), a program that was signed into law by President Bush in October 2008 to address the subprime mortgage crisis by buying assets and equity from financial institutions. President Obama's 2010 budget proposal also addressed the overhaul of the nation's healthcare system and called for investments in clean energy, education, and the country's infrastructure (Calmes, 2009).

One of the issues facing the Obama administration early on was whether to extend the tax cuts enacted under President Bush, which were set to expire in December 2010. Critics of the cuts argued that these cuts spurred an increase in income inequality, that they played a pivotal role in the budget deficits that began in 2002, and that, contrary to predictions, they failed to encourage economic growth. Others, however, contended that the tax cuts created higher marginal rates for the very wealthy and actually generated an increase in federal tax receipts from 2004 to 2007. After a great deal of debate, during which it was projected that extending the cuts through 2020 would add more than $3 trillion to the national debt, these cuts were extended for two years.

The Obama budget proposal for FY 2013, released early in 2012 and totaling $3.8 trillion, called for $4 trillion in cuts over ten years and $1.5 trillion in tax hikes for households earning more than $250,000. It included $7.5 billion in administrative cuts and increased funding for education, rail and road construction, electric cars, and general research and development. Provisions included ending the Bush tax cuts, restoring the estate tax to 2009 levels, increasing the tax rate on dividends for the wealthy, and instituting the "Buffet Rule," which would subject those earning more than $1 million to a tax rate of at least 30 percent (Lee & Paletta, 2012). The budget also called for elimination of tax breaks for oil and gas companies; caps on discretionary spending; reforms to Medicare, Medicaid, and other health programs; and mandatory savings in a variety of areas. An analysis by the Congressional Budget Office noted that under the 2013 budget proposal, the deficit for 2012 would equal $1.3 trillion, or 8.1 percent of GDP. This would decline to $977 billion in 2013, or 6.1 percent of GDP; fall further relative to GDP in subsequent years to 2.5 percent in 2017; and then increase to 3.0 percent of GDP by 2022. The estimated accumulated federal debt as of the end of FY 2011 (September 30, 2011) was $14.8 trillion, for which the government incurred $454 billion in interest expenses during FY 2011 (United States Department of the Treasury). President Obama's proposed 2013 budget put forward a balanced plan of spending cuts and revenue increases that reduce the deficit by more than $4 trillion over the next decade, including $1 trillion in spending cuts he signed into law in the summer of 2012.

For an outline of the issues that these presidents have struggled with, see the box "Exploring Concepts: Issues in Budgeting."

Exploring Concepts

ISSUES IN BUDGETING

1. The fiscal health of the federal government, particularly in light of unprecedented deficits
2. The struggles of state and local governments to balance their budgets in both the short term and the longer term
3. Pressures on spending at all levels of government, particularly focused on two areas—health care spending, which affects all levels of government, and education spending, the effects of which are felt primarily at the state and local level
4. Concerns about revenue structure and reliance on various sources, particularly intergovernmental revenues and sales tax revenues
5. The problems created by the need to deal with (and finance) an aging infrastructure
6. The influence of financial and performance data on budgeting decisions
7. Institutional and organizational responses to the management of the finance and budget function

SOURCE: Phillip G. Joyce and Scott Pattison, "Public Budgeting in 2020: Return to Equilibrium, or Continued Mismatch between Demands and Resources?" *Public Administration Review* 70 (2010): s24–s32.

State and Local Expenditures

Expenditure comparisons at the state and local levels are complicated by our system of intergovernmental transfers. In education, for example, the federal government provides money directly to individuals (in the form of student grants and loans), but it also transfers large sums to state and local governments. States spend money directly (for colleges and universities), but they also transfer money received from the federal government and some raised at the state level to local governments, primarily to support education. Consequently, local governments provide less than 30 percent of the money spent on education in this country and actually are involved in spending 70 percent of that money.

State and local revenues come from several sources, taxes being foremost among these (see Figure 5.2). The majority of tax receipts collected for state and local governments are sales and gross receipts taxes (34.1 percent), property taxes (33.4 percent), and individual income taxes (21.3 percent) (U.S. Census, 2009). But, of course, as we would expect, state and local revenues declined significantly during the recession. Overall, tax revenue declined 4.5 percent in 2009, to $1.3 trillion. Individual and corporate income taxes saw the largest declines in 2009, at 11.3 percent and 19.2 percent, respectively (U.S. Census, 2009). This has caused governments at the state and local level to experience significant fiscal stress and to limit spending in vital areas such as education and health care.

Other areas of spending are significant, too. If we include intergovernmental transfers spent at the state and local levels in our calculations of state and local spending, the following patterns emerge: States spend the greatest portion of their funds on education, with public welfare next, followed by highways, health, and natural resources. At the local

FIGURE 5.2
State and Local Revenues, Fiscal Year 2009

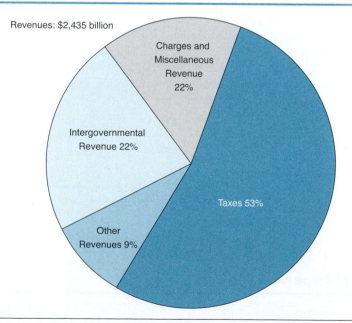

NOTE: Total exceeds 100 percent because of sampling errors.

SOURCE: U.S. Census Bureau, Appendix Table A-1, State and Local Government Finances Summary 2009, retrieved March 19, 2012, from http://www2.census.gov/govs/estimate/09_summary_report.pdf.

level, the largest amount again is spent on education, with health, public works, and social welfare next. Because of intergovernmental transfers, federal fiscal policies can have a significant impact on state and local governments. Cuts at the federal level directly affect not only federal agencies, but also state and local governments that depend on federal funding. In fact, in a statement by the National Council of State Legislatures, states have an "incalculable stake" in the manner in which the federal government balances its budget (see www.ncsl.org/statefed/fedbud.htm#FederalGrants).

The Budget as a Managerial Tool

As a public manager, you will find that the budget process is critical to your success and that of your agency, quite simply because it establishes the level of funding for your programs. A variety of steps are required to enable an agency to spend money. First, legislation must be passed and signed by the chief executive to authorize the program. This *authorizing legislation* permits the establishment or continuation of a particular program or agency. (Authorizing legislation usually covers multiple years or is even open-ended, although some programs, such as the space program, require new authorization each year.) Next come *appropriations*, whereby the legislature sets aside funds and creates budget authority for the funds' expenditure. Only after both steps have been taken can an agency spend money in pursuit of its stated objectives.

In most cases, governments use a *fiscal year* as their basic accounting period. The federal fiscal year begins on October 1 and runs through September 30 of the following year. The fiscal year carries the name of the year in which it ends; thus, fiscal year 2013, or FY 2013, begins October 1, 2012, and ends September 30, 2013. States and localities differ widely in terms of fiscal years; some follow the federal pattern, whereas others start July 1 (as did the federal government until 1976). Still others match the fiscal year to the calendar year. Kentucky and a few other states actually have a two-year-long fiscal year because their legislatures meet and pass a budget only every other year.

The fiscal year is the key period in which money is spent, but a variety of steps must be taken before and after the fiscal year that can affect an agency's expenditures. The budget must be developed, typically by the chief executive (president, governor, mayor) and transmitted to the legislature; it must be approved by the legislature (hopefully) prior to the beginning of the fiscal year; it must be executed during the fiscal year; and it must be reviewed and audited following the fiscal year. At any given point in the budget cycle, there are actually several budgets being worked on. While one budget is being executed (say, FY 2012), another (FY 2013) is being formulated and approved, while another, (FY 2011) is being audited.

Budget Formulation

In the federal government and in many state and local jurisdictions, the chief executive has primary responsibility for preparing the budget. The budget cycle (see Figure 5.3) typically begins with a letter from a central budget office to agencies outlining the timetable for

FIGURE 5.3

The Budget Cycle at the Federal Level

Major Steps in the Budget Process

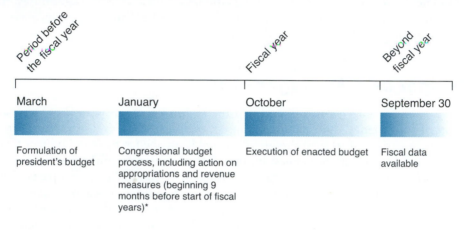

Period before the fiscal year		Fiscal year	Beyond fiscal year
March	**January**	**October**	**September 30**
Formulation of president's budget	Congressional budget process, including action on appropriations and revenue measures (beginning 9 months before start of fiscal years)*	Execution of enacted budget	Fiscal data available

*If appropriation action is not complete by September 30, Congress enacts temporary appropriations (i.e., a continuing resolution).

© Cengage Learning

preparing the budget, transmitting forms for use in the process, and indicating any policy concerns of special priority for the fiscal year. The agencies then prepare their own budget requests and forward them to the central budget office for review (see the box "Take Action: Financial Management: The Program Manager's Role"). Often a series of meetings (or sometimes hearings) are held to negotiate differences in the views of the central budget office (reflecting the priorities of the chief executive) and the agencies. Finally, the budget document is prepared by the central budget office and transmitted by the chief executive to the legislature for approval.

In some jurisdictions, responsibility for preparing the budget may not lie completely with the chief executive, and the budget cycle may vary accordingly. In many states, for example, responsibility for budget formulation may be shared among the governor, other elected officials, and members of the legislature. Cities with a strong mayor form usually give responsibility to the chief executive, whereas cities that operate under other forms tend to disperse budget authority. The city manager usually prepares the budget in council-manager cities, though typically with substantial input from the mayor and other council members.

The Office of Management and Budget (OMB) is the central budget office at the federal level and has evolved from an office established in 1921. Originally called the Bureau of the Budget, it was renamed by President Nixon in 1970 to reflect an emphasis on management concerns in addition to budgetary responsibilities. At the outset of the budget process, OMB collects information on projected revenues for the coming fiscal year and on the outlook for the economy. In addition, OMB develops information on the progress of the current year's budget, as well as the budget being considered

Take Action

FINANCIAL MANAGEMENT: THE PROGRAM MANAGER'S ROLE

Many in government think financial management is the responsibility of financial offices, accountants, and the like. Most program managers, in particular, feel they do not have to be concerned with financial management.

WRONG. Nothing could be further from the truth. Successful program managers appreciate that, in government, they have the responsibility for financial management. They understand what this entails, and thus have a far better chance of successfully delivering their programs despite reduced budgets.

What is financial management? It is nothing more than obtaining and effectively using funds and other resources to accomplish the goals and objectives of the organization. It typically entails:

- Defining people, materials, and services for achieving a program's goals and objectives.
- Defining the sources of resources that can be used to fund the program's costs.
- Obtaining the resources.
- Managing and minimizing the costs.
- Obtaining results from the expenditure of the resources.
- Preventing waste in the expenditure of the resources.
- Reporting accountability for both the use of resources and delivery of the results.

SOURCE: Harold I. Steinberg, "Improving Financial Management: The Program Manager's Role," *PA Times* 20, no. 11 (November 1997): 1. Reprinted by permission of the author.

by Congress. After a beginning consultation with the agencies to assess their program priorities, OMB works with the president to establish basic policy guidelines for developing the budget.

Networking

Federal organizations involved in budgeting and financial management include the Office of Management and Budget at www.whitehouse.gov/omb, the Congressional Budget Office at www.cbo.gov, and the Government Accountability Office at www.gao.gov.

These guidelines are communicated to the agencies, along with detailed forms for budget requests. In turn, managers in the various agencies assess their program priorities and decide on the necessary level of funding for accomplishing objectives in the next fiscal year. Starting about September, a period of negotiation occurs with OMB. The central budget office represents the president's policy concerns and usually takes a generalist perspective, in contrast to the more narrow, specialized interests of the agency representatives. About November or December, the president becomes more actively involved in the budget process and makes final decisions with respect to both revenue and fiscal considerations and individual program needs.

The final budget document, which is submitted to Congress early in the new year, represents the culmination of a long process of analysis and interaction among a wide variety of groups. Obviously, given the magnitude and complexity of the federal government, the process of budget formulation at that level is the most complex in this country. But the difficulties of reconciling different and competing interests in the budget process are significant at all levels of government. In addition, chief executives at the state and local levels face constraints not found at the federal level. For example, as we noted above, almost all governors are required by constitution or statute to submit a balanced budget to the legislature, making it essential that they project anticipated revenues as closely as possible.

Budget Approval

The budget approval phase begins with submission of the budget to the legislature and ends with approval of the budget. The legislature, in most cases, can approve, disapprove, or modify the chief executive's budget proposal; it can add or eliminate programs; and it can alter methods of raising revenues. Remember that first programs must be authorized and then money appropriated for their implementation. In some cases, appropriations are contained in one bill that is debated, amended, and passed by the legislative body. In other cases, appropriations may be divided among several different appropriations bills.

The budget submitted to the legislative body is first sent to the committee or committees responsible for appropriations. These committees review the submitted document and hold hearings involving agency personnel, representatives of interest groups, other legislators, and private citizens. After consideration by the full legislative body, the bill as amended is passed and sent to the chief executive for signature (where approval is required). In the case of bicameral legislatures, the bill is sent to the other legislative body for similar consideration. If there are differences in the bills produced by the two houses of the legislature, the differences are worked out in a conference committee, and the bill is passed again by the two houses and sent to the chief executive.

Again, there are wide variations in the approval process from jurisdiction to jurisdiction. At the federal level, granting budget authority—the authority to obligate funds for immediate or future *outlays* (government spending)—can come about in several ways. Budget authority for most programs must be granted annually through passage of an appropriations bill. Congress has voted permanent budget authority for some programs, so funds become available each year without further congressional action.

In addition, within any given fiscal year, some outlays will be based on obligations made in previous years. Thus, total budget outlays for any fiscal year include previously granted budget authority, authority granted through appropriations for the current year, and money obligated in previous years for spending in the upcoming fiscal year, minus outlays deferred to later years.

Under procedures established by the Congressional Budget Act of 1974, Congress considers budget totals before considering individual appropriations measures. Based on work by the budget committees of both houses, a first *concurrent resolution* (a resolution of both houses not requiring the president's signature) is passed by May 15. It establishes targets for total revenues and total spending authority within various functional areas for the upcoming fiscal year. Although the president is not formally involved in this part of the budget process, consultation frequently occurs so that all parties will be informed of developments in the approval process. In some cases, the various parties even agree on a set of budget totals to be honored by both the president in his budget submission and Congress in its approval process.

Congressional review of appropriations requests begins in the House of Representatives, where the Ways and Means Committee considers revenue estimates and the Appropriations Committee (through various subcommittees) reviews spending recommendations. Appropriations are considered within twelve different appropriations bills covering groups of departments and agencies within related functional areas. After initial passage by the House, all tax bills and the twelve appropriations bills are forwarded to the Senate for consideration. Differences in the appropriations measures coming from the two houses are worked out in conference committee and, following approval by both houses, are forwarded to the president for signature. The two budget committees are charged with drawing up a second concurrent resolution—this one binding in nature—setting limits on total spending. Finally, a separate *reconciliation bill* attempts to reconcile individual actions in taxes, authorizations, or appropriations with the totals.

While the budget process as outlined here seems fairly straightforward, in practice, there are many variations. Indeed, arguing that the budget process has become more policy-laden or politicized over the last decades, Irene Rubin writes, "At the national level, in recent years, the term *budget process* has become oxymoronic, because a process suggests a list of rules, followed in sequence, known by the participants, and repeated from year to year. But the reality is that the budget process has been invented on the fly, during the year" (Rubin, 2011). If action on appropriations for the fiscal year is not completed by the beginning of the fiscal year (October 1), Congress enacts a continuing resolution, which permits the government to keep operating until an appropriations measure is passed.

What Would You Do?

The budget of the Parks and Recreation Department that you head is stretched to the limit. The city council seems unwilling to add any resources to support new programs you think would benefit the community. You have called a staff meeting to consider alternative sources of revenue, but now you are wondering if the council will be offended if you try to come up with funds on your own to do something they chose not to support. What would you do?

Throughout its consideration of the budget, Congress is aided by the work of budget committee staff members (whose numbers have grown substantially in recent years) and by the Congressional Budget Office. This agency provides basic budget information and its own economic forecasts and indicates to Congress how its conclusions differ from those of the executive branch. Such differences have, in several years, led the Congressional Budget Office to predict a more substantial budget deficit than that anticipated by the administration.

An increase in staff capabilities has been among the most important developments in the legislative approval process in most states and some larger cities. Legislative budget staffs vary in structure and composition—partisan or nonpartisan, centralized or decentralized, joint (both houses) or single house, and so on. Their responsibilities usually include analyzing the governor's budget, forecasting revenues and expenditures, and developing alternatives to the executive budget. In all cases, greater staff capabilities have considerably aided the resurgence of state legislative involvement in the budget process.

One important feature of the approval process at the state level is the existence in most states of the *line-item veto*. (The line-item veto allows the executive to veto specific items in an appropriations bill rather than having to decide between "all or nothing.") Such authority has been sought at the federal level by recent presidents, and President Clinton became the first chief executive granted such capacity when the federal Line-Item Veto Act (Pub. L. 104–130) took effect in January 1997. The act, though stopping short of extending full constitutional line-item veto power, gave the president authority to strike items from a federal appropriations bill without having to veto the entire piece of legislation. The Clinton administration, like its Republican predecessors, argued that the powers granted under the act would enable the president to make significant cuts in federal spending. Proponents added that a great deal of time and energy would be saved because the executive and legislative branches would not have to renegotiate an entire budget when only specific items were at issue.

Despite the value inherent in such a measure, the Supreme Court invalidated the federal act in *Clinton v. City of New York* (1998), stating that although there may be procedures for amending or repealing federal statutes, the process must be consistent with the constitutional powers afforded each branch of government (see *Immigration and Naturalization Services v. Chadha* [1983]). In the case of the line-item veto, the president simply did not have the constitutional authority to amend or repeal a spending bill passed by Congress. In the absence of any suitable formulation that would meet the constitutional test, it appears that the federal line-item veto will wind up a historical anomaly (Joyce, 1998).

Budget Execution

The budget execution stage, generally coinciding with the fiscal year, is that part of the budget cycle in which the agencies of government carry out agreed-upon programs and policies. The execution stage involves public administrators in all aspects of the management process—planning, analysis, personnel management, communication, and other interpersonal skills.

Basic financial controls are exercised during the budget execution phase through the mechanism of *apportionment*, a process by which funds are allocated to agencies for specific portions of the year. Typically, the central budget office asks for submission of spending plans indicating what money the agencies anticipate spending in each quarter of the year. Because the agencies may not have received all they wanted in the appropriations process, the apportionment mechanism also acts as the basis for required changes in programs and policies. As soon as there is agreement between the central budget office (acting on behalf of the chief executive) and the agencies on the changes embodied in the apportionment plan, agencies begin receiving *allotments* to spend within a given period.

To ensure that funds are expended for the purposes for which they were intended and that there is enough money budgeted to cover a proposed expenditure, a *preaudit* (a review in advance of an actual expenditure) is usually required. Depending on the jurisdiction, the preaudit may be conducted by an agency's own budget office, by an independent agency, or even by an elected state official. Once approval has been given, the treasurer will "write a check" for the expenditure.

Even though budgets are not passed until just before (or even well into) the fiscal year, important changes may occur during the year that require changes in an agency's budgeted expenditures. Some changes may require greater funding—for example, when an unexpected natural disaster, such as a drought, places special burdens on farmers. If the need must be met prior to the next budget cycle, the president and Congress can work together to provide a *supplemental appropriation,* a bill passed during the fiscal year to add new money to an agency's budget for that fiscal year. Such a bill may simply provide more money for existing programs or money for a newly authorized program.

There are also devices, used primarily by chief executives as a matter of administrative discretion, to restrict agencies' spending below budgeted amounts. Presidents throughout the nation's history have sought to limit agency spending by *impoundment*—withholding—of funds authorized and appropriated by law, typically in the case of emergencies or where the purpose of the money had been achieved and budgeted funds still remain. At the state level, governors regularly withhold agency funds when revenue projections fall below levels on which the budget was based.

The 1974 Budget Act sought to clarify matters by defining two types of legal impoundments. The first, a *deferral,* is a decision by the president to withhold funds for a brief period. In such circumstances, the president must inform Congress, and either house of Congress may veto the action. The second, a *rescission,* is a presidential decision to withhold funds permanently; a rescission must receive the positive approval of both houses of Congress. Through these devices, Congress has sought to maintain its involvement in budget execution while at the same time allowing some administrative discretion to the president. (Not surprisingly, recent presidents, including President Clinton and President Bush, have argued for expanded rescission authority.)

Because situations change, public managers are often accorded some flexibility in the use of allocated funds. Money originally allocated for salaries and wages, for example, might be shifted (with appropriate approvals) to an equipment and expense category. On a broader scale, some agencies engage in *reprogramming*—that is, taking money appropriated for one program and diverting it to another that emerges as a higher priority. This strategy must be undertaken with great care because of legal and ethical implications and because efforts to subvert the legislature's intention are likely to incur retribution in the next year's budget process.

Audit Phase

The final phase of the budget process is the postexecution or audit phase. *Postaudits* take place following the end of the fiscal year and are concerned with verifying the correctness and propriety of agency operations. These audits were originally designed to ensure financial control; as such, they focused on accuracy of record keeping; compliance with statutes; and uncovering of fraud, waste, and mismanagement. More recently, the concept of auditing has been broadened to include *performance auditing*—analyzing and evaluating the effective performance of agencies in carrying out their objectives. Three purposes are served by postaudits: (1) financial viability, as indicated by efficient use of resources; (2) compliance with statutes and other limitations; and (3) program performance, including the results of program operations.

Agencies themselves can carry out audits; we have already seen how the auditing work of inspectors general has revealed waste and fraud in some agencies. There is a clear trend toward broader use of independent agencies. Moreover, to maintain detachment in the review of executive agencies, the postaudit function is increasingly being attached to the legislative rather than the executive branch. In 1921, for example, the federal government created the General Accounting Office (GAO) as a support agency of Congress, although President Wilson had previously vetoed such legislation on the grounds that the officers of such an agency should be answerable to the executive rather than the legislature. Recall that the GAO was originally concerned primarily with the financial auditing of selected federal agencies; however, more recently, it has not only changed its name—to become the Government Accountability Office—but it has extended its activities to include program evaluations as well.

At the state level, organizational arrangements vary; however, the trend toward having postaudit agencies attached to the legislature is clear. In 1938, there were five states in which the audit function was part of the legislative branch; in 1960, there were fifteen; today, there are more than forty. A large number of states retain an elected state auditor, whose office often goes beyond detached analysis and becomes embroiled in political controversy. Finally, a number of large cities, including Dallas and Seattle, have developed legislative postaudit functions.

Approaches to Public Budgeting

To be an effective tool in management and decision making, the budget must present information about the purposes of the proposed activity and resources to be expended. There are a variety of different ways to present such information. Some approaches to budgeting, for example, are based on the assumption that budget decisions are (and should be) largely *incremental*—policy makers start with the given situation (last year's budget) as a base and make only marginal adjustments to that base. Following this approach, managers build budgets by asking for limited increases in spending rather than focusing on major programmatic concerns. Similarly, the legislature focuses on individual expenditures rather than the "big picture." According to proponents of incrementalism, this approach is an accurate representation of the actual behavior of decision makers and is an appropriate way to maintain balance among different interests represented in the budget.

In contrast, other budget theorists argue for a more rational, comprehensive, and programmatic approach.

Budgets can be categorized according to the purposes they serve. In a classic work, Allen Schick (1987) suggested that budgets can have at least three different purposes, all of which are reflected in any approach to budgeting. These purposes are planning, management, and control.

Planning involves the determination of organizational objectives and the development of strategies to meet those objectives; *management* involves the design of organizational means by which approved goals can be translated into action, as well as developing the staffing and resources necessary for execution; *control* refers to the process of ensuring that operating officials follow the policies and plans established by their superiors. According to Schick, each attempt at budget reform changes the balance among the three purposes—sometimes inadvertently, sometimes deliberately. Understanding how budgets are put together will help you present an effective case for program changes.

The Line-Item Budget

Those who established the first systematic governmental budgeting schemes were concerned primarily with assuring the public that expenditures were properly made and accounted for. Consequently, the systems they designed emphasized the control function. Because all agencies purchase essentially the same kinds of goods and services, it was argued, account classifications could be designed that would be broadly applicable to various agencies or departments. It would then be possible for auditors to apply uniform criteria to evaluate the expenditures of all.

In what is called a *line-item budget*, categories of expenditures are listed with amounts allocated to each. Typically, line-item budgets are organized by departments, so that the budget for one agency might look something like this:

Organizational Unit: XXXXX

Expenditure Code	Category/Subcategory	2011	2012
100	Salaries and wages	2,585,400	2,879,000
200	Other operating expenses	887,250	1,102,000
2100	Travel	150,000	200,000
2200	Supplies	250,000	370,000
2300	Utilities	88,000	93,000
2400	Maintenance	78,500	89,000
2500	Other	320,750	350,000
Total		3,472,650	3,981,000

The cost of each object of expenditure is generally based on the agency's past experience and analysis of expected changes during the budget year. Because personnel costs (salaries, wages, and other personal services) typically constitute over half the budget, special attention is given to projected staffing changes, and such changes are often appended to the budget. (Our example projects, among other things, the addition of new personnel during the upcoming year.)

The line-item budget continues to be widely used because it is easy to understand and offers political leaders the more palatable option of reducing items (such as travel) rather than eliminating "programs." Moreover, it is well suited to incremental decisions, which make only minor modifications in the previous budget. However, because the line-item budget focuses on expenditures and not on their results, it is of little benefit to planning or management.

The Performance Budget

The 1930s proved a turning point with respect to public budgeting. The federal budget grew tremendously, the Bureau of the Budget became attached to the White House, and, in general, greater attention was paid to the executive management of government agencies. This interest in management was paralleled at the state and local levels, where efforts to relate budget presentations to programmatic activities had been under way for some time. The result was a new approach to budgeting: the performance budget.

The *performance budget* is organized around programs or activities rather than departments. It includes various performance measurements to indicate the relationship between the work actually done and its cost. As the Hoover Commission described it, a performance budget "would analyze the work of government departments and agencies according to their

CourseReader Assignment

Log in to **www.cengage.com** and open CourseReader to access the reading:

Read "What Do We Talk about When We Talk about Performance? Dialogue Theory and Performance Budgeting," by Donald P. Moynihan.

As we have noted in this chapter, there is a great deal of emphasis on performance measurement and performance budgeting in public organizations today. The PART program was one effort to emphasize performance in the federal government. Here it provides the opportunity for the author to explore the concept of performance in more detail.

Moynihan writes that what constitutes performance to some might mean something quite different to others. Try to come up with examples of where this might be the case in public policy in your local area. How would you expect the different meanings of performance to affect the measurement of performance? And how would you expect the measurement of performance to affect the development of new policies?

functions, activities, or projects. It would concentrate attention on the work to be done or the service to be rendered, rather than the things to be acquired." Because it focuses on the relationship between available resources and the work to be done, performance budgeting is well suited to the purposes of management.

To construct a performance budget, the manager must first determine appropriate program categories, such as highway safety, and then break down that program into appropriate subprograms, such as school visitations or advertising programs. It is then necessary to establish detailed work measures for each activity—for example, a highway safety program might anticipate twenty-seven school visitations during the course of the year. These data would then be related to the cost of making such visits. In its most detailed presentation, a performance budget requires identifying the work activity, establishing an output unit, calculating the cost of each unit, and projecting the units required and the associated costs for the coming year.

Although performance measures are obviously helpful in making budgetary decisions, not all organizations can easily develop such information. A license bureau can report the number of licenses issued and fairly easily calculate the cost per license issued, but a research unit or a group promoting civil rights would find its work much more difficult to measure. Performance budgeting also tends to concentrate on quantity of work rather than quality.

Finally, performance budgeting somewhat diffuses organizational responsibility because one program or function may be located in several different units. "Public information," for example, may involve work in the mayor's office, police department, fire department, and elsewhere. To sort out costs by department, one would need to construct a crosswalk or matrix of expenditures. A matrix might place various activities on one dimension and departments on another.

Activities	1	2	3	Total
Division A	$10,000	$20,000	$15,000	$45,000
Division B	12,000	16,000	10,000	38,000
Division C	5,000	12,000	13,000	30,000
Total	27,000	48,000	38,000	

© Cengage Learning

A matrix could also be constructed relating activities to traditional objects of expenditure; such calculations are typical in performance budgets.

Program Budgeting

Another approach to budgeting had its origins in the Department of Defense in the early 1960s. Soon after taking office as secretary of defense, Robert McNamara discovered that his ability to manage the department was severely restricted by the lack of coordination between planning and budgeting. Each service (army, navy, air force) prepared its own annual budget, reflecting its own priorities, and then submitted the documents to the secretary. This plan failed to give proper attention to systemwide issues. But, equally important, because the budgeting system was based on a one-year time frame, it bore little relation to the multiyear projections of the department's planning and analysis staff. The development of major weapons systems, for example, involves research and development, assembly, and operations over many years. Yet, this fact was not clearly reflected in the annual budget submissions.

McNamara instituted a new approach, which came to be known as the *planning-programming-budgeting system (PPBS)*, an effort to connect planning, systems analysis, and budgeting in a single exercise. In the Department of Defense, PPBS began with the identification of nearly 1,000 program elements, each grouped under one of nine major programs or missions—that is, strategic retaliatory forces, continental air and missile defense forces, civil defense, and so on. Not only was extensive study required to identify the right combination of program elements to support each mission, but, once having established the combinations, units in the department were required to submit detailed analyses of proposed program changes. In addition, the new budget system was designed to cover a nine-year period and to show detailed projections for the first six years.

President Johnson was so impressed with the operation of PPBS in the Department of Defense that he ordered the new system extended to all federal agencies. Each cabinet-level department was asked to identify a limited number of purposes to be served by the agency and then to organize budget requests around those themes. The Department of Health, Education, and Welfare (HEW), for example, chose topics such as "social and rehabilitation services" that cut across several agencies within HEW. Costs for each program element were projected five years into the future, and extensive documentation justifying each element was required, especially in areas undergoing significant changes. Most agencies were able to develop their budgets using the new approach, but there was considerable confusion in the implementation of PPBS. As a result of this confusion, and for a variety of other political reasons, President Nixon formally terminated PPBS in 1971.

During its relatively short tenure, PPBS attracted great attention, with many cities, states, and other countries embracing the new technique. PPBS not only emphasized the planning aspect of budgeting, but it appeared to bring greater rationality and comprehensiveness to the budget process. These goals, however, were accomplished at great cost. Substantial numbers of new staff members were needed, both in the central budget office and in the various agencies, to provide the kind of analysis PPBS required. The process proved extraordinarily time-consuming. Consequently, very few full-blown PPBS systems remain, although many of the principles of PPBS have been incorporated into other approaches, often under the more general label *program budgeting*.

There are important differences between performance budgeting and program budgeting. "As a general rule, performance budgeting is concerned with the *process of work* (what methods should be used), while program budgeting is concerned with the *purpose of work* (what activities should be authorized)" (Schick, 1987, p. 53). Moreover, although both systems urge measurement of work being done, performance budgeting is more likely to employ measures related to the work (for example, the number of tons of garbage collected) and a program budget might concentrate instead on measures related to the purpose of the work (for example, the rate of infectious disease in the community). Performance data are of great interest to individual managers who seek to improve productivity, but legislators and other policy makers are more likely to be interested in the purposes of various activities.

Outcome-Based Budgeting

A recent trend in government budgeting involves increasing the level of accountability for public resources. Citizens, elected officials, and administrators want to be able to determine how much is being spent on each program or agency and the return on the public's investment—that is, the substantive impact of each policy. In practical terms, this requires linking budget information with some type of a performance measurement system. The resulting budget enables administrators to track levels of expenditures and report on the outcomes being achieved.

Unlike performance budgeting mentioned previously, outcome-based budgeting goes beyond looking at mere issues of productivity and unit cost and assesses the long-term impact of each policy, program, or agency within its targeted area. Though based on quantitative measures, *outcome-based budgeting* determines the qualitative results of government initiatives. Many government agencies have incorporated outcome-based budgeting within their strategic planning processes, making it possible to observe the level of resources needed to reach goals and objectives and then use that information for budget decision making.

In Catawba County, North Carolina, local officials used outcome-based budgeting to enhance their government's system of service delivery. The county in the past few years had experienced limited growth in revenues; yet, during this time the call for human services continued to rise. County leadership responded by handing decision-making authority to agency administrators, challenging them to reduce costs while more effectively meeting citizen demands. Those who achieved 90 percent of their goals would be able to apply their savings to unrestricted needs. Catawba County administrators embarked on a citizen-driven, outcome-based system of budgeting to ensure that resources were targeted to meet specific community goals. Over time, they not only saved money but also enhanced government responsiveness (and received an award from the Government Finance Officers Association in 2010 for their efforts).

We will see later the way performance or outcome measurement has affected the conduct of the public's business at all levels of government. For now, we should simply note that the current federal budgeting system, like most at the state and local levels, is a combination of elements from several of the approaches we have discussed. What is most important is not whether one particular system or another is being used, but rather what political and administrative choices underlie the selection of a particular budget approach. That is, what are decision makers trying to emphasize by using the type of budget they select?

Budgetary Strategies and Political Games

Despite all attempts to rationalize the budget process, public budgeting is an inherently political activity. The changing demands on government and its programs, the shifting interests that are brought to bear in policy decisions, and the many different actors (and personalities) that are part of the budget process mean that budget decisions will always occur in a highly charged political environment. Because agency managers typically (and properly) believe in the programs they operate and would like to see the programs be of even greater benefit to the public, they tend to become advocates of an agency position, often seeking to expand the size and scope of the agency's work.

If you can deal effectively with the political environment in which budgeting occurs, you will likely be more successful in expanding, or at least maintaining, your agency's programs. (There are, of course, many cases in which you will be judged on your capacity to hold the line on expenditures or to manage program reductions.) Whatever your intent, understanding the politics of the budgetary process will be helpful.

In discussions of budgetary strategies, two basic concepts will help orient your thinking. The first is the notion of program base. The *base* refers to those elements of an agency's program that everyone expects will be continued from year to year. Under normal circumstances, the program's base is assumed to remain pretty much the same from one year to the next and is not subject to special scrutiny. Having an activity approved for one year is one thing; having that activity considered a part of your agency's base budget is far more important. A second concept is that of receiving a *fair share* of the overall budget. Managers often measure success in terms of whether their program receives a proportionate amount of any increases or decreases that the government generally supports. Agency personnel often work for years to build a base that they consider a fair share of the overall budget.

As we saw earlier, budget requests typically originate with the agencies. They are then reviewed and often changed by a central budget office (acting in behalf of the chief executive) and submitted to the legislature for approval. In constructing a budget request, you need to take into account several different types of expenditures. As mentioned previously, many departments at the federal level have a large budget component that is essentially uncontrollable or fixed. The Department of Health and Human Services (HHS), for example, which administers many entitlement programs, has a large percentage of its budget that is fixed. A second part of an agency's budget is likely to be devoted to *adjustments for inflation*. The rising cost of utilities, telephones, postage, and other essential services must be taken into account, either absorbed in the base or covered by increased expenditures. Finally, some part of the agency's budget is discretionary, subject to increase or decrease according to the agency's priorities. The discretionary portion of the budget allows you to decide which new programs to propose and which existing activities to recommend for more (or less) funding. Understanding these categories will help you argue for changes in a particular budget.

Strategies for Program Development

These choices lead to strategic questions you must answer in building a budget—including the important question of what total amount to request. Although an overall budget is likely to differ only incrementally from that of the previous year, some agencies are clearly more assertive in their requests than others. They are more willing to request large increases rather than small ones. How assertive an agency should be, however, is conditioned by several factors.

Support from the chief executive (the president, governor, mayor, and so on) is highly important, whether the support is advocacy for a particular program or more generally interest in a particular field, such as law enforcement. Legislative support is also highly important. Agency personnel work throughout the year to maintain contact with key legislative leaders and to build the kinds of alliances that will be helpful in supporting programs of mutual interest. Finally, your personality—especially your willingness to take risks and defend risky choices—will play a strong role in deciding how much to request.

Aaron Wildavsky, who wrote a landmark study of the politics of the budgetary process (1988), suggested three other strategic elements that affect the nature of the request and help build political support for it. The first of these is *clientele support*. The support of client groups and other associations interested in the agency's work will be helpful in developing testimony and lobbying in behalf of programs. An agency that is confident of the testimony of "satisfied customers" or able to show support for proposed changes will likely fare much better than others. Obviously, the most effective way to build support is to serve a client group well, but agencies may also try to stimulate supportive clientele to communicate with legislators about the agency's good work.

Wildavsky's second element of political support is the *confidence* of higher executives and legislative officials in your character and ability. The magnitude of government budgets is so great that higher officials or legislators simply cannot know all the details necessary for making a purely rational analysis. At some point, they must simply trust the manager. Managers who enjoy a good reputation are typically more successful, especially in dealings with the legislature. One administrator commented, "If you have the confidence of your [appropriations] subcommittee your life is much easier and you can do your department some good; if you don't have confidence you can't accomplish much and you are always in trouble" (Wildavsky, 1988, p. 105). There are many ways to build confidence, but highly successful managers seem to agree that integrity (telling the whole truth) and responsiveness (keeping in touch and responding completely to inquiries) are particularly important.

Third, agency officials can take certain tactical positions to attempt to develop or protect their favorite programs. One approach, verging on the unethical but nonetheless common, is *budget padding*—that is, proposing a higher budget than is actually needed. Agency officials assume that after the central budget office and legislature cut the budget, you will have what you wanted in the first place. Another strategy is one Wildavsky terms the "camel's nose." The manager asks for a small amount to begin a program, then later treats this program as part of the base and argues that it would be unfortunate to lose the money already invested by not finishing the job (Wildavsky, 1988, p. 115).

Over the past couple of decades, many programs at all levels of government have experienced lower revenues and more limited funding. In some cases, such as in the social services, programs have been reduced or eliminated. In other cases, changes such as the termination of revenue sharing at one level of government have resulted in lower revenues at another. In still other cases, popular efforts to limit either revenues or expenditures, such as Proposition 13 in California, have limited government funds. Many public managers have had to turn their attention from developing new programs to maintaining or even reducing existing ones. This has been referred to as managing fiscal stress or, where serious reductions have occurred, cutback management.

As you would expect under retrenchment conditions, many managers have used budgetary tactics of the sort outlined by Wildavsky to lessen the impact of fiscal stress on their agencies (Wildavsky, 1988, p. 113). Any attempt to resist cuts is risky because it can quickly undermine the manager's credibility. Under conditions of long-term fiscal limitations, resistance to cuts is simply not a realistic option for many managers. Other ways of dealing with fiscal stress have been tried with some success:

- Following a *multiyear plan* to preserve the administrative capacity and the capital investment of the jurisdictions.
- *Targeting* cuts in specific programs rather than cutting across the board (all programs cut at the same percentage).
- *Smoothing out* the impact of the cuts (lessening their immediate effect). Smoothing out may occur by improving productivity, so the organization can accomplish more with less, or by generating new revenues, such as imposing new user charges for services.

Aspects of Financial Management

Although those in public organizations need to budget their resources, they must also attend to other aspects of managing the public's money. They must be concerned with the long-term financing of buildings, roads and highways, and equipment; they must carefully plan and manage borrowing; they must ensure against future losses; and, in all cases, they must try to get the most for the money they spend.

Networking

Professional associations for budgeting and financial management can be found at www.aabpa.org, www.abfm.org, and www.gfoa.org.

Capital Budgeting

In addition to budgeting annual expenditures, public policy makers and managers need to invest in facilities and equipment that will be used over a period of time. For example, government is primarily responsible for developing and maintaining the country's public works *infrastructure*—streets and highways, tunnels and bridges, sewers and water treatment facilities, and so on. Governments invest in a variety of major facilities, including schools and universities, hospitals and mental health centers, public housing, and correctional institutions. Innumerable equipment purchases (especially military equipment at the federal level) are intended for long-term use. Expenditures on items that will be used over a period of several years are called *capital expenditures*.

Budgeting for capital expenditures is similar to the process of budgeting for annual expenditures, but it differs in some ways. In most jurisdictions, except the federal government, capital expenditures are treated in a separate budget called a *capital budget*.

Most states have a separate capital budget, and nearly all give special treatment to capital expenditures in budget presentations. Nearly all major cities and most local governments use a capital budget. For many years, the federal government treated capital spending merely as part of the regular budget. Only recently has it begun to provide a special analysis of capital spending. There is still not a separate capital budget at the federal level, though the issue continues to be debated.

The primary argument in favor of separate consideration of capital items is that the benefits of these items are spread over future generations, so it is not unreasonable to share the burden of repaying the money borrowed. A separate capital budget may also encourage more long-term thinking—the lack of which is often decried in the annual budget process. On the other hand, the capital budget can become a political "pork barrel," in which each legislator seeks to gain his or her share of projects (and their funding). A capital budget can become a device for avoiding fiscal responsibility by pushing expenditures that should be faced immediately into an indefinite future. Whether a separate budget is developed or not, one should keep in mind the relationship between capital and operating expenditures. Building a new swimming pool, for example, implies that annual expenditures will be forthcoming in future years to keep it operating.

What Would You Do?

A friend who is a city manager once commented that he liked to put a "radio" item in each budget—an item that would make a lot of noise and attract attention but could be "unplugged" easily. He said that after the council focused all its attention on that item and it was finally removed, everything else would be approved with little question. You are preparing your budget for presentation to the council. What would you do?

Ideally, a capital budget develops in the context of a fairly comprehensive planning process, undertaken either for the government as a whole or by the various agencies within their functional areas (such as health or criminal justice). Whether or not a planning process is in operation, an important intermediate step (and one followed by nearly all governments considering capital projects) is development of a capital investment program—a timetable indicating various projects to be undertaken, schedules for their completion, and methods of financing. A capital investment plan is usually written to cover a three- to five-year period and is moved forward each year. Georgia, for example, has a capital budget that is mainly a gathering of capital outlays by agency and project category, as these have been requested by various agencies' submissions to the budget office. For each category, budget makers identify the financing source and also the sources of funding over the length of the request.

To undertake such a plan, government decision makers often solicit proposals from agencies and then try to bring order to the resulting submissions. Among the criteria they might use would be whether the project is essential, especially for health and safety; whether the project fills a gap in existing services; whether it builds effectively on existing services; and whether it meets an unforeseen emergency need. Because financing for capital projects is usually spread over many years, as are the benefits, complete analysis of each project is likely to involve detailed consideration of both costs and benefits over time.

Debt Management

One part of the capital budgeting process is careful consideration of the source of funding. Some jurisdictions try to operate on a "pay as you go" basis, paying in full for all projects during the fiscal year in which they are authorized. (One variation of this idea is the accumulation of money in a sinking fund, something like a Christmas Club account, which is then used to pay for the needed improvement.) Other jurisdictions may be willing to borrow money for a project, either because waiting to accumulate funds would simply take too long or because the costs as well as the benefits of the project should be spread over a period of years—a "pay as you use" approach.

Borrowing is often used to finance capital improvement projects; but borrowing may be employed to meet a variety of other needs as well. In some cases, anticipated revenues will simply not be available at the time spending is necessary. To solve the resulting cash flow problem, governments undertake short-term borrowing. (In more questionable cases, money is borrowed from future years' revenues to pay operating expenses within the current year.) Borrowing is also used for emergency needs; for example, a natural disaster, such as fire or flood, might require funds far beyond the capacity of the annual budget. Especially when such spending will be used to reconstruct facilities that will have long-term benefits, borrowing may well be justified. Finally, at least at the federal level, borrowing is sometimes justified as a way of stimulating the economy.

Governments may undertake various types of borrowing. The primary mechanism for financing government debt is the issuance of a *bond*—that is, a promise to repay a certain amount (*principal*) at a certain time (*maturity date*) at a particular *rate of interest*. One of the most common bonds is the *general obligation bond*, which pledges the "full faith and credit" of the jurisdiction—in other words, the government provides as security all its revenues and resources. In contrast, *revenue bonds* promise as security the anticipated revenues that a capital project will produce. Revenue bonds might be issued based on the future toll receipts of a new highway or on the gross receipts of a new municipal sports complex.

Both from the standpoint of a jurisdiction and of potential investors who might purchase the bonds, it is helpful to know something about the jurisdiction's *debt capacity*. For example, you would want to know the value of a city's resources combined with the ability of its government to provide payment. As a service to investors, several firms provide bond ratings for cities and other jurisdictions. The ratings are also important to the jurisdiction because a lower rating means higher costs of borrowing for the government. Standard and Poor's reference guides rate bonds in descending quality from AAA to AA to A to BBB to BB, and so on. Cities or other government units that carry high ratings will be more successful than others in selling their bonds. (The effect of credit rating reductions at the federal level was recently demonstrated when Standard and Poor's lowered the U.S. credit rating to one level below AAA. The credit rating company said "political brinkmanship" in the 2011 debate over the debt had made the U.S. government's ability to manage its finances "less stable, less effective and less predictable" (*Washington Post,* 2011).

Risk Management

Public organizations are subject to a variety of risks that can prove extremely costly. For example, in one city an individual lost control of his car, bounced off a guardrail, and ran into a ditch. The driver suffered serious injuries and then sued the city for several million dollars, arguing that the guardrail had been improperly installed. Similarly, a city employee with no previous health problems began to suffer back pain on the job. After several operations, high medical bills, and physical therapy, he was given disability retirement at age twenty-six. Another city was sued by residents who lived near the municipal airport because the noise of aircraft landing and taking off supposedly lessened the value of their property. Over the years, cases such as these involving civil damages, breach of contract, workers' compensation, and related legal problems have cost cities, states, and other jurisdictions millions of dollars.

Risk management is concerned with how public organizations anticipate and cope with these risks. A first step in risk management is to identify potential areas of loss and then to attempt to reduce the probability of losses occurring. Risk reduction programs might include improved work safety, periodic inspections of physical property owned by the city, and employee health programs. But, whatever the success of risk reduction efforts, losses do occur. The government has a variety of options for meeting losses: paying from operating funds or financial reserves, levying special taxes to cover the loss, or even floating bonds.

In anticipation of losses, many public organizations purchase insurance from private firms. In recent years, this option has become more difficult, as insurance rates for governments and other public organizations have risen dramatically and put many traditional forms of insurance beyond reach. (The difficulty of purchasing insurance has also led some jurisdictions to eliminate uninsured services such as recreation programs.) Another possibility, however, is *self-insurance*, the development of an insurance pool by the jurisdiction itself. Many governments are larger than insurance companies, so such an undertaking is not only financially feasible but also provides some administrative control and flexibility that is not present when private firms are used. An increasingly popular means of self-insurance involves pooling risks in a shared program operated by several municipalities.

Purchasing

A final aspect of financial management in public organizations is the purchase of goods and services. Because public organizations are typically not equipped to produce all the goods and services they require (and in most cases would not find it financially feasible to do so), they must acquire some goods and services from the private sector. Like individuals and businesses, public organizations want to get the most for their money. But at the same time, because government purchasing involves such substantial sums of money and is capable of influencing the structure of the market generally, public purchasing must also take into account social and political goals.

Governments have often found that centralizing purchasing in one agency, rather than having each agency buy what it needs, results in considerable savings. For one thing, a central purchasing unit can buy in sufficient volume to get better prices; for another, those in the purchasing unit can develop expertise with respect to pricing, business conditions, and market practices. Finally, experts in purchasing are likely to be more successful in the negotiating process. Although individual agencies occasionally complain that their specific needs are not met by the purchasing unit, most state and local jurisdictions use centralized purchasing operations.

In most cases, a purchasing unit circulates and advertises the government's needs and solicits bids for the required goods and services. The resulting bids are evaluated in terms of cost, and the lowest bid is usually, though not automatically, chosen. Consideration is also given to the quality of the product and to the ability of the firm to actually deliver the goods or services in a timely fashion. In addition, purchasers are often required to give special preference to certain groups, such as minority-owned firms or in-state companies. Several jurisdictions often join together to cooperate in purchasing activities. In some instances, several local governments may form a common purchasing unit; in other cases, prices negotiated by the state purchasing office are available to local governments as well.

Accounting and Related Information Systems

Keeping track of the revenues and expenditures of government and other public organizations is an enormously complex task. Not only are there billions of dollars to record and report, but the presentation of financial information must serve several purposes at once. Certainly financial data should be developed and reported in such a way that public officials can be held accountable for the use of public funds. At the same time, the accounting and reporting system should provide managers with information they can use to operate their organizations more efficiently and effectively. This dual requirement means that financial information should correlate closely with other managerially relevant material, such as personnel data or productivity measures.

Government Accounting

Accounting, whether in the public or private sector, is simply "the process of identifying, measuring, and communicating economic information to permit informed judgment and decision making by users of the information" (Berne & Schramm, 1986, p. 12). But because the purposes of public organizations differ from those of private organizations, accounting practices also differ. Those in public organizations are generally not concerned with making a profit; rather, they tend to focus on achieving a balance between revenues and expenditures—what comes in and what goes out. There are some exceptions, such as public corporations, hospitals, and water companies, which are more like profit-seeking groups; however, in nearly all public organizations, accountability is more important than profit maximization.

Governmental accounting systems reflect these different purposes. The cornerstone of accounting in the public sector is the allocation of resources to various funds, each of which is designed to record transactions within a particular functional area and to ensure that funds are used in accordance with the purposes sought. (Use of such funds is uncommon in the private sector.) The funds typically reflect policy makers' intent in authorizing certain activities and appropriating funds for them. The legislature may decide, for example, that certain gasoline taxes should be used exclusively for highway maintenance—in which case a separate fund might be created to keep track of money produced by the tax and spent for highways. In all cases, a primary concern is that the accounting system show whether the organization's activities have been consistent with the purposes for which they were created. Several broad types of funds are used in public organizations:

1. *General government funds* are used to account for most of the ordinary or routine functions of government. Most important among the general government funds is what is called the *general fund*, which handles the "unrestricted" funds of government, those not restricted to specific purposes (and typically allocated to other funds). The general fund is the dominant fund in most jurisdictions and handles most of the government's operational activities. Related general government funds might include those that account for special revenues, like a dedicated gasoline tax, or those that monitor expenditures for capital projects.

2. *Proprietary funds* are used to account for government activities or enterprises that more closely resemble private business in their orientation toward profit. This does not mean that all agencies employing funds are required to make a profit; indeed, they may break even or perhaps require a subsidy. What is implied is that a measure of profit is possible and usually desirable in such operations; examples include a local transit system or a state printing operation.

3. Finally, *fiduciary funds* are used when the government must hold assets for individuals (such as those in a pension fund) or when the government holds resources to be transmitted to another organization (such as property taxes that a county collects for a city).

Within each fund there is an accounting of the resources available and the flow of funds in and out of the account. There are *assets*—what the government *owns*; and, there are *liabilities*—what the government *owes*. Assets include items such as cash, capital facilities, equipment, and money owed to the government; liabilities include items such as bills that the government has yet to pay. When the organization's liabilities are subtracted from its assets, the remainder is called a *fund balance* (and may be expressed either in positive or negative terms). An organization with $2,525,000 in assets and $2,300,000 in liabilities has a fund balance of $225,000. Note that a fund balance does not mean the amount of cash on hand, but rather signifies a relationship between all assets (including cash) and all liabilities. Broadly, the fund balance is the key measure of the viability of the operation monitored by the fund and is one of many items contained in financial reports issued by governments and other public organizations.

Both accounting practices and financial reporting are guided by standards referred to as "generally accepted accounting practices." The Governmental Accounting Standards Board (GASB) was established in 1984 to develop standards for accounting and financial reporting at the state and local levels. The GASB has been especially attentive to multiple users of public financial information, including citizens, taxpayers, legislative bodies, upper-level executives, labor and employee groups, interest groups, contractors, and the press. Again, an important characteristic of governmental accounting is that it must serve multiple purposes, including accountability within a democratic system.

Computer-Based Information Systems

The emergence and widespread use of computers in tracking financial data as well as other program-relevant information has led to a "quiet revolution" in the analysis and use of information in public organizations. Not only do computers make easier the accumulation and manipulation of vast amounts of data, but they also greatly facilitate analysis of those data in terms that are meaningful to decision makers at all levels. Computers have also increased the probability that information can be provided when it is needed, not weeks later. Consequently, a great deal of attention is being given to the design and implementation of computer-based information systems in the public sector and to the political and organizational implications of such systems. Applications in the area of financial management have led the way in these efforts.

A distinction is often made between management information systems and decision support systems. *Management information systems* collect and summarize routine information as a basis for structuring decision making. Relevant databases might include budgetary information, expenditures for salaries and wages, and personnel data. The system might be asked, for example, to produce a list of employees eligible for salary increases based on length of service in the agency. *Decision support systems*, on the other hand, are interactive systems that can assist in the solution of unstructured or nonroutine problems. These systems allow the manager to manipulate data within the system to produce a specific analysis for a particular decision, or provide optimization models to use in analyzing a particular policy recommendation. Although most public organizations are developing management information systems of various sorts, the development of decision support systems is receiving increased attention.

Applications of computer-based information systems are as wide-ranging as the work of public organizations. Most organizations are quickly becoming familiar with the use of spreadsheets and statistical packages for budget analysis, financial management packages for revenue and expenditure forecasting, and accounting packages for fund accounting and analysis. But far more extensive applications of information technology (IT) have been developed in government agencies, as we will see later.

At the state and local levels, one of the most interesting developments in information technology has been the design and implementation of information systems integrating budgeting, personnel, performance reporting, and auditing. Several states have led this process of integration, including Michigan, Oregon, Texas, Wyoming, and Washington. Efforts of this nature reflect an overall shift on the part of states toward more sophisticated systems of accounting. State governments over the past decade have used information technology to enhance their capacity to generate more detailed financial and productivity data, thus allowing for extensive analyses at a programmatic level and a link between expenditures and actual performance.

To the extent that budgetary and performance data are made available to the chief executive and other top managers on a timely basis, more effective management decisions may be possible. In addition, freeing budget analysts from the more mundane aspects of budgetary procedures should allow more attention to planning and analysis.

Similar developments have occurred at the local level. Baltimore, Maryland, has implemented a comprehensive accounting and performance measurement system, called Citistat, to track (virtually in real time) the productivity and fiscal efficiency of city departments. In a room lined with large projection screens and computer terminals, Baltimore's mayor, Stephanie Rawlings-Blake, meets biweekly with top aides and department heads to hear the latest reports on the city's service delivery. If a department's numbers lag behind its performance targets, the manager must account to his or her peers for the difference. "If we only looked at performance every year at budget time, I'd be old and gray before anything would change. Citistat brings the sense of urgency we need around here," said previous mayor Martin O'Malley (cited in Swope, 2001, p. 20). Thus far, the information system has contributed to significant improvements in public safety and public health, as well as opened new doors for collaboration between city departments.

Whether Citistat or similar IT initiatives will create across-the-board improvements for public organizations remains to be seen. Some argue that change of this nature requires far more than increased capacity to handle information. Moreover, the implementation of these types of systems may have negative consequences on the organizational culture and relationships within affected agencies.

Summary and Action Implications

Budgeting and financial management in public organizations have a lot in common with those activities elsewhere. But there are also important differences, most of which flow from the necessity for public organizations to be accountable to elected officials and, ultimately, to the people.

The centrality of the budget to any organization can hardly be underestimated; if you want to know what's going on in an organization, look at where the money is going. Establishing budget processes that reflect the organization's priorities, while securing appropriate levels of involvement from those who want to affect the budget, is extremely important. Finding ways to present budgetary information clearly and comprehensibly is a great aid to decision makers and to the public. Finally, developing mechanisms to ensure that the public's money is being spent both efficiently and responsibly is essential. You will find that knowing the technical side of the budget

process—being able to follow the budget process and clearly understand preparation, administration, and review—will be extremely helpful as you try to influence the
operations of your organization.

If you work in a central budget office, you will find that the period during which
the budget is formulated is intense, and your technical expertise will be put to the test.
But you will also recognize that you are playing an important role in shaping public
policies. Similarly, if you are managing an agency, you will place your imprint on the
policies and directions of your organization through the budget process. Your skill in
presenting and supporting requests for programs may determine whether or not they
are undertaken.

The budget process at the federal level, and in some state and local jurisdictions, is integrated with a process for long-range planning. Federal agencies are asked to provide certain projections for the two-year period following the year for which the budget is being
prepared, thus adding an element of long-range planning to the process.

Budgets and financial management systems are important tools for planning, prioritiz-
ing, and operating public programs, as well as important mechanisms for accountability
and control. Public access to budgets and financial statements allows citizens to see how
their interests are reflected in the actual conduct of government. Budgets and other financial documents that clearly show what is happening in an agency are a necessary part of
operating in the public interest.

STUDY QUESTIONS

1. Discuss how government uses the budget to affect fiscal policy.

2. Describe some of the ways government obtains funds for operation. Identify the various types of taxes that governments use.

3. How does the government spend the money it collects?

4. The budget cycle consists of four major phases. Discuss government's role in the
budget cycle and the components of each phase.

5. Allen Schick suggests three different purposes of the budget. Identify and define these
purposes.

6. Compare and contrast the different types of budgeting processes.

7. Explain the two basic concepts of budgetary strategies.

8. Political influence has a major impact on the budgetary process. What are some
of the strategies managers use to influence the budget process?

9. Financial management is an important part of fiscal activities. Discuss some of the concerns fiscal managers deal with, including capital budgeting, debt management, risk management, and purchasing.

10. Discuss the broad types of funds that public organizations use.

CASES AND EXERCISES

1. Figure 5.4 contains several pages from the City of Tempe's budget document. Analyze these budget pages from the perspective of (1) a city council member who will have to make decisions about which city services to fund; (2) the public works department director, who wants to improve services to the community; and (3) an average citizen interested in seeing whether the city's tax dollars are being put to good use. For the purposes of each viewpoint, how complete and clear is the information? Does the budget tell you what you want to know in order to act? How might the budget presentation be improved? To what extent is any local government's budget a reflection of the particular locality?

2. Consider the following case: You are Mike Smith, chief procurement officer for a major university. Work generated by your staff of twenty procurement specialists includes writing proposals to vendors and evaluating the vendors' bids. To write those bids, the procurement specialist works with someone from the university agency who is knowledgeable about the project. Tom Drake, a procurement specialist, is currently working with Kathy Kline of the Communications Department to develop a bid proposal to purchase a new campuswide telephone system that includes a quick-dial feature. The university's current telephone system was installed fifteen years ago by Regional Telephone. Over the last few years, Regional and one other vendor have sold add-on equipment to five of the university's fifteen departments. This add-on equipment is expensive and represents a major investment to the five departments, one of which is the Communications Department. Departments that have the quick-dial equipment are pleased with the results; departments that do not have quick dial cannot afford it and are unhappy with Regional.

    Tom has updated you on the status of the proposal. The communications office has insisted throughout the proposal process that the new phone system must be capable of using the existing quick-dial equipment. Tom tells you that if that is the case, only Regional and two or three other vendors would be able to bid on the system. Six other vendors with their own quick-dial equipment would not be able to respond to the bid. Tom explains that in some cases, a whole new system was less expensive than hooking up one of Regional's systems to existing quick-dial equipment. Tom also tells you he has heard that several staff members from the Communications Department have threatened to quit if the bid goes to a company other than

SOURCE: Case 2 was provided by Bill Carney.

FIGURE 5.4
City of Tempe: Water Utilities Department

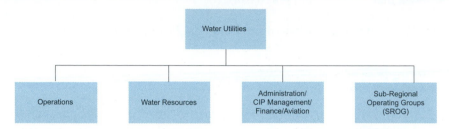

Department Purpose:
To provide the residents, businesses and visitors of Tempe with a reliable and economical supply of drinking water that meets or exceeds all federal, state and local standards of quality, and to protect the health, safety and overall environment of our community through wastewater and storm water management and the collection and disposal of household hazardous materials.

Department Description:
The Water Utilities Department is responsible for Operations, Water Resources, Administration, and SROG. The Operations Division is comprised of Plant Operations, Field Operations, Environmental Services, Environmental Health & Safety, and Security. Water Resources is responsible for the water conservation program, Tempe Town Lake, and hydrology services. The Administration Division includes Capital Improvement Program (CIP) management, Finance, and Aviation. The Sub-Regional Operating Groups (SROG) division is responsible for administration of the SROG program.

FY 2006-07 Budget Highlights:
Funding was approved for laboratory supplies and testing, compound meter replacement, sewer cleaning, and a rate study for water, sewer and irrigation. In addition, funding for two temporary intern positions was approved to address an increased workload at the Household Products Collection Center (HPCC).

Expenditure by Type	2004-05 Actual	2005-06 Budget	2005-06 Revised	2006-07 Budget
Personal Services	$ 9,878,309	$10,846,863	$10,805,993	$11,510,134
Supplies and Services	12,055,360	12,825,110	13,348,528	14,036,150
Capital Outlay	229,835	222,100	384,933	283,200
Internal Services	3,684,064	3,375,861	3,372,724	3,309,785
Contributions	1,000			
Expenditure Total	**$25,848,568**	**$27,269,934**	**$27,912,178**	**$29,139,269**
Per Capita	**$158.65**	**$165.91**	**$169.82**	**$175.75**

Expenditures by Division	2004-05 Actual	2005-06 Budget	2005-06 Revised	2006-07 Budget
Operations	$16,327,978	$17,574,531	$18,175,519	$19,079,336
Water Resources	607,459	1,073,629	892,387	1,052,672
Administration/CIP Management/Finance/Aviation	4,516,225	4,216,435	4,444,003	4,604,428
SROG	4,396,906	4,405,339	4,400,269	4,402,833
Total	**$25,848,568**	**$27,269,934**	**$27,912,178**	**$29,139,269**

	2004-05 Actual			2005-06 Revised			2006-07 Budget		
Authorized Personnel	Full Time	Perm FTE	Temp FTE	Full Time	Perm FTE	Temp FTE	Full Time	Perm FTE	Temp FTE
Operations	113	0.50		117	1.00		116	1.00	
Water Resources	4			4			4		
Admin./CIP Mgt./Finance/Aviation	12		0.49	11	0.50	0.49	12	0.50	0.49
SROG	1			1			1		
Total	**130**	**0.50**	**0.49**	**133**	**1.50**	**0.49**	**133**	**1.50**	**0.49**

(Continued)

FIGURE 5.4 *(Continued)*

Related Strategic issue: Neighborhood Quality of Life and Public Safety

Goal: To provide a safe and adequate domestic water supply to all citizens in Tempe, while at the same time minimizing cost

Objective: 1) To monitor increases in water treatment costs for the Johnny G. Martinez and South Tempe Water Treatment plants; and 2) maintain an Operating and Maintenance Cost per 1,000 gallons treated under eighty cents

Measures *(Comparative Benchmark)*	2004-05 Actual	2005-06 Budget	2005-06 Revised	2006-07 Budget
Total Water Treatment Operating and Maintenance Cost	$9,186,874	$10,995,858	$10,995,858	$10,849,927
Number of Customer Accounts	41,532	41,532	41,532	42,000
Total Gallons Treated (Million Gallons)	15,152	18,800	17,563	17,900
Operating and Maintenance Cost per 1,000 gallons treated	*$0.61*	*$0.59*	*$0.63*	*$0.61*
Operating and Maintenance Cost per customer account	$221.20	$264.76	$264.76	$258.33

Related Strategic issue: Neighborhood Quality of Life and Public Safety

Goal: To reduce operating and maintenance costs of the wastewater collection system

Objective: To achieve wastewater collection costs that are less than $10,000 per mile

Measures	2004-05 Actual	2005-06 Budget	2005-06 Revised	2006-07 Budget
Total Wastewater Collection Operating and Maintenance Cost	$3,153,522	$3,445,996	$3,445,996	$3,453,689
Miles of Mains in Collection System	500.0	502.2	502.2	502.2
Operating and Maintenance Cost per mile	$6,307	$6,862	$6,862	$6,877

Related Strategic issue: Neighborhood Quality of Life and Public Safety

Goal: To minimize the number of resident complaints related to water quality and respond to those complaints within twenty-four hours

Objective: To maintain low resident complaints and to respond within twenty-four hours

Measures	2004-05 Actual	2005-06 Budget	2005-06 Revised	2006-07 Budget
Taste and Odor Complaints	6	N/A	17	<17
Hardness Complaints	2	N/A	1	<1
Other Complaints	9	N/A	5	<5
Response within twenty-four hours of the complaint	100%	N/A	100%	100%

SOURCE: City of Tempe Annual Budget, July 1, 2006, through June 30, 2007, Performance Budget (pp. 194–195). Retrieved April 7, 2007, from www.tempe.gov/budget/FY%2006–07%20docs/5%20Performance%20Budget.pdf.

Regional. After fifteen years, they feel Regional is the best and only qualified vendor. Tom wants to know how he should proceed to satisfy both the university's needs and the vendors' rights to a fair bidding process.

a. How should Tom proceed to ensure that all bidders have an equal chance to participate in the bid process?

b. How can the procurement office avoid the practice of vendors helping buyers to write a bid proposal?

c. What about Tom's responsibility to taxpayers? (Thousands of dollars would be wasted if the quick-dial equipment that has already been purchased was scrapped.)

3. The following simulation reenacts a series of budget discussions held at the University of Southern Anonymous (USA) during a time of significant budget reductions. To conduct the simulation, divide the class into five groups, each of which will represent one character in the simulation. All students in the class should read the following general description of the situation facing USA. Then members of each group should read only the character description assigned to their group. (It is important that you read only the description assigned to you.) The role descriptions of the following characters can be found after the general description of the situation in the following pages:

Vice President Cooper
Dean Berryderry, College of Liberal Arts
Dean Stevens, dean of Science
Dean Dudley, dean of Education
Dean Dollar, dean of Business

After all participants have had a chance to read the general description of the situation and the specific information pertaining to their character, each character group should meet separately for fifteen to twenty minutes. During this period, the group should (1) select a representative to play the character at a meeting to be held in Vice President Cooper's office, and (2) develop detailed strategies and information for that person to use in representing the group's interests in the meeting.

Following the individual group meetings, the five individuals selected to play the five characters should meet around a table near the middle of the room. Vice President Cooper will call the meeting to order, present any opening remarks he or she wishes to make, and then preside over the remainder of the discussion. All other students should remain quiet during this part of the simulation. During the course of the meeting, any member may request a recess to consult with his or her group (for no longer than five minutes). When the meeting in Vice President Cooper's office reconvenes, the person who called the recess will have the floor. The meeting should continue until a consensus is reached concerning the reductions or until Vice President Cooper feels the meeting is stalled and he or she will have to make a decision independently. Enjoy the discussion!

General Description of the Situation

The University of Southern Anonymous (USA) has been informed by the state administration that its budget for the current year will be reduced by several million dollars. The president of the university, I. M. Fearless, has informed Vice President for Academic Affairs Cooper that the various colleges in the university will be required to reduce their budgets by an average of 8 percent. In turn, Vice President Cooper has chosen not to implement across-the-board cuts of 8 percent for all colleges, but has discussed different target percentage reductions with each of the deans of the four colleges—Liberal Arts, Science, Education, and Business. In response to a request from several of the deans, Vice President Cooper has called a meeting of the four deans to get their reactions to his targeted amounts for each college and to find out how each college plans to implement the required reduction.

USA is a medium-sized midwestern university whose mission is providing students with a broad-based liberal arts education as well as a limited graduate program, primarily in business and education. The school serves a regional constituency in the southern part of the state, though it draws students from around the country, many of whom first heard of USA because of its reputation as a leader in intercollegiate billiards. (In fact, some cynics refer to USA as "Cue U.")

Though the university has traditionally enjoyed a good relationship with the governor and members of the legislature, President Fearless has antagonized many in the state capital with his rough and abrasive manner. Many on campus see the president as bringing the university the same administrative style he employed as a colonel in the Marine Corps. Despite these difficulties, most academic programs at the university are considered sound, with some exceptions. Similarly, many feel some programs are not suited to the mission of a regional midwestern university, notably the school's long-standing program in oceanography, which some feel is out of place because the university is seven hundred miles from the nearest ocean.

Character Descriptions

Vice President Cooper In your five years as vice president at USA, you have never faced such a difficult situation. You recognize that the university's president is in some political trouble and may be asked to resign soon. As a ploy to reduce the heat on his office, he has passed on the largest part of the budgetary reductions to you. If you can come through this situation in good shape, you will receive considerable praise and be a likely candidate for the presidency should the president be forced to resign. You will, however, need to be sure that you maintain the support of all the deans of the colleges, because their support is essential for your promotion. On the other hand, a major disruption at the university, in which you might lose support of the deans, would end any chances of your attaining your ambition. In fact, you might be fired along with the president!

Given the instructions from the president, there seems to be little you can do other than assign reductions to the colleges. After reviewing the various programs within the colleges, however, you have decided that across-the-board cuts would be inappropriate and that some colleges could indeed stand to be cut more than others. You have, therefore, assigned different reductions to each college, with Education receiving the greatest reduction (20 percent), Liberal Arts receiving the second greatest reduction (10 percent), Science next (7 percent), and Business last (2 percent). You have chosen these figures based on your assessment of the quality of programs, the quantity of students (faculty/student ratios), the nature of the programs, and their suitability to the mission of your university.

The total reductions you have assigned to the deans exceed the total the president has required you to complete. Your reasons for this strategy are twofold: (1) if any of the deans complain too loudly, you can fall back to the figure you actually need as a compromise; and (2) if you persuade all the deans to accept the assigned reduction, then you will have some money available for internal reallocations, which you would like to achieve anyway.

For the most part, you are willing to let the various deans assign reductions within their colleges as they see fit, as long as each seems to be doing a thorough job in the assignment. Later, if there is money available, you can make other reallocations to add needed new programs or strengthen others.

However, you are personally interested in a couple of particular areas. First, your favorite uncle chairs the oceanography program. Second, your own degree is in higher education administration, and you have enjoyed periodic classroom visits to that department. Third, the governor has expressed a strong interest in the integrity of the public administration program.

Dean Berryderry   College of Liberal Arts (target reduction—10 percent). You approach the meeting with the vice president with some trepidation, because you realize that your college is likely to be high on the list of cuts. You would prefer across-the-board cuts that would not place a special burden on your college. Several of your programs, however, are of minimal quality and simply have not been attracting students over the years. For example, your program in German has graduated an average of two majors per year over the past several years, with a faculty of only three. Several other programs, such as anthropology and geography, are showing similar results. These programs, however, are important to a broad-based liberal arts education. You feel that students should at least have the opportunity to enroll in such programs if they see fit.

On the other hand, there are some programs currently housed in your college you would just as soon see ended. For example, the graduate program in public administration is a professional program that you feel is inconsistent with the liberal arts perspective of the college. The total faculty salaries in this department would just about equal the total by which you need to reduce your budget. This is an obvious area to eliminate.

Next, it has occurred to you that your staff of professional advisers could be eliminated and all academic advising performed by members of your faculty. This could be accomplished with no faculty or program reductions.

You feel a natural alliance with the College of Science and would prefer to see reductions occur in either Education or Business rather than in Liberal Arts or Science. However, Dean Stevens of the College of Science has always been somewhat antagonistic toward you, perhaps because of your critical remarks about the oceanography program, which you think should be eliminated.

Finally, several personal considerations enter into your thinking. First, if the vice president were to become president, you would probably be the leading candidate for the vice presidency. You find that very attractive. Second, although you don't want to appear to favor any department, your home department, the Department of Political Science, is putting strong pressure on you to support expansion of the program. Across-the-board cuts *within* your college would make that impossible. Third, a member of your faculty was recently offended by sexual advances from the dean of the School of Business, Dean Dollar.

Dean Stevens   Dean of the College of Science (target reduction—7 percent). You have conducted a thorough analysis of the possibilities for reduction within your college. You feel that by eliminating one visiting professorship, four graduate teaching assistantship positions, and two staff positions, you'll be able to accommodate the reductions. You are quite aware, however, that others see your Department of Oceanography as a primary target for elimination. This is, however, one of your oldest and strongest programs, certainly one of the leading oceanography programs in the Midwest. You want to protect the program as it is; however, even if you are required to reduce that program, you wish to do so only by eliminating several faculty positions rather than the entire department. You also feel this program will be protected because the chair of that department is the vice president's uncle.

Several other personal considerations affect your thinking. First, you feel that the entire College of Education could be eliminated with no real loss to the university. Other programs within the state clearly produce enough graduates in that field. Eliminating the entire college would mean that no reductions would be needed in any other college. Second, you think Dean Berryderry is an idiot. You were especially incensed by Berryderry's comments about oceanography. If Berryderry can't run his own college, why should he try to run yours? Third, one of your faculty members recently was offended by sexual advances from the dean of the School of Business, Dean Dollar.

Dean Dudley Dean of the College of Education (target reduction—20 percent). You know you are in trouble! Over the past several years, enrollments have been dropping in Education to the point that you are considerably overstaffed. At the same time, other programs in the state have developed and now have better reputations. This is especially true for your Department of Higher Education Administration. Another campus in the state boasts one of the country's leading programs in this area. Your best hope is to argue for across-the-board cuts that would affect all colleges equally. Your suspicion is that the College of Business will receive the lowest reduction, and the College of Liberal Arts and the College of Science will be somewhere above. One of them would probably benefit from across-the-board cuts as opposed to targeted reductions; the other would probably lose—but you don't know which one.

In addition, several personal considerations guide your thinking. First, nearly all the athletes who are part of the school's winning billiards program are students in your college. You doubt if they could pass their coursework elsewhere. Second, the chair of the Department of Higher Education Administration has been one of your strongest critics over the years, and eliminating that department would eliminate one of your biggest problems. Third, a member of your faculty was recently offended by sexual advances from the dean of the School of Business, Dean Dollar.

Dean Dollar Dean of the School of Business (target reduction—2 percent). Though you realize that your college will have to take a token reduction, you are certain that your reduction is far less than that required from other schools. Consequently, you are highly supportive of the vice president's selective reduction and opposed to across-the-board cuts. Your college has grown by leaps and bounds in the past several years, and you are in desperate need of more faculty, not fewer. At the same time, salaries have increased dramatically in your field, and retention of capable faculty is a problem. You can probably accommodate the reductions assigned to you through minimal staff changes and will not have to fire faculty.

You see all this as a possibility for considerable reorganization of programs. One program that you would particularly be interested in bringing into the college is that in public administration. This program is viewed with great favor by the governor and, consequently, by those higher in the university's administration. Moreover, the program would seem to be consistent with the interest of your college in management. You wonder if perhaps somewhere in all of this redistribution of money you might be able to acquire a new program. If you can discredit Dean Berryderry's interest in public administration and champion that field, you should stand a good chance of receiving support from the higher administration. All in all, you see this process as opening the possibility of adding to your college rather than reducing it. This result, however, depends on selective reductions rather than across-the-board cuts and upon reallocations *beyond* the amount required for the president's stated budget reduction.

You also have several personal concerns. First, you think both the College of Education and the Department of Oceanography (in the College of Science) could be eliminated outright and you could use the money. Second, you have heard that the chair of the Department of Oceanography is the vice president's cousin. Third, you have just met a very attractive person who is an adviser in the College of Liberal Arts. You think you are falling in love—again!

Do Not Read This Paragraph until after the Simulation.

Following the simulation, the entire class should discuss each group's strategies and tactics. Sometimes it is helpful to ask first what others thought each dean was trying to do and then ask that group to describe its strategy. Pay particular attention to strategies of cooperation and competition, as well as to strategies that have little to do with actual budget reductions. (For example, shifting a program from one location to another doesn't save the university any money.) Note also the inevitable lack of information, as well as the roles of rumor and false impressions in the budget process. (Both these features are more typical of budget decisions than you might think!) Finally, just for fun, have Dean Berryderry read the last line of his or her description, then have Dean Stevens do the same, then Dean Dudley, and then Dean Dollar.

FOR ADDITIONAL READING

Briffault, Richard. *Balancing Acts.* Washington, DC: Brookings Institution Press, 1996.

Clynch, Edward J., and Thomas P. Lauth, eds. *Governors, Legislatures, and Budgets: Diversity across the American States.* Westport, CT: Greenwood Press, 1991.

Ellig, Jerry, Maurice McTigue, and Henry Wray. *Government Performance and Results.* Boca Raton, FL: CRC Press, 2011.

Frank, Howard A. *Forecasting in Local Government: New Tools and Techniques.* New York: Quorum Books, 1993.

Garner, C. William. *Accounting and Budgeting in Public and Non-Profit Organizations: A Manager's Guide.* San Francisco: Jossey-Bass, 1991.

Gosling, James J. *Budgeting Politics in American Governments.* White Plains, NY: Longman Publishing Group, 1992.

Gross, Malvern, and Richard Larkin, eds. *Financial and Accounting Guide for Non-Profit Organizations*. New York: John Wiley & Sons, 1999.

Guess, George M., and Lance T. LeLoup. *Comparative Public Budgeting: Global Perspectives on Taxing and Spending*. Albany: State University of New York Press, 2010.

Jones, Vernon Dale. *Downsizing the Federal Government*. Armonk, NY: M.E. Sharpe, 1997.

Joyce, Philip G. *The Congressional Budget Office: Honest Numbers, Power, and Policymaking*. Washington, DC: Georgetown University Press, 2011.

Kettl, Donald F., and John Dilulio, Jr. *Cutting Government*. Washington, DC: Brookings Institution Press, 1995.

Lee, Robert D., Ronald Wayne Johnson, and Philip G. Joyce. *Public Budgeting Systems*. 8th ed. Sudbury, MA: Jones and Bartlett Publishers, 2008.

Light, Paul. *Thickening Government*. Washington, DC: Brookings Institution Press, 1995.

Maddox, David. *Budgeting for Not-for-Profit Organizations*. New York: John Wiley & Sons, 1999.

Mikesell, John L. *Fiscal Administration*. 2nd ed. Pacific Grove, CA: Brooks/Cole, 1986.

Miller, Gerald J. *Government Budgeting and Financial Management in Practice*. Boca Raton, FL: CRC Press, 2011.

Miller, Gerald J. *Government Financial Management Theory*. New York: Marcel Dekker, 1991.

Reed, B. J., and John Swain. *Public Finance Administration*. Englewood Cliffs, NJ: Prentice-Hall, 1990.

Reischauer, Robert D. *Setting National Priorities*. Washington, DC: Brookings Institution Press, 1997.

Rubin, Irene S. *The Politics of Public Budgeting*. Chatham, NJ: Chatham House, 1990.

Schick, Allen. *The Federal Budget*. Washington, DC: Brookings Institution Press, 1995.

Scott, David, John D. Martin, and Arthur J. Keown. *Basic Financial Management*. Upper Saddle River, NJ: Prentice-Hall, 1999.

Swain, John W., and B. J. Reed. *Budgeting for Public Managers*. Armonk, NY: M.E. Sharpe, 2010.

Wildavsky, Aaron B., and Naomi Caiden. *The New Politics of the Budgetary Process* (Longman Classics in Political Science). 5th ed. New York: Pearson/Longman, 2004.

THE MANAGEMENT OF HUMAN RESOURCES

Nothing is more critical for an administrator than to effectively manage the people who work in his or her organization. Yet, the hiring and treatment of public employees often seem so bound up in rules, regulations, and "red tape" that effective management is extremely difficult. Many managers feel that civil service systems (and central personnel offices), originally designed to attract and retain competent personnel, exist merely to complicate the manager's life and make it more difficult to manage. Instead of simply hiring someone for a job, the manager must advise an applicant to take a competitive examination and join many other candidates on a register for the position (some of whom may be given special preferences in the hiring process) and then to wait until all the paperwork clears. After someone has been hired, the manager finds there are limits to the "rewards and punishments" that can be offered to encourage improved job performance. And, should the person fail to perform adequately, the paperwork and justifications required to terminate his or her employment seem endless. You may wonder how anything else gets done!

But there are good reasons for the way human resources or personnel management in government has developed. Even though it is true that some civil service systems have become overly rigid, even "fossilized," most of the requirements relating to government employment are deeply rooted in important political and ethical principles. An understanding of how government personnel systems operate includes a knowledge of personnel techniques and a sensitivity to the values that underlie human resources management in public organizations.

Nowhere is the contest between the competing values of efficiency and responsiveness played out more clearly than in the area of human resources or personnel. On the one hand, staffing government agencies with the most competent people available is essential to effective management. On the other hand, those who staff the offices of government should be responsive to the citizenry. In any case, the human resources or personnel system for any public organization ultimately reflects the political priorities of the particular public involved. In certain cases or at certain times, managerial concern for efficiency may receive preference; in others, the democratic concern for responsiveness may be paramount.

Networking

For general information on personnel issues, see the International Personnel Management Association at www.ipma-hr.org. For jobs and recruiting, see http://www.publicservicecareers.org/, www.fedworld.gov, www.careersingovernment.com, and www.govtjob.net.

Griggs v Duke Power Co

Merit Systems in Public Employment

Because the Constitution made little mention of either administrative structures or how they would be staffed, early leaders at all levels of government experimented with many different approaches to hiring, working with, and firing personnel. In the late 1800s, however, growing concern about the composition of the civil service led to a new focus on competence and professionalism and, in turn, to legislation establishing the merit principle in public employment. The *merit principle*, though widely varied in its application, generally means that selection and treatment of government employees should be based on merit or competence rather than on personal or political favoritism. Despite the apparent simplicity and appeal of this notion, the development of public personnel systems has been infused with controversy.

Spoils versus Merit

Most of the early American presidents followed George Washington's lead in seeking people of high competence and integrity—what he called "fitness of character"—to hold governmental positions. This approach resulted in a stable and fairly skilled government workforce, but not without several problems. Because there were few well-educated people in society and because those with education tended to be from the wealthier classes, the newly formed civil service soon took on a somewhat elitist character. Moreover, partisan considerations began to enter into the process. Presidents and members of Congress began to recognize not only that government employees needed to be loyal to the new government (and presumably the party in power), but also that public offices (and salaries) could be rewards to the party faithful. Finally, there was the question of tenure: should civil servants hold office for life, thus providing experience and continuity, or should they change with each administration, providing loyalty (and jobs) to the incoming party?

All these concerns were dramatically illustrated in the administration of Andrew Jackson. Jackson was swept into office on a strong wave of democratic sentiment and was especially concerned with making government more accessible to those previously excluded: the "common people." Though Jackson was not the first to employ the *spoils system* (the notion that "to the victor belong the spoils"—in this case, the ability to give government jobs to the party faithful), his administration was notable for its expansion of the system and for its elaborate justification of it. Jackson argued that the common people had as much right to government jobs as the wealthy and that most government jobs could be done without special training.

Jackson is sometimes portrayed as something of a villain for his defense of the spoils system, though far greater abuses occurred later at all levels of government. At the same time, however, Jackson made several positive contributions to democratic government; for example, there is no question that he democratized the civil service of his era and set a tone for greater representativeness within government agencies for decades to come.

Even Jackson could not have foreseen the corruption and abuse that would soon become associated with the spoils system (see the box "Public Administration in

History: The Spoils System"). Succeeding presidents went far beyond Jackson in applying the system, as did political bosses at the state and local levels. The quality of the civil service rapidly declined, and even those who found jobs in government became disenchanted with the financial contributions exacted from them each election year. The system also became a problem for each new president, as thousands of office-seekers came to press their claims for patronage positions, and presidents soon grew weary of the long lines of people seeking jobs.

Public Administration in History

THE SPOILS SYSTEM

By the late 1800s, the spoils system was firmly a part of political life in most jurisdictions. One aspect of the system was collecting funds from appointees to help sustain the party in power. Although such practices persisted in some jurisdictions well into the 1950s and even the 1960s, they were hardly as blatant as the tribute requested in the letter from a state party committee in 1870.

> Dear Sir:
>
> (We) have great and imperative need of funds at once, to carry the campaign to successful issue. An assessment of one percent on the annual gross receipts of your office is therefore called for, and you will please enclose that amount, without delay, to the treasurer, E. S. Rowse, in the envelope enclosed. This assessment is made after conference with our friends at Washington, where it is confidently expected that those who receive the benefits of Federal appointments will support the machinery that sustains the party which gives them pecuniary benefit and honor. The exigencies are great, and delay or neglect will rightly be construed into unfriendliness to the Administration. We do not look for such a record from you, and you will at once see the propriety and wisdom of the earliest attention to the matter.
>
> Isaac Sheppard
>
> Chairman of Committee

SOURCE: Reprinted with the permission of Simon & Schuster Adult Publishing Group, from *The Republican Era: 1869–1901, A Study in Administrative History* by Leonard D. White. © 1958 by the Macmillan Company. All rights reserved.

These factors set the stage for reform, but even more important in eventually bringing about change was the increasing corruption in government. There were kickbacks from contractors, private sales of surplus public property, skimming of tax receipts, and many other abuses. Corruption was becoming a normal way of doing government business.

The various ills that grew from the spoils system eventually led to a strong and active reform movement, spearheaded by such groups as the National Civil Service Reform League. The reformers made vigorous and eloquent appeals, but their eventual success was ensured more by a historical accident—the assassination of President Garfield—than by eloquence. Though Garfield had hardly been a proponent of civil service reform and had drawn criticism from reform groups for his failure to support a reform bill, the fact that he was killed by a disappointed office-seeker made him a martyr for the reform cause.

A man named Charles Guiteau had hoped to be consul to Paris. After weeks of making his case and after repeatedly being turned away from Garfield's office, he followed Garfield into a train station and shot him twice in the back. As he did so, he shouted that now Chester Arthur, a noted spoilsman, would be president. The reformers capitalized on this comment, portraying the situation as the obvious result of the evil spoils system. In a sudden change of heart (and reality), they described Garfield as a proponent of reform. After two more years of pressure, the Republican Congress finally acknowledged the rising sentiment for reform and passed the Pendleton Act, which was signed into law in January 1883.

The Pendleton Act is one of two landmark pieces of legislation in federal personnel administration (the other being the Civil Service Reform Act of 1978). The Pendleton Act was primarily an effort to eliminate political influence from administrative agencies and, secondarily, an effort to ensure more competent government employees. It pursued these aims through the following major provisions:

1. A bipartisan commission, the U.S. Civil Service Commission, was created within the executive branch to establish and implement personnel rules and procedures for the federal government.
2. Open and competitive examinations to test job-related skills were developed wherever practical within the agencies covered by the law and were to become the primary basis upon which to make hiring decisions.
3. Employees were given protection against political pressures, such as assessments (mandatory contributions) or "required" participation in campaign activities.
4. *Lateral entry* into government positions (that is, entry at any level as opposed to only the beginning level) was encouraged, thus maintaining an important element of Jacksonian openness.
5. Positions in Washington offices were to be apportioned among the various states, in an effort to provide geographical representation in the civil service.
6. The president was given authority to extend coverage to other groups of government employees beyond the approximately 10 percent of federal employees covered by the act.

These provisions, especially the last, provided the basis for the gradual extension of the idea of a merit system throughout most of the federal government as well as state and local governments (see the box "Exploring Concepts: Principles of Civil Service"). The concept of merit is so central to the American approach to public personnel administration that "merit system" and "civil service system" have become almost synonymous.

Exploring Concepts

PRINCIPLES OF CIVIL SERVICE

1. The selection of subordinate government officials should be based on merit…rather than…political favoritism;
2. that since jobs are to be filled by weighing the merits of applicants, those hired should have tenure regardless of political changes at the top of organizations;
3. that the price of job security should be a willing responsiveness to the legitimate political leaders of the day.

SOURCE: Hugh Heclo, *A Government of Strangers* (Washington, DC: Brookings Institution, 1977), p. 20.

The Pendleton Act, although important in establishing the notion of a merit system of public employment, merely provided a framework within which a more full-blown system might develop. Unfortunately, development of the system was not well coordinated. Although the merit system was gradually extended to more and more government employees, its values were not always the primary motivation for extension. For example, one unlikely set of agents for the extension of personnel reforms turned out to be outgoing presidents. Many of them sought to "blanket in" those they had appointed to patronage positions by making the positions subject to the merit system. In this way, merit coverage was extended from its original 10 percent of all federal employees in 1883 to approximately 70 percent by the end of World War I and some 90 percent today.

Other changes in the system also occurred slowly. The Pendleton Act contained provisions for examinations, but other devices for improving the quality of the workforce, such as position classification, standard pay schedules, and objective performance appraisals, had not yet been developed. Over the next decades, these ideas too became a part of the federal system of civil service. The Classification Act of 1923, for example, established a system for classifying jobs according to the qualifications needed to carry them out and tying them to various pay grades, thus providing uniformity throughout the system.

Changes were also required to respond to a newly professionalized workforce and a larger and more activist government. In the early days, the main jobs in government were essentially clerkships, but as government grew and entered new fields, there was a need for more professional and more highly specialized people. Similarly, especially through the Roosevelt years, a multitude of new agencies were created, each placing different demands on the personnel system. Prior to this time, the Civil Service Commission had assumed the role of the government's central personnel agency; now it was necessary to decentralize personnel responsibilities to the various agencies, with the commission setting regulations and monitoring implementation.

The merit system has now become firmly established at the federal level. Nine out of ten federal employees are covered by either the general merit system or by one of several special systems created by law to pursue merit principles within specific agencies: the Postal

Service, the Federal Bureau of Investigation, the Foreign Service, and so on. The remaining positions are exempt because they are not amenable to competitive selection or to regular personnel procedures; they include seasonal workers, those in intelligence, and a limited number of policy-making and confidential positions. Any incoming president now has over 2,500 positions to fill on a purely political basis—a number that has actually risen substantially in the last fifteen years. Questions about the background and preparation of political appointees were raised with the resignation of Michael Brown, a former commissioner of the Arabian Horse Association, as director of the Federal Emergency Management Agency (FEMA) after Hurricane Katrina. In addition, both the head of the recovery division and the FEMA chief-of-staff were political appointees, whose counterparts in the Clinton administration were career officials with decades of experience.

Many questions have been raised in recent years about whether there are too many political appointees in the federal government or, in other words, whether the federal bureaucracy has become too highly politicized. Others, however, argue that political appointees help in controlling the bureaucracy. In any case, this argument has intensified as the growth in numbers of political appointees has been accompanied by increasing centralization of the appointment process in the White House. At present, nearly all the political appointments that occur at the federal level—executives, members of boards and commissions, ambassadorships, and judgeships—are cleared through the White House personnel office.

The Civil Service Reform Act and Its Aftermath

For nearly one hundred years, the Pendleton Act provided the primary statutory basis for federal civil service. That changed with the passage and implementation of the Civil Service Reform Act of 1978. During the 1960s and 1970s, it became increasingly clear that there were serious problems in the federal personnel management system. The problems were in large part a result of the fairly haphazard pattern through which the system had been established. Responsibilities for personnel management were spread among the president, Congress, the courts, the Civil Service Commission, and various agencies; but there was often not agreement on the basic principles that should guide the development of the system.

Even within the Civil Service Commission itself, there was confusion about the direction of personnel policy. On the one hand, the commission existed to execute the president's personnel directives; on the other hand, it was also responsible for protecting employees from political abuse. At times, the two objectives came into conflict. As a result, the numbers of rules and regulations were not only excessive, but they often directly conflicted with one another.

President Carter made reform of the personnel system one of the central themes of his administration and targeted at least five problem areas:

1. *Technical overkill.* Critics charged that those in charge of the personnel function had, in their drive to achieve political neutrality, created overly detailed regulations for recruiting, testing, selecting, classifying, and releasing employees. In many cases, these technical rules became a maze that prevented rather than aided action, and sorting through the procedures to replace a key manager could take as long as two years.

2. *Excessive protection of employees.* Similarly, many felt that the drive to achieve political neutrality created excessive protections for employees. Although these protections were initiated for the best of reasons—so that employees would not be unduly or arbitrarily punished or dismissed—they sometimes resulted in incredible outcomes, such as an award of almost $5,000 in back pay to a postal employee who had been fired for shooting a coworker in the stomach! On the other hand, protections were needed in other areas. For example, employees who pointed out cases of waste, fraud, and abuse in public agencies—"whistle-blowers"—were often subjected to harassment or even dismissal.

3. *Lack of management flexibility.* Managers, especially political appointees, claimed that civil service regulations were so inflexible that they could not manage effectively. In an effort to counter this tendency, one official in the Nixon administration prepared a document, known as the Malek Manual, suggesting 130 ways that managers could subvert the intent of the merit system and do what they wanted to do. One entry described how to get rid of someone who doesn't enjoy traveling: "[He] is given extensive travel orders crisscrossing the country to towns (hopefully with the worst accommodations possible) of a population of 20,000 or under. Until his wife threatens him with divorce, unless he quits, you have him out of town and out of the way. When he finally asks for relief you tearfully reiterate the importance of the project and state that he must continue to obey travel orders or resign."

4. *Inadequate incentives to eliminate inefficiencies.* It was also charged that a system that seemed to grant raises according to longevity rather than performance and that made raises and promotion appear almost automatic encouraged inefficiency. Over 99 percent of the nearly 3 million federal employees regularly received satisfactory performance ratings that entitled them to raises. Alan Campbell, a leading advocate of reform, wrote: "The current system provides few incentives for managers to manage or for employees to perform."

5. *Discrimination.* Many—notably women and minorities—felt the federal personnel system was not adequately promoting their representation within the bureaucratic ranks. They wanted to make sure that any new system would be more attentive to their interests and better able to cope with the increasing number of complaints in this area.

The Civil Service Reform Act was proposed to "restore the merit principle to a system which has grown into a bureaucratic maze" (Carter, 1978). The act sought to deal with the often contradictory roles of the Civil Service Commission by creating a new Office of Personnel Management (OPM) responsible for policy leadership and a Merit Systems Protection Board to handle investigations and appeals. OPM is "the President's principal agent for managing the federal workforce"; it has responsibility for human resource management and enforcement of personnel regulations (Campbell, 1978, p. 100). The Merit Systems Protection Board, on the other hand, is the "watchdog" of the personnel system, hearing and resolving complaints, as well as protecting whistle-blowers from reprisals. The previously conflicting responsibilities of the Civil Service Commission were split between the two new agencies.

Beyond establishing the two new agencies, perhaps the most striking feature of the Civil Service Reform Act was the creation of the Senior Executive Service (SES). Following ideas that had been discussed for nearly forty years and specifically proposed but not adopted in the Nixon years, the SES created a separate personnel system for the highest-ranking civil service officials, permitting greater flexibility in assignments and establishing a new system of incentives for top-level managers. Basically, eligible managers would apply for positions in the SES and, if accepted, would hold SES rank as individuals, rather than being limited to the rank of a particular position. This meant that, within certain limitations, SES managers could be moved from agency to agency depending on their talents and the needs of the agencies. A new system of performance evaluations and pay increases closely tied to performance was also developed, along with an elaborate system of bonuses for exceptional executives. A 1991 "deal" involving pay plans and performance measures required SES members to be "recertified" every three years.

In addition to these major features, the Civil Service Reform Act made several other changes: giving agencies greater flexibility to administer their own personnel systems, establishing a new and more sophisticated performance appraisal system, creating a merit pay system for managers just below the SES range, providing protection for whistle-blowers, assigning the federal Equal Employment Opportunity program (previously with the Civil Service Commission) to the Equal Employment Opportunity Commission, and creating a more independent Federal Labor Relations Authority.

After more than three decades, the Civil Service Reform Act is still receiving mixed reviews. The most favorable opinion is that there is little wrong with the act itself, but that implementation has been flawed by lack of funding and administration pressures to increase the number of political appointees. Others suggest the act was based on questionable assumptions about the nature of the federal workforce and was doomed from the beginning. In any case, the Civil Service Reform Act represented the first major change in personnel policy at the federal level since the Pendleton Act. Its confirmation of the principle of merit, its effort to sort out the multiple responsibilities of the personnel system, and its attempt to produce greater managerial flexibility have been significant.

Networking

The Office of Personnel Management is located at www.opm.gov.

Reinvention and the National Performance Review

During the 1990s, Vice President Gore's National Performance Review (NPR), and the "Reinventing Government" movement generally, had a dramatic impact on personnel systems within the federal government. The goal of NPR was to enhance government productivity by streamlining processes, increasing accountability, and decentralizing authority to encourage entrepreneurial behavior. Decentralization and the focus on results instituted a fundamental change in the way government agencies, and thus personnel systems, work. Public employees are now held accountable for customer service and productivity and are rewarded based on their agency's efficiency and performance. While the NPR has given way to other reforms, and other administrations, its impact on the culture of the federal government has been substantial.

The Bush administration had its own approach to administrative reform in the federal government. In August 2001, President George W. Bush introduced the President's Management Agenda (PMA), which focused on management and performance measurements. Among the five areas of improvement, human capital development was the first to be emphasized. As an MBA business-oriented administrator, President Bush saw the need for competent and competitive personnel as a key to effectively delivering government services to citizens (Breul, 2007). Agencies were given the flexibility to "use their performance management and awards programs to develop results-based elements and standards, to align employee performance plans with organizational goals and objectives, and to design recognition and incentive programs that reward employees for accomplishing those goals and objectives to develop a strong performance culture within their organizations" (Office of Personnel Management [OPM], n.d., p. 35). While Bush continued the practice of giving chief operating officers the responsibility for day-to-day operations, he strengthened the requirements for performance-oriented management, focusing primarily on the results achieved by each individual department and agency (Breul, 2007, p. 22).

In 2002, the OPM established the Human Capital Assessment and Accountability Framework (HCAAF). According to the HCAAF, each agency had to "maintain a current human capital plan and submit to OPM an annual human capital accountability report" (Office of Personnel Management, Human Capital Assessment and Accountability Framework, n.d.). Human capital management in every organization was followed by the level of achieving certain merit standards in five key human capital areas: (1) strategic alignment (planning and goal setting), (2) leadership and knowledge management (implementation), (3) results-oriented performance culture (implementation), (4) talent management (implementation), and (5) accountability (evaluating results).

One of the six themes of President Obama's plan for building a high-performance government was "transforming the federal workforce" (OMB, 2009, p. 10). Noting that nearly half the federal workforce was projected to retire in the coming decade, the Obama administration described it as an opportunity to "reform and re-energize" the federal workforce and transform its capacity to address the challenges of the twenty-first century by implementing new systems and processes to "acquire, develop, engage, compensate, recognize, and effectively retain talented employees" (OMB, 2009, p. 10).

Under the leadership of the OPM, the federal hiring process would be reformed. Agencies would develop strategic workforce plans; post brief, clear job announcements in plain language; provide timely notification to applicants about the status of applications; measure the average length of the hiring process; and evaluate the effectiveness of hiring efforts and reforms. President Obama's plan also called for greater investments in the existing workforce, allowing workers to build skills and expertise. Agencies would increase and improve training and implement measures to evaluate training effectiveness; increase the rotation of managers within and between agencies to help individuals build a wide range of experience and skills; and put in place a "healthy leadership pipeline" by identifying potential successors for mission-critical positions well before incumbents retire. Methods of evaluating employee performance also would be improved; agencies would implement processes for rewarding success and "smart risk-taking" for both individuals and teams; and incentives would be created to retain talented workers.

In 2010 OPM was specifically charged with five high-priority performance goals that are measurable commitments to deliver specific results. The first is to reform federal recruiting, hiring, and retention policies and procedures, a multiyear process to streamline and improve the hiring process. The second is to increase the strategic use of telework to improve continuity of operations, reduce management costs, and increase employee job satisfaction. The third is to maintain or exceed OPM-related goals of the Intelligence Reform and Terrorism Prevention Act (IRTPA) of 2004 and provide deliverables necessary to ensure that security clearance reforms are substantially operational across the federal government. The fourth is to ensure that every agency establishes and begins to implement a plan for a comprehensive health and wellness program that would achieve a 75 percent participation rate over five years. Finally, OPM was charged with increasing the number of retirement records it receives that are complete and require no development actions to 81 percent by the end of 2012.

State and Local Personnel Systems

Many of the same problems that led to institution of the federal civil service system in the late 1800s also existed at the state and local levels—indeed, the problems were often more severe. Although the federal government was certainly influenced by politicians interested in maintaining power through patronage, it was never so completely dominated by political bosses and machines as were the states and, especially, the cities.

Even after the federal government created its civil service system, states and localities were slow to follow. New York adopted the first state civil service law in 1883, followed by Massachusetts in 1884. It was twenty years, however, before another state joined these two. By 1935, only twenty states had adopted merit systems. Today nearly all states have relatively sophisticated civil service merit systems, although those systems don't cover everyone. Even now, only about 60 percent of state government employees are covered by merit systems.

The story is much the same at the local level: Albany, New York, was the first city to adopt a civil service system (1884), and a few other cities and counties followed prior to the turn of the century, but reform came slowly at the local level. Moreover, even where formal systems were adopted, patronage practices and political manipulation of the government workforce continued. Chicago and Cook County were among the first to adopt civil service systems. Yet, even today, mayoral candidates often run on a platform of reducing machine control in Chicago. Today almost 90 percent of local jurisdictions with populations of over 50,000 have some type of merit system on the books.

What Would You Do?

A department director that reports to you has had six sexual harassment claims filed against him over the last four years. All six have been investigated but dismissed. What would you do?

Over the years, a primary motivator for adopting merit systems at state and local levels has been the number of federal laws requiring such systems in order for states and localities to receive federal funds. By 1980, every state and thousands of local governments had federal grants that required personnel systems that met a set of federal standards. The result has been that most state agencies receiving large amounts of federal funding are now covered by merit systems; those that receive limited or no federal funds are much less likely to have a merit system. In addition to these requirements, the courts have extended due process protections to many public employees and have supported affirmative action and other personnel-related actions that place greater burdens on state and local governments for detailed testing, classification, and reporting. Many states have thus found it advisable to establish or to extend merit concepts for their own protection.

Though these regulations have been somewhat relaxed in recent years, it seems unlikely that state and local governments will return to massive use of the spoils system. Indeed, there is some evidence that governments are pursuing many of the same reforms pursued at the federal level in the late 1970s, which some charge have led to greater politicization of the public workforce. For example, states and localities are experimenting with decentralization of personnel functions, greater responsiveness of managerial and political authority, and closer ties between performance appraisals and merit pay. It remains to be seen whether elected officials at state and local levels will be subject to the same temptation as were those at the federal level to employ the new devices in a more politicized approach to public personnel.

Hiring, Firing, and Things in Between

Most provisions of public personnel systems exist to protect public employees from excessive political interference; however, in some cases, they appear to make public personnel actions unduly complicated. Knowing the "rules of the game" will be a considerable help in your administrative work and if you are looking for a job in a government agency.

Classification Systems

The key to most public personnel systems is the notion of *position classification:* the arrangement of jobs on the basis of duties and responsibilities and the skills required to perform them. A position classification system usually begins with a set of job descriptions, each based on a thorough analysis of the work and the required capabilities. A *job description* typically contains the following elements: job title, duties required, responsibilities associated with the position, and qualifications needed to carry out the job. A clerk-typist position, for example, might be described as including duties such as typing reports, maintaining correspondence records, answering telephone and walk-in inquiries, arranging for meetings and conferences on behalf of the supervisor, and other duties "as assigned." Qualifications might include a high school diploma or the equivalent, typing speed of forty words per minute, and two years of clerical experience.

Typically, sets of jobs that are closely related are then grouped together in classes that indicate increasing levels of difficulty—Clerk-Typist I, Clerk-Typist II, Clerk-Typist III, and so on. In larger jurisdictions, such as the federal government, classes may also be grouped into grade schedules that group jobs of varying levels of difficulty. For example, the federal General Schedule, which covers clerical and professional positions, lists a variety of different occupations under the grade GS-11.

Organizations use personnel classification systems for several reasons: to maintain an objective inventory of positions, to provide equity across similar jobs, to connect tasks and the skills required to perform them, and to provide standards for judging the work of specific employees. Historically, such systems developed out of a concern for objectivity and equity consistent with the idea of protecting employees from political abuse. The Position Classification Act of 1923, for example, required grouping jobs into classes on the basis of duties and responsibilities and, in language sounding much more contemporary, committed the federal government to providing "equal compensation for equal work, irrespective of sex." With this early impetus, most public organizations have developed rather sophisticated classification systems that are usually more advanced than their private-sector counterparts.

Although most people agree that the objective of current classification systems—equal pay for substantially equal work—is basically sound, many have argued that classification systems have become burdensome, inflexible, and unfair. Specifically, many argue that the complexity of the system creates excessive requirements that interfere with agency performance. The National Academy of Public Administration (NAPA) developed an alternative classification scheme that groups hundreds of federal job categories into occupational "families" based on similarities in career progression, basic skills, recruitment training, and performance measurement. Families might include such areas as general support, office services, technical, engineering, health, or law enforcement. NAPA has also recommended the adoption of broadbanding for pay classification. (In broadbanding, the upper and lower limits are defined, but the number of different levels in between is reduced.)

The Recruitment Process

Having objective statements of duties, responsibilities, and qualifications makes it possible to recruit personnel based not on who one knows, but on what one knows and what one can do. Recruitment efforts in the public sector must also be concerned with ensuring fairness, openness, and representativeness. Typically, the recruitment process involves the following steps:

1. Advertising or giving notice of a vacancy to be filled
2. Testing or otherwise screening applicants
3. Preparing a list of qualified candidates
4. Selecting someone to fill the position

In most jurisdictions, a personnel officer within a particular agency or someone from a central personnel department is significantly involved in the first three steps. Testing or screening processes have been subject to special scrutiny in recent years. Screening can occur through a review of written applications and recommendations, aptitude or ability testing, performance examinations, interviews, or assessment centers. Of the aptitude or ability tests that public organizations use, some measure general knowledge, others measure personality characteristics, and still others measure specific job-related knowledge or abilities. Performance examinations, such as typing tests, measure specific job capabilities.

The method of testing should relate to the job to be filled. Though individual interviews are a common part of the hiring process, for example, they tend to be poor predictors of eventual job performance. Generally speaking, *structured interviews*, in which a previously developed set of questions is used with each applicant, and *panel interviews*, which involve more than one interviewer, are preferable. Similarly, carefully constructed assessment centers using several independent raters may be used. (An *assessment center* puts several job applicants through a series of job-related simulations to observe their performance under "real-life" conditions.)

After testing or screening, a small number of eligible applicants are certified and forwarded to the hiring agency, often with rankings based on the candidates' qualifications. Most merit systems require that at least the top three names be forwarded to the agency so the manager will have some flexibility to consider personal or subjective characteristics in the final selection. This *rule of three* provision has proven controversial, however; many claim that it has been used as a device to discriminate against women and minorities. (Under this provision, for instance, a sexist employer could hire a male even if a woman candidate were objectively more capable.) An equally controversial provision of many merit systems requires that veterans (or sometimes even relatives of veterans) receive extra points in the ranking system. Obviously, such a provision works against the interests of nonveterans, most of whom are women; however, it is strongly supported by veterans' groups and has been upheld by the courts.

What Would You Do?

One of your employees, whose work is otherwise quite good, has annoyed many of her fellow employees with her arrogant attitude. You don't want to lose her, but her behavior is clearly bothering others and, they claim, affecting the quality of their work. What would you do?

The centralized process of recruitment traditionally underlying public personnel systems itself has come under fire in recent years. Many suggest that it places decision-making authority in the hands of human resources staff as opposed to public managers. For example, many have recommended that federal agencies be given the power to establish their own recruitment and examining programs. The argument suggests that managers in each policy area can be more effective in recognizing the skills and abilities needed to make the agency more productive and that they are in the best position to determine when to increase hiring levels.

As a result, the trend toward decentralized recruitment has gained in popularity even in larger, more diverse agencies within the federal government. Decentralized processes may rely on similar selection criteria as a centralized system, but the primary difference is that agency heads, rather than personnel managers, select the viable candidates. Those with the greatest knowledge of the policy field, therefore, choose the individuals they believe will enhance the organization. Moreover, by not having to engage in the selection process, personnel staff members are free to concentrate on broader concerns, such as diversity, affirmative action, and other factors affecting the organization.

Networking

For employment opportunities in the federal government, go to the Office of Personnel Management at www.opm.gov, or USAJOBS at www.usajobs.opm.gov/infocenter/howjobsgetfilled.asp, or www.careersingovernment.com, or visit any of the federal agencies online. Those interested in employment at other levels of government can go to www.PublicServiceCareers.org, or www.govtjobs.com. For nonprofit-sector jobs, go to www.philanthropy.com or www.opportunitynocs.org.

For those interested in applying for positions in the federal government, or in other levels of government, and the nonprofit sector, the Internet has become a vital resource. Applicants can complete the necessary forms and submit their materials online, and in some cases the entire recruitment process can occur without the candidate ever visiting the hiring organization. The federal Office of Personnel Management in 2011 launched a new website called USAJobsRecruit, an online tool for showing best practices and advertising hiring events. The one-stop shop gives managers and human resources personnel access to recruiting and communication tools, such as discussion forums, chats, and blogs. Whether it's done in person or online, be sure to submit the appropriate application materials. In some cases this may be as simple as sending in a current resume with the vacancy number and level. Usually, however, resumes should be accompanied by the proper application forms. Many recruiters will not consider application materials unless they are submitted in a style and format consistent with those called for in the vacancy announcement.

One aspect of the recruitment process that is receiving increasing attention is the matter of succession planning (Riccucci, 2011, p. 135). The question here is how government can adequately recruit sufficient talent to overcome several structural difficulties it faces in the recruitment process. In the 1970s, with the growth of government, a large number of baby boomers were recruited to the public service. Those people have now reached or will soon reach retirement age. "By some estimates, up to 70% of the Senior Executive Service (SES) is currently eligible to retire" (PriceWaterhouseCoopers, 2006, p. 6.) Another challenge to the system is the large drop in government employment propelled by the recession. John Berry, head of the Office of Personnel Management, recently told Congress, "As agencies are looking at increasing their buyouts and other options to tighten their belts, it's increasing our retirement pressure" (*Federal Times,* 2010). As a result of these two factors, federal retirements jumped 24 percent in the first ten months of 2011 as compared with the previous year.

Even while there are challenges brought about by replacing retiring federal executives, there are other demographic concerns faced by federal recruiters as well. According to the Census Bureau, by the year 2050, current minorities will be the majority in America and the percentage of the population over sixty-five will more than double. In addition, other demographic patterns, including immigration and shifting patterns of migration, will challenge government agencies to find the appropriate mechanisms for recruiting populations different from those that currently staff the upper levels of government. Succession planning is the process of attracting, developing, and retaining appropriate executive talent at the upper levels of government. In this process, agencies are trying to match human resources decisions with their strategic objectives and, in turn, exploring new avenues for recruitment, training, job rotation, and performance evaluation to meet evolving circumstances. Clearly, succession planning will be a growing concern for public executives at all levels over the coming decades.

Pay Systems

Naturally, both the recruiting process and the individual's job performance are affected by compensation patterns, including wages and benefits. Generally speaking, pay is determined by the nature of the work and the quality of job performance. But pay plans in the public sector are difficult to construct, for they must embody two often contradictory principles. To be fair and equitable, they must be highly structured; to be competitive, they must be responsive to changing political and economic conditions.

Most large government personnel systems (including states and big cities) base their pay plans on classification systems that usually define a series of grades, each containing a set of jobs that are comparable in terms of difficulty, and a number of steps within each grade. These steps represent approximately equal increments of pay, with the highest about 20 to 30 percent above the lowest. In most cases, the grades are slightly overlapping, so the first step in one grade is equal to one of the higher steps in the grade below. Individuals are assigned to a particular grade and step depending on the position description and individual qualifications for the position.

Employees in this type of system may receive pay increases in several ways. One way is to change grades; however, for an employee to change grades, either the position has to be reclassified or all equivalent positions have to be moved to a higher range. For an employee to receive increases within a grade, either the entire pay plan must be adjusted upward—for example, through a legislative action to improve overall pay (such as through cost-of-living increases)—or the individual may receive a raise. Raises can be based on several factors, ranging from seniority to merit pay (pay for performance).

The idea of *merit pay* is simply that increases in salaries and wages should be tied to the actual quality of the work being done, so that those who perform better or more productively receive greater rewards. Although governments have used various merit pay systems, such systems have not always worked well. In many cases, the money available for merit raises for a few is spread so thinly that meritorious employees aren't differentiated from others. Part of the reason for this is the difficulty of objectively measuring an individual's performance and the fact that many managers find it awkward to evaluate their employees' work.

Recall that the Civil Service Reform Act of 1978 sought to remedy this situation by requiring merit pay based on formal performance appraisal systems. Although agencies have been given considerable flexibility as to what systems they adopt, efforts have been made to base evaluations on critical elements of the individual's job or to develop results-oriented systems that tie evaluation to specific job outcomes. Any system of performance appraisal must be both accurate and fair.

> Performance-appraisal systems must be based on the real requirements of the task. They must reflect realistic levels of performance, and be couched in terms that the workers understand, while at the same time providing workers with some insights on where and how performance improvements need to be made. (Siegel & Myrtle, 1985, p. 337)

One aspect of compensation policy that has received substantial attention over the years is the comparability of wages and salaries in the public and private sectors. Efforts to make such comparisons are similar to comparing apples and oranges; thus early studies tended to show public-sector salaries considerably below those in the private sector—today ranging between 22 and 38 percent, depending on grade level. (Incidentally, the greatest differences are at top-level positions.)

Under these conditions, the federal Pay Comparability Act of 1990 required the federal government to close the gap between the public and private sectors, beginning by closing the gap 20 percent in 1993 and then 10 percent in subsequent years. Both Presidents Reagan and Bush in the 1990s cited the country's economic problems as reason to impose lower wages than those suggested by comparability studies. President Clinton, although proposing some increases, rejected the comparability targets, arguing that the law's formulas were based on flawed methodology. More recently, President George W. Bush argued that full statutory pay raises would interfere with the nation's ability to fight terrorism. President Obama has frozen federal pay as one part of an effort to reduce the budget deficit.

In any case, the comparison remains difficult. A *USA Today* analysis concluded that, overall, federal government employees in 2008 earned about $7,000 more that their private-sector counterparts in similar jobs. Countering that analysis, a public union spokesperson argued that the study compares apples and oranges, because federal jobs require a higher set of skills. "When you look at the actual duties, you see that very few federal jobs align with those in the private sector" (*USA Today*, 2010). Meanwhile, a 2010 study by the Center for State and Local Government Excellence, based on data from the Bureau of Labor Statistics, concluded that wages and salaries of state and local employees are lower than those for private-sector employees with comparable education and work experience. And the gap is getting bigger (http://slge.org/publications/out-of-balance-comparing-public-and-private-sector-compensation-over-20-years). Others, however, argue that government benefits offset any differences.

Conditions of Employment and Related Matters

There are several contemporary issues in personnel management that relate either to conditions under which employees are hired or under which they must work. For example, increasing numbers of employers in both the public and private sectors are recognizing that substance abuse is responsible for greater absenteeism, higher accident rates, and generally lower productivity. Consequently, programs have been established to identify and aid or dismiss employees who have problems with drugs or alcohol.

Testing for drugs, primarily through urinalysis, has become quite common. Despite the fact that such programs violate personal dignity and have a variety of technical problems, a substantial number of private companies now use drug testing. But that number is declining. According to the American Management Association, the percentage of employers with testing programs has dropped steadily since 1996, from 81 percent to 62 percent in 2004 (http://www.time.com/time/nation/article/0,8599,1211429,00.html). The decline may be due to people searching out employers who don't test. But the decline may also be due to agency calculations of costs and benefits. "According to a 1999 ACLU study, the federal government spent $11.7 million to find 153 drug users among almost 29,000 employees tested in 1990, a cost of $77,000 per positive test" (http://www.time.com/time/nation/article/0,8599,1211429,00.html).

Employees in private firms have little protection from testing and, in the absence of collective bargaining agreements to the contrary, may be tested at management discretion. Because public employees (at least civilian employees) are more clearly protected against illegal search and seizure and are guaranteed equal protection and due process, programs to test public employees have frequently been challenged in the courts. For the most part, the courts have held that random mandatory testing is a violation of employee rights, but that testing may be required where there is reasonable suspicion of abuse or where testing is made a part of the hiring process. But questions continue to be debated. For example, what type of testing is appropriate for those in "sensitive positions," such as air traffic controllers or those in contact with nuclear or chemical weapons?

Networking

The following sites track contemporary issues in personnel management. Many others are available.

www.ipma-hr.org (International Public Management Association for Human Resources; benefits)

www.shrm.org (Society for Human Resource Management)

www.hr.com (general information relating to human resource management)

www.hr-guide.com (index of subjects relating to personnel management)

Sexual Harassment

Another contemporary concern is establishing a work environment that is supportive of and sensitive to the needs of all people, regardless of gender. One aspect of this concern is sexual harassment, a topic that has received considerable national attention in the wake of several highly publicized cases. *Sexual harassment* may be defined as any unwanted and nonreciprocal verbal or physical sexual advances or derogatory remarks that the recipient finds offensive or that interfere with job performance. Sexual harassment especially includes (though is not limited to) situations in which one person in a position of power or influence uses his or her position to encourage or coerce a subordinate or coworker into undesired sexual activity, even to the point of withholding or taking away promotions or raises. The courts consider sexual harassment a type of inequality that employers must deal with, both by eliminating offensive behaviors and by creating a less hostile or intimidating work environment for both men and women.

Although sexual harassment appears to be a common problem, many instances remain unreported. (The number of reported incidents rose dramatically during the last two decades with the increase in public awareness.) One reason for unreported cases may be the complex and often ambiguous procedures many organizations have for dealing with complaints. Most tend to be lengthy, expensive, and psychologically draining. For this reason, public organizations are currently reviewing their policies on sexual harassment, establishing more clearly the seriousness of the offense and developing strong enforcement and disciplinary measures, including dismissal. The goal is to eliminate specific instances of harassment and create a work environment that is fully supportive of the potential of all employees. In fiscal year 2006, the federal Equal Employment Opportunities Commission received about 12,000 charges of sexual harassment, with 85 percent of those charges filed by women. EEOC resolved nearly all of these sexual harassment charges and recovered $48.8 million in monetary benefits for the charging parties (www.eeoc.gov/types/sexual_harassment.html).

Networking

For discussions of sexual harassment and other personnel issues, see http://www.eeoc.gov/.

AIDS Policy

Other issues relating to a positive work environment arise as public organizations, like others, work to protect the rights of individuals with HIV/AIDS. The Office of Personnel Management provided one of the first directives for federal agencies, setting a policy that prohibits the discrimination against employees with AIDS and that allows managers to take disciplinary action against anyone who refuses to work with an employee who has AIDS. The guidelines said that employees with AIDS "should be allowed to continue working as long as they are able to maintain acceptable performance and do not pose a safety or health threat to themselves or others in the workplace." Moreover, because there is no medical basis for refusing to work with employees with AIDS, where managers feel the refusal is "impeding or disrupting the organization's work, [the manager] should consider appropriate corrective or disciplinary action against the threatening or disruptive employees" (Havemann, 1988a, p. 34).

These considerations have become even more important with the passage of the 1990 Americans with Disabilities Act (ADA), which considers those infected with HIV/AIDS as disabled individuals. (The ADA will be discussed in more detail later in this chapter.) Consequently, many agencies are developing HIV/AIDS plans for the workplace. Despite this attention, much work remains to be done to create a positive work environment for this protected group.

Workplace Violence

In recent years, incidents of violence in the public workplace have had a dramatic effect on work environments. Although multiple murders and acts of terrorism, such as the 1995 Oklahoma City bombing, tend to capture the public's attention, other forms of violence pose an equally significant threat to workplace safety and quality. Violent crime affects organizations in all sectors; however, the government remains a primary target. In 2005 alone, the U.S. Department of Labor reported that 32 percent of all state employees reported some type of workplace violence as compared to 15 percent of local government employees and 5 percent of employees in private industries (www.bls.gov/iif/oshwc/osnr0026.pdf). The increase in violence over the past decade has prompted administrators to implement strategies for reducing the risk of workplace crime. While the Department of Labor reported in 2006 that 70 percent of public workplaces do not have any formal plan to address workplace violence, preventive measures include improving the physical environment, adding security and related staff, and reducing hours of operation during high-risk periods (www.bls.gov/opub/ted/2006/oct/wk5/art02.htm). However, as we noted, many public administrators have yet to realize the actual threat of violence that affects their organization. Some continue to view occupational violence as someone else's problem. Recent research on violent crime, though, suggests otherwise. The political nature of government, the deterioration in public perception of government workers, and the increase in stress loads among public employees combine to make public organizations likely targets for workplace violence.

One particular aspect of workplace violence that deserves attention is violence against women, something that has been egregious in the military. An estimated 17 percent of women in the general population become victims at some point in their lives, while the number in the military is estimated to be between 23 and 33 percent. Defense Secretary Leon Panetta has estimated that, since victims are too often afraid to come forward, the actual number may be close to 19,000, more than six times the number of reported attacks in 2011. Mr. Panetta has announced reforms, including training in the prosecution of sexual assault cases, increased opportunities for reporting abuse, and greater support for victims (*New York Times*, 2012).

Removing Employees

Occasionally things don't work out on the job. An employee may not live up to expectations or may become unproductive. In cases such as these, your first step as a manager is to try to improve the individual's work (a strategy that is far easier than recruiting and training a replacement). You may encourage or counsel the employee, either personally or, better, through an employee assistance program. In a surprising number of cases, you may be able to restructure the job to better motivate the employee. Concerns about an employee's work can often be addressed in positive and productive ways that are helpful to both the individual and the organization.

But if your efforts to help the employee fail, you may have to resort to disciplinary action: formal reprimands, reduction of pay, suspension without pay, or outright dismissal. In all cases, it is important to be able to demonstrate that there is adequate cause for disciplinary action. Simply firing someone for personal reasons unrelated to the job opens both you and the organization to possible lawsuits; and firing someone for political reasons is contrary to the whole concept of merit employment in the public sector.

There is a strong presumption that public-sector employees are entitled to notice and an opportunity to be heard before disciplinary action or before dismissal. This does not mean that a person cannot be demoted, suspended, or terminated but rather that the employer cannot take such action in an arbitrary way.

At the federal level, the Civil Service Reform Act encourages development of performance appraisal systems that make it easier for managers to document employee incompetence and remove employees from the organization. At the state and local levels, various court cases have indicated that employees being terminated have certain due process rights, such as advance notice and the opportunity for a hearing. In any case, if you decide to pursue disciplinary action, you should build a clear case to demonstrate the underlying reasons for your action.

Personnel Reform Efforts

There have been a number of efforts to reform the federal personnel management system. Two recent experiments have underscored the importance of agency flexibility in personnel matters. In November 2002, when the Department of Homeland Security (DHS) was created, it was given authority to work with the Office of Personnel Management to create a personnel system unique to its needs. DHS responded by creating a system with more open pay ranges, performance pay pools, and specific market-based pay adjustments. Similarly, in November 2003, the Department of Defense (DOD) was asked to create a National Security Personnel System, again one unique to its needs. The flexibilities that DOD incorporated included a broadband pay system, performance-based pay, and a simplification of the employee appeals process.

Similar recommendations have come from other sources. In 2001, a National Commission on the Public Service, chaired by former Federal Reserve chairman Paul A. Volcker, was convened to analyze and report on the state of the public service at the federal level. The commission released its report, titled "Urgent Business for America," in January 2003, commenting that "the organization of the federal government and the operation of public programs are not good enough: Not good enough for the American people, not good enough to meet the extraordinary challenges of the century just beginning, and not good enough for the hundreds of thousands of talented federal workers who hate the constraints that keep them from serving their country with the full measure of their talents and energy." The commission made a series of recommendations to improve the quality of management of the federal government (see the box "Public Administration Reform: Urgent Business for America").

Public Administration Reform

URGENT BUSINESS FOR AMERICA

The Organization of Government

Fundamental reorganization of the federal government is urgently needed to improve the capacity for coherent design and efficient implementation of public policy:

- The federal government should be reorganized into a limited number of mission-related executive departments.
- The operating agencies in these new departments should be run by managers chosen for their operational skills and given the authority to develop management and personnel systems appropriate to their missions.
- The President should be given expedited authority to recommend structural reorganization of federal agencies and departments.
- The House and Senate should realign their committee oversight to match the mission-driven reorganization of the executive branch.

Leadership for Government

Effective government leadership requires immediate changes in the entry process for top leaders and the long-term development of a highly skilled federal management corps:

- The President and Congress should develop a cooperative approach to speeding and streamlining the presidential appointments process.
- Congress and the President should work together to significantly reduce the number of executive branch political positions.
- The Senior Executive Service should be divided into an Executive Management Corps and a Professional and Technical Corps.
- Congress should undertake a critical examination of "ethics" regulations imposed on federal employees, modifying those with little demonstrated public benefit.
- Congress should grant an immediate and significant increase in judicial, executive, and legislative salaries to ensure a reasonable relationship to other professional opportunities.
- Congress should break the statutory link between the salaries of members of Congress and those of judges and senior political appointees.

Operational Effectiveness in Government

The federal workforce must be reshaped, and the systems that support it must be rooted in new personnel management principles that ensure much higher levels of government performance:

- More flexible personnel management systems should be developed by operating agencies to meet their special needs.
- Congress and the Office of Personnel Management should continue their efforts to simplify and accelerate the recruitment of federal employees.

(Continued)

(Continued)

- Congress should establish policies that permit agencies to set compensation related to current market comparisons.
- Competitive outsourcing should follow clear preset standards and goals that advance the public interest and do not undermine core competencies of the government.

SOURCE: The National Commission on the Public Service, *Urgent Business for America* (http://www.brookings .eduresearch/reports/2003/01/01governance).

The Changing Character of Labor-Management Relations

An interesting issue that cuts across the field of public personnel management is the rise and decline of public-sector unions. At the federal level, many rather narrow issues, having to do primarily with working conditions, are resolved through collective bargaining, though more controversial issues, such as compensation and hiring practices, are rarely considered. At state and local levels, there is a patchwork of labor relations practices, ranging from highly restrictive to extremely permissive labor legislation.

The early development of public-sector unions was tied to the reform of the patronage system. With the establishment of merit principles in public employment, employees had greater protection from political intrusions, but they also had fewer direct ways to get the attention of political leaders. To combat the possibility that they might simply be ignored, public employees began organizing in the late 1800s and early 1900s. At first, political leaders strenuously opposed these efforts; at least two presidents issued gag orders to prevent federal workers from pursuing wage demands except through departmental channels. In response, the newly organized employees, led by the postal workers, pressed Congress for recognition, which they finally received in the Lloyd-LaFollette Act of 1912. The only statutory basis for public-sector unionization for more than half a century, this act permitted federal employees to join unions (that did not advocate the right to strike) and to appeal directly to Congress.

With the early emergence of unions at the federal level, a few agencies, such as the Tennessee Valley Authority, developed advanced patterns of labor-management relations; elsewhere, however, public unions emerged slowly, especially in comparison to their counterparts in the private sector. The slow development of public unions can be explained in part by several difficult questions.

First, there was the issue of sovereignty, the notion that the ultimate power to decide issues of public policy in a democracy lies with the people or their elected representatives and cannot properly be delegated, even partially, to some nongovernmental group such as a union. Illustrating this position, President Franklin Roosevelt wrote, "The process of collective bargaining, as usually understood, cannot be transplanted into the public service.... The very nature and purpose of Government makes it impossible for administrative officials to represent fully or bind the employer in mutual discussions. The employer is the whole people who speak by means of laws enacted by their representatives in Congress" (Klingner & Nalbandian, 1985, p. 292).

A second set of factors restricting the growth of public unions concerns the nature of governmental services, which are considered either essential to the community (police, fire, national defense) or unprofitable (systems of mass transportation). In the case of essential services, the ultimate union weapon—the strike—may be seen as holding the public interest hostage and can backfire. In the case of low-profit undertakings, the balancing factor of the market—the fact that a company may go out of business if pressed too far—does not appear to operate. In either case, the private-sector model of collective bargaining seems to apply only loosely.

A third factor limiting the growth of public-sector unions through much of this century is the varied nature of government employment and the difficulties this presents for unionizing. Traditionally, unions have organized around occupational groups, such as truck drivers or garment workers. But government employs people in thousands of occupational groups; to have a union for each group would lead to endless and unsuccessful bargaining for both sides. The federal government is also characterized by geographic dispersion (only about 10 percent of the federal workforce is located in the Washington area) and the fact that there are so many white-collar workers in government, workers who have been historically reluctant to organize. Thus, finding an appropriate focus for union activity has been especially difficult at the federal level.

Networking

For information on labor-management issues, see www.labornet.org and www.dol.gov. On specific unions, see www.afge.org and www.afscme.org.

Yet, unions have been able to organize. Sparked at least partly by the success of unions in the private sector, where the right to bargain collectively was never seriously questioned after passage of the Wagner Act in 1935, public employees continued to press for recognition of their right to negotiate labor-management disputes. Soon even the sovereignty argument was eroded; Secretary of Labor Willard Wirtz commented, "This doctrine is wrong in theory; what's more, it doesn't work" (Levitan, 1983, p. 6). Bills providing recognition for unions in the public sector were introduced (although unsuccessfully) in every session of Congress from 1949 to 1961.

Just as another such bill seemed stalled in Congress, President Kennedy took the initiative in reforming public labor-management relations by issuing Executive Order 10988 in 1962. Kennedy's order affirmed the right of federal employees to form and join unions, set up conditions under which unions would be recognized for purposes of "meeting and conferring" (discussing, not necessarily negotiating) with management on certain issues, and established limits on the kinds of issues that could be discussed. Though the order placed a great deal of administrative authority in the hands of the various agencies, it did seek some uniformity in application through the Civil Service Commission.

The Kennedy order was expanded somewhat by several executive orders during the Nixon and Ford administrations. Principally, Executive Order 11491, issued in 1969, sought a more coherent labor policy at the federal level through establishment of the Federal Labor Relations Council (FLRC) and slightly expanded the scope of bargaining. The essential items of wages and benefits, however, remained outside the bargaining process.

The next landmark in federal employee unions was the Civil Service Reform Act of 1978. Though the CSRA did little to expand areas of bargaining or to alter administration of federal labor practices (other than replacing the FLRC with a Federal Labor Relations Authority separate from the Office of Personnel Management), the act was important in that it based federal labor relations on a single, comprehensive statute rather than a series of executive orders.

Currently, about a third of all federal workers are represented by unions, the largest of which is the American Federation of Government Employees (AFGE), a part of the AFL-CIO, which has 600,000 federal employees as members. But because Congress has refused to permit a "union shop" among federal workers, though it exists in the private sector, the actual membership of federal unions is significantly less than it might otherwise be. (A *union shop* is an arrangement under which all members of an agency are required to join the union that represents them.) The AFGE, for instance, negotiates agreements that apply to three times its actual membership. Despite that fact, the percentage of federal workers who pay dues to unions compares quite favorably to that among workers in the private sector; public unions have done quite well in terms of membership. Indeed, overall, public-sector union membership is higher than that in the private sector. In 2010, for example, the membership rate among public employees was over four times that of private-sector employees. While government union membership has remained fairly stable over the last thirty years, that in the private sector has declined significantly. Most public employees in unions are at the local level, many in highly unionized occupations of teachers, firefighters, and police officers (ftp://ftp.bls.gov/pub/news.release/Hirstory/union2.01212004).

At state and local levels, there is incredible variety in the kinds of labor-management relations permitted by law. Though there has been occasional talk of uniform federal statutes to govern state and local practices, the case of *National League of Cities v. Usery* (1976) seemed to indicate that states have considerable sovereignty over public employees. More recently, however, the case of *Garcia v. San Antonio Metropolitan Transit Authority* (1985) again opened the possibility of further federal intervention. But until federal legislation is passed, states will continue to exercise control over labor relations in widely varying ways. At present, some states follow the "meet and confer" model of the Kennedy program, while others establish a "negotiations" process similar to the private-sector model. Some states differentiate between state and local employees, while others differentiate among various occupational groups as well. Some states require enforced arbitration of one kind or another, and eight states permit strikes by public employees.

In all, forty-three states have comprehensive labor-relations laws, most of which are more favorable to unions than the existing federal legislation. Over the last thirty years, in fact, the two most rapidly growing unions in this country were the American Federation of State, County, and Municipal Employees and the American Federation of Teachers, both of which operate exclusively at the state and local levels.

Steps in the Bargaining Process

The first and major steps in the bargaining process are recognizing the union's right to exist, determining the type of bargaining permitted, and determining the scope of bargaining. Scope of bargaining is a source of continuing debate in many jurisdictions. Legislation may prescribe areas where negotiation is permitted, where it is prohibited, and where it is required. But the applicable legislation may range from a prohibition on negotiating wages and salaries (as exists at the federal level) to situations in which wages and salaries are at the heart of the process (as in many states and localities). Even beyond these questions, many other issues are less clear. For example, does inclusion of "work methods and procedures" in a bargaining arrangement for public schools mean that teachers can negotiate class sizes?

The typical procedure requires that organizers who wish to represent employees petition the administrative authority to establish a *bargaining unit* that will represent the employees in conferring or negotiating various issues. (The decision to include or exclude certain groups in the bargaining unit is called *unit determination.*) Whereas the traditional standard for setting unit boundaries has been to establish a "community of interests," governments have loosely applied this concept, in some cases recognizing agency-based units (the Department of Social Services or the Department of Mental Health) and in others recognizing units based on occupational classes (nurses, custodians, or security officers). After deciding on the bargaining unit, some mechanism must be established to ensure coordination among the various groups and to prevent *whipsaw tactics* (arguing that pay or benefits negotiated by one group should apply to others as well).

A similar concern is where to draw the line between managers and workers; for example, are first-line supervisors part of the bargaining unit or part of management? The importance of this issue was illustrated in the case of *NLRB v. Yeshiva University* (1980), in which it was determined that faculty at Yeshiva University, a private university, are management personnel, participating in decisions such as curricula and scheduling, and therefore outside the coverage of federal labor laws. Similar questions are raised in almost any unit determination; inclusion or exclusion of supervisors in the bargaining process varies greatly from place to place.

After appropriate bargaining units have been established, the administrative authority may either voluntarily recognize a particular union, essentially by petition, as representing a group of employees, or it may conduct an election to determine which, if any, union will represent the employees. Once a union has been recognized, it is usually granted exclusive representation of employees in the unit, including the ability to bargain on all issues required or permitted by law. (The reverse of this process, decertification, is rare, though it can occur.) Bargaining may then begin, typically with both sides bargaining in good faith—attempting to resolve the issues at hand even while following the strategy they feel will be most advantageous to them. In most cases, the bargaining process results in an agreement; occasionally it does not. Where an *impasse* occurs, there are several possibilities for resolving the issue: mediation, fact-finding, and arbitration.

1. *Mediation* involves the use of a neutral third party to attempt to work out a settlement. The work of the mediator is to assist the parties in communicating and clarifying their positions, but not to impose solutions. Though the mediator's recommendations are not binding, professional mediators are remarkably successful in helping parties reach agreements.

2. *Fact-finding* employs the third party in a somewhat more investigatory and judicial role: to examine evidence on both sides of the issue, present the evidence, and, in most cases, make specific recommendations for a settlement. Some jurisdictions require making the recommendations public on the assumption that public pressure will then lead toward an agreement.

3. *Arbitration* is a form of impasse resolution involving fact-finding followed by specific recommendations that are usually binding on the parties. One form of arbitration that has received attention recently is *final-offer arbitration*, a technique in which both parties must present their best offer with the understanding that the arbitrator will choose one or the other without modification. Presumably, since both parties know that unreasonable proposals will lead to the arbitrator choosing the opposing proposal, it is in the interest of both parties to submit their most reasonable position.

A significant recent development in labor-management relations in the federal government has been the increasing use of alternative dispute resolution (ADR). As we noted earlier, ADR was encouraged in federal legislation passed in the early 1990s and reaffirmed in the Administrative Dispute Resolution Act of 1996. ADR typically involves the use of a neutral third party, often a mediator, who can help the disputing parties arrive at some agreement, short of imposing legal remedies. In addition, ADR may involve conciliation, problem solving, dispute panels, fact-finding, and facilitation. While ADR is not intended to replace more traditional approaches, it often can lead to solutions that are not only quicker and less costly, but also have significant buy-in from the parties involved. The Bureau of the Treasury's Engraving and Printing Bureau began using ADR in 1997 and, in its first five years, processed over 165 cases with an estimated cost avoidance of $3 million to $4 million (www.opm.gove/er/adrguide_2002). More recently the Federal Labor Relations Authority has created a Collaboration and Alternative Dispute Resolution Program, which provides interest-based dispute resolution assistance in cases of unfair labor practices or impasse bargaining. CADR also provides training for labor and management to create more collaborative workplaces and to provide the basis for dispute resolution efforts.

Change in labor-management relations also has been targeted in the culture and leadership styles that characterize public organizations. Many public agencies have opted for a more participatory form of management, thus precluding the legalistic, not to mention lengthy, process of collective bargaining. Administrators work to dismantle bureaucratic hierarchies and distribute power throughout the organization. Public employees enjoy a more meaningful form of empowerment than could ever have been facilitated through traditional channels. The result is a more effective and productive organization.

Of course, such an alternative does not completely resolve the issue. The structural factors that pit the two sides against each other, for the most part, remain in place. Public unions still hold a level of power in government personnel administration, and the gains made on behalf of workers through lobbying and court decisions continue to influence the administrative process. However, the relationship is changing. Though the direction of this change remains to be seen, reform of the system and the search for alternative forms of communication between labor and management appear necessary.

To Strike or Not to Strike

If impasse resolution fails, the employee organization may consider a strike. Although most governmental jurisdictions prohibit strikes by public employees, they do occur. There are usually several hundred work stoppages in public agencies each year. These strikes raise difficult questions for public-sector labor-management relations. Certainly public employees have the right to form associations, and one might argue that they should have the right to withhold services just as employees in the private sector do. On the other hand, the importance of public services, especially those such as fire or police protection, may justify different standards in the public sector.

Experts make the following arguments against public employee strikes:

1. Strikes violate sovereignty (conceding authority to any special-interest group contravenes the public interest).
2. Public services are essential and cannot be interrupted. In effect, all government services are vital.
3. Traditional channels of influence on public policy exist for unions: lobbying and voting.
4. Whereas strikes in the private sector are usually of an economic nature, those in the public service are political. They are strategies that use the leverage of public inconvenience to cause a redirection of budgetary priorities (Siegel & Myrtle, 1985, pp. 377–378).

On the other hand, advocates of public employees' right to strike make these points:

1. Public employee strikes occur whether or not they are illegal and regardless of heavy penalties prescribed by law.
2. In strike situations, labor-management conflict becomes channeled and socially constructive: both labor and management gain greater understanding of each other and of the consequences of work stoppages.
3. The right to strike enhances a union's strength as a bargaining agent. Lack of the ultimate ability to withdraw services weakens labor's position at the bargaining table.
4. Many private workers doing the same work that public employees do (for example, in transit, health care, garbage collection, and communications) have the right to strike, and for many other public employees (clerks, for instance), the public consequences of striking would be little different from what they are when private-sector clerks strike.

Though strikes at the state and especially at the local level are more frequent, two landmark strikes at the federal level were especially dramatic. The postal workers' strike of 1970 occurred when members of the Manhattan-Bronx Branch of the National Association of Letter Carriers voted to strike against the U.S. Postal Service. The immediate issue was the low wage scale for carriers—a scale that left a substantial number of postal workers on welfare. Beyond this concern, the postal workers desired the right to negotiate wages and benefits, especially if the Nixon administration followed its plans to make the post office a government corporation. The strike began with about 25,000 postal work- ers in New York City, but soon spread up and down the East Coast and to several major cities around the country, ultimately involving some 200,000 union members. As the situ- ation became more intolerable, President Nixon sent 27,500 National Guardsmen into New York to sort and deliver the mail. He also broke a long-standing precedent, however, and agreed to permit postal workers to bargain for wages. Following this agreement, the postal workers returned to work, most claiming victory in the strike. Eventually, the Postal Reorganization Act was passed, setting up the government corporation Nixon sought, and also providing for a bargaining pattern similar to that in the private sector.

A quite different result occurred when members of the Professional Air Traffic Controllers Organization (PATCO) went on strike in August 1981. PATCO had earlier established itself as one of the most powerful and most militant of the public unions, boasting 90 percent of the air traffic controllers in the Federal Aviation Authority (FAA) as members (probably the highest percentage among federal-level unions at the time). Early in the year, the FAA was pressured into negotiating with the union concerning issues of wages and working conditions, even though it had no statutory power to do so and could only recommend wage increases to Congress. The union, arguing that the controllers were underpaid and subject to severe job stress, presented several demands, including a $10,000 across-the-board annual salary increase for the controllers and a four-day, 32-hour work week. Although the FAA did not meet these demands, Secretary of Transportation Drew Lewis agreed to support a $40 million package of improvements, including a $4,000 wage increase. However, 95 percent of the union membership rejected this proposal.

After a final round of negotiations was unsuccessful, the union decided to strike; union leader Robert Poli declared, "The only illegal strike is one that fails" (Steele, 1982, p. 38). As it turned out, this strike was to fail. What had begun as a confrontation between the union and the FAA now became a confrontation between the union and the White House.

President Reagan acted decisively, fining the union and firing nearly 11,500 striking controllers for participating in an illegal strike. Although there was severe disruption in the air transportation system for several days, new controllers were hired, airline sched- ules were altered, and training programs were accelerated. The situation soon gave at least the appearance of a return to normalcy. Beaten in the strike and decertified by the Federal Labor Relations Authority (FLRA), less than a year later PATCO filed for bankruptcy.

Unions Redefined

While the PATCO example has made strikes by public employees extremely difficult, unions still exert significant influence, especially at the state and local levels. But, in many ways, the character and role of organized labor have undergone a fundamental change during the last three or four decades, as efforts to reinvent government and reform person- nel processes have redefined the ties between labor and management. In some respects, the influence of unions has been diminished by the more businesslike approach taken by government agencies. Contracting out and privatization, too, have contributed to labor's troubles, due to more and more services being delivered by private or nongovernmental organizations. The net result has been a drop not only in the power of unions, but also, depending on how you count, in some cases in the level of union membership. Quoting the Bureau of Labor Statistics, the *Washington Post* reported in 2010 that as a percentage of the total federal workforce, union membership remained essentially flat between 2008 and 2009. "Twenty-eight percent of federal workers were union members in 2009, compared with 28.1 percent in 2008...." At the same time, the total number of "unionized workers climbed slightly to more than 1 million, versus 994,000 the year before. The number surpassed the percentage growth because the federal workforce grew by more than 50,000 in 2009" (*Washington Post*, 2010). What remains the same, however, is the often confrontational nature of the labor-management relationship, with many identifying collective bargaining as a key contributor to bitter contests between management and staff personnel. As a result, an adversarial climate has often prevailed. Public organizations often spend months, or sometimes years, trying to reach agreements or attempting to effectively manage existing contracts. Meanwhile, the relationship between managers and union employees becomes bogged down over what amounts to minuscule matters.

During the past decades, however, both labor and management have sought more peaceful, less adversarial alternatives to bargaining and dispute resolution. A major step toward this goal came in 1993 when President Clinton issued Executive Order 12871, which encouraged the two sides to form partnerships and take a cooperative approach to labor issues. This executive order was augmented by congressional passage of the Alternative Dispute Resolution Act in 1996. The order created the National Partnership Council, with representatives from public unions, management, and the Public Employee Department of the AFL-CIO. However, in 2002, President George W. Bush used Executive Order 13203 to eliminate the requirement for partnerships in federal agencies, preferring a less structured form of labor-management cooperation. Interestingly, the Obama administration recently cleared the way for unionization of employees of the Transportation Security Administration, including airport screeners and others, an action that will add 50,000 to 60,000 union members to federal employment. Many take this action to portend greater support for union activity at the federal level.

Unions, however, have not gained as much favor at the state and local levels. The economic recession brought on by the near collapse of the financial sector in 2008 created significant budget deficits at all levels of government. As state officials wrestled with ways to rein in spending and save money, they took aim at government workers' salaries and benefits as a means to help ease their budget crises. Pension funds and collective bargaining rights were specific targets in several states as governors and other elected officials introduced legislation to cut benefits, increase workers' pension contributions, and curb the bargaining power of public-sector unions as ways to control costs.

One of the most notable of these efforts took place in Wisconsin. Governor Scott Walker, a Republican who won office in the 2010 midterm elections, proposed as part of a "budget repair bill" a measure that would increase public employees' health-care and pension contributions while eliminating most of their collective bargaining rights. Despite widespread public protests and questions about the legality of the Wisconsin State Assembly's process of approving the measure, the law went into effect on July 1, 2011. Opponents of the measure subsequently gathered enough signatures to force recall elections for Governor Walker, Lieutenant Governor Rebecca Kleefisch, and four Republican state senators in May 2012.

Despite the Wisconsin controversy, several other governors, such as John Kasich of Ohio and New Jersey's Chris Christie, also advocated plans to limit collective bargaining rights for public employees. The state of Michigan in March 2011 passed a measure giving unelected emergency financial managers, who are appointed to financially struggling municipalities and schools, the power to dissolve local governments, void union contracts, and impose new union agreements. In Florida, a law passed in 2011 mandated that, for the first time, public workers contribute to the state's pension system. New York governor Andrew Cuomo negotiated a three-year salary freeze and increased health-care contributions with the state's largest public employee union in 2011, while California's Jerry Brown proposed sweeping changes to the pension system for public employees that included a hike in current worker contributions and a cut in benefits for new hires.

Correcting Patterns of Discrimination in Public Employment

Whereas civil service systems have traditionally emphasized the concept of merit in public employment, other values have become increasingly important. Most prominent is a concern for correcting patterns of discrimination in hiring and treatment of workers in public agencies. The two terms that have been central to that debate are *equal employment opportunity* and *affirmative action*. Equal employment opportunity refers to efforts to eliminate employment discrimination on the basis of race, ethnic background, sex, sexual orientation, age, or physical handicap. It simply seeks to ensure that all people have an equal chance to compete for and hold positions of employment based on their job qualifications. Affirmative action, on the other hand, involves the use of "positive, results-oriented practices to ensure that women, minorities, handicapped persons, and other protected classes of people will be equitably represented in the organization" (Hall & Albrecht, 1979, p. 26).

The concept of equal opportunity has a firm basis in constitutional and legal history, but the primary piece of federal legislation guiding current practices is the Civil Rights Act of 1964. (Many states had passed equal employment legislation in advance of the federal act.) Title VII of the Civil Rights Act banned employment discrimination in areas such as selection, promotion, and training based on race, national origin, sex, or religion and created the Equal Employment Opportunity Commission to investigate complaints of discrimination in the private sector. In 1972 the act was amended through the Equal Employment Opportunity Act to extend coverage to all public-sector employees (at the federal, state, and local levels) and to provide for stronger actions, including filing suits, against those who did not comply with the act.

The original Civil Rights Act did not require affirmative action to correct past patterns of discrimination; this requirement was included in an executive order issued by President Johnson. Executive Order 11246 sought to secure compliance with the Civil Rights Act by requiring that federal contractors not discriminate on the basis of race, creed, or national origin and that they develop affirmative action programs leading to equal employment practices. President Johnson's Executive Order 11375 later added women to the list of protected groups and specified requirements for affirmative action plans.

These requirements were first applied to federal contractors but were soon adopted elsewhere in government and the private sector. The Civil Rights Act of 1964 had declared "that it shall be the policy of the United States to ensure equal employment opportunities for federal employees," but it was an executive order issued by President Nixon in 1969 that required agency heads to create "affirmative programs" in eliminating patterns of discrimination (Shafritz, Hyde, & Rosenbloom, 1981, pp. 185–186). Similarly, state and local governments were brought under the provisions of the Civil Rights Act in 1972 and were threatened with loss of federal funds in the event of noncompliance. Title IX of the Higher Education Act of 1972 was interpreted to require universities to provide equal athletic opportunities for both sexes in intercollegiate sports; the penalty was withdrawal of federal funds from universities found not in compliance.

During the past two decades, however, there has been a waning of support for equal employment opportunity programs. Beginning in 1984, with the Supreme Court's ruling in *Grove City v. Bell* (1984), limits on the applicability of civil rights legislation have been the source of considerable controversy. In *Grove*, the Court narrowly interpreted the law as it regarded sex discrimination to mean that federal funds were to be restricted from the particular program receiving funds rather than from an educational institution as a whole. This meant that if an English department was found guilty of discrimination, its federal funds would be cut off, but funds to other parts of the institution would not be.

Obviously, the effect of the *Grove* case was to severely limit the enforcement power of federal legislation dealing with sex discrimination and, by implication, similar legislation dealing with discrimination based on race, age, or handicap. Barely a week after the *Grove* ruling, for example, the Department of Education dropped charges against the University of Maryland's athletic programs because they did not receive federal aid—though the institution as a whole received substantial federal funding in scholarships, research money, and so on. Not surprisingly, legislation was soon introduced in Congress to put teeth back into the various civil rights laws. The Civil Rights Restoration Act, passed by an overwhelming bipartisan majority, applies not only to educational institutions, but also to a wide range of other public and private organizations receiving federal funds.

The act, in many respects, proved to be the last of Congress's progressive stances on civil rights. Since then, equal opportunity legislation has come under fire from a conservative judiciary as well as from a conservative trend in legislatures at all levels of government. The result has been a shift in the balance of power toward employers and away from those petitioning on the grounds of discrimination.

Americans with Disabilities Act

In 1990, the Americans with Disabilities Act (ADA) was passed. The purpose of the ADA is to prohibit discrimination against 54 million Americans who live with some type of disability (and with the aging of the population that number can be expected to rise). Beginning in 1992, the ADA prohibited employers of twenty-five or more people from discriminating against those with disabilities who can satisfactorily meet the expectations of the job they hold or seek, with or without reasonable accommodation. A disabled person must be qualified, meet educational and skill requirements, and be able to perform the essential functions of the position. However, the employer is required to make reasonable accommodations to the work environment so that the disabled person can perform to the best of his or her ability (Bishop & Jones, 1993, p. 122).

With respect to public services, the ADA prohibits excluding a person from participating in programs or activities of a public entity or denying an individual benefits of its services. A public entity is defined to include not only the federal government but also any part of state or local government. Other sections of the act deal with transportation, public accommodations, and telecommunications.

Although the ADA has substantially changed both employment patterns and the design of public facilities, Supreme Court decisions dealt a major blow to the enforceability of the law. In *Sutton v. United Airlines* (1999), the Court ruled that mitigating devices such as medical therapies and supplies (other than eyeglasses) could be used by employers as the basis for arguing against ADA enforcement. In *University of Alabama v. Garrett* (2001), the Court reviewed a petition brought by employees of the state who claimed to have been discriminated against under the ADA. The Court ruled against the plaintiffs, stating that suits of this nature abrogate states' immunity under the Eleventh Amendment. In doing so, the Court effectively blocked the rights of state employees to file suit for monetary damages in federal court for discrimination under the ADA.

As a result of these and other Supreme Court cases, lower courts have found that people with a range of substantially limiting impairments are not people with disabilities. To correct that situation, Congress passed the ADA Amendments Act of 2008, which became law January 1, 2009. Directly citing the Supreme Court decisions that Congress felt were inappropriate, the Amendments Act revises the definition of "disability" to more broadly encompass impairments that substantially limit major life activity. Congress also decided that mitigating measures have no bearing in determining whether disability qualifies for ADA protection and that impairments that are episodic but substantially limit one's activities when active (for example, epilepsy or post-traumatic stress disorder) can also be used to define disability.

Questions of Compliance

Early efforts to prove discrimination against an employer required proof of "evil intention": evidence that the employer was knowingly discriminating. The difficulty of proving intent led to a new focus on "unequal treatment": proof that an employer used different selection procedures for different groups or used the same procedure in different ways. Still, under this definition, minorities made little progress entering the workforce.

In 1971, however, the Supreme Court, in *Griggs v. Duke Power Company*, settled on a new definition: *adverse or disparate impact*. The *Griggs* decision held that it was no longer necessary to prove discriminatory motive or differential treatment; it was simply necessary to show that employment practices affect one group more harshly than another. The Court stated, "Practices, procedures, or tests neutral on their face, and even neutral in terms of intent cannot be maintained if they operate to 'freeze' the status quo of prior discriminatory practices" (Hays & Reeves, 1984, p. 354).

The notion of adverse impact has been articulated more fully in a set of Uniform Guidelines agreed upon by federal agencies. Under the Uniform Guidelines, employers are required to keep records indicating the relationship between those hired and minorities, including women, and the comparative success of various groups in selection for a position. If, for example, women constitute 50 percent of the labor market, yet only 20 percent of the workforce are women, there is evidence of adverse impact. (Actual figures show that about 41 percent of employees in local government are women, 41 percent in state government are women, and 43 percent in federal government are women. Women are disproportionately represented in lower-paying positions, such as secretarial or clerical jobs.)

The guidelines also follow another aspect of the *Griggs* case. Employers whose practices are found to have adverse impact are required to demonstrate the job relatedness of tests or procedures used in hiring or promotion decisions. That is, if a screening test cannot be shown to relate specifically to job performance, then it cannot be used as a criterion in making employment decisions. Elimination of the Professional and Administrative Career Examination (PACE) is a classic case of the job-relatedness issue. In a court challenge, it was ruled that the PACE exam, at that time the primary test given to applicants for federal managerial positions, was not related to the eventual jobs these people would hold and had an adverse impact on African Americans and Hispanics. For this reason, the exam was shelved.

A conservative shift in the Supreme Court, however, led to an end to these protective standards. In *Wards Cove v. San Antonio* (1989), the Court reversed the *Griggs* interpretation of Title VII and ruled that plaintiffs, not employers, must substantiate their position in discrimination cases. In particular, the Court deemed unconstitutional the earlier ruling that allowed the establishment of a prima facie case based on the "four-fifths rule"—that is, when minority hires constitute less than 80 percent of the nonminority hires. Although the Wards Cove packing plant paid minority employees less and segregated their living and dining quarters, justices said that the workers would have to prove that such practices created a gap between the percentage of minorities actually employed and the percentage in the workforce.

Federal lawmakers tried repeatedly to counter the Wards Cove ruling and restore the more progressive provisions of *Griggs*, finally adopting the Civil Rights Act of 1991. In many respects, though, the act only confused the issue of Title VII protection. Progressive critics argued that too much had to be sacrificed to gain the act's approval. Although it contained several important provisions, such as extending the definition of discrimination to personnel decisions other than hiring and promotion, the act still placed in the Court's hands the final decision on what can be considered discrimination in the workplace.

Consequently, the courts have continued to narrow the bounds on what constitutes discrimination. The Supreme Court's decision in *University of Alabama v. Garrett* (2001) was discussed previously, but another example of this trend can be seen in *Kimel v. Florida Board of Regents* (2000). In *Kimel*, the Court considered a challenge to the Age Discrimination in Employment Act (ADEA) that allows suits to be filed against state governments for monetary damages on the grounds of discrimination in employment decisions. The case was filed by three sets of petitioners in Florida, who claimed to have experienced discrimination on the basis of age during the employment process. However, the Court not only ruled against the plaintiffs, but also criticized Congress for passing the ADEA in the first place. The Court held that (1) "age is not a suspect classification under the Equal

Protection Clause, and so states may discriminate on the basis of age without offending the Fourteenth Amendment, if the age classification in question is rationally related to a legitimate state interest," and (2) Congress had "failed to identify a widespread pattern of age discrimination by states," and it concluded that "this failure confirms that Congress had no reason to believe that broad prophylactic legislation was necessary in this field" (Wise, 2001, p. 348).

Two other cases are likely to confuse matters even further. The *Ricci v. DeStefano* (2009) case concerned a lawsuit brought against the city of New Haven, Connecticut, by a number of white and Hispanic firefighters. The city had used a test for promotion in which none of the black firefighters who passed the exam had scored high enough to be considered for the new positions. After seeing the results the city invalidated the exam, feeling it might be accused of discriminating against the black firefighters. The Supreme Court ruled that New Haven's decision to ignore the test results violated the Civil Rights Act. On the other hand, in *Staub v. Proctor Hospital* (2011), the Court ruled that an employer may be liable for discrimination even when the person who takes the action has no discriminatory intent, if it can be demonstrated that the person was acting in behalf of a supervisor who did have such intent.

The long-term impact of these decisions remains to be seen, but in general the immediate effect is that the burden of proof now lies with the plaintiff on matters of discrimination. Moreover, given the underlying message in the Court's rulings, it appears that even the statutory foundation of equal opportunity employment has come under scrutiny, leaving us to wonder if our days of formal protection against discrimination may be numbered.

Affirmative Action and Reverse Discrimination

Another area of intense controversy involves attempts to correct past patterns of discrimination against minorities and women through the use of affirmative action programs. Such plans typically include (1) a statement of policy indicating a commitment to correct discrimination in employment practices, (2) an analysis of existing practices and their results, and (3) a statement of goals to improve those practices.

Unfortunately, a great deal of popular and legal confusion has developed around the notion of goals and quotas, often resulting in charges of *reverse discrimination* against white males. Although quotas require hiring specific numbers of people from specific groups (and are rarely used in actual practice), goals or timetables are intended to be flexible and are to be established internally by the employer. Both goals and quotas may involve numbers (and this causes some of the confusion), but the goals are merely intended to show a direction in which an employer wishes to move. Generally, a good faith effort in that direction will be viewed as satisfactory in terms of providing opportunities for equal employment and the advantages diversity brings. Even the Supreme Court has found it difficult to clarify exactly what is acceptable and what constitutes reverse discrimination. In *Bakke v. The Regents of the University of California* (1978), the Supreme Court ruled that it was illegal for a university to reserve a specific number of slots in its medical school for minority applicants who were less qualified than other students who were rejected. The Court agreed that race could be considered one factor in an admissions decision, but only one among several.

On a slightly different issue, the Court held in *United Steel Workers of America v. Weber* (1979) that a training program that admitted black workers before white workers with more seniority was acceptable. The key here seemed to be that the company initiated the program voluntarily to eliminate obvious patterns of discrimination and that it did not necessitate the discharge of white workers (Stewart, 1983). On the other hand, in *Firefighters Local Union #1784 v. Stotts* (1984), the Court held that a lower court could not order an employer to lay off more senior employees in favor of less senior employees on the basis of race to preserve a specific percentage of minority employees. Most recently, as we saw earlier, the Court ruled in *Ricci v. DeStefano* (2009) that a hiring test could not be used as a justification for discrimination against those in the majority. The emerging consensus seems to be that affirmative action programs will be limited to specific needs and circumstances. Broad-scale programs are not likely to be accepted.

Federal courts have begun to hear challenges to affirmative action programs used by universities to increase student diversity. The Supreme Court sought to clarify the use of race in admissions in two University of Michigan decisions. In *Grutter v. Bollinger* (2003), the Court upheld the law school's policy of narrowly tailoring the use of race in admissions policy, but in *Gratz v. Bollinger* (2003) the same Court upheld *Bakke* in ruling that the use of a point system awarding minorities extra points in undergraduate admissions was illegal given that it, in effect, was a quota system.

Given this trend, as well as the increasingly conservative view in Washington and in many states as evident in California's Proposition 209 (1996), which ended affirmative action programs, the future of affirmative action seems questionable. Some suggest that although preferences and so-called set asides have leveled the playing field, they no longer offer what the nation needs to ensure a diverse workforce. Unfortunately, the discourse on the issue often degenerates into political rhetoric, with both sides losing sight of an important principle: not only must all people have an equal opportunity to serve, but also the distinct contribution made by each person must be appreciated. By pursuing an agenda to enhance diversity, organizations may gain important contributions from a broader range of viewpoints. (See the box "Take Action: Advantages of Diversity.")

CourseReader Assignment

Log in to **www.cengage.com** and open CourseReader to access the reading:

Read "Diversity in the US Federal Government: Diversity Management and Employee Turnover in Federal Agencies," by Sungjoo Choi. This article specifically explores the relationship between diversity management and employee turnover. However, in the process it raises interesting issues about diversity more generally.

What do you see as the advantages of diversity in public organizations? What does it mean to "manage" diversity? In addition to its effect on employee turnover, what other relationships do you think we might find between diversity and other organizational factors? How might those be "managed"?

Take Action   ADVANTAGES OF DIVERSITY

1. More democratic decision making and better decisions from the number and diversity of views brought to bear on policy making;
2. Improved bureaucratic operations and outputs from decisions and services that are more responsive to the needs of all citizens, particularly members of minority groups;
3. Better human talent development and management decisions;
4. An increase, both symbolically and actually, in the legitimacy of public service and other governance institutions; and
5. Elevation of social equity and justice to prime administrative values on par with other values in public administration paradigms

Adapted from Harvey L. White and Mitchell F. Rice, "The Multiple Dimensions of Diversity and Culture," in *Diversity and Public Administration: Theory, Issues, and Perspectives,* ed. Mitchell F. Rice (Armonk, NY: M.E. Sharpe, 2010), pp. 3-22.

A few alternatives have been offered for promoting and sustaining diversity, including several strategies that target the underlying culture of organizations. The process begins with creating a shared sense of purpose toward diversity and then empowering those at all levels to contribute action steps for achieving this goal. Periodic assessments can be used to determine how successful the organizational change has been and to identify any future barriers the group may need to overcome. As Walter Broadnax comments, "Diversity of individuals and diversity of public organizations once kept us apart. Increasingly, it is the benefits of diversity that will bring us closer together" (Broadnax, 2010, p. S-179).

The Glass Ceiling

Unfortunately, extending diversity throughout the organization, especially at the highest levels of management, has proven difficult. Although the representation of women and minorities in the federal workforce has generally improved along with their representation in the middle- and upper-management levels, certain groups remain underrepresented in the overall workforce, and white women and all minorities remain underrepresented in the key jobs that lead to middle- and upper-management positions. Similarly, at the state and local level, about 51 percent of government employees are women, but they still fill only 40 percent of the management positions (Equal Employment Opportunity Commission, 2009).

The "glass ceiling" encountered by many women and minorities has been recognized in several recent studies. Data from OPM revealed that "women were promoted less than men who had comparable amounts of formal education and experience and who entered government at the same grade levels as the women; and women face obstacles to advancement at lower levels in the pipeline. For those women who have advanced, it usually meant staying late, relocating, or working longer hours" (Desky, 1992, p. 1). Recognizing these concerns, the Civil Rights Act of 1991 set up a "glass ceiling" commission to study the barriers to the advancement of women and minorities in the private sector.

However, efforts to remove the glass ceiling have been thwarted by similar trends affecting affirmative action, and only rarely does the issue of equitable treatment for women in the workplace receive its share of the national spotlight. Congress in 2000 addressed the issue by passing the Equity Contracting for Women Act, which encourages contractors to do business with women-owned businesses in industries where women are underrepresented. The downside of the legislation is that it relies mainly on market forces to achieve parity, meaning that firms are not obligated to contract with women contractors.

The result of these trends is that despite some gains made by women to achieve equal treatment, they still experience a significant gap in pay, job status, and overall employment opportunity (Guy, 1993). The ratio of women's to men's earnings, for all occupations, was 81.2 percent in 2010. The ratio varies by occupation and by industry.

> In 1964, about 19 million of the nation's nonfarm employees were women; the three industries that employed the most women—manufacturing; trade, transportation, and utilities; and local government—accounted for 54 percent of these women. By 2010, nearly 65 million women had jobs, and 53 percent of these women worked in the three industries that employed the most women: education and health services; trade, transportation, and utilities; and local government. During this period, the growth of the education and health industry, and the number of women employed in it, has been notable. (http://www.bls.gov/spotlight/2011/women/)

The political debate in Washington, and in communities across the country, has shifted so far away from any type of "set asides" or "preferential treatment" that even advocates for women find themselves sidestepping the labels outright in their efforts to lobby for new legislation. In fact, even some advocates for protection on the basis of race, sexual preference, and other factors have turned away from protection of women, arguing that women have achieved equal opportunity and that continuation of affirmative action would not only provide an undue advantage but would soon negatively affect women's self-perception.

Relations between Political Appointees and Career Executives

The tension between political responsiveness and managerial effectiveness that characterizes public management is especially well illustrated in the relationship between political appointees and career executives. Each newly elected administration, whether at the federal, state, or local level, has a certain number of top-level managerial positions to fill with people of its choosing. These appointees become the "bosses" of career civil servants who staff the various agencies of government. As you might imagine, there is occasionally some tension between the two groups. Incoming presidents are usually elected on a platform of change and view career employees as representing opposition to change. The political executive wants to move in new policy directions but often has little experience in government operations; the career executive, on the other hand, has both knowledge and expertise but, aware of potential problems, may appear reluctant to change. At the same time, the legality of using political appointments, or patronage, for certain kinds of positions has been challenged in the courts. Political patronage practices were declared unconstitutional by the U.S. Supreme Court in three cases between 1976 and 1990. In *Elrod v. Burns* (1976), the Court held that the Sheriff's Office of Cook County, Illinois, could not fire employees because of their political affiliation. It would be a violation of their First Amendment rights to freedom of belief and association. Similarly, in *Branti v. Finkel* (1980), the Court found that assistant public defenders in Rockland County, New York, could not be terminated because of their party affiliation. These protections were extended to include politically motivated transfers, promotions, recalls from layoffs, and hires in *Rutan v. Republican Party* in 1990. The only exception to this prohibition against patronage is when a position can be shown to have partisan affiliation as a necessary requirement for effective performance. As a practical matter, this still allows appointment of political executives, but it curtails the use of non–civil service appointments for other types of employees.

What Would You Do?

You are the top civil service official in a large federal agency. The new administration has just appointed the cabinet secretary and her top political appointees. You want the agency to work well but are afraid that the new appointees, all drawn from large corporations, may not understand how government works and may make some mistakes that could be damaging to some of your most important programs. What would you do?

In any case, sorting out the relationship between politically appointed executives and career executives brings us back to the old question of politics and administration. One interpretation suggests that the role of the career executive is solely to execute orders given by superior authorities—elected officials and their appointees. In the most extreme formulation of this view, the career executive should be isolated from any involvement in policy development and should concentrate on implementing policies handed down from above.

In contrast to this extreme position, career executives and many others find another interpretation of the politics-administration issue more appealing. This view holds that there are important reasons for career executives' involvement in policy development. Certainly, career executives have the background and expertise to contribute substantially to developing practical and effective public policies. In addition, these executives are likely to be more effective in implementing policy if they have been involved in developing it, if they understand the need for policy changes, and if they feel some sense of ownership of the new policies.

Political appointees, on the other hand, generally come to government with relatively little knowledge about their subject matter (at least compared to career bureaucrats) and certainly with little understanding of how policies are developed in a governmental setting.

While the average tenure of career civil servants is over thirteen years, political executives last an average of only eighteen to twenty-two months. If the stereotype of the bureaucrat is one of hostility to any change, the stereotype of the political appointee is of someone brash, inexperienced, and intent on bringing about change.

There appear to be at least three areas in which further improvements might be made in the relationship between political appointees and career executives. First, political appointees must receive the training and orientation they need to effectively manage public organizations and to work with career executives in both developing and implementing policies. Second, an exchange of views between political leaders and careerists, including team-building sessions, may help to develop greater understanding between the groups and forge more effective working relationships. Third, Congress should reassess the structure of executive management in government and make whatever structural changes are needed to establish a more balanced politics-career interface. But the basic dilemma continues: the political appointee must make sure that the bureaucracy is responsive to the policy directives of the current president; the career executive must maintain high standards of professionalism so that the work of the organization is carried out in the best way possible.

Summary and Action Implications

Personnel systems in the public sector have evolved in response to a variety of competing demands. Much of the earliest personnel legislation at the federal level was directed toward ensuring a neutral and competent bureaucracy protected from the potentially corrupting influences of politics. More recent efforts have sought greater responsiveness on the part of the bureaucracy to political leadership. Personnel systems in the public sector—like systems of budgeting and financial management—reflect important, though sometimes changing, values.

The development of merit systems for public employment reflects such concerns. Basically, policies governing recruitment and classification in the public sector reflect the fact that public organizations must, by definition, operate in the public interest. Similar concerns significantly affect the way contemporary issues such as conditions of employment (drug testing, etc.), labor-management relations, and pay equity are played out in the public sector.

As a manager, you must be concerned with recruitment, training, and retention of the best possible people to work in your organization. You may often feel that public personnel systems and the people who monitor them are simply roadblocks to effective management. Fortunately, in many jurisdictions, the relationship between manager and personnel officer is shifting in a more positive direction.

Personnel managers have been given the responsibility of protecting the merit system from abuse by maintaining detailed records of personnel transactions and enforcing personnel rules and procedures. Personnel officers have thus often been placed in the position of exercising control over the activities of program managers. But public personnel officers, like their private-sector counterparts, have always had another role as well—helping managers employ and utilize personnel effectively.

Although this service aspect of the personnel officer's role has often been treated as a secondary function, there is every reason to believe that the more progressive personnel systems will increasingly emphasize this aspect. Increasingly, personnel officers are shifting from the traditional emphasis on compliance to a new emphasis on consultation. In this role, those in personnel will be available to help with human resource management questions of all kinds. For example, a personnel specialist might be called in to help develop a productivity improvement program or to advise on legal questions. As this new orientation becomes established, line managers will tend to view the personnel officer more as an ally than as a protagonist.

Consequently, you are likely to be more effective as a public manager if you are able to develop a good understanding of the technical details of personnel transactions and an effective working relationship with the personnel professionals in your agency. The support of trained experts in the field of personnel management can help improve your organization's performance and, in turn, its service to the public.

STUDY QUESTIONS

1. "To the victor belong the spoils" was a phrase used to define the spoils system for filling vacancies of government jobs. Discuss the historical use of this system and its contemporary manifestations.

2. What was the Pendleton Act, and how did it help to reform federal personnel procedures?

3. Explain the basic principles of the civil service system.

4. Discuss some of the basic problems President Carter faced regarding personnel and civil service reform.

5. The Civil Service Reform Act provided for various changes in personnel procedures. Explain the importance of this legislation and discuss the impact of its major provisions on the civil service system.

6. What are some of the criticisms of the Civil Service Reform Act?

7. List the steps in recruiting for a government position.

8. Identify various methods of testing and screening applicants.

9. Discuss government methods to combat discrimination in employment activities.

10. What are some of the tools governments use to ensure compliance with equal employment opportunity regulations?

11. With changing labor-management relations, public unionization has become an issue. Explain the factors public managers must recognize to unionize the public sector.

12. Discuss the major components of the bargaining process.

13. Identify arguments against strikes by public employees and give a few examples of strikes that have occurred.

14. Discuss the relationship between political appointees and career executives and how it might be improved.

CASES AND EXERCISES

1. Consider the following case: You are Steve Style, a programming director in a large city's data-processing department. You manage five sections of computer programmers, each made up of a senior programmer and three to four trainees. The department generates computer systems for the other city departments, thus requiring you and your staff to spend a lot of time with the users of the systems. Your staff has a reputation throughout the city for being highly professional. For some time, your boss, Isabel Info, has been talking about the need to expand the programming staff by adding a database administrator.

A few months ago, a new police chief was hired, brought in from another city. In the past, when a new department head came in, if he or she were married, the spouse also found a job somewhere in city government. You had heard that the police chief's wife has a degree in computer science. On Monday, Isabel calls to tell you she has just hired Theresa Topcop as the database administrator in your area. Isabel is happy to get someone with Theresa's education and background, which includes working for several software companies. Isabel also tells you that Theresa is the police chief's wife and that she will be making more money than any of your current senior programmers.

Excited about the addition of a database administrator, you go to tell the staff about the program expansion. Rather than the positive reaction you had expected, theirs is quite negative. David Denman, the most experienced programmer, is upset for two reasons: First, isn't she the police chief's wife? It sounds to him like a deal was made. And second, why didn't any of the current staff have a chance to interview for the new position? Another staff member leaves the meeting grumbling about how much money Theresa will be making in comparison to the other senior programmers.

You go back to your office trying to figure out how to deal with this problem. You're looking forward to having a database administrator, and from what Isabel tells you, Theresa is well qualified. You are concerned about the staff's reaction. You know you will face an uphill battle to convince the users that Theresa is qualified for the position.

- As a practical matter, how does an administration deal with the problem of a "qualified spouse"?
- How do you justify to your staff the fact that Theresa is making a higher salary than any of them and that they didn't have the chance to interview for the position?
- How does the personnel office handle this problem in light of the city's civil service system?

SOURCE: The preceding case was provided by Perri Lampe.

2. Through contacts with the U.S. Office of Personnel Management, the state's personnel office, and the city's personnel office, learn as much as you can about finding employment in a government agency in your area. Ask the following questions:
   - What kinds of positions are typically available?
   - What should you expect in terms of the salary range for entry at the bachelor's or master's level?
   - What benefits and salary increments are associated with these positions?
   - What is the hiring process (how do you apply; what types of tests or interviews are required; who makes the final decision)?

   In addition, contact a variety of nonprofit organizations in your community or a representative of the American Society of Association Executives to discuss career possibilities in the nonprofit sector. Make your report available to students on campus through your academic department and through your school's placement center.

3. Obtain a copy of your school's policy (or policies) on sexual harassment regarding administrators, faculty, staff, and students. Based on conversations with knowledgeable faculty and other school officials, as well as your own reading and research, analyze the policy in terms of the following questions:
   - Does the policy define sexual harassment in terms that are generally understandable?
   - Does the policy specify particular types of actions that will be considered harassment?
   - Are there clearly defined procedures through which charges of harassment can be brought and heard?
   - Are there specific penalties, including dismissal from the school, for prohibited actions?
   - Has the policy been employed in actual cases with success?
   - Does the policy act as a deterrent to sexual harassment?
   - Are there training programs or other educational materials available to help administrators, faculty, and students understand the issue of sexual harassment specifically and gender sensitivity more generally?
   - What would you suggest to strengthen, clarify, or more easily enforce the policy?

SOURCE: The preceding exercise was adapted from material provided by Charles Sampson of the University of Missouri-Columbia.

4. Form small groups to complete the following exercise.

You have just accepted membership on the Energy Resources Commission (ERC) Recruitment Task Force. This task force was recently created by the newly elected governor. The purpose of the task force is to develop recruitment strategies to staff the ERC, which has just been established to fulfill the following functions:

- Determine the future energy needs for the state
- Develop strategies to meet these needs
- Provide technical assistance to the public utilities and agencies involved in meeting these needs

Special recruitment problems are anticipated because this is a completely new agency that will require a significant number of professional and technical personnel. The task force has been charged with the responsibility for developing specific action plans to recruit the required personnel over the next three years. The ERC will require approximately 250 employees by the end of this three-year period, in the following categories:

(1) Management and management staff (50 employees)
(2) Clerical support staff (65 employees)
(3) Professional/technical personnel (100 employees)
(4) Blue-collar/maintenance-type personnel (35 employees)

Factors that may or may not complicate the recruitment effort include the following:

(1) The primary sources of employment in the state are in agriculture, mining, and transportation.
(2) The population of the state totals 10 million, but almost 40 percent of the population resides in a single upstate metropolitan district.
(3) The political environment has traditionally been characterized by conflict between upstate Democrats and downstate Republicans.
(4) This political competition has produced extensive reliance on patronage as the means for staffing most public agencies.
(5) Control of state government has just shifted to the Republicans after twelve years of Democratic control, but one of the new governor's major campaign promises was to professionalize the personnel system and expand civil service coverage to most state employees.
(6) During the campaign, the governor also committed himself to hiring within the state whenever possible.
(7) The state is currently involved in two employment discrimination lawsuits: one brought by the National Organization for Women and the other by the NAACP.
(8) Racial minorities compose 15 percent of the population, but most of these individuals reside in the upstate metropolitan area.
(9) Of the total state workforce, 22 percent are women and 4 percent are classified minority.
(10) The unemployment rate for the state is 12 percent, but most of the unemployed reside in the upstate area.
(11) The unemployment rate by occupational class is as follows: 18 percent blue-collar, 7 percent white-collar, and 3 percent professional/technical.

(12) The unemployment rate for minorities is 21 percent, and the rate for women is 16 percent.

(13) Public-sector unionization is in its early stages of development in the state. Unions are competing for membership and becoming more and more militant. A key demand, which is currently before the legislature, is to establish an "agency shop" for public utility employees.

(14) Citizens' groups and professional associations actively lobbied for the creation of the ERC.

(15) The ERC is being partially funded by a federal grant-in-aid program that, in addition to requiring 50 percent matching funds from the state, also requires establishment of a merit system to ensure nondiscrimination in employment.

The task force is to design a specific recruitment strategy to meet all the staffing needs of the new Energy Resources Commission. Besides paying particular interest to the preceding characteristics, you might also consider the following in your deliberations:

(1) Need and approach for determining the commission's specific staffing requirements

(2) Characteristics of the labor market geographically and by occupational field

(3) Level and availability of the state's labor resources

(4) Extent of search process for candidates geographically and occupationally; type of institutions/organizations/agencies to be covered in recruitment process

(5) Qualification standards (education, training, work experience, residency, physical characteristics, and so on) that should be required for each occupational category in the commission

(6) Implications of these standards for the recruitment effort

(7) Selection devices (practical or aptitude tests, credentials examination, interviews, and so on) and their effect on recruitment

(8) Whether recruitment should be for specific jobs or for a career (and the implication of this decision for qualification standards, selection devices, and so on)

(9) Recruitment approaches for each occupational category—for example, job announcements, written brochures and materials, recruitment visits (and institutions that will be covered, if any), use of professional/collegial contacts (whose?), and so on

(10) Consideration of the factors to emphasize to prospective candidates (that is, what would be the attractive aspects of a job/career in this agency in this locale?)

FOR ADDITIONAL READING

Bowman, J. S., J. P. West, and M. A. Beck. *Achieving Competencies in Public Service: The Professional Edge.* Armonk, NY: M.E. Sharpe, 2009.

Capozzoli, Thomas, and R. Steven McVey. *Managing Violence in the Workplace.* Delray Beach, FL: St. Lucie Press, 1996.

Cayer, N. Joseph. *Public Personnel Administration*. Belmont, CA: Wadsworth/Thomson Learning, 2003.

Coleman, Charles J. *Managing Labor Relations in the Public Sector*. San Francisco: Jossey-Bass, 1990.

Condrey, Stephen E., and James L. Perry. *Handbook of Human Resource Management in Government*. San Francisco: Jossey-Bass, 2005.

Dresang, Dennis L. *Public Personnel Management and Public Policy*. Dallas: Pearson Publications, 1999.

Durant, Robert F. *The Oxford Handbook of American Bureaucracy*. New York: Oxford University Press, 2010.

Farazmand, Ali. *Strategic Public Personnel Administration: Building and Managing Human Capital for the 21st Century*. Westport, CT: Praeger Publishers, 2007.

Farnham, David. *Managing People in the Public Service*. Basingstoke, UK: Macmillan Business, 1996.

Huddleston, Mark, and William Boyer. *The Higher Civil Service in the United States*. Pittsburgh: University of Pittsburgh Press, 1996.

Ingraham, Patricia, and Carolyn Ban, eds. *Legislating Bureaucratic Change: The Civil Service Reform Act of 1978*. Albany: State University of New York Press, 1984.

Jackson, Susan E., ed. *Diversity in the Workplace: Human Resource Initiatives*. New York: Guilford Press, 1992.

Kearney, Richard C. *Public Sector Performance: Management, Motivation and Measurement*. Boulder, CO: Westview Press, 2000.

Klingner, Donald E., John Nalbandian, and Jared Llorens. *Public Personnel Management: Contexts and Strategies*. New York: Longman, 2009.

Maranto, Robert, and David Shultz. *A Short History of the United States Civil Service*. Lanham, MD: University Press of America, 1991.

Menzel, Donald C., and Harvey L. White. *The State of Public Administration: Issues, Challenges, and Opportunities*. Armonk, NY: M.E. Sharpe, 2011.

National Academy of Public Administration. *Modernizing Federal Classification: An Opportunity for Excellence*. Washington, DC: National Academy, 1991.

Nigro, Lloyd G., and Felix A. Nigro. *The New Public Personnel Administration*. 4th ed. Itasca, IL: F. E. Peacock Publishers, 1993.

Pynes, Joan E. *Human Resources Management for Public and Nonprofit Organizations*. 2nd ed. San Francisco: Jossey-Bass, 2004.

Riccucci, Norma. *Public Personnel Administration and Labor Relations*. Armonk, NY: M.E. Sharpe, 2007.

Riccucci, Norma, Katherine C. Naff, Jay M. Shafritz, and David H. Rosenbloom. *Personnel Management in Government: Politics and Process*. Boca Raton, FL: CRC Press, 2007.

Rice, Kenneth W. *Strategic Diversity: How to Leverage the Differences within the New Workforce for Improved Organizational Performance*. Bloomington, IN: Xlibris Corp., 2009.

Rice, Mitchell F., ed. *Diversity and Public Administration: Theory, Issues, and Perspectives*. Armonk, NY: M.E. Sharpe, 2010.

Risher, Howard, Charles H. Fay, et al. *New Strategies for Public Pay*. San Francisco: Jossey-Bass, 1997.

Robinson, Dana Gaines, and James C. Robinson. *Performance Consulting*. San Francisco: Berrett Koehler Publishers, 1995.

Selden, Sally Coleman. *The Promise of Representative Bureaucracy*. Armonk, NY: M.E. Sharpe, 1997.

Shafritz, Jay M., Albert C. Hyde, and David H. Rosenbloom. *Personnel Management in Government: Politics and Process*. 4th ed. New York: Marcel Dekker, 1991.

Sloane, Arthur A., and Fred Witney. *Labor Relations*. 8th ed. Englewood Cliffs, NJ: Prentice-Hall, 1994.

Stivers, Camilla. *Gender Images in Public Administration: Legitimacy and the Administrative State*. 2nd ed. Thousand Oaks, CA: Sage Publications, 2002.

Sylvia, Ronald D., and C. Kenneth Meyer. *Public Personnel Administration*: Fort Worth, TX: Harcourt College Publishers, 2002.

THE ETHICS OF PUBLIC SERVICE

So far we have focused on the context of public administration—the values, structures, and relationships you need to act effectively and responsibly in public organizations. Now we begin a transition to more skill-based issues by exploring the ethical issues raised in public service. An ethical posture toward work in public organizations requires not only knowing the right answers, but also being willing and able to do what is right. You must be prepared to act.

As a public manager, you will often face difficult ethical choices. These choices may present themselves in several ways. "It is certainly true that in many administrative ethics dilemmas, multiple rationales for action can be considered. It is also true there is no science or set of fixed rules for resolving the dilemmas. Without question, ethical tensions are inevitable" (Goodsell, 2006, p. 136). Understanding the moral implications of your actions and resolving the dilemmas they pose are some of the most difficult problems you will face when working in the public sector. Consequently, your ability to understand the context in which public problems arise and to work them out in a careful, reasoned, and ethical fashion will be essential to your success (and your own sense of personal well-being).

In this chapter, we examine a variety of ethical issues faced by public managers. Some involve concerns that might arise in any organization—cases of lying, cheating, or stealing, or questions about what to do when you feel compelled to refuse an order from your boss. Others are more directly connected to the special values that underlie public service, involving the relationship between political leaders and career civil servants or between competing demands for efficiency and responsiveness.

Approaches to Ethical Deliberation

Ethics is a branch of philosophy concerned with the study of moral principles and action. To properly define *ethics*, therefore, we must first understand the meaning of morality. *Morality* is concerned with those practices and activities that are considered right or wrong; it is also concerned with the values those practices reflect and the rules through which they are carried out. The morality of a society, a political system, or a public organization concerns what is considered to be right or wrong within that group. Morality expresses certain values that members of the group hold to be important and is reflected in laws, rules, and regulations, or in policies and procedures. Moral action, in turn, is action that is consistent with the group's morality—that which expresses the group's most basic commitments about what is right and what is wrong.

Ethics, on the other hand, can be defined as "a systematic attempt through the use of reason to make sense of our individual and social moral experience in such a way as to determine the rules which ought to govern human conduct" (DeGeorge, 1982, p. 12). Ethics is concerned with the process by which we clarify what is right and wrong and by which we act on what we take to be right; it involves the use of reason in determining a proper course of action. Ethics is the search for moral standards.

Though we have defined ethics as the study of morality, the two terms are often used interchangeably. For example, we often call an action that is morally correct an ethical action. Similarly, we speak of codes of moral conduct as codes of ethics. Despite the overlapping uses of the terms, the distinction between morality and ethics is important not only for philosophical reasons, but also because focusing on ethics emphasizes the individual's active involvement in searching out morally correct positions. Ethics calls us into action; it requires us to reason, to analyze, and to seek guidance as to the proper course of action.

This deliberative aspect of ethics is important because the issues you will face in public organizations are rarely black or white. Should you lie to a legislator so as to carry out a policy you think is correct? Should you bend the rules to benefit a client in need? Should you follow orders from an organizational superior even if you know you are being asked to do something wrong? These questions and the thousands of others you may encounter in public organizations don't have easy answers. To act properly, you must be able to sort through the many and often competing values that underlie your work, and you must be able to come to a reasoned conclusion that will form the basis for action.

It's not enough to simply say, "It depends," and then go about your business, though such a position has gained widespread currency in our society. *Ethical (or moral) relativism* is the belief that actions that are immoral in some places or circumstances are moral in others and that one can make moral judgments only by taking into account the context in which an action occurs. According to this view, there are no universal rules of conduct that apply in all situations, as we will see in our discussion of postmodern ethics. A defense of the relativist position is that different cultures have different rules of conduct. One culture may consider it proper to leave elderly people to die in solitude, whereas another may give them considerable care and attention.

Such arguments, however, may fail to take into account larger and more unifying moral principles, such as respect for the elderly. Furthermore, the relativist position seems at odds with our moral experience. When we make the judgment that murder is immoral, we don't mean that it is immoral for some individuals and not others. We don't even mean that murder is immoral in some countries and not in others. We claim that murder is immoral for all people at all times—and we can defend our statement on both rational and emotional grounds. This position suggests that there is only one right answer to moral questions (even though that answer may be hard to find!). The postmodern position is quite different but also compelling. In either case, by understanding the context in which an action occurs, working through the various arguments in behalf of one position or another, and arriving at a set of guidelines for action, one can at least act with greater clarity and confidence.

What are the steps in ethical deliberation? First, as displayed in the box "Take Action: Steps in Ethical Deliberation," you should attempt to *clarify the facts*. Although most ethical issues involve both facts and values, and the facts alone are not likely to resolve the issue, it is important to establish the facts as clearly as possible. A pollution control policy may require precise measurements of pollutants released into the air; knowing the exact measurements, rather than speculating about them, may resolve the issue. In other cases, merely clarifying the facts will help resolve certain ethical problems.

Second, it is easier to resolve ethical issues if those involved come to some agreement about *basic principles*. These may be broad moral standards (such as freedom or justice), laws or rules accepted by society, or standards of behavior appropriate to a particular group or organization. These ideas are, of course, deeply held by members of any society or organization, so disagreements may be marked. For example, two detectives may have dramatically different views about how to treat criminals, but if they clarify their agreement on the basic goal of fighting crime, they may be able to reconcile their differences. Generally speaking, any progress you can make in establishing a common ground or in bringing about agreement on basic principles will help resolve the issue.

Third, one of the central aspects of ethical deliberation is the *analysis of arguments* presented in behalf of various viewpoints. The arguments may be articulated by different individuals or different groups, or they may simply be arguments and counterarguments you think through yourself. In either case, you will need to consider the evidence presented, the justifications for various viewpoints, and possible fallacies of the justifications. Throughout the process of argumentation, dialogue is extremely helpful in clarifying one's position. (If the problem is one you are considering alone, finding someone to talk through the issues with you is a good idea.)

Ultimately, however, you will need to *make a decision and act on it*. Ethical deliberation will lead you to a decision, but acting in a way that is consistent with that decision is also important, though often difficult.

Take Action   STEPS IN ETHICAL DELIBERATION

1. Clarify the facts.
2. Agree on basic principles.
3. Analyze the arguments.
4. Make a decision and act on it.

Reasoning, Development, and Action

You will be better prepared to deliberate if you become familiar with some basic approaches to ethical reasoning: moral philosophy, moral psychology, and moral action. In each case, we will present only a brief overview. You should be aware that there are varying and sometimes conflicting interpretations of these issues, and you may find others (perhaps including your teacher) who disagree with the formulation presented here. Consider this material merely an invitation for further learning!

Moral Philosophy Regarding *moral philosophy*, we can ask: given a particular set of circumstances, how do we determine what is right and what is wrong? In other words, how do we go about figuring out the proper course of action? One approach is to consider who will benefit and who will suffer from various alternative actions, then ask which course of action provides the greatest benefit at the least cost. Another approach is to search for a moral principle or rule against which to measure aspects of the particular case. In the first approach, one focuses on the consequences of the action; in the second, one looks for universal rules of conduct.

One of the most common forms of ethical deliberation is *utilitarianism,* which focuses on the consequences of actions. Utilitarianism holds that an action is right, compared to other courses of action, if it results in the greatest good (or at least the minimum harm) for the greatest number of people. Proponents of this view contend that there are no universal principles guiding action, but rather the likely benefits and costs associated with any action must be calculated to judge the action either moral or immoral.

Obviously, this view leans toward relativism; according to a utilitarian, telling the truth cannot be judged a priori either right or wrong. Rather, the rightness or wrongness of telling the truth depends on a calculation of who is helped and who is harmed. Only then can a moral judgment be rendered. In the utilitarian view, "Actions themselves have no intrinsic values. They are simply means to attain things which do have value" (DeGeorge, 1982, p. 40).

An administrator employing a utilitarian approach to moral reasoning in a specific situation would ask what the likely outcomes of one course of action or another might be. If building a new highway through a particular neighborhood would inconvenience a few people but benefit many others, then building that highway in that location would be considered a proper course of action. The administrator would not follow any predetermined moral principle (such as that citizens should not be arbitrarily displaced), but would calculate costs and benefits relative to the specific case. Moreover, the administrator would not generalize beyond the specific case; each act would be judged on its own merits.

A contrasting approach to moral reasoning based on the search for general rules or principles of conduct is often called deontological. *Deontology* holds that broad principles of rightness and wrongness can be established and that these principles are not dependent on the consequences of a particular action. Those who hold this view tend to focus on duties or responsibilities (*deontology* derives from the Greek word for "duty"). Quite simply, one's duty is to do what is morally correct and avoid doing that which is morally wrong, regardless of the consequences. Deontologists thus tend to focus on broad principles of right and wrong, such as those embodied in concepts like "rights" or "justice."

Using the deontological approach, an administrator would act in accord with generally accepted moral precepts, such as honesty or benevolence. Administrators are expected, for example, to tell the truth, keep their promises, and respect the dignity of the individual. Doing so does not derive from laws or codes of ethics, but from generally accepted moral principles. In particular situations, these actions might even be harmful to the overall interests of the organization or the society, but because the actions could be justified as consistent with a shared sense of moral order, the administrator should feel strongly compelled to act in that way.

Philosopher John Rawls presents one contemporary deontological theory that has received considerable attention. His approach emphasizes fairness or equity in policy decisions (Rawls, 1971). Rawls's theory suggests that if decisions were made under conditions in which the decision maker had no knowledge of whether they would personally accrue harm or benefit by choosing one way or another, then fairness would likely prevail. Imagine a city council committee deciding where to spend $1 million on street improvements. If all members of the committee acted in their own interest, they might spend the money in their own neighborhoods (and those would likely be the more affluent neighborhoods). On the other hand, if all members of the committee acted under a "veil of ignorance," not knowing where they lived or whether or not they were affluent, they would most likely spend the money to bring the poorer streets up to some standard level (and in doing so, they would likely spend more in less affluent neighborhoods). If all public decisions were rendered by acting out of concern for fairness rather than self-interest, Rawls argues, a far different moral order would prevail—one that was much more consistent with the basic principles of liberty and justice.

Moral Psychology Psychologist Lawrence Kohlberg devised a scheme outlining three levels of moral development through which people pass: the preconventional, conventional, and postconventional stages (Kohlberg, 1971). According to Kohlberg, most people operate on one of the first two levels of moral development, and no one operates exclusively on the third level.

At the *preconventional level*, children begin to develop certain ideas about right and wrong. They interpret these ideas in terms of the consequences of their actions or the physical power of those around them. At an early stage, the ideas are associated with punishments; for example, if the child writes on the wall with a crayon, the child will be scolded. To avoid the negative consequences associated with writing on the wall, the child avoids that behavior. Later on, the child begins to behave in certain ways to receive rewards, such as parental praise.

Whether to avoid negative consequences or to receive praise, the child begins to behave in ways that we characterize as right rather than wrong. Of course, from the child's point of view, there is no moral code; the child is merely doing things to avoid punishments or to seek rewards. At this level of moral development, therefore, the consequences of our actions—the rewards or punishments we receive—determine whether we consider our actions right or wrong. The preconventional orientation is, of course, one that we all carry into adulthood.

At the *conventional level* of moral development, people behave morally in terms of conformity to various standards or conventions of the family, group, or nation. The individual seeks to conform to given moral standards and, indeed, to actively support and maintain those standards. This level involves two stages. Kohlberg calls the first the "Good Boy/Nice Girl" stage, at which we conform to expectations of parents, teachers, or peers and to the norms we learn at home, church, or school. We develop moral rules or codes, standards of right and wrong; however, what we think of as good behavior is really just that which meets the expectations of others.

A second stage in the conventional level of moral development is the "Law and Order" orientation. At this stage, we develop an orientation toward authority and the social order.

We learn what it means to be a "good citizen" and accept the importance of living by the conventional rules of society. Notions of duty and honor tend to dominate one's moral perspective at this level. We recognize that certain behaviors are wrong—lying, cheating, stealing—but if asked why, we can only answer, "Because everyone knows they are wrong" (DeGeorge, 1982, p. 25). Most adults continue to operate, at least in part, at this level of moral development.

Few adults reach the final level, the *postconventional*, but some do. At this level, people accept moral principles and behave according to those principles, not merely because someone says they should, but because they know themselves what makes these principles right. The individual seeks to define moral principles and to understand how those values operate independently of any group or society. A first postconventional stage is called the "social-contract" or "legalistic" stage, which has a strong utilitarian bias. The individual recognizes the rights of other individuals, including the right to one's own beliefs and values, and how societies are constituted to support those rights. The result is a legalistic viewpoint, though it recognizes the possibility of changing the legal order (rather than freezing it, as in the previous level). Changes of this sort are often supported based on the greatest good for the greatest number.

What Would You Do?

You were recently appointed city manager in a small community in Tennessee. Yesterday, the mayor gave you an envelope filled with receipts from a recent trip he took to an economic development conference. Included were receipts from a four-day vacation that the mayor and his wife took at a resort near the conference city. It was clear the mayor wanted the city to reimburse him for everything that was included in the envelope. What would you do?

The second stage of the postconventional level represents the highest stage of moral development. At this stage, the individual freely chooses to live by a particular set of abstract moral principles, such as justice, equality, and respect for individual dignity. One chooses to follow these precepts not for reward or punishment and not to meet others' expectations, but because one understands why the principle should be supported and chooses to live by that standard. The actual standards may be the same in both the conventional and postconventional levels, but there is an important difference in the *reason* one holds an action to be right or wrong.

Although we have focused on Kohlberg's work here, we should point out that there are several alternatives to his interpretation that have been voiced recently. One important alternative, for example, is that suggested by Carol Gilligan. Gilligan argues that, in contrast to the rational and impartial perspective of Rawls and Kohlberg, one may interpret moral theory in terms of care and relationships. According to Gilligan, a final and mature morality involves an interaction between the concerns of impartiality and those of personal relationship and care (Blum, 1988, pp. 472–491).

As you work in and with public organizations, you will come to recognize that many of the ethical decisions you make are based in a level of moral development. We do certain things because they will lead to rewards or punishments, and we do other things because we must adhere to laws or organizational standards of conduct. For example, you may obey an order from a superior so that you won't be fired, or you may purchase a new piece of equipment through a bidding process rather than from a friend because that's the law. But you will also encounter cases that will require you to think more carefully and personally about the standards you are willing to live by. For example, purchasing a piece of equipment might be complicated by the fact that your supervisor *ordered* you to purchase the equipment from a friend without other bids. In cases such as these, postconventional or principled reasoning may be essential. Certainly if you recognize that not all answers come from the power or expectations of others and that careful deliberation concerning moral principles is often quite appropriate, you will be better positioned to make the correct ethical decisions, time after time.

Moral Action Knowing the proper and correct course of action is not enough. You must act in a way that is consistent with what you consider to be right. (After all, we describe people as having "integrity" not merely on the basis of what they believe, but on the basis of how they act.) This concern is especially significant for a public manager (or, for that matter, any other professional) who wishes to act ethically. Questions of ethics in the public service are not abstract; they are real. And they have immediate and sometimes serious human consequences. It is thus important to consider how we can ensure moral actions in public organizations.

A long-standing philosophical tradition holds that putting principles (whether utilitarian, deontological, or otherwise) into action requires the development of "character" on the part of the individual. In other words, it is necessary to apply a complex set of general principles to specific cases—something that requires more than abstract knowledge. Aristotle spoke of the importance of gaining "practical wisdom" so as to make morally correct judgments in specific situations. This practical wisdom or "virtue" requires that the individual not simply know how to apply given principles, but rather why to do so. That is, to bring moral knowledge to bear in the "real world," the individual needs a strong sense of what is ideal in human conduct. Terry Cooper, for example, argues that virtues are character traits acquired through reflection and conduct. They involve an integration of both thought and feeling by which potentially conflicting tendencies are brought under control (Cooper & Wright, 1992, p. 6).

This "ethics of virtue," then, is not merely another philosophical approach but a way of developing the skills one brings to the problem of ethical decision making. Aristotle speaks of developing the skills of virtue in the same way we develop other skills—that is, by practice: "The virtues we get first by exercising them....For the things we have to learn before we can do them, we learn by doing them....We become just by doing just acts, temperate by doing temperate acts, brave by doing brave acts" (McKeon, 1941, p. 952).

But what are the virtues that we must practice? Obviously, this question has challenged philosophers over the centuries. Answers range from honesty, courage, and trustworthiness to kindness, fairness, and dependability, but most seem to center around concerns for benevolence and justice. If this is the case, then all persons should practice these virtues, whereas members of specific professions (such as public administrators) should practice applications of these virtues in their specific situations (Tong, 1986, pp. 91–92).

How then, does one sort out the various philosophical and psychological approaches one might employ to make ethical choices in the "real world"? First, if you set about solving difficult moral problems through the application of broad moral principles in specific situations, you need to understand the principles and moral reasoning that underlie them. Second, you must engage in careful and consistent ethical deliberation, through self-reflection and dialogue with others. Third, you must understand how virtues such as benevolence or justice are played out in public organizations; that is, you must recognize the political and ethical context that conditions the moral priorities of the public service.

James Svara has suggested an approach to ethics that takes various considerations into account. The first is the duty-based approach, which emphasizes the responsibilities of public administrators and the idea of public service (Svara, 2007, p. 28):

1. Put the public interest over personal interest.
2. Display a service orientation and commitment to serve.
3. Have a commitment to procedural fairness.
4. Exercise fiduciary responsibility.
5. Be bound by and uphold the law.
6. Support the democratic process.
7. Be responsive to the policy goals of political superiors while fairly examining all policy options and exercising leadership appropriate to position.

The duty-based approach is a useful tool for public administrators, but if used alone, it may impose unanticipated problems. It also may be used as a loose guide for administrators who often face complicated situations that cannot be easily resolved if virtue, principle, and consequences are not taken into account.

The virtue-based approach concentrates on what "a good person would do" and is highly intuitive. It reflects the values and norms widely accepted in society. But when used alone, this approach could put the administrator in a dilemma because what is good for one person is not always considered good for others.

The principle-based approach guides the administrator in what is right to do (unlike duty, which says what is obligatory). While this approach may be useful for the public administrator because it relies on a broader perception of what is good and what is bad (external source), it still should not be used alone for many reasons. Some principles are contradictory, such as the principle of doing no harm and the principle of honesty.

The consequential approach is the least used approach in public administration. Also called the utilitarian approach, the idea is that an ethical outcome produces "the greatest good for the greatest number." On the surface, this seems right but is difficult to implement. What if the greatest good for the greatest number harms minorities in an unethical way? Can we justify that? Are the means used for the ends ethical?

The questions that come from any approach used alone indicate that public administrators should use a comprehensive approach that would put duty in the center but also would take into account virtues, principles, and consequences. For this reason, Svara proposes an ethical triangle model, which according to the author "conveys the idea that administrators should act on their duty to promote public interest by seeking a balance of virtue, principle, and good consequences" (Svara, 2007, p. 67). The use of an ethical triangle prevents under- and overutilization of any approach taken alone, and it also "helps to prevent the shortcomings of using any of the approaches alone" (Svara, 2007, p. 68). Rather, it allows one to benefit from the advantages of separate approaches while avoiding the worst disadvantages of the "pure" approaches. For example, if we have the intent to achieve the greatest good for the greatest number, the ethical triangle reminds us to look also at our duties (serve the public interest), principles (no harm for anyone), and virtues (being fair and just).

As you approach ethical questions, it may be helpful to consider first the utilitarian position: what are the costs and benefits, and which alternative will bring the greatest benefits? Next, you might ask whether the alternative you chose will infringe upon the rights of others and, if so, whether there are overwhelming factors that justify such an outcome. Then, you might ask whether the chosen alternative violates principles of equity and fairness and, if so, whether again there are overwhelming factors that would justify the outcome. Finally, you might ask whether the alternative is consistent with your ideals with respect to human conduct (especially the conduct of public affairs) and whether by choosing this alternative you will be acting in a way you consider virtuous. At any point, you may find that the alternative comes up short, and you must search for another. Remember that your ultimate goal is the development of virtue and the application of sound ethical reasoning to public problems.

Postmodern Ethics

The *conventional* or *modernist* approach to administrative ethics has been recently challenged by public administration theorists Michael Harmon and O. C. McSwite. In their book, *Whenever Two or More Are Gathered* (2011), they argue that modernist administrative ethics carries two basic assumptions that are increasingly being called into question. The first assumption is that human beings are consciously rational creatures, an assumption that underlies not only administrative ethics but also much of Western philosophical thinking. This assumption is being challenged by contemporary psychoanalysis and psychology, both of which see human behavior as driven by largely unconscious motivations. This position is being reinforced by recent brain research that emphasizes the importance of affective or nonrational processes. Indeed, human intention often appears to be constructed retrospectively, more as a rationalization of actions chosen through the unconscious working of the brain. The second assumption of modernist administrative ethics is that language carries stable meanings. An increasingly vibrant challenge to this position holds that language is much more contingent, very much dependent on context.

An alternative to conventional administrative ethics is *postmodernism*, put forward by Harmon and McSwite (2011) in what they term "relationship-based ethics." Recognizing that human circumstances are inherently "messy" means that social situations and social institutions are at best incomplete and therefore open to development and transformation (p. 217). Developing ways in which ethical questions can be dealt with in a contingent but stable and creative way is the task of relationship-based ethics. While many theorists have proposed approaches to this issue, Harmon and McSwite especially note the work of Carl Jung, the Swiss psychoanalyst, and his development of a "dialectical ethics," bringing together ego and shadow to create a synthesis of both (p. 220). This mode of ethical decision making does not simply fall on the continuum between principle or duty versus situational or relativist schools of thought. Indeed, a relationship-based ethics would propose a way of bringing people together to deliberate in such a way as to arrive at shared meaning and just outcomes.

Similarly, Zygmunt Bauman, who takes an explicitly postmodernist stance, argues that in contemporary society, morality has come to be defined largely through the philosophical search for absolutes, universals, and foundations. The search for absolutes is seen as problematic because of the fragmentation of today's world and the resulting difficulty that any one person or group or culture has establishing truth or reality. In such a fractured society, one in which the language of any group or culture reflects its own circumstances and cannot be generalized to others, there is no basis for privileging one version of the truth over another. "The choice is not between following the rules and breaking them, as there is no one set of rules to be obeyed or breached. The choice is, rather, between different sets of rules and different authorities preaching them" (Bauman, 1993, p. 20).

The plurality of views means that there are different and competing criteria for evaluating various positions. For example, something might be evaluated either as aesthetically pleasing or economically advantageous. But neither can be given priority over the other. Thus, we are left with the dilemma that "actions may be right in one sense, wrong in another" (Bauman, 1993, p. 5). We are left to wonder which action ought to be measured by what criteria. There is no basis for choice because there is no absolute code or set of rules that can be demonstrated to be binding in all circumstances. "Rules would tell me what to do and when; rules would tell me where my duty starts and where it ends" (Bauman, 1993, p. 60). But no universal rules are possible.

In proposing an alternative to traditional approaches, Margaret Urban Walker distinguishes two models of morality. The first, which she calls the *theoretical-juridical* model, includes utilitarian, contract, Neo-Kantian, or rights-based theories, all of which see "morality as a compact, propositionally codifiable, impersonally action-guiding code with an agent, or as a compact set of law-like propositions that 'explain' the moral behavior of a well-formed moral agent" (Walker, 1998, pp. 7–8). Presumably all such codes would be universal. (This is the approach found in most studies of administrative ethics.)

The alternative she calls the *expressive-collaborative* model, a model that she argues is increasingly necessary today because it is extremely difficult to find a specific moral code that applies in all, or even most, situations. People have different ideas about what constitutes ethical behavior depending on their position in society, their cultural background, or the accepted practices of their groups, their organizations, their "tribes," or their communities. People find that their interactions make sense within one frame of reference but make no sense to those outside that frame. "An expressive-collaborative model looks at moral life as a continuing negotiation *among* people, a practice of mutually allotting, assuming, or deflecting responsibilities of important kinds, and understanding the implications of doing so" (Walker, 1998, p. 60). The resolution of a moral problem then may not be an appeal to authority or even precedent but rather the interactive process of constructing a narrative, one that is not at all set at the beginning and only takes shape as the negotiation continues. The answer is not set in stone waiting to be discovered. Consequently, in Walker's words, "the resolution of a moral problem may be less like the solution to a puzzle or the answer to a question than like the outcome of a negotiation" (Walker, 1998, p. 70).

Issues of Administrative Responsibility

People who work in or with public organizations face literally dozens of ethical dilemmas. Some—like lying, cheating, or stealing—are the same problems that many others face. But some, like the public manager's commitment to democratic standards or feelings about the political involvement of public employees, are peculiar to public organizations.

One of the most troublesome "broad-range" issues in the field of public administration is that of administrative responsibility. (In the section that follows, we focus much more specifically on issues where personal values, such as honesty, equity, and justice, become deeply intermingled with the broader values of public service.) As a public manager, you may often confront the potentially conflicting demands of operating as efficiently as possible while, at the same time, being fully responsive to administrative superiors, to the legislature, to the citizenry, and to the principles of democratic governance generally. This tension between *efficiency* and *responsiveness* characterizes many of the problems public managers face.

As we have seen, the tension between efficiency and responsiveness grows from two other issues that are deeply rooted in the history of public administration: those of politics and administration, and of bureaucracy versus democracy. Early writers in the field sought a clear distinction between *politics* and *administration*, arguing that, wherever possible, administrative activities should be insulated from the potentially corrupting influence of politics. Obviously, this idea was based on the assumption that policy making could be distinguished from policy implementing. Making such an assumption allows easy resolution of questions of democratic responsibility: the legislature, charged with making policy, should be responsive to the people; the administrative agencies, charged with implementing policy, should be responsive to the legislature. The requirements of democracy will be met by a neutral and competent public bureaucracy that follows the mandates of the legislative body. This is called the doctrine of *neutral competence*. Most writers and practitioners clearly preferred this somewhat narrow view of administrative responsibility. Indeed, the doctrine of neutral competence, and the politics-administration dichotomy on which it is based, continue to influence the field. But there were and are many who recognize the difficulty of maintaining a neutral public bureaucracy. Some even argue that the more active role that administrative agencies play in the policy process is not only inevitable but also proper.

Networking

For general discussions of ethics in government, see the Center for Public Integrity at http://www.iwatchnews.org/; the Institute for Philosophy and Public Policy at http://policy.gmu.edu/Home/ResearchPublications/ResearchCenters/InstituteforPhilosophy andPublicPolicy/tabid/464/Default.aspx; and the Josephson Institute of Ethics at www.josephsoninstitute.org.

The Limits of Administrative Discretion

We have noted that administrators take their primary cues from the actions of legislatures that initiate programs and from executives who are charged with carrying out the programs. If you are hired to manage a new agency, one of your first priorities will be to familiarize yourself with the legislation that created the agency and with any executive orders or directives outlining the agency's responsibilities. But if your situation is typical, you will find that neither the legislation nor the directions you receive from the executive are sufficiently detailed to answer all the questions your work raises. There will be a need to develop policies regarding these issues—policies that are, in effect, merely more detailed pieces of "legislation." In addition, as you get into the work, you may find it necessary to ask the legislature or the chief executive to make certain changes in the rules and regulations under which you operate.

The problem, of course, is to make sure that your policies or recommendations for change are consistent with the wishes of the citizenry (see the box "Exploring Concepts: Today's Leadership Challenge"). In most jurisdictions, of course, the legislature and the chief executive are popularly elected, and their reelection depends on their response to the public's perceived needs and interests. For them, the electoral process ensures responsiveness, at least in theory. As long as you are acting in a way that is clearly consistent with legislative intent, you are likely to be considered appropriately responsive. But because most situations aren't that clear, the question becomes "How can we ensure that the administrator is exercising discretion in a way consistent with the will of the people, whether expressed in the Constitution, the laws of the land, or the preferences of citizens?" Historically, two answers to this question have been offered. In an important debate in the pages of the *Public Administration Review* and other journals some forty years ago, Herman Finer argued that, to maintain responsiveness to the public, managers in public organizations should be subjected to strict and rigid controls by the legislature. His question was straightforward (though perhaps overdrawn): "Are the servants of the public to decide their own course, or is their course of action to be decided by a body outside themselves?" (Finer, 1972, p. 8). His answer was equally direct: only through specific and detailed legislation carefully limiting the work of public managers could responsiveness to the legislature be maintained. This interpretation of how to ensure responsiveness is often called *objective responsibility*, depending as it does on objective external controls.

Exploring Concepts

TODAY'S LEADERSHIP CHALLENGE

Citizen engagement is part of a family of democratic reform ideas—an aspect of our political culture—that includes public participation, public involvement, participatory democracy, deliberative democracy, and collaborative governance. These terms make distinctions about the purpose, scope, and techniques of participation, but they all recognize and build upon a belief that citizens have the right to participate in decisions that affect their lives. Citizen participation policies and programs thus reflect a basic commitment to this principle and invite citizens to engage in policy development and decision-making activities. Citizen participation activities revolve around six general aims:

- Inform and educate the public on important policy issues.
- Improve government decisions by supplying better information upward from citizens to decision makers.
- Create opportunities for citizens to shape and, in some cases, determine public policy.
- Legitimate government decisions by ensuring that the voices of those impacted by government policy have been heard, considered, and addressed.
- Involve citizens in monitoring the outcomes of policy for evaluation.
- Improve the quality of public life by restoring trust and engagement of citizens in public life.

Since the modern era of citizen participation in federal policy decision making was entered…government is being asked to adopt a more active stance toward involving citizens in service-delivery; democratic activists are saying this is not enough.

As a result of these influences, citizen participation is being recast as an instrument to improve the quality and legitimacy of government action. "One of the powerful things about citizen engagement," a senior manager told us, "is that it takes government out of the middle role—as a broker for all information in techniques where people don't get to hear each other's point of view." We see this shift as the establishment of a new role for government in the twenty-first century: convener of the public. To fulfill and sustain this role, public agencies need to adapt existing policy and administrative processes and support the development of new national mechanisms to share knowledge, promote practice, and evaluate results of citizen engagement in ways that improve outcomes over time. Another participant in our June conference observed, "The public voice should not be echoing alone in one out of several silos of variables in a project; it should be the overarching sound that integrates all the silos." As convener, government's role is to help create that "overarching sound."

SOURCE: Carolyn J. Lukensmeyer and Lars Hasselblad Torres, "Today's Leadership Challenge—Engaging Citizens," *Public Manager* 35, no. 3 (Fall 2006): pp. 26–31.

CourseReader Assignment

Log in to www.cengage.com and open CourseReader to access the reading:

Read "Creating a Decision Architecture," by Raymond Cox. Earlier we discussed administrative discretion from a legal standpoint. We saw how the courts interpret discretion. Here we examine the ethical and managerial dimensions of discretion.

How does the author define discretion? Are there other aspects of discretion that you would add to his definition? To what extent is discretion capable of being delineated in advance through decision rules? To what extent must administrators rely on an analysis of particular cases as they arise? Is discretion an ethical issue or a managerial issue? Both? Neither?

Carl Friedrich, on the other hand, argued that the increasing complexity of modern society made such detailed legislation difficult, if not impossible. Consequently, Friedrich felt that the administrator's own concern for the public interest was often the only real assurance that his or her actions would be responsive to the electorate. Fortunately, wrote Friedrich, the growing number of professionals in government increases the likelihood that a sense of democratic responsibility will be part of the administrator's makeup (Friedrich, 1972).

Others, following Friedrich's lead, noted the growing number of governmental officials in schools of public affairs and public administration. These schools take quite seriously the need to expose students to the ethical issues they may encounter in public organizations and to ways these issues might be resolved. This way of ensuring responsiveness is often called *subjective responsibility*, depending as it does on the subjective nature of the individual. Recently, Terry Cooper has argued that citizenship involves both rights and responsibilities and that the citizen must assume a positive role in the betterment of society as a whole. In doing so, he or she acts in pursuit of the common good and in accord with values such as political participation, political equality, and justice. When a citizen becomes a public administrator, he or she assumes the role of "citizen-administrator, both a citizen and someone working for the citizenry." In this case, the administrator's ultimate obligation is to deliver public goods and services "in ways that enhance the common good of community life through which character and civic virtue are formed" (Cooper, 1991, p. 161).

One approach to ensuring responsiveness that cuts across the objective/subjective distinction is *representative bureaucracy*—the idea that public agencies whose employees reflect certain demographic characteristics of the population as a whole are likely to operate more in line with the policy preferences of the general citizenry. According to this view, an agency with a substantial number of women or minority employees is more likely to take into account the views of women and minorities in the population than would an agency of white males. Experience with representative bureaucracy has produced mixed results. Whereas we might indeed expect greater responsiveness with respect to race and gender, there is no reason to think that such an agency would be more or less representative on other types of issues. Moreover, there is no real assurance that a person from one particular group would necessarily or always reflect that group's policy preferences. Those preferences might well be displaced by the professional or bureaucratic norms that person adopts.

Avenues for Public Participation

Another way to ensure that public managers and employees act in a way consistent with the desires of the public is to involve citizens directly in the decision-making process through membership on advisory boards, open hearings, or direct polling. Such techniques, which have now become widespread, took their initial impetus from passage of the Economic Opportunity Act of 1964, legislation that required the "maximum feasible participation" of the poor in the design and conduct of antipoverty programs. In this case, the question of involvement itself became quite an issue, especially as the representatives of the poor came into direct confrontation with those holding established positions of power. The movement toward widespread citizen participation was soon well established, however, and spread quickly to local school boards, universities, and other government agencies. Today, for example, the practice of holding hearings prior to administrative decisions is commonplace at all levels of government.

There are questions, of course, as to whether real power is transferred to the citizens or whether citizen involvement is merely a device for defusing protests. Some use the term *co-optation* to describe situations in which citizens are given the feeling of involvement but little real power. On balance, it is probably accurate to say that there are some cases in which citizens have been co-opted through involvement in advisory boards or even public hearings, but in most cases, administrators are truly interested in receiving input from the public that will help them make difficult decisions.

The complexities of public involvement in administrative decision making are illustrated in the following "classic" case, actually a continuation of one we encountered in Chapter 2. The Clean Air Act required the EPA to set national emissions standards for hazardous air pollutants to protect the public health. But no definition was given as to what would be considered "an ample margin of safety."

The issue received national attention in 1983 when EPA was trying to decide what, if anything, should be done about inorganic arsenic, a cancer-causing pollutant produced when arsenic-content ore is smelted into copper. The problem was particularly serious in the area around Tacoma, Washington, where the American Smelting and Refining Company (ASARCO) operated a copper smelter. The EPA had concluded that, in the absence of any controls on ASARCO's arsenic emissions, approximately four new cases of lung cancer would be contracted each year in the Tacoma area.

Even after installation of the "best available" pollution-control equipment, there would still be one new case of cancer per year. But there was an important consideration on the other side of the issue as well. If the EPA were to impose any more onerous conditions on ASARCO—for example, that it use ore containing less arsenic or install a new and far more expensive electric smelter—the company could not afford to continue to operate the plant. ASARCO employed 570 workers, with an annual payroll of approximately $23 million; the company bought an additional $12 million worth of goods from local suppliers. Closing the plant therefore would pose serious economic problems for the local economy.

William Ruckelshaus, then administrator of the EPA, decided that the citizens of the Tacoma area ought to wrestle with the problem. Accordingly, Ruckelshaus flew to Tacoma to announce a series of three public workshops to be held during the summer of 1983. The purpose was to acquaint residents with the details of the pollution problem, help them prepare for subsequent formal hearings, and enable them to deliberate about what should be done.

Some questions concerned technical matters, like the reliability of the proposed control equipment and the risk figures and epidemiological studies on which the EPA had based its estimates. Other questions revealed the inadequacy of the EPA's explanation of the relative health risk posed by the smelter: One resident asked whether that risk was greater than the risk posed by auto emissions.

Residents were not solely concerned, however, with the factual basis for the agency's claims. Several residents wanted to discuss the effects of the arsenic emissions on their gardens, their animals, and on the overall quality of life. Several residents expressed hostility toward the EPA for involving them in this difficult decision making in the first place. These issues are very complex, and the public is not sophisticated enough to make these decisions. This is not to say that the EPA doesn't have an obligation to inform the public, but information is one thing—defaulting its legal mandate is another.

These numerous workshops, together with the national attention that Ruckelshaus had deliberately drawn by traveling to Tacoma, created considerable and often unfavorable press coverage. In an editorial on July 16, 1983, entitled "Mr. Ruckelshaus a Caesar," the *New York Times* argued that "Mr. Ruckelshaus has it all upside down....What is inexcusable is for him to impose such an impossible choice on Tacomans." An article in the *Los Angeles Times* pointed out the difficulties "in taking a community's pulse....[Should one] poll the community...[or] count the pros and cons at the massive hearing?" Ruckelshaus was not surprised by the controversy. He said, "Listen, I know people don't like these kinds of decisions....Welcome to the world of regulation. People have demanded to be involved and now I have involved them, and they say, 'Don't ask that question.' What's the alternative? Don't involve them? Then you are accused of doing something nefarious" (Reich, 1985).*

The outcome of the case is anticlimactic: before the EPA promulgated its regulations, declining copper prices led to the closing of the ASARCO smelter anyway. The case does, however, point out some of the difficulties in designing adequate programs for public participation. Certainly there is every reason to think that Ruckelshaus really wanted to test the pulse of the citizens before making regulations. But his attempt was met not only with ambivalence, as is often the case, but with outright hostility. Moreover, despite his efforts,

---

*EXTRACT SOURCE: Reprinted by permission of the Yale Law Journal Company and William S. Hein Company. From *The Yale Law Journal*, Vol. 94, pp. 1617–1641.

there were few clear signals to the agency about what to do. The ethical issues posed by the requirements of administrative responsibility are indeed complex.

Transparency in Government

Recently there have been calls for nations around the world, including the United States, to become more attentive to the issues of transparency and accountability in government. To be transparent, something must be capable of being seen through. In government, transparency means that we are able to see clearly the workings of government, how public processes are carried out, and how successful these policies are in meeting their objectives. Government that is not transparent lacks public oversight and is more likely to be corrupt and yield to undue influences.

Openness and transparency are significant democratic values—they are the right thing to do and essential to accountability—but they also aid in the efficiency and responsiveness of public actions. Transparency, for example, supports informed decision making and gives all parties access to information important to their interests and concerns, thereby leveling the playing field. Disclosure promotes full participation in the governance process. In contrast, corruption, which by its nature is private and concealed, limits public engagement in the governance process, decreases public confidence in the institutions of governance, and increases the cost of public services, something that is especially troubling in a time of scarce resources. Transparency, on the other hand, can lead to many positive public outcomes. Certainly the notion of the public interest and that of citizenship and civic engagement require openness and transparency to be successful.

On his first full day in office, President Obama issued a memorandum for heads of executive departments and agencies related to transparency in government (see the box "Exploring Concepts: Obama's Elements of Open Government"). The memo read in part: "My Administration is committed to creating an unprecedented level of openness in Government. We will work together to ensure the public trust and establish a system of transparency, public participation, and collaboration. Openness will strengthen our democracy and promote efficiency and effectiveness in Government" (Obama, 2009).

Exploring Concepts

OBAMA'S ELEMENTS OF OPEN GOVERNMENT

1. Transparency
2. Public participation
3. Collaboration

Over the next several months, the Office of Management and Budget conducted a series of forums involving federal employees and the public in discussing ways to improve government transparency as well as greater public participation and collaboration.

In December 2009, the administration released another memorandum, an Open Government Directive that included more detailed instructions as to how agencies should proceed in pursuit of the president's policy. Among other things, the directive required a high-level official in each agency to be accountable for information made public about the agency's spending, material often published through such government websites as USAspending.gov or Recovery.gov (Ginsberg, 2011). Other uses of technology to provide results-oriented information to the public were also pursued.

While the president's initial memo focused on participation and collaboration as well as transparency, the effort to improve transparency has clearly been the most important in the years immediately following the directive. The most significant actions have been oriented to releasing information previously inaccessible to the public. "By the beginning of 2011, agencies had released more than 300,000 data sets for public consumption through Data.gov" (Lukensmeyer, Goldman, & Stern, 2011, p. 11). As time goes by, we would expect that there would be increasing attention given to matters of participation and collaboration as well. As is apparent, all three elements—transparency, public participation, and collaboration—reinforce one another in pursuit of open government.

The Ethics of Privatization

We noted in Chapter 3 the increasing involvement of for-profit and nonprofit organizations in the delivery of public programs. Especially as governments have contracted for or otherwise sought to "privatize" services, private and nonprofit organizations have become major providers of public services. But, as we also saw, transfer of responsibility may raise significant ethical questions regarding equity and accountability. The government might find it necessary or expedient to contract out for garbage collection, for example, but neither necessity nor cost savings would justify allowing contractors to engage in discrimination or other unethical practices.

The issue is particularly critical for private-sector providers, who could have a tendency to maximize profits even at the sacrifice of some other public value. A private organization might be tempted to provide either more services than necessary for clients (to increase payments and therefore revenues) or fewer services than necessary (to cut costs). Actions such as these, clearly motivated by concern for profit, are less likely to occur in service delivery by nonprofit organizations, simply by virtue of their service ethos, but even they require mechanisms to ensure equity and accountability (Rubin, 1990).

In any privatization arrangement, the government's responsibility is not only to ensure quality and cost consistent with stewardship of public resources, but also to promote democratic ideals and ensure constitutional protections. There are at least two different types of delegation to consider: those that involve no transfer of discretionary authority and those that do. Obviously, many contracts involve no transfer of authority. Public works contracts, for example, can usually be standardized and highly specified so as to grant virtually no discretionary public authority to contractors (though there are exceptions). The government retains responsibility for exercising public authority (such as determining eligibility for and frequency of garbage collection or street repair) and for holding contractors accountable for quality, quantity, and cost of work.

Other arrangements may involve transfer of discretionary authority—for example, the authority to determine details of eligibility requirements for student loans or the authority to decide what services to provide to inmates of a privately operated prison. In situations such as these, appropriate accountability structures must be in place to ensure responsiveness to the government agency that administers the contract as well as to the public generally. Developing contractual arrangements that fully incorporate appropriate concerns for the public interest presents one of the most significant challenges in privatizing public services.

Ethical Problems for the Individual

Even the most straightforward ethical problems may be problematic, especially in the context of work in public organizations. Think for a moment about telling the truth. At first glance, nothing could seem more obvious than to tell "the truth, the whole truth, and nothing but the truth." But is that really the proper ethical position (outside a courtroom)? Should you be prepared to lie to protect matters vital to the national defense? Should you tell the whole truth in response to questions from the press about confidential matters affecting your clients? Is it proper to "stretch" research findings so they better support a policy position you feel is in the public interest? These are just a few of the most pressing and difficult questions you may face that will test not only your principles but also your willingness to act in accord with those principles.

Interacting with Elected Officials

The relationship between public managers and elected officials, either chief executives (such as mayors or governors) or members of a legislative body, presents a unique but nearly pervasive set of issues for the public manager. Whether as a department head working with a legislative committee, a city manager working with a city council, or an executive director working with the board of a nonprofit organization, the relationship between manager and the legislative body presents special problems.

We have examined some of the implications of this relationship for the development of public policy, but we should also be aware of possible ethical implications. On the one hand, an administrator should be accountable to the legislative body, but on the other hand, responding blindly to legislative decree may not always be in the public interest.

The latter situation might arise in several ways. Certainly, differing strongly with members of the legislature on policy questions presents great difficulties. As an administrator, to what extent should you seek to persuade the legislature to your position? Is it proper for a manager to try to build a power base in the legislature to enable special consideration of legislation favorable to the agency? If the legislature acts contrary to your strong beliefs, should you continue in your position or should you resign? If you continue, is it proper to try later to shape implementation of the legislation to fall more closely in line with your beliefs?

Similarly, difficult questions might arise if the manager is asked to do something improper. For instance, what would you do if a legislator asked you to do something illegal, such as permitting health-care payments to an ineligible client? How would your decision change if the legislator only asked you to "bend the rules" a little bit? How would your decision change if the legislator chaired the committee that passed on your agency's appropriation?

These issues may arise in any public organization; however, they are especially well illustrated at the local level with the council-manager form of government, which is built around the distinction between policy and administration. Theoretically, the council is responsible for determining policy and the manager is responsible for carrying it out. In practice, however, the line between policy and administration is never so clear; inevitably, the manager becomes involved in policy matters and the council in administrative matters.

Because of this overlap, the Code of Ethics of the International City Management Association contains several statements that influence the council-manager relationship. The code's first item emphasizes the manager's dedication to "effective and democratic local government by *responsible elected officials*" and recognizes the contribution professional management can make in this regard. More specifically, on the manager's policy role, the code suggests that the manager "submit policy proposals to elected officials; provide them with facts and advice on matters of policy as a basis for making decisions and setting community goals, and uphold and implement municipal policies adopted by elected officials." Similarly, the manager is advised to "recognize that elected representatives of the people are entitled to the credit for the establishment of municipal policies; (while) responsibility for public execution rests with the members" (Code of Ethics, 2004).

Despite these helpful guidelines, city managers often face difficulties in relationships with city councils. One city manager disagreed strongly with a council move to limit widening a particular city street, an improvement the manager felt was essential to local economic development, another felt that a council member was acting irresponsibly in proposing legislation that would help his contracting business, and still another was asked to process travel vouchers that included payment for personal vacation expenses. Simply figuring out how to respond effectively to these situations is hard enough, but the problem is even greater when you remember that the city manager who forces an issue of policy or ethics may be seen as "attacking" the boss—and may, at any time, be summarily fired. It's no wonder that the average tenure of city managers in this country is four to five years!

Following Orders

Another problem has to do with limits to organizational authority. What would you do if your boss asked you to do something you felt was morally wrong? Suppose you are asked to "bury" a report on toxic wastes you consider potentially dangerous to the public or that, under pressures of time, you are asked to give quick approval to a piece of equipment that might be unsafe. Imagine that you are asked to approve an expense reimbursement for your boss, when you know the amount has been "padded."

In such cases, you face difficult choices—choices made even more difficult by the very logic that causes us to employ bureaucratic means of organizing. Bureaucratic organizations are attractive because they enable people to accomplish large-scale tasks they would not otherwise be able to undertake, but bureaucracy as a social form also demands a certain amount of obedience to authority. Presumably, if orders are not obeyed, the whole system falls apart—so there are strong pressures for individuals to follow orders rather than their consciences.

The most dramatic example of unquestioning obedience to authority comes from Hitler's attempt to exterminate the European Jews during World War II. Although the killings were ordered by political leaders, they were carried out through German bureaucracy. The problem faced not only those at the top of the organization but also those throughout. Raul Hilberg, author of a classic study of the Holocaust, wrote the following:

> Most bureaucrats composed memoranda, drew up blueprints, signed correspondence, talked on the telephone, and participated in conferences....However, these men were not stupid; they realized the connection between their paperwork and the heaps of corpses in the East. And they realized, also, the shortcomings of those rationalizations which placed all evil on the Jew and all good on the German. That was why they were compelled to justify their individual activities. The first rationalization was the oldest, the simplest, and therefore the most effective: the doctrine of superior orders. First and foremost there was duty. No matter what objections there might be, orders were given to be obeyed. A clear order was like an absolution; armed with such an order, a perpetrator felt that he could pass his responsibility and his conscience upward. (Hilberg, 1961, p. 649)

This manner of justifying one's actions became central to the defense of those accused at the Nuremberg trials. Many defendants argued, as did General Alfred Jodl, that it is "not the task of a soldier to act as a judge over his superior commander" (Arendt, 1963, p. 133). But despite the rationale of "superior orders" for the German bureaucrats and their more contemporary counterparts, the moral dilemma posed by such orders remains.

One might argue, of course, that the German example is overdrawn—that such a thing could never happen in a democratic society such as ours. But perhaps it could. Indeed, a remarkable series of studies conducted by Yale psychologist Stanley Milgram many years ago suggests that Americans are often quite willing to obey, even when doing so causes them extreme moral discomfort.

What Would You Do?

The dean at the university where you are a department chair forwards an e-mail to you that is clearly an advertisement for a consulting firm's seminar on grant writing and asks you to send the note on to your faculty. You are concerned about using the university's e-mail for commercial purposes. What would you do?

In an elaborate series of experiments, Milgram asked subjects to administer shocks to a person supposedly involved in a memory experiment. Even though the person receiving the shocks writhed in pain (he was actually an actor and an accomplice), the subjects continued to follow Milgram's orders to administer the painful shocks—simply because they were told to do so! Milgram concluded that "a substantial proportion of people do what they are told, irrespective of the content of the act and without limitations of conscience as long as they perceive that the command comes from a legitimate authority" (Milgram, 1974, p. 189).

Contemporary examples of problems with orders from above are perhaps less dramatic than the German illustration, but they present equally difficult choices for the individual. You may, of course, protest the action, either directly to your superiors or more indirectly, although in doing so, you may place yourself in jeopardy. Or you may leave the organization, resigning in protest, even though the available alternatives—such as unemployment—may not be attractive. Or you may simply keep quiet and do what you are told. The latter alternative is certainly the easiest in most cases. By obeying orders, you feel you have someone else (your superior) to blame if something goes wrong. In any case, many feel that if people in large organizations fail to follow orders, things won't get done. Unfortunately, rationalizations such as these don't allow you to escape the moral consequences of your actions.

Conflicts of Interest

Another area of potential ethical difficulties for public officials involves conflicts of interest. Finding ways to avoid conflicts of interest, especially financial, has been central to federal, state, and local ethics legislation for the past twenty-five to thirty years. At the federal level, legislation detailing the ethical behavior expected of public officials has deep historical roots; however, the tone of modern ethics legislation was set by Executive Order 11222 issued by President Johnson in 1965. In part, the policy reads as follows:

> Where government is based on the consent of the governed, every citizen is entitled to have complete confidence in the integrity of his government. Each individual officer, employee, or advisor of government must help to earn and must honor that trust by his own integrity and conduct in all official actions.

The executive order then provides a set of "standards of conduct" that covers such topics as accepting gifts, financial conflicts of interest, misuse of federal property, and limitations on outside employment. The policy also bars use of public office for personal gain or for the gain of those with whom the individual has family, business, or financial ties.

The Johnson policy also initiated public disclosure of financial statements, something that was given greater prominence in the Ethics and Government Act of 1978. This act codified many of the previously established standards and created the Office of Government Ethics to establish more detailed regulations to monitor the behavior of public servants and provide ethics training for managers and other officials.

Under existing legislation, officers of the executive branch of the federal government are required to refrain from participating "personally and financially" in deciding, approving, recommending, or advising with respect to matters in which they, family members, or close associates have a financial interest. An official facing a possible conflict of interest has a number of avenues available. First, the official can simply withdraw from participating in the particular case. Second, the official may seek a waiver, especially when his or her interest is not considered substantial or the relationship is too remote to affect the integrity of the action. Third, the official may choose to place his or her assets in a "blind trust." Finally, the official can sell, give away, or otherwise divest himself or herself of the financial interest in question.

What Would You Do?

Your wife's brother has applied for a job in the state-level department that you head. What would you do?

Other parts of the federal ethics legislation restrict outside income and the acceptance of gifts or favors. For example, as a federal employee, you are prohibited from accepting any salary or contribution from any source other than the federal government. The law also limits the acceptance of meals, entertainment, and gifts. For example, meals can usually be accepted if offered during the course of a working meeting, but there are prohibitions on "one-on-one" meals in which you are being treated.

There are also prohibitions on what a federal employee can do after leaving a government position. Sections of the Ethics and Government Act prohibit former officials from representing outside parties before the federal government with respect to matters in which they had some personal involvement or official responsibility for a period of two years. There is also a one-year "cooling-off period," during which you cannot represent parties before your agency even on matters that were not your responsibility while working for the government. A commission created by President George H. W. Bush recommended strengthening provisions dealing with activities of former federal officials by requiring a prohibition not only against personally representing outside interests before government agencies but also against "aiding or advising any other person." The proposal would eliminate not only direct representation, but "behind the scenes" advice and counsel as well.

Legislation such as this is obviously intended to prevent "influence peddling" by those who have recently left government and to limit the "revolving door" phenomenon, wherein people move in and out of government to acquire knowledge and information valuable to external groups. This issue became particularly prominent during the Reagan administration, when several officials, including Michael Deaver and Lynn Nofziger, were accused of using their previous contacts to unduly influence the governmental decision process.

Finally, the potential for conflicts of interest is decreased by requirements for financial disclosure on the part of executive officials. The Bush commission, for example, wrote that "financial disclosure has been variously described as the linchpin of the ethical enforcement system, as the disinfectant sunlight which makes possible the cleaning up of abusive practices" (President's Commission, 1989, p. 5). Though financial reporting requirements have sometimes been criticized as excessively detailed and intrusive, they have been, in the view of most ethics experts, highly valuable in maintaining public confidence in the integrity of government. If nothing else, the reports have meant that individuals are forced to carefully review potential conflicts of interests that they may bring to government, and thus be more aware of those interests should conflicts arise.

The recommendations of the Bush commission led, in February 1993, to new standards creating greater uniformity across all agencies of the federal government. The rules cover seven areas: (1) gifts from outside sources, (2) gifts between federal employees, (3) conflicts of financial interests, (4) impartiality in performing official duties, (5) other employment, (6) misuse of position, and (7) outside activities. In many respects, these standards reflected the new president's pledge for a return to values-based leadership. As a candidate, President Clinton had voiced sharp criticism against the ethical shortcomings of preceding administrations. Then, on Inauguration Day, he used his first executive order to require new ethics commitments of executive branch appointees, restricting an appointee's lobbying or attempts to influence an agency where he or she worked.

However, despite the efforts of the Clinton administration to set a high moral tone, it is unlikely that the Clinton presidency will be remembered for its stance on ethics. As mentioned in Chapter 2, President Clinton was impeached by Congress for lying under oath to a federal grand jury, and even though the Senate later acquitted the president, the fact that President Clinton lied to the grand jury (and to the public) to protect his political career was never disputed. President George W. Bush's administration was not immune from ethical conflicts. His actions against terrorism, while supported in general, opened the administration to harsh criticism. Specific actions, such as the USA PATRIOT Act (adopted 2001), which gives permission for "warrantless searches of phone and Internet records," raised concerns about protecting the basic civil liberties. Questions were also raised about the honesty of the president's justifications for the war in Iraq and the political motivations for firing federal attorneys.

The Obama administration has placed its greatest emphasis on openness and transparency in government, a topic we reviewed previously. One particular noteworthy element of the Obama approach is the unveiling in March 2012 of a new website, Ethics.gov. The website allows users "to cross-check several federal databases for information about lobbyists and their activities, contribution and spending records for candidates for federal office and political action committees, [and] travel by administration officials and visitors to the White House" (http://thecaucus.blogs.nytimes.com/2012/03/08/white-house-ethics-hub-goes-live-online/). The new website provides searchable and downloadable information related to issues that frequently cause ethical concerns in government in order to move such concerns out of the shadow into public light.

Networking

The primary federal agency dealing with ethics issues is the Office of Government Ethics at www.usoge.gov.

Many of the same provisions for preventing conflict of interest in federal ethics legislation have been paralleled at the state level. Many states have passed detailed ethics legislation, often using financial disclosure as a chief mechanism for preventing abuse. Indeed, almost all states have some form of financial disclosure provision for some state employees. In addition, more states have adopted ethics codes and ethics commissions. Similarly, given the influence of money in politics, other states have sought to establish controls on political money. Florida, for example, reduced the limits on campaign contributions and created a fully funded public campaign finance system. Many states have adopted similar versions of the federal conflict of interest legislation passed during the Bush administration, and many have also pursued the open government policies of the Obama administration.

Whistle-Blowing

There has been a marked increase over the last twenty years in employee disclosure of problems in public organizations. Public employees have exposed defense contract overruns; spoken out against corruption in local police departments; and revealed abuses of the merit system, improper enforcement of toxic waste legislation, and other matters. Alan Campbell, director of the Office of Personnel Management during the Carter administration, described these public disclosures, or whistle-blowing, in this way: "Quite simply, I view whistle-blowing as a popular short-hand label for any disclosure of a legal violation, mismanagement, a gross waste of funds, an abuse of authority, or a danger to public health or safety, whether the disclosure is made within or outside the chain of command" (Bowman, 1983, p. 91). In other words, the *whistle-blower* reveals information about fraud, waste, or abuse in government, including actions that might endanger the safety or liberty of other government employees or citizens at large.

Generally, employees who decide to blow the whistle move through several stages. First, the employees become aware of an organizational practice that is unethical or dangerous. Second, they express concern to their immediate supervisor or those further up in the hierarchy; and third, unsatisfied that anyone in the organization will take appropriate action, they take the issue outside, either through leaks to the press or to external public interest groups. (The press, of course, may independently play an important role in revealing instances of wrongdoing.)

Unfortunately, whistle-blowers in both government and industry have often been subjected to abuse and retaliation by superiors. One study of whistle-blowers shows a large number who were fired or forced to resign or retire, as well as others who were refused promotions or given less desirable work assignments. Others felt excluded from communication within the organization and were avoided by both supervisors and coworkers (Truelson, 1986, p. 9). Studies show that, as a result, many public employees who have knowledge of corruption don't bother to report it (Bowman, 1983, p. 91).

If you discover improper actions on the part of persons in your organization, you have a strong obligation to report those actions; however, you should be careful that your allegations are based on fact and are properly reported. James Bowman suggests that an act of whistle-blowing can be justified if the following conditions are met:

1. If it is done with an appropriate moral motive
2. If all internal channels of dissent have been exhausted

3. If it is based on evidence that would persuade a reasonable person
4. If analysis has been made of the seriousness, immediacy, and specificity of the problem
5. If it is commensurate with one's responsibility
6. If it has some chance of success (Bowman, 1983, p. 91)

At the federal level, codes of conduct have encouraged public servants to expose corruption wherever it is discovered, and protection for whistle-blowers has been provided through the Civil Service Reform Act. Moreover, some agencies have established formal *dissent channels*, confidential patterns of communications outside the normal chain of command that allow a potential whistle-blower or someone who merely disagrees with a proposed policy to express a dissenting opinion without fear of reprisal. Consequently, whistle-blowing has become somewhat more common at the federal level. But wherever you work, if you decide to blow the whistle, you should be fully aware not only of potential dangers, but also of the protection available to you based on rights of free speech and on prohibitions against discriminatory actions. Encouraging greater communication by providing freer and more open channels of dissent is one way to ensure more ethical behavior in public organizations (see the box "Take Action: Ten Tips for Potential Whistle-Blowers").

Take Action   TEN TIPS FOR POTENTIAL WHISTLE-BLOWERS

1. Consult your loved ones. Blowing the whistle is a family decision. Before taking any irreversible steps, talk to your spouse, your family, or close friends—the support group you will need to depend upon in the coming days—about your decision to blow the whistle. If they are not with you, you may want to rethink your path.
2. Check for skeletons in your closet. Any personal vulnerability or peccadillo you possess can, and most likely will, be used by the agency against you. One practical step is to make a copy of the complete contents of your personnel file as insurance that new but backdated "dirt" cannot be later slipped in.
3. Document, document, document. Keep copious records and a daily diary of relevant information, memorialize conversations with letters to the file, and maintain a separate set of documents outside of work in a safe place. Your chances of success will likely depend on how powerful a paper trail you produce. After you blow the whistle, your access to agency records may be immediately cut off.
4. Do not use government resources. Do not engage in whistle-blowing activity on agency time, even to defend yourself in a retaliation case unless you have specific approval, such as through a union collective bargaining agreement.

(Continued)

(Continued)

5. Check to see who, if anyone, will support your account. Gauge the level of concern among your coworkers for the concerns you might raise. If you can't count on others to later testify as supporting witnesses, you may be well advised to wait before challenging misconduct. Try to stay on good terms with administrative staff members who may be in a position to know of impending agency actions.

6. Consult an attorney early. Do not wait until you are in the "career emergency room" before seeking professional help.

7. Choose your battles. Pick favorable terrain for highlighting your issue. Don't sweat the small stuff. In any personnel action, the advantage is with the employer, not the lone employee.

8. Identify allies. There is strength in numbers. Do not wait to be isolated by the agency. If possible, line up the assistance of sympathetic interest groups, elected officials, or journalists. The strength of your support coalition may determine the outcome of the battle ahead.

9. Have a well-thought-out plan. Be clearheaded about precisely what you expect to accomplish and how. Try to prepare for agency countermoves by anticipating agency responses to your charges and mapping out the counter argument to those charges.

10. Get yourself a little career counseling. Map out where your actions will leave you a year from now, two years from now, five years, and so on. Plan out the route you want to take and how you reasonably expect your professional path to proceed. There is no doubt that you are about to embark upon a professional journey.

SOURCE: POGO/GAP/PEER 2002, 4–7, in Svara, James. (2007). *The Ethics Primer for Public Administrators in Government and Nonprofit Organizations*. Sudbury, MA: Jones and Bartlett Publishers, p. 127.

Prohibitions on Political Activities

Political neutrality has traditionally been considered important to effective democratic governance. President Jefferson, for example, issued an order against federal government employee partisanship, an order whose essence was repeated by Presidents Grant and Hayes. Legislative action occurred with the adoption of the Pendleton Act in 1883, which "prohibited political assessment, solicitations, subscriptions, or contributions from or by any employee of the United States." The most sweeping ban on political activity, however, occurred during Theodore Roosevelt's administration. He declared that classified civil service employees "shall take no active part in political management or in political campaigns" (Masters & Bierman, 1985, p. 519). Later, Congress passed the Hatch Political Activities Act in 1939, stating that "no officer or employee of the executive branch of the federal government, or any agency or department thereof, shall take any active part in political management or in political campaigns." (A set of amendments passed in 1940 extended the ban on political management and campaigning to state and local employees whose programs were financed fully or in part by federal funds.)

Under the Hatch Act, public employees can register to vote, contribute money to campaigns, assist in voter registration drives, and express opinions about candidates and issues; however, for activities not allowed, see the box "Exploring Concepts: Activities Prohibited under the Hatch Act."

Exploring Concepts

ACTIVITIES PROHIBITED UNDER THE HATCH ACT

1. Endorsing partisan candidates
2. Listing or raising money for political action committees
3. Participating in partisan voter registration and get-out-the-vote drives
4. Distributing campaign material on behalf of candidates
5. Serving as a delegate to a political convention
6. Making campaign speeches
7. Seeking public office in partisan elections

SOURCE: Masters & Bierman, 1985, pp. 519–520.

Although the Hatch Act seeks to protect public employees from political harassment and the political process from special influence, it has been subject to various interpretations and has proven confusing in its application. Moreover, many have claimed that it unduly restricts public employees' political freedoms by disenfranchising them from important political activities during the time they are employed by the government. Others have pointed out that the Hatch Act's restrictions on U.S. government employees are more stringent than those placed on employees in Great Britain, Canada, and Australia. For this reason, there have been recent efforts in Congress to change the Hatch Act so as to permit a greater range of political activities by employees in government. Many support the proposed legislation, especially those in public employee unions, who feel that public employees should be able to run for office and solicit campaign funds on their own time. Others, however, have argued that the Hatch Act is still necessary to prevent coercion of political officials. Reform of the Hatch Act was considered for a number of years, with Congress passing major reform legislation in 1991 (though it was vetoed by President Bush).

In 1993, Congress changed the Hatch Act, generally strengthening those sections dealing with activities while on duty and expanding the off-duty activities of federal employees. Basically, with the exception of running for office, which is still prohibited, the new act permits federal workers to participate in a full range of political activities on their own time, not while on the job (*Congressional Quarterly Weekly*, 1993, p. 511).

Managing Ethics

How does a manager promote more ethical practices in an organization? First, of course, there are a variety of formal controls, including legal, on the behavior of those in public organizations—the courts may direct public officials to undertake specific actions or to "cease and desist" from certain courses of action. They may also be required, on behalf of their agencies, to provide individuals with damages or other compensation. And, of course, any public employee may be prosecuted for breaking the law. But what if you are sued as an individual for actions you have undertaken in the course of your official duties?

Actually, this question has been the subject of considerable legal debate throughout our country's history. Early interpretations of the law generally protected public officials against suits, claiming they violated an individual's rights in the course of one's duties. Recent interpretations have severely limited the immunity granted to public officials. Speaking broadly, there are two types of immunity: absolute immunity and qualified (or "good faith") immunity. Absolute immunity, which means that an official is not liable for damages under any circumstances, has been granted to certain legislative and judicial officers and, in limited cases, to members of the executive branch. (The president has been granted absolute immunity, but state governors have not.)

Most other officials have only qualified immunity; they may be sued, but they can defend themselves by showing they were acting in good faith. They must show that they were unaware of impropriety at the time and that any reasonable person might have acted similarly. Although the current legal position allows most officials to be sued, relatively few suits have been successful; most public managers have been found to have acted in good faith. In any case, knowing something about public officials' liability for their actions will better enable you and those in your organization to avoid problems in the first place or to respond to them when they arise.

Besides legal proceedings, other formal devices are available to protect against waste or fraud by public officials or the private individuals or groups with which they interact. For example, most major federal agencies have an Office of the Inspector General to investigate cases of fraud, waste, and abuse in government. The inspectors general are charged with looking into situations in which federal employees or funds are used improperly. Targets of investigations may be either public employees or private individuals, such as contractors, who might attempt to defraud the government.

Through their internal investigations of federal agencies, the inspectors general have occasionally revealed major problems. For example, the Office of the Inspector General of the Department of Health and Human Services initiated several studies related to excessive billings for Medicaid payments. Selling samples, billing Medicaid at higher prices than charged the public, and billing for brand-name drugs while dispensing generic drugs are among the suspected abuses. Similarly, the inspector general's office in the Department of Defense announced plans to probe the military fastener industry—makers of bolts, screws, and other hardware—to see if substandard parts contributed to military accidents. In a related case, two Maryland defense contractors pleaded guilty to a decade-long scheme to sell cheap, low-grade fasteners for military equipment. The contractors admitted to substituting commercial-grade bolts, screws, and other fasteners for more expensive military-grade hardware ordered by defense contractors for radar and sonar systems, satellites, Trident submarines, and armored earthmovers like those used in the Persian Gulf War (*Washington Post*, 1992).

Establishing an Ethical Climate

In addition to using formal controls, you can help promote ethical behavior by providing strong ethical leadership, creating a climate in which ethical behavior is valued, and encouraging free and open communications throughout the organization. "Managing ethics involves more than making public statements espousing a particular set of values and more than selecting employees with good moral character. Managing ethics also involves careful analysis of the organizational culture, working to develop a cultural environment that places high value on ethical integrity and developing policies and procedures and systems that enable organization members to act with ethical integrity" (Denhardt, 1989, p. 1). See the box "Take Action: Intervention Techniques for Integrating Ethics into Agency Operations."

Take Action
INTERVENTION TECHNIQUES FOR INTEGRATING ETHICS INTO AGENCY OPERATIONS

- Do both compliance and integrity training and counseling.
- Give briefings on common ethical problems on the job for new hires.
- Give termination briefings on potential postemployment problems.
- Designate senior manager(s) for integrity issues, separate from compliance/investigative unit.
- Require annual sign-off on prospective commitment and compliance.
- Consider ethical values and character in recruitment.
- Integrate ethical performance into promotional exams and annual reviews; link ethical behavior to incentives.
- Publicize positive, noteworthy role models.
- Raise ethical concerns at meetings and through regular communication channels.
- Train middle managers to recognize and commend subordinates' statements about ethical concerns.
- Review management practices and administrative routines at every level and in every type of unit in the organization.
- Get the whole team—all employees, all levels, all units to participate; ethics is not a spectator sport.
- Give earnest attention to ethical treatment of subordinates, clients, and others.

SOURCE: Carol W. Lewis, *The Ethics Challenge in Public Service.* © 1991 by Jossey-Bass. This material is used by permission of John Wiley & Sons, Inc.

Many organizational members feel that, in the absence of an ethics program, the requirements of large bureaucracies tend to promote unethical, dishonest, and inhumane behavior. "Managers perceive that the bureaucratic environment is less ethical than their own values and beliefs, that they are under pressure to compromise personal standards to achieve organizational goals, and that their supervisors are interested only in results, not how they were obtained" (Bowman, 1983, p. 74).

A first step in promoting more ethical practices in your organization is to analyze the basic ideas, beliefs, and attitudes that guide the behavior of the organization's members. One device for assessing the prevailing beliefs of your organization is an *ethics audit*, an assessment of the value premises that guide action in the organization. The audit provides a methodical review of the organization's activities and the implicit values that underlie the activities. Importantly, these values may not turn out to be those contained in public pronouncements. One student of organizational behavior concluded that "the key to learning the ethics of individuals or organizations is simple: *Do not listen to what they say about ethics; observe what they do*" (Pastin, 1988, p. 92). By clearly establishing the values that guide behavior in the organization, you and other members can more consciously and clearly begin to alter those values that seem inappropriate.

As an example, after numerous incidents of defense contract violations, the General Dynamics Corporation brought in an outside consultant to help establish an ethics program. The consultant conducted an ethics audit, which helped members of the organization recognize that they shared a basic, though unstated, assumption that the government was their adversary and that taking advantage of an adversary was quite acceptable. Once this assumption was understood, it could be addressed openly and replaced with more appropriate assumptions about the relationships between government and its contractors. An example of an ethics audit conducted by a public agency is contained in Carol Lewis's book, *The Ethics Challenge in Public Service* (1991, pp. 199–202).

Following an ethics audit, your organization may wish to develop a clearer statement of values to guide individual behavior. The statement should include general moral guidelines but also articulate a vision of the organization's mission—what it stands for, what it seeks to achieve, and how it plans to go about its business. Developing such a statement should involve many members of the organization and have the full support of top management.

Besides developing a statement of management philosophy for your organization, you may also wish to employ more general codes of ethics developed by other organizations. The federal government, for example, has promulgated a Code of Ethics for Federal Service, and many state and local government organizations have developed similar codes. Professional organizations such as the International City Management Association (ICMA) also have codes of ethics related to members of their profession. Perhaps the most comprehensive code of ethics for public-sector managers is that of the American Society for Public Administration (ASPA). The ASPA Code of Ethics and accompanying guidelines illustrate the variety of ethical concerns public managers face and provide guidance for resolving ethical issues (see Appendix at the end of this chapter).

After assessing values and adopting statements to express the desired values, you might wish to develop training programs or other devices for communicating these ideals within the organization. The Office of Government Ethics, for example, conducts frequent seminars for federal managers on ethics in the public service. Similarly, organizations such as ASPA and ICMA have developed training programs that are available nationally or can be adapted to local circumstances. Training programs are also available for executives in nonprofit organizations.

As a manager, however, you should not neglect the fact that your own actions will be taken as a model of appropriate behavior. The example you set will be one of the most important training devices to members of your organization. If you wish them to take the moral "high road," you must demonstrate by example that ethics is a substantial concern and that unethical conduct will not be tolerated.

Summary and Action Implications

As we move from the context of public administration to the ethics of public service, we also move from areas where abstract knowledge is helpful to areas where the ability to act is important. In dealing with the many ethical dilemmas that confront public officials, you must not only know what the correct action is but also be able to act in a way consistent with that judgment. Understanding how ethical choices are made is helpful, as is recognizing the importance of deliberation in making ethical decisions. But what will ultimately make the difference will be your willingness to act on the basis of moral principles.

The particular ethical issues you may face range from matters of individual integrity to those that derive from the special value commitments associated with working in the public interest. Most of the latter are associated with the tension between efficiency and responsiveness that seems to pervade public organizations. That tension, as well as issues of accountability and responsiveness to public demands, is especially intense in the relationship between administrators and the legislative branch.

Many of the concerns you may encounter as a public manager are similar to those other managers face, but some are especially conditioned by the fact that you are operating "in the public interest." In either case, you must exhibit the virtues of benevolence and justice (including honesty, trustworthiness, and fairness) in your behavior. As you face some of the difficulties that arise, careful self-reflection and dialogue with others about ethical concerns will be especially helpful.

It is within your power as an administrator to undertake programs to encourage and facilitate a more ethical climate within your organization. Conducting an ethics audit, developing a statement of organizational philosophy or a code of ethics, and establishing training programs to deal with ethical issues will help improve your organization's ethics.

As a manager, however, perhaps the most important message you can send is that communicated by your own actions. If you seem to attach great importance to ethical concerns, others in the organization will attach similar importance. The model you provide can make an important difference in the ethics of your organization.

STUDY QUESTIONS

1. Although *ethics* and *morality* are similar, what is the distinction between the terms?

2. Discuss the steps in ethical deliberation.

3. Compare the two approaches commonly used in moral philosophy.

4. Discuss the three levels of moral development devised by psychologist Lawrence Kohlberg.

5. What is meant by an "ethics of virtue"?

6. Discuss the conflict between efficiency and responsiveness.

7. Explain the limitations on administrators' discretion with regard to responsiveness and efficiency.

8. Discuss some of the ethical problems individuals who work in public organizations encounter and how they can deal with them properly.

9. The Hatch Act defines prohibited activities of public employees. Explain the significance of these prohibitions with regard to an individual's political actions.

10. Explain ways to improve the ethical behavior of those in a public organization and provide examples of managing ethics.

CASES AND EXERCISES

1. To illustrate various aspects of ethical deliberation, read and discuss the following case.

There is a raging river that can be crossed only by boat. The only boat is owned and operated by a person we shall call A (in order to protect the innocent as well as the guilty). On the tame side of the river, X is deeply and sincerely in love with a person, C, on the other side of the river. X goes to A and asks to be taken across the river, offering to pay for the service. A declines any money, but agrees to take X across the river if X will sleep with A. Person X refuses, of course (!), but argues and then pleads with A to name some other price. A, however, remains firm.

Person X leaves, but returns a second day to seek a way across the river. A remains as adamant as before. In frustration, X seeks out a third person, B, who hears the situation sympathetically, agreeing that A is certainly a rogue. But B says, "I have other matters to deal with just now and cannot help you."

In desperation, X goes to A a third time, only to be met with the same deal for the trip across the river. X finally agrees to the price and sleeps with A, who then delivers X across the river as promised.

X and C are joyously reunited, until C asks how X got across the river. X truthfully replies, "I had to sleep with A to earn the trip across the river." C replies indignantly, "Out of my life! I will have nothing to do with one who holds honor and principle so lightly!"

X, of course, is frustrated and desperate again, and appeals to another person, D, who replies, "I understand and am deeply sympathetic. I'd do anything I can to help you." (The curtain falls.) (ASPA, n.d.)

Following your discussion of the case itself, consider to what extent the discussion reflected moral relativism, utilitarianism, or deontology. Then, reconsider the case, following the steps of ethical deliberation presented in this chapter. Clarify the facts, find basic principles, and analyze the arguments. How could you establish a moral action?

2. A random check of long-distance telephone calls at the Department of Housing and Urban Development, conducted by the agency's inspector general, indicated that some 30 percent were personal calls (though charged to the government). The cost of the calls was estimated at $73,000 for the sample and, by extrapolation, $290,000 for the agency as a whole. Many calls were placed to the homes of employees or their relatives; others were calls to prerecorded messages, such as time and temperature, horoscopes, and financial information. Penalties for unauthorized use of federal telephone lines include fines, suspension, and dismissal.

Why do you think employees at HUD, and presumably elsewhere, misuse official telephone lines? What, if anything, should be done to limit such excesses? How do you respond to employees who argue that using agency telephone lines for personal business is necessary from time to time? What about those who argue that telephone use is an essential benefit the organization should provide? If you crack down on unauthorized calls, what will happen to morale in the agency?

To put the case in a more intense, real-world setting, imagine that you are secretary of Housing and Urban Development. You have just finished testifying at a congressional hearing. On your way out the door, a senator corners you and waves a copy of the inspector general's report in your face, saying, "This is an outrage! These people are stealing from the public, and you've been letting it happen! I want some action on this right away!" Next, a reporter, who has seen the report and heard the exchange with the senator, shoves a microphone in your face and asks, "Well, what are you going to do?" What is your response, both immediately and over the next several days?

3. Consider the following case: Sidney Franklin knew that one of his most valued employees, Anderson Hayes, was stealing from the organization—not much, and in a way that no one but Sidney would ever know—but he *was* stealing. Sidney also knew that without Anderson, his unit could never complete a newly assigned task on

time. He decided to do nothing about the stealing incident and secretly hoped that success in the new assignment would bring about a long-desired promotion and get him out of this awkward situation.

Analyze and discuss this case in terms of the moral position that the individual involved should have taken. Then consider the nature of your own ethical reasoning. What types of moral philosophy, moral psychology, or moral action have you been using?

4. As a class, conduct an ethics audit (or survey) of your college or university and recommend ways the institution might begin to develop higher standards of ethical conduct.

Begin by considering in detail what might be expected from such an audit (or survey) in any organization and what is practical and ethical to expect from such a project conducted by students within the institution. Recognize your available resources, but also the limitations on your work. (You might even want to discuss your project with several university officers before proceeding.)

As a practical matter, consider basing your work primarily on interviews with important decision makers throughout the institution, including administrators, deans and department chairs, members of the faculty (especially members of the faculty council or faculty senate), representatives of the school's athletic programs, and staff support in areas such as budget and accounting and personnel or human resources. Also consider interviews with members of the school's governing board. You might also want to collect material based on public record: newspaper reports, magazine articles, editorials, and so forth. *The Chronicle of Higher Education* and other materials dealing with higher education show what kinds of efforts other schools have undertaken.

Throughout your interviews and other research, you should first seek to determine the major ethical concerns facing institutions of higher education. Topics you will likely encounter are plagiarism and other forms of academic dishonesty (on the part of both faculty and students), the integrity of the research process, matters of institutional governance, questions of equal opportunity and affirmative action, institutional policies toward drugs and alcohol, the school's position on certain political issues, and athletic recruiting policies—just to name a few. You may find that your institution has taken strong moral positions in some areas (perhaps many areas). You may even find parts of the institution that have undertaken serious and detailed appraisals of their ethical positions. You may also find, however, that many of these issues simply haven't been considered, at least in terms of ethical implications.

If you can simply develop an inventory of ethical issues that should receive greater attention from members of the institution, you will have done a great service. But you may also identify cases where actual behavior seems to imply an ethical position different from the position espoused by those with whom you talk. If you discover such cases, be prepared not only to document your findings, but also to present your report in such a way that will be helpful and constructive. Remember that you are seeking to provide a service to the institution, not an exposé.

Based on your research and analysis, prepare a written report for the school's president or chancellor and offer to have a delegation meet with him or her (or a representative) to discuss your findings. Again, your approach should be to provide preliminary findings that will be useful in terms of institutional ethics. It may be helpful to think of yourself as a member of the president's or chancellor's staff, developing a report upon which constructive action can be taken. As in any such situation, you should be prepared to suggest specific action steps that will enable the school to give serious and sustained attention to its ethical posture.

After you finish, spend some time considering as a class what you have learned from this exercise—about institutional ethics and the administrative process, and what will make you a more effective and responsible administrator in the future. Try to develop specific action-oriented statements to guide your actions. Finally, consider whether there were any ethical questions you faced in the course of this project. How did you resolve them? Or did you?

FOR ADDITIONAL READING

Adams, Guy B., and Danny L. Balfour. *Unmasking Administrative Evil*. 3rd ed. Armonk, NY: M.E. Sharpe, 2009.

Bowman, James S., ed. *Ethical Frontiers in Public Management: Seeking New Strategies for Resolving Ethical Dilemmas*. San Francisco: Jossey-Bass, 1991.

Bowman, James S., ed. *Public Integrity Annual*. Lexington, KY: Council of State Governments, 1997.

Bruce, Willa. *Classics of Administrative Ethics*. Boulder, CO: Westview Press, 2001.

Burke, John P. *Bureaucratic Responsibility*. Baltimore: Johns Hopkins University Press, 2000.

Cooper, Terry L. *An Ethic of Citizenship for Public Administration*. Englewood Cliffs, NJ: Prentice-Hall, 1991.

Cooper, Terry L. *Exemplary Public Administrators: Character and Leadership in Government*. San Francisco: Jossey-Bass, 1992.

Cooper, Terry L. *The Responsible Administrator: An Approach to Ethics for the Administrative Role*. 3rd ed. San Francisco: Jossey-Bass, 1990.

Cooper, Terry L., ed. *Handbook of Administrative Ethics*. New York: Marcel Dekker, 1994.

Cox, Raymond W. *Ethics and Integrity in Public Administration: Concepts and Cases*. Armonk, NY: M.E. Sharpe, 2009.

Denhardt, Robert B. *Theories of Public Organization*. 5th ed. Belmont, CA: Thomson/Wadsworth, 2007.

Frederickson, George H., and Richard K. Ghere, eds. *Ethics in Public Management*. Armonk, NY: M.E. Sharpe, 2005.

Guy, Mary E., Meredith A. Newman, and Sharon H. Mastracci. *Emotional Labor: Putting the Service in Public Service*. Armonk, NY: M.E. Sharpe, 2008.

Harmon, Michael M. *Public Administration's Final Exam: A Pragmatist Restructuring of the Profession and the Discipline*. Tuscaloosa: University of Alabama Press, 2006.

Harmon, Michael M. *Responsibility as Paradox*. Thousand Oaks, CA: Sage Publications, 1995.

Harmon, Michael M., and O. C. McSwite. *Whenever Two or More Are Gathered: Relationship as the Heart of Ethical Discourse*. Tuscaloosa: University of Alabama Press, 2011.

Hodgkinson, Christopher. *Administrative Philosophy.* Oxford: Pergamon Press, 1996.

Jun, Jong S. *The Social Construction of Public Administration: Interpretive and Critical Perspectives.* Albany: State University of New York Press, 2006.

Jurkiewicz, Carole L. *The Foundations of Organizational Evil.* Armonk, NY: M.E. Sharpe, 2012.

Martinez, J. Michael. *Public Administration Ethics for the 21st Century.* Santa Barbara, CA: Praeger, 2009.

Menzel, Donald C. *Ethics Management for Public Administrators: Building Organizations of Integrity.* 2nd ed. Armonk, NY: M.E. Sharpe, 2012.

Menzel, Donald C. *Ethics Moments in Government: Cases and Controversies.* Boca Raton, FL: CRC Press, 2010.

O'Leary, Rosemary. *The Ethics of Dissent: Managing Guerrilla Government* (Public Affairs and Policy Administration Series). Washington, DC: CQ Press, 2006.

Pasquerella, Lynn, Alfred G. Killilea, and Michael Vocino. *Ethical Dilemmas in Public Administration.* Westport, CT: Praeger, 1996.

Richardson, William D. *Ethics and Character: The Pursuit of Democratic Virtues.* Durham, NC: Carolina Academic Press, 1999.

Rohr, John. *Ethics and Public Administration.* Armonk, NY: M.E. Sharpe, 1993.

Rohr, John. *Ethics for Bureaucrats.* New York: Marcel Dekker, 1978.

Rohr, John. *To Run a Constitution.* Lawrence: University Press of Kansas, 1986.

Stivers, Camilla. *Governance in Dark Times: Practical Philosophy for Public Service.* Washington, DC: Georgetown University Press, 2008.

Svara, James. *The Ethics Primer for Public Administrators in Government and Nonprofit Organizations.* Sudbury, MA: Jones and Bartlett Publishers, 2007.

Tong, Rosemarie. *Ethics in Policy Analysis.* Englewood Cliffs, NJ: Prentice-Hall, 1986.

Walker, Margaret Urban. *Moral Understandings: A Feminist Study in Ethics.* New York: Routledge, 1998.

Washington, Sally. *Ethics in the Public Service.* Paris: OECD, 1996.

Wolff, Jonathan. *Ethics and Public Policy.* New York: Routledge, 2011.

APPENDIX

Code of Ethics of the American Society for Public Administration (ASPA)

I. Serve the Public Interest

Serve the public, beyond serving oneself. ASPA members are committed to

1. Exercise discretionary authority to promote the public interest.

2. Oppose all forms of discrimination and harassment, and promote affirmative action.

3. Recognize and support the public's right to know the public's business.

4. Involve citizens in policy decision-making.

5. Exercise compassion, benevolence, fairness, and optimism.

6. Respond to the public in ways that are complete, clear, and easy to understand.

7. Assist citizens in their dealings with government.

8. Be prepared to make decisions that may not be popular.

II. Respect the Constitution and the Law

Respect, support, and study government constitutions and laws that define responsibilities of public agencies, employees, and all citizens. ASPA members are committed to

1. Understand and apply legislation and regulations relevant to their professional role.

2. Work to improve and change laws and policies that are counterproductive or obsolete.

3. Eliminate unlawful discrimination.

4. Prevent all forms of mismanagement of public funds by establishing and maintaining strong fiscal and management controls, and by supporting audits and investigative activities.

5. Respect and protect privileged information.

6. Encourage and facilitate legitimate dissent activities in government and protect the whistle-blowing rights of public employees.

7. Promote constitutional principles of equality, fairness, representativeness, responsiveness, and due process in protecting citizens' rights.

III. Demonstrate Personal Integrity

Demonstrate the highest standards in all activities to inspire public confidence and trust in public service. ASPA members are committed to

1. Maintain truthfulness and honesty and to not compromise them for advancement, honor, or personal gain.

2. Ensure that others receive credit for their work and contributions.

3. Zealously guard against conflict of interest or its appearance: e.g., nepotism, improper outside employment, misuse of public resources, or the acceptance of gifts.

4. Respect superiors, subordinates, colleagues, and the public.

5. Take responsibility for their own errors.

6. Conduct official acts without partisanship.

IV. Promote Ethical Organizations

Strengthen organizational capabilities to apply ethics, efficiency, and effectiveness in serving the public. ASPA members are committed to

1. Enhance organizational capacity for open communication, creativity, and dedication.

2. Subordinate institutional loyalties to the public good.

3. Establish procedures that promote ethical behavior and hold individuals and organizations accountable for their conduct.

4. Provide organization members with an administrative means for dissent, assurance of due process, and safeguards against reprisal.

5. Promote merit principles that protect against arbitrary and capricious actions.

6. Promote organizational accountability through appropriate controls and procedures.

7. Encourage organizations to adopt, distribute, and periodically review a code of ethics as a living document.

V. Strive for Professional Excellence

Strengthen individual capabilities and encourage the professional development of others. ASPA members are committed to

1. Provide support and encouragement to upgrade competence.

2. Accept as a personal duty the responsibility to keep up to date on emerging issues and potential problems.

3. Encourage others, throughout their careers, to participate in professional activities and associations.

4. Allocate time to meet with students and provide a bridge between classroom studies and the realities of public service.

SOURCE: www.aspanet.org.

CHAPTER 8

DESIGNING AND MANAGING ORGANIZATIONS

A public administrator needs a good understanding of the values and principles underlying work in the public and nonprofit sectors, knowledge of how public policy is developed and executed, and familiarity with a number of administrative techniques peculiar to public and nonprofit organizations. But the real key to managerial success is not what you know, but what you can do. How effectively and how responsibly can you deal with the seemingly endless series of problems and opportunities that confront you in an organizational setting? For example, a legislator or foundation program officer calls to ask for an immediate report on a matter you know will require a week to examine properly; a subordinate confesses that he has grown dependent on drugs and needs your help; someone in a meeting becomes outraged over what you perceive as a minor matter and threatens to have you fired; your boss asks your assistance in designing a completely new program and asks if you would be interested in running it. These situations and many more like them constitute the real challenges of public administration.

Your response to each event, of course, is spontaneous; yet, your actions will soon add up to a pattern that reflects your knowledge, values, and most of all, skills in dealing with other people. Organizations create the environment or context for these actions and set the stage for how your choices and behaviors will be seen and reacted to by others. An understanding of organizations—how they are structured, how they influence behavior, how they both limit the range of possibilities and facilitate new opportunities at the same time—is crucial to success in public administration. If, time after time, you act effectively and responsibly in situations that arise unexpectedly and require immediate answers with little time to think through the "theoretical" possibilities, you will be considered a highly successful manager.

Fortunately, the skills required for managerial effectiveness can be developed over time. In this and the following chapter, we examine how your knowledge and values can be brought to bear in real-world situations. We focus on the nature and structure of organizations, the specific personal and interpersonal skills a manager requires, and some ways you might further develop those skills. In this chapter, we look at several broad approaches to understanding the structure and design of public and nonprofit organizations, as well as people's behavior within those organizational settings.

The Organizational Context

To gain the ability to function well within organizations, it is useful to begin by asking some basic questions about how and why we create organizations in the first place. What are the reasons for and advantages of formal organizations? What do we gain and lose by creating organizations? Is there a best way to organize or reorganize public and nonprofit programs? We all have certain ideas and assumptions about how to organize and structure work. For instance, you may have preferences about how you would organize a group project for a school assignment or how you would organize tasks if you and several of your friends decided to throw a party. Where do these ideas about organizing come from, and what have we learned about how these structures work?

Organizations are as necessary as they are unavoidable in the modern world. When you think about all the organizations that you are connected to and rely on, the list can seem endless: your school, the businesses you buy goods and services from, the power company, the government organizations that you depend on for services and programs ranging from streets and fire protection to national defense and education. Yet, because we sometimes get frustrated with these organizations, we forget why people create them in the first place. Because they are so much a part of our lives, almost all of us can relay personal "horror stories" about dealing with organizations and how an organization was slow, rigid, or unresponsive. So why don't we just get rid of them?

The simple answer is that organizations exist because we need them. Think of what school would be like without an organization with job descriptions, multiple offices, schedules, rules, procedures, regulations, and all the features that can make organizations such as universities seem very frustrating at times. How would you know when classes are offered? Would each professor get to decide who gets to take his or her class and when and where it would be held? Imagine if the number of classes you were required to take in order to graduate depended on whom you asked? What if there wasn't any particular department or procedure for applying for financial aid? What if the library was open only when the library staff felt like it and people could just take books without checking them out and keep them as long as they wanted?

Obviously, there are advantages to organizing formal structures for getting things done. At the most basic level, we can often accomplish more by working together with other people than we can alone. But there are other advantages as well. By organizing, we can achieve cooperation between people and coordination between tasks. Organizational structures, and the rules and procedures that go with them, create predictability and regularity for the people who work in those organizations and those that interact with them. When you create schedules and processes, then people are not dependent on the whim of any particular individual. When rules are formally established, then we can increase consistency and fairness. Organizational structure allows people to know what to expect and what is expected of them. Organizations also provide the framework for dividing work so people can develop skills in a particular area—not everyone in the organization has to be an expert in everything the organization does.

At the same time, there are disadvantages to formal organizations. Putting limits on individual choice is unavoidable if you are to gain the advantages of formal organization structure. The same procedures that ensure fairness and consistency in the treatment of individuals in organizations often keep individuals from getting what they want when they want it. Although, in our interactions with organizations, we would like to bypass the rules on occasion, if there were no rules, each of us would be forced to act alone and beg, bribe, or convince individuals to help us. As individual employees of organizations, we may feel limited in our freedom to decide when we will go to work and the tasks we will (or will not) accomplish. If we were completely free to do so, however, it would be very difficult to accomplish shared tasks, much less be fair to the needs of the people we are supposed to be serving. When we create, design, and manage organizations, we want to gain the advantages of predictability and fairness while being mindful of the disadvantages and limits we are placing on individuals. Given this challenge, what are some ways to evaluate the alternative ways of managing and designing organizations?

Images of Organizing in the Public and Nonprofit Sectors

All managers carry around in their heads ideas or images of how public and nonprofit organizations should operate and how individual managers should act. These images, built up through experience, reading, discussion, and reflection, include notions about the most effective structures for public agencies, the best way to manage employees, and the proper relationship between elected and appointed officials. Depending on your particular view, you will tend to look for and emphasize certain things and ignore others. The images you carry in your head will lead you to emphasize certain aspects of organizational life and to de-emphasize others.

Some of these images derive from our experiences in our families, others come from school experiences, and still others are a result of work in other organizations. Some are general lessons we learned about topics such as power and authority, communications and cooperation, and so forth. Others are more specific to the world of work or the public service. Some are fairly conscious; others lie far beneath the surface.

Whatever their form, these images direct our actions in specific ways. They make us see the world in a particular way and, correspondingly, act in a particular way. So it is important to carefully consider how individuals think about public and nonprofit organizations. What images do we have, and how do they direct us to act? Which images allow us to be most successful, and which hold us back or get in the way?

As you begin to think more carefully about the images that shape your work, and especially as you begin to accumulate experiences, you will begin to identify areas where your insight (and consequently your actions) might be improved. One way to sharpen your images of public and nonprofit organizations is to consider what scholars and practitioners in the field of general management, particularly public and nonprofit management, have said and written. Fortunately, there is a considerable and growing body of material to draw upon that offers many categories and approaches you might use in thinking about your involvement.

For the most part, this literature has developed out of the experiences of practicing managers. (Because the literature on nonprofit management is still in its early stages, much of the following discussion relates to public-sector management.) Reflective practitioners and thoughtful academics have asked over and over how public and nonprofit managers can be helped to select those features of organizational life that will be most helpful to them. Many students and practitioners of public administration have contributed to our understanding of the management of public agencies. They have developed "word pictures" (often simply called theories) to suggest what will be most helpful when you approach similar problems. Each theoretical approach directs attention toward certain topics or ideas and away from others. It is up to you to select the most relevant and most helpful approaches to your particular situation. In this chapter, we review some of the most influential ways of thinking about organizations and management in the public sector. Some early approaches focused on fairly obvious points, but more recent approaches are more complex and sophisticated.

The Functions of Management

In the twentieth century, French management theorist and practitioner Henri Fayol (1949) identified five general functions managers should perform: planning, organizing, commanding, coordinating, and controlling. Several years later, Luther Gulick compiled a similar list. Gulick, an adviser on federal government reorganization, described the functions of public management in terms of an acronym, POSDCORB: planning, organizing, staffing, directing, coordinating, reporting, and budgeting (Gulick, 1937a). To Fayol and Gulick, these activities were the essence of management and identified functions that had to be performed if organizations were to be managed effectively. They constituted advice to managers about what they should be doing.

Planning involves preparing yourself and your organization to move effectively into the future. All managers engage in planning at least to some extent, and for some managers, such as those on strategic planning staffs, planning is almost a full-time activity. Some managers make plans for the entire organization, while others make plans for the units they directly supervise, but all managers plan for their own activities. Unfortunately, as we noted earlier, planning is one managerial function that is often easy to overlook. Managers get caught up in the hectic pace of conversations, meetings, and deadlines and often neglect planning. Yet, the most effective managers are aware that time taken out for planning, whether for the organization or for oneself, pays rich dividends.

Planning is closely related to decision making, an aspect of managerial work that cuts across many of the other areas. The ability to make thoughtful decisions seems to distinguish the more successful managers. Because decision making is so fundamental to managerial work, it has been studied intensively for many years. In most organizations, decision making is a central activity.

Organizing refers to many different activities, including dividing the organization into different departments, creating levels in the organization's hierarchy, and deciding who reports to whom. In a specific department or division, organizing also includes the task of defining specific positions and jobs. Note that organizing includes job design, but the assignment of individuals to specific jobs involves the staffing rather than the organizing function.

Staffing is the process of acquiring, training, and developing the personnel to conduct the organization's activities. It is generally described as "personnel management" or sometimes "human resources management." As we saw in Chapter 6, specific tasks such as hiring, training, firing, and so forth are examples of the staffing or personnel function. Obviously, dealing with people involves important skills in communication and motivation, as well as the ability to make sound decisions about whom to hire.

Directing is often the most dynamic and most visible management function. It includes three critical management activities: leading, motivating, and changing things when necessary. Providing direction to an organization is a subtle and complex task that involves the full range of personal and interpersonal skills.

What Would You Do?

You have been given the assignment of managing a brand new federal program designed to ensure an adequate supply of flu vaccine each year. Your first task will be to explore whether provision of vaccine should become a public function or remain in private hands (or something in between). You are then to prepare a plan for organizing the transition to whatever new system you recommend. What would you do?

Coordinating the work of many different people in many different places is also a central managerial function. The complexity and diversity of most modern organizations mean that a great deal of time must be spent making sure that all the "pieces" fall into place at the right time. Coordinating involves special skills in problem solving—how to make things work—but it also involves skills in communicating and negotiating.

Reporting provides the basis for accountability. It involves analyzing and keeping records of organizational activities and performance, and then providing meaningful and useful information to elected officials, citizens, and others to whom the manager is accountable. Reporting and record keeping are also important so that the manager and others can keep track of tasks and activities, analyze performance and progress toward goal attainment, identify problems in a timely fashion, and find opportunities for improvement.

Budgeting involves managing the organization's resources, especially financial. It also involves securing, planning for, and managing the organization's funds. As we saw in Chapter 5, budgeting is a technical field, but it also involves human skills, especially those of developing funding for one's programs and allocating scarce resources among competing programs and people.

In addition to these standard management functions, there are also a number of miscellaneous tasks that are usually considered managerial work. One of the most important is dealing with people from outside the organization. Skills in presenting your organization and point of view to others are becoming increasingly important as the relationships among organizations at different levels become more intense. Representing your organization before outside groups and organizations has come to be known in the literature on management as *boundary spanning*.

The Early Writers: A Concern for Structure

The question of how to best organize and manage work has occupied theorists and practitioners for many years. When you think about setting up an organization, you might think, for example, about establishing who will be "in charge" of what, making assignments and delegating tasks, and maybe even setting up some rules and timetables. Although this may feel like the "natural" or obvious way to organize, many of these ideas can be traced to the work of a German sociologist named Max Weber, who observed the emergence of large-scale organizations in the late nineteenth and early twentieth centuries. He was the first to use the term *bureaucracy* and to write comprehensively about the structure of these large-scale organizations. According to Weber, bureaucracy meant any large organization, public or private, characterized by a clearly defined hierarchy of impersonal offices and employment of qualified people who are subject to strict discipline and control (Gerth & Mills, 1946, p. 328). More specifically, Weber said that bureaucracies could be characterized as follows:

1. There is a fixed and stable structure for dividing tasks and responsibilities established and operated according to rules and regulations.
2. The authority to give orders related to these duties is set forth in official rules.
3. Only people who are qualified to do the work are employed in order to provide consistent and ongoing accomplishment of organizational tasks.
4. There is a system of graded authority or hierarchy in which each level of the organization, from bottom to top, is supervised by the next higher level.
5. Management is based on written records and documents to keep track of correspondence, decisions, financial matters, and other items of importance.
6. Office management is based on thorough and expert training.
7. Working in a bureaucracy is a vocation or profession. It is generally a full-time activity, not a secondary activity.

Though we now often use *bureaucracy* pejoratively, Weber's more technical use of the term carries no negative connotation. In fact, Weber argued that bureaucracy is the most efficient way to organize: "Experience tends to universally show that the purely bureaucratic type of administration [is] capable of attaining the highest degree of efficiency and is formally the most rational known means of carrying out imperative control over human beings" (Gerth & Mills, 1946, p. 337). On the other hand, Weber was also concerned about some of the drawbacks of the bureaucratic form. First, he cautioned that fully developed bureaucratic power and expertise could come to "overtower" or surpass democratic controls. Second, he was concerned about the effects of bureaucracy on individual freedoms.

Despite these concerns, the bureaucratic form of organization has long served as the foundation for many of our ideas about organizational design and structure. Early writers on public administration thought of management in highly mechanical terms and considered questions of organizational structure and design of paramount importance. Recall that the birth of public administration as a separate field of study occurred during a time of impressive gains in science and industry. New ideas and new products were changing society almost overnight, as were the industrial and organizational processes that made them possible. It was a time of rigid control by "captains of industry"; it was also a time of the birth of the assembly line.

In such an era, the machine became the leading image for how to organize technical and human processes. Just as the machine was precise, mechanical, and efficient, so should be the organizations that built the machines. The result was a highly mechanical approach to organization that valued the idea of developing proper structures and operating them with great efficiency.

This orientation was epitomized in the influential work of Frederick W. Taylor, who developed what he termed *"scientific management,"* an approach based on carefully defined "laws, rules, and principles" (1923, p. 7). Taylor focused first on the individual worker, designing detailed measurements of time and motion to discover how the worker might become more efficient. For example, one might measure the distance from where a particular piece of equipment was stored to where it was used and then try to reduce the distance, time, and motion required to use the equipment. (In one example, Taylor sought to develop a "science of shoveling" based on the premise that the size of each individual shovel load would affect the daily output of "first-class shovelers." After careful and detailed experiments, it was determined that the greatest tonnage per day would be achieved with an average shovel load of about twenty-one pounds!)

Taylor's approach could be applied to a wide variety of work-process problems, from the design of assembly lines to the arrangement of items on one's desk. But beyond these efforts to turn workers into highly tuned machines, Taylor's work provided guidance for managers throughout the organization. The manager's role became that of making the organization more efficient through the application of detailed "scientific" information. The smooth-running organization was to be highly mechanical, with the human elements strictly controlled to contribute to overall efficiency. The manager's job was to ensure the efficient operation of the system.

Just as Taylor and others emphasized the efficient operation of industrial systems, others soon applied this emphasis in public administration. Leonard White wrote, "The objective of public administration is the most efficient utilization of the resources at the disposal of officials and employees" (1926, p. 2). "In the science of administration, whether public or private, the basic 'good' is efficiency," Luther Gulick concurred (1937b, p. 192). Though several writers objected, pointing out that other values such as responsiveness come into play and that mechanical efficiency is "coldly calculating and inhuman" (Dimock, 1936, p. 120), efficiency was clearly the primary interest of most early public administrationists.

Early writers in public administration transferred other lessons from the field of business to the design and structure of organizations, specifically the importance of establishing single centers of power controlling basically top-down structures. At the top of the organization there was to be one single authority to whom all subordinate personnel ultimately reported. Though the organization would be characterized by many managers, and perhaps many organizational units, the ultimate responsibility and authority lay at the top.

Networking

The Academy of Management Online at www.aomonline.org, the Society for Industrial and Organizational Psychology at www.siop.org, and the Institute for Operations Research and the Management Sciences at www.informs.org offer research and information sources concerning the general principles of organization theory and behavior. For an alternative, visit the *Electronic Journal of Radical Organisation Theory* at www.mngt.waikato.ac.nz/ejrot. This site is published by the University of Waikato School of Management Studies in Hamilton, New Zealand.

To reconcile this view with the democratic requirement that public organizations be responsive to the popular will, early writers suggested that the organization's head, the single source of power and authority, should simply be accountable to the legislative body in much the same way a corporate chief executive officer is accountable to a board of directors. (Recall this idea as "the doctrine of neutral competence.") In describing the role of an agency chief executive, early writers advised to vest all administrative authority in a single executive who would be given power to carry out the work and the responsibility for seeing that the work was done. According to W. F. Willoughby, this was the first step in making the executive branch a "single, integrated piece of administrative machinery" (1927, p. 37). (This advice was at odds with the standard political practice of that period: the election of many administrative officers and the use of many large executive boards. As we saw earlier, even today, most states elect officers such as secretary of state or treasurer rather than having such officers report to a single chief executive—in this case, the governor.)

The early writers who put forth the administrative management viewpoint were practical people who drew on their experience in managing public agencies. Consequently, when they described their work, they tended to emphasize how organizational structures might be built. Luther Gulick, for example, wrote extensively about the formation of agencies. After the agency was created and an executive chosen, Gulick saw the next task as one of dividing the necessary work and then establishing proper means of coordination and control. The new organization would move through four phases in which the legislature or chief executive would (1) define the job, (2) select a director, who would (3) determine the nature and number of required units, and (4) establish a structure of authority through which he or she would coordinate and control activities of the units (1937a, p. 7).

The division of labor, which amounted to creation of an organizational structure, was a critical element. The logic was compelling: because people differ in knowledge and skills, and because the amount of time any one person can contribute to the solution of large-scale problems is limited, it is necessary to divide the work of the organization into manageable portions. As we saw earlier, division of labor could be accomplished in a limited number of ways. Gulick suggested organizing on the basis of (1) the major purpose served (such as education or welfare), (2) the process (engineering or medicine), (3) the persons or things being dealt with by the unit (veterans or convicts), or (4) the place or geographic location where the work is done (1937a, pp. 21–29).

FIGURE 8.1

Typical Organization Chart Showing Line and Staff

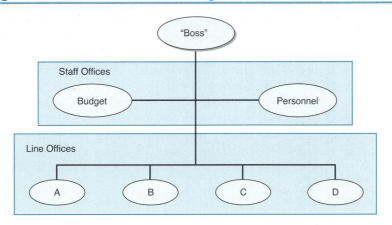

© Cengage Learning

Having established a division of labor, the next problem facing the new director or manager was to create a structure of authority to coordinate and control the various parts of the organization. Gulick's answer to this question, like others during this period, was again drawn from orthodox practice in business: the organization should feature unity of command exercised through a hierarchical structure of authority. By the early 1900s, hierarchical organizations, like those symbolized in the standard organization chart (see Figure 8.1), had become models for industry (as they had previously been in the military and the Catholic Church). Gulick and many other early scholars and practitioners in public administration suggested a similar approach in the public sector.

Guidance for creating such structures was given by two former General Motors executives, James Mooney and Alan Reiley (1939). Mooney and Reiley described four main principles for structuring large organizations. The first, *coordination through unity of command,* emphasized the importance of strong executive leadership exercised through a specific and formal chain of command. In this structure, each person would have only one boss, and each boss would have a limited span of control—that is, a limited number of people reporting to him or her. Mooney and Reiley argued that there should be no question about whose orders to obey.

The second principle was the *scalar principle,* which described the vertical division of labor among various organizational levels. (In military terms, the difference between a general and a private reflects the scalar principle.) Third was the *functional principle,* describing a horizontal division of labor. (Again, in military terms, the difference between Infantry and Air Force would be a functional difference.) Finally, Mooney and Reiley discussed the relationship between *line* and *staff,* with line offices representing the direct flow of authority, and staff offices (such as personnel or finance) available to advise the chief executive but not exercising direct authority over line offices.

The language of hierarchical structures became somewhat standard. Just as distinctions were often drawn between line and staff, managers were (and are today) often classified as top, middle, or supervisory. Supervisory managers are at the bottom of the hierarchy, top managers at the peak, and middle managers in between. A supervisory manager directly manages the people involved in producing the organization's output. The supervisory level is the first level of management, so supervisors are sometimes called first-line managers. Normally, no managers are below the supervisory level. An example of a supervisory manager is the person to whom your mail carrier reports at the post office.

Supervisors report to middle managers, usually defined as "managers who manage other managers." If the organization is small, there may be only one level of middle managers; large organizations usually have more than one middle-management level. The highest level of management, the top level, usually has the fewest managers. Top managers, often called "executives," are responsible for entire organizations, whereas middle-and supervisory-level managers focus on increasingly smaller sections of the organization. Top managers are usually the most involved in relationships with other groups and agencies.

It is easy to distinguish supervisory-level from middle-level managers, but it is often ambiguous where middle management stops and top management begins. Titles often confuse things more than they help. The title of vice president, for example, indicates a top manager in some organizations; in others, the vice president is only a middle manager. Banks are particularly well known for having many vice presidents, most of whom are obviously not part of top management. Similarly, titles in public organizations, such as division director, branch chief, and department head, are used in different ways and are usually only meaningful if you understand the conventions of the organization.

In any case, early writers on public administration generally sought to apply what they saw as the correct "principles" of administrative management to the conduct of public organizations. They implied that the problems and solutions facing government were much the same as those in industry: centralization of authority and the development of hierarchical structures. But this assumption sidestepped several important issues essential to the operations of public agencies. Is the criterion of efficiency the only criterion by which the work of public organizations should be evaluated? Is it incompatible to create highly authoritarian structures to carry out the work of a democracy?

There were also questions about whether approaches to organization based on structural analysis alone were even the most efficient. In both the public and private sectors, for example, managers and researchers began to ask whether the rigid structures described in the principles of administrative management could effectively adapt to change. And, perhaps most important, where does the individual enter into the equation, other than as a potential machine? The structural lens through which many early scholars and practitioners viewed the world proved to be somewhat limiting; something else was needed.

Recognizing Human Behavior

In the mid-1920s, an impetus to further investigation of informal or human factors in organizational life came from studies conducted by Harvard researchers at the Hawthorne Works of the Western Electric Company. The studies, which became known as the Hawthorne studies, began in a way largely consistent with the scientific management tradition and were designed to measure the relationship between working conditions (such as lighting, temperature, and humidity) and worker productivity (such as monotony and fatigue). In the experiment, certain groups were isolated from their coworkers and placed in carefully controlled environments where conditions could be varied systematically. But as the experiment developed, regardless of the changes in environmental conditions—lighter or darker, hotter or colder, more or less humid—the productivity of the experimental group tended to increase. Can you guess why?

Researchers discovered that the experimental group was responding not to the conditions around them, but to the fact that they had been singled out for special attention. As a result, the researchers developed a new interest in the human aspects of organizational life. Those in the Hawthorne study began to see organizations as not only meeting the stated goals of producing goods or services, but also as being concerned, even if implicitly, with the distribution of "satisfactions"—some monetary, others social and psychological—to members of the organization. The informal organization (in other words, the human interactions that paralleled those prescribed by the organizational structure) was viewed as important or even more important than the formal organization. If this were the case, then it made sense that the manager's role involved attention to both the formal structure of the work process and the pattern of informal relationships among the workers. Either one could affect efficiency and effectiveness.

CourseReader Assignment

Log in to **www.cengage.com** and open CourseReader to access the reading:

Read "Transformational Leadership in the Public Sector: Does Structure Matter?" by Sanjay K. Pandey and Bradley E. Wright. This article concerns the possibility of achieving transformational leadership in public organizations. Specifically, it explores some of the structural constraints on transformational leadership. But it also points out some of the structural opportunities that public organizations present.

What do we mean by transformational leadership? Can you think of leaders in government, in private organizations, or nonprofit organizations whom you would consider transformational? What is it about their work that seems to distinguish them from other leaders? Do you think the structure of government affects the possibility of transformational leadership? Or can leaders be transformational in any circumstance?

There was abundant advice on how to manage the formal structure, but only speculation on how to manage the informal or human side of organizations. Consequently, a number of studies were undertaken that dealt with the critical human relationship between manager and worker. Many of the studies suggested that changes in one's approach to managing, or management style, could lead to important differences in productivity. By treating workers differently, you could affect the work they did.

An example of this orientation was Douglas MacGregor's (1960) discussion of Theory X and Theory Y. After reviewing other work on management, MacGregor suggested that a better theory of human behavior (not structure) might make it possible to more effectively control workers in organizations. MacGregor contrasted a set of assumptions about human behavior that appeared to form the basis for traditional management techniques (Theory X) with a set of assumptions he felt would underlie a new, more enlightened approach (Theory Y). Traditionally, MacGregor argued, managers assume that human beings are lazy and dislike work, that they must therefore be coerced to produce, and that most in fact want such direction. MacGregor suggested in contrast that work is quite natural, people do not need to be coerced, they will devote energy to objectives to which they are committed, and they will make commitments to objectives that, when completed, will lead to rewards. As a consequence, MacGregor suggested that most workers were not being utilized to their full potential. The lesson was straightforward: managers must take care to determine the needs and desires of their employees and then help orient the individual's objectives so that they are met by work that fulfills the organization's objectives.

Closely associated with this viewpoint is a "hierarchy of needs" proposed by the psychologist Abraham Maslow. Maslow's hierarchy is most often pictured as a pyramid with basic needs at the bottom and more complex needs near the top. The idea is that basic needs need to be satisfied first, but, after that, needs such as love, friendship, and intimacy become more important. There are five levels to Maslow's hierarchy of needs: physiological needs, security needs, social needs, esteem needs, and self-actualization needs. Those at the top, those who are closest to fulfilling their potential and have already completed the other levels in the hierarchy, are self-aware and concerned with personal growth. They have reached the level of self-actualization (Maslow, 1954).

Two Classic Works

Two writers on organizational behavior, both stimulated by the new attention to human factors in organizational life, wrote "classics" on the subject during the 1940s and 1950s. One author, Herbert Simon, came from the field of public administration; the other, Chris Argyris, began his work in industrial psychology. Both have influenced all fields of management even to the present.

Simon suggested that the reason we have large organizations in the first place is that human beings are limited or "bounded" in their rationality or capacity to solve the complex problems of the modern world. "The capacity of the human mind for formulating and solving complex problems is very small in comparison with the size of the problems whose solution is required for objectively rational behavior in the real world or even for a reasonable approximation to such objective rationality" (1957, p. 198). Organizations are seen as devices for molding our sometimes erratic behavior to rational patterns of obtaining our objectives.

In the abstract, it's not difficult to design a rational system for reaching organizational objectives. The difficulty comes when human beings, with all their emotions and interests, are inserted into the system. Because they are human, they often appear "irrational" in terms of the system, even though what they are doing, from their point of view, may be perfectly rational. The chief problem for Simon, therefore, became how to understand and direct human behavior in such a way that it aids in pursuit of the organization's objectives in a rational (that is, efficient) way.

Simon described the organization as a decision-making system involving two primary sets of decisions on the part of the individual: the decision to be a part of an organization and the decision to contribute desired behaviors to the organization. Simon approaches each problem through a rational calculation of costs and benefits. For example, a person may be expected to remain a member of an organization as long as the benefits exceed those that might be obtained elsewhere.

The same approach is used with respect to the individual's contributions to the organization, an issue closely tied to the question of authority. Simon argued that each individual establishes "an *area of acceptance* within which the subordinate is willing to accept the decisions made for him by his superior" (Simon, 1957, pp. 74–75). But because it is in the interest of the organization to have the "zone" or area of acceptance as wide as possible, the organization, through its managers, offers certain "inducements" designed to increase the individual's "contributions." Inducements include money and status, but they also involve creating a state of mind in which individuals tend to obey rather than disobey.

Simon argues that you cannot expect people to make perfectly rational decisions. Indeed, most human beings act with *bounded rationality*; they seek the best possible solution, though not necessarily the most rational from a purely economic standpoint. Members can be made to fall in line with the organization's expectations by means of inducements that are just good enough to elicit the desired contributions. In this way, what Simon terms "administrative man" (in contrast to "economic man") becomes a part of a rationally behaving system.

Rather than focusing on rational systems, Chris Argyris focused on the interaction of the individual and the organization. He suggested, like MacGregor, that formal organizational structures and traditional management practices were inconsistent with a natural human striving for growth and development. Individuals in our society, Argyris concluded, develop from infancy through adulthood along several important dimensions: from passivity to activity, dependence to independence, a limited to greater range of behaviors, shallow to deeper interests, shorter to longer time perspectives, positions of subordination to those of equality or superordination, and lack of awareness to greater awareness. Movement along each dimension contributes to what we know as the healthy adult personality.

Yet, argued Argyris, these goals are exactly those that traditional management practices prevent. For example, standard patterns of management give the individual little control over his or her work. Workers are expected to be passive, submissive, and limited in the range of their responses. They are expected to behave like children. Moreover, if individuals express frustration at such a situation, managers often see their behavior as hostile and dysfunctional. The typical managerial response is to crack down, to assert even more severe methods of control.

A healthier approach, suggests Argyris, would be to understand the basic tendencies of the human personality for growth and development and then to "fuse" these tendencies with the objectives of the organization. Achieving this congruence or fusion is the task of the manager. This requires that the manager develop "skill in self-awareness, in effective diagnosing, in helping individuals grow and become more creative, in coping with dependent-oriented…employees, and in surviving in a competitive world of management" (1962, p. 213).

Both Simon and Argyris shift from concerns with structure to concerns with human behavior. Each offers a new way of looking at organizations and the people in them. The manager, according to this new view, needs to take structure into account (for that will affect human behavior), but the "bottom line" is how people behave. And, of course, the behavior of human beings is affected by more than the structures in which they reside. The attention of the manager is redirected from structure to behavior, in Simon's and Argyris's works. In this new view, the job of the manager is to mold human behavior toward the purposes of the organization.

The Organization and Its Environment

The early emphasis on structure and the later emphasis on human behavior proved helpful in focusing attention on important aspects of life in complex organizations. But neither viewpoint considered the relationship between the organization and its environment. This missing element began to appear, however, as writers in the field of public administration returned to issues of structure, though they viewed structure in quite a different way. The new concern for structure was stimulated by two emerging approaches to public organizations: systems theory and the political economy approach. The *systems approach* suggested that public (or other) organizations could be viewed in the same way as biological or physical systems as whole "organisms," independent of their parts and pursuing specific purposes within a complex environment. The *political economy approach* focused on politics and economics as categories for analyzing organizational behavior.

Systems Theory

The systems model suggests that the organization receives from its environment the human and material resources it requires to function, as well as requests and directives about how it should operate. These resources, requests, and directives are processed through the organization and transformed by it. The resulting outputs (products, services, and so on) are transmitted back into the environment. In turn, these outputs are taken into account as new inputs are developed, and, over time, a balancing point is reached that makes possible the survival of the organization.

A classic study of the relationship between an agency and its environment was Selznick's analysis of the Tennessee Valley Authority (TVA) in the 1940s. Selznick argued that, in contrast to the closed, mechanical systems implied in many approaches to public organization, organizations are in fact open systems. That is, they exist within an institutional framework, which includes political parties, pressure groups, and special interests. Though the groups' demands may appear "irrational" from the perspective of the organization, they simply cannot be ignored.

The TVA sought to involve already existing local agencies in planning power distribution systems and other programs, in order to anticipate potential demands and be prepared to respond. Additionally, the TVA wanted to get local groups committed to the TVA program by making them feel part of the organization. By bringing outside groups into the structure of the organization (by placing persons on advisory groups or negotiating service contracts with them), TVA sought support for its own programs. You will recall this idea as co-optation, a term Selznick defined as "the process of absorbing new elements into the leadership or policy-determining structure of the organization as a means of averting threats to its stability or existence" (Selznick, 1949, p. 13).

What Would You Do?

You have been taking doctoral-level classes at a local university while continuing to work as a mid-level manager in state government. Some of your fellow workers have been teasing you lately about your "theoretical" approach to management, which, they say, just doesn't work in the "real world." You are beginning to wonder yourself whether theoretical ideas really make a difference in practice. What would you do?

Another study examining the influence of environmental factors on the operations of public agencies was Herbert Kaufman's analysis of the U.S. Forest Service (Kaufman, 1960). The Forest Service faced the problem of how to secure compliance and consistency from forest rangers scattered across the country who were subjected to pressure from their local communities. Rangers often served, of course, in isolated locations. Although they sought to carry out the policies of the Forest Service, they also developed loyalties to their local communities. They often had to carry out regulations that would adversely affect their friends and neighbors and, in such cases, might be tempted to deviate from central office directives. The agency's response was to devise a series of training programs, procedural devices, inspections, and sanctions as efforts to reduce the influence of the local environment and to ensure that central office orders were actually carried out.

Looking at how environmental factors influence public organizations led other writers to characterize public agencies as interdependent systems operating in a complex environment. No longer could one agency's work be viewed in isolation from that of other public and private agencies. One would simply not be able to understand how an agency operated without understanding the myriad external influences on the agency. Imagine, for example, the difficulty of implementing a new set of standards for water quality in a city located on a state boundary, such as Cincinnati. Think of all the agencies, public and private, that would have to be notified and would wish to express their views. Think of the various political jurisdictions—states, cities, counties, and special districts. Think of the various bodies within each jurisdiction that might want input: the mayor, legislature, and administrative agencies.

The complexity of administrative activities has led some scholars to suggest that it is no longer meaningful to focus on a specific agency's contribution to implementing policy, but to think in terms of programs. Recall that many federal programs operate through a pattern of funding in which money, rules, and guidelines are established for programs that are delivered at the state and local levels through both public and private agencies.

For example, in the delivery of social services, such as drug prevention efforts, state and local governments use federal money to fund private or nonprofit providers of the services. In many cases, the money goes to fund programs, not specific agencies, so that these programs operate through rather diffuse networks of loosely joined groups rather than through traditional hierarchical structures. In such ill-structured "structures," older notions of organizational control give way to new emphasis on bargaining and negotiation, in which the systems perspective has much to offer.

From Political Economy to Organization Development

Interest in interorganizational policy networks was further stimulated by the emergence of the political economy approach to understanding public organizations. Wamsley and Zald (1976) suggest that public organizations can best be understood in terms of the conjunction of political and economic factors influencing their operation. These factors affect the organization both internally and externally, leading to four categories through which we might view organizations. First, the external political environment involves the interplay of various interest groups and other organizations that affect the organization's political climate. Second, the external economic environment consists of market exchanges that influence the available supply of resources. Third, the internal political category focuses on the distribution of power and authority. Fourth, the internal economy concerns the allocation of resources and how they are used.

The Wamsley-Zald approach is related to a more sophisticated, complex approach most often associated with Vincent Ostrom. Ostrom's public choice approach begins with examining how individuals might make choices if they were free to act rationally and in their own self-interest. Under some circumstances, people might be expected to engage in collective action, especially where "public goods" are involved or where situations are neither purely public nor purely private. (Public goods are distinguished from private goods—those that can be measured, marketed, and maintained—by the fact that they are highly indivisible; a public good such as the national defense is available to all once it is provided for one.)

Following this logic, Ostrom sees public organizations as "a means for allocating decision-making capabilities in order to provide public goods and services responsive to the preferences of individuals in different social contexts" (Ostrom & Ostrom, 1971, p. 207). Ostrom argues that the best structures for satisfying individual preferences are not centralized bureaucratic agencies, but rather more fragmented, multiorganizational arrangements.

Although earlier behavioral studies like Simon's and Argyris's were important in countering the field's dependence on a structural interpretation of organizational life, they were limited in certain ways. First, most of the behavioral literature failed to question the top-down pattern of organizational authority; many people thought it merely provided more sophisticated mechanisms for managerial control. Second, there seemed little interest in organization change processes, at a time when rapid social change was becoming a dominant feature of the landscape. Third, as open systems theorists pointed out, the perspective failed to comprehend the complexity of interorganizational bargaining and negotiation.

Similarly, the political economy approach seemed to unnecessarily limit creativity and communication and seemed, at least to some, to place values in a secondary position.

Among major critics of earlier approaches were a group of scholars in the early 1970s whose collective work came to be known as "the New Public Administration." In contrast to older approaches that emphasized efficiency and control, the New Public Administration heralded openness and change, equity and involvement. In a rapidly changing society populated by diverse groups, the New Public Administrationists felt the key element in the survival of organizations—indeed, of society—was the capacity to adapt to rapid social change. Organizations would have to find ways to deal with an increasingly "turbulent" environment.

Doing so would require stimulating the creativity of everyone involved in any public program, both within the agency and in the environment. Involving the organization's members and its clients in the decision-making process would, the New Public Administrationists felt, foster creativity. Moreover, such an approach seemed far more consistent with democratic norms and practices than operating through top-down structures of control. The key words in the New Public Administration were *equity* and *involvement*.

Many of those associated with the New Public Administration became students of organizational change processes and sought ways to help organizations implement needed changes. One of the most important approaches they employed was *organization development*, a process-oriented approach to planned change. Organization development suggests many techniques for change that we will examine later, but it also offers another approach to view the work of organizations.

Robert Golembiewski, a leader in the application of organization development strategies and techniques to the public sector, points out that organization development represents a particular philosophy of management that is considerably at odds with traditional top-down tendencies and values the following:

1. Mutual accessibility and open communications
2. A willingness to experiment with new behaviors and to choose those that seem most effective
3. A collaborative concept of authority that emphasizes cooperation and willingness to examine conflicts openly
4. Helping relationships involving a sense of community and acceptance of responsibility for others
5. Authenticity in interpersonal relationships (Golembiewski, 1972, pp. 60–66)

Decision Making in Organizations

As suggested in our discussion of the public policy process, decision making represents one of the most critical functions of public and nonprofit organizations. Although the scope and nature of decision making vary from issue to issue, the process itself is a daily activity. Some have even suggested that organizations can be viewed as living histories of their decision-making processes. To better appreciate this important function, it may be helpful to examine some of the core concepts of organizational decision making and to understand how leaders use these concepts in their management practice (Hatch, 1997, pp. 270–281).

Scholars of organizations traditionally followed an economic view of decision making, which assumed that decisions were the result of rational, well-informed selection procedures. (Much of our discussion to this point reflects this traditional viewpoint.) In the rational model, management recognizes the problem, identifies alternatives, selects and implements the most efficient alternative, and monitors the results.

However, a series of works, beginning with March and Simon (1958) and Cyert and March (1963), challenged this rational viewpoint, arguing that decision making can be viewed as rational only in certain circumstances. Most often, organizations lack the information and capacity needed for making rational decisions. Simon, who received a Nobel Prize for his work in artificial intelligence, referred to this phenomenon as a "bounded rationality," as discussed previously. He identified five of the most common constraints:

1. Imperfect and incomplete information
2. The complexity of the problem
3. Human information-processing capacity
4. The time available for decision-making processes
5. The conflicting preferences decision makers have for organizational goals
   (Hatch, 1997, p. 274)

Despite attempts on the part of managers to use more rational processes, these factors pose insurmountable barriers to rational decision making. The implications are twofold. First, managers will never have enough data to adequately inform decision-making processes. Second, even if they did, they would face conflicting goals from stakeholders, to the point that they would be unable to make a truly rational selection of the most efficient alternatives. For Simon, the best that managers can do involves what he called "satisficing"—that is, making do with the most information possible at the time and attempting to balance between competing demands.

But what happens when the goals of a particular decision-point are relatively clear and the only true variable lies in the uncertainty of the policy direction or outcome? Henry Mintzberg and his colleagues (1976) referred to this as the "trial-and-error" model of decision making. Managers take an incremental approach to implementing policy alternatives, assess the impact, and then move to the next decision-point. Over time, the belief is that a comprehensive solution to the issue will be attained, but the process will allow decision makers to proceed with caution.

Often the opposite may also be true. Decision makers may (and will!) face a variety of competing demands from stakeholders, which they must balance before even moving to the decision stage. Handling the complexity of these situations requires what organization theorists refer to as the "coalition model" of decision making. The coalition model involves a search for "interest-accommodating alternatives" as opposed to the "problem-solving information" in the rational model. Policy leaders recognize that what may be the most efficient alternative will not be acceptable to different interest groups. The best option is the one they can "sell" to their key constituencies. Although some believe that the coalition model implies some sort of breakdown in "normal" decision making, in today's dynamic, multicultural world (particularly in the public and nonprofit sectors) it tends to be the rule more than the exception.

Of course, both the trial-and-error and coalition models of decision making assume that either the certainty of approach or the goals of the process have been determined. All that's left is "filling in the blank" of the other variable. Anyone who has served in a public or nonprofit organization will tell you that many times both sets of questions need to be answered. In these situations, which are characterized by a continuous ebb and flow of leadership, ongoing change in the policy environment, and shifting sets of coalitions among stakeholders, leaders find themselves using the "garbage can model" of decision making. (Does this sound familiar? If not, it will very soon!) Randomness replaces rationality. Indeed, Cohen, March, and Olsen (1972) used the term *organized anarchies* to describe organizations that practice the garbage can model as normal policy.

The approaches to organizational decision making described here should not be taken as mutually exclusive. Leaders in public and nonprofit organizations should explore a variety of methods, depending on the changing conditions in the policy environment. In fact, the most effective managers will be able to "read" the shifting conditions and balance their desire for rationality with a sensitivity to their "political barometers."

Organizational Culture, Organizational Learning, and Strategic Management

During the past generation, many discussions of management and organizations, especially in the private sector, have emphasized the importance of understanding the "culture" of the organization. Most writers refer to *organizational culture* as the basic pattern of attitudes, beliefs, and values that underlie the organization's operations. An organization's culture consists of shared assumptions that members of the organization hold. Edgar H. Schein (1997, pp. 8–10) notes that culture can be manifested in many ways, including the following:

1. *Observed behavioral regularities when people interact.* The language they use, the customs and traditions that evolve, and the rituals they employ in a wide variety of situations.
2. *Group norms.* The implicit standards and values that evolve in working groups, such as the particular norm of a "fair day's work for a fair day's pay" that evolved among workers in the Hawthorne studies.
3. *Espoused values.* The articulated, publicly announced principles and values that the group claims to be trying to achieve.
4. *Formal philosophy.* The broad policies and ideological principles that guide a group's actions toward stockholders, employees, customers, and other stakeholders.
5. *Rules of the game.* Implicit rules for getting along in the organizations and "the ropes" that a newcomer must learn to be an accepted member—"the way we do things around here."
6. *Climate.* The feeling that is conveyed in a group by the physical layout and the way in which members of the organization interact with each other, customers, or outsiders.
7. *Embedded skills.* The special competencies group members display in accomplishing certain tasks, the ability to make certain things that gets passed on from generation to generation without necessarily being articulated in writing.

8. *Habits of thinking, mental models, and/or linguistic paradigms.* The shared cognitive frames that guide the perceptions, thought, and language used by the members of a group and are taught to new members in the early socialization process.
9. *Shared meanings.* The emergent understandings that are created by group members as they interact with each other.
10. *"Root metaphors" or integrating symbols.* The ideas, feelings, and images groups develop to characterize themselves that may or may not be appreciated consciously, but that become embodied in buildings, office layout, and other material artifacts of the group.

As these manifestations suggest, some of the most important aspects of an organization lie outside of the explicit characteristics shared in normal group interaction. The unique ways in which an organization communicates internally and externally, its system of reward and punishment, and the way group members perceive themselves and the outside world all stem from the deeper, mostly undiscussed system of values and beliefs that define the group as a whole (Schein, 1997).

What Would You Do?

As a newly hired city manager, you want to shift the culture of your organization to reflect a greater commitment to citizen service. What would you do?

These layers of culture represent key concerns in their own right. They yield insight in very different ways about the nature of the group. However, organizational culture becomes even more critical as it relates to planned organizational change. Organizations face dynamic conditions in their internal and external environments—a variety of social, economic, and political factors impact group performance. The successful organization remains flexible to meet these changing conditions. Yet, given the multiple levels of organizational culture, change within the group cannot simply occur on the surface. The organization's underlying system of beliefs and values must be transformed if change is to be sustainable (Schein, 1997; Senge, 1990).

In this context, the notion of organizational culture becomes closely related to another important management concept: *organizational learning.* Learning organizations recognize that the primary contributors to error, or the disparity between what the group intends to happen and what actually occurs (Argyris, 1993) and thus barriers to change, are embedded deep within the organization's collective consciousness. They are not talked about, or even immediately acknowledged by group members. Therefore, groups that succeed in becoming learning organizations, those that are able to correct error and overcome their barriers, can successfully bring about change both in surface behavior and in the underlying levels of culture in the organization.

For example, say an organization's performance has started to suffer because of a decline in employee satisfaction and infighting among staff members. An immediate response may be to alter the group's behavior to reduce the infighting and improve the quality of work life. This type of surface-level change would be a form of single-loop learning. However, such behavioral change more than likely would not resolve the deeper problem that produced the infighting in the first place. To resolve this more tacit concern, double-loop learning, or a change in the underlying system of beliefs, would need to occur. Both the actions and values of the group would need to be affected. Peter Senge, writing in *The Fifth Discipline*, suggests five elements that contribute to building a learning organization:

1. *Personal mastery.* A discipline that connects individual learning, personal skills, and spiritual growth with organizational learning. It involves one's inherent capacity to continuously focus on what's most important, while ensuring that the view of reality remains clear and truthful (Senge, 1990, p. 141).

2. *Mental models.* A discipline that links the way in which we view the world—our assumptions about "how things work"—with innovation and learning. Our mental models may pose substantial barriers to new ideas, those that conflict with our current understanding of reality, or they may become a source of new knowledge and creative learning (Senge, 1990, pp. 174–178).

3. *Shared vision.* A discipline in which an image or idea becomes transformed into a powerful force that is shared throughout the organization or group. The organization that has a shared vision is "connected, bound together by a common aspiration" (Senge, 1990, p. 206).

4. *Team learning.* A discipline that reflects the capacity of a group of individuals to coalesce, to engage their respective energies into an integrated team. The team remains connected through its shared vision, thus ensuring that the individual learning that occurs becomes translated into a group—indeed, a shared—experience (Senge, 1990, pp. 234–235).

5. *Systems thinking.* A discipline that shows how human action—whether in business, government, or other pursuits—represents a systemic, interrelated set of events. Thus, we may understand and effect change by recognizing the interconnectedness of our actions and their consequences in the broader system. Those who are able to achieve this type of systems thinking—what Senge calls "the fifth discipline"—have embodied the concept of individual and organizational learning (Senge, 1990, p. 7).

Networking

Visit MIT's Society for Organizational Learning at www.solonline.org. This site discusses research about organizational culture and change.

The convergence of the concepts of organizational culture and organizational learning provides an important foundation for understanding organizational change. Yet these concepts also relate to an older concept, one that remains crucial in contemporary society: *strategic management.* Peters and Waterman's *In Search of Excellence* (1982) introduced this concept in its analysis of implicit philosophies that guide most successful American companies. Much of the work remains just as valuable today as it was nearly three decades ago.

In particular, Peters and Waterman state the importance of establishing a core set of values that comprise the organization's mission and shape decisions throughout the structure. They suggest the importance of constant interchange between managers and workers, the organization and its clients. Though terms like "MBWA," or Management by Walking Around, may seem dated, the supporting principle of leadership maintaining close contact with members of the organization has even grown in significance.

These criteria for excellence can be translated into a public-sector context without great difficulty. For example, the International City Management Association and the Center for Excellence in Local Government adapted Peters and Waterman's criteria to define "excellence in local government."

1. *Action orientation.* Excellent local governments identify problems and deal with them quickly, fighting through structural, political, legal, and environmental constraints that make action more difficult than in the private sector.

2. *Closeness to citizens.* This criterion includes establishing and maintaining a variety of close links with citizens who are served by the local government, including those who are regulated against their will. Excellent local governments listen and are sensitive and responsive to public input.

3. *Autonomy and entrepreneurship.* Excellent local governments have developed climates conducive to conceiving ideas and doing new things to solve problems. They have track records for implementing creative solutions, even in the face of declining resources.

4. *Employee orientation.* This criterion demands more than lip service to employees and their needs. Excellent local governments insist on intensive, pervasive treatment of employees as human beings and adults.

5. *Values.* Excellent local governments have a defined set of values. Their overall focus is on being the best by providing superior service to the public. Their values are communicated clearly and demonstrated regularly to employees. Those values also provide the source of enthusiasm and pride among employees.

6. *Mission, goals, and competence.* Mission is the underlying premise of the organization. Excellent local governments have evaluated their missions based on changing resource levels and citizen demands, and they have used mission statements as the foundation for establishing community and organizational goals. Within their defined mission, excellent local governments provide consistent, uniform service levels.

7. *Structure.* In excellent local governments, the potential negative effects of antiquated, bureaucratic structures have been minimized. These organizations have fewer management levels and fewer centralized support staffs. They provide firm central direction while giving maximum autonomy to employees.

8. *Political relationships.* Political relationships refer to more than how the elected governing body and management staff work together. In excellent local governments, managers and policy makers are tuned in to the political environment; have established positive, open, and respectful relationships with each other; and have established political stability (Barbour et al., 1984).

Even more recently, Jim Collins, an author well known in the field of business management, built a concept for reaching "great" levels of achievement in the public service.

His book *Good to Great: Why Some Companies Make the Leap…and Others Don't* (2001) and the subsequent *Good to Great and the Social Sector: A Monograph to Accompany Good to Great* (2005), make it clear that public organizations should not blindly follow business practices for a simple reason: public organizations' achievement cannot be measured though earned profit. While for the "great" private companies, it is perfectly legitimate to measure the input and output in monetary terms, for the "great" public organizations, money is the measure for the input, but delivering "superior performance" and "a distinctive impact over a long period of time" are legitimate measures for successful output (Collins, 2005, p. 5). **See the box "Take Action: Top 10 Tips to Rediscover Your Staff."**

Take Action   TOP 10 TIPS TO REDISCOVER YOUR STAFF

1. Dump contingency management practices. Read up on the subject and identify how contingency manifests itself in tangible ways in organizations; set about changing habits and processes.

2. Embrace complexity. Complexity management practices are the antithesis of contingency management. Complexity is a nonlinear management model. It is not just a theory. Learn what it means in practice and develop staff to work in new ways.

3. Make plans and stick to them. All the unpredictability and uncertainty around contingency management in practice is unsettling for staff. It gives the impression of a lack of direction, lack of conviction, and inconsistency. Learn to have plans that can absorb and accommodate challenges rather than plans that keep attuned to outside demands. Plan for the unexpected and expect the unpredictable.

4. Reassess your approach and attitudes toward organizational culture. Know that organizational culture can be influenced but not controlled by senior managers. Do not mistake quiet compliance for cultural change. It is a staff survival mechanism; fury may be bubbling beneath!

5. Find ways to involve all staff in culture renewal, evaluation, and development initiatives. Remember that your staff creates the culture, so getting them positive and excited leads to a positive and exciting culture.

6. Look carefully at your cultural messages and symbols, and ask whether you and your top team are really delivering on them. Would I, as an outsider coming to your place for the first time, see that you mean what you preach or is it just more empty rhetoric? Take the time to make your values mean something.

7. Think about how you can stop talking about empowering work practices and begin enshrining them so that people believe you mean it. A charter is one good idea.

(Continued)

(Continued)

8. Remember that delegation is not empowerment. Review your approach and make sure managers do not pass on work to others as a "development opportunity." Staff always sees this for what it really is, and it does only damage.

9. Invite staff to take the initiative. Real empowerment is about creating the space for people to empower themselves. Support and encourage this but do not dictate it.

10. Retain your awareness that the changes managerialism dictates might make the organization meaner and leaner but that the effects on people policies must be carefully managed.

SOURCE: Paul Davis, "Too Busy Managing to Lead? A View from 'Down Under,'" *Public Management* 89, no. 1 (January/February 2007): 28–32.

Collins (2005) offers five essential elements for building "great" public organizations:

1. *Defining "great"—calibrating success without business metrics* (p. 4). Public organizations should strive for excellence in delivering services. According to the author, "what matters is not finding the perfect indicator, but settling upon a *consistent and intelligent* method of assessing your output results, and then tracking your trajectory with rigor" (Collins, 2005, p. 8). His advice to public organizations is to actually be concentrated on great outputs.

2. *Level 5 leadership—getting things done within a diffuse power structure* (p. 9). A level 5 leader is the leader who can "build enduring greatness through a paradoxical blend of personal humility and professional will" (Collins, 2005, p. 12, "Level 5 Leadership/Level 5 Hierarchy"). True leaders, as the author implies, are those who empower people. These leaders are followed by the people when people have the freedom not to follow them (Collins, 2005, p. 13).

3. *First who—getting the right people on the bus, within social-sector constraints* (p. 13). True leaders also know who should be "on the bus" and how to attract the right people to "get on the bus"; that is, they know how to overcome social-sector constraints and recruit motivated and competent "great" (not good or average) people.

4. *The hedgehog concept—rethinking the economic engine without a profit motive* (p. 17). In order to be effective with all the constraints in the social sector, social-sector managers should concentrate on three elements: "passion," "best at," and "resource engine" (Collins, 2005, p. 19). "Passion" refers to the organization's values and core mission; "best at" refers to the activities that are unique to the organization; "resource engine" refers to the appropriate combination of time, money, and brand.

5. *Turning the flywheel—building momentum by building the brand* (p. 23). Organizations in the social sector should build brand, by which they are recognized in a positive manner. The brand helps these organizations achieve superior performance. But organizations will be able to build the brand only if they recognize that they should make a change within the organization. In other words, while the sector itself may face huge challenges, social-sector organizations should recognize what is their (own) advantage and work on building and advancing their "pocket of greatness" (Collins, 2005, pp. 28–31).

Guidelines for Public Management

What lessons can you draw from these various perspectives that might guide your actions as a public manager? One way to begin to answer that question is to summarize some of the thinking about management in terms of guidelines for practice. The recent literature on strategic management seems to suggest the following guidelines:

1. *Maintain clarity about organizational priorities, goals, and objectives.* Although some ambiguity is often unavoidable in stating organization priorities, goals, and objectives, most organizations are far too confused on these issues. This confusion leaves people throughout the organization, including people who are required to make frequent decisions about organizational direction, without an appropriate basis for making such decisions. The direction of the organization should be stated as clearly as possible and widely communicated to all members.

2. *Make decisions today in terms of the most likely future circumstances.* Strategic management implies making all organizational decisions in terms of "futurity"—that is, how they will meet expected changes in the environment. It suggests taking every action in light of anticipated conditions, thus putting the organization in the best position to take advantage of future opportunities.

3. *Be attentive to the context in which you operate, especially relationships with other actors in the governmental system.* There is a natural but unfortunate tendency toward "tunnel vision" in most organizations. Actions are viewed in immediate terms, without duly considering who will be affected by the action. Acknowledging the importance of the environment is essential to strategic thinking.

4. *Understand clearly the organization's capacities and limitations.* New programs and policies can be effectively implemented only if they fall within the existing capacity of the organization or provide sufficient opportunity to build capacity. There are dangers in both underutilization of resources and becoming overextended.

5. *Balance program goals with attention to organizational values and processes.* It is important to state programmatic objectives clearly; however, the organization's culture and the prevailing norms, beliefs, and values of its members are equally important. Organizational processes, such as leadership, communications, motivation, group dynamics, and so forth, need constant attention, because they are essential to goal accomplishment.

6. *Create diverse mechanisms, both temporary and permanent, for constantly renegotiating programs and processes.* Both programmatic concerns and organizational processes are constantly changing in ways that affect persons throughout the organization. Thus, clarity with respect to priorities, goals, and objectives must not lead to rigidity. Mechanisms must permit and, in fact, encourage the entire membership of the organization to contribute regularly to refining programs and processes.

7. *Build trust and commitment through open communications and genuine participation.* Guidelines by which we measure the degree of participation the organization encourages include members' access to information and to forums of decision making, their ability to open any issue without fear of retaliation, and their feeling that their ideas will at least be considered by major decision makers (Redford, 1969, p. 8).

Much of the work reviewed here applies equally to management in the public and private sectors. But it is interesting to note that some of the most recent general trends in management have been anticipated in public-sector management. Public organizations' dependence on pluralistic decision processes—that is, processes through which different people and groups are likely to be involved—makes the process of managing change in the public sector quite complicated. It also means that a high degree of ambiguity and uncertainty is likely to surround most efforts to implement or alter programs. Managers must be especially skillful in negotiating across organizational boundaries rather than expecting to control circumstances "from the top." In addition, public organizations must have a service orientation—specifically, an understanding of and an attempt to act in accord with the public interest. We noted that organizations seeking public purposes must operate openly, be cognizant of client interests, and understand the political context within which they operate.

Under these circumstances, it is not at all surprising that the values and perspectives that now seem so much a part of "modern management," such as those associated with strategic management or Total Quality Management, have always been central (if not dominant) in public administration theory. Thus, for example, Marshall Dimock's (1936, p. 120) comment that "successful administration is warm and vibrant. It is human" sounds very much like a quotation from Peter Senge or Jim Collins. One might thus argue that, in contrast to Woodrow Wilson's admonition that public agencies should operate like businesses, it seems that public organizations and the values and interests they represent today should be and are becoming models for organizations of all types.

However, in this age of reinvention and managerialist government, there are reasons to be concerned that business values have overshadowed the ethic of citizenship that accompanies our theory of democracy. Public administration sometimes seems to be more concerned with promoting the entrepreneurial spirit than fostering meaningful engagement and sustaining citizen participation in civil society. There is a danger of devoting ourselves to satisfying the customer while neglecting to ensure equity, justice, and equality for citizens.

We will note later, in discussing recent critiques of the reinvention movement, that citizens are more than mere customers of government; they are its owners. Placing this relationship in economic terms reduces the role (and responsibility) of the citizen in the governance process. This critique carries important implications for our notions of public management. Specifically, in the current framework, public administrators cannot afford to view citizens in instrumental terms, and thus believe that by achieving an efficient, market-oriented system of service delivery that citizen trust and participation will be maintained. Citizen engagement, in this context, may be limited to a source of legitimation for public decisions that have already been made in more rational forms (for different perspectives, see Bryson & Crosby, 1992; Chrislip & Larson, 1994; Thomas, 1995).

Such a limited concept of engagement not only weakens our systems of public management and administration—it removes decision-making processes from the public realm—but it also threatens to destroy the remaining level of citizen trust we as public servants enjoy. Citizens have expressed that their confidence is less contingent on managerial pursuits, such as efficiency and performance, and more on the values of responsiveness and equity. Yet, sometimes it is tempting to forget this important message and to continue to strive simply for greater productivity.

The question we encounter once again is "How can we balance efficiency and responsiveness in the operation of public programs?" The field of public administration has generally leaned toward the efficiency side of the equation. Now, however, there is growing evidence that emphasizing responsiveness is not only consistent with democratic principles, but, in the long run, may also be the most effective way of operating. Whereas a structural view of organizations tends to emphasize internal efficiency, it is apparent that greater attention to external relationships and the ability to negotiate across organizational boundaries will become more and more necessary in our increasingly complex society, as will an organizational environment that fosters creativity (Denhardt & Denhardt, 2011).

Developing a "democratic" approach to management has often been attractive to public administration theorists because it seems only proper that government institutions in a democracy should operate democratically. What we are finding more and more is that such an approach is not only appealing but also necessary for organizations of all types— not only those in the public sector—to survive.

Postmodern Narratives on Management

In recent years, the images of organizations just discussed have come under criticism from a variety of standpoints. Some challenge the notion of a single, unifying concept of management and organizations. Others bring into question the overly functionalistic nature of management theory. And still others attempt to counter the political context of traditional theory, particularly the use of power by elites to marginalize the powerless. We will now discuss these contrary perspectives on organizations under the heading of postmodernism, which was discussed in Chapter 7. But as we will see, even this term is problematic, because postmodernism defies our tendency for categorizing diverse viewpoints into a single, definitive theory.

Postmodernism

The philosophical roots of what we call postmodernism can be traced to the late 1960s and a school of French philosophy known as *poststructuralism*. Poststructuralists took issue with many of the core assumptions underlying modernist philosophy. For example, the poststructuralists opposed modernity's primacy of rationality, objectivity, and the application of scientific principles in the development of a universal explanation of the social world. They argued for more diverse "readings" of society—that is, for new ways of knowing, based on the view that any particular interpretation of society has as much validity as any other because all such views are based on an individual's or group's view of what is real.

In management theory, a key theme underlying the postmodernist critique centers on the multiple sources of knowledge that confront us in our organizational experience— what we may refer to as *fragmentation*. As Hatch explained, "Postmodernists challenge the modernist desire for unifying views with their belief that knowledge is fundamentally fragmented—that is, knowledge is produced in so many different bits and pieces that there can be no reasonable expectation that it will ever add up to an integrated and singular view" (Hatch, 1997, p. 44). Consequently, we are faced with this question: given the increasingly global, networked nature of public and nonprofit organizations, how can we cling to a belief in a central, complete theory of management?

A second important theme involves a postmodernist challenge to what is called the *progress myth*. This stems from modernity's premise that our scientific knowledge is the result of a cumulative process, with one theory building uniformly on previous theories toward a shared end of advancing the human condition. Rather than some altruistic enterprise, postmodernists argue that modernity proved to be a wholesale abuse of scientific knowledge by the powerful for the purpose of maintaining the status quo. Indeed, even the notion of a common human goal reveals the power-saturated, neocolonial character of modernism. So how can we presume to be in a position to determine what's in the best interest of societies around the world, much less to impose a particular form of knowledge to identify and evaluate policy alternatives? In other words, this new perspective casts doubts on anyone's claim to understand reality and casts doubt on anyone's claim to hold power over others.

To counter these tendencies, postmodern theorists employ a narrative device known as *discourse analysis*. It begins by viewing presentations of organizational inquiry—such as oral, textual, or visual narratives—as forms of discourse and then using what they call discourse analysis to deconstruct the narratives to reveal modernist assumptions underlying the content. Discourse analysis exposes (and challenges) any attempt on the part of the "author(s)" to provide some type of *grand narrative*, in the modernist tradition, of organizations or society. Another purpose, however, is more action-oriented and involves the use of discourse analysis to reverse the power-saturated state of language in the organizational context. It opens the door for more diverse "voices" in organizational narratives—that is, the inclusion of traditionally dispossessed participants in social experiences of management.

Issues of Gender and Power

Feminist scholars have used elements of discourse analysis, as well as the liberating experience of postmodernism generally, to launch a sustained critique against traditional organization and management theory. At the heart of their critique is the segmentation of power along gender lines in organizational hierarchies—what the feminist scholar Jane Flax refers to as a "sexual division of labor" in modern management.

In Chapter 6, we discussed the "glass ceiling" that limits the advancement of women in the workplace. However, Flax points out that the corollary to such structural barriers is that women tend to be employed in occupational areas that consist overwhelmingly of other women, jobs that are paid less and subject women workers to gender-stereotyped roles, like child care, schoolteachers, housecleaning, secretaries, and other forms of "women's work" (cited in Hatch, 1997, p. 293).

Mary Guy and Meredith Newman (2004), along with Sharon Mastracci (Guy, Newman, & Mastracci, 2008), have explored this issue by asking what it is about women's jobs that causes them to pay less. They employ the term *emotional labor* to indicate that some tasks require "the emotive work thought natural for women, such as caring, negotiating, empathizing, smoothing troubled relationships, and working behind the scenes to enable cooperation" (p. 298). This work is largely invisible and not fully compensated, whether such positions are held by men or women. Public service relies heavily on such skills, yet pay and promotion systems fail to acknowledge and compensate this work.

This concern for the powerless provides perhaps the most compelling argument of feminist theories. From a foundation in neo-Marxian critical theory, feminist scholars draw into question the very legitimacy of our ways of organizing in the postindustrial era. To them, studies of organization and management theory have become little more than sources of intellectual justification for an abuse of power by elites whose only purpose is to maintain social, political, and economic order. Even postmodernism itself has come under attack from feminist critics, who see these theories as shifting the concern away from substantive issues of power and inequality in daily work life.

Moreover, contrary to what advocates depict as a democratization of economic and political space in the global marketplace, feminist critics argue globalization and the imposition of new forms of governance by industrialized nations have done nothing but take the Northern, Western drive for power and economic supremacy to new frontiers (Stivers, 2002). The result has been a further marginalization of women, especially in what the development community refers to as "third world" societies.

Summary and Action Implications

As we have seen, your behavior is guided by the images you carry around in your head: images that have to do with the role of public agencies in a democratic society, with the most effective and responsible way to run a complex public organization, and with the relationships you establish with other actors, both within and outside the governmental system. Over your career, you will develop and refine your images based on experience, careful reflection, and self-critique. You will also benefit from comparing your images (and approaches) to those that other people recommend.

Through the years, students and practitioners of public administration have spent considerable time reflecting on the nature of their work and sorting out the factors that make for successful public management. Each resulting theory represents an attempt to suggest where you should cast your attention. Because you can't attend to all things at once, a certain amount of selectivity goes into theory building. Each theory implies evaluating what is most important to be aware of and to do to manage successfully.

Early writers thought that issues of organizational structure were most important, so they spent considerable time detailing concerns for structure. Later theorists (some of them practitioners) felt that structural issues should be balanced, if not outweighed, by a concern for the behavior of individuals in the organization. Still others sought further refinements, moving from behavior to structure and back again. More recent approaches have emphasized the organization's culture or value structure, but others have challenged the very notion of our ways of organizing in contemporary society.

For the time being, however, we should note the special sensitivity that those in public organizations have always shown for value questions. We have seen time and again how the values of public service—the pursuit of the public interest—affect the work of those in public organizations. The concern of contemporary writers in business and related fields of service and human values is something that those in public administration have always had to contend with, especially as they have been challenged to find a form of management compatible with the requirements of a democratic society.

STUDY QUESTIONS

1. Discuss the approaches to public management espoused by early writers.

2. Explain Douglas MacGregor's Theory X and Theory Y management concepts.

3. Compare the management approaches of Herbert Simon and Chris Argyris.

4. Two management approaches combine the human element with the structural aspect of the organization. Discuss the differences between the systems approach and the political economy approach.

5. What shared assumptions, as outlined by Edgar H. Schein, seem consistent in organizational cultures? What features do Peters and Waterman contribute to the list?

6. What basic philosophies underlie recent work in organizational culture and strategic management?

CASES AND EXERCISES

1. In four small groups (or multiples of four), analyze your class as an organization, taking into account questions of power and authority, communications, motivation, group dynamics, and so on. One group should employ only a structural perspective, the second group should employ only a behavioral perspective, and the third group should employ only a systems perspective. The fourth group should employ whatever perspective (or combination of perspectives) that its members consider most modern and most complete. Have each group (or a representative of each type of group, depending on the numbers) report their conclusions to the entire class. Think of each perspective as allowing you to see certain things and preventing you from seeing others. What do you see from the structural perspective? What about the behavioral perspective? The systems perspective? The combination perspective is likely to seem most complete, but consider the possibility that this modern viewpoint overlooks a great deal, and that, though we think it is complete (as those using earlier perspectives considered them complete), there may be much left to understand about organizations, even small ones. What other questions might we encounter in the future?

2. As a class, study the interorganizational relationships of one small organization. The organization might be a unit at the university (either an academic or a staff unit); a unit in city, state, or federal government; or a local nonprofit organization. Pick an organization that is clearly identifiable and, if possible, that appears to have considerable autonomy. Based on interviews with its top administrators and top staff people, develop a chart showing the organization's relationships with others in its environment. (A model resembling a molecular structure might be appropriate.) Indicate the importance of each relationship, the degree to which that relationship is considered positive or negative, and the degree to which it is considered essential. Try to develop some sense for how much time administrators and staff members spend on external relations versus internal organizational work.

3. The following statement is a mission statement from the City of Oakland (California): "The City of Oakland is committed to the delivery of effective, courteous, and responsive services. Citizens and employees are treated with fairness, dignity, and respect. Civic and employee pride are accomplished through constant pursuit of excellence and a workforce that values and reflects the diversity of the Oakland community." First, this statement permeates the organization. For something that is well established, what elements would you wish to add to the statement? Second, think about the relationship between a city and its citizens. What statements of philosophy dealing with the relationship between city and citizens would be appropriate to add? Third, given the statement and your modifications, what specific steps would you recommend to the elected and appointed officials in the city for putting their commitments (and yours) into practice?

FOR ADDITIONAL READING

Ban, Carolyn. *How Do Public Managers Manage?* San Francisco: Jossey-Bass, 1995.

Baum, Howell S. *The Organization of Hope.* Albany: State University of New York Press, 1997.

Bennis, Warren, Jagdesh Parikh, and Ronnie Lessem. *Beyond Leadership.* Cambridge, MA: Basil Blackwell, 1994.

Block, Peter. *Stewardship.* San Francisco: Berrett Koehler Publishers, 1993.

Boje, David M., Robert P. Gephart, Jr., and Tojo Joseph Thatchenkery, eds. *Postmodern Management and Organization Theory.* Thousand Oaks, CA: Sage Publications, 1996.

Box, Richard C. *Critical Social Theory in Public Administration.* Armonk, NY: M.E. Sharpe, 2005.

Caiden, Gerald. *Administrative Reform Comes of Age.* Berlin: W. de Gruyter, 1991.

Carnavale, David G. *Trustworthy Government.* San Francisco: Jossey-Bass, 1995.

Catlaw, Thomas J. *Fabricating the People: Politics and Administration in the Biopolitical State.* Tuscaloosa: University of Alabama Press, 2007.

Cohen, Steven, and Ronald Brand. *Total Quality Management in Government.* San Francisco: Jossey-Bass, 1993.

Collins, Jim. *Good to Great: Why Some Companies Make the Leap…and Others Don't.* New York: HarperBusiness, 2001.

Collins, Jim. *Good to Great and the Social Sectors: A Monograph to Accompany Good to Great.* New York: HarperCollins, 2005.

Crosby, Barbara C., and John M. Bryson. *Leadership for the Common Good: Tackling Public Problems in a Shared-Power World.* 2nd ed. San Francisco: Jossey-Bass, 2005.

Davis, Charles R. *Organization Theories and Public Administration.* Westport, CT: Praeger, 1996.

Denhardt, Janet Vinzant, and Robert B. Denhardt. *The New Public Service: Serving, Not Steering.* 3rd ed. Armonk, NY: M.E. Sharpe, 2011.

Denhardt, Robert B. *The Pursuit of Significance.* Belmont, CA: Wadsworth, 1993.

Denhardt, Robert B. *Theories of Public Organization.* 6th ed. Boston: Wadsworth, Cengage Learning, 2011.

Diamond, Michael A. *The Unconscious Life of Organizations: Interpreting Organizational Identity.* Westport, CT: Quorum Books, 1993.

Dunn, Delmer. *Politics and Administration at the Top.* Pittsburgh: University of Pittsburgh Press, 1997.

Farmer, David John. *The Language of Public Administration: Bureaucracy, Modernity, and Postmodernity.* Tuscaloosa: University of Alabama Press, 1995.

Farmer, David John. *To Kill the King: Post-Traditional Governance and Bureaucracy.* Armonk, NY: M.E. Sharpe, 2005.

Fox, Charles, and Hugh Miller. *Postmodern Public Administration.* Thousand Oaks, CA: Sage Publications, 1995.

Fredrickson, H. George. *New Public Administration.* Tuscaloosa: University of Alabama Press, 1980.

Frost, Peter J., Arie Y. Lewin, and Richard L. Daft, eds. *Talking about Organization Science: Debates and Dialogue from Crossroads.* Thousand Oaks, CA: Sage Publications, 2000.

Guy, Mary E., Meredith A. Newman, and Sharon H. Mastracci. *Emotional Labor: Putting the Service in Public Service.* Armonk, NY: M.E. Sharpe, 2008.

Ingraham, Patricia W., Philip G. Joyce, and Amy Kneedler Donahue. *Government Performance: Why Management Matters.* Baltimore: Johns Hopkins University Press, 2003.

Kee, James Edwin, and Kathryn E. Newcomer. *Transforming Public and Nonprofit Organizations: Stewardship for Leading Change.* Vienna, VA: Management Concepts, 2008.

Kettl, Donald, et al. *Cutting Government.* Washington, DC: Brookings Institution Press, 1995.

Lee, Dalton M. *The Basis of Management in Public Organizations.* New York: R. Long, 1990.

Mastracci, Sharon H., Mary E. Guy, and Meredith A. Newman. *Emotional Labor and Crisis Response: Working on the Razor's Edge.* Armonk, NY: M.E. Sharpe, 2011.

McSwite, O. C. *Legitimacy in Public Administration: A Discourse Analysis* (Advances in Public Administration). Thousand Oaks, CA: Sage Publications, 1997.

Milakovich, Michael. *Improving Service Quality.* Delray Beach, FL: St. Lucie Press, 1995.

Morgan, Gareth. *Images of Organization.* 2nd ed. Thousand Oaks, CA: Sage Publications, 1997.

Peters, B. Guy. *The Future of Governing.* Lawrence: University Press of Kansas, 1996.

Peters, B. Guy, and Bert Rockman. *Agenda for Excellence 2.* Chatham, NJ: Chatham House, 1996.

Rainey, Hal G. *Understanding and Managing Public Organizations.* San Francisco: Jossey-Bass, 1997.

Schein, Edgar H. *Organizational Culture and Leadership.* San Francisco: Jossey-Bass, 1987.

Senge, Peter M. *The Fifth Discipline.* New York: Currency Doubleday Dell Publishing, 1990.

Senge, Peter M., et al. *The Fifth Discipline Fieldbook*. New York: Currency Doubleday Dell Publishing, 1994.

Stivers, Camilla. *Gender Images in Public Administration: Legitimacy and the Administrative State*. Newbury Park, CA: Sage Publications, 2002.

Terry, Larry D. *Leadership of Public Bureaucracies: The Administrator as Conservator*. 2nd ed. Armonk, NY: M.E. Sharpe, 2003.

Wamsley, Gary, et al. *Refounding Democratic Public Administration*. Thousand Oaks, CA: Sage Publications, 1996.

White, Jay D. *Taking Language Seriously: The Narrative Foundations of Public Administration Research*. Washington, DC: Georgetown University Press, 1999.

CHAPTER 9

LEADERSHIP AND MANAGEMENT SKILLS IN PUBLIC ORGANIZATIONS

All the ideas and approaches we have examined are helpful in understanding what is going on in public and nonprofit management. But putting those ideas into practice requires the ability to lead and work effectively with other people. Ideas about what leadership is, who can be a leader, and the roles that leaders serve have changed over time. While early perspectives on leadership focused on those holding top-level positions, more modern views recognize that leadership can and should be exercised at all levels of organizations. By carefully considering and constantly practicing good leadership, you can become more effective in whatever position you occupy in an organization.

Effective leadership and management involve decision making, communication, self-awareness, and the ability to motivate others and manage group dynamics. It should be recognized, however, that leadership and management in practice are often complex and fluid, demanding both a strong skill set and enormous flexibility. For instance, you may be called upon to clear up a situation and take appropriate action, often within a matter of seconds. As a leader, you will necessarily and appropriately analyze and understand the situation in terms of your own approach or theory. But you will also have to act and engage with others in decision making. In doing so, you need to have the ability to influence others and to exercise power constructively and responsibly.

Putting ideas into action requires that you have the ability not only to make decisions and delegate tasks but also to do so in a manner that energizes and engages others. Such decision making requires both confidence and self-awareness. Employees look to leaders not only for direction, but also for cues about how to feel about their work and their part in achieving organizational goals. Interestingly, however, successfully exercising these leadership skills depends on several essential "personal" skills that are part of one's social and psychological makeup. Some of these personal skills reflect your approach to the world, others have to do with your capacity for creativity or effective decision making, and still others have to do with how you deal with ambiguity or lack of clarity. For example, the manager suddenly promoted to the directorship of a mental health department will certainly have important (and immediate) decisions to make, perhaps involving creative solutions to organizational problems left by the departing director. The new manager will also have to operate, perhaps for months, in a highly ambiguous situation.

Leadership and Power

Many commentators have argued that improved leadership is essential for us to success-fully meet the challenges of the coming century. Public opinion data reveal widespread loss of faith in the leadership of business, government, labor, and other private and public institutions. But many argue that the problem relates not merely to formal positions of power but also to a pervasive failure of leadership throughout society. Because effective leadership sometimes involves the use of power, the capacity to understand power, espe-cially the capacity to recognize and use the resources one has available to influence others, is essential in modern organizations of all types. But *power* is a far narrower term than *leadership*. We will consider power as one aspect of the larger question of how one might develop greater skills in public leadership.

Early leadership studies attempted to identify and understand the attributes of "great men." Such approaches focused on the personal characteristics of existing or historical leaders, assuming that leaders were "born, not made." These so-called "trait studies" were reviewed in the 1940s by Ralph Stogdill (1948), who found that although leaders do appear to possess traits that make them different from other people, there was a lack of agreement about exactly what those traits were. For example, some of the studies that Stogdill reviewed found that leaders were more intelligent and active, while others found that leaders were taller and more dependable. Overall, Stogdill (1974) concluded that leaders encouraged cooperative behavior, were sensitive to others, exercised initiative, and had self-confidence. But having those traits did not necessarily mean that you would be an effective leader.

Although the trait approach to leadership offered some insights, it became evident over time that it left a number of important questions unanswered. For example, beyond per-sonal characteristics, what did leaders actually do? Why was it that the same leaders might be effective in one situation but not another? These questions led researchers to focus on the behavior of leaders and the exercise of leadership in particular contexts. One of the more important studies of leadership behavior was initiated at Ohio State University in the 1940s. Leadership was conceptualized as based on two types of behaviors. The first type was called "consideration," which was behavior focused on relationships and con-cern for others. The second type was called "initiation of structure," which was behavior aimed at task definition and completion (Bass, 1990). A similar study at the University of Michigan referred to these same sets of behaviors as "employee orientation" and "job or production orientation." Based on these dimensions, Blake and Mouton (1964) came up with a Managerial Grid that plotted behaviors associated with production and people on a scale of 1 to 9. The ideal in their model was to be a "9.9" manager—that is, a manager with a high concern for both people and production.

Other researchers began to focus on the context of leadership, trying to match different types of organizational situations with the appropriate mix of leadership behaviors. One such "situational" leadership model was developed by Hersey and Blanchard (1988). In this model, the key to assessing a situation was the readiness and ability of the follower to accomplish a particular task. For example, a person lacking in ability needs the leader to use high-task behavior to provide instruction and guidance. Then, once that person begins to show a willingness to try, the leader should be encouraging, using high-relationship behavior. On the other hand, a person who is ready and willing to accomplish a task needs neither high-task or high-relationship behavior—in this case, the leader should just get out of the way!

Networking

For different perspectives on leadership, visit the James MacGregor Burns Academy of Leadership at http://www.academyofleadership.org/, the Research Center for Leadership in Action at http://wagner.nyu.edu/leadership/, the Center for Integrative Leadership at http://www.leadership.umn.edu/, or the Centre for Advanced Studies in Leadership at www.casl.se.

More contemporary perspectives on leadership embrace the idea that leadership is not just the responsibility of those in the executive suite, but can and should be exercised throughout an organization. John Gardner, the former cabinet secretary and founder of Common Cause, stated, "In this country leadership is dispersed among all the segments of society and down through all levels, and the system simply won't work as it should unless large numbers of people throughout society are prepared to take leaderlike action to make things work at their level" (Gardner, 1987, p. ix). In this view, leadership is a pervasive phenomenon occurring in families, work groups, and businesses and at all levels of government, society, and culture. Leadership, then, should be seen not merely as a position someone holds, but rather as something that happens in a group or organization, something that comes and goes, something that ebbs and flows as the group or organization does its work.

As we have seen, modern society can be described as (1) highly turbulent, subject to sudden and dramatic shifts; (2) highly interdependent, requiring cooperation across many sectors; and (3) greatly in need of creative and integrative solutions to problems. Under such circumstances, ambiguity is increasingly a hallmark of decision making, and the involvement (rather than the control) of many individuals in group decisions will be necessary. "Leadership...will become an increasingly intricate process of multilateral brokerage, including constituencies both within and without the organization. More and more decisions will be public decisions; that is, the people they affect will insist on being heard" (Bennis, 1983, p. 16). Leadership for the future cannot be equated merely with the exercise of control by those in formal positions of power.

So what do we know about leadership, especially shared or public leadership? What do we know about leadership in the increasingly common situations where no one is really "in charge"—student organizations, churches, political groups, and so on? Often, much of their work is done through committees or other even less formal groups. And those committees seem to waste a lot of time and energy, partly because of lack of leadership. Even though one person may be designated the "leader," rarely does he or she exercise much control. Usually, things drift for a while—maybe a long while—until someone finally puts forth a suggestion that people pick up on and get excited about. At that point, we can say that someone has exercised leadership.

Somewhat more formally, then, we can define leadership as "the character of the relationship between the individual and a group or organization that stimulates or releases some latent energy within the group so that those involved more clearly understand their own needs, desires, interests, and potentialities and begin to work toward their fulfillment" (Denhardt & Prelgovisk, 1992, pp. 33–44). Where leadership is present, something occurs in the dynamics of the group or organization that leads to change. What is central to leadership is the capacity of the leader—whether or not he or she is called a leader—to "energize" the group.

What Would You Do?

The state government division that you head is going through several significant changes in a very short period of time. You are moving to a new location and at the same time embarking on some major new programs. All of this is occurring in a year in which your staff has been substantially reduced by retirements and transfers and you are in the midst of hiring replacement personnel. It promises to be a really difficult year, filled with change and uncertainty. You want to make things go as smoothly as possible for your staff. What would you do?

The leader merely taps and reshapes the "consciousness" of the group. Acts of leadership express a new direction, but one that is determined by the emerging interests of all members of a group. We can say that someone exercises public leadership when he or she (1) helps the group or organization understand its needs and potential; (2) integrates and articulates the group's vision; and (3) acts as a trigger or stimulus for group action. The essence of leadership, therefore, is its energizing effect. But often the people we formally refer to as leaders don't really lead; at best, they manage things successfully by keeping the group running more or less smoothly.

To energize the group, for example, the leader must know how to sense its underlying desires, sometimes even before those desires are clear to the group members themselves. The leader must also be able to act in ambiguous situations and to take risks; leadership involves change, and change is often difficult for both group and leader. Developing the personal strength to face change is important. Leadership has often been viewed in terms of the exercise of power by one person or group over another— getting people to do what one wants them to do by manipulating power and influence. Leadership in the future will be more and more independent of power, and the most critical leadership skills will be the personal (rather than interpersonal) skills associated with correctly empathizing with and "reading" a group, acting with a sense of direction in the presence of ambiguity, and having the courage to take risks when change is warranted.

Sally Helgesen (1996) calls this new approach "grassroots leadership." She argues that today's organizations differ dramatically from those created in past generations. Power becomes shared throughout the group and, in turn, leaders "are to be found not only among those at the top, the 'lead horses,' but also among those who constitute what in the industrial era we called the rank and file" (p. 21). Accordingly, each individual plays a key role in shaping the organization; each helps the group deal with issues of organizational change.

In fact, although power may be an important resource to the leader, one need not exercise traditional power to bring about change (see the box "Exploring Concepts: Bases of Social Power"). Efforts to control a group are often ultimately destructive of leadership. On the other hand, when the direction of the group or organization is selected through a developmental process that gives priority to group members' needs and desires, leadership is much more likely to be enduring. Leadership, in this context, relates more to sharing power among the group rather than using power for the purpose of control. So for the new knowledge-based organizations of today to be successful, greater autonomy and decision-making capacity should be distributed to the front line, with those closest to the situation serving as the leaders of change.

Exploring Concepts

BASES OF SOCIAL POWER

Power is really much more complex than we often think. For example, the power we exercise is based on a number of different factors that operate in social situations. A classic research article describes the following "bases of social power":

1. *Reward power.* The ability to meet the needs of another or control the other by rewarding the desired behavior. Pay, promotions, or bonuses may be ways that organizations exert reward power over employees.
2. *Punishment power.* Coercive power, or the ability to deliver a painful or punishing outcome to others, and hence control them by their desire to escape the punishment. Firing, ridiculing, or disciplining an individual are common techniques of punishment.
3. *Expert power.* Power based on the ability to understand, use, and deliver information that others need. Engineers or scientists may exert great influence in an organization based on their knowledge of scientific techniques for manufacturing a product, and so forth.
4. *Legitimate power.* Control or influence exerted by virtue of one's holding a particular position in the organizational structure. The "power" is vested in the rights and responsibilities of the position, not the person. Thus, a company president or chairman of the board has power by virtue of the rights and responsibility given to whoever holds the office. Compliance with legitimate power occurs because other individuals in the organization respect the organizational structure and the rights and responsibilities that accompany particular positions.
5. *Referent power.* Charisma, or the ability to motivate others to comply with one's wishes because of one's personal attractiveness. Control based on referent power depends on the power-holder's ability to have others like and be attracted to him or her and to follow his or her leadership because of this attraction.

SOURCE: Adapted from John R. P. French, Jr., and Bertram Raven, "The Bases of Social Power," in *Dorwin Cartwright and Alvin F. Zander, eds., *Group Dynamics*, 2nd ed., New York: HarperCollins Publishers, 1962. © 1962 by Dorwin Cartwright and Alvin F. Zander. Reprinted by permission.

Perhaps most importantly, leadership is not just about doing things right, but also about doing the right things (Bennis & Nanus, 1985). Particularly in the public sector, the goals sought by leaders inevitably involve important public values. Public leaders, at all levels, must play a "transformational" role in helping people to articulate and act on shared ideals and values within the context of democratic governance. Transformational leaders understand and support the needs of followers, work with them to define and seek higher-level needs, and engage followers as whole people. "The result of transformational leadership is a relationship of mutual stimulation and elevation that converts followers into leaders and may convert leaders into moral agents" (Burns, 1978, p. 4). In fact, leadership in the public sector involves attention not only to the needs and values of those within the organization, but also to the values and preferences of citizens.

In *The Leadership Challenge*, James Kouzes and Barry Posner (2007) assert that *credibility* is the foundation of leadership. Constituents must trust that their leader "will do as they say they will do." They expect their leader to be honest, forward-looking, competent, and inspiring. The five practices of credible leaders are to (1) model the way, (2) inspire a shared vision, (3) challenge the process, (4) enable others to act, and (5) encourage the heart.

First, leaders "model the way" (Kouzes & Posner, 2007, chs. 3–4). Successful leaders understand and are able to articulate their personal values and find their unique voice; identify the shared values among their constituents; reinforce shared values through meaningful verbal and nonverbal communication, such as artifacts, symbols, metaphors, and storytelling; and act consistently with those personal and shared values. Values serve as the anchor, motivation, and compass by which individuals authentically lead their own life and guide others.

From this source of authenticity, leaders "inspire a shared vision" (Kouzes & Posner, 2007, chs. 5–6). A successful leader imagines the possibilities, rather than the probabilities, of "*an ideal and unique image of the future for the common good*" (Kouzes & Posner, 2007, p. 105). This vision is value-oriented and introduces meaning and purpose into our lives. Leaders articulate their initial vision; educate their constituents to their vision through meaningful verbal and nonverbal communication; and engage the constituents in continuous dialogue to collectively discover, clarify, and commit to the common goals of the vision.

Inspiring a vision naturally requires that leaders "challenge the process," that is, request that constituents change from the status quo (Kouzes & Posner, 2007, chs. 7–8). In *Leadership on the Line*, Ronald Heifetz and Marty Linsky (2002) argue that leadership is fundamentally concerned with adaptive challenges. As opposed to *technical challenges,* which require a change in the knowledge, skill, procedure, or structure of a given situation, *adaptive challenges* exist when social conflict or crisis demands that the current beliefs, attitudes, and behaviors of people must change in order to realize a more just and equitable collective future.

Beliefs, attitudes, and behaviors inform the identity and competence of a person. When leaders move beyond their position of authority and request that people risk their identity to adaptively work toward an uncertain future, they will naturally face resistance from those people who feel discomforted by and resistant to change. Leaders and their vision constantly face the danger of being marginalized, diverted, attacked, or seduced by people who resist change. Thus, the challenge of leadership is to orchestrate conflict in a way that ennobles people and engages them in adaptive work at a rate that they can handle (Heifetz & Linsky, 2002; Helgesen, 2005). Leaders learn to build momentum on small wins.

According to Heifetz and Linsky (2002), in order to manage conflict and change, leaders must continuously maintain a holistic and realistic understanding of the context of change. To appropriately evaluate and successfully orchestrate the situation, the leader must iteratively alternate between the objective vantage point of standing on "the balcony" and the subjective vantage point of acting on the stage. The balcony allows the leader to view and assess the entire stage in order to (a) distinguish the adaptive from the technical challenges; (b) attentively listen to and interpret the underpinnings of the words and behaviors of various actors to gain an understanding and appreciation of their perceived risks, fears, and conflicts; and (c) assess the reaction of the authority figure(s), such as the director, for clues that indicate the cast's level of tolerance for change (Heifetz & Linsky, 2002, ch. 3).

With a holistic and realistic understanding of the situation, a leader returns to the stage to partake in the production and to "enable others to act" (Kouzes & Posner, 2007, chs. 9–10). That is, a leader must empower constituents to mobilize and engage in adaptive work. Empowerment acknowledges that power is expandable and reinforcing and that it originates from sources such as talents, knowledge, experience, ideas, personal relationships, and personal authority (Helgesen, 2005; Kouzes & Posner, 2007). Leaders empower their constituents when they provide them with the competence and confidence to assume the control and responsibility needed to collaboratively work toward a shared vision. Leaders "become more powerful when [they] give [their] own power away" (Kouzes & Posner, 2007, p. 251).

Finally, according to Kouzes and Posner, leaders "encourage the heart"—that is, they appeal to the passions of their followers and their emotional commitments so that there are not only rational reasons for following, but followers have a deeper although more abstract commitment to the leader's path. Leaders persuade others not only by appeals to the "head," but also by appeals to the "heart."

A new approach to understanding leadership is to consider leadership as an art. This view opens the possibility that both music and leadership shape and are shaped by similar patterns of human experience and human energy, that the best leaders display a certain "musicality" that distinguishes them from others, and that actual artistic expressions, skillfully facilitated, can be employed to tap and evoke significant aspects of the leadership experience and help to unveil its mysteries.

What do transformational leaders do that causes others to follow? Denhardt and Denhardt (2006) argue that the best leaders *connect with us emotionally in a way that energizes us and moves us to act*. Transformational leadership engages others in a very special way, touching elements of desire, commitment, and possibility that are deeply seated in the inner lives of potential followers. Leaders facilitate a reshaping of human energy, restructuring the narratives of human experience and bringing alive a new progression of possibilities, even in spite of ambiguity, complexity, and uncertainty.

Interestingly, this is similar to the role of music in our lives. Music connects with us emotionally, communicating a certain energy that resonates with one or another emotional state.

It touches us physically, emotionally, even spiritually and primes us for what might be called a *feeling-based exploration* of our personal condition. In this way, music relaxes us, assures us, consoles us, inspires us, excites us, or calms us as its rhythms and harmonies interact with our own. In a very real way, we are *moved* from wherever we might have been to a new condition, noticeably more in tune with something we value, and definitely a couple of notches removed from any of our default states. The music's progressions and transitions—its changes in harmony, melody, and rhythm—become progressions and transitions in our own feeling states, and, indeed, over time we are primed for analogous progressions in other aspects of our lives, more or less at ease with complexity, dissonance, ambiguity, dramatic emotion, and more.

It's easy to think of music as a metaphor for leadership. For example, many have illustrated leadership by referring to the role of an orchestra conductor or the leader of a jazz ensemble. On this point, Denhardt (1993) argues that leaders are rarely able to write and conduct a "symphony" that others play. More often they are called on to be fully integrated into the performance themselves, to play along with others, like the leader of a jazz ensemble improvising a tune. "By establishing the theme, the leader of the ensemble…can chart the basic pattern and direction in which the performance will move. By setting the tone and the tempo, the leader gives focus to the spirit and energy of the group. By modeling effective and responsible performance in their own solos, leaders can energize and articulate the performance of others. But it is the performance of others that is critical" (pp. 180–181).

More importantly, leaders confront many of the same issues faced by musicians and do so in ways that go beyond metaphorical parallels. For example, leaders, like musicians, are concerned with rhythm and timing, and leaders can learn a great deal about rhythm and timing from musicians. We understand that groups and organizations have rhythmic patterns that organize the experiences of those in the group. We understand the different cycles of group life and the varying pace at which different groups work. Many have experienced what happens when a group accustomed to a particular rhythm in its work gets a new "boss," someone with a completely different rhythm, typically resulting in chaos and frustration. And there is the matter of improvisation: leaders, like musicians, often improvise (though they rarely think of their work in this way), and they can certainly learn the basics of improvisation from musicians (see Denhardt & Denhardt, 2006). In all these ways leadership might be considered an art rather than a science (Cimino & Denhardt, forthcoming).

Communication

All the good ideas in the world are worth very little if they cannot be shared with others. Communication is the basis for setting goals, engaging others, and ensuring cooperation. Hales (1986) found that between two-thirds and four-fifths of a manager's day is spent giving or receiving information, and that most of this giving and receiving takes place in face-to-face interactions. In fact, the ability to communicate well is necessary for any adult to function successfully in virtually any role in American society. Early research showed that, on the average, adult Americans spent 70 percent of the waking day in some form of communication activity (Rankin, 1929): 9 percent of the time was spent writing, 16 percent reading, 30 percent speaking, and 45 percent listening. In the following sections we will discuss the communication modes of listening, speaking, and writing. (We will not address reading, except to note that the special skill known as "speed reading" is probably one a manager might find useful.)

Listening

We spend more time in listening than in any other form of communication. Recent research focusing exclusively on managers reveals that managers spend a greater-than-average portion of their time listening—about 63 percent of a typical day. But doing a lot of listening does not mean that managers listen well. Listening is not the same as hearing, and although hearing cannot be altered without medical or technical intervention, one can substantially improve the quality of one's listening with proper motivation and training. Let us first review some basics of effective listening (see the box "Take Action: Principles of Effective Listening").

Take Action   PRINCIPLES OF EFFECTIVE LISTENING

1. Have a reason or purpose.
2. Suspend judgment initially.
3. Resist distractions.
4. Wait before responding.
5. Rephrase what you listen to in your own words.
6. Seek the important themes.
7. Use the thinking-speaking differential to reflect and find meaning.

Have a Reason or Purpose   This is the most important principle of those we will discuss. Having a purpose or a reason to listen provides the motivation to listen, and, generally speaking, you will do things you are motivated to do better than if you are not motivated. Listening is no exception. One must be motivated to listen well; it does not just happen. Without motivation, you will not use the other six principles, or you will not use them as well as you could.

But, you ask, what if I don't have a reason to listen? In such cases, it is a good idea to actively search for a reason to listen to what is being said. Ask yourself, "How can this information help me do my job better?" or "How can I use this information in some way, on the job or elsewhere?" Finding a reason to listen will provide the motivation to use all the other principles and techniques.

Suspend Judgment Initially   The key word in this phrase is "initially." You will obviously need to evaluate the material you listen to, but you should wait until you hear the entire message before you begin the evaluation. This can be difficult. In an election year, for example, if we know a particular candidate's party, we are likely to evaluate what the candidate is going to say before he or she even begins speaking. It is not coincidental that television and radio advertising for many candidates does not prominently identify the candidate's party. The advertisers want to increase the chances of having the message heard rather than losing half the audience immediately by identifying the speaker as a Democrat or a Republican. To make a judgment before listening carefully to what someone is saying is the opposite of the "suspension" principle.

Resist Distractions   Many things can distract us when we are trying to listen. The "distraction" principle tells us to fight back, to actively resist whatever may be distracting us. Among the many things that distract us, various sounds are usually the most powerful. The sound may be a nonverbal noise, such as the siren from a passing fire engine or ambulance; the voices of several people speaking at once; or something about the way the speaker talks. Regardless of what type of sound is creating the distraction, the remedy is to resist, to try harder. In this case, "trying harder" means that you should increase your concentration. If you are in a face-to-face situation with a speaker, make sure you maintain constant eye contact. You can also lean a little bit in the direction of the speaker. By increasing your level of concentration, you can resist distractions you would have thought impossible to overcome. And that is the problem with distractions—they become an excuse for not even trying to listen because "it's impossible to hear what she's saying."

A common classroom demonstration in listening skills illustrates the "distraction" principle (as well as others). Two volunteers are positioned in front of the class, about fifteen feet away from each other. Each reads aloud a brief paragraph (that only takes thirty to forty seconds to read). Each student in the class is assigned to listen to one or the other of the volunteers, but not to both. The students are instructed not to take notes while the paragraphs are being read, but at the end of the reading they are to write down something about each of the major points in the paragraph they listened to. The trick is that the volunteers not only read different paragraphs, but they read them simultaneously! After the first round of the exercise usually only a small number, and sometimes none, of the students in the class are able to write down something about every major point their speaker read.

The instructor then reviews the eye contact and leaning points, picks two new volunteers, gives them two new paragraphs, and repeats the exercise. The second time around it is not unusual to find that 20 percent to 25 percent of the class has written down something about each major point. This exercise demonstrates that there is variability in the quality of listening, both between and within individuals. It also shows that it is possible to resist even a major distraction, that our ability to resist distractions is much higher than we realize, and that we can overcome a great deal to improve the quality of our listening.

Some distractions are less obvious and are perceived only semiconsciously. One such distraction for many Americans is listening to English spoken with a foreign accent or with a different regional accent. In a personal conversation, Professor Allen Bluedorn told of learning this in a listening course that he took while he was in the U.S. Army. Bluedorn wondered if he had been using people's accents as an excuse not to listen to them. (He was stationed at Fort Bliss in El Paso, Texas, and frequently heard English spoken with a Spanish accent.) He tested his theory by concentrating harder the next time he conversed with someone with a Spanish accent. To his surprise, he found that he clearly understood everything the person said. He concluded that he had indeed been succumbing to the distraction of the accent, and it had become an excuse not to listen well. This lesson is important in today's increasingly multicultural organizations, where English is often spoken with a wide variety of accents. But the larger and more important lesson is that even substantial distractions can be overcome.

Wait before Responding The "response" principle suggests that one relax and wait for natural opportunities to speak instead of jumping into the conversation immediately. When we are burning to contribute to a discussion, we may get so excited about what we want to say (as soon as we get the chance) that we don't listen to the person who is speaking. Instead, we can wait for a natural opportunity to contribute and try to flow with the conversation as an event rather than interrupting.

Rephrase What You Listen To in Your Own Words The "rephrasing" principle suggests an incredibly simple, yet powerful, way to check one's understanding. The idea is merely to take something you hear (an opinion, instructions, and so on) and put it into your own words. You then repeat it to the person who gave you the information and ask if that is what was meant. As easy as it seems, this is an excellent way to check understanding and avoid mistakes. When you give instructions, you can ask the person who is receiving them to do the same thing. You can say, for example, "I'm not sure I explained that very well. Please tell me what you got out of that."

Seek the Important Themes The "thematic" principle indicates that the main ideas are more important than facts—so important that they are the general keys to understanding and retaining what is said. Understanding the main ideas provides a framework for organizing the facts, which makes the facts themselves easier to remember.

The man usually credited with starting the listening movement over thirty years ago, Ralph Nichols, demonstrated this point in his research (Nichols & Stevens, 1957). He discovered that A and B students reported different listening habits than C and D students.

In surveys of hundreds of students, he discovered that the A and B students gave a much different response to the question "What do you listen for first when you attend a lecture?" than did the C and D students. The A and B students predominantly gave a response like "I listen for the main ideas first," whereas C and D students said, "I listen for the facts." (This finding probably does not entirely explain the differences in these students' GPAs, but it is undoubtedly part of it.)

Use the Thinking-Speaking Differential to Reflect and Find Meaning   The "meaning" principle reflects the fact that people think faster than they speak. Although it varies by region, people in the United States speak at a rate of about 150 words per minute, but in terms of language, they think at a rate of about 500 words per minute. Thus, we normally think more than three times faster than we speak. This differential creates an opportunity to listen more effectively, but the opportunity can also be a temptation to do things that interfere with our listening. The extra time can also be used for things that distract from the listening process—concentration lapses, daydreaming, thinking about something other than what the speaker is saying, and so forth. All of these can interfere with good listening, so extra time can be a two-edged sword—both opportunity and temptation.

Listening is both the most widely used and most widely misused communication skill. It is also the skill least often taught in the American education system at all levels (Steil, Barker, & Watson, 1983).

Speaking

Most of the speaking that managers do is informal, in one-on-one or small-group communications in their offices, on the phone, and in meetings. To demonstrate how we can improve our speaking, we will focus on giving instructions, because a significant amount of manager-initiated communication consists of giving instructions to others. The managerial activity of delegation, in fact, would be virtually impossible without being able to properly give instructions. The key to doing so successfully is the ability to put yourself in the position of the person who is getting the instructions. Ideally, you want to give exactly the right amount of information—neither too much nor too little. (If one must depart from the ideal, however, it is usually better to give too much rather than too little.) The following two questions can help you put yourself in the position of the individual to whom you are giving the instructions:

1. What does the person *need* to know to carry out the instructions?
2. What does the person *want* to know to carry out the instructions?

The ability to decide what information is necessary is, incidentally, a justification for promoting from within—making managers out of those who have done the jobs they will be managing. People who have done the job should be able to determine more accurately what their subordinates need to know when they receive instructions. Unfortunately, not everyone who is promoted to the management level takes full advantage of this knowledge.

To demonstrate how difficult it is to identify what information to transmit, we'll look at another classroom exercise on how you can put yourself in the position of the person who will be receiving the instructions. Students form pairs, and one member of each pair is given a diagram. The students are seated back to back, and the one with the diagram gives the other one instructions for drawing the diagram on a piece of paper. Only the instruction giver is allowed to speak and may not look at the partner's drawing. After the drawing is completed, it is evaluated with a set of scoring rules. The partners then switch roles, a new diagram is used, and verbal instructions are again given to draw the diagram.

It has been found that the scores in the second round are usually higher than those in the first, even if the second diagram is more complex. Why? The answer seems to be that the instruction giver in the second round has been in the position of receiving instructions already and thus has a better idea of what information is really helpful. Furthermore, the instruction givers during the second round know the scoring rules and can focus on what elements of the diagrams will be scored when the copies are evaluated. Most important, however, the instruction giver who understands what information someone needs is better able to provide that information.

Writing

Writing is a less common form of managerial communication than speaking and listening, but it is important nevertheless. Most managerial writing is brief, often one or two pages. The memo is the most common type of written communication for many managers. Sussman and Deep (1984) offer six rules for effective managerial writing that they call the "Six Cs."

1. *Clarity.* To be clear, one must put oneself in the reader's position—much as the instruction giver must put himself or herself in the receiver's position. Write in the active voice (such as, Dave painted the house) rather than the passive (such as, The house was painted by Dave); avoid jargon; and try to use the simple format of introduction, body, and conclusion.
2. *Courtesy.* Courtesy involves knowing your readers, adapting to their moods, and writing at their level, providing neither too much nor too little information. Again, there are clear parallels with instruction giving.
3. *Conciseness.* This is the rule of brevity: be short and to the point. Sometimes you may want to repeat something for emphasis, but the general rule is, the shorter the better. Think of it this way: which are you more likely to read—a fifty-word memo or a ten-page report? You are likely to read the fifty-word memo on the spot; the ten-page report goes into the "when I get a chance" pile.
4. *Confidence.* Always write with confidence. Confidence is really a matter of the writer's judgment, based on one's knowledge of one's readers. Judgment is especially important in avoiding two extremes: overbearing (too confident) and wishy-washy (not confident enough).
5. *Correctness.* You must be correct in following the technical rules of writing: grammar, composition, spelling, and punctuation. Inaccurate spelling is especially conspicuous.
6. *Conversational tone.* To achieve a conversational tone, write the way you talk, and try to imagine one specific person to whom you are writing. Thinking of a specific individual rather than an abstract category makes it much easier to write. (It is much easier to write to John Jones than to "all economics professors.") Occasionally, conversational writing calls for violating some formal rules of grammar, but this breach can make things smoother, more understandable, and easier to follow.

Communication will affect nearly every aspect of your work as a public manager. Your ability to persuade others of your position, your clarity in sharing ideas, and your ability to deal effectively with difficult people will shape your image as an administrator (see the box "Take Action: Secret Weapons for Organizational Communication"). Fortunately, you can improve your ability to listen, to speak, and to write. Practicing your communication skills whenever possible will pay dividends in every career.

Take Action   ## SECRET WEAPONS FOR ORGANIZATIONAL COMMUNICATION

Here are several methods for dealing with difficult situations in the work setting:

1. Remember that people do things for their own reasons, not yours. Someone's anger may mean he or she actually sees the situation from a completely different perspective, so try to understand that view.
2. When under attack, use a calm, even tone of voice and low-key body language. The content of what you say can be the same—just modify your delivery; in face-to-face communication, words carry 7 percent of your message, tone of voice 38 percent, and body language 55 percent.
3. Use conversational fantasy to anticipate a really sticky situation by saying exactly what you want to say. Then tone it down to what you know you should say.
4. Remember to rehearse so that you are prepared to cope with the situation when it arises. Practice receiving and returning "verbal hardballs."
5. If necessary, use emotional jujitsu. The principle of jujitsu is to flow with your opponent's strength, to turn his own force against him by redirecting it rather than resisting it. Rather than defending yourself, agree. Your critic will be instantly disarmed, and then you can begin to deal with the causes of the emotion rather than the emotion itself.

SOURCE: Excerpted from "Personal Productivity: Organizational Communication," *Government Productivity News* 3 (September 1989): 4.

Delegation and Motivation

Management can be defined as "the process of getting things done through others." To get things done through others, it is necessary to communicate with others and, often, to motivate them as well. Much of the time, those "others" are the people you supervise. After all, if you can do all the work yourself, you should just go ahead and do it. As a manager, however, you are not there to do the actual work but to do the managerial work.

Delegation

Delegation is the process of assigning tasks to others. Like so many other managerial tasks, it may be done poorly or it may be done well. Poor delegation can be nearly fatal.

To delegate well, you need to try to delegate an equal amount of authority and responsibility for a job. Authority is the legitimate power to do the job, and responsibility is the accountability the individual has to you for getting the job done. The idea that an individual should have equal amounts of both is the *parity principle*. Managers often complain that they will be held responsible for something but have not been given enough authority to get the job done. Less frequent, but equally troublesome, is an individual who has authority but is not held responsible for its use.

Generally speaking, you should delegate jobs with complete and clear instructions, and you should delegate tasks to the appropriate level. Holding everything else equal, the appropriate level is the lowest level in the hierarchy where the task can be accomplished competently. You should also provide support for the delegated tasks. This support can take many forms, including delegation of authority in a public statement (such as saying at a meeting, "Betty is in charge of inspections in the northern district now").

It is often helpful to involve subordinates in the process of delegation, encouraging them to make suggestions about the kind of work they can or should be doing. Delegation should be a two-way process. On the other hand, do not fall victim to the upward delegation phenomenon. Upward delegation occurs when subordinates bring problems to their managers that the subordinates should be solving themselves. This is the opposite of effective delegation, and you should refuse to take on such problems. An effective technique is to insist that any subordinate who wants advice about an issue (the way the upward delegation attempt is often presented) should first think of at least one potential solution before coming to you to discuss it. To allow for creativity and motivation in the delegation process, it is best to hold subordinates accountable for results and leave the "how" up to them. This principle assumes, of course, that the "how" will be within the constraints of legal and ethical behavior as well as the constraints of public or organizational policies. Finally, tasks should be delegated consistently when the workload is light as well as heavy and when the jobs are fun as well as unpleasant.

Besides getting things done through others, delegation helps to develop employees, thereby making them more valuable to you and to the organization. Some managers are threatened by the idea that they may be developing possible replacements (that is, competitors). But there is another way to look at this situation. Unless you are at the very top of the organization, you probably want to be promoted. But you cannot be promoted if you cannot be replaced. Developing your subordinates through delegation is a way of providing, to your advantage, your own potential replacements!

Motivation

Whether members of an organization perform well depends partly on ability and partly on motivation. A person must already possess or be able to learn the right mix of skills and abilities to do a job and must be motivated to do the job well. When you can help develop your employees' skills through instruction, training programs, and so forth, you are likely to have a significantly greater impact on their motivation.

Pay and Job Satisfaction   When one thinks of motivation in a managerial context, monetary compensation is a subject that naturally comes to mind. Frederick Taylor (1923) based the entire incentive system of his scientific management program on economic factors. Contemporary thinking about motivation is more sophisticated than Taylor's, however, as pay is seen to interact with other motivators in complex ways.

Even as early as the 1950s, Frederick Herzberg developed a model of motivation known as the *two-factor theory*. Herzberg (1959) argued that two sets of variables were relevant to the question of motivation: "hygiene factors," which impact job dissatisfaction, and "motivators," which impact job satisfaction.

Hygiene factors included variables such as pay and working conditions; motivators were factors such as chances for achievement, recognition, and advancement. Herzberg argued that improvements in hygiene factors such as pay would not increase job satisfaction; instead, any improvements would simply reduce dissatisfaction. If an individual's pay got worse or did not increase fast enough, dissatisfaction would increase. Conversely, motivators such as achievement or advancement would not affect dissatisfaction, but would increase or decrease job satisfaction. The lesson for managers was that motivating employees is a far more complex task than simply changing salary levels.

Controversy about the effect of job satisfaction goes back at least as far as the Hawthorne studies conducted during the mid-1920s and early 1930s. Recall from Chapter 8 that these studies began as a research project to investigate the effects of physical working conditions, such as lighting, on workers' productivity. Given some unexpected findings early in the studies, the investigators changed the focus of the research to investigate the impacts of social and supervisory variables on performance. Some authors interpreted the results of the later studies as indicating that higher levels of job satisfaction led to higher levels of worker performance, a conclusion that some argue was never present in the original research reports and is thus a misinterpretation (Organ, 1986). But misinterpretation or not, the Hawthorne studies are usually credited for the "discovery" that a "happy worker is a productive worker." Other studies of the job satisfaction–performance relationship produced mixed results. Some theorists argued that the job-satisfaction-leads-to-better-performance thesis was wrong in terms of the causal ordering—that it was actually the other way around, with higher levels of performance causing higher levels of job satisfaction.

Although there is still not complete agreement on this issue, support is accumulating for a third interpretation of the job satisfaction–performance relationship: that there will only be a relationship between job satisfaction and performance if the rewards one receives are based on one's performance. If rewards are based on performance, there should be a positive correlation between job satisfaction and performance (the higher the performance, the higher the job satisfaction) because higher performance will lead to higher rewards, which will produce higher job satisfaction. If this is true, one part of the manager's job will be to make sure that performance is directly linked to rewards—monetary as well as others. One method to achieve this linkage is reinforcement theory.

Reinforcement Theory   Reinforcement theory and related approaches have been given various labels, including behaviorism, operant conditioning, stimulus-response psychology, and Skinnerian psychology. All of the labels refer to more or less the same thing: an approach to explaining behavior based on Thorndike's law of effect, which states,

"Of several responses made to the same situation, those which are accompanied or closely followed by satisfaction (reinforcement)…will be more likely to occur; those which are accompanied or closely followed by discomfort (punishment)…will be less likely to occur" (Daft & Steers, 1986, p. 51).

The law of effect as it relates to learning in both animals and human beings has been studied for more than a century. Results of this research have produced a number of generalizations about the specifics of reinforcement. There are four basic scenarios or results that may follow a specific behavior. If a reward follows the behavior, the individual is more likely to repeat the behavior; this is called positive reinforcement. Reinforcement will also occur when behavior is followed by the removal of something unpleasant, called negative reinforcement.

On the other hand, if an unpleasant event or punishment follows the behavior, the individual is less likely to repeat it. Note that negative reinforcement is not the same as punishment, even though the terms have become synonymous in ordinary usage. From the standpoint of the recipient, punishment would be considered a bad outcome, whereas negative reinforcement would be considered a good outcome. The final possibility is that nothing will happen following a behavior, or at least no reinforcement will occur in connection with it. When this is the case, the individual is less likely to repeat the behavior and will eventually stop doing it altogether. This cessation of behavior is called extinction.

Regardless of which of the four possibilities one is considering, a common theme, and one of the key principles of the reinforcement approach, is that whatever response is given to the behavior, the response should follow the behavior as soon as possible. If there is too long a delay following the behavior, the response (reward, removal of an unpleasant situation, and so on) may be misinterpreted and associated with other behaviors that have occurred in the interval.

Other important considerations of the reinforcement approach are the patterns, frequency, and basis for providing the response. In terms of frequency, responses can be given every time the behavior occurs (continuous reinforcement schedule) or for only a certain proportion of occurrences (partial reinforcement schedule). The basis for making the responses can be either the number of times an event occurs (ratio schedules) or the passage of time (interval schedules). The pattern of responses can be either consistent (fixed schedules) or random (variable schedules). Research indicates that while fixed schedules lead to faster learning, they also lead to quicker unlearning or forgetting when the schedule is abandoned. Conversely, variable schedules lead to slower learning, but once the behavior is learned, the unlearning or forgetting is much slower when the schedule is abandoned.

This description of reinforcement approaches probably conjures up images of laboratory animals running through a maze to earn food or to avoid electric shocks, and these are indeed how reinforcement has been studied in the laboratory. An obvious and natural parallel applying reinforcement theory in a managerial context is to link pay in some way to an individual's performance. This can be done, but pay (wages or salaries) tends to be set only once a year, and because organizational policies often dictate pay scales, many managers have only a partial impact on establishing their subordinates' salaries. This limits the extent to which the manager can use pay as a motivational tool.

An article in the *PA Times* identified several assumptions underlying pay-for-performance forms of motivation:

1. An individual's performance could be accurately or reasonably measured according to some criteria.
2. This system could affect an employee's decision to leave or remain with his or her organization and influence an employee's willingness to work harder for his or her organization than those who are not under the system.
3. An employee will place high value on monetary rewards in the workplace (Lee, 2001, p. 3).
4. Beginning with the first assumption, though, we can see the challenges faced by public and nonprofit managers in employing such a system in practice. As the author found, "It [a performance-based system] may work in private companies, since they have a clear goal (maximization of profit) that can be measured in quantitative ways. However, this doesn't seem to be working in most public agencies" (Lee, 2001, p. 3). Unclear goals, combined with the need to balance between competing interest groups, tend to make establishing such clear-cut objectives impossible in the delivery of public services.

Moreover, the author found in his study of public employees in New Jersey that people who work in public and nonprofit organizations tend to seek more than financial incentives: "If a public-sector employee is committed to his or her supervisor, he or she is more likely to remain with the agency and make an extra effort on behalf of the organization. In other words, a major motivating factor is not monetary reward, but an effective personal relationship among employees" (Lee, 2001, p. 3). Pay-for-performance may boost some forms of productivity, but it shouldn't be viewed as a building block for a truly high-impact organization.

Goal Setting   Goal setting is another method of motivating that can be used by itself or in conjunction with reinforcement techniques. In fact, you can use it to motivate yourself as well as other people. A goal is a desired state of affairs one attempts to achieve, and, as research has shown, just the act of setting goals seems to increase the probability of success. But some ways of setting goals are better than others in terms of motivational impact. Research indicates there are at least twelve ways in which you can shape a goal to have maximum motivational impact:

1. Write down a goal rather than just keep it in mind. In a technical sense, one does not "do" a goal, but *achieves* a goal. Therefore, the proper way to write a goal statement is with the word *to* followed by an action verb—for example, "To finish reading this chapter by 5 o'clock." Something about writing down a goal creates greater commitment on the part of the writer. It is harder to ignore, and seeing it on your desk or in your notebook constantly makes the goal harder to forget. Writing down a goal can also facilitate planning because you are consciously identifying the actions you must take to achieve the goal.
2. Because specific goals are much better motivators than general goals, a properly stated goal should be very clear. For example, a field experiment on goal setting at the Weyerhaeuser Company in Oklahoma several years ago tested the relative impacts

of general and specific goals. The objects of the experiment were truck drivers who hauled logs from one location to another. The federal government established safety standards for how much weight the truckers could carry, and this amount was taken to be the maximum capacity of the trucks, or 100 percent. The researchers and managers at Weyerhaeuser noted that the truckers normally only hauled about 62 percent of capacity. The first part of the experiment consisted of management informing the truckers that they wanted more weight to be carried on each load and that the truckers were to do their best to achieve this goal.

3. The truckers' performance was tracked for the next three months, and there was little or no improvement (1 or 2 percent at most). The truckers were then informed that a goal had been set for them: to haul 94 percent of capacity on each load—a much more specific goal than "Do your best." After three months, the truckers were averaging over 90 percent of capacity per load, very close to the 94 percent goal the managers had set for them.

4. No pay increases were given for the increase in weight hauled, although the truckers were told they would not be asked to make any more runs than they normally did as a result of hauling more weight. This remarkable change in behavior saved Weyerhaeuser over $250,000 annually, and subsequent checks on the truckers have found they have maintained this level of performance for several years. So a specific goal indeed makes a difference.

5. The means for verifying whether a goal has been achieved should be specified. In the study at Weyerhaeuser, the truckers weighed in at the delivery location for the logs, which provided a precise way to measure the amount of weight they were hauling and, in turn, how close they were to the goal. (Incidentally, the weigh-in procedure was not added by the experiment; the truckers had been following it for many years as part of their job.)

6. A date or time by which the goal is to be accomplished should be specified. The presence or absence of a deadline is a critical attribute of any goal-setting exercise. Deadlines stimulate action, and the closer the deadline, the more motivation to act. The absence of a deadline makes the urgency of the goal indefinite and hence less motivating. For example, there are a disproportionately large number of plays during the last few minutes of a football game because the team that is behind faces a deadline for scoring more points or losing the game. Similar increases in activity occur toward the end of the trading period each day on the New York Stock Exchange. Think of your own behavior when a test date is rapidly approaching, and you begin to increase your preparation activities.

7. A goal should be perceived as attainable. Impossible goals often are demotivating because there is no reason to try if they cannot, by definition, be attained. (Problems may also occur, however, if the goal is too attainable.)

8. Although a goal should be attainable, it should also be challenging. There is little or no satisfaction in achieving a goal that presents little challenge. The best goal in terms of motivation is one that is perceived as attainable yet challenging, that can be achieved, but only with significant effort.

9. Psychologist David McClelland (1985) demonstrated this phenomenon many years ago. Children were asked to throw beanbags into a box from various distances,

including a position located right next to the box. After they had thrown from various distances, they were asked from which position they preferred to throw. Very few picked the location next to the box; most picked a position farther away—a decision consistent with the properties of attainability and challenge. In effect, the children were setting their own goals, and the goals they set were challenging but attainable.

10. When setting goals for others, the goals must be understandable to the people for whom you are setting them. If they cannot understand the goals, how can you expect them to achieve them? As in so many areas, clarity is extremely important.

11. It was originally believed that if the participants were not involved in setting the goals, they would reject them. Subsequent research, such as in the Weyerhaeuser study, in which the truck drivers did not take part in establishing the goals, has shown that people are quite willing to accept goals that others set for them. This does not mean, however, that involving people in establishing goals is a waste of time. Among other things, if the people who will actually be trying to accomplish the goals take part in formulating them, there is a greater chance that they will more completely and accurately understand the goals. And although people may be willing to accept goals established by others, there may be greater motivation if they participate.

12. Managers often worry about involving subordinates in decision making, including decisions about goals and goal levels. A study comparing goals that managers set for their subordinates to goals for the same activities set by the subordinates themselves revealed that the subordinates set more difficult goals (Hitt, Middlemist, & Mathis, 1983, p. 289). Although this may not happen all the time, it is an intriguing finding that supports the notion of including subordinates in the goal-setting process.

Individual Decision Making

One could argue that decision making is the most universal managerial activity because it is involved in all the other functions of management. It is impossible to plan, control, staff, direct, organize, or perform any of the miscellaneous management functions without making decisions. All management involves either explicit or implicit decisions. We will examine decision making at the individual level and explore several models of how decisions should be made and how decisions are actually made.

A great deal of research has been conducted concerning rational processes for decision making, some of which we discussed in terms of rational policy analysis. In its purest form, the rational model of decision making suggests the following steps:

1. Find an occasion for decision making ("decide to decide") and then formulate the problem in the best way possible.
2. Develop as many alternative solutions as possible.
3. Choose the alternative that maximizes the possibility that we will attain our goals or standards.

In essence, analyze the problem, generate alternative solutions, and choose from among the solutions. For our purposes, the most important lesson of the rational decision model lies at the beginning—becoming aware that a problem exists and correctly defining the problem. If you are not aware of a problem, you will not go through the rest of the process to solve it. Your chances of solving the problem are obviously low. (The probabilities are not zero, however, because problems are sometimes solved by accident.) Even if you are aware that a problem exists, if you do not identify the problem correctly, your chances of solving it do not increase very much. How you define the situation is the result of your own perception of reality. Human beings need to make sense of things. We do not tolerate chaos well, and thus are continually defining and redefining situations in which we find ourselves. Aside from our need to make sense of things, defining the situation is important because that will be the basis for our actions and decisions. All mentally healthy individuals behave in a way consistent with their definitions of situations.

When it comes to problem solving, incorrect diagnosis of the problem (that is, an incorrect definition of the situation) can be disastrous. A good example of this can be seen in the Cold War days of the early 1960s. During this period, the United States and its allies had installed long-range radar systems to monitor the Soviet Union and to give warning of any Soviet attack by either missile or bomber. Soon after the radar systems were installed, the commander of an installation in England was made aware of a set of images on the station's screens that looked as if the Soviet Union were launching a massive missile assault against the United States. It was the commander's job to evaluate the information, report it to Washington, and include a recommendation and an evaluation of the accuracy of the information.

Obviously, since missiles travel pretty fast, the commander did not have a great deal of time to contemplate the situation. But, being a calm and collected individual, the commander thought things over for a few minutes before he made his report. He remembered that Nikita Khrushchev, then premier of the Soviet Union, was in New York City addressing the United Nations that day. He thought it would be an unlikely time for the Soviets to attack. He also took into consideration the fact that the radar system was new and that new systems sometimes have "bugs" in them. Putting all this together, he made his report, including in it his relatively low confidence in the information on his screens. He stated that he believed there was a malfunction somewhere in the system and recommended that the radar images not be interpreted as an attack on the United States. Obviously he was correct; there was no attack by the Soviet Union. But what was actually happening?

It turned out that the radars were so powerful that some of the radiation they broadcast traveled far out into space. The system operated smoothly for about a week, but then the moon orbited into position and was hit by some of the radiation, which it reflected back to the radar antennas, creating images on the screens that looked very much like a group of missiles heading toward the United States. The computers in the radar system had not been programmed to disregard radiation bouncing back from the moon.

The commander was presented with a problem: the decision of interpreting the images and making his report. He had two interpretations. One was that the Soviet Union had started World War III, and the other that he had a malfunctioning system. One definition of the situation might have actually started World War III, but the other would prevent that catastrophe. So you can see why correctly identifying the problem is critical in a problem-solving situation.

The rational decision model is often presented as the way people actually go about making decisions (or at least the way they should), and this is probably true to a certain extent. It is also clear that, in many cases, solutions to problems are arrived at in a far different way. The basis of the rational problem-solving process is the economic assumption that people attempt to maximize their outcomes when they make choices (that is, decisions). Theoretically, people select a criterion, such as income or profit, then evaluate all decision alternatives in terms of that criterion, and finally select the alternative that will produce the best results.

As we discussed in Chapter 8, Herbert Simon, in his studies of organizational decision making, found that the rational model rarely describes human problem-solving or decision-making behavior in real life. He argued that maximizing outcomes is simply not possible in most situations and identified several reasons that it is usually impossible (Simon, 1957, p. xxvi). All the reasons Simon offers add up to constraints on human beings' abilities to acquire and process information. There are time limits for making most decisions, and there are only so many resources available to gather information. Moreover, because we care more about some problems than others, our motivation to solve problems varies. We are willing to spend more mental and physical energy on some problems than on others.

Even if we had access to unlimited information about any problem, there are cognitive limits to how much information we can process at any given time. Furthermore, particularly in managerial situations, we seldom have the luxury of being able to deal with just one problem at a time. Other problems compete for our attention, time, and energy, further taxing our cognitive limits.

Putting all these constraints together, Simon argues that human beings attempt to be rational, but they can be rational only within certain limits or bounds. What Simon calls "bounded rationality" (see Chapter 8) suggests that choices will be evaluated, but only within the bounds of these constraints. This results in a "satisficing" criterion for evaluating alternatives, rather than in a maximizing one.

A *satisficing decision* is one that is just "good enough" in terms of some criterion. Bounded rationality leads to satisficing decisions, and the process, in its pure form, operates as follows: When an individual faces a choice situation in which a decision must be made, rather than attempting to gather all possible information, generate all possible alternatives, and choose the alternative likely to produce the best results, the decision maker decides what level of outcome (in terms of some criterion) will be satisfactory or "good enough." The individual then examines choice alternatives one at a time and selects the first one that equals or exceeds the minimal ("good enough") criterion level. The process stops at this point, and the choice becomes the decision. No attempt will be made to examine other, potentially better, options.

That human beings vary in attempts to maximize suggests something of a continuum between satisficing and maximizing. But Simon's work suggests that most decisions, most of the time, fall much closer to the satisficing end of the continuum than the maximizing end, even where we are making important (and potentially costly) decisions. Marketing research shows, for example, that people tend to seek out most of the information they acquire about new cars after they purchase a new car rather than before.

Thus, the rational decision-making process can be considered a prescriptive model that tells us what we should do to make better decisions, but it does not give us an accurate picture of how human beings actually make decisions. Because we tend to satisfice rather than maximize, a modified and more limited version of this process, the satisficing model, provides the more accurate description. Hence, we can call it a descriptive model, which attempts to describe how things actually happen without regard to how they should happen. Given the nature of managerial work, satisficing may be the only way a manager can deal with the constant stream of problems and choice situations that arise daily.

Interestingly, one alternative model of decision making in the public sector claims to be both prescriptive and descriptive. Charles Lindblom's incremental model of decision making assumes that most governmental decisions (and others) usually begin by analyzing the existing situation and then move marginally or incrementally away from that position. In making a case for new programs, for example, managers often talk about how a new idea "builds on" existing strengths. This descriptive aspect of the model has a familiar ring. But, in a curious twist, Lindblom also suggests that the incremental model may even make sense normatively: because incremental proposals focus on well-known experiences, they reduce the number of alternatives to be considered and thus reduce the complexity of the problem at hand (Lindblom, 1968, p. 27).

Group Dynamics

Individuals acting alone make a majority of organizational decisions, but sometimes two or more people combine efforts to solve a problem or make a decision. Research has shown that sometimes a group should make a decision and that certain advantages come from group decision making, but there are also disadvantages. Similarly, studies of group dynamics have established fairly predictable patterns of interactions.

Advantages of Group Decision Making

An old cliché has it that two heads are better than one—probably because two heads hold more information than one. Put any two people together, and it is very likely that each knows something the other does not. Create a group of five or six, and there is even more information available. We have already seen that generating alternatives is one of the fundamental steps in the rational decision-making process, even under satisficing conditions. Because there is more information in a group, there is greater potential for generating more alternative solutions to a problem than could be generated by a single decision maker. But these advantages will surface only if the group is managed properly.

Groups may also benefit from synergy: the notion that the whole is greater than the sum of the parts. Synergy can occur in a group, but it is a precious commodity that is not easy to create. Consider the following case. Three people get together to solve a problem. Bob proposes a solution, and Allen proposes a different solution. Betty has been listening to the proposals, which gives her an idea about how to solve the problem in a completely new way. The idea represents something new that was not present before in the group. If it were possible to quantify the information in the group at the beginning of the discussion, the total information would equal the sum of the information held by the individual members. With Betty's new idea—an idea stimulated by the group discussion—the sum is now greater than the sum of the individual parts.

We want to do more than just make a good decision. The final step in the decision-making process is always implementation. If the people who make the decision are the ones who will be implementing it, commitment to the decision should help with implementation. Research also reveals that satisfaction with the group and its processes increases as the networks become more decentralized. Satisfaction is not exactly the same thing as commitment, but the two are closely related. In most cases, then, as participation in making the decision increases, so should commitment to the final decision.

What Would You Do?

You are the leader of a task force composed of a dozen members, each selected for his or her significant expertise in the field. Drawn from several different professional areas, these are "the best and the brightest" your organization has available. As your meetings progress, however, you recognize that, although these are very smart people, many of them take a rather narrow view of the world and are almost contemptuous of anyone who sees things differently. You recognize that unless something changes, the task force will fail to achieve its goal. What would you do?

An interesting property of group decision making, the *risk shift*, can be either an advantage or a disadvantage. The risk shift refers to how daring the decisions would be if made as a group compared to the average risk of the same decision if each member made it alone. It was originally thought that groups would always make riskier decisions than would individual members. As more research was conducted, however, it was discovered that sometimes the shift works in the opposite direction: that groups sometimes make decisions that are less risky than those made by members working alone.

Sometimes a daring decision produces better results, but sometimes it makes things worse. Because the same can be said about more conservative decisions, the dilemma is that it is often impossible to predict whether a more conservative or more daring decision will yield better results. The most we can say is that a group decision will normally be either more daring or more conservative than the average riskiness of a decision made by each member acting individually.

Disadvantages of Group Decision Making

Along with the advantages of group decision making, there are potential problems. One of the obvious constraints on human beings that results in our "bounded rationality" is the constraint of time. Time not only limits the efforts of individual decision makers to acquire and process information, but it also limits the possibilities for groups to make decisions. Normally, it takes a group much longer to make a decision than it takes an individual to make a decision about the same problem. Time thus becomes an important constraint on a manager's ability to use group decision making.

Another constraint may be cost. Even if group decision making and individual decision making were equally fast, the group is still more expensive. Compare a single decision maker whose pay is $100 per hour who takes one hour to reach a decision with a committee of five managers who are paid $100 each and also reach a decision in one hour. The cost to the organization for the single decision maker is $100, whereas the cost of the committee is $500.

Another property of groups is groupthink, which is the opposite of synergy. If synergy is the concept that the whole is greater than the sum of the parts, groupthink makes the whole (the group) less than the sum of the parts. Groupthink was first defined and analyzed by Irving Janis as "a mode of thinking that people engage in when they are deeply involved in a cohesive in-group, when the members' strivings for unanimity override their motivation to realistically appraise alternative courses of action" (Janis, 1983, pp. 8–9). Because the group is so cohesive, greater emphasis is given to conformity than to making good decisions.

Janis identified characteristics of groups victimized by groupthink and cautioned managers to interpret the presence of these characteristics in a group carefully. For example, groups experiencing groupthink have an illusion of morality, a belief that the group's position, whatever it may be, is inherently ethical and moral in comparison to positions held by other individuals and groups. Such groups also engage in negative stereotyping of other people and groups, often viewing outsiders as the "enemy" and as being too different to negotiate with. Groupthink tends to produce an illusion of invulnerability, which makes decisions seem less risky than they really are. Rationalization is commonly employed as a way to discredit information critical of the group or its decisions, and there is frequent self-censorship of dissenting views, which minimizes the amount of critical or contrary information to which the group is exposed. A strong conformity pressure permeates the group and puts further pressure on group members to agree with the dominant position. Finally, an illusion of unanimity results in the belief that everyone in the group has confidence in the group's decisions and judgment. Obviously, groups that are victimized by groupthink are limited in their constructive abilities.

Groupthink has been used to explain flawed decision-making processes in situations such as the Bay of Pigs, Watergate, and the *Challenger* space shuttle disaster. In the case of the *Challenger* disaster, a Presidential Commission investigated the accident and identified faulty decision making as a primary cause. Moorehead, Ference, and Neck (1991) analyzed the testimony of those involved and found the situation had many characteristics associated with groupthink. For example, the Commission found that those testifying displayed a strong sense of overconfidence because of the extraordinarily successful history of NASA (National Aeronautics and Space Administration). Even though engineers predicted during the final launch approval process that critical joints would fail, flight center officials discounted the analysis and rationalized that the conclusions were faulty or questionable. Two of the three top NASA officials stereotyped and criticized the views of others, particularly the engineers who warned them about the dangers of proceeding with the launch. Dissenters were pressured to either change their minds or remain silent. As a result of these and other problems, the launch was authorized and the shuttle exploded, killing all seven astronauts.

Interpersonal Dynamics in Groups

Interpersonal relationships affect the work of groups or teams. To illustrate the problems that can arise, imagine that two people who despise each other are assigned to the same committee. Obviously, these two individuals will not work as well together as two people who are neutral toward each other or who like and respect each other. Even if the conflict is not manifested, personal animosity may contribute to building a *hidden agenda,* where privately held goals and priorities motivate actions more directly than the overt and publicly stated reasons. Obviously, the operation of hidden agendas disrupts the group and diminishes its effectiveness.

But the interpersonal dynamics of groups in action are much more subtle and complex than these examples suggest (Gardner, 1974, pp. 8–11). For example, groups often follow a fairly predictable pattern of development. Typically, at the outset of the group's work, its members are highly dependent on the leader of the group. They ask for direction and become quite frustrated if they don't get it. If the leader allows the group to become overly dependent, however, its productivity will suffer in the long term. The leader can resist dependency by referring questions back to the group's members for input.

Often, however, a period of counterdependency will often follow, in which members may show hostility toward the leader. Although still wanting some direction, the group's members are now also experiencing a need for independence, just as an adolescent may simultaneously love and hate his or her parents. Counterdependency seems especially likely to occur in authoritarian work environments, where members' actions are too closely regulated.

On the other hand, in a group where members feel they can openly express themselves and their ideas without fear of retaliation, feelings of interdependence may develop. At this stage, group members recognize the purposes they hold in common and come to have greater trust and respect for one another. The group will probably be most effective when it reaches this stage.

As the group moves through these stages of development, certain patterns of behavior are likely to occur. Early in the group's development, some members may seek flight, actually withdrawing from the work of the group, being silent, or giving irrelevant or self-serving remarks. Most flight behavior is an implicit attempt to say that nothing significant will happen unless the leader gives in to the group's desire for explicit direction. In the counterdependent stage, members may engage in flight behavior or in pairing. Fighting the group's leader in some symbolic fashion is, of course, a fairly straightforward act of rebellion; pairing or breaking off into small groups or alliances is somewhat more subtle, but it expresses the same emotion.

Finally, as the group reaches the stage of interdependence, the actual work of the group can be accomplished in reasonable and satisfying ways. At this stage, a variety of leadership functions must occur for the group to maintain its effectiveness (see the box "Take Action: Leadership Roles in Group Dynamics"). These functions can all be performed by a single person, typically the group's formal leader, but they can also be performed by a variety of different people active at different times in the group's development. In either case, if you wish to help the group meet its objectives, you should be attentive both to the stages of group development and to the extent to which the various leadership functions are being fulfilled.

Take Action LEADERSHIP ROLES IN GROUP DYNAMICS

1. *The coordinator role.* Communicate to all members about meetings, schedules, tasks, procedures, and similar matters; act as an information clearinghouse for all group members and as a contact person with other groups or outsiders.
2. *The facilitator role.* Set up procedures and a structure for group work; assist members in identifying problems, defining issues, summarizing progress, and working together. (This role involves minimal direct influence on the group task. It concentrates on establishing an interpersonal network that helps members work together to solve problems.)
3. *The trainer role.* Teach group members ways of approaching problems; provide the group with methods of learning from their own experiences; arrange for outside consultants to train the group.
4. *The observer role.* Be alert to how the group is functioning and particularly to which functions are not being met; describe to members what is happening in terms of the group process; show the group areas in which change might facilitate their work.
5. *The gap filler role.* Fulfill those functions that are not being handled by anyone else, particularly the functions of summarizing, clarifying, synthesizing, or facilitating compromise.
6. *The monitor role.* Once the group has determined a procedure to follow or a solution to a problem, see to it that the group is reminded of responsibilities, functions, and assignments necessary for implementation of the decision; provide copies of budgets, schedules, assignment sheets, and agendas to members so they can complete their work on schedule.

SOURCE: Excerpted from Ernest Stech and Sharon Ratliffe, *Working in Groups* (Lincolnwood, IL: National Textbook Company, 1976), pp. 220–221. Reprinted by permission of The McGraw-Hill Companies.

Specialized Techniques for Group Decision Making

Brainstorming is a technique that was developed to enhance the alternative-generating portion of the decision-making process. The goal is to generate as many ideas about some problem as possible, although suspending judgment about each idea. The task before the group is to develop ideas about a problem, or even solutions to the problem, and the more of them generated, the better.

Once the assignment is announced, group members begin to propose ideas. The ideas are described orally, and someone records each idea on a chalkboard or flipchart for everyone to see. No evaluations of ideas are permitted during brainstorming. The session continues until everyone is out of ideas or the leader feels the session has lasted long enough. The purpose is to bring out the information held by different group members and to encourage synergy by stimulating new ideas.

Whereas brainstorming helps enrich the alternative-generating portion of the decision-making process, the nominal group technique generates both alternatives and solutions. A major purpose of the design is to avoid groupthink. A *nominal group* is a face-to-face meeting that allows only very limited interaction among participants. A problem is presented, but unlike in brainstorming, the group is expected to make a decision about how to solve the problem. After the problem has been presented, each member, working alone, writes down as many solutions to the problem as he or she can formulate. When everyone is finished writing, the leader calls for the solutions. Each person in the room presents one solution until all the possible solutions have been heard.

The solutions are recorded publicly as they are presented, again usually on a whiteboard or a chart paper. Other members may ask questions for clarification if they do not understand a solution, but only clarifying questions are allowed. Members may not debate the merits of particular solutions. After every solution has been presented and all questions answered, the group makes a decision by means of a written poll, taken as a secret ballot. Each member rank-orders the different solutions from best to worst. The rankings are submitted to the meeting leader without any identifying material on the ballot. The leader or someone assisting the leader tabulates the ballots, and the solution that receives the highest average preference becomes the group's decision.

Quality circles are the most comprehensive specialized technique for group decision making in that they are explicitly concerned with every step in the decision-making process, from recognition that a problem exists through implementation of solutions. Quality circles also incorporate other specialized techniques such as brainstorming.

One specialized approach that is often helpful in group dynamics is the helping relationship, which has been explored in great detail by Edgar Schein in his recent book, *Helping* (2009). A helping relationship can be informal (as when we seek help from a friend, a spouse, or a coworker), semiformal (as when we go to a computer consultant), or formal (as when we hire a management consultant), but all of these involvements bear certain features in common. Most importantly, the helping relationship occurs between people, and an effective human interaction must occur for effective helping to take place.

Initially, the helping relationship must be based on conditions of mutual trust. "Trusting another person means, in this context, that no matter what we choose to reveal about our thoughts, feelings, or intentions, the other person will not belittle us, make us look bad, or take advantage of what we have said in confidence" (Schein, 2009, p. 18). Trust equates to emotional safety. Beyond that, we understand certain rules that govern our behavior and our relationships. For example, building an effective relationship requires that both parties get something out of it and it feels "fair." Over time, we learn the different roles we play and the expectations associated with those roles. But we also recognize that confusing roles can be detrimental to an effective relationship. For example, though we may be a parent, if we act in a parental way toward others at work, we may appear patronizing, and trust in the relationship will be undermined.

Conflict, Bargaining, and Negotiation

Differences and conflicts inevitably arise in public and nonprofit organizations. But as Richard Box (1998) explains, finding a way to equitably resolve differences is a key interpersonal skill, opening the door to more citizen-oriented governance. "For elected leaders and public service practitioners, this means a flexible attitude toward change, shedding of protective feelings about personal turf, and a willingness to engage in open dialogue on issues facing the community" (p. 12).

What Would You Do?

Your division of purchasing is composed of two sections, one that acquires goods and another that acquires services. Over time, the two section heads have developed an intense rivalry that has increasingly turned ugly. The two are basically at war, with insults flying back and forth at every occasion. They are forcing you into the position of having to choose sides—which you don't want to do. What would you do?

Roger Fisher and William Ury (1991) of the Harvard Negotiation Project have suggested that negotiation is a natural process that occurs where two parties share certain interests but are opposed with respect to others. Negotiations often move quickly to positions that are held by one party or another. For example, a union representative requests a 10 percent raise, but the city negotiator takes the position that only a 2 percent raise is possible. Moving quickly to a position and allowing it to become hard and fast not only produces undesirable results but also damages the continuing relationship between the parties. Positional bargaining seems to move participants to one of two postures: a soft posture that emphasizes the ongoing relationship and seeks agreement among participants, or a hard posture that assumes an adversarial relationship and in which each party seeks victory over the other.

Fischer and Ury suggest an alternative method called "principled negotiation." Principled negotiation is based on four elements of negotiation: people, interests, options, and the criteria for solution. Four guidelines emerge from these elements (see the box "Take Action: Guidelines for Successful Negotiations").

According to Fischer and Ury, following these guidelines leads to negotiated settlements that are more equitable and more likely to lead to continued effective working

---

Take Action   GUIDELINES FOR SUCCESSFUL NEGOTIATIONS

1. Separate the people from the problem.
2. Focus on interests, not positions.
3. Generate a variety of possibilities before deciding what to do.
4. Insist that the result will be based on some objective standard.

SOURCE: From *Getting to Yes*, 2nd ed., by Roger Fisher, William Ury, and Bruce Patton. © 1981, 1991 by Roger Fisher and William Ury. Reprinted by permission of Houghton Mifflin Company. All rights reserved.

relationships than are more traditional modes of bargaining. Remember that negotiations occur in all kinds of situations, from deciding which movie to see to resolving matters of war and peace. However, the same general guidelines may be employed in all negotiations to generate more effective and responsible solutions (Fischer & Ury, 1991).

More recently, managers of public and nonprofit organizations have adopted systems for alternative dispute resolution (ADR). ADR can be thought of as any conflict management strategy outside of formal adjudication. Approaches range from preventative measures, such as building consensus and setting clear parameters on interpersonal (and interorganizational) relationships, to more formal approaches, such as court-based mediation and arbitration (Constantino & Sickles-Merchant, 1996). Recall that earlier in Chapter 2 we discussed the increasing use of ADR in the federal government.

Networking

For information on conflict resolution, visit the Conflict Resolution Center at http://www.crnhq.org/, the National Association for Community Mediation at www.nafcm.org, or Illinois's Center for Conflict Resolution at http://www.ccrchicago.org/, which offers insight into specific examples of ADR at the state level.

Summary and Action Implications

Leadership involves more than power and control. To lead others, you must first know yourself. Thus, understanding yourself is an essential prerequisite to acting effectively and responsibly in public organizations. Moreover, to the extent that you are able to learn about yourself—your strengths and weaknesses, your desires and frustrations—you will be much more effective in your work with others. Whereas power may be a resource, leadership capabilities are more likely to arise from the ability to understand the emerging desires of a group, to articulate the vision or direction the group wishes to follow, and to stimulate the group to action. Leadership unquestionably requires social or interpersonal skills, but it is based in empathetic understanding, the ability to express the aspirations of the group, and the confidence to undertake the risks associated with change.

All the knowledge, values, and skills you possess are expressed in the moment of action. Whether you are a manager or a policy analyst or hold some other position in a public organization, your ability to act effectively and responsibly "in the real world" will determine your success. Your actions will usually occur in social settings and require working with others. Especially in a managerial position, you will engage in almost constant interaction with other people, so no matter how much you know or how proper your values, your effectiveness will be limited if you cannot work well with others.

Today we recognize that interpersonal skills, like other skills, can be developed and improved over time. Just as artists or athletes can improve proficiency, so can you improve your skills in areas of communications, delegation, negotiation, and group dynamics. The key to improving your skills in public management, as in other areas, is practice and repetition, accompanied by self-reflection and self-critique.

If you want to be a better communicator, for example, you should seek opportunities to practice communicating with others. Find opportunities to make presentations; practice listening with special concentration and sensitivity; try to develop your writing skills. As you practice, be conscious of your own and others' reactions. Reflect upon your successes and failures and try to learn from both. Over time, you'll improve your skills and find that you are far more effective.

Throughout this book, we have described public management as involving cognitive, conceptual, technical, and human skills. In the moment of action, however, the areas cannot be separated. Indeed, your capacity to bring together knowledge, technique, and interactive skills at the moment of action will determine success or failure in most situations. Public management can be studied in the abstract, but it must be lived in the real world—a world of stress, complexity, and uncertainty. In few other fields do so many aspects of the human personality have to come together. But it is this very difficulty that makes public service so challenging and rewarding.

STUDY QUESTIONS

1. What are the seven basics of effective listening?

2. Why is speaking an important interpersonal skill?

3. Discuss the "Six Cs" for effective written communication.

4. Management can be defined as "the process of getting things done through others." Discuss how delegation and motivation enable the work of management to occur.

5. Explain reinforcement theory and its four basic scenarios or results.

6. Goal setting is another motivation technique. Discuss what characteristics a goal should have for maximum motivational impact.

7. What features are present in rational decision making?

8. What are the elements of "principled negotiation"?

9. Discuss the advantages and disadvantages associated with group decision making.

10. Explain the fundamentals of managing group dynamics.

11. Identify and discuss various techniques for group decision making.

CASES AND EXERCISES

1. Although power should not be equated with leadership, it can certainly be an important resource to public managers. To illustrate some types of power, think back over the past week or two as you attended class and worked in various groups and organizations, and answer the following questions:

   a. Who were the two or three people during this period who exercised the greatest power over you?
   b. Who were the people during this period over whom you exercised the most power? Now return to the box "Exploring Concepts: Bases of Social Power" on page 327. What was the basis for the power that others exercised over you? What was the basis for the power that you exercised over others? How might you most effectively build up your power base in groups and organizations to which you belong?

2. Chapter 1 discusses the management skills identified by the U.S. Office of Personnel Management (see pages 11–12). Some of those skills are listed here. Go through the list and assess your level of development in each of the skills. You might want to verify your evaluations by talking with others who know you well and have seen you operate in groups and organizations. After you have a sense of your own level of skill development, try to identify the activities (classes, workshops, readings, and so on) that would help you improve your skills in areas that need some work.

   ### The "How" of Management Effectiveness Characteristics

   - *Broad perspectives:* Broad, long-term view; balancing short- and long-term considerations.
   - *Strategic view:* Collecting, assessing, analyzing information; diagnosis; anticipation; judgment.
   - *Environmental sensitivity:* "Tuned in to" the agency and its environment; aware of the importance of nontechnical factors.
   - *Leadership:* Individual; group; willingness to lead, manage, and accept responsibility.
   - *Flexibility:* Openness to new information; behavioral flexibility; tolerance for stress, ambiguity, change; innovativeness.
   - *Action orientation:* Independence, proactivity; calculated risk-taking; problem solving; decisiveness.
   - *Focus on results:* Concern with goal achievement; follow-through, tenacity.
   - *Communication:* Speaking; writing; listening.
   - *Interpersonal sensitivity:* Self-knowledge and awareness of impact on others; sensitivity to needs, strengths, and weaknesses of others; negotiation; conflict resolution; persuasion.
   - *Technical competence:* Specialized expertise (such as, engineering, physical science, law, accounting, social science).

3. Divide your class into groups of three. Taking turns, have one person choose a topic from the following list and begin a conversation with the group. Follow the rules of effective communication.

   a. You are short of cash and want to take a winter vacation to an island off the coast of Mexico. You need to borrow at least $300 for the trip. You are pretty sure you can pay it back in three months.

   b. The two classmates you are talking with have been working with you on a class project. Actually, the problem is that they haven't been working! You have to do something to get them busy, or your grade will suffer. You need at least a "B" in the course to graduate.

   c. You have been working in behalf of the homeless in your community for the past two years. A march on Washington has been scheduled for next week, and a bus has been chartered to take people from your community to Washington at a cost of $83 each. The problem is that unless you can find two more people to make the trip, the bus won't go. You want to convince your two friends to go with you.

4. Imagine that you are an administrative assistant to the director of the Department of Social Services in your state government. The director is interested in starting a new strategic planning process and wants to send a letter to all the managers and employees in the department describing the new process and enlisting their support. You have been asked to draft the letter. Using the information about strategic planning in Chapter 4, draft an appropriate letter.

   After everyone in the class has drafted a letter, each draft should be shared with and analyzed by at least one other student. Your analysis should take into account the specifics of the situation (what should be said, how much should be said, how it should be said) as well as the more general Six Cs of effective communications listed in this chapter.

5. Divide the class into groups of three. Have one person in each group play the role of Chris, the supervisor, and another play the role of Brett, the employee. (Each person should read only his or her own role description and not that of the other person.) The third person in each group should observe the discussion between Chris and Brett and then comment on the motivation strategies employed. The scene begins as Brett walks into Chris's office and says, "Someone said you wanted to see me."

   Chris You are twenty-eight years old and recently received your MPA from a fairly prestigious school in the East. You have worked for the federal government for four years, moving rapidly from a presidential management internship to your current position supervising a small unit that produces health and safety brochures for industry. Brett has worked with the agency for twenty-three years as a design specialist. Throughout this period, from what you understand, Brett has done an excellent job. In the few months you have been with the agency, however, you have noticed a decided drop in both the amount and quality of Brett's work. With a heavy workload anticipated over the next several months, you decide that you have to do something to improve Brett's performance. You have asked Brett to come and speak with you.

Brett You have worked for twenty-three years as a design specialist for a small federal government unit that produces health and safety brochures for industry. Throughout your career, you have taken great pride in your work and have done an excellent job. Over the last few months, however, you have been increasingly troubled by painful back spasms, the source of which you have not been able to identify. The problem with your back has triggered a lot of concerns about your health, your age, and your work. Although you haven't shared these concerns with anyone, you find that you spend long periods daydreaming about them. Even drinking a few martinis each evening hasn't calmed your fears. You still enjoy your design work, but somehow the projects you have had recently just don't seem all that exciting. What's worse, your supervisor, a kid probably half your age, has been hinting that your work may not be up to par.

6. Consider the following case. You have recently been appointed head of a new agency established to monitor pollution emissions from coal-fired power plants throughout the Midwest. The data you collect will have a direct impact on an anticipated presidential decision concerning acid rain in the Northeast and Canada. You must try to develop the most comprehensive and precise measures possible and then monitor as many plants as you reasonably can during the relatively short period prior to the presidential decision. Most of your staff have been in the pollution control field much longer than you and are highly committed to the goals of your agency. They have been arguing that a new piece of equipment, an Emission Systems Monitoring Instrument (ESMI), is the only device that is capable of taking precise measurements of the particular pollutants with which you are concerned. The problem is that the ESMI is both extremely expensive and would require nearly half the time you have available just to be delivered. You are skeptical about whether the ESMI is worth the cost, but even more concerned that its limited availability will mean that you will fail to meet your deadline. You also think, though you are not sure, that the rough estimates generated by the existing equipment are sufficient for the purposes of your report to the president. Do you go ahead with the existing equipment, or do you buy the ESMI?

7. Divide the class into task groups of five people each, with three observers assigned to each group.

   The task groups should list what they consider the five most important guidelines for effectively managing a large organization. After each task group completes its work, the observers should lead a discussion of the group dynamics they observed in the work of the task group.

   For observers only: During the discussion, you should silently watch the discussion and take notes about the operation of the group. Try to identify patterns of group development such as those presented in the chapter. Pay special attention to shifting patterns of leadership and communications. If this same group were to perform a similar task, what would you suggest to improve its effectiveness?

8. The following "classic" exercise in group problem solving will illustrate several important aspects of the decision-making process.

Your spaceship has just crash-landed on the moon. You were scheduled to rendezvous with the mother ship 200 miles away on the lighted surface of the moon, but the rough landing has ruined your ship and destroyed all the equipment on board, except for the fifteen items listed below.

You and four to seven other people should take this test individually, without knowing one another's answers, then take the test as a group. Share your individual solutions and reach a consensus—one ranking for each item that best satisfies all group members.

Your crew's survival depends on reaching the mother ship, so you must choose the most critical items available for the 200-mile trip. Your task is to rank the fifteen items in terms of their importance for survival. Place 1 by the most important item, 2 by the second most important, and so on through 15, the least important.

- box of matches
- food concentrate
- fifty feet of nylon rope
- parachute silk
- solar-powered portable heating unit
- two .45-caliber pistols
- one case of dehydrated evaporated milk
- two 100-pound tanks of oxygen
- stellar map (of the moon's constellation)
- self-inflating life raft
- magnetic compass
- five gallons of water
- signal flares
- first-aid kit containing injection needles
- solar-powered FM receiver-transmitter

SOURCE: Jay Hall, "Decisions, Decisions, Decisions," *Psychology Today* 5 (November 1971): pp. 51–88. Reprinted with permission from *Psychology Today*. © 1971, www.psychologytoday.com by Sussex Publishers, Inc.

Note: NASA experts have determined the best solution to this task. Their answers appear in the chapter appendix.

FOR ADDITIONAL READING

Allison, Graham, and Philip Zelikow. *Essence of Decision: Explaining the Cuban Missile Crisis.* 2nd ed. New York: Longman, 1999.

Bass, Bernard M., and Bruce J. Avolio, eds. *Improving Organizational Effectiveness through Transformational Leadership.* Thousand Oaks, CA: Sage Publications, 1993.

Bechard, Richard. *Changing the Essence: The Art of Creating and Leading Fundamental Change in Organizations.* San Francisco: Jossey-Bass, 1992.

Bingham, Richard D., et al. *Managing Local Government: Public Administration in Practice.* Newbury Park, CA: Sage Publications, 1991.

Bozeman, Barry, and Jeffrey D. Straussman. *Public Management Strategies: Guidelines for Managerial Effectiveness*. San Francisco: Jossey-Bass, 1990.

Burns, James MacGregor. *Leadership*. New York: Harper & Row, 1978.

Cohen, Stephen R. *Principle-Centered Leadership*. New York: Simon and Schuster, 1991.

Conger, Jay A. *Learning to Lead: The Art of Transforming Managers into Leaders*. San Francisco: Jossey-Bass, 1992.

Covey, Stephen R. *The Seven Habits of Highly Effective People: Restoring the Character Ethic*. New York: Simon and Schuster, 1990.

Denhardt, Robert B., and Janet Vinzant Denhardt. *The Dance of Leadership: The Art of Leading in Business, Government, and Society*. Armonk, NY: M.E. Sharpe, 2006.

Denhardt, Robert B., Janet Vinzant Denhardt, and Maria Pilar Aristigueta. *Managing Human Behavior in Public and Nonprofit Organizations*. Thousand Oaks, CA: Sage Publications, 2001.

Fischer, Roger, and William Ury. *Getting to Yes*. 2nd ed. New York: Penguin Books, 1991.

Garnett, James L. *Communicating for Results in Government: A Strategic Approach for Public Managers*. San Francisco: Jossey-Bass, 1992.

Heifetz, Ronald A., and Martin Linsky. *Leadership on the Line: Staying Alive through the Dangers of Leading*. Boston, MA: Harvard Business School Press, 2002.

Helgesen, Sally. *The Web of Inclusion: A New Architecture for Building Great Organizations*. New York: Currency/Doubleday, 1995.

Holzer, Mark, ed. *Public Service: Callings, Commitments, and Contributions*. Boulder, CO: Westview Press, 2000.

Kee, James Edwin, and Kathryn E. Newcomer. *Transforming Public and Nonprofit Organizations: Stewardship for Leading Change*. Vienna, VA: Management Concepts, 2008.

King, Cheryl Simrell, and Camilla Stivers, eds. *Government Is Us: Public Administration in an Anti-Government Era*. Thousand Oaks, CA: Sage Publications, 1998.

Kouzes, James M., and Barry Z. Posner. *The Leadership Challenge*. 4th ed. San Francisco: Jossey-Bass, 2008.

Murray, Nancy. *An Inner Voice for Public Administration*. Westport, CT: Praeger Publishers, 1997.

National Academy of Public Administration. *Leading People in Change: Empowerment, Commitment, Accountability*. Washington, DC: National Academy, 1993.

Raffel, Jeffrey A., Peter Leisink, and Anthony E. Middlebrooks. *Public Sector Leadership: International Challenges and Perspectives*. Cheltenham, UK; Northampton, MA: Edward Elgar, 2009.

Schein, Edgar H. *Helping: How to Offer, Give, and Receive Help*. San Francisco: Berrett-Koehler, 2009.

Vroom, Victor H., and Arthur G. Jago. *The New Leadership*. Englewood Cliffs, NJ: Prentice-Hall, 1988.

APPENDIX

"Lost on the Moon" Exercise: Answers from NASA Experts

1. Two 100-pound tanks of oxygen: most pressing survival need

2. Five gallons of water: replacement for tremendous liquid loss on lighted side

3. Stellar map of the moon's constellation: primary means of navigation

4. Food concentrate: efficient means of supplying energy requirements

5. Solar-powered FM receiver-transmitter: for communication with mothership; but FM requires line-of-sight transmission and short ranges

6. Fifty feet of nylon rope: useful in scaling cliffs, tying injured together

7. First-aid kit containing injection needles: needles for vitamins, medicines, and so forth; will fit special aperture in NASA spacesuits

8. Parachute silk: protection from sun's rays

9. Self-inflating life raft: Carbon monoxide bottle in military raft may be used for propulsion

10. Signal flares: distress signal when mothership is sighted

11. Two .45-caliber pistols: possible means of self-propulsion

12. One case of dehydrated evaporated milk: bulkier duplication of food concentrate

13. Solar-powered portable heating unit: not needed unless on dark side

14. Magnetic compass: magnetic field on moon is not polarized; worthless for navigation

15. Box of matches: no oxygen on moon to sustain flame; virtually worthless

CHAPTER 10

ADMINISTRATIVE REFORM, PRODUCTIVITY, AND PERFORMANCE

The history of public administration is a history of reform. When Woodrow Wilson and his contemporaries wrote about the separation of politics and administration, signaling the emergence of the field of public administration, they did so in the context of political and institutional reform. The Progressive Reform Movement, which began in the late 1880s, sought to reduce corruption and enhance professionalism in public service, in part by reducing the power of political parties. Although this movement marks an important time in the history of the field of public administration, the truth is that the field has been in the process of being "reformed" ever since. Recent history has been no exception. As Kettl (2009) notes, "Government reform has been a staple of presidential management for the last 50 years," from President Kennedy's "whiz kids" and President Johnson's planning-programming-budgeting system (PPBS) to President George Bush's performance system tied to the budget (p. 39). In the broadest sense, all of these reforms represent, at least in part, an ongoing attempt to reconcile the need for administrative efficiency and democratic accountability. This chapter will focus on major reforms that have emphasized increasing administrative efficiency as well as look at the role of technology in changing the way government works.

Over the past twenty years, a primary focus of reform has been the "New Public Management," or "reinventing government." As we will see, the New Public Management is significantly different from the New Public Administration described in Chapter 8. The New Public Management (NPM) is based on a belief that public organizations—or, more accurately, the systems underlying public organizations—lack the capacity to meet the challenges and opportunities of the twenty-first century and need to be thoroughly reformed. Again, the concept of reinvention and the broader effort of NPM in many ways can be considered approaches to a rather old question: how can we improve government performance and accountability?

However, the reform movement in the public and nonprofit sectors should not be equated simply with a call for increased productivity. Proponents of reform recognize that public and nonprofit agencies, particularly in America, constitute some of the most productive institutions in the world, even more so than private institutions. (For example, over the past generation, government productivity has increased at double the national average.) Instead, NPM and other reformist themes suggest that government should not account merely for its own activities but should be assessed on its capacity to achieve substantial public outcomes.

NPM and reinvention are, however, closely related to issues of quality and productivity in government. The two stem from similar sources. Concern about government productivity centers on issues of efficiency and accountability. These issues have, of course, been debated throughout the country's history; modern expression is typically dated back to the passage of Proposition 13, a tax limitation initiative passed by California voters in the late 1970s. Following the California example, other states and localities also began efforts to limit what voters perceived as the excessive cost of government services.

At the federal level, the desire to avoid new taxes meant the reduction or elimination of numerous domestic programs. Many of these programs provided aid to state and local governments. When the reductions were combined with the desire to limit state and local taxation, many governments were severely constrained in trying to provide sufficient revenues to support important, even basic, services. But despite these limitations, these governments were often asked to "do more with less," to provide increased services with the same or even with reduced funding.

We examined some of the implications of this situation in Chapter 5 with respect to budgeting and financial management, as many governments were forced to search for alternate funding methods, including privatization and so forth. But the same governments also sought new ways to improve both the quality and quantity of work without extra cost. Many governments and agencies at all levels initiated new solutions or at least intensified efforts to find them, tried to break from the traditional assumptions, and searched for more effective means of meeting their objectives.

Public organizations started to lose their traditional bureaucratic structure, becoming instead more lateral systems of shared power and teamwork. Systems of management, too, were transformed into more equitable, less controlling forms of leadership. And government agencies began to form meaningful partnerships with other institutions and citizens in response to public problems. Nongovernmental organizations (NGOs) also underwent a transformation of sorts. During the 1990s, NGOs became drivers of policy issues in a variety of areas, such as human rights, economic development, urban revitalization, and even governmental reform.

Advances in information technology (IT) played an integral role in transforming public and nonprofit organizations worldwide. The impact was twofold. First, increased capacity for communication and information sharing redefined the distribution of authority within institutions. Every member of the organization had access to the latest news and information, and so shared one of the more important sources of power. Second, IT enabled public and nonprofit organizations to engage more effectively with their counterparts in other sectors and around the world, as well as with citizens. Such change restructured the ways in which governments and other public service agencies responded to opportunities and challenges.

So whether we call it an effect of NPM, reinvention, or efforts to improve quality and productivity, public and nonprofit administration at the beginning of the twenty-first century is quite different from that of merely a generation ago. The ways in which we organize ourselves, engage with others, and respond to public concerns have undergone a huge change or, to use Kettl's phrase, "a transformation in governance" (Kettl, 2000, p. 488). Yet, as we explore the various aspects of reform, keep asking these questions: Have we improved service to the public? Is the work we are doing today consistent with our expectations for a system of democratic governance? Are we truly acting in the interest of citizens?

New Public Management, Reinvention, the Management Agenda, and Nonprofit Reform

The current reform agenda in public administration can be traced to several worldwide trends. First, and perhaps most significant, the social, political, and economic dialogue in industrialized countries underwent a rightward shift during the late 1970s and early 1980s, as political leaders recognized the unsustainable nature of comprehensive, centralized systems of public service delivery. Leaders in Europe, Asia, and North America started to examine more cost-efficient, effective ways of providing public services, including public welfare, transportation, health care, and others. Second, fiscal challenges brought on by the changing nature of the global economy prompted scholars and practitioners to explore new ways of thinking about public administration. By the early 1990s, many public managers around the world, using slogans like NPM and reinvention, had embarked on a journey to restructure bureaucratic agencies, streamline agency processes, and decentralize policy decision making.

The New Public Management

The New Public Management, or NPM, is a term used to describe a set of principles and practices in the public service that has emerged during the past several decades in a variety of countries around the world (Barzelay, 2001, p. xi). Although the application of NPM has varied country by country, the reform agenda has remained consistent in its drive to create organizations that are mission-driven, decentralized, and incentive-based. Reformers strive for more flexible public organizations and more responsive interorganizational networks, guided by the key principles of accountability, responsiveness, and a commitment to outcome-based governance (Boston, 1996; Peters, 1994).

Perhaps the best example of the NPM principles at work can be seen in New Zealand's administrative reforms. Beginning in 1985, New Zealand's national government took several bold steps aimed at transforming its system of public administration. Among the most significant reforms, the government redeveloped its personnel system as an attempt to make top executives more performance-oriented; instituted a comprehensive performance measurement system based on a new process of measuring the productivity and effectiveness of government agencies; and reengineered its departmental systems to reflect the Labour administration's commitment to governmental accountability (Boston, 1996).

The effectiveness of New Zealand's reform agenda, as well as parallel activities in Canada, Great Britain, and the United States, prompted public administration reformers around the world to adopt many of the principles from NPM, as well as use these principles as a new framework for public policy and governance (Barzelay, 2001, pp. xi–xv; see also Kettl, 1997). For example, reports from the United Nations' Commission on Global Governance and other international bodies reinforced this international movement, advocating decentralized decision making, civil society, empowerment, and a reliance on third-sector organizations for achieving public outcomes (Commission on Global Governance, 1995).

Reinventing Government

In the early 1990s, Osborne and Gaebler's (1992) landmark work, *Reinventing Government*, brought many of the NPM principles to American shores. For Osborne and Gaebler, the reform agenda represented a response to what they call "the bankruptcy of bureaucracy"—that is, the ineffectiveness of government organizations. The authors believed that public agencies had failed to keep pace with changing conditions in the postindustrial society, with government still attempting to respond to public issues with a "one-size-fits-all" approach. As a result, the systems in which public administrators function had become the problem, not the solution, and consequently citizens had begun to lose faith in the capacity of government to serve their needs.

A central theme in reinvention is that only more entrepreneurial forms of government will enable public administrators to effectively deal with problems and capitalize on opportunities in contemporary society. Yet, in contrast to most interpretations, Osborne and Gaebler actually avoided the more traditional view that government should be run like a business: "Government and business are fundamentally different institutions. Business leaders are driven by the profit motive; government leaders are driven by the desire to get reelected.... Differences such as these create fundamentally different incentives in the public sector" (p. 20). Although encouraging public administrators to derive insights from successful experiences in all sectors, Osborne and Gaebler maintain that public- and private-sector organizations face a distinct array of challenges.

What Would You Do?

You are a top-level manager in a state transportation department. You have been planning to widen and realign an existing highway that runs through some of the most picturesque countryside in the state, part of which is in a national forest and the remainder of which is in two different resort communities and the county. There are several businesses along the route, all of which could be hurt if the new highway pulls traffic away. Some of your staff have suggested a lengthy process of public involvement in the design of the highway. You are concerned, however, that such a process could raise major controversies and take at least an extra year. You think the highway is needed now. What would you do?

Entrepreneurial government, then, refers to more streamlined, flexible, and responsive systems of public policy and administration. Osborne and Gaebler cite example after example of public organizations that had chosen innovative strategies for doing more with less, thus increasing the value of public services without raising costs for public consumers. These strategies ranged from privatization efforts in Phoenix, Arizona, that enhanced competition among service providers, thus significantly raising performance standards, to public school initiatives in East Harlem, New York, that empowered residents with greater choice for students' learning opportunities. The authors suggest that the common themes of competition and empowerment, combined with more attention to public outcomes and action based on customer priorities rather than bureaucratic imperatives, represent the future of successful government.

To carry out the reform agenda, Osborne and Gaebler provide ten principles underlying reinvention and public entrepreneurship:

1. Catalytic government: steering rather than rowing
2. Community-owned government: empowering rather than serving
3. Competitive government: injecting competition into service delivery
4. Mission-driven government: transforming rule-driven organizations
5. Results-oriented government: funding outcomes, not inputs
6. Customer-driven government: meeting the needs of the customer, not the bureaucracy
7. Enterprising government: earning rather than spending
8. Anticipatory government: prevention rather than cure
9. Decentralized government: from hierarchy to participation and teamwork
10. Market-oriented government: leveraging change through the market

Osborne and Gaebler intended these ten principles to serve as a new conceptual framework for public administration—an analytical checklist to transform the actions of government. "What we are describing is nothing less than a shift in the basic model of governance used in America. This shift is under way all around us, but because we are not looking for it—because we assume that all governments have to be big, centralized, and bureaucratic—we seldom see it. We are blind to the new realities, because they do not fit our preconceptions" (p. 321). By applying the ten reinvention principles in the context of any given policy area, a new universe of opportunity, an altogether different system of governance, would evolve.

Networking

> Global perspectives on NPM are available from the OECD Public Management and Governance Service at www.oecd.org.

The Management Agenda

The "reinvention" movement was the centerpiece of the Clinton administration's effort to bring about administrative reform. But, as we have already mentioned in previous chapters, George W. Bush also initiated several managerial reforms in the executive branch of the federal government—though these efforts continue to build on the basic ideas of NPM. The President's Management Agenda (PMA) emphasized five core initiatives:

- Strategic management of human capital
- Competitive sourcing
- Improved financial performance

- Expanded e-government
- Budget performance integration

For each of these reforms, President Bush appointed four political appointees in the Office of Management and Budget (OMB), and one in the Office of Personnel Management (OPM), as "owners" who should be held accountable for the success of the initiatives (Breul, 2007). In addition, the Bush administration developed an "Executive Branch Management Scorecard to track the implementation of the PMA," known as the Program Assessment Rating Tool (PART). PART is essentially a questionnaire designed to follow the implementation of the executive programs in terms of meeting the requirements imposed by the PMA. It is discussed in more detail later in this chapter.

President Obama has continued the focus on performance management, but also has emphasized governmental transparency as a key strategy to improve governmental performance. As noted in Chapter 7, Obama issued a memorandum on "Transparency and Open Government" with the statement "Openness will strengthen our democracy and promote efficiency and effectiveness in government" (Obama, Presidential Memorandum, 2009). The Obama administration has also emphasized the role of citizen involvement in government. Both of these developments are discussed more fully later in this chapter with regard to technology and in Chapter 11 in relation to democratic reforms.

Nonprofit Management Reform

Since the 1990s, the reform agenda in government has had a substantial impact on the nonprofit sector. We have discussed the interconnected nature of public-nonprofit relations, but as governments use contracts, grants, and other strategies to devolve public services to nonprofits, they also have begun to hold their not-for-profit counterparts accountable to many of the same performance and outcome objectives. Consequently, nonprofit organizations in today's world find themselves buoyed by the "tides of reform" affecting the public sector (Light, 2000).

The factors precipitating reform in the nonprofit sector, of course, go beyond those that are government-imposed. In fact, Paul Light (2000, pp. 17–43) has identified several important trends influencing the nonprofit reform movement, including "nationalizing trends" relating to productivity, recruitment, resource development, and technology, combined with "local realities" of ensuring consistency, building patterns of shared responsibility, and enhancing nonprofit capacity for public service delivery.

Unfortunately, nonprofit organizations have experienced less of the tides of reform and more of a tidal wave! "The nonprofit sector has never been under greater pressure to improve. Despite two decades of phenomenal growth, the sector suffers from a general impression that it is less efficient and more wasteful than its government and private competitors. Even if the sector could prove that it has achieved 'ordinary excellence,' spending money wisely and producing measurable results as a natural by-product of organizational design, it faces a serious public relations problem among clients and funders alike" (Light, 2000, p. 1). As a result, nonprofits have been flooded with demands to reform systems of administration, service delivery, and accountability, with each set of demands often reflecting divergent philosophies.

As Light explains, the movement to enhance productivity and accountability in nonprofit organizations can be categorized into these four reformist principles:

1. Scientific Management—Management should be based on the "one best way," with individual organizations seeking to implement codes of internal conduct and basic best practices of administration.
2. War on Waste—Management should be based on a drive for external efficiency, with organizations and alliances reengineering to achieve efficient, streamlined systems for administration and service delivery.
3. Watchful Eye—Management should be based on creating more transparent patterns of administration, with organizational stakeholders holding agencies accountable for openness and compliance.
4. Liberation Management—Management should be based on achieving positive outcomes, with agencies working together in the public interest (pp. 46–71).

While on a theoretical level these philosophies may not seem incompatible, the struggle to apply such principles in management practice has taken a toll on nonprofits. Indeed, when faced with competing demands by funders and donors, a single nonprofit may find itself swept away in attempts to implement multiple reform strategies at the same time. Foundations, government grant-makers, and other institutions that provide financial support to nonprofit organizations, even at the local level, have a poor track record for engaging in a substantive dialogue concerning policies and procedures, much less for coordinating funding programs and reporting standards. As a result, nonprofits must be prepared to structure their administrative practices and reporting systems to correspond with each funder's demands.

The problem here, though, is that few can agree on what constitutes a "good" nonprofit, this despite an emerging trend for foundations and government grant-makers to fund "capacity-building" activities (for discussion, see Greene, 2001, pp. 1–12). Although scholars, management consultants, and program officers have attempted to bring order out of chaos, the results have amounted to little more than platitudes. The *Chronicle for Philanthropy,* for example, offered the following "expert tips":

- Management challenges are normal for nonprofit organizations.... There are no quick fixes....
- Ideas are nothing, thinking is everything.... Proffer the pole, not the fish....
- In times of great change, our support can reap great dividends.... Don't redesign the kitchen while the house is on fire....
- Speak the truth....
- Change demands a champion....
- Building a nonprofit organization is a long, hard haul.... We don't know enough yet.... (Kibbe, 2001, p. 10)

Even the application of a particular reformist agenda may be carried out in different ways, depending on those implementing the strategy and on what level the implementation occurs. For example, a United Way–based "outcome measurement" system in one community may vary significantly from another just miles away; or the definition of "impact" as interpreted at the state level may be off the mark with agencies at the grassroots.

The challenge for nonprofit management in the future will be to balance the drive to adopt sound management practices from the private sector with a dedication to public service. Such a balance will be difficult, though, as demands for reform seem to be increasing, and the tides appear to be toward the former rather than the latter. Perhaps even more important, greater attention needs to be placed on those activities that fall outside of the individual nonprofit. Foundations, government agencies, and other funders, in conjunction with the nonprofits they support, must begin a more substantive dialogue around ways to coordinate grant-making and reporting requirements, as a way of bringing a level of consistency and coordination to an increasingly fragmented public policy process, and of easing the administrative burden on nonprofit organizations. Indeed, reforming the nonprofit sector will be as much about improving the dialogue among leaders in philanthropy, business, and government as it is about building the capacity of nonprofit organizations.

The Results of NPM and Reinvention

It will be some time before we can fully assess the impact of NPM, reinvention, and the drive to improve nonprofit organizations. However, many have begun to question the lessons learned from the reform movements. Proponents point out that some of the key reform-oriented initiatives, such as the Government Performance and Results Act (GPRA), have helped improve public service. Kathryn Newcomer and Aaron Otto (2000) recently summarized some of GPRA's benefits at the federal level:

- Amplifying conflicting/polarizing expectations—GPRA has raised consciousness over some of the terms and concepts underlying management reform (p. 1).
- Strengthening programmatic communities—Federal agencies have started working more collaboratively on achieving shared objectives (p. 2).
- Asking the right questions about program performance—GPRA has helped to enhance the quality of the discourse around performance measurement (p. 2).
- Effectively reporting performance—Federal officials have improved their agencies' capacity for accurately and appropriately measuring program impacts (pp. 2, 6).

On the other hand, critics of NPM and reinvention suggest that even though certain aspects of the reform agenda have contributed to meaningful improvements in public service, the application of these principles has produced a variety of negative externalities not envisioned by early reformers. In practice, the adoption of business practices and the reliance on market forces by public organizations have degenerated into a sense of *managerialism*—a belief that government could and should be run like a business based on strictly economic principles. As public managers began to apply their reform agendas, many focused on administrative efficiency more than on the democratic principles of effective governance.

Another point of concern is that the reform movement has concentrated on customer-centered instead of citizen-centered public administration. Critics argue that "citizens are not the customers of government; they are its owners who elect leaders to represent their interests. A customer-centered model puts citizens in a reactive role limited to liking or disliking services and hoping that administrators will change delivery if enough customers

CourseReader Assignment

Log in to **www.cengage.com** and open CourseReader to access the reading:

Read "Reforming Public Management: Analyzing the Impact of Public Service Reform on Organizational and Managerial Trust," by R. Paul Battaglio, Jr., and Stephen E. Condrey. In this chapter we have discussed the New Public Management (NPM), which this article explores in more detail. While the NPM has been advocated as a way of improving quality and productivity in public organizations, there are some unintended consequences that cause more concern. One is the impact on organizational and managerial trust.

What do you see as the advantages and disadvantages of the NPM? What are the values that underlie the NPM? How do those square with the values of democratic administration?

object" (Schachter, 1995, p. 530, citing Frederickson, 1994). In contrast, citizen-centered public administration restores the public to an ownership position—a proactive relationship in which citizens engage with the institutions of governance to achieve public outcomes.

Despite this criticism, however, the NPM and reinvention movements have had a pervasive impact on public administration in this country and around the world. As we will see later in the chapter, the principles underlying these reform efforts have contributed to major initiatives to enhance government performance and accountability. Public organizations at all levels have employed a variety of strategies to streamline work processes and enhance the public service.

Information and Communication Technologies

Advances in information and communication technologies (ICT) over the last two decades have permeated nearly every aspect of public organizations, revolutionizing the way in which government and citizens interact. An explosion of digital information is being shared in a multitude of ways in order to create value, and a proliferation of communication networks allows interaction that spans the globe regardless of time or location (Dawes, 2010). Beginning with the personal computer revolution in the early 1980s, technology has been a central part of the drive to increase performance in public organizations. By the beginning of the twenty-first century, advances in technology and the rise of the Internet had governments turning to online resources for many of their core functions, including economic development, human and social service delivery, health care, and citizen engagement. In less than a generation, advances in ICT and the Internet have helped reshape our notions of government and public space.

These advances represent a new paradigm for governments that focuses on applying technology in a way that "will make the citizen-government relationship more inclusive and more direct" (Deloitte, 2002, p. 21). In this new paradigm, government is more accountable, more transparent, and more trustworthy (Chun et al., 2010). This new paradigm, however, has not been fully realized. Dawes (2010), for example, points out that "the networked society is fraught with complexity and vulnerable to new threats—threats to stability, privacy, security, and stewardship" (p. s86). Others suggest that while the use of technology in government will continue to increase, with more sophisticated websites, better applications, and the availability of more services and information, it has not yet fulfilled "the promise of a more efficient, effective, and democratic public administration" (Helbig, Gil-García, & Ferro, 2005, p. 1), nor has it led to any meaningful transformation or reform of government and its relationship with citizens (Norris, 2010).

Technology and Management Reform

From a management perspective, the most immediate impact of ICT has been to redefine our concept of organization. Intranets, e-mail, and other networking resources have allowed, or in some cases forced, agencies to transform work processes and integrate strategies for meeting public objectives. The Internet, global e-mail, and increasingly sophisticated mobile devices have transformed communication not only within but also with government. Public records now are "born digital" rather than on paper, and information is made widely available across a variety of networks, resulting in boundaries between organizations, sectors, and levels of government "becoming more permeable as information is used and reused in interconnected, overlapping organizational networks that often reach deeply into the nonprofit and private sectors" (Dawes, 2010, p. s86). Governments interact with citizens, business, and other governments much more routinely through electronic means such as e-mail, websites, and interactive voice systems than in person or on paper, and they also are beginning to cross the boundary between the physical and the digital by becoming involved in "virtual electronic worlds" (Dawes, p. s86).

The application of technology has not been limited to the federal government, as state and local authorities also have made the move to take the "business of government" online (Swope, 2004). State governments across the country are capitalizing on advancements in ICT to create seamless systems of service delivery in areas such as health care, education, public safety, and corrections. At the local level, public agencies are using ICT to manage the regulatory process, interact with citizens, and increase the efficiency of public services. We mentioned the city of Baltimore's use of Citistat in Chapter 7 in our discussion of financial management systems. Another role of Baltimore's Citistat has been to track the effectiveness of interagency partnerships in addressing important health and human service concerns. For example, as part of its "Leadstat" initiative, city officials use GIS technology to pinpoint actual cases of lead poisoning, using a red "dot" on a GIS map, and then assess the effectiveness of their abatement strategies by monitoring the number of dots that change from red to green, which indicates a successful abatement (Swope, 2001, p. 23).

Advances in ICT and the rise of the technology sector also have made a significant impact on the philanthropic sector, opening new doors for resource development and performance measurement. During the late 1990s, the boom in high-tech firms created a new generation of philanthropists. The Bill and Melinda Gates Foundation of Seattle, for example, which was established by the family of Microsoft's multibillion-dollar chairman, became the nation's largest foundation, which controlled approximately $37 billion in assets as of 2010.

Many nonprofits also began using the new technologies as a way of expanding their strategies for fund-raising. Some charities now use their websites to take in direct contributions, and many more have turned to e-mail, social media, and other forms of electronic engagement to solicit gifts from more e-savvy philanthropists. Goodwill Industries has taken this to new ends, using an eBay-type online auction house to raise money for its education, training, and job placement programs for people with disabilities. The Internet also has spawned a number of online fund-raising collaboratives that raise money on behalf of several philanthropic organizations (Hruby, 2001). One such collaborative, Network for Good (www1.networkforgood.org), enables individuals and organizations to research charities, make donations, and find volunteer opportunities. As of 2012, Network for Good had collected and distributed more than $500 million to more than 60,000 nonprofit organizations via its website.

E-Government and E-Governance

The term *electronic government* has come to refer to the government's use of technology to provide information, deliver services, support operations, and interact with citizens, businesses, and other governments at any time from any place. The evolution of e-government has been described as occurring in stages, moving from a basic electronic presence providing web-based information to simple interactions with external stakeholders via e-mail and interactive forms, to the provision of electronic transaction services (such as licenses, permits, and tax payments), and, finally, to a transformative process of shared governance through the seamless flow of information, opportunities for meaningful dialogue and citizen participation, and collaborative decision making (Chun et al., 2010).

Although the terms *e-government* and *e-governance* often are used interchangeably in reference to the use of technology in government, there are those who argue that the latter represents a broader, more normative view that includes "not only services and administration but also democratic processes and the relationships among citizens, civil society, the private sector, and the state" (Dawes, 2010, p. s87). E-governance can be considered in terms of five goals: developing a policy framework that addresses the way in which information is gathered, used, protected, and shared; enhancing public services; improving the quality and cost-effectiveness of government operations; engaging citizens in democratic processes; and creating administrative and institutional reform. To date, e-governance in the United States has been most successful in enhancing public services

Networking

Check out the National Center for Digital Governance at http://www.umass.edu/digitalcenter/index.html, the Center for Technology in Government at www.ctg.albany.edu, and the National Science Foundation Digital Government Research Program at www.digitalgovernment.org.

and improving operations, as governments have been most heavily focused on management and service improvements. There has been some progress in policy development, while relatively few government entities have pursued citizen engagement and administrative and institutional reform goals in e-governance (Dawes, 2010).

Despite concerns over progress toward the more transformational goals of e-governance, it is clear that the use of ITC to provide information and services has become a way of life at all levels of government. Virtually all federal agencies and states and most local governments have established websites, although they may vary in quality and ease of use. In 2000 the White House launched FirstGov.gov, which has now been changed to USA .gov. This site provides citizens, businesses and organizations, and federal employees access to a wide variety of information and government services, including those for finding a government job, applying for a passport, finding the cheapest gas prices, shopping government auctions, and replacing personal records. USA.gov also offers links to websites for federal agencies and state, local, and tribal governments. The White House also maintains its own website, www.whitehouse.gov. States are using e-government approaches as well. For example, the Texas Health and Human Services Commission's "2-1-1 Texas" program allows citizens to connect with more than 60,000 state and local health and human services programs through a single web portal or by dialing 2-1-1. In Kansas, the Department of Health has established a web-based Health Information Exchange to share confidential information among public health professionals across the state. The city of Seattle's website, which the Center for Digital Government named as the best municipal website in the United States in 2011, links citizens to information about government processes, programs, events, service opportunities, online neighborhood communities, and more and allows users to create their own customizable city web portals through My.Seattle.Gov. It also provides access to a wide variety of data generated by city departments through data.Seattle.gov. For an up-to-date list of state and local government websites, visit www.statelocalgov.net/index.cfm.

Governments may be lagging in the creation of opportunities for citizen engagement through technology; however, more and more citizens are using ICT to access government information and services at all levels. According to a 2010 study conducted by the Pew Internet and American Life Project, 82 percent of all American adults who use the Internet said they had looked for information or completed a transaction on a government website in the past twelve months. Recent efforts by government agencies to increase transparency by making data about a variety of activities available online have not gone unnoticed, as 40 percent of online adults visited at least one site that provides access to government data, such as www.recovery.gov. Internet users also are seeking ways to share their views on government policies and issues, as nearly a quarter (23 percent) participated in online discussions, many of which occurred in nongovernment arenas. The Pew report also noted that about a third of online adults are going beyond government websites, turning to blogs, social networking sites, e-mail, online video, or text messaging to find information about the government (Smith, 2010).

The move beyond the use of traditional websites in order to interact has come about through a set of technologies known collectively as "Web 2.0," which, in addition to allowing users to access information, enables them to share information, connect and collaborate with others, and become actively involved in creating content. These interactive technologies include social media such as Facebook, Twitter, and other networks; YouTube; open data portals (such as the Seattle site mentioned earlier); blogs; wikis, mashups, widgets, and virtual worlds; and more. These technologies are being adopted at all levels of government at a rapid pace. For example, in 2011, 87 percent of the largest cities in the United States used Twitter, compared with 25 percent in 2009. Facebook use in these cities rose to 87 percent from 13 percent in the same period, and the appearance of YouTube links on these cities' websites jumped from 16 percent in 2009 to 75 percent in 2011. The use of open data portals has been less prevalent, with only 12 of the 75 largest cities having created such a tool as of 2011 (Mossberger & Wu, 2012). This rise in the use of interactive technology obviously presents the potential to expand citizen engagement; however, some argue that this potential is being limited by the fact that these tools are still used primarily in the traditional one-way manner of communication (Bryer & Zavattaro, 2011). There is some evidence that governments are hesitant to "give up control or power of the message, using the platforms as public relations and marketing tools to craft and shape an image" (Bryer & Zavattaro, 2011, p. 332). If this is the case, these technologies are simply another way for government to provide information to citizens, rather than driving a fundamental change in the relationship between government and citizens.

There are other limitations and challenges to interactive technologies as well. ICT almost always involves significant resource commitments. Even though federal, state, and local government have invested billions of dollars in technology over the last two decades, budget restrictions often make it difficult for jurisdictions to develop and maintain websites and technology-related services. Security is of primary concern as well. Not only must systems be protected from viruses and hacking, but sensitive information and transactions must be safeguarded so they are not revealed or used inappropriately. Privacy also is an issue. The Privacy Act of 1974 limits the amount of information the federal government can collect about individuals and regulates how that information can be used. For platforms launched by a government entity, administrators need to control any information collected and stored. This process becomes more complicated when jurisdictions use the services of a third-party provider, such as Facebook. A jurisdiction may have less control over what is done with information in this case, as it is not clear who owns the information (Bryer & Zavattaro, 2011). Other concerns include ethical implications; ensuring broad-based access; and the management of electronic records and archives.

Despite these challenges, there is great potential in e-government and e-governance. At the very least, the quality and range of services are likely to grow, and the use of ICT to provide access to and interact with citizens "will be largely institutionalized and routinized within governments—so much so that we may no longer refer to it as e-government at all, but will view [it] as just another way of accessing government information and services" (Norris, 2010, p. s181). Beyond the routine provision of information and services, however, there is great potential for coordination and collaboration in addressing public problems at all levels. The use of Web 2.0 platforms and tools offers the possibility of a new role for government in which "government opens its doors to the world; co-innovates with everyone, especially citizens; shares resources that previously were closely guarded; harnesses the power of mass collaboration; drives transparency throughout its operations; and behaves not as an isolated department or jurisdiction, but something new—a truly integrated system" (Roberts, 2011, p. 687). In order to realize this potential, both government and citizens must be willing to adopt new behaviors to go along with new technology. Rather than continuing to use ICT in the traditional one-way model, what will be needed is a conscious effort by government to create ICT policies and procedures that bring citizens together, giving them a more central role and enabling and encouraging them to become actively engaged in the process of finding solutions to public problems.

Performance Measurement

Over the last two decades, *performance measurement* has "emerged as the most important form of public sector management reform in many years" (Gilmour & Lewis, 2006, p. 742), as citizens, legislators, and advocacy groups have begun demanding more value from public organizations. Government increasingly has been under pressure to prove that substantive results, or outcomes related to a program's public effectiveness, are generated by its activities. However, because of the lack of profit motive in most government programs, it can be difficult to assess which programs generate desirable outcomes and which ones do not. Performance measurement offers a means to produce quantitative evidence about program outcomes that show how well a program is meeting its goals.

A distinction should be made here between inputs, outputs, and outcomes: inputs are resources—financial, human, and otherwise—available to the organization; outputs are actual goods or services produced by an organization; and outcomes are long-term objectives that the organization wants to achieve. As an illustration, the Federal Aviation Administration issues regulations, which constitute one type of its outputs. But someone measuring the performance of this organization would be only moderately interested in the number of regulations it issues. More important would be the effect of the regulations on desired goals, such as improved air safety. Improved air safety would be an outcome. Generally speaking, objectives are likely to be narrow and specific, directly tied to each organization's particular activities; outcomes, on the other hand, are related to the larger purposes to be served by the organization's work.

As the call for "reinventing government" gained strength in the early 1990s, the move toward performance measurement occurred at all levels of government. Federal agencies developed performance standards at the program level and in their management and administrative functions. State and local governments followed suit, both as a means of assessing their activities and of enhancing their reporting under federal programs (Wholey, Hatry, & Newcomer, 1994). In 1993, performance measurement became law at the federal level under the Government Performance and Results Act (GPRA), which was designed to push agencies to link planning and performance outcomes to budgeting. GPRA required federal agencies to develop long-term strategic plans and annual performance plans, both outlining the strategies and resources needed to meet performance goals and to produce annual reports on the outcomes achieved (Rubin & Willoughby, 2011). Within these plans, federal agencies identified *performance indicators*—specific, quantifiable goals that the agency strives for in pursuit of its objectives—that reflected each agency's outputs and outcomes.

Networking

Information about the performance outcomes of federal agencies is available through Performance.gov (www.performance.gov/). Information about government performance issues is available from the Office of Management and Budget (www.whitehouse.gov/omb/performance), OMB Watch (www.ombwatch.org/government_performance/), and the Congressional Institute (www.conginst.org/).

Concerned that data generated by GPRA were not being used to assess performance in order to guide program funding decisions, President George W. Bush, as mentioned earlier, instituted the Program Assessment Rating Tool (PART) in 2002 as part of his President's Management Agenda (PMA). Intended to link performance information with decisions about program funding, PART was used to rate programs in four areas: program purpose and design, strategic planning, program management, and program results. "The goal was not simply to measure inputs and outputs—how many children, for example, stepped through the doors of a Head Start program—but to evaluate outcomes, such as whether they left it healthier and smarter" (Zeller, 2009, p. 708). Whereas GPRA focused on agencies, PART was aimed at programs. It went beyond GPRA in that it made judgments about whether programs were effective by assessing their management and results; it also allowed decision makers to impose budgetary and management consequences on programs that were unable to demonstrate their effectiveness (Breul & Kamensky, 2008).

Although PART was used under the Bush administration to assess more than 1,000 federal programs, its impact on decision making was limited. One problem was the fact that while many programs could not demonstrate results according to PART criteria, that did not necessarily mean that these programs were ineffective (Joyce, 2007). Another issue was that a "one size fits all" approach to the evaluation process did not take into account the diversity in how federal programs are structured, resulting in programs that had problems in meeting PART stipulations (Radin, 2010). Politics also played a role in limiting the use of PART evaluations to make budget decisions, as political considerations sometimes kept alive programs that had been deemed as wasteful or unnecessary (Vlk, 2011).

Soon after taking office, President Obama announced as part of the 2010 budget his plans to "fundamentally reconfigure" the way in which the federal government assesses program performance by replacing PART with a new performance improvement and analysis framework that would move the focus from grading programs on their level of success to requiring agency heads to set priority goals, demonstrate progress in achieving goals, and explain performance trends (OMB, 2009, p. 9). The Obama administration argued that while GPRA and PART had led to the development of better performance measures, performance data still were not being used to improve program performance. The administration's initial strategy for improving performance and the use of data focused on creating consistent leadership in the Office of Management and Budget (OMB), appointing a chief performance officer and an associate OMB director for performance and personnel management, directing all major federal agencies to identify a limited number of high-priority goals, and making a commitment to "maximize the productive use of performance data" (Newcomer and Caudle, 2011, p. 118).

In 2010, Congress amended GPRA through the GPRA Modernization Act (GPRAMA), which created "a more defined performance framework by defining a governance structure and by better connecting plans, programs, and performance information" (Kamensky, 2011, p. 141). GPRAMA mandates the setting of long-term federal priority goals and requires agencies to set performance goals consistent with the priority goals. Agency performance goals require quarterly, rather than annual, reporting and reviews aimed at increasing the use of performance data in program decision making, made public through a government website (www.performance.gov). GPRAMA also expands opportunities for congressional involvement in setting goals and measuring performance; formalizes the use of agency performance improvement officers; and requires OMB "to coordinate the development of outcome-priority goals in a limited number of crosscutting policy areas" (Rubin & Willoughby, 2011, p. 16).

The long-term impact of GPRA, PART, and GPRAMA remains to be seen. As Rubin and Willoughby point out, even though observers have noted an improvement in integrating performance data in the budget process, "there is still a long way to go before performance information is the main driver used to allocate government's increasingly scarce resources" (p. 17). However, Kamensky (2011) argues that the shift from a traditional agency- and program-based model of performance to "one premised on portfolios of services and results" brought about by the Obama administration and congressional initiatives constitutes a "performance revolution," one that is likely to change roles and relationships in both the executive and legislative branches (pp. 143–144). "The implications . . . are profound. To remain relevant, the performance community will need to transition from its traditional emphasis on standardized, periodic reporting models, where analysis is performed by a central staff, to a new model that embraces collaborative elements" (pp. 144–145). We may expect President Obama to continue this approach to performance reporting in his second term.

The move toward performance measurement goes well beyond GPRA and its requirements for federal agencies. Public organizations at all levels, as well as organizations in the nonprofit sector, increasingly are tying evaluation research to their planning and implementation functions. Most state governments and many local governments, for instance, now use performance measurement as a means of assessing their activities in terms of both outputs and outcomes. Accordingly, these states can associate budget decisions and program directives with the specific performance standards set by each agency. And, as a result, the states enjoy a more effective system of accounting for their efficiency and effectiveness to citizens and other stakeholders.

Melkers and Willoughby (2007) noted that, as of 2004, "33 states had maintained, amended, or added legislation that prescribe performance-based application, while 17 states had an administrative requirement or executive mandate for such application" (p. 80). Despite these requirements, in most states there is neither a legislative nor an administrative requirement for comprehensive performance-based applications. Only eleven states have some type of statewide performance-based requirements: Arizona, Delaware, Louisiana, Maryland, Minnesota, Missouri, New Mexico, Oregon, South Dakota, Virginia, and Wyoming (p. 83). But nearly all states are taking some measures to move in this direction.

Several years ago, for example, Texas instituted a performance-budgeting system as a means of enhancing agency accountability and productivity. Under the new system, state agencies must determine the resources necessary to accomplish performance goals and then negotiate the goals and resources with the state legislature. Once the outcomes and allocations have been established, lawmakers grant spending authority based on the performance goals. The move away from program categories and line items, thus, gives administrators in Texas greater flexibility in meeting their performance objectives (see Chapter 5). And the budget system ensures that evaluation and measurement are based on productivity rather than on agency processes. However, as we see in the box "Exploring Concepts: Seeing Eye to Eye: Performance Measures That Matter to Citizens," the task of identifying measures is not always easy.

Exploring Concepts

SEEING EYE TO EYE: PERFORMANCE MEASURES THAT MATTER TO CITIZENS

Citizen participation has often been the square peg that public administrators try to squeeze into the round holes of government, whether it is for strategic planning, budgeting, land-use planning, or other key processes. This is especially true when it comes to performance measurement. Most participation is input driven (citizen satisfaction surveys) or output driven (annual performance reports). While both are important components of a performance measurement system, neither impacts the design of the system or influences what is actually measured. Barbara J. Cohn Berman's Listening to the Public presents the results of a multi-year research project conducted by the Fund for the City of New York that provides local governments with a rounder peg that has the potential to greatly influence the design of their performance measurement systems.

Taking its cue from private sector market research practices, the Fund's Center on Municipal Government Performance set out to listen to the citizens of New York City

(Continued)

(Continued)

through focus groups, surveys, and interviews over a six-year period between 1996 and 2001 to determine how the public perceived local government performance. Overall, researchers found participants to be knowledgeable about public services and realistic in their expectations. Their opinions were shaped by their own personal experiences and most critically influenced by their interactions with government employees and agencies.

The value of Berman's work is her methodology and its potential widespread application and impact. During the focus groups, participants were provided brief descriptions of thirty different city responsibilities so that all had an equal base level of understanding. Participants then ranked how familiar they were with each service, how important they believed each service to be, and how well each service is performed. While not scientific, these ratings provide insight into the public's perception of city services, allowing researchers to draw the conclusions mentioned.

From focus group discussions stimulated by this activity and subsequent phone interviews, Berman extrapolates common themes and presents potentially new performance measures that are important to citizens. For example, one person had this comment: "I called 911 for my grandmother. They came quickly, knew what to do, and got her to the right hospital on time." From this one comment Berman derived three potential performance measures: (1) the initial response time to reach the patient, (2) the elapsed time to transport the patient to the appropriate hospital, and (3) the knowledge, compassion, competence, and responsiveness of personnel. Berman documents comments and potential performance measures for each of the thirty services ranked. Such an exercise could be easily replicated by jurisdictions and used to validate their current measures and/or provide new ones that are more important to citizens.

The Center also identified governmental functions regarded by citizens as very important, but for which there was no performance data. The Center then developed new tools to produce reliable performance information and applied them to New York City. The first tool was concerned with the quality of the roads—roadway maintenance ranked second in the 2001 focus groups for being very important but low performing. Berman describes how the Center adapted a pavement-roughness measurement technology known as profilometry to produce a smoothness score and jolt score for city streets. Volunteers and focus groups were used to calibrate the technology to easy-to-understand performance measures, and maps were produced to spatially depict the results and observe changes over time. Since this technology was first deployed in New York, other cities have begun conducting similar studies.

As noted, Berman discovered that citizens perceive government much differently than does government itself. For citizens, problems do not fit neatly into departmental structures. Consider street-level issues such as garbage, vacant lots, unsafe buildings, and graffiti that together influence citizen perception of government but are not the responsibility of a single department. The Center developed a system called Computerized Neighborhood Environment Tracking (ComNet) to provide a means for citizens to easily communicate these problems to the appropriate local authority without having to know departmental responsibilities. Citizens or government employees use handheld computer devices while walking

(Continued)

predetermined routes to record observable problems. Detailed summaries are tabulated and the problems are automatically routed to the correct department. This also provides data that can be mapped to determine service level disparities and note changes over time. Numerous cities across the country have now used ComNet for similar systems.

The final tool developed by the Center is an online survey instrument called Citizen-Gauge, which allows citizens to rate their interactions with government employees based on the qualities the Center found to be most important during its research: accessibility, courtesy, knowledge, timeliness, and responsiveness. While CitizenGauge offers an additional feedback mechanism that should be welcome to agencies concerned about their performance, it also carries the weaknesses inherent in a "suggestion box" system—feedback that is anecdotal and not representative. Local governments might receive more useful data through community surveys and use CitizenGauge to pinpoint interim problems between surveys.

SOURCE: John Ruggini, "Seeing Eye to Eye: Performance Measures That Matter to Citizens," *Government Finance Review* 21, no. 6 (December 2005): 62–63.

Local governments are also working to improve performance management. For example, public officials in Portland, Oregon, have implemented several performance measurement tracking systems aimed at enhancing the productivity and effectiveness of government programs. Underlying Portland's system is the use of benchmarks, which provide performance standards and points of comparison for the city's leadership and staff. The city also has integrated productivity and outcome targets in its strategic planning and budget decision-making processes.

City officials at all levels have a key role to play in Portland's performance management system. Because of the decentralized nature of the city government, department heads, middle managers, and staff share responsibility for setting strategic objectives, tracking effectiveness, and reporting to key stakeholders on the performance results. Moreover, the city uses its community outreach to bring citizens into the performance management process. Portland relies on both informal approaches to citizen engagement and formal mechanisms of public participation, with citizens who initially served on the Portland-Multnomah Progress Board, which developed the early benchmarking program, who then later became involved in Mayor Tom Potter's 2005 effort to create a "vision PDX." In that project which lasted more than two years, some 17,000 citizens participated in developing "Portland 2030," a report summarizing the views and aspirations of Portland's citizens on the built, economic, environmental, learning, and social future of the city

Besides the benefits for productivity, Portland's performance measurement system and its strong commitment to public participation have given the city government exciting new forums for sharing progress and facilitating organizational learning. The city's report stated, "Communicating results is seen as a driving force behind the intent and expectations of Portland's performance measurement efforts, involving both communication within the government as well as communication to stakeholders and the public"

(Bernstein, 2000, pp. 2–3). City officials use a variety of messaging strategies to inform their colleagues internally on performance issues and to connect with the public on citizen priorities.

However, the Portland experience has not come without its share of obstacles. Among the most significant roadblocks have been (1) setting solid, measurable performance targets; (2) ensuring the quality and reliability of performance data; and (3) covering the time and cost required to maintain the reporting and tracking under the new system. The result has been concerns relating to the agency-by-agency consistency of the system and the capacity of city departments to continue tracking performance over time.

The principal strength of the Portland initiative is the high degree of ownership for the system throughout the city government. If staff had seen this initiative as something imposed by department heads or elected officials, there might have been a higher level of resistance. Under such conditions it would be questionable if the performance management approach would be sustainable in the future. But in Portland the city government as a whole appears to have embraced this new system as a way of serving more effectively in the public interest; as a result, performance management seems to be a key part of the city's policy and administrative decision making.

Similarly, the United Way of America implemented a comprehensive *performance measurement* program to foster a consistent, effective system of performance management across United Way–funded agencies (Hatry et al., 1996). The United Way approach concentrates on a logical chain—linking program inputs, activities, outputs, and outcomes—with outcomes measured by specific points of information, referred to as "indicators." The goal for the United Way is to encourage agencies to move away from traditional, efficiency-related measures to more meaningful assessments of program impact, based on the number and percentage of clients, to achieve the program outcomes (Hatry et al., 1996, pp. 1–2).

In identifying performance standards, public and nonprofit organizations may pull from a variety of sources. This is usually done in a process called *benchmarking*, through which they target specific goals based on previous performance levels, standards set by similar organizations, objectives created through a strategic planning process, or any combination of these. Public administrators then assess agency performance using comparisons with these predetermined indicators. Through benchmarking, administrators are able to connect their evaluation research directly with the agency's planning and implementation strategies (Jennings, 2010).

The most effective application of performance measurement integrates evaluation and measurement within the broader context of performance management. A report on one successful performance management exercise was developed by Jay Hakes (1997), at the time the administrator of the Energy Information Administration (EIA) of the U.S. Department of Energy. Based on his EIA experience, Hakes suggests that organizations that attempt to pattern assessment strategies without first sequencing these strategies in the overall process of organizational change may lose sight of important organizational barriers, both to performance measurement and to the change itself. These groups may fall into the trap of monitoring activities without linking them to the targeted goals and outcomes of the organization.

To prevent this occurrence, Hakes suggests several action steps that lay a foundation for successful performance measurement:

- Analyzing goals deriving from statutes and historic practices
- Discussing desired outputs and outcomes with major customers in and out of government
- Writing a strategic plan
- Drawing an input/output map of the organization (Hakes, 1997, p. 10)

It is important to note that these steps represent merely the beginning of successful performance management. Commitments from top leadership, organizational members, stakeholders, and those overseeing agency resources must be gained for the change strategy to be effective. The performance measures themselves must be linked with the organization's budget allocations and reward systems. In this regard, creating an effective measurement strategy means transforming the organization into a performance-based organization.

The next steps in the process involve integrating the measures throughout the organization. This can be done, according to Hakes, by involving organizational members in the process and by gaining feedback to enhance the measures. Data sources, complete with baseline indicators, should be established and a benchmarking process initiated to ensure that the goals will be measurable and the activities geared toward predetermined performance standards.

Finally, clear decisions must be reached on how the performance measurement system will be used. Some may opt for a more punitive application of assessment, choosing to use the techniques to play a watchdog role. Hakes encourages public administrators to employ measurement strategies in a more constructive way: "If workers can use measures for self-correction and continuous improvement without risk of punishment or with some prospect for reward, progress on providing value for dollar (maximum outputs and outcomes for minimal inputs) will surpass the expectations of most observers" (1997, p. 17). As with any successful approach to organizational change, Hakes reveals that the most meaningful attempt at performance management will occur when leadership engages members throughout the organization and, in turn, connects the assessment strategy to the organization's long-term outcomes. More importantly, Hakes suggests that public administrators must become less concerned with only quantitative indicators and more concerned with creating a culture of success within their organizations. (The challenges of applying performance management in practice are discussed in the box "Exploring Concepts: Performance Management: Theory and Practice.")

Exploring Concepts

PERFORMANCE MANAGEMENT: THEORY AND PRACTICE

In theory, measures of performance are thought to be answers to questions. In practice, performance measures are often themselves questions, or at least they raise as many questions as they answer. Performance measures are exactly that, quantitative representations

(Continued)

(Continued)

of some reality. Because performance measures are represented quantitatively, they have the appearance of fact and convey impressions of objectivity and neutrality. In practice, such measures are quantitative interpretations of reality in exactly the same way words are narrative interpretations of reality. In practice, very little is judged to be neutral and objective; all performance measures may be used as arguments and weapons in policy debates.

MEASURING PERFORMANCE

	In Theory	In Practice
Measures of performance are...	answers, objective, neutral, questions, interpretations, arguments	facts, evidence, slanted, weapons
Results are...	aggregated for everyone	aggregated for some but not others
Performance is...	long term	short term
Policy is moved by...	data and analysis	rhetoric
What to measure...	the important	the measurable
Program domain...	comparable	particular
Causal assertions can be...	demonstrated	unclear
This program...	performs poorly	performs poorly, but things would be worse without it

SOURCE: Adapted from H. George Frederickson, "Measuring Performance in Theory and Practice," *PA Times* 23, no. 8 (August 2000): 8–10. Reprinted by permission.

Another interesting approach to performance measurement that has made its way into the public and nonprofit sectors is Kaplan and Norton's (1996) "Balanced Scorecard." The Balanced Scorecard balances concerns for financial performance and internal business processes with customer service and organizational learning. This enables decision makers to track various dimensions of an organization's performance and communicate more effectively with stakeholders. Kaplan and Norton point out, however, that the Balanced Scorecard is not just a technique to control behavior or evaluate past performance. Rather, it should be used to communicate, to inform, and to enable learning and growth. Through the use of this technique, managers should be able to monitor and adjust the implementation of their strategies and to make fundamental changes in the way the organization operates (Kaplan & Norton, 1996, pp. 18–24).

The Government Accountability Office (GAO) completed a comprehensive survey of twenty-five federal and state regulatory agencies to determine best practices for performance-based management and measurement. Agencies selected for participation had been identified either by the GAO or other sources as leaders in designing and implementing performance management systems. The GAO study provided twelve recommendations based on best practices shared across the various sites:

1. Focus on building effective performance management strategies by making managing-for-results a top priority and dedicating resources to enhance core organizational competencies.
2. Ensure ownership of performance management and measurement activities throughout the agency.
3. Redesign work processes, internal structures, and lines of responsibility to be consistent with the new performance measurement systems.
4. Forge solid alliances—in this particular case, with regulated agencies, as well as with partners in service delivery.
5. Develop ties with counterparts, which in the case of regulatory agencies were other organizations in programs with crosscutting jurisdictions.
6. Adopt a systems-thinking approach to understand the influences and impacts of individual programs.
7. Establish clear, measurable performance goals and objectives that are in line with the new performance measurement rationale.
8. Identify appropriate performance targets for each of the goals and objectives in the system.
9. Select appropriate, reliable data sources to support the performance goals and objectives.
10. Focus analysis on specific functions—in this case, regulatory interventions—with an emphasis on maximizing results and targeting action at all phases of action.
11. Integrate into the performance analysis consideration of internal and external factors affecting the agency and its interventions.
12. Engage in processes of continuous improvement to ensure ongoing appropriateness in performance measurement systems (Government Accounting Office, 1999).

Although the study focused on regulatory agencies, the GAO anticipates that its findings can be used by nonregulatory organizations at all levels to enhance productivity and performance (for discussion, see the CAP Corner, *PA Times*, December 1999, p. 10).

Not only those in the United States, but government agencies around the world have begun to develop strategies to help them evaluate how well they are meeting programmatic goals and outcomes. A recent study examined reform efforts in member states of the Organisation for Economic Co-operation and Development (OECD) and selected nonmember nations. Nations such as Canada, Spain, and Sweden were singled out for their efforts to develop and implement performance measurement techniques on a nationwide basis. Other countries, like the United States, Germany, Korea, Mexico, and the Netherlands, were cited for implementing performance monitoring in specific policy areas. The areas sampled included health care, police and public safety, and policy advice.

The findings from this research suggested that several requirements influence the success of performance monitoring by public organizations: the need for "strategic leadership from central units," "the establishment of the proper organizational incentives which support and encourage results-based management," and "the use of program evaluation as a complement to ongoing performance measurement systems to address performance issues that performance measurement cannot well deal with so as to make the best use of these two measurement tools" (Mayne, 1997, p. 16).

The research showed that the dynamic environments in which the organizations functioned had a significant impact on each agency's capacity for performance and its measurement. In fact, the study found that the ability of an organization to adapt to changing conditions exceeded raw performance as the primary indicator of organizational success. Mayne (1997) wrote, "Maximizing flexibility may be more important than maximizing short-term utility" (p. 16). The study concluded that organizational survival depended on each group's ability to integrate performance measurement with the organization's overall capacity for problem solving and strategic management.

Of course, such a capacity depends on each agency's ability to monitor both the broader organizational performance and the effectiveness of individual programs. We have noted the significance of these evaluation strategies in our discussion of performance measurement. However, additional attention should be given to program evaluation, which generates valuable insight into organizational processes and the programmatic impacts produced by policies and initiatives. If performance measurement connects the organization as a whole to specific results and outcomes, then program evaluation reveals how actions by an organization contribute to the objectives within each policy area.

Implementation Issues in Quality and Productivity

Whatever approach to improving quality, productivity, and performance you undertake, the design of your intervention will be important to its success.

Productivity in public organizations, as in others, can often be improved through technological innovations. Many areas of federal, state, and local governmental activity rest on a strong technical base. In areas such as the design and construction of waste-to-energy plants, development of pollution control devices (including hazardous waste treatment centers), or building of public housing, new technologies may help governments to be not only more effective in meeting their objectives but also more cost-efficient.

What Would You Do?

As head of a state agency, you are concerned that your employees have fallen into the old trap of assuming that "the way things have always been done" is the way they should be done in the future. You would like your agency to be one known for its innovation practices, for being on the cutting edge of what's happening in your field. What would you do?

Think for a moment about the changes that are likely to occur in the country's transportation system over the next twenty years. In the not-too-distant future, high-speed intercity rail systems or vehicles that move on cushions of air may well displace planes, cars, and trains as the primary means of transportation between major urban areas. Designing the systems, regulating them, coordinating among various systems, providing communications and control—all these and many more functions will fall at least in part to government, and all will benefit from advanced technology. Other efforts, such as those associated with the reinventing government movement, are more concerned with changing the culture and practices of organizations, but these can vary in scope. Some programs simply require you to undertake new efforts to motivate your employees. Others are more programmatic; for example, you might emphasize greater responsibility on the part of lower-level personnel through a job enrichment strategy, or you might develop a recognition program within the unit.

You might also work with a broader program, such as by undertaking a reinvention effort throughout a local government or establishing a governmentwide employee suggestion award system.

Steps to Productivity Improvement

Whatever the level or organization of the quality and productivity effort, there are certain basic issues to consider:

1. *Identify ripe areas.* Identify areas that are "ripe" for productivity improvement. Any program, however great its ambitions, must start small. It makes sense to start where you are most likely to achieve immediate gains, because you will identify savings most quickly here, and because a few early successes will encourage productivity improvement efforts elsewhere. To identify areas, managers should be particularly attentive to:
   - functions continually faced with large backlogs of work or slipping deadlines.
   - operations where visible problems have already been hinted at (citizen complaints, high employee turnover).
   - operations that appear to be using an unusually large percentage of resources.
   - operations where large numbers of employees perform essentially repetitive tasks (payoffs will be especially evident here because of the effect of multiplying any increase by the number of employees).
   - availability of new techniques or technology already proven workable elsewhere (for example, computer installation to improve police response time).
   - receptivity of managers and supervisors to new ideas coupled with an ability to follow through (Holzer, Rosen, & Zalk, 1986, pp. 9–15).

2. *Locate models in other jurisdictions.* Whatever your organization, it is likely that there are others like it and that others have experienced similar problems. Having some idea of how others approached the issues you are now confronting is especially helpful. Fortunately, such information is readily available, either through publications such as the *Governmental Productivity News* or through professional organizations such as the American Society for Public Administration or the International City

Management Association. From these sources, you may discover new approaches to productivity improvement, or you may find that approaches you are considering have either been successful or have failed elsewhere.

3. *Define roles.* Define the roles of those who will be involved in planning and implementing the program. Some programs are oriented to a particular department, while others cut across several departments within a jurisdiction; in either case, some staffing for the productivity effort will be necessary. Staffing at the department level will provide a specific focus to the productivity program and will allow you to build technical expertise (such as in fire or police work). A centralized productivity staff will enable you to give broad impetus to the program and to build general expertise in productivity techniques. Presumably, this general knowledge can then be applied in various departments.

4. *Set realistic goals and objectives.* As noted, productivity programs in public organizations have been stimulated by public demand for "doing more with less." You may thus be tempted to set high expectations for a new productivity improvement effort; resist the temptation. Setting realistic goals and objectives and actually meeting them is more helpful in the long run than setting too-high expectations and falling short.

5. *Choose among alternative programs.* Different approaches range from changes in management style to technological innovations to specific productivity efforts, such as quality circles or incentive programs. In implementing a productivity program, it is advisable to fit the solution to the problem rather than the other way around. Though this advice seems obvious, you may find yourself tempted to pursue an immediate opportunity rather than engage in more careful planning. For example, a vendor might herald a new telecommunications system as the solution to all your problems. Even though you may not view communications issues as your highest priorities in terms of productivity improvement, you may be tempted to adopt the new technology "just because it's there." A more reasonable approach, of course, is to establish a prioritized list of problems, then seek to develop solutions that match your most important concerns.

6. *Anticipate problems.* Many problems can arise in implementing a productivity improvement program, especially one of high visibility. Many of the problems are based on misconceptions about what productivity improvement is all about and can be anticipated and dealt with early in the program. Employees might feel that a quality circles program will lead to elimination of jobs, or they may feel that safety standards will be lowered; in fact, neither outcome is likely. But these are serious concerns that should be thoroughly discussed as the program is begun. To the extent possible, all participants and all people likely to be affected by the program should have a chance to learn about and comment on the proposed program. Dealing with questions up front minimizes confusion and disruption later.

7. *Implement the program.* After carefully analyzing the need for a productivity improvement program and deciding on a course of action that will address the identified needs, you will face the difficult task of implementation. Implementation may, in fact, be the most difficult phase. Expectations may be too high; needed legislation may be difficult to pass; organization "turf" issues may interfere; there may not be enough money to invest in the program.

You can avoid some of the difficulties by starting the program on a modest basis and then expanding to other areas. Limiting objectives at the outset can help keep expectations from rising too high and will make it easier to demonstrate the viability of the effort. Beginning the program in an area where you might reasonably expect quick and identifiable gains will enable you to claim early success and in turn make the program more likely to be adopted elsewhere. Similarly, keeping a low profile for the program in its early days will make it less threatening to labor and management. Whatever publicity is accorded to the program (and many political leaders will want high-profile efforts), you should monitor the program carefully in its early days to avoid misconceptions.

The most serious limitations, however, are the difficulties in institutionalizing the program. Implementation is not merely a short-term concern; you should be concerned from the beginning about how durable the program is likely to be. Several factors work against institutionalization of productivity improvement programs. Programs may be dependent on a particular individual, such as a governor or mayor or a particular department head, and may be discontinued when that person leaves office. Many programs lack an organizational home and thus find it difficult to sustain support over a period of years.

8. *Evaluate the program.* Most productivity improvement programs require an initial investment of money and time; you have to spend money to save money, and many people may be skeptical of the program's value. Skeptics are likely to be unconvinced by general statements of program advocates; they will want to see specific, objective data. Types of information you should collect from the beginning are documented cost savings, increased output that has been achieved at a similar or reduced cost, or increased citizen satisfaction with the agency's services. This information can be made public through periodic reports to legislators or other decision makers or through press conferences or news releases. An aspect of evaluation that needs special attention is the development of an appropriate measurement system to ensure that the proper information is being acquired at an appropriate time. You must be sure that information is gathered on a timely basis and that it is accurate. The information must also be fully relevant to measuring the improvement effort. It is difficult to develop a measurement system, but it may be critical to sustaining your program over time.

We have already discussed ways to measure objectives. For example, a social service agency might measure the number of clients served, a police department might measure response time, or a public works department might measure numbers of miles of streets and highways paved. Matters are complicated, of course, by the fact that most organizations seek several objectives simultaneously. The social services agency is not concerned only with screening clients, but may also make referrals to other agencies or distribute money to certain clients. Each of these multiple objectives, and each of the activities that contribute to the objectives, may require its own separate measure.

Even more important, those who measure the effects of productivity improvement programs need to be attentive to what properly reflects the quality of work performed. Obtaining an increase in cost savings at the expense of courtesy or promptness is questionable at best. Responding to requests for information or help "when it is convenient" to the agency may be less costly, but it will probably not be acceptable in terms of quality. You may wish to consider either a separate measure of quality or the implementation of a quality control system. You might also be able to develop composite measures that combine considerations for output and quality. For example, the streets department might measure repairs made within a certain number of working days, or the revenue department might measure the number of tax returns processed without error.

Three conditions appear to be required for productivity improvements to occur: "(a) the performance of individuals or groups must be assessed in a valid, objective manner, emphasizing the public purposes of the services provided by those employees; (b) such assessment should be closely linked to some type of reward or penalty, whether monetary or nonmonetary; and (c) there should be both early meaningful involvement by employee organizations as well as adequate advance participation and training for those affected, including supervisory as well as nonsupervisory employees" (Greiner et al., 1981, p. 411). Developing programs with these considerations in mind will not only help ensure early successes in productivity improvement but will also help sustain the program through the years.

Summary and Action Implications

Technical innovations are often dramatic in their impact, sometimes saving thousands, even millions, of dollars. But technological innovations do not occur independently of the skills and attitudes of those who work in an organization. Innovations seem to flourish in a climate where human creativity is encouraged and usually require human changes— what one group calls "orgware"—to be successfully implemented.

Improved productivity appears to depend at least in part on a shift from the traditional authoritarian approach to management to a more open and participatory approach. This shift has been especially apparent in implementing productivity improvement programs at all levels of government. In many cases, we find a shifting orientation toward management that places greater emphasis on the involvement of all employees. (The resulting orientation was perhaps best expressed by the head of a state productivity council who described his philosophy this way: "Those who do the work know the work best and know best how to improve the work.") The result is an approach to management that not only seems more human in scale and perspective, but that many authorities are coming to believe is far more productive as well.

A study by the Canadian government of "well-performing" governmental organizations in that country twenty years ago outlines some of the basics of this approach in terms that are still relevant today. That study identified five factors leading to organizational success that we may take as recommended patterns of action for managers to seek in trying to improve productivity:

Emphasis on people. People are challenged, encouraged, and developed. They are given power to act and to use their judgment. There is a belief that high performance is a product of people who care rather than systems that constrain. People do not preoccupy themselves with the risk of failure, but are confident they can tackle virtually any challenge.

Participative leadership. Leadership is not authoritarian or coercive, but participative whenever possible. The leaders envision an ideal organization, define purpose and goals, then articulate these and foster commitment. Staff communicate easily. They feel comfortable consulting peers as well as those above and below them. Although formal levels exist for administrative purposes, there are no boundaries that inhibit collaboration in achieving goals.

Innovative work styles. Staff reflect on their performance. They learn from the effects of their actions. They seek to solve problems creatively. They maintain strong monitoring, feedback, and control systems as useful tools. They are self-reliant, rather than dependent on control from an outside authority.

Strong client orientation. These organizations focus strongly on their clients, deriving satisfaction from serving the client rather than the bureaucracy. There is an alignment of values and purpose between the well-performing agency and [its] political and central agency masters.

A mindset that seeks optimum performance. People hold values that drive them to always seek improvement in their organization's performance. When conditions change, they adjust their methods, not their values. Because of this orientation toward performance and adaptability, the organization performs well even in a changing environment. This mindset may be the most important feature of all.

SOURCE: Extract originally from the *Report of the Auditor General of Canada to the House of Commons for Fiscal Year Ending 31 March 1988*, Chapter 4: "Attributes of Well-Performing Organizations." Minister of Supply and Services, Canada, 1990.

As a manager, one of the primary technical concerns you will face is improving your organization's productivity. Whereas you may be able to accomplish great gains through technological innovations, the most significant long-term gains will come from a proper emphasis on the human factors in organizational effectiveness. To be judged successful, you will always have to balance your concern for the technical side of your agency's work and your attention to the human side of the organization.

STUDY QUESTIONS

1. What is the New Public Management reform movement? How has it changed the way government operates and its role in the governance system?

2. How have advances in information and communication technology changed public organizations in terms of management, service delivery, and relationships with citizens?

3. What are some of the key benefits and barriers to effective performance management systems in government? What factors contribute to success?

CASES AND EXERCISES

1. Complete the following exercise: The newly elected governor of a large Middle Atlantic state has asked you to assist in developing a plan to revise the method of patrolling the highways. The problem stems from a report by the federal Department of Transportation showing that an independent sampling of traffic in the state indicates that far too many motorists are exceeding the federally mandated speed limit. The report goes on to threaten a cutoff of all federal highway funds to the state if something is not done. Perhaps of greater urgency, however, is the finding that the number of accidents per 1,000 miles driven is rising dramatically.

   The governor's office has provided you with a set of alternative strategies for patrolling the highways and the associated costs and probable reductions in both accidents and speeders. Also included in the materials is a study of the revenue generated by the issuance of citations. You are asked to write a report indicating the various payoffs associated with each strategy.

   These are the types of patrols:
   - stationary radar trap patrol
   - cruising car patrol
   - airplane/chase car patrol

   These are the costs per shift for each patrol type:
   - stationary = $600 per patrol
   - cruising = $800 per patrol
   - airplane = $1,500 per patrol

   The cost of servicing each accident that occurs during a patrol is $250. The likelihood of accidents, however, differs depending on the type of patrol: the stationary patrol results in a 50 percent probability of two accidents; the cruising patrol results in a 30 percent probability of two accidents; and the airplane patrol results in a 25 percent probability of two accidents. Finally, the number of citations issued varies by type of patrol: stationary patrols issue eight citations on average; cruising patrols issue five citations on average; and airplane patrols issue three citations on average.

   A previous study indicated that accident rates of less than an average of one per patrol were typical of states where the Department of Transportation found acceptable levels of speeding.

   In a concluding paragraph, the governor indicates that it costs the state $50 to process a citation (which averages a fine of $85), but the governor goes on to say that may not be relevant to the choice of patrol type because the whole idea is to prevent accidents by slowing traffic to the legal speed limit (and preventing a cutoff of federal money).

   How would you go about developing the report to the governor?

2. The governor of a large midwestern state has recently introduced a performance management initiative to enhance the activities of state agencies and, more specifically, to reverse downward trends in educational achievement and increases in juvenile crime. The governor, responding to increasing public outcry, has encouraged her

cabinet to develop ten outcomes in the area of human and social services and then to identify performance indicators that can be used in monitoring the state's progress in achieving these outcomes. As a senior cabinet member, you have been called upon to play a leadership role in this process. What are the primary outcomes that the state would need to accomplish in order to reverse the downward trends? What performance indicators could be used to help keep the statewide initiative on track? How would you ensure that these performance measurement strategies are implemented throughout the state and that the necessary organizational change has occurred to ensure their effectiveness?

FOR ADDITIONAL READING

Altshuler, Alan A., and Robert D. Behn, eds. *Innovation in American Government: Challenge, Opportunities and Dilemmas.* Washington, DC: Brookings Institution Press, 1997.

Balutis, Alan P., Terry F. Buss, and Dwight Ink. *Transforming American Governance: Rebooting the Public Square.* Armonk, NY: M.E. Sharpe, 2011.

Barzelay, Michael. *The New Public Management: Improving Research and Policy Dialogue.* Berkeley: University of California Press/Russell Sage Foundation, 2001.

Berman, Evan M. *Performance and Productivity in Public and Nonprofit Organizations.* 2nd ed. Armonk, NY: M.E. Sharpe, 2006.

Bevir, Mark. *The Sage Handbook of Governance.* Thousand Oaks, CA: Sage Publications, 2011.

Borins, Sandford F. *Innovations in Government: Research, Recognition, and Replication* (Innovative Governance in the 21st Century). Washington, DC: Brookings Institution Press, 2008.

Cohen, Steven, and Ronald Brand. *Total Quality Management in Government: A Practical Guide for the Real World.* San Francisco: Jossey-Bass, 1993.

Dilulio, John, Jr., Gerald Garvey, and Donald Kettl. *Improving Government Performance.* Washington, DC: Brookings Institution Press, 1993.

Dubnick, Melvin J., and H. George Frederickson. *Accountable Governance: Problems and Promises.* Armonk, NY: M.E. Sharpe, 2011.

Eggers, W. D. *Government 2.0: Using Technology to Improve Education, Cut Red Tape, Reduce Gridlock, and Enhance Democracy.* Lanham, MD: Rowman and Littlefield, 2007.

Frederickson, David G., and H. George Frederickson. *Measuring the Performance of the Hollow State.* Washington, DC: Georgetown University Press, 2006.

Garson, David G., ed. *Handbook of Public Information Systems.* 2nd ed. Boca Raton, FL: Taylor & Francis, 2005.

Gore, Albert. *Businesslike Government.* Washington, DC: Government Printing Office, 1997.

Gore, Albert. *Common Sense Government.* New York: Random House, 1995.

Gore, Albert. *Serving the American Public.* Washington, DC: Government Printing Office, 1997.

Julnes, Patria de Lancer, and Marc Holzer. *Performance Measurement: Building Theory, Improving Practice* (Aspa Classics). Armonk, NY: M.E. Sharpe, 2008.

Kamensky, John M., and Albert Morales, eds. *Competition, Choice, and Incentives in Government Programs.* Lanham, MD: Rowman and Littlefield, 2006.

Kelman, Steven. *Unleashing Change: A Study of Organizational Renewal in Government.* Washington, DC: Brookings Institution Press, 2005.

King, Cheryl Simrell. *Government Is Us 2.0.* Armonk, NY: M.E. Sharpe, 2011.

Lane, Jan-Erik. *New Public Management.* London: Routledge, 2000.

Leighninger, Matthew, and Bill Bradley. *The Next Form of Democracy: How Expert Rule Is Giving Way to Shared Governance—and Why Politics Will Never Be the Same.* Nashville, TN: Vanderbilt University Press, 2006.

Light, Paul C. *The Tides of Reform.* New Haven, CT: Yale University Press, 1997.

Moynihan, Donald P. *The Dynamics of Performance Management: Constructing Information and Reform.* Washington, DC: Georgetown University Press, 2008.

National Performance Review. *From Red Tape to Results: Creating a Government That Works Better and Costs Less.* Washington, DC: Government Printing Office, 1993.

O'Leary, Rosemary, and Lisa B. Bingham. *The Collaborative Public Manager: New Ideas for the Twenty-First Century.* Washington, DC: Georgetown University Press, 2009.

Osborne, David, and Ted Gaebler. *Reinventing Government.* Reading, MA: Addison-Wesley, 1992.

Osborne, David, and Peter Plastrik. *Banishing Bureaucracy.* Reading, MA: Addison-Wesley, 1997.

Pollitt, Christopher, and Geert Bouckaert. *Public Management Reform: A Comparative Analysis.* 2nd ed. New York: Oxford University Press, 2004.

Pollitt, Christopher, and Colin Talbot, eds. *Unbundled Government: A Critical Analysis of the Global Trend to Agencies, Quangos and Contractualisation.* London: Routledge, 2004.

Radin, Beryl. *Challenging the Performance Movement: Accountability, Complexity, and Democratic Values.* Washington, DC: Georgetown University Press, 2006.

Roberts, Nancy Charlotte. *The Age of Direct Citizen Participation* (Aspa Classics). Armonk, NY: M.E. Sharpe, 2008.

Rocheleau, Bruce. *Public Management Information Systems.* Hershey, PA: Idea Group, 2006.

Salamon, Lester M. *The State of Nonprofit America.* Washington, DC: Brookings Institution Press, 2002.

Schachter, Hindy L. *Reinventing Government or Reinventing Ourselves.* Albany: State University of New York Press, 1997.

Sirianni, Carmen. *Investing in Democracy: Engaging Citizens in Collaborative Governance.* Washington, DC: Brookings Institution Press, 2009.

Stanton, Thomas H., ed. *Meeting the Challenge of 9/11: Blueprints for More Effective Government.* Armonk, NY: M.E. Sharpe, 2006.

Svara, James H., and Janet V. Denhardt. *The Connected Community: Local Governments as Partners in Citizen Engagement and Community Building.* Phoenix: Alliance for Innovation, 2010.

White, Jay D. *Managing Information in the Public Sector.* Armonk, NY: M.E. Sharpe, 2007.

OPPORTUNITIES FOR THE FUTURE: GLOBALIZATION, DEMOCRACY, AND THE NEW PUBLIC SERVICE

For those of you considering work in public service, whether for a relatively short period or for an entire career, several considerations may shape your thinking. The challenges and complexities of public service provide a special excitement that comes from being a part of unfolding major events—local, state, national, or even international. If you want to be a part of what's happening in a changing society, then public service is the place for you. Think about the incredible variety of work in the public sector. Public managers are key actors in foreign affairs, the human services, environmental policy, educational reform, the space program, and an endless variety of other important areas. Indeed, it is fair to say that every major local, state, national, or international issue now being discussed will provide challenges and opportunities for public managers in the future. If you are interested in meaningful work—work that makes a difference in people's lives—then you should find involvement in public service quite appealing.

The Importance of Public Service

Throughout most of our country's history, public service has been recognized as an important undertaking that contributes to the betterment of society, supported by citizens and politicians alike. Unfortunately, for the past twenty-five years or so, support has wavered. From the late 1960s through the middle 1980s, public service seemed to be under fairly constant attack. Through the candidacies of both Jimmy Carter and Ronald Reagan, national politicians of both parties organized their campaigns at least in part around attacks on Washington and the bureaucracy. Public administrators were criticized as both unresponsive and overly responsive—unresponsive to the common citizen and overly responsive to special interests. Public organizations were accused of being highly ineffective and inefficient, failing to achieve their objectives and wasting enormous sums of public funds.

Fortunately, the environment of public service has changed considerably over the past several years, leading us to be somewhat more optimistic about its future image. The first President Bush and President Clinton were more supportive of federal public service, and Presidents George W. Bush and Barack Obama appeared to be continuing this trend. President Obama continues to be as supportive of the federal service as any chief executive should be supportive of his employees, but budgetary issues may make this difficult.

In policy areas, over the past decade, Americans have seen tax reductions and tax reform at the federal level, as well as tax limitations at the state and local levels. These actions have helped to mitigate the view that the government tax machine is running wild. The political climate has also been changing, even to the point that we might suggest the reemergence of a positive view of government. It must be said, however, that such a view has been most evident at the state and local levels. In several important areas—notably education, economic development, and environmental concerns—the states are taking positive actions. And at the same time, public confidence in state and local governments is growing.

Efforts in support of public service return our country to a long-standing tradition. At other periods—and even today in other countries—public service has been considered a proud and honorable profession. John F. Kennedy's inaugural statement continues to have relevance today. Recall that Kennedy said, "Ask not what your country can do for you; ask what you can do for your country." In another speech, Kennedy amplified the point: "Let the public service be a proud and lively career. And let every man and woman who works in any area of our national government, in any branch at any level, be able to say with pride and honor in future years: I served the United States Government in that hour of our nation's need." Those who work in the field of public administration at all levels of government carry forward that long and proud tradition (see the box "Public Administration in History: Main Conclusions of the Volcker Commission").

Trends in Public Service

The opportunities and challenges that will face those in public service over the coming years are substantial. Public servants will not only work to resolve important public policy problems, but they will also do so in a manner that maintains public confidence and the values of citizenship. Efforts to restore meaning and integrity to public service are much needed in our society and in societies around the world, but they should be accompanied by a clear understanding of several important trends in our field that are reshaping the values and commitments of public service. Two major worldwide trends are particularly important: (1) globalization and (2) increasing democratization and the expanding role of citizens in the governance process. Before explaining these trends in more detail, it must first be noted that these trends are taking place against a backdrop of worldwide economic scarcity and instability.

Economic Changes and Redefining Government

Changing economic conditions are affecting both the mission and structure of public organizations and governance systems. Our economy has been transformed in several ways: from a production base to a service base, from a national base to a global base, and from a growing public commitment to a limited commitment. In each case, there are direct implications for those in public service:

- Public managers face challenges in areas where traditional industries, such as steel or timber, have suddenly declined, as "high tech and high touch" has become a banner for economic growth.

Public Administration in History

MAIN CONCLUSIONS OF THE VOLCKER COMMISSION

The central message of this report of the Commission on the Public Service is both simple and profound, both urgent and timeless. In essence, we call for a renewed sense of commitment by all Americans to the highest traditions of public service—to a public service responsive to the political will of the people and also protective of our constitutional values; to a public service able to cope with complexity and conflict and also able to maintain the highest ethical standards; to a public service attractive to the young and talented from all parts of our society and also capable of earning the respect of all our citizens.

A great nation must demand no less. The multiple challenges thrust upon the Government of the United States as we approach the twenty-first century can only reinforce the point. Yet, there is evidence on all sides of an erosion of performance and morale across government in America. Too many of our most talented public servants—those with the skills and dedication that are the hallmarks of an effective career service—are ready to leave. Too few of our brightest young people—those with the imagination and energy that are essential for the future—are willing to join.

Meanwhile, the need for a strong public service is growing, not lessening. Americans have always expected their national government to guarantee their basic freedoms and provide for the common defense. We continue to expect our government to keep the peace with other nations, resolve differences among our people, pay the bills for needed services, and honor the people's trust by providing the highest levels of integrity and performance.

At the same time, Americans now live in a stronger, more populous nation, a nation with unprecedented opportunity. But they also live in a world of enormous complexity and awesome risks. Our economy is infinitely more open to international competition, our currency floats in a worldwide market, and we live with complex technologies beyond the understanding of any single human mind. Our diplomacy is much more complicated, and the wise use of our unparalleled military power more difficult. And for all our scientific achievements, we are assaulted daily by new social, environmental, and health issues almost incomprehensible in scope and impact—issues like drugs, AIDS, and global warming.

Faced with these challenges, the simple idea that Americans must draw upon talented and dedicated individuals to serve us in government is uncontestable. America must have a public service that can both value the lessons of experience and appreciate the requirements for change; a public service that both responds to political leadership and respects the law; a public service with the professional skills and the ethical sensitivity America deserves.

SOURCE: Excerpted from the National Commission on the Public Service, *Leadership for America: Rebuilding the Public Service* (Washington, DC, 1989), pp. 1–2.

- Those at the state and local levels must play new and important roles in economic development, including international economic development, which may require them to know as much about business decisions in Japan as in their own state capital.
- There are also challenges for those operating public programs, especially in the human services, who have found government spending severely restricted at a time when the need for those services seems ever increasing.

The last five years have created even greater challenges to the U.S. and global economies. In 2008, the fallout from a combination of low interest rates and high levels of liquidity in the U.S. financial system precipitated "the deepest slump in the world economy since the 1930s" (Altman, 2009, p. 6). This combination had spurred the release of a flood of money into the subprime mortgage sector in 2005 and 2006, primarily in the United States and to some extent in other countries, driving real estate prices up dramatically. Subprime and near-prime mortgages were offered to buyers who historically had not been able to qualify because of low credit scores or insufficient resources for a down payment, often with little or no documentation of income. Banks also made it easier for homeowners to refinance loans and withdraw cash from homes that had gone up in value. This expansion of credit fueled global speculation in real estate and mortgage-backed securities, reinforcing risky lending practices as the lines between traditional investment banks and mortgage lenders were blurred by government deregulation. This economic boom, however, was not sustainable. U.S. real estate prices peaked early in 2006 and then began to plummet. The collapse in prices undermined the value of the subprime mortgage pool, and as cheap introductory loans began to convert to more expensive terms that many borrowers could not afford, subprime loan losses mounted, exposing other risky lending and triggering a financial crisis (Altman, 2009).

By December 2007, according to the National Bureau of Economic Research (2008), the United States already was in a recession, and in the fall of 2008 the collapse of the investment banking firm Lehman Brothers triggered a crisis that rocked global financial markets and led to unprecedented levels of government intervention in "rescuing" other major financial institutions. Housing markets worsened, with sharp increases in foreclosures. Unemployment rose sharply as well. Across the globe economies shrank as international trade declined and credit tightened. In the United States and around the world, governments and central banks attempted to arrest the downturn through the use of bailouts, fiscal stimulus packages, and changes in monetary policy (IMF, 2009). A Financial Crisis Inquiry Commission, created as part of the Fraud Enforcement and Recovery Act passed by Congress and signed by President Obama in May 2009, spent a year investigating the cause of the crisis and concluded that it was "an 'avoidable' disaster caused by widespread failures in government regulation, corporate mismanagement and heedless risk-taking by Wall Street" (Chan, 2011, p. 1).

While there are hopeful signs of economic recovery, the economic downturn continues to present formidable challenges to government. Fortunately, in responding to these challenges, government is not alone. Public service work is no longer the work only of government, but an effort in which governmental agencies, nonprofit and third-sector organizations, and corporate and business interests participate. Consider these examples:

- In many states, the number of people employed by private security forces exceeds the number employed by local police departments.
- In some cities, the chamber of commerce is so involved in public programs that it receives more funding from government than it receives from private business.
- In major urban areas, fewer than half of human services are delivered by government; the majority are delivered by nonprofit and private agencies.

Some of these trends, such as privatization and contracting for specific goods and services, are becoming familiar; others are quite distinctive because they involve third parties' discretion in the use of public authority and in spending of public funds. This development suggests a significant reshaping of public service and raises serious questions about equity and accountability in the management of public programs.

Trends associated with the reform agendas in the public and nonprofit sectors reflect more recent responses to our changing social and economic condition. We have noted that the reform agenda stems from the belief that government has failed to keep pace with the dynamic environment in the postindustrial world. Consequently, the reform movement already has had a dramatic impact on the character and processes of government organizations at all levels. And given the current global, economic, and political realities, such trends promise to continue into the future.

An important consideration with respect to the reform movements relates to the application of entrepreneurial practices and business values in public service. Although transforming the relationship between a government and its citizens in economic terms—that is, viewing the citizen as a customer—may generate cost savings and lead to more streamlined public organizations, the question remains as to what the long-term impact will be for issues of citizenship and public participation. Although creating a government that "does more with less" may produce a stronger bottom line, it could also have harmful effects on citizen engagement with the institutions of governance.

Globalization

The international dimensions of public administration are more important than ever, in terms of both the world economy and political trends. Some argue, in fact, that globalization "defines the fundamental challenge to the role of government and public administration in the twenty-first century" (Abonyi & Slyke, 2010). Understanding the activities of political and administrative officials in other countries is important not only for those who will spend part of their careers outside the United States, but also for those who will work at home. Increasingly, city managers, for example, find that to be effective in local economic development activities, they must be experts in international business. But global interdependencies will affect us in other ways as well; for example, the deforestation in Brazil, Africa, and the Philippines will directly affect the quality of our own environment. And, of course, we cannot overlook our obligation to help reduce poverty and hunger throughout the world.

Several diverse—indeed, competing—views have emerged relating to this globalization trend. They range from a critical perspective, in which the trend is seen as an attempt by developed nations to introduce Western values into other regions, to what supporters believe to be a chance to extend employment opportunities and wealth creation into impoverished nations. This latter view suggests that, over time, all of us in the global village will benefit from the forces of globalization and the internationalization of economic markets.

The impact of globalization on public administration should not be underestimated. However, relating to the internationalization process is a pattern that carries perhaps even greater implications: decentralization. Central governments increasingly are handing over new powers and responsibilities to local and regional authorities.

Networking

For information concerning international perspectives on governance and public administration, visit the Organisation for Economic Co-operation and Development (OECD) at www.oecd.org or the United Nations at www.un.org/esa. Local issues on a global scale, including decentralization and sustainable development, can be researched online at the International City Management Association (ICMA) at www.icma.org/resources/index.htm or at the International City Government Resource Centre at www.geocities.com/Paris/9925.

Whether triggered by declining revenues at the national level or the nation-state's diminished power base, the result has been growing demand for services and decision making by subnational administrations. And in many cases, these administrations lack the capacity and resources to deal effectively with their newfound authority.

To better understand these trends and what they mean for public administration, we will need to develop more globalized, comparative forms of analysis. Such analysis will lead to an understanding of international issues and enhance the way we deal with issues in our own communities. So as we continue to live in our "global village," we will be challenged to deal with opportunities and threats that defy national boundaries. Our systems of governance, consequently, will need to reflect our concern for the public interest—both at home and abroad.

The Role of Citizens in the Governance Process

In the United States and around the world, the movement toward democratization has been growing increasingly evident. According to the United Nations Development Programme, "More countries than ever before are working to build democratic governance. Their challenge is to develop institutions and processes that are more responsive to the needs of ordinary citizens, including the poor, and that promote development" (http://www.und3p.org/content/undp/en/home/ourwork/democraticgovernance/overview.html). This is not only an international trend; more and more communities across the United States are working to find ways to engage citizens in defining problems, making policy decisions, and implementing policy. Moving beyond their role as recipients of government services, citizens increasingly are involved in helping shape the policies and programs that affect their lives. In many ways, this emerging form of citizen participation represents a return to important principles that underlie our system of democracy, such as becoming more concerned with equity and justice as opposed to merely efficiency and performance.

Yet the shift from the more traditional representative democracy to a direct form poses unique challenges for elected and administrative officials, particularly as many public administrators view citizen participation as a source of tension. Often they associate civic engagement with public hearings, legal and administrative arbitration, and other formal mechanisms that tend to be time-consuming and highly confrontational. Public involvement, accordingly, comes to represent a hindrance to efficient management. In turn, public involvement is limited to being a source of legitimacy, through hearings and similar forums, of decisions that have already been made through more rational approaches. However, such limited forms of civic engagement not only result in policies that are detached from the actual needs of affected populations but also, over time, create barriers between the local institutions of government and citizens.

Despite these concerns, public officials at all levels have established open governance processes to encourage more substantive forms of engagement. For example, the federal government, whose agencies and departments issue nearly 8,000 regulations each year, encourages citizen participation in the rule-making process through the website www.regulations.gov. The site provides interested citizens the opportunity to help shape federal rules and regulations by reviewing and commenting on proposed or final regulations in any federal agency. Visitors to the site also can comment on other comments and sign up for alerts about particular regulations. The Ohio Department of Aging created a Civic Engagement Initiative that is aimed at involving citizens fifty years and older in their communities. It focuses on lifelong learning and volunteerism as a means of increasing the capacity to help meet community needs and to build personal employability among this population. In Portsmouth, New Hampshire, the mayor and city council brought together small groups of citizens in "study circles" to help develop the city's strategic master plan. This grassroots effort became an ongoing collaboration known as Portsmouth Listens, through which citizens partner with the city to help shape decisions on budgets and local issues on an ongoing basis, thus taking an active role in preserving and enhancing their local quality of life.

The move to more direct forms of civic participation opens the door for effective and responsible citizenship, but in order for these forms to be successful, those in government must be willing to listen and act in a responsive manner. In addition, the creation and organization of more direct forms of engagement cannot be accomplished by administrators alone, as citizen participation may look very different from the perspective of the citizen versus that of government. Consequently, administrators need to understand the process from both points of view and involve a wide range of individuals, groups, and organizations in any efforts to foster citizen participation. Further, in order to achieve effective participation, both public administrators and citizens need to change their behavior, adapting the roles they play in the governance process, which will require new skills. For example, not only do administrators need to listen, but they also need to begin to confer and work in partnership with citizens, while citizens must be willing to ask questions, actively participate, and take responsibility for their communities. While citizens are more likely to participate when invited and welcomed to do so, when their actions match a need, and when their contributions are used, administrators are used to treating citizens as consumers of government service rather than consulting and collaborating with them (Denhardt & Denhardt, 2011; Svara & Denhardt, 2011). Only through the pursuit of this "two-way street" between citizens and government will the most healthy relationship be brought about.

For those in public administration, the challenge will be to sustain these meaningful forms of engagement and civic society. To guide public administrators in this capacity, Janet and Robert Denhardt (2011) offer seven principles of what they call "the New Public Service." Rather than attempting to control or steer government by deciding upon its goals and directions and choosing the ways in which to reach them, the New Public Service urges that administrators focus on building public institutions marked by integrity and responsiveness that serve and empower citizens by integrating citizen discourse and the public interest into the decision-making process. To do so, administrators need to consider the following:

1. The primary role of the public servant is to help citizens articulate and meet their interests rather than to attempt to control or steer society in new directions.
2. Public administrators must make the creation of a collective, shared notion of the public interest paramount. Rather than finding quick solutions driven by individual choices, administrators aim to create shared interests and shared responsibility.
3. Policies and programs to meet public needs can be most effectively and responsibly achieved through collective efforts and collaborative processes.
4. The public interest is the result of a dialogue about shared values rather than the aggregation of individual interests. Consequently, public servants should not simply respond to the demands of "customers" but instead should focus on building relationships of trust and collaboration with and among citizens.
5. Public servants must be attentive to more than the market; they also must attend to statutory and constitutional law, community values, political norms, professional standards, and citizen interests.
6. Public organizations and the networks in which they participate are more likely to be successful in the long run if they are operated through processes of collaboration and shared leadership based on a respect for all people.
7. The public interest is better advanced by public servants and citizens committed to making meaningful contributions to society than by entrepreneurial managers acting as if public money were their own.

These principles suggest that the public interest will be defined through a dialogue about shared values and interests and that facilitating this dialogue and acting on the results should be of primary concern to public administrators. This might mean, for example, building coalitions of public, private, and nonprofit agencies to meet mutually agreed-upon needs. In this process, public servants will be accountable not only to the public interest but also to statutory and constitutional law, other agencies and levels of government, the media, professional standards, community values, democratic norms, professional standards, and citizen interests.

Restoring and maintaining public trust requires more than improvements in efficiency, which is what the "run government like a business" efforts of the New Public Management and the "reinventing government" movement have tried to do. After all, while treating citizens as customers may lead administrators to answer the phone by the third ring, it doesn't teach them to be responsive to the needs of the caller. Consequently, the New Public Service raises important concerns about pushing government toward the adoption of the values of business. Adopting business practices is one thing, but, as we have seen, many of the contemporary efforts to reform the management of government have gone well beyond adopting business *practices*. Instead, the focus has been on adopting a wide variety of business *values*, such as self-interest, competition, the market, and the entrepreneurial spirit. Unfortunately, consideration of important values such as participation, deliberation, leadership, expertise, responsibility, justice, and equity is minimized or lost altogether in this approach. The New Public Service argues that if citizens are to regain their confidence in government, they must perceive public institutions as responsive. And the best way to appear to be responsive is to be responsive.

This idea has important implications for the role of government. Instead of giving the traditional government response of "Yes, we can provide that service" or "No, we can't," administrators will need to respond to citizens' needs and concerns by saying such things as "Let's work together to figure out what we're going to do, and then to make it happen." In a world of active citizenship, in which community members are engaged in helping to shape policies and programs to meet their needs, public administrators must do more than simply deliver services, no matter how efficiently they do so. They must also take on a facilitating, conciliating, or mediating role. These are new roles that will require new skills; rather than exerting management control, administrators will need to learn and practice skills such as brokering, negotiating, and conflict resolution and to focus on issues of responsiveness and integrity rather than simply striving for efficiency. The New Public Service contends that the government shouldn't be run like a business; it should be run like a democracy, and the most important criteria for assessing administrative performance should be to examine how effectively the work of public officials has engaged citizens in the governance process and advanced the public interest.

To help public administrators learn the skills necessary to foster engagement and build "a culture of democratic governance" (NLC, 2011, p. 1), the National League of Cities (NLC) outlined seven actions designed to promote shared responsibility and engage more citizens in efforts to build and strengthen their communities. First, government leaders and administrators should model civility, working to ensure that decision making is conducted in a civil, responsible way. Second, they need to sharpen skills, developing proficiency in convening and facilitation, conflict resolution, mediation, and cultural competence. Third, they must create opportunities for informed engagement, giving citizens a firsthand look at how government works. Fourth, they must support a culture of community involvement, helping citizens understand that public problems cannot be solved by government alone. Fifth, they must make the most of technology, using the kinds of tools we discussed in Chapter 10 to inform and educate, solicit feedback, and conduct community conversations. Sixth, they must include everybody, involving citizens who traditionally have not been engaged and reaching out to future voters and leaders. Finally, they must make it last, making participation an ongoing process rather than a one-time product (pp. 2–6). As NLC notes, "The best examples of democratic governance are those that engage a diverse assortment of people and institutions in learning more about community issues and working together to arrive at solutions" (p. 1).

Public administrators can draw from a variety of means to educate citizens, invite them to share their views, and encourage their involvement in making recommendations, solving problems, assessing performance, delivering services, and mobilizing others. This process involves various combinations of four broad activities—generating information, deliberating, sharing delivery of services, and organizing—with different kinds of involvement stressing different combinations (Svara & Denhardt, 2011, pp. 21–22). Thus, developing an engaged community includes both citizen "exchange" activities that inform, collect information, and solicit input and consultations; and citizen "engagement" activities that promote collaboration, create dialogue, build relationships, and empower citizens in making decisions and taking responsibility for their community. To make such efforts successful, it is important to match the method to the intended purpose, be clear about the citizens' role and potential impact, listen, and be honest about how citizens' views and contributions have been used (Svara & Denhardt, 2011, pp. 25–26). As Denhardt and Denhardt (2001) argue, "While it's important to maintain a concern for legal and political standards and economic criteria, it is imperative that we place at the center of our work a concept of the public service based on and fully integrated with citizen discourse and the public interest. We should put democracy first" (p. 399).

Ethics and the Imperatives of Good Governance

Perhaps the most important purpose of public service is to work with others to foster good governance across administrative, political, and economic spheres. But what is "good governance"? While there are surely multiple answers to that question, establishing a proper ethical basis for public action is foundational. If the generation now in their teens and twenties has one significant contribution to make to the development of public service, it may be to identify and elaborate the moral and ethical dimensions of public administration and to assert moral leadership.

As we have seen, early writers in the field portrayed public administration primarily as managers' concern with the technical processes of implementing public policy. Over the years, public administrators have developed considerable skill in managing public programs—probably more than they are usually given credit for.

Others soon came to recognize that public administration is also a political concern— that administrators at all levels are deeply involved in shaping public policy. Despite recent rhetoric in Washington, there is every reason to expect that those in public organizations

CourseReader Assignment

Log in to **www.cengage.com** and open CourseReader to access the reading:

Read "The State of Social Equity in American Public Administration" by H. George Frederickson. The field of public administration has been described as being concerned with efficiency, effectiveness, and responsiveness. The notion of social equity fits nicely with these principles of public administration. It serves as a reminder that, whatever actions they take, whether in the design or implementation of public policy, public administrators act in terms of values.

What are the values that define the field of public administration for you? How does the notion of social equity fit into your response? Do you agree that public administrators have a responsibility to close the gaps between the haves and have-nots? How might that be possible?

will increasingly be called upon to do more than simply respond to legislative mandates; they will be asked to identify and to articulate important public interests.

Beyond a view of public administration as a managerial or a political concern, public administration today is increasingly an ethical concern. Indeed, all the "spontaneous" little actions you will take as an administrator will carry important value implications. At the root of every act of every public servant, whether in developing or executing public policy, lies a moral or ethical question.

What does it mean, then, to recognize public service as not only a managerial and political concern but also as a moral and ethical concern? For one thing, it means that public administrators must demonstrate in their own actions the highest standards of behavior. Beyond that, to see the public service as a moral and ethical concern requires recognizing that every action an administrator takes involves an effort to discover or to clarify the public interest.

The future public servant will likely be both active in policy development and responsive to the public interest. Our constitutional structure not only permits but also encourages an active executive and administrative role. Even more important is the implicit philosophical directive of the Constitution that public service is a special calling in a democracy and that those who participate in the public service, regardless of background or occupation, are guardians of a public trust.

This point is most critical at a time when our definition of public service is shifting. As we have noted, the public service is no longer merely that group of political and administrative officials employed by government agencies. Public service today involves a wide range of private and nonprofit organizations in the delivery of public goods and services. This development raises managerial concerns, political concerns, and most of all, moral and ethical concerns. Under these conditions, public administrators must assume leadership in establishing a high moral tone for the public service generally. In contrast to the often-heard advice that public administrators should follow the model of business, we might propose just the opposite: that public organizations and the values and commitments they represent should become models for all organizations, at least those involved in the management of public programs.

Ethical considerations have become a central theme in public administration around the world. In Japan, for example, lawmakers at the national level recently passed comprehensive legislation to ensure ethical practices by governmental officials. Among other provisions, the National Public Service Ethics Act, which took effect in April 2000, established a national ethics board to continuously monitor the compliance of government officials and to oversee investigations and punishment for violations of ethical standards.

For the public service to regain its proper role in our society, we will have to establish and maintain throughout government and the public service a true commitment to the values of democracy. Trust in the public service and the public's willingness to participate in the work of government will occur only if the public is convinced that those in office, whether political or administrative, seek the public interest (not merely their own) and do so with skill and responsibility. Only when our commitment to democratic practices and ideals is clear to all will we once again be able to establish public service as the highest calling in our society.

Commitment to democratic ideals involves concerns such as responsiveness and involvement, but also commitment to equity and justice. Consider for a moment the reasons that bring people to public service. No doubt high on the list would be "concern for the well-being of others." At one point in our history, we seemed to feel that the primary measure of success in the public service was the elimination of human suffering. Public officials are still at the forefront of dealing with the complex and difficult issues of homelessness, poverty, and drug addiction. Perhaps more than any other group, public administrators are uniquely situated to see and understand these concerns. They certainly should be able to pinpoint the failures of past policies, to suggest alternatives, and to work actively toward implementation with elected leaders. Indeed, they have a moral responsibility to do so.

While "good governance" is difficult to define, Jreisat (2011, pp. 432-434) offers a list of core values that are useful in thinking about what might be considered the ultimate purposes of public service. He suggests that good governance:

- Is ethical and accountable
- Creates trust and promotes broadly shared values, particularly accountability and sustained openness and transparency
- Is based on effective leadership both within government and across society
- Is where rules and legal standards for orderly conduct and progressive social transformation are constructed
- Is based on new and modified political and administrative forms to replace hierarchical, command and control systems.

At the center of public service, of course, is the ideal of service in the public interest. The opportunity and challenge are not necessarily to define what the public interest "is" at a particular point in time, but to make a centerpiece of our search for shared values and good governance in any era.

A Final Note

The challenges to public service are substantial and pose managerial, political, and ethical questions for all who participate in public programs. They will require careful analysis and effective action on the part of academics and practitioners in the field of public administration and beyond. Most of all, they are challenges that will require responsibility, both in the sense of acting responsibly and in the sense of accepting responsibility for our ideas and actions. The frontiers of public service will present quite difficult personal and professional choices. But responsible public servants will find their solution very rewarding. Albert Schweitzer once said, "I don't know where you will go or what you will do, but the ones among you that will be most happy will be those who serve." We would only add that especially happy will be those who serve the public, well and faithfully.

STUDY QUESTIONS

1. Discuss some of the changes in the image of public service over the last thirty years.

2. What would you recommend to attract and retain "the best and the brightest" in public service?

3. Discuss future trends in the field of public administration.

CASES AND EXERCISES

1. By most objective measures, public agencies are, on average, highly productive—at least in comparison to their private-sector counterparts. (Obviously, there are wide variations in both sectors, but the general conclusion seems valid.) The general public, however, seems to have exactly the opposite impression: that government agencies are hopelessly inefficient and unproductive. Part of the problem seems to be that people are more critical of government in the abstract than where it directly touches their lives. In fact, one study found that most people are highly critical of the coldness and inefficiency of government in general, but highly complimentary of specific government employees with whom they had dealt most recently.

In any case, there seems to be some disparity between image and reality—a disparity that is often quite damaging to the morale of the public workforce. Write an essay explaining why you think governments are considered less productive and less efficient than they really are. Consider the issue from several viewpoints. How would the issue appear from the perspective of a legislator? A public manager? A citizen? On the basis of your analysis, what should be done to improve the image of public service?

2. In this chapter, we have considered a number of trends that are likely to affect public service over the next decade or more. What do these trends mean in terms of the skills that individual public managers will require? Review once more the set of public management skills in Chapter 1, and then in small groups discuss the following questions: What specific skills will public managers likely utilize more frequently in the future than in the past? What, if any, will be de-emphasized? To what extent will the demands of future public service change the mix of conceptual, technical, and human skills needed for effective public management? Finally, how will the values that underlie the work of public managers shift as we move through the coming years?

3. Divide the class into groups ranging from seven to ten members each. Have each group describe a citizen engagement program that could be used by local government for actively involving citizens in defining environmental and sustainability issues, establishing policy, and/or implementing solutions. What are some of the specific steps that could be taken to facilitate broad-based participation and meaningful involvement?

FOR ADDITIONAL READING

Denhardt, Janet V., and Robert B. Denhardt. *The New Public Service*. 3rd ed. Armonk, NY: M.E. Sharpe, 2011.

Donahue, John D., and Joseph S. Nye, eds. *For the People: Can We Fix Public Service?* Cambridge, MA: Visions of Governance in the 21st Century, 2003.

Frederickson, George. *The Spirit of Public Administration*. San Francisco: Jossey-Bass, 1997.

Hesse, Joachim Jens, Christopher Hood, and B. Guy Peters, eds. *Paradoxes in Public Sector Reform: An International Comparison*. Berlin: Duncker & Humblot, 2003.

Ingraham, Patricia W., and Donald F. Kettl. *Agenda for Excellence: Public Service in America*. Chatham, NJ: Chatham House, 1992.

Ingraham, Patricia W., and Laurence E. Lynn, Jr., eds. *The Art of Governance: Analyzing Management and Administration*. Washington, DC: Georgetown University Press, 2004.

Ingraham, Patricia W., and Barbara Romzek. *Governance and the Public Service: Rethinking the Research Agenda for Public Sector Change*. San Francisco: Jossey-Bass, 1994.

Johnson, Norman J., and James H. Svara. *Justice for All: Promoting Social Equity in Public Administration*. Armonk, NY: M.E. Sharpe, 2011.

Kettl, Donald F. *The Global Public Management Revolution*. 2nd ed. Washington, DC: Brookings Institution Press, 2005.

King, Cheryl Simrell, and Camilla Stivers. *Government Is Us*. Thousand Oaks, CA: Sage Publications, 1998.

Lane, Jan-Erik. *Public Administration and Public Management: The Principal-Agent Perspective*. London: Routledge, 2005.

National Commission on the Public Service. *Leadership for America*. Washington, DC: National Commission, 1989.

Nye, Joseph S., Jr., Philip D. Zelikow, and David C. King, eds. *Why People Don't Trust Government*. Cambridge, MA: Harvard University Press, 1997.

Organisation for Economic and Co-operative Development (OECD). *Government of the Future*. PUMA Policy Brief No. 9. Paris: OECD, June 2001.

Thomas, John C. *Public Participation in Public Decisions*. San Francisco: Jossey-Bass, 1995.

Tummala, Krishna K., ed. *Comparative Bureaucratic Systems*. Lanham, MD: Lexington Books, 2003.

GLOSSARY

Accounting: The process of identifying, measuring, and communicating economic information to permit informed judgment and decision making.

Adverse or disparate impact: Criterion for showing that employment practices affect one group more harshly than another.

Affirmative action: Use of positive, results-oriented practices to ensure that women, minorities, individuals with disabilities, and other protected classes of people will be equitably represented in an organization.

Agenda setting: Phase in public policy process when certain problems come to be viewed as needing attention.

Allotments: Amounts that agencies are authorized to spend within a given period.

Apportionment: Process by which funds are allocated to agencies for specific portions of the year.

Appropriation: Legislative action to set aside funds and create budget authority for their expenditures.

Area of acceptance: Area within which the subordinate is willing to accept the decisions made by the supervisor.

Authorizing legislation: Legislative action that permits establishment or continuation of a particular program or agency.

Autocracy: Government by one.

Bargaining unit: The organization that will represent employees in conferring and negotiating various issues.

Block grants: Grants in which the money can be used for nearly any purpose within a specific functional field.

Bond: Promise to repay a certain amount (principal) at a certain time (maturity date) at a particular rate of interest.

Boundary spanning: Representing an organization to outside groups and organizations.

Bounded rationality: Seeking the best possible solution, but not necessarily the most rational, from a purely economic standpoint.

Brainstorming: Technique for enhancing the alternative-generating portion of the decision-making process.

Budget padding: Proposing a higher budget than is actually needed.

Business cycle: Periods of economic growth featuring inflation and high employment followed by periods of recession or depression and unemployment.

Capital budget: A separate budget tracking capital expenditures.

Capital expenditures: Spending for items that will be used over a period of several years.

Capital grants: Grants for use in construction or renovation.

Categorical or project grants: Grants requiring that the money may be spent for only a limited purpose; typically available on a competitive basis.

Charter: Local government's equivalent of a constitution.

Coercive federalism: The use of mandates and preemptions of state and local authority by the federal government.

Commission: A form of local government in which the citizens elect a set of commissioners, each of which acts as director of a particular department.

Concurrent resolution: A resolution of both houses of Congress not requiring the president's signature.

Confederation: A system of government in which constituent units grant powers to the central government.

Constituent policy: Policy designed to benefit the public generally or to serve the government.

Continuing resolution: Resolution permitting the government to continue operating until an appropriations measure is passed.

Contracting: Actions by governments to work with nongovernmental organizations or businesses under contract to deliver services.

Cooperative federalism: Greater sharing of responsibilities between federal and state governments.

Co-optation: Situations in which citizens are made to feel involved but are allowed to exercise little real power.

Coproduction: Using volunteer activity to supplement or supplant the work of government officials.

Cost-benefit: Identifying and quantifying both negative impacts (costs) and positive impacts (benefits) of a proposal, then subtracting one from the other to arrive at a net benefit.

Cost-effectiveness technique: An evaluation technique that compares policies by quantifying their total costs and effects.

Council-manager: A form of local government in which the council is elected and appoints a professional administrator to manage the day-to-day affairs of the city.

Councils of government: Oversight bodies representing various localities to help coordinate local affairs.

Cross-cutting requirements: Rules that apply to most grant programs.

Debt capacity: Value of a city's resources combined with the ability of the government to draw on them to provide payment.

Decision analysis: Technique wherein decisions are likely to be made sequentially and under some degree of uncertainty.

Decision support system: Interactive system that can assist in the solution of unstructured or nonroutine problems.

Decision tree: Technique that identifies various possible outcomes, given the risk associated with each.

Deferral: Decision by the president to withhold expenditure of funds for a brief period.

Delegation: Assigning tasks to others.

Democracy: A political system in which decision-making power is widely shared among members of the society.

Deontology: Belief that broad principles of rightness and wrongness can be established and are not dependent on particular circumstances.

Dillon's Rule: Municipalities have only those powers granted in their charters; cities are creatures of the state.

Direct orders: Requirements or restrictions that are enforced by one government over another.

Discretionary spending: That portion of the budget still open to changes by the president and Congress.

Distributive policy: Policy involving use of general tax funds to provide assistance and benefits to individuals or groups.

Dual federalism: Pattern in which federal and state governments are struggling for power and influence with little intergovernmental cooperation.

Effectiveness: Extent to which a program is achieving or failing to achieve its stated objectives.

Efficiency: Relationship between inputs and outputs.

Enterprise zone: Designation of an area within a city permitting special tax incentives and other benefits for businesses willing to relocate there.

Entitlement grants: Grants that provide assistance to persons who meet certain criteria.

Entitlement programs: Programs that provide a specified set of benefits to those who meet certain eligibility requirements.

Equal employment opportunity: Refers to efforts to eliminate employment discrimination on the basis of race, ethnic background, sex, age, or physical handicap; ensures that all persons have an equal chance to compete for employment and promotions based on job qualifications.

Equality: The idea that all persons have an equal claim to life, liberty, and the pursuit of happiness.

Ethical or moral relativism: Belief that moral judgment can be made only by taking into account the context in which action occurs.

Ethics: Process by which we clarify right and wrong and act on what we take to be right.

Ethics audit: Evaluation of the value premises that guide an organization's action.

Excise tax: Tax applied to the sale of specific commodities.

Executive order: A presidential mandate directed to and governing, with the effect of law, the actions of government officials and agencies.

Expert systems: Computer programs that mimic the decision-making processes of human experts within a particular field.

Exploratory evaluation: Investigating a variety of hunches or intuitions about program operations.

Federal: Refers to a system of government involving a division of powers between two levels of government, typically federal and state.

Fiduciary funds: Funds used when government must hold assets for individuals or when government holds resources to be transmitted to another organization.

Final-offer arbitration: Technique in which both parties must present their best offer with the understanding that an arbitrator will choose one or the other without modification.

Fiscal policy: Public policy concerned with the impact of government taxation and spending on the economy.

Fiscal year (FY): Government's basic accounting period.

Formula grants: Grants that employ a specific division rule to indicate how much money any given jurisdiction will receive.

Franchise: Exclusive award to one firm (or a limited number) to operate a certain business within a jurisdiction.

Functional principle: Horizontal division of labor.

Fund balance: The remainder when an organization's liabilities are subtracted from its assets.

Gainsharing plan: Monetary award for a group of employees based on savings generated by the group.

General fund: Fund that handles "unrestricted" funds of government.

General obligation bond: A bond pledging the full faith and credit of the governmental jurisdiction.

Grants: Transfers of money (and/or property) from one government to another.

Grantsmanship: Skills needed to compete successfully in the grant process.

Gross domestic product (GDP): Measure of total spending in the economy; includes total personal consumption, private investment, and government purchases.

Hidden agenda: Privately held goals and priorities.

Home rule: Provision allowing cities greater autonomy over local activities.

Impoundment: Withholding of funds authorized and appropriated by law.

Incremental: An approach to budgeting that takes last year's budget as a base and makes only marginal adjustments to that base.

Independent agencies: Agencies intentionally created outside the normal cabinet organization.

Individualism: The idea that the dignity and integrity of the individual are of supreme importance.

Institutional subsystem: System responsible for adapting the organization to its environment and for anticipating and planning for the future.

Intergovernmental relations: All the complex and interdependent relations among various levels of government.

Interorganizational networks: Relationships within and among various groups and organizations working in a single policy area.

Interorganizational relations: Relationships between governments and other governments and between governments and private and nonprofit agencies.

Interstate compact: Agreement among states to resolve disputes or work together on common problems.

Interventionist: External consultant brought in to reveal dysfunctional patterns of behavior and to try to develop more effective working relationships.

Iron triangle: Term given to a coalition of interest groups, agency personnel, and members of Congress created to exert influence on a particular policy issue.

Job description: A thorough analysis of the work to be done and the capabilities for a job; typically contains these elements: job title, duties required, responsibilities, and job qualifications.

Lateral entry: Entry into government positions at any level.

Legislative casework: Review and advocacy by legislators or their staff members with respect to constituents' interactions with government.

Legislative veto: Statutory provision that gives Congress the authority to approve or disapprove certain executive actions.

Liberty: The idea that individual citizens of a democracy should have a high degree of self-determination.

Line-item budget: Budget format for listing categories of expenditures along with amounts allocated to each.

Line-item veto: An executive function allowing the executive to veto specific items in an appropriations bill rather than choosing between "all or nothing."

Management information system: System that collects and summarizes routine information as a basis for structuring decision making.

Managerial subsystem: System concerned with providing necessary resources for accomplishing a technical task and mediating between the technical and institutional subsystems.

Managerialism: Belief that government could and should be run like a business based strictly on economic principles and management prerogative.

Mandate: Order requiring a government to do something.

Mayor-council: A form of local government in which both the mayor and council are elected.

Merit pay: Increases in salary and wages that are tied to actual quality of work performed.

Merit principle: Concept that selection and treatment of government employees should be based on merit or competence rather than personal or political favoritism.

Morality: Practices and activities considered right or wrong and the values those practices reflect.

Neutral competence: The belief that a neutral public bureaucracy following the mandates of a legislative body will meet the requirements of democracy.

Nominal group: Face-to-face meeting that allows only limited interaction among participants.

Nonprofit organizations: Organizations prohibited by law from distributing surplus revenues to individuals.

Objective responsibility: Assurance of responsiveness through external controls.

Oligarchy: Government by the few.

Ombudsman: Permanent office that receives complaints and acts on behalf of citizens to secure information, request services, or pursue grievances.

Operating grants: Grants for use in development and operation of specific programs.

Organization development: Process-oriented approach to planned change.

Organizational culture: Basic patterns of attitudes, beliefs, and values that underlie an organization's operation.

Outcome evaluation: Evaluation focusing on the results of program activity and the extent to which a program meets its objectives.

Outlays: Another term for government spending.

Parity principle: Idea that an individual should have equal amounts of authority and responsibility.

Participant-observer: Someone in either the target population or the agency who makes observations and draws conclusions based on firsthand experience.

Performance appraisal: Specific evaluation with respect to an individual's progress in completing specified tasks.

Performance auditing: Analysis and evaluation of the effective performance of agencies in carrying out their objectives.

Performance bonus: One-time monetary award based on superior performance on the job or in a particular task.

Performance budget: Budget format organized around programs or activities; includes various performance measurements that indicate the relationship between work actually done and its cost.

Performance measurement: The process of measuring individual, group, and organizational performance against strategic goals or targets.

PERT: A way to monitor the time or costs of various activities required to complete a project, showing the sequence in which the activities must be completed.

Picket-fence federalism: Pattern of intergovernmental relations in which the horizontal bars represent levels of government and the vertical slats represent various substantive fields.

Piecework bonus: Incentive that ties the worker's productivity in a given task to the monetary rewards he or she receives.

Planning-programming-budgeting system (PPBS): Effort to connect planning, systems analysis, and budgeting in a single exercise.

Policy: Statement of goals and intentions with respect to a particular problem or set of problems.

Policy analysis: Process of researching or analyzing public problems to provide policy makers with specific information about the range of available policy options and the advantages and disadvantages of different approaches.

Policy analysts: Persons who provide important information about public programs through research into the operations and impacts of the programs.

Policy entrepreneur: A person willing to invest personal time, energy, and money in pursuit of particular policy changes.

Political economy approach: Focus on politics and economies as categories for analyzing organizational behavior.

Position classification: Analyzing and organizing jobs on the basis of duties, responsibilities, and knowledge and skills required to perform them.

Postaudit: An audit or review of agency actions that takes place after the fiscal year and is concerned with verifying the correctness and propriety of agency operations.

Preaudit: Review in advance of an actual expenditure.

Preemption: Federal government efforts to take over an area traditionally associated with state government.

Privatization: Use of nongovernmental agencies to provide goods and services previously provided by government.

Process charting/flowcharting: Graphically demonstrating the various steps in an operation, the people who perform each step, and relationships among those elements.

Process evaluation: Evaluation that focuses on improvements and organizational processes that will result in more efficient and effective results.

Program design: The process of formulating measurable program goals and objectives, as well as developing organizational processes that can effectively meet these goals and objectives.

Program managers: Persons ranging from the executive level to the supervisory level who are in charge of particular governmental programs.

Progressive tax: One that taxes those with higher incomes at a higher rate.

Proportional tax: One that taxes everyone at the same rate.

Proprietary funds: Used to account for government activities that more closely resemble private business.

Public corporation: An essentially commercial agency in which work requires greater latitude and which acquires at least a portion of its funding in the marketplace (e.g., Tennessee Valley Authority).

Public policy: Authoritative statements made by legitimate governmental actors about public problems.

Reconciliation bill: Legislative action that attempts to reconcile individual actions in taxes, authorizations, or appropriations with the totals.

Redistributive policy: Policy designed to take taxes from certain groups and give them to another group.

Reengineering: One approach to redefining work processes and organizational structures to be in line with agency outcomes.

Regressive tax: One that taxes those with lower incomes at a proportionally higher rate than those with higher incomes.

Regulatory commission: Group formed to regulate a particular area of the economy; usually headed by a group of individuals appointed by the president and confirmed by the Senate.

Regulatory policy: Policy designed to limit actions of persons or groups to protect all or parts of the general public.

Representative bureaucracy: The idea that public agencies whose employees reflect certain demographic characteristics of the population as a whole are likely to operate more in line with the policy preferences of the general citizenry.

Reprogramming: Taking money appropriated for one program and diverting it to another that emerges as a higher priority.

Rescission: Presidential decision to permanently withhold funds.

Revenue bond: Bond that promises the anticipated revenues of the project as security.

Revenue sharing: Grant pattern in which the money can be used any way the recipient government chooses.

Risk management: Ways that public organizations anticipate and cope with risks.

Risk shift: Difference in the daringness of decisions group members make as a group, compared to the average risk of the same decision if each member made it alone.

Role ambiguity: Occurs when the rights and responsibilities of the job are not clearly understood.

Role conflict: Occurs when one faces two different and incompatible sets of demands.

Rule making: Administrative establishment of general guidelines for application to a class of people or a class of actions at some future time.

Rule of three: Provision of most merit systems that requires at least the top three applicants' names to be forwarded to the hiring official to allow some flexibility in selection.

Sales tax: Tax applied to goods and services at either the retail or wholesale level.

Satisficing decision: One that is just "good enough" in terms of some criterion.

Scalar principle: Vertical division of labor among various organizational levels.

Scientific management: Approach to management based on carefully defined laws, rules, and principles.

Self-insurance: The development of an insurance pool by the jurisdiction itself.

Sexual harassment: Any unwarranted and nonreciprocal verbal or physical sexual advances or derogatory remarks that the recipient finds offensive or that interfere with his or her job performance.

Span of control: Number of people that one individual can supervise effectively.

Special districts: Local governments created for a specific purpose within a specific area.

Spoils system: The ability to give government jobs to the party faithful; "to the victor belong the spoils."

Staff managers: Persons who support the work of program managers through budgeting and financial management, personnel and labor relations, and purchasing and procurement.

Stakeholder: Any individual, group, or organization that has a serious interest—or a stake—in program outcomes.

Strategic planning: Matching organizational objectives and capabilities to the anticipated demands of the environment to produce a plan of action that will ensure achievement of objectives.

Structured interviews: Those in which a previously developed set of questions is used with each applicant.

Subjective responsibility: Assurance of responsiveness based on an individual's character.

Suggestion award programs: Incentives for employees who make specific suggestions that result in savings for the organization.

Sunset law: Provision that sets a specific termination date for a program.

Sunshine law: Provision that requires agencies to conduct business in public view.

Supplemental appropriation: Bill passed during the fiscal year that adds new money to an agency's budget for the same fiscal year.

Supply-side economics: Argument that decreased taxes and government spending will stimulate capital investment and economic growth.

System: Set of regularized interactions configured or "bounded" in a way that differentiates and separates them from other actions that constitute the system's environment.

Systems approach: Suggestion that public (or other) organizations can be viewed in the same general way as biological or physical systems.

Systems theory: Effort to identify the interactions of various internal and external elements that impinge on an organization's operations.

Task forces: Groups brought together to work on specific organizational problems.

Technical subsystem: System concerned with the effective performance of an organization's actual work.

Time series analysis: Making a number of observations about the target population both before and after program intervention.

Two-factor theory: Model of motivation involving two variables: job satisfaction and job dissatisfaction.

Uncontrollable expenditures: Expenditures or commitments made previously that are off-limits for current legislation.

Union shop: An arrangement under which all members of an agency are required to join the union that represents them.

Unit determination: Decision to include or exclude certain groups in a bargaining unit.

Utilitarianism: Philosophy of the greatest good for the greatest number of people.

Vouchers: Coupons citizens redeem for goods or services.

Whipsaw tactics: Argument that pay or benefits negotiated by one group should be applied to others.

Zero-base budgeting: Budget format that presents information about the efficiency and effectiveness of existing programs and highlights possibilities for eliminating or reducing programs.

REFERENCES

Chapter One

Appleby, Paul. *Policy and Administration.* Tuscaloosa, AL: University of Alabama Press, 1949.

Blumenthal, W. Michael. "Candid Reflections of a Businessman in Washington." In *Public Management,* edited by James L. Perry and Kenneth L. Kraemer. Palo Alto, CA: Mayfield Publishing, 1983.

Flanders, Loretta R., and Dennis Utterback. "The Management Excellence Inventory." *Public Administration Review* 45 (May/June 1985): 403–410.

Katz, Robert L. "Skills of an Effective Administrator." *Harvard Business Review* 52 (September/October 1974): 90–102.

Kettl, Donald F. *The Next Government of the United States: Why Our Institutions Fail Us and How to Fix Them.* New York: W.W. Norton, 2009.

O'Leary, Rosemary, and Lisa Bingham. *The Collaborative Public Manager: New Ideas for the Twenty-First Century.* Washington, DC: Georgetown University Press, 2009.

Redford, Emmette S. *Democracy in the Administrative State.* New York: Oxford University Press, 1969.

Rosenbloom, David. *Public Administration.* New York: McGraw-Hill, 1993.

Simon, Herbert A., Donald W. Smithburg, and Victor A. Thompson. *Public Administration.* New York: Knopf, 1950.

White, Leonard D. *The Study of Public Administration.* New York: Macmillan, 1948.

Willoughby, W. F. *Principles of Public Administration.* Baltimore, MD: Johns Hopkins University Press, 1927.

Wilson, Woodrow. "The Study of Public Administration." *Political Science Quarterly* 2 (June 1887): 197–222.

Chapter Two

Archibald, Samuel J. "The Freedom of Information Act Revisited." *Public Administration Review* 39, no. 4 (July/August 1979): 311–317.

Barry, Donald D., and Howard R. Whitcomb. *The Legal Foundations of Public Administration.* 3rd ed. Lanham, MD: Rowman and Littlefield, 2005.

Boris, Elizabeth T. "Nonprofit Organizations in a Democracy: Varied Roles and Responsibilities." In *Nonprofits and Government: Collaboration and Conflict,* edited by Elizabeth T. Boris and C. Eugene Steuerle, pp. 3–29. Washington, DC: Urban Institute Press, 1999.

Bowman, Ann, and Richard C. Kearney. *The Resurgence of the States.* Englewood Cliffs, NJ: Prentice-Hall, 1986.

Buss, Terry F., Alan Balutis, and Dwight Ink. "American Governance 3.0: Issues and Prospects." In *Transforming American Governance: Rebooting the Public Square,* edited by Alan P. Balutis, Terry F. Buss, and Dwight Ink, pp. 3–39. Armonk, NY: M.E. Sharpe, 2011.

Caldwell, Lynton. *Administrative Theories of Hamilton and Jefferson.* New York: Russell & Russell, 1964.

Cooper, Phillip J. "Conflict or Constructive Tension: The Changing Relationship of Judges and Administrators." *Public Administration Review* 45, special issue (November 1985): 643–652.

Cooper, Phillip J. *Public Law and Public Administration.* Palo Alto, CA: Mayfield Publishing, 1983.

Cooper, Phillip J. *Public Law and Public Administration.* 3rd ed. Itasca, IL: F.E. Peacock Publishers, 2000.

"Council-Manager System." *American City and County,* 121, no. 10 (September 2006):16.

Crenson, Matthew A. *The Federal Machine.* Baltimore, MD: Johns Hopkins University Press, 1975.

DeMuth, Christopher. "Contemporary Conservatism and Government Regulation." In *Crisis of Conservatism? The Republican Party, the Conservative Movement, and American Politics after Bush,* edited by Joel D. Aberbach and Gillian Peele, pp. 303–334. New York: Oxford University Press, 2011.

Drajem, Mark, and Catherine Dodge. "Obama Wrote 5% Fewer Rules Than Bush While Costing Business." *Bloomberg* (October 25, 2011), http://www.bloomberg.com/news/2011-10-25/obama-wrote-5-fewer-rules-than-bush-while-costing-business.html.

Dudley, E. Susan. "The Bush Administration Regulatory Record." *Regulation* 27, no. 4 (Winter 2004–2005): 4–9.

The Economist. "Regulation and the Obama Administration: Red Tape Rising" (January 20, 2011).

Funk, William F., Jeffrey S. Lubbers, and Charles Pou, Jr., eds. *Federal Administrative Procedure Sourcebook.* 4th ed. Chicago: ABA Publishing, 2008.

Gilmour, Robert S. "Agency Administration by Judiciary." *Southern Review of Public Administration* 6, no. 1 (Spring 1982): 26–42.

Hall, Daniel E. *Administrative Law: Bureaucracy in a Democracy.* 3rd ed. Upper Saddle River, NJ: Pearson Prentice Hall, 2006.

Harrison, John, and Olga Khazan. "Obama Adds Cabinet Seat for SBA Administrator, Proposes Merging Commerce Agencies," *Washington Post* (January 13, 2012), http://www.washingtonpost.com/blogs/on-small-business/post/obama-adds-cabinet-seat-for-sbaadministrator-proposes-merging-commerce-agencies/2012/01/13/gIQAd00KwP_blog.html.

Heinzerling, Lisa, and Mark V. Tushnet. *The Regulatory and Administrative State: Materials, Cases, Comments.* New York: Oxford University Press, 2006.

ICMA. "Form of Government Statistics" (2010), http://icma.org/en/icma/knowledge_network/documents/kn/Document/302186/Form_of_Government_Statistics_2010.

Karl, Barry D. Executive Reorganization and Reform in the New Deal. Cambridge, MA: Harvard University Press, 1963.

Kessler, David. *A Question of Intent: A Great American Battle with a Deadly Industry.* New York: Public Affairs, 2001.

Kettl, Donald F. "Obama's Stealth Revolution: Quietly Reshaping the Way Government Works." In *Transforming American Governance: Rebooting the Public Square,* edited by Alan P. Balutis, Terry F. Buss, and Dwight Ink, pp. 285–289. Armonk, NY: M.E. Sharpe, 2011.

Kettl, Donald F. "The Transformation of Governance: Globalization, Devolution, and the Role of Government." *Public Administration Review* 60, no. 6 (2000): 488–497.

Kingdon, John W. *Agendas, Alternatives, and Public Policies.* 2nd ed. New York: HarperCollins, 1995.

Kraft, Michael E., and Scott R. Furlong. *Public Policy: Politics, Analysis, and Alternatives.* 2nd ed. Washington, DC: CQ Press, 2007.

Leonhardt, David. "In Health Bill, Obama Attacks Wealth Inequality." *New York Times* (March 23, 2010).

Light, Paul C. *Making Nonprofits Work: A Report on the Tides of Nonprofit Management Reform.* Washington, DC: Brookings Institution/Aspen Institute, 2000.

Lowi, Theodore. "Four Systems of Policy, Politics, and Choice." *Public Administration Review* 32 (July/August 1972): 298–310.

Meckler, Laura, and Carol E. Lee. "White House Regulation Shift Is a Political Bet." *Wall Street Journal* (September 12, 2011).

Meier, Kenneth J. *Politics and the Bureaucracy.* Monterey, CA: Wadsworth, 1987.

Moe, Ronald C. "The Emerging Federal Quasi Government: Issues of Management and Accountability." *Public Administration Review* 61, no. 3 (2001): 290–312.

Nelson, Michael. "A Short, Ironic History of American National Bureaucracy." *Journal of Politics* 44, no. 3 (August 1982): 747–778.

Niskanen, William A. "The Clinton Regulatory Legacy." *Regulation* 24, no. 2 (Summer 2001): 42.

Pfiffner, James P. "The First MBA President: George W. Bush as Public Administrator." *Public Administration Review* 67 (2007): 6–20.

Reich, Robert B. "Public Administration and Public Deliberation: An Interpretive Essay." *Yale Law Review* 94 (1985): 1617–1641.

Ripley, Randall, and Grace A. Franklin. *Congress, Policy, and the Bureaucracy.* Chicago: Dorsey Press, 1987.

Salamon, Lester M. *America's Nonprofit Sector: A Primer.* 2nd ed. New York: Foundation Center, 1999.

Villalobos, Jose, and Justin S. Vaughn. "More Czars than the Romanovs? Obama's Czars in Historical and Legal Context." Paper for the APSA 2010 Annual Meeting.

Vlk, Bruce. "Post–New Public Management under the Obama Administration: An Early Snapshot." *Michigan Journal of Public Affairs* 8 (Spring 2011): 3–17.

Walsh, Annmarie Hauck. *The Public's Business.* Cambridge, MA: MIT Press, 1978.

White, Leonard D. *The Federalists.* New York: Macmillan, 1948.

U.S. Census Bureau. *Statistical Abstract of the United States.* Washington, DC: Government Printing Office, 2011.

Chapter Three

Berman, David. "State/Local Relations." In *Municipal Yearbook.* Washington, DC: International City Management Association, 1992.

Berrios, Ruben. "Government Contracts and Contractor Behavior." *Journal of Business Ethics* 63 (2006): 119–130.

Bevir, Mark. *The Sage Handbook of Governance.* Thousand Oaks, CA: Sage Publications, 2011.

Bowman, Ann O'M., and Michael A. Pagano. "The State of American Federalism, 1991–1992." *Publius* 22 (Summer 1992): 1–20.

Bryson, John. *Strategic Planning for Private and Nonprofit Organizations.* San Francisco: Jossey-Bass, 1995.

Carver, John, and Miriam Mayhew Carver. *Basic Principles of Policy Governance.* Vol. 1 of *CarverGuide Series on Effective Board Governance.* San Francisco: Jossey-Bass, 1996.

Cohen, Steven, and William B. Eimicke. *The Responsible Contract Manager: Protecting the Public Interest in an Outsourced World.* Washington, DC: Georgetown University Press, 2008.

Conlan, Tim, and John Dinan. "Federalism, the Bush Administration, and the Transformation of American Conservatism." *Publius* 37 (Summer 2007): 279–303.

Conlan, Tim, and John Dinan. "Inflection Point? Federalism and the Obama Administration." *Publius* 41 (Summer 2011): 421–446.

Cooper, Phillip J. *Governing by Contract.* Washington, DC: CQ Press, 2003.

Eadie, D. C. *Extraordinary Board Leadership: The Seven Keys to High-Impact Governance*. New York: Aspen Publishing, 2001.

Eggers, William D. *Government 2.0*. Lanham, MD: Rowman and Littlefield, 2007, pp. 106–107.

Fredericksen, Patricia, and Rosanne London. "Disconnect in the Hollow State: The Pivotal Role of Organizational Capacity in Community-Based Development Organizations." *Public Administration Review* 60, no. 3 (May/June 2000): 230–239.

Goldsmith, Stephen, and William D. Eggers. *Governing by Network*. Washington, DC: Brookings Institution Press, 2004.

Greene, Stephen G. "Getting the Basics Right." *Chronicle of Philanthropy* 13, no. 14 (May 3, 2001): 1, 9–12.

Gullo, Theresa. "History and Evaluation of the Unfunded Mandates Reform Act." *National Tax Journal* 57, no. 3 (September 2004): 559–570.

Gurwitt, Rob. "The Lonely Leap." *Governing* 13, no. 10 (July 2000): 38–44.

Hernandez, Shawn. "Power of Partnerships." *Governing* 14, no. 9 (June 2001): 10.

Hult, Karen M., and Charles Walcott. *Governing Public Organizations*. Pacific Grove, CA: Brooks/Cole, 1990.

Kettl, Donald F. *The Next Government of the United States: Why Our Institutions Fail Us and How to Fix Them*. New York: W.W. Norton, 2009.

Kettl, Donald F. "Transformation of Governance: Globalization, Devolution and the Role of Government." *Public Administration Review* 60, no. 6 (November/December 2000): 488–497.

Kincaid, John. "From Cooperative to Coercive Federalism." *Annals of the American Academy of Political and Social Science* 509 (American Federalism: The Third Century, May 1990): 139–152.

Light, Paul. *Making Non-Profits Work*. Washington, DC: Brookings Institution Press, 2000.

Liu, Amy, Roland Anglin, Jr., Richard Mizelle, and Allison Plyer, eds. *Resilience and Opportunity*. Washington, DC: Brookings Institution Press, 2011.

Mariani, Michele. "e-Permitting 101." *Governing* 14, no. 7 (April 2001): 86–88.

Matthews, Trudi. "The Medicare Prescription Drug, Improvement and Modernization Act of 2003: Health Care Changes." *The Book of the States* (2004): 544–548.

Metzger, Gillian E. "Federalism under Obama." *William and Mary Law Review* 53 (November 2011): 567–619.

Nathan, Richard P. "There Will Always Be a New Federalism." *Journal of Public Administration Research and Theory* 16 (2006): 499–510.

Nathan, Richard P., Fred C. Doolittle, and associates. *Reagan and the States*. Princeton, NJ: Princeton University Press, 1987.

Nice, David C. *Federalism: The Politics of Intergovernmental Relations*. New York: St. Martin's Press, 1987.

The Nonprofit Sector in Brief—Facts and Figures from the Nonprofit Almanac 2007. Center on Nonprofits and Philanthropy at the Urban Institute, p. 5, www.urban.org/UploadedPDF/311373_nonprofit_sector.pdf.

Office of Management and Budget, *Budget of the United States Government, 2012*, ch. 18. Washington, DC: Government Printing Office, 2012.

Osborne, David, and Ted Gaebler. *Reinventing Government: How the Entrepreneurial Spirit Is Transforming the Public Sector*. Reading, MA: Addison-Wesley, 1992.

PA Times, 27, no. 8 (August 2004): 1.

Pittman, James E. *21st Century Issues in America: An Introduction to Public Administration Theory and Practice*. Bloomington, IN: Author House Publications, 2009.

Plotnick, Robert, Marcia Meyers, Jennifer Romich, and Stephen Rathgab Smith, eds. *Old Assumptions, New Realities*. New York: Russell Sage, 2011.

Posner, Paul. "The Politics of Coercive Federalism in the Bush Era." *Publius* 37 (Summer 2007): 390–412.

President Obama, Presidential Memorandum, May 20, 2009.

"The Pros and Cons of Privatizing Government Functions," *Governing Magazine* (December 2010), http://www.governing.com/topics/mgmt/pros-cons-privatizing-government-functions.html#.

"Reducing Waste and Wartime Contracts," *Washington Post* (August 28, 2011), http://www.washingtonpost.com/opinions/reducing-waste-in-wartime-contracts/2011/08/26/gIQAyqQhlJ_story.html.

Rosenau, Pauline Vaillancourt, ed. *Public-Private Policy Partnerships*. Cambridge, MA: MIT Press, 2000.

Sagawa, Shirley, and Eli Segal. *Common Interest, Common Good: Creating Value through Business and Social Sector Partnerships*. Boston: Harvard Business School Press, 2000.

Smith, Bucklin & Associates. *The Complete Guide to Nonprofit Management*. 2nd ed. New York: John Wiley & Sons, 2000.

Smucker, Bob. *The Nonprofit Lobbying Guide*. 2nd ed. Washington, DC: Independent Sector, 1999.

Stone, Charles F., and Isabel V. Sawhill. *Economic Policy in the Reagan Years*. Washington, DC: The Urban Institute, 1984.

Sunderman, Gail L. "The Federal Role in Education: From the Reagan to the Obama Administration." *Voices in Urban Education* 24 (Summer 2009): 6–14.

Walker, David B. "The Advent of an Ambiguous Federalism and the Emergence of New Federalism III." *Public Administration Review* 56 (May/June 1996): 271–280.

Walters, Jonathan. "The Welfare Bonanza." *Governing Magazine* (January 2000), http://www.governing.com/topics/health-human-services/Welfare-Bonanza.html.

Wise, Charles R. "Judicial Federalism: The Resurgence of the Supreme Court's Role in the Protection of State Sovereignty." *Public Administration Review* 58, no. 2 (March/April 1998): 95–98.

Wise, Charles R. "The Supreme Court's New Constitutional Federalism: Implications for Public Administration." *Public Administration Review* 61, no. 3 (May/June 2001): 343–358.

Wright, Deil S. *Understanding Intergovernmental Relations*. 3rd ed. Pacific Grove, CA: Brooks/Cole, 1988.

Chapter Four

Andrews, Rhys. *Strategic Management and Public Service Performance*. New York: Palgrave Macmillan, 2012.

Bardach, Eugene. *The Implementation Game*. Cambridge, MA: MIT Press, 1977.

Beland, Daniel, and Alex Waddan. *The Politics of Policy Change*. Washington, DC: Georgetown University Press, 2012.

Birkland, Thomas A. *An Introduction to the Policy Process*. 3rd ed. Armonk, NY: M.E. Sharpe, 2011.

Bryson, John M. *Strategic Planning for Public and Nonprofit Organizations: A Guide to Strengthening and Sustaining Organizational Achievement*. 3rd ed. San Francisco: Jossey-Bass, 2004.

Chelimsky, Eleanor. *Program Evaluation: Patterns and Directions*. Washington, DC: American Society for Public Administration, 1985.

Fischer, Frank, Gerald Miller, and Mara S. Sidney. *Handbook of Public Policy Analysis: Theory, Politics, and Methods* (Public Administration and Public Policy). Boca Raton, FL: CRC/Taylor & Francis, 2007.

Geva-May, Iris. *Thinking like a Policy Analyst*. New York: Palgrave Macmillan, 2005.

Greiner, Larry E., and Thomas G. Cummings. *Dynamic Strategy-Making: A Real-Time Approach for the 21st Century Leader*. San Francisco: Jossey-Bass, 2009.

Gulick, Luther. "Notes on the Theory of Organization." In *Papers on the Science of Administration*, edited by L. Gulick and L. Urwick, pp. 1–46. New York: Institute of Public Administration, 1937.

Hammer, Michael, and James Champy. *Reengineering the Corporation: A Manifesto for Business Revolution*. New York: Harper, 1993.

Jennings, Edward T., Jr., Dale Krane, Alex N. Pattakos, and B. J. Reed, eds. *From Nation to States*. Albany: State University of New York Press, 1986.

Kraft, Michael E., and Scott R. Furlong. *Public Policy: Politics, Analysis, and Alternatives*. Washington, DC: CQ Press, 2009.

Latane, Henry A. "The Rationality Model in Organizational Decision Making." In *The Social Science of Organizations*, edited by Harold J. Leavitt. Englewood Cliffs, NJ: Prentice-Hall, 1963.

Linden, Russell. *Seamless Government*. San Francisco: Jossey-Bass, 1994.

Pressman, Jeffrey, and Aaron Wildavsky. *Implementation*. Berkeley: University of California Press, 1973.

Quade, E. S. *Analysis for Public Decisions*. 2nd ed. New York: North-Holland, 1989.

Sabatier, Paul A. *Theories of the Policy Process*. Boulder, CO: Westview Press, 2007.

Stokey, Edith, and Richard Zechauser. *A Primer for Policy Analysis*. New York: Norton, 1978.

Stone, Deborah. *The Policy Paradox*. New York: W.W. Norton, 2011.

Thompson, James D. *Organizations in Action*. New York: McGraw-Hill, 1967.

Chapter Five

Berne, Robert, and Richard Schramm. *The Financial Analysis of Governments*. Englewood Cliffs, NJ: Prentice-Hall, 1986.

Calmes, Jackie. "Obama, Breaking 'From a Troubled Past,' Seeks Budget to Reshape U.S. Priorities." *New York Times* (February 27, 2009), A1.

Congressional Budget Office. *The Long Term Budget Outlook*. Washington, DC: CBO, 2007.

Goldfarb, Zachary, "S and P Downgrades U.S. Credit Rating for the First Time." *Washington Post*, August 5, 2011.

Joyce, Philip G. "The Federal Line Item Veto Experiment: After the Supreme Court Ruling, What's Next?" *Public Budgeting and Finance* 18 (December 1998): 3–21.

Joyce, Phillip G., and Scott Pattison. "Public Budgeting in 2020: Return to Equilibrium, or Continued Mismatch between Demands and Resources?" *Public Administration Review* 70 (2010): s24–s32.

Lee, Carol E., and Damian Paletta. "Obama Seeks New Taxes on Rich." *Wall Street Journal* (February 14, 2012), A1.

Office of Management and Budget (OMB). *A New Era of Responsibility: Renewing America's Promise*. Washington, DC: Government Printing Office, 2009.

Rubin, Irene. *Public Budgeting: Policy, Process, and Politics* (ASPA Classics). Armonk, NY: M.E. Sharpe, 2008.

Rubin, Irene S. "New Directions in Public Budgeting." In *The State of Public Administration: Issues, Challenges, and Opportunities*, edited by Donald C. Menzel and Harvey L. White, pp. 142–155. Armonk, NY: M.E. Sharpe, 2011.

Schick, Allen. "The Road to PPB: The Stages of Budget Reform." In *Perspectives on Budgeting*, edited by Allen Schick. 2nd ed. Washington, DC: American Society for Public Administration, 1987.

Stevenson, Richard W. "Congress Passes Tax Cut, with Rebates This Summer." *New York Times* (May 27, 2001), A1–A26.

Tritch, Teresa. "How the Deficit Got This Big." *New York Times* (July 24, 2011), SR11.

Uchitelle, Louis. "Taxes, the Market, and Luck Underlie the Budget Surplus." *New York Times* (October 20, 2000), A1.

United States Department of the Treasury, Bureau of the Public Debt. *The Debt to the Penny and Who Holds It*. www.treasurydirect.gov/NP/BBPlogin?application=np.

U.S. Census Bureau, *Statistical Abstract of the United States: 2012*. State and Local Governments Revenue and Expenditures. http://www.census.gov/compendia/statab/2012/tables/12s0436.pdf.

Wildavsky, Aaron. *The Politics of the Budgetary Process*. Glenview, IL: Scott, Foresman, 1988.

Chapter Six

Bishop, Peter C., and Augustus Jones, Jr. "Implementing the Americans with Disabilities Act of 1990." *Public Administration Review* 53 (March/April 1993): 121–128.

Breul, Jonathan D. "Three Bush Administration Management Reform Initiatives: The President's Management Agenda, Freedom to Manage Legislative Proposals, and the Program Assessment Rating Tool." *Public Administration Review* 67, no. 1 (2007): 21–26.

Broadnax, Walter D. "Diversity in Public Organizations." *Public Administration Review* 70 (2010): s177–s179.

Campbell, Alan K. "Civil Service Reform: A New Commitment." *Public Administration Review* 38 (March/April 1978).

Carter, Jimmy. "State of the Union Address." January 19, 1978.

Cauchon, Dennis. "Federal Pay Ahead of Private Industry." *USA Today* (March 4, 2010).

Desky, Joanne. "Glass Ceiling Slows Down Women in Government." *PA Times* (December 1992): 1.

Equal Employment Opportunity Commission, State and Local Government Information, National Employment Survey (2009), http://www.eeoc.gov/eeoc/statistics/employment/jobpat-eeo4/2009/table3/table3_1_state_.html.

Guy, M. E. "Three Steps Forward, Two Steps Backward: The Status of Women's Integration into Public Management." *Public Administration Review* (1993): 285–292.

Hall, Francine, and Maryann H. Albrecht. *The Management of Affirmative Action*. Santa Monica, CA: Goodyear, 1979.

Havemann, Judith. "The Government Takes a Stand on AIDS in Its Office." *Washington Post National Weekly Edition* (March 28–April 3, 1988): 34.

Hays, Steven W., and Zane T. Reeves. *Personnel Management in the Public Sector*. Boston: Allyn & Bacon, 1984.

Heclo, Hugh. *A Government of Strangers*. Washington, DC: Brookings Institution Press, 1977.

Klingner, Donald E., and John Nalbandian. *Public Personnel Management*. 2nd ed. Englewood Cliffs, NJ: Prentice-Hall, 1985.

Losey, Stephen, "Retirements Surge 24% over Last Year," *Federal Times* (December 2010), http://www.federaltimes.com/article/20111212/PERSONNEL02/112120301/1001.

Office of Management and Budget. *Analytical Perspectives: Budget of the U.S. Government Fiscal Year 2010.* Washington, DC: Government Printing Office, 2009.

Office of Personnel Management. "Human Capital and Assessment Framework," n.d., http://www.opm.gov/hcaaf_resource_center/2-2.asp.

Office of Personnel Management. "Post Reform: Gains, Losses, and Constant Change," n.d., www.opm.gov/BiographyofAnIdeal/docs/Bio1979-Present.pdf.

O'Keefe, Ed. "Number of Federal Union Workers Rose Slightly." *Washington Post* (January 25, 2010).

PriceWaterhouseCoopers. *The Crisis in Federal Government Succession Planning*, 2006, http://www.pwc.com/en_US/us/public-sector/assets/wfp-succession-planning-final-a.pdf.

Riccucci, Norma M. "Human Resources Management." In *The State of Public Administration: Issues, Challenges, and Opportunities*, edited by Donald C. Menzel and Harvey L. White, pp. 127–141. Armonk, NY: M.E. Sharpe, 2011.

Shafritz, Jay M., Albert C. Hyde, and David H. Rosenbloom. *Personnel Management in Government.* 2nd ed. New York: Marcel Dekker, 1981.

Siegel, Gilbert B., and Robert C. Myrtle. *Public Personnel Administration: Concepts and Realities.* Boston: Houghton Mifflin, 1985.

Steele, Randy. "Strike Zone." *Flying* (March 1982): 34–41.

Stewart, Debra W. "Assuring Equal Employment Opportunity in the Organization." In *Handbook of Public Personnel and Labor Relations*, edited by Jack Rabin, Thomas Vocino, W. Bartley Hildreth, and Gerald J. Miller. New York: Marcel Dekker, 1983.

White, Harvey L., and Mitchell F. Rice. "The Multiple Dimensions of Diversity and Culture." In *Diversity and Public Administration: Theory, Issues, and Perspectives*, edited by Mitchell F. Rice. Armonk, NY: M.E. Sharpe, 2010.

Wise, Charles R. "The Supreme Court's New Constitutional Federalism: Implications for Public Administration." *Public Administration Review* 61, no. 3 (May/June 2001): 343–358.

Chapter Seven

American Society for Public Administration. *Ethical Dilemmas.* Washington, DC: ASPA, n.d.

Arendt, Hannah. *Eichmann in Jerusalem.* New York: Viking Press, 1963.

Bauman, Zygmunt. *Postmodern Ethics.* Oxford, UK: Cambridge, MA: Blackwell, 1993.

Blum, Lawrence A. "Gilligan and Kohlberg: Implications for Moral Theory." *Ethics* (April 1988): 472–491.

Bowman, James S. "Ethical Issues for the Public Manager." In *Handbook of Organization Management,* edited by William B. Eddy, pp. 69–102. New York: Marcel Dekker, 1983.

Code of Ethics, International City Management Association, Washington DC (July 2004).

Congressional Quarterly Weekly (March 6, 1993), 511.

Cooper, Terry L. *An Ethic of Citizenship for Public Administration.* Englewood Cliffs, NJ: Prentice-Hall, 1991.

Cooper, Terry L., and N. Dale Wright, eds. *Exemplary Public Administrators.* San Francisco: Jossey-Bass, 1992.

DeGeorge, Richard T. *Business Ethics.* New York: Macmillan, 1982.

Denhardt, Kathryn G. "Managing Ethics." Unpublished manuscript, 1989.

Finer, Herman. "Administrative Responsibility in Democratic Government." In *Bureaucratic Power in National Politics,* edited by Frances Rourke, pp. 165–175. Boston: Little, Brown, 1972.

Friedrich, Carl J. "Public Policy and the Nature of Democratic Responsibility." In *Bureaucratic Power in National Politics,* edited by Frances J. Rourke, pp. 176–186. Boston: Little, Brown, 1972.

Ginsberg, Wendy R. *The Obama Administration's Open Government Initiative*. Washington: Congressional Research Service, 2011.

Goodsell, Charles T. "Conflating Forms of Separation and Administrative Ethics." *Administration and Society* 38, no. 1 (March 2006): 135–141.

Harmon, Michael M., and O. C. McSwite. *Whenever Two or More Are Gathered: Relationship as the Heart of Ethical Discourse*. Tuscaloosa: University of Alabama Press, 2011.

Hilberg, Raul. *The Destruction of the European Jews*. Chicago: Quadrangle Books, 1961.

Kohlberg, Lawrence. "From Is to Ought." In *Cognitive Development and Epistemology,* edited by T. Mishel, pp. 151–235. New York: Academic Press, 1971.

Lewis, Carol. *The Ethics Challenge in Public Service*. San Francisco: Jossey-Bass, 1991.

Lukensmeyer, Carolyn J., Joe Goldman, and David Stern. *Assessing Public Participation in an Open Government Era*. Washington: IBM Center for the Business of Government, 2011.

Masters, Marick F., and Leonard Bierman. "The Hatch Act and the Political Activities of Federal Employee Unions." *Public Administration Review* (July/August 1985): 518–526.

McKeon, Richard. *Basic Works of Aristotle*. New York: Random House, 1941.

Milgram, Stanley. *Obedience to Authority*. New York: Harper & Row, 1974.

Obama, Barack. Presidential Memorandum, January 21, 2009 Presidential Documents. 4685. Federal Register. Vol. 74, No. 15. Monday, January 26, 2009.

Pastin, Mark. "The Thinking Manager's Toolbox." In *Ethical Insight, Ethical Action,* pp. 91–104. Washington, DC: International City Managers Association, 1988.

President's Commission on Federal Ethics Law Reform. *To Serve with Honor: Report and Recommendations to the President*. Washington, DC: U.S. Department of Justice, 1989.

Rawls, John. *A Theory of Justice*. Cambridge, MA: Belnap Press of Harvard University Press, 1971.

Reich, Robert B. "Public Administration and Public Deliberation: An Interpretive Essay." *Yale Law Review* 94 (1985): 1617–1641.

Rubin, Hank. "Dimensions of Institutional Ethics." In *The Nonprofit Organization,* edited by David Gies, J. Steven Ott, and Jay Shafritz. Pacific Grove, CA: Brooks/Cole, 1990.

Svara, James. *The Ethics Primer for Public Administrators in Government and Nonprofit Organizations*. Sudbury, MA: Jones and Bartlett Publishers, 2007.

Tong, Rosemary. *Ethics in Policy Analysis*. Englewood Cliffs, NJ: Prentice Hall, 1986.

Truelson, Judith A. "Protecting David from Goliath: On Blowing the Whistle on Systematic Corruption." *Dialogue* (Spring 1986): 1–23.

Walker, Margaret Urban. *Moral Understandings: A Feminist Study in Ethics*. New York: Routledge, 1998.

Chapter Eight

Argyris, Chris. *Interpersonal Competence and Organizational Effectiveness*. Pacific Grove, CA: Brooks/Cole, 1962.

Argyris, Chris. *Knowledge for Action: A Guide to Overcoming Barriers to Organizational Change*. San Francisco: Jossey-Bass, 1993.

Barbour, George, P., Jr., Thomas W. Fletcher, and George A. Sipel. *Handbook: Excellence in Local Government Management*. Washington, DC: International City Management Association, 1984.

Bryson, John M., and Barbara C. Crosby. *Leadership for the Common Good: Tackling Public Problems in a Shared-Power World*. San Francisco: Jossey-Bass, 1992.

Chrislip, David D., and Carl E. Larson. *Collaborative Leadership*. San Francisco: Jossey-Bass, 1994.

Cohen, Michael D., James G. March, and Johan P. Olsen. "A Garbage Can Model of Organizational Choice." *Administrative Science Quarterly* 17 (1972): 1–25.

Collins, Jim. *Good to Great and the Social Sector: A Monograph to Accompany Good to Great*. Boulder, CO: 2005.

Collins, Jim. *Good to Great: Why Some Companies Make the Leap . . . and Others Don't*. New York: HarperBusiness, 2001.

Cyert, Richard M., and James G. March. *A Behavioral Theory of the Firm*. Englewood Cliffs, NJ: Prentice-Hall, 1963.

Denhardt, Janet Vinzant, and Robert B. Denhardt. *The New Public Service: Serving, Not Steering*. 3rd ed. Armonk, NY: M.E. Sharpe, 2011.

Dimock, Marshall E. "The Criteria and Objectives of Public Administration." In *The Frontiers of Public Administration*, edited by John M. Gaus, Leonard D. White, and Marshall E. Dimock. Chicago: University of Chicago Press, 1936.

Fayol, Henri. *General and Industrial Management*. Translated by C. Storrs. London: Isaac Pitman and Sons, 1949.

Gerth, H. H., and C. Wright Mills. *From Max Weber: Essays in Sociology*. New York: Oxford University Press, 1946.

Golembiewski, Robert T. *Renewing Organizations*. Itasca, IL: Peacock, 1972.

Gulick, Luther. "Notes on the Theory of Organization." In *Papers on the Science of* Administration, edited by Luther Gulick and L. Urwick, pp. 1–46. New York: Institute of Public Administration, 1937a.

Gulick, Luther. "Science, Values, and Public Administration." In *Papers on the Science of Administration*, edited by Luther Gulick and L. Urwick, pp. 189–195. New York: Institute of Public Administration, 1937b.

Guy, Mary Ellen, and Meredith A. Newman. "Women's Jobs, Men's Jobs: Sex Segregation and Emotional Labor." *Public Administration Review* 64, no. 3 (2004): 289–298.

Guy, Mary, Meredith Newman, and Sharon Mastracci. *Emotional Labor: Putting the Service Back in Public Service*. Armonk, NY: M.E. Sharpe, 2008.

Hatch, Mary Jo. *Organization Theory: Modern, Symbolic and Postmodern Perspectives*. Oxford: Oxford University Press, 1997.

Kaufman, Herbert. *The Forest Ranger*. Baltimore, MD: Johns Hopkins University Press, 1960.

MacGregor, Douglas. *The Human Side of the Enterprise*. New York: McGraw-Hill, 1960.

March, James G., and Herbert Simon. *Organizations*. New York: John Wiley, 1958.

Maslow, Abraham H. *Motivation and Personality*. New York: Harper, 1954.

Mastracci, Sharon H., Mary E. Guy, and Meredith A. Newman. *Emotional Labor and Crisis Response: Working on the Razor's Edge*. Armonk, NY: M.E. Sharpe, 2011.

Mintzberg, Henry, Duru Raisinghani, and Andre Theoret. "The Structure of Unstructured Decision Processes." *Administrative Science Quarterly* 21 (1976): 246–275.

Mooney, James, and Alan C. Reiley. *The Principles of Organization*. New York: Harper & Row, 1939.

Ostrom, Vincent, and Elinor Ostrom. "Public Choice: A Different Approach to the Study of Public Administration." *Public Administration Review* 31 (March/April 1971): 203–216.

Peters, J. Thomas, and Robert H. Waterman. *In Search of Excellence*. New York: Harper & Row, 1982.

Redford, Emmette. *Democracy in the Administrative State*. New York: Oxford University Press, 1969.

Schein, Edgar H. *Organizational Culture and Leadership*. 2nd ed. San Francisco: Jossey-Bass, 1997.

Selznick, Philip. *TVA and the Grass Roots*. Berkeley: University of California Press, 1949.

Senge, Peter M. *The Fifth Discipline: The Art and Practice of the Learning Organization*. New York: Currency Doubleday, 1990.

Simon, Herbert A. *Models of Man*. New York: Wiley, 1957.

Stivers, Camilla. *Gender Images in Public Administration: Legitimacy and the Administrative State*. Newbury Park, CA: Sage Publications, 2002.

Taylor, Frederick W. *Scientific Management*. New York: Harper & Row, 1923.

Thomas, John Clayton. *Public Participation in Public Decisions*. San Francisco: Jossey-Bass, 1995.

Wamsley, Gary, and Mayer Zald. *The Political Economy of Public Organizations*. Lexington, MA: Lexington Books, 1973.

White, Leonard. *Introduction to the Study of Public Administration*. New York: Macmillan, 1926.

Willoughby, W. F. *Principles of Public Organization*. Baltimore, MD: Johns Hopkins University Press, 1927.

Chapter Nine

Bennis, Warren. "The Artform of Leadership." In *The Executive Mind*, edited by Suresh Srivastya. San Francisco: Jossey-Bass, 1983.

Bennis, Warren, and Burt Nanus. *Leaders: The Strategies for Taking Charge*. New York: Harper & Row, 1985.

Blake, Robert R., and Jane Mouton. *The Managerial Grid: The Key to Leadership Excellence*. Houston: Gulf Publishing, 1964.

Burns, James MacGregor. *Leadership*. New York: Harper & Row, 1978.

Cimino, John, and Robert B. Denhardt. "Music, Leadership, and the Inner Work of Art." In *Being the Change: 21st Century Thinking for Transformational Leaders*, edited by Carol Pearson. San Francisco: Barrett-Koehler, forthcoming.

Constantino, Cathy A., and Christina Sickles-Merchant. *Designing Conflict Management Systems*. San Francisco: Jossey-Bass, 1996.

Daft, Richard L., and Richard M. Steers. *Organizations: A Micro/Macro Approach*. Glenview IL: Scott, Foresman, 1986.

Denhardt, Robert B. *The Pursuit of Significance: Strategies for Managerial Success in Public Organizations*. Belmont, CA: Wadsworth, 1993.

Denhardt, Robert B., and Janet Vinzant Denhardt. *The Dance of Leadership: The Art of Leading in Business, Government, and Society*. Armonk, NY: M.E. Sharpe, 2006.

Denhardt, Robert B., and Kevin Prelgovisk. "Public Leadership: A Developmental Perspective." In *Executive Leadership in the Public Service*, edited by Robert B. Denhardt and William H. Stewart. Tuscaloosa: University of Alabama Press, 1992.

Fisher, Roger, and William Ury. *Getting to Yes*. 2nd ed. New York: Penguin Books, 1991.

Gardner, John. Remarks to the National Conference of the National Association of Schools of Public Affairs and Administration, Seattle, October 23, 1987.

Gardner, Neely. *Group Leadership*. Washington, DC: National Training and Development Service, 1974.

Hales, Colin P. "What Do Managers Do? A Critical Review of the Evidence." *Journal of Management* 23 (1986): 88–115.

Heifetz, Ronald A., and Martin Linsky. *Leadership on the Line: Staying Alive through the Dangers of Leading.* Boston, MA: Harvard Business School Press, 2002.

Helgesen, Sally. "Leading from the Grassroots." In *The Leader of the Future: New Visions, Strategies, and Practices for the Next Era,* edited by Frances Hesselbein, Marshall Goldsmith, and Richard Beckhard. San Francisco: Jossey-Bass, 1996.

Helgesen, Sally. *The Web of Inclusion: A New Architecture for Building Great Organizations.* Washington DC: Beard Publishers, 2005.

Hersey, Paul, and Kenneth H. Blanchard. *Management of Organizational Behavior.* 5th ed. Englewood Cliffs, NJ: Prentice-Hall, 1988.

Herzberg, Frederick. *The Motivation to Work.* New York: Wiley, 1959.

Hitt, Michael A., Dennis R. Middlemist, and Robert L. Mathis. *Management Concepts and Effective Practice.* St. Paul, MN: West, 1983.

Janis, Irving. *Groupthink.* 2nd ed. Boston: Houghton Mifflin, 1983.

Kouzes, James M., and Barry Z. Posner. *The Leadership Challenge.* 4th ed. San Francisco: Jossey-Bass, 2007.

Lee, Seok-Hwan. "Does Performance-Base Pay Motivate? Maybe, Or Maybe Not . . ." *PA Times* 24, no. 4 (April 2001): 3.

Lindblom, Charles E. *The Policy-Making Process.* Englewood Cliffs, NJ: Prentice-Hall, 1968.

McClelland, David. *Human Motivation.* Glenview, IL: Scott, Foresman, 1985.

Moorhead, Gregory, Richard Ference, and Chris P. Neck. "Group Decision Fiascoes Continue: Space Shuttle Challenger and a Revised Groupthink Framework." *Human Relations* 44, no. 6 (1991): 539–550.

Nichols, Ralph G., and Leonard A. Stevens. *Are You Listening?* New York: McGraw-Hill, 1957.

Organ, Dennis H. "A Review of Management and the Worker." *Academy of Management Review,* 11, no. 2 (April 1986): 459–464.

Rankin, Paul. "Listening Ability," proceedings of the Ohio State Educational Conference, Ninth Annual Session, 1929.

Schein, Edgar H. *Helping: How to Offer, Give, and Receive Help.* San Francisco: Berrett-Koehler, 2009.

Simon, Herbert A. *Models of Man.* New York: Wiley, 1957.

Steil, Lyman K., Larry L. Barker, and Kittie W. Watson. *Effective Listening.* Reading, MA: Addison-Wesley, 1983.

Stogdill, Ralph M. *Handbook of Leadership.* New York: Free Press, 1974.

Stogdill, Ralph M. "Personal Factors Associated with Leadership: A Survey of the Literature." *Journal of Psychology* 25 (1948): 35–71.

Sussman, Lyle, and Samuel Deep. *Comex.* Cincinnati, OH: Southwestern, 1984.

Taylor, Frederick W. *Scientific Management.* New York: Harper & Row, 1923.

Chapter Ten

Barzelay, Michael. *The New Public Management: Improving Research and Policy Dialogue.* Berkeley, CA: University of California Press/Russell Sage Foundation, 2001.

Bernstein, David J. *Portland, Oregon: Pioneering External Accountability, a GASB SEA Research Case Study.* Portland, OR: City of Portland and Governmental Accounting Standards Board, 2000.

Boston, Jonathan, ed. *Public Management: The New Zealand Model*. Auckland, New Zealand: Oxford University Press, 1996.

Breul, Jonathon D. "Three Bush Administration Management Reform Initiatives: The President's Management Agenda, Freedom to Manage Legislative Proposals, and the Program Assessment Rating Tool." *Public Administration Review* 67, no. 1 (2007): 21–26.

Breul, Jonathan, and John M. Kamensky. "Federal Government Reform: Lessons from Clinton's 'Reinventing Government' and Bush's 'Management Agenda' Initiatives." *Public Administration Review* 68 no. 6 (November/December 2008): 1009–1026.

Bryer, Thomas A., and Staci M. Zavattaro. "Social Media and Public Administration: Theoretical Dimensions and Introduction to the Symposium." *Administrative Theory and Praxis* 33, 3 (September 2011): 325–340.

Chun, Soon Ae, Stuart Shulman, Rodrigo Sandoval, and Eduard Hovy. "Government 2.0: Making Connections between Citizens, Data and Government." *Information Polity* 15 (2010): 1–9.

Commission on Global Governance. *Our Global Neighborhood*. Report issued to the United Nations. Oxford, UK: Oxford University Press, 1995.

Dawes, Sharon S. "The Evolution and Continuing Challenges of E-Governance." *Public Administration Review* 70, Supplement 1 (December 2010): s86–s102.

Deloitte Research. *At the Dawn of e-Government: The Citizen as Customer*. New York: Deloitte Consulting LLC, 2002.

Frederickson, H. George. "Some Policy Implications of the Federal Reinventing Government Report." *Policy Currents* 4,1 (February 1994): 1–3.

Gilmour, John B., and David E. Lewis. "Does Performance Budgeting Work? An Examination of the Office of Management and Budget's PART Scores." *Public Administration Review* 66, no. 5 (September/October 2006): 742–752.

Government Accounting Office. *Managing for Results: Strengthening Regulatory Agencies' Performance Management Practices*. Washington, DC: Government Printing Office, 1999.

Greene, Stephen G. "Getting the Basics Right." *Chronicle of Philanthropy* 13, no. 14 (May 3, 2001): 1–12.

Greiner, John M., Harry P. Hatry, Margo P. Koss, Annie P. Millar, and Jane P. Woodward. *Productivity and Motivation: A Review of State and Local Government Initiatives*. Washington, DC: Urban Institute, 1981.

Hakes, Jay E. "Performance Measurement and Organization Change." *PA Times* 20 (July 1997): 10, 17.

Hatry, Harry, Therese van Houten, Margaret C. Plantz, and Martha Taylor Greenway. *Measuring Program Outcomes: A Practical Approach*. Alexandria, VA: United Way of America, 1996.

Helbig , Natalie C., J. Ramón Gil-García, and Enrico Ferro. "Understanding the Complexity in Electronic Government: Implications from the Digital Divide Literature." Paper presented at the Eleventh Americas Conference on Information Systems, Omaha, NE (August 2005).

Holzer, Marc, Ellen Doree Rosen, and Constance Zalk. "Steps in Productivity Improvement." In *Productivity Improvement Techniques,* edited by John Matzer, Jr. Washington, DC: International City Management Association, 1986.

Hruby, Laura. "All Aboard." *Chronicle of Philanthropy* 13, no. 17 (June 14, 2001): 8–13.

Jennings, Edward T. "Strategic Planning and Balanced Scorecards: Charting the Course to Policy Destinations." *Public Administration Review* 70 (2010): s224–s226.

Joyce, G. Philip. "Linking Performance and Budgeting: Opportunities in the Federal Budget Process." In *Integrating Performance and Budgets: The Budget Office of Tomorrow,* edited by Jonathan Breul and Carl Moravitz. New York: Rowman and Littlefield, 2007.

Kamensky, John M. "The Obama Performance Approach: A Midterm Snapshot." *Public Performance and Management Review* 35, no. 1 (September 2011): 133–148.

Kaplan, Robert, and David Norton. *The Balanced Scorecard: Translating Strategy into Action.* Boston: Harvard Business School Press, 1996.

Kettl, Donald F. "The Global Revolution in Public Management: Driving Themes, Missing Links." *Journal of Policy Analysis and Management* 16 (Summer 1997): 446–462.

Kettl, Donald F. "The Transformation of Governance: Globalization, Devolution, and the Role of Government." *Public Administration Review* 60, no. 6 (November/December 2000): 488–497.

Kettl, Donald F. "Obama's Stealth Revolution: Quietly Reshaping the Way Government Works," *The Public Manager* 38, no. 4 (January 2009): 39-42.

Kibbe, Barbara. "Improving Non-Profit Operations." *Chronicle of Philanthropy* (May 3, 2001), www.philanthropy.com/free/articles/v13/i14/14001001.htm.

Light, Paul C. *Making Nonprofits Work: A Report on the Tides of Nonprofit Management Reform.* Washington, DC: Brookings Institution Press, 2000.

Mayne, John. "Public Sector Reforms: International Perspectives on Performance Monitoring." *PA Times* (July 20, 1997): 1, 16.

Melkers, Julia, and Katherine Willoughby. "Staying the Course: The Use of Performance Measurement in State Governments." In *Integrating Performance and Budgets: The Budget Office of Tomorrow,* edited by Jonathan Breul and Carl Moravitz. New York: Rowman and Littlefield, 2007.

Mossberger, Karen, and Yonghong Wu. *Civic Engagement and Local E-Government: Social Networking Comes of Age.* Urbana: University of Illinois Institute for Policy and Civic Engagement (February 13, 2012).

Newcomer, Kathryn, and Sharon Caudle. "Public Performance Management Systems: Embedding Practices for Improved Success." *Public Performance and Management Review* 35, no. 1 (September 2011): 108–132.

Newcomer, Kathryn, and Aaron A. Otto. "Is GPRA Improving Federal Government?" *PA Times* 23, no. 1 (January 2000): 1–6.

Norris, Donald F. "E-Government 2020: Plus ça change, plus c'est la meme chose." *Public Administration Review* 70, Supplement 1 (December 2010): s180–s181.

Obama, Barack. "Transparency and Open Government," Presidential Memorandum (January 21, 2009), http://www.whitehouse.gov/the_press_office/TransparencyandOpenGovernment.

Office of Management and Budget. *Analytical Perspectives: Budget of the U.S. Government Fiscal Year 2010.* Washington, DC: Government Printing Office, 2009.

Osborne, David, and Ted Gaebler. *Reinventing Government.* Reading, MA: Addison-Wesley, 1992.

Peters, B. Guy. "New Visions of Government and the Public Service." In *New Paradigms for Government: Issues for the Changing Public Service,* edited by Patricia W. Ingraham and Barbara S. Romzek. San Francisco: Jossey-Bass, 1994.

Radin, Beryl A. "Overhead Agencies and Permanent Government: The Office of Management and Budget in the Obama Administration," paper presented at the Annual Meeting of the American Political Science Association, Washington, DC (September 2010).

Roberts, Nancy C. "Beyond Smokestacks and Silos: Open-Source, Web-Enabled Coordination in Organizations and Networks." *Public Administration Review* 71, no. 5 (September/October 2011): 677–693.

Rubin, Marilyn, and Katherine Willoughby. "Measuring Government Performance: The Intersection of Strategic Planning and Performance Budgeting." Paper presented at the 7th Transatlantic Dialogue Conference, Newark, NJ (June 2011).

Schachter, Hindy Lauer. "Reinventing Government or Reinventing Ourselves: Two Models for Improving Government Service." *Public Administration Review* 55 (November/December 1995): 530–537.

Smith, Aaron. *Government Online: The Internet Gives Citizens New Paths to Government Services and Information.* Washington, DC: Pew Internet & American Life Project (April 27, 2010).

Swope, Christopher. "E-Government's New Gear." *Governing Magazine* (March 2004), 52.

Swope, Christopher. "Restless for Results." *Governing Magazine* (April 2001), 20–23.

Vlk, Bruce. "Post-New Public Management under the Obama Administration: An Early Snapshot." *Michigan Journal of Public Affairs* 8 (Spring 2011): 3–17.

Wholey, J. S., H. P. Hatry, and K. E. Newcomer, eds. *Handbook for Practical Program Evaluation.* San Francisco: Jossey-Bass, 1994.

Zeller, Shawn. "Performance Anxiety for 'New' Federal Standards." *CQ Weekly* (March 30, 2009), 708–709.

Chapter Eleven

Abonyi, George, and David M. Van Slyke. "Governing on the Edges." *Public Administration Review* 70, Supplement 1 (December 2010), 543–545.

Altman, Roger C. "The Great Crash, 2008: A Geopolitical Setback for the West." *Foreign Affairs* 88, 1 (January/February 2009): 1–14.

CAP Corner, *PA Times*, December 1999, 10.

Chan, Sewell. "Financial Crisis Was Avoidable, Inquiry Finds." *New York Times* (January 25, 2011).

Denhardt, Janet V., and Robert B. Denhardt. *The New Public Service: Serving, Not Steering.* 3rd ed. Armonk, NY: M.E. Sharpe, 2011.

Denhardt, Robert B., and Janet V. Denhardt. "The New Public Service: Putting Democracy First." *National Civic Review* 90, no. 4 (Winter 2001): 391–400.

International Monetary Fund (IMF). *World Economic Outlook April 2009: Crisis and Recovery.* Washington, DC: International Monetary Fund, Publication Services, 2009.

Johnson, Norman J., and James H. Svara. *Justice for All: Promoting Social Equity in Public Administration.* Armonk, NY: M.E. Sharpe, 2011.

Jreisat, Jamal. "Issues in Concept and Practice." In *The State of Public Administration: Issues, Challenges, and Opportunities*, edited by Donald C. Menzel and Harvey L. White, pp. 422–438. Armonk, NY: M.E. Sharpe, 2011.

National Bureau of Economic Research. *Determination of the December 2007 Peak in Economic Activity* (December 1, 2008), http://www.nber.org/dec2008.html.

National League of Cities (NLC). *Beyond Civility: From Public Engagement to Problem Solving— An Action Guide for City Leaders.* Washington, DC: National League of Cities Center for Research and Innovation, 2011.

Svara, James H., and Janet Denhardt. "The Connected Community." In *The Connected Community: Local Governments as Partners in Citizen Engagement and Community Building,* edited by James H. Svara and Janet Denhardt, pp. 4–49. Phoenix, AZ: The Alliance for Innovation, 2011.

INDEX

NOTE: Italic *b* following page number indicates box; italic *f* following page number indicates figure; italic *n* following page number indicates networking information; and italic *t* following page number indicates table.